Gregorian and Old Roman Eighth-Mode Tracts

Gregorian and Old Roman Eighth-Mode Tracts

A Case Study in the Transmission of Western Chant

Emma Hornby

Routledge
Taylor & Francis Group
LONDON AND NEW YORK

First published 2002 by Ashgate Publishing

Reissued 2018 by Routledge
2 Park Square, Milton Park, Abingdon, Oxon OX14 4RN
711 Third Avenue, New York, NY 10017, USA

Routledge is an imprint of the Taylor & Francis Group, an informa business

A Library of Congress record exists under LC control number: 2001053593

ISBN 13: 978-1-138-72501-0 (hbk)
ISBN 13: 978-1-138-72497-6 (pbk)
ISBN 13: 978-1-315-19208-6 (ebk)

Contents

Preface

This study uses detailed musical analysis of the eighth-mode tracts in addressing some of the still unresolved questions of chant scholarship. The first question is that of the relationship between Old Roman and Gregorian chant. Although the common origin of the two chant traditions is generally acknowledged, the nature of their relationship remains uncertain because the melodic dialects had greatly diverged by the time they were notated. Parallel analysis of these chants in the two traditions promotes a deeper understanding of this relationship.

The second question is that of the relationship between oral and written modes of transmission in the ecclesiastical culture of the Middle Ages. The Mass Proper chants were introduced to Francia from Rome in the middle of the eighth century, but do not appear in manuscripts with musical notation until the late ninth century. It is possible to construct a model showing how the eighth-mode tracts may have been transmitted before notation was widely used, stabilised by the memory prompts of the text, the form, and the melodic outlines of the genre. The closeness of the readings of these chants in the earliest manuscripts may be the result of a stable oral genre, rather than an early ninth-century neumed exemplar.

The Middle Ages saw a transition to a culture more dependent on writing. An investigation is made of the effect this transition had on the way the eighth-mode tracts were understood by those who performed and notated them. This draws on three types of evidence: the manner in which the eighth-mode tracts were notated; the forms and structures of eighth-mode tracts composed after the development of musical notation; and the relationship between the eighth-mode tracts and theoretical descriptions of the eighth-mode.

The history of the eighth-mode tracts before they were written down has been the focus of much speculation, because they are generally regarded as being very old, and because they are so closely related to each other. Many scholars have argued that certain eighth-mode tracts are older, or retain more archaic elements, than others. The musical and historical evidence used in support of such chronologies is critically examined.

The findings of this study are closely based on the versions of the eighth-mode tracts found in medieval manuscripts: on the melodic outlines encountered in different manuscripts, and on the manner in which the eighth-mode tracts are notated. For this reason, transcription has been avoided as far as possible and the musical examples and appendices consist largely of reproductions of the relevant portions of the manuscripts. The reproductions have been scanned, and Corel Photo House software has been used to remove sufficient background 'noise' to render them legible. The responsibility for any inadvertently removed puncta is entirely my own. The appendices consist of:

(i) the manuscript versions of a representative tract, *Iubilate*, presented phrase by phrase, so that the manuscripts may easily be compared;

(ii) the core repertory of eighth-mode tracts in two manuscripts, one from each tradition, arranged phrase by phrase according to phrase type;

(iii) the core repertory of eighth-mode tracts in two manuscripts, presented tract by tract, to allow easy comparison of each chant in the two traditions;

(iv) the eighth-mode tracts of *DIJ1*, a manuscript whose notation and layout are of particular interest;

(v) the eighth-mode tracts that appear in eleventh- and twelfth-century manuscripts but which are not part of the core repertory, presented tract by tract.

For conciseness, references to melodic outlines in the text use the a-p letter notation of *DIJ1*. The notation is interpreted as follows:

The texts of the tracts are given in standardised versions based on the manuscripts used in this study; 'ae' is replaced throughout by 'e', and the cedilla is ignored.

Individual phrases within tracts are referred to within this study by means of the first word or first few words of the tract title together with a number (for example, *Iubilate 7*). Tables indicating the texts and musical phrases to which these abbreviations refer may be found in Chapter 3, between pages 99 and 123.

I gratefully acknowledge financial assistance during this project from the British Academy, the Worshipful Company of Musicians, the Ian Karten Charitable Trust, Worcester College, Oxford, and my grandparents. I wish to thank Jane Bellingham, John Caldwell, Janet Hornby and Rebecca

Maloy, who read and commented on part or all of the text, and members of the *IMS Cantus Planus Study Group* for stimulating and supportive conversations. Thanks are due to Thornton College, Buckingham for the use of computing facilities. I wish also to thank John Wagstaff in the Music Faculty Library at Oxford for his expertise and kind support, and my family and friends, especially Tom, for their seemingly inexhaustible patience.

Acknowledgements

I wish to thank the following for their kind permission to reproduce portions of the manuscripts in their possession:

The Bodleian Library, University of Oxford (MS. Canon. Liturg. 350: fols. 27v, 31v [*STM*]; MS. Canon. Liturg. 340: fols. 26r, 28r [*MOG4*]; MS. Canon. Liturg. 341: fol. 14v [*TYR*]; MS. Canon. Liturg. 366: fols. 4v, 5r, 8v, 9v, 9r, 10r, 22r [*BRE*]; MS. Canon. Liturg. 354: fols. 10v, 11v, 12r, 12v, 15v, 19r [*PAS2*]; MS. Rawl. C. 892: fols. 16v, 18r, 18v [*IRI*]; MS. Laud Misc. 358: fols. 34r, 34v, 35r, 42r, 52v, 53r [*SAB*])

The Vatican Library (San Pietro F22: 17v [*ORP*] and Vat. Lat. 5319: 37r-v [*ORJ*])

The Bibliothèque Nationale, Paris (BN lat. 776:10r, 24r, 31r, 32v, 36v [*ALB*] and BN lat. 1087: 23v, 25v [*CLU1*])

I am grateful to:

Bärenreiter for permission to reproduce examples from *Monumenta Musica sacrae 5* (1981) (pp 55, 56, 59, 63, 64 [*DEN1*]);

Fondation Martin Bodmer for permission to reproduce examples from Lütolf (ed.), *Das Graduale von Santa Cecilia in Trastevere* (1987) (8v, 18r, 27r, 27v, 30r, 31v, 32r, 32v, 34r, 34v, 35v, 36v, 47v, 52r, 52v, 57v, 58r, 63v, 64r, 77r, 77v, 78r [*ORC*]);

The Abbaye St Pierre de Solesmes for permission to reproduce pages of *Paléographie Musicale* (*PM 2/2* (*GAL2*): pp 59, 61, 62, 85; *PM 1* (*GAL1*): pp 29, 32; *PM4* (*MUR3*): pp 82, 89, 203; *PM 8* (*DIJ1*): pp 127-138; *PM 10* (*LAN*): pp 16, 30, 32, 35, 101, 102; *PM 11* (*CHA1*): pp 20, 22; *PM 13* (*YRX*): pp 12, 50, 55, 56, 59, 62, 75, 151; *PM 14*: Plate XLV (Chieti fragment); *PM15* (*BEN5*): 10r, 26v, 45r, 46r, 49r, 50r, 50v, 51v, 52v, 54v, 55v, 56r, 56v, 57r, 58r, 58v, 59v, 60r, 74r, 82v, 90r, 97v, 98r, 119r, 119v, 120r, 120v, 214v, 215r; *PM 16* (*NOY4*): 12r, 13r; *PM18* (*LAV*): 36r, 52r, 54r, 58r, 58v, 60v, 107r, 107v, 150r, 151r, 151v; *PM 19* (*KLO1*): 38v, 40r, 42v).

Several examples are reproduced from H. Loriquet, J. Pothier and A. Colette (eds.), *Le Graduel de l'église cathedrale de Rouen au XIIIe siècle* (Rouen, 1907) [*ROG1*]. Every effort has been made to trace the publisher of this volume, but without success. Ashgate would be pleased to hear from the publisher.

Abbreviations

AM	*Acta Musicologica*
AMS	René-Jean Hesbert, *Antiphonale Missarum Sextuplex* (Brussels, 1935)
CP: Tihany	László Dobszay *et al.* (eds.), *International Musicological Society Study Group 'Cantus Planus'. Papers read at the Third Meeting, Tihany, Hungary, 1988* (Budapest, 1990)
CP: Eger	László Dobszay *et al.* (eds.), *International Musicological Society Study Group 'Cantus Planus'. Papers read at the Fifth Meeting, Eger, Hungary, 1993* (Budapest, 1995)
CP: Sopron	László Dobszay (ed.), *International Musicological Society Study Group 'Cantus Planus'. Papers read at the Seventh Meeting, Sopron, Hungary, 1995* (Budapest, 1998)
CP: Visegrad	*International Musicological Society Study Group 'Cantus Planus'. Papers read at the Ninth Meeting, Visegrad, Hungary, 1998* (forthcoming)
EG	*Études Grégoriennes*
EMH	*Early Music History*
GR II	*Le Graduel Romain: Édition critique par les moines de Solesmes.* II: *Les Sources* (Solesmes, 1957).
IMS 1977	Daniel Heartz and Bonnie Wade (eds.), *Report of the Twelfth Congress of the International Musicological Society, Berkeley, 1977* (Basel, 1981)
IMS 1987	Angelo Pompilio, Donatella Restani, Lorenzo Bianconi, and F. Alberto Gallo (eds.), *Atti del XIV congresso della Società Internazionale di Musicologia: Trasmissione e recezione delle forme di cultura musicale, Bologna, 27 agosto–1 settembre 1987* (Rome, 1990)
JAMS	*Journal of the American Musicological Society*
JM	*Journal of Musicology*
JPMMS	*Journal of the Plainsong and Medieval Music Society*
KmJb	*Kirchenmusikalisches Jahrbuch*
MQ	*Musical Quarterly*
NCMH	Rosamund McKitterick (ed.), *The New Cambridge Medieval History*, vol. II (Cambridge, 1995)
NG	Stanley Sadie (ed.), *The New Grove Dictionary of Music and Musicians* (London, 1980)

PM	*Paléographie Musicale*
PMM	*Plainsong and Medieval Music*
PRMA	*Proceedings of the Royal Musical Association*
VD	S. J. P. Van Dijk, *Handlist of the Latin Liturgical Manuscripts in the Bodleian Library, Oxford* (typescript, 1957)
WP	David Hiley, *Western Plainchant: A Handbook* (Oxford, 1993)

Sigla of Manuscripts Referred to in this Study

Sigla	Provenance	Date	Manuscript signature	Notation
ALB	Saint Michel in Gaillac	eleventh century; before 1079	PARIS, BN lat. 776	Aquitanian neumes with lines
BEC	Bec	thirteenth century	PARIS, BN lat. 1105	Square notation
BEN1	Salerno?	tenth–eleventh century	BENEVENTO, Bibl. Cap. 33	Beneventan neumes
BEN5	Benevento	1100–1150	BENEVENTO, Bibl. Cap. 34	Beneventan neumes on lines
BRE	Brescia	eleventh century	OXFORD, Bodl. Canon. Liturg. 366	N. Italian neumes
CHA1	Brittany	tenth century	CHARTRES 47	Breton neumes
CLU1	Cluny	c1000–1050	PARIS, BN lat. 1087	French neumes
DEN1	Saint Denis	eleventh century	PARIS, Bibl. Mazarine 384	French neumes
DIJ1	Saint Bénigne, Dijon	c1000–1025	MONTPELLIER, Faculté de Médecine H 159	French neumes with alphabetical pitch notation

GAL1	Saint Gall	late–ninth to early–tenth century	SAINT GALL, Stiftsbibl. 359	Saint Gall neumes
GAL2	Saint Gall	early eleventh century	SAINT GALL, Stiftsbibl. 339	Saint Gall neumes
IRI	Ireland	c1150–1200	OXFORD, Bodl. Rawl. C. 892	Anglo-Norman point neumes on lines
KLO1	Klosterneuburg	twelfth century	GRAZ, Univ. 807	Messine Klosterneuburg notation on lines
LAN	Laon region	c930	LAON 239	Messine notation
LAV	Bologna	c1025–1050	ROME, Bibl. Angelica 123	N. East Italian neumes
LEW	Lewes	c1250–1300	CAMBRIDGE, Fitzwilliam 369	Square notation
MOG4	Saint-Gall in Moggio	c1216	OXFORD, Bodl. Canon. Liturg. 340	German neumes
MUR3	Saint Gall, Einsiedeln, or Mürbach	c970	EINSIEDELN, 121	Saint Gall neumes
NOV2	Novalese	eleventh century	OXFORD, Bodl. Douce 222	Novalese neumes
NOY4	Corbie or Noyon	tenth century	The Mont-Renaud manuscript (private collection)	French neumes

ORC	Saint Cecilia in Trastevere	1071	Private collection (Martin Bodmer)	Beneventan neumes on lines
ORJ	Saint John in the Lateran	eleventh–twelfth century	ROME, Vat lat 5319	Beneventan neumes on lines
ORP	Saint Peter's in the Vatican	thirteenth century	ROME, San Pietro F22	Beneventan neumes on lines
PAS2	Saint Paul in Carinthia (diocese of Salzburg)	twelfth century	OXFORD, Bodl. Canon. Liturg. 354	German neumes
RAG	Ragusa	thirteenth century	OXFORD, Bodl, Canon. Liturg. 342	Beneventan neumes on lines
ROG1	Rouen Cathedral	thirteenth century	PARIS, BN lat. 904	Square notation
ROP	Meulan	late–twelfth century	SAINT PETERSBURG, O v I 6	Anglo-Norman point neumes on lines
SAB	Saint Albans Abbey	c1160	OXFORD, Bodl. Laud Misc. 358	Anglo-Norman point neumes on lines
STM	Aquileia or Moggio	twelfth century	OXFORD, Bodl. Canon. Liturg. 350	German neumes
TOU	Toulouse	eleventh century	LONDON, BL Harleian 4951	Aquitanian neumes with lines
TYR	Innichen (north west of Aquileia)	twelfth century	OXFORD, Bodl. Canon. Liturg. 341	Saint Gall neumes

YRX	Saint Yrieix	eleventh century; before 1060	PARIS, BN lat. 903	Aquitanian neumes with lines

Manuscript sigla are derived from *GRII* except for: *MOG4, RAG* and *SAB*, which have no sigla despite appearing in *GRII*; *LEW*, *STM* and *TYR*, which are not in *GRII*; and *ORC*, *ORJ* and *ORP*, which are Old Roman manuscripts, and are therefore not included in *GRII.*

Textual Origins and Liturgical Placing of the Core Repertory of Eighth-Mode Tracts

Ember Saturday in Advent	*Qui regis*	Psalm 79: 2–3*
Saint Agatha (5th February)	*Qui seminant*	Psalm 125: 5–6
Saint Valentine (14th February)	*Desiderium*	Psalm 20: 3–4
Saint Gregory (25th February)	*Beatus uir*	Psalm 111: 1–3
Septuagesima	*De profundis*	Psalm 129: 1–4
Sexagesima	*Commouisti*	Psalm 59: 4–6
Quinquagesima	*Iubilate*	Psalm 99: 2–3*
Ember Saturday in Lent	*Laudate*	Psalm 116
Quadragesima III	*Ad te leuaui*	Psalm 122: 1–3
Quadragesima IV	*Qui confidunt*	Psalm 124: 1–2
Passion Sunday (Quadragesima V)	*Sepe*	Psalm 128: 1–4
Holy Saturday	*Cantemus*	Exodus 15: 1–2
	Vinea facta est	Isaiah 5: 1–2
	Attende	Deut. 32: 1–4
	Sicut ceruus	Psalm 41: 1–4

* These tracts begin at the start of their respective psalms. The first verse consists of the title (in *Qui regis*: 'In finem pro his qui commutabuntur testimonium Asaph psalmus', and in *Iubilate*: 'Psalmus in confessione').

Chapter 1
Introduction

Historical Background

In 751, the Frankish throne was seized from the Merovingians by Pippin III. His military successes, and those of his Carolingian forebears, had made this move 'impossible to resist'.[1] To consolidate his power, Pippin turned to the Church for endorsement. He was anointed as king by the bishops in Francia and subsequently by Pope Stephen II, showing that he was acclaimed not only by the secular powers, but also that he had been granted ecclesiastical and divine approval.[2] This was a novelty in Francia, and marked the beginning of a theocracy, in which the king wielded both temporal and spiritual power, and was consequently responsible for both the temporal and spiritual welfare of his flock.[3]

The pattern of Carolingian kingship was in stark contrast to the ruling powers previously seen in Western Europe since the collapse of the Roman Empire. Most rulers at this time preserved their kingship by military strength, supporting this by constructing elaborate genealogies reaching back to Woden and other Germanic gods. Such habits were hard to break: after their conversion in the seventh century, Anglo-Saxon kings began to trace their genealogies back to saints instead of to pagan figures.[4] The assertion of the Carolingian kings that they had instead been divinely chosen to lead the *communitas fidelium* (community of the faithful) had far-reaching consequences. If divinely inspired, their authority could not be questioned. As spiritual as well as temporal rulers, the Carolingians had

---

[1] Fouracre, P., 'Frankish Gaul to 814', in *NCMH*, 85–109; 96.

[2] Anti-Merovingian propaganda was also an important factor in 'legitimising the Carolingian usurpation'. See Hen, Y., *Culture and Religion in Merovingian Gaul, AD 481–751* (Leiden, 1995), 198.

[3] Nelson, J., 'Kingship and Empire in the Carolingian World', in R. McKitterick (ed.), *Carolingian Culture: Emulation and Innovation* (Cambridge, 1994), 52–87.

[4] Rollason, D., *The Mildrith Legend: A Study in Early Medieval Hagiography in England* (Leicester, 1982).

licence to interfere in many spheres of daily life that had previously been the exclusive preserve of ecclesiastical powers.[5]

For example, the Frankish aristocracy had dominated the Frankish Church in the early eighth century. In the name of spiritual reform, Pippin confiscated many of their estates and revenues, and granted privileges of immunity to monasteries, thereby bringing much of the wealth and power of the church under his direct control.[6] It was not only in the interests of the Carolingian rulers to take an active part in reforming the patterns of worship and religious life in order to maintain and extend their power over ecclesiastical institutions; such interventions also promoted cultural and political unity among a diverse populace as well as demonstrating concern for the spiritual welfare of the flock. Charlemagne's *Admonitio generalis* (789), perhaps the most famous intervention of the king in ecclesiastical matters, is a clear example of this. As well as outlining the behaviour and duties expected of bishops, priests, deacons, and the laity, and the extent of their jurisdiction, it gives instructions for the training of the clergy and for the religious education of the laity.

The Carolingian desire to replace the existing Gallican liturgical customs with the authoritative practices of Rome should be understood within this culture, where religious uniformity aided political stability, and where the king bore responsibility for the spiritual welfare of the people. There had been Frankish interest in Roman liturgical practice before this time: '[the Gelasian Sacramentary] circulated widely in the Kingdom of the Franks, even before the reforms undertaken by Pepin III, and was one of the principal agents of Romanization there long before any royal initiatives on that score'.[7] However, it was in the Carolingian era that such interest was combined with the intention of securing widespread liturgical unity. Such liturgical unity was not easily achieved: despite Charlemagne's efforts, including depositing an exemplar of the Hadrianum (or Gregorian) Sacramentary in the palace library in Aachen, no uniform and authoritative version of the Sacramentary became the Frankish standard in his lifetime.[8]

The Carolingians' concern for the unity and standardisation of Sacramentaries parallels their efforts with liturgical chant, even to the extent of identifying the authoritative practices of Rome with Pope Gregory

---

[5] McKitterick, R., *The Frankish Church and the Carolingian Reforms, 789–895* (London, 1977), xx. See also Nelson, J, 'Kingship and Royal Government', in *NCMH*, 383–430; 422–30.

[6] McKitterick, R., *The Frankish Kingdoms under the Carolingians 751–987* (London, 1983), 41.

[7] Vogel, C., *Medieval Liturgy: An Introduction to the Sources,* trans. and rev. W. Storey and N. Rasmussen (Washington DC, 1986), 70.

[8] Brown, G., 'Introduction: The Carolingian Renaissance', in McKitterick (ed.), *Carolingian Culture,* op. cit., 1–51; 22.

the Great in both cases. With both Sacramentaries and chant, the Carolingians encountered difficulties in persuading people to replace their existing liturgical customs with the centrally endorsed Roman ones. The first evidence pertaining to the adoption of Roman chant in Francia coincides with that of the wider process of Romanising the liturgy, instigated by Pippin soon after the visit of Pope Stephen II in 754.[9] The *Admonitio Generalis* warns that the clergy should 'learn and practise the Roman chant correctly, in conformity with Pippin's attempt to abolish the Gallican chant for the sake of unanimity with the Roman church'.[10] There is extensive documentary evidence that Metz was the centre from which the new chant was disseminated, and Chrodegang of Metz is identified as one of the principal agents of liturgical and musical reform.[11]

However, Frankish writers of the 830s make it clear that the Roman chant tradition had not been adopted in Francia as successfully as the reformers might have wished. Amalar of Metz and Helisacher, Abbot of St. Riquier, both recorded their distress at the continuing differences between Roman and Frankish practice.[12] By the later–ninth century, commentators such as John the Deacon and Notker Balbulus had begun to apportion blame for the continuing discrepancies between Roman and Frankish chant. While John the Deacon maintained that the barbaric Franks had been unable to manage the subtleties of Roman chant,[13] Notker Balbulus took the view that the Roman cantors were wilfully obstructive.[14] Wherever the blame really lay, Roman and Frankish practice were noticeably different, even though 'the will to Romanize and standardize was… a central goal of the Carolingian reform'.[15]

---

[9] For accounts of the adoption of Roman chant in Francia, see *WP*, 514–18; Levy, K., 'Toledo, Rome and the legacy of Gaul', *EMH* 4 (1984), 49–99; 49–50; Van Dijk, S. J. P., 'Papal Schola "versus" Charlemagne', in P. Fischer (ed.), *Organicae Voces: Festschrift J. Smits van Waesberghe* (Amsterdam, 1963), 21–30; Jeffery, P., 'Rome and Jerusalem: From Oral Tradition to Written Repertory', in G. Boone (ed.), *Essays on Medieval Music in Honor of David G. Hughes*: *Isham Library Papers* 4 (Harvard: Cambridge, Mass., 1995); 207–47; 234–42; Rankin, S., 'Carolingian Music', in R. McKitterick (ed.), *Carolingian Culture*, op. cit., 274–316; 275–9; Rankin, S., 'Ways of Telling Stories', in Boone, op. cit., 371–94; 371–6.

[10] Emerson, J., 'Plainchant' in S. Sadie, (ed.), *The New Grove Dictionary of Music and Musicians: Second Edition* (London, 2001) [Hereinafter *NG2*], vol. 19, 828.

[11] *WP*, 516–17.

[12] See J. McKinnon's articles in *NG2*, vol. 1; 441–2 (Amalar of Metz) and vol. 11; 340 (Helisacher).

[13] *Vita Sancti Gregorii Magni* (Rome, 872–75), edited in *Bibliotheca Patrum Latina* 75 (Paris, 1849), 62–242.

[14] *De Carolo Magno* (St. Gall, 883–84), edited in *St. Gallische Geschichtsquellen* 6 (St. Gall, 1918). See also the English translation in A. Grant, (ed. and transl.), *Early Lives of Charlemagne by Einhard and the Monk of Saint Gall* (New York, 1966)

[15] Jeffery, op. cit., 236.

The Roman origin of Gregorian chant[16] is made clear by the texts, which derive not from a version of the psalter common in Francia, but instead from the Roman psalter.[17] Further, 'the repertory of [the] Roman Mass Proper is virtually identical to that of the standard or so-called Gregorian repertory. The texts of the two are the same [and] they are similarly assigned throughout the year.'[18] These factors indicate that the Frankish repertory of Mass Proper chants originated in Rome. Furthermore, McKinnon has suggested that the spiritual and political stability needed for the development of an organised annual cycle of *schola* music was unlikely to have arisen in pre-Carolingian Francia. Instead, Mass chants in Merovingian Gaul are referred to as scriptural readings, they were sung by soloists, and there appears to have been some freedom in the choice of psalms for a given occasion.[19] McKinnon argues that the organisation of the chant repertory into a liturgical cycle was undertaken in Rome: 'The bulk of the Gregorian Mass Proper repertory appears to have been constructed within the Roman *schola cantorum*, probably during the later decades of the seventh century and the earlier decades of the eighth, and then, after being transmitted across the Alps by members of Pope Stephen's clerical entourage in the winter of 753–74, it was recreated, so to speak, by some body of Frankish singers, quite possibly the canons of Metz, who were

[16] Although the connection with Pope Gregory the Great is now widely regarded as being spurious, the term 'Gregorian chant' is generally associated with the chant tradition first found in Frankish manuscripts of the late–ninth century. See *WP*, 503–13; McKinnon, J., *The Advent Project: The Later–Seventh–Century Creation of the Roman Mass Proper* (Berkeley, 2000), 2; 96–8.

[17] Dyer, J., 'Latin Psalters, Old Roman and Gregorian Chants', *KmJb* 68 (1984), 11–30; 13. The Gallican Psalter is part of St. Jerome's Latin version of the Septuagint and was current in Francia throughout the period. St. Jerome also translated the Psalter directly from the Hebrew. The oldest complete Latin Bibles have this, known as the Psalterium Iuxta Hebraeos, but it did not replace the well-established Gallican version when the Vulgate was adopted in Francia in Alcuin's recension of the Bible in the ninth century. The Roman Psalter was Jerome's rapid correction of an ancient Latin version, undertaken during his stay in Rome. This version, exported to England at the time of its conversion by Gregory the Great, was also in use in Rome and Italy and is the version from which the texts of Roman and Gregorian chants are derived. See R. Weber, *Le Psautier Romain* (Rome, 1953).

[18] McKinnon, J., 'Vaticana Latina 5319: Witness to the Mid-Eighth-Century Roman Proper of the Mass', in *CP: Sopron*, 403–11; 403.

[19] McKinnon, J., 'Lector Chant versus Schola Chant: A Question of Historical Plausibility', in J. Szendrei and D. Hiley (eds.), *Laborare Fratres in Unum : Festschrift László Dobszay* (Hildesheim and Zurich, 1995), 201–11; 205–6; McKinnon, J., 'Centuries of Silence: Gaul', in *The Advent Project*, op. cit., 60–76.

organised by Bishop Chrodegang in 754–55 after the model of the Roman *schola.*'[20]

Although the evidence that the Gregorian Mass Proper chants had a Roman origin is conclusive, 'The Central Question of Gregorian Chant'[21] remains unanswered. While Gregorian chant is found in notated liturgical manuscripts right across Western Europe, dating from the late-ninth century onwards, the surviving manuscripts from the city of Rome itself, dating from the eleventh century onwards, preserve a different melodic tradition, known as Old Roman. As McKinnon has noted, 'the task facing Western chant scholars is the immensely difficult one of trying to determine which extant melodic version, the Old Roman or the Gregorian, is closer to the Roman original of the mid-eighth century'.[22]

As early as 1967, Cutter pointed out the limitations of the purely historical approach, remarking that the relationship between the two traditions would only be discovered if the evidence of the musical manuscripts was considered as well.[23] While this was a salutary warning, at least one musical analysis in this manner had already been undertaken. In 1955, Hucke analysed a sample of graduals in the two traditions and concluded that 'die Redaktion der fränkischen Überlieferung der Form und der Aufbau der altrömischen Vorlagen im allgemeinen sehr getreu folgt; dass die fränkische Überlieferung sehr fest und unveränderlich ist; dass die altrömische Überlieferung weniger fest ist, und Variantenbildung und Umsingungserscheinungen um kleinerem Rahmen erkennen lässt'.[24] He found also that 'die fränkische Fassung zeigt eine Neigung für weite, emphatische, raumgreifende Melodiezüge, die altrömische eher für kleingliedrige Melodik'.[25] These findings – the close relationship between musical form and structure in the two traditions and the differentiated melodic dialects, with an ornamented Roman style and a more emphatic Gregorian one – have been echoed by many scholars since.[26]

Many theories about the relationship between the two repertories have been promulgated since Bruno Stäblein first outlined a possible

---

[20] McKinnon, 'Lector Chant', op. cit., 202; McKinnon, *The Advent Project,* op. cit., 76; 402–3.

[21] See Apel's article of the same name in *JAMS* 9 (1956), 118–27.

[22] 'Vaticana Latina 5319', op. cit., 403.

[23] Cutter, P., 'The Question of the "Old Roman" Chant: A Reappraisal', *AM* 39 (1967), 2–20; 20.

[24] Hucke, H., 'Gregorianischer Gesang in altrömischer und fränkischer Überlieferung', *Archiv für Musikwissenschaft* 12 (1955), 74–87; 84.

[25] Ibid., 77.

[26] McKinnon, *The Advent Project,* op. cit., 380–81.

interpretation of the evidence in 1950.[27] Hucke was the first to argue that the differences between the repertories may be due to the alteration of the imported Roman chants to a Frankish singing style. 'Es ist offenbar, dass die Römer dem andersartigen Singen der Franken nicht mit ihren musikalischen Begriffen beikommen konnten... Hier ging es nicht mehr um Feinheiten beim Vortrag der dulcis modulatio. Es ging um eine Fremdartige Art und Weise des Singers, die dem Römer als "barbarisches Gebrüll" erscheinen mochte.'[28] This hypothesis is consistent with the complaint of John the Deacon about the lack of singing skills among the Frankish cantors, and with the Frankish records of the repeated attempts to learn the repertory from the Romans. The claim of scholars such as Lipphardt that Gregorian chant is the Roman chant of the eighth century, and that it was instead the Old Roman chant that changed, appears to be based on a desire to consider the Gregorian repertory as authoritative, rather than on an objective reading of the historical evidence.[29] The third, and perhaps most likely, alternative is that both traditions changed between the eighth century and the first extant notated manuscripts, but the question of which tradition is closer to the eighth-century original is still open.[30]

The current study uses parallel analysis of a specific group of chants, the eighth-mode tracts, in order to establish a body of concrete musical evidence with which to assess the way in which the Gregorian and Old Roman traditions are related. Other valuable comparative studies have been

---

[27] Stäblein, B., 'Zur Frühgeschichte des römischen Chorals', in H. Anglès (ed.), *Congresso Internazionale di Musica Sacra, Rome, 1950* (Tournai, 1952), 271–5. See also 'Zur Entstehung der gregorianischen Melodien', *Kirchenmusikalisches Jahrbuch* XXXV (1951), 5–9. The ensuing debate is summarised in many places, including: Cutter, 'The Question of the "Old Roman" Chant', op. cit.; Stäblein, B., 'Die Gesänge des altrömischen Graduale Vat. Lat. 5319: Einführung', in *Monumenta Monodica Medii Aevi* 2 (1970), 31*–83*; van Deusen, N., *An Historical and Stylistic Comparison of the Graduals of Gregorian and Old Roman Chant* (PhD, Indiana University, 1972); 7–21; Hughes, A., *Medieval Music – The Sixth Liberal Art* (Toronto, 1974), 89–93.

[28] 'It is clear that the Romans could not reconcile the Franks' different way of singing with their own musical ideas... Here it was not a question of subtleties in the performance of the *dulcis modulatio*. It was a question of the strange manner of the singers, which appeared to the Romans to be "barbaric bellowing"' (Hucke, H., 'Die Einführung des gregorianischen Gesanges im Frankenreich', *Römische Quartalschrift* 49 (1954), 172–87).

[29] Lipphardt, W., 'Gregor der Grosse und sein Anteil am römischen Antiphonar', in H. Anglès (ed.), *Congresso Internazionale di Musica Sacra, Rome, 1950* (Tournai, 1952), 248–54. See also Cutter, 'The Question of the "Old Roman" Chant', op. cit., 14.

[30] For a recent detailed account of this, with the conclusion that the Gregorian dialect generally reflects the eighth-century version more closely, see McKinnon, *The Advent Project*, op. cit., especially 375–403. Hiley (*WP*, 560–62) comes to the opposite conclusion.

undertaken by (for example) Nowacki on the antiphon,[31] van Deusen on the gradual,[32] and Maloy on the offertory.[33] By focusing on a small group of chants in the current study, it is possible to come to very detailed conclusions about how these chants were accurately transmitted before the development of pitched notation, and about the relationship between the Old Roman version, the Gregorian version, and the eighth-century version that was the ancestor of both.

The Eighth-Mode Tracts

Tracts came to be sung between the readings of the Mass in Lent and at other penitential times of year, such as the Ember Saturdays – that is, when it would be inappropriate to sing an alleluia.[34] There are two kinds of tract; those in the second mode and those in the eighth. The tracts within each mode fall into a distinct melodic family but both types are soloists' chants, sung through directly without a refrain. This distinguishes them from the gradual, alleluia and offertory, which are sung responsorially and have refrains that are sung both first and last. These refrains usually derive from a passage later in the psalm than the verse text. The eighth-mode tracts are fundamentally *in directum* chants: the textual structure makes it clear that these were not originally responsorial chants which were adapted at a late date to their present form. Consecutive verses of a psalm or canticle are always used to provide the text of an eighth-mode tract, often beginning with the first verse.[35]

In the Old Roman and Gregorian traditions, the same Feasts are assigned eighth-mode tracts, and they use the same texts. The 'core repertory' of eighth-mode tracts consists of those found regularly in the

---

[31] Nowacki, E., *Studies on the Office Antiphons of the Old Roman Manuscripts* (PhD, Brandeis University, 1980).

[32] van Deusen, N., *An Historical and Stylistic Comparison of the Graduals of Gregorian and Old Roman Chant* (PhD, Indiana University, 1972).

[33] Maloy, R., *The Offertory Chant: Aspects of Chronology and Transmission* (PhD, Cincinnati University, 2001).

[34] McKinnon believes that the origin of the tract lies in fourth-century Fore-Mass psalmody. See *The Advent Project*, op. cit., 282–3.

[35] For a detailed appraisal of this, and of the other characteristics indicating that the eighth-mode tracts were originally *in directum* psalmody, see Cullin, O., *Le Trait dans les Répertoires Vieux-Romain et Grégorien: Un Témoin de la Psalmodie sans Refrain* (PhD, University of Paris (Sorbonne), 1990), chapter 1: 'Les Fondaments du Style sans Refrain', 15–46.

ninth-century unnotated Graduals,[36] and in all notated Gregorian and Old Roman manuscripts, unless the relevant folios of a manuscript have been lost. These are the chants that form the basis of the analysis in Chapter 3. A small group of non-standard eighth-mode tracts does not appear in any of the unnotated ninth-century Graduals, in the earliest notated Graduals, or in many later Graduals; these chants are considered in Chapter 6. There are no chants in either the Gregorian or the Old Roman tradition whose identification as an eighth-mode tract is difficult: these chants are sung in a specific liturgical context and have a clearly defined musical structure.

In the eighth-mode tracts, the psalm verses are delineated, not by the alternation of solo and choral singing, but by a clear verse structure articulated by the use of six basic phrase shapes, each of which is associated with a specific formal context. The Gregorian and Old Roman traditions have closely related phrase shapes for each of these formal contexts, and they generally use the equivalent phrase for a given portion of text. Although the melodic outlines are usually the same in the two traditions, the Old Roman melodies are generally more decorated (Example 1.1).[37]

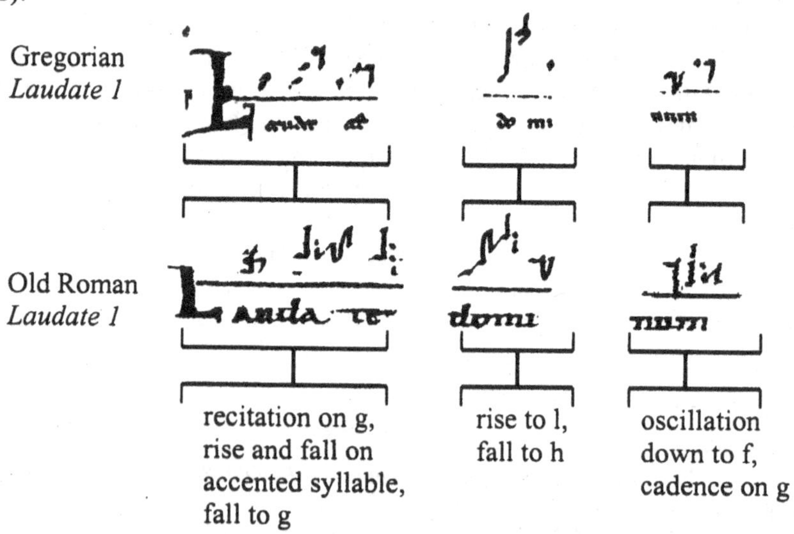

Example 1.1

[36] Published in *AMS*. 'Hesbert's Datierung der Handschrift Monza in das 8. Jahrhundert ist zu früh' (Hucke, H., 'Der Übergang von mündlicher zu schriftlicher Musiküberlieferung im Mittelalter', in *IMS 1977*, 180–91; 187).

[37] The a-p letter notation of *DIJ1* is adopted in this study for the concise indication of pitches.

Analytical Procedure

For the purposes of this analysis, each tract has been divided into verses and phrases according to the structure of the text. New verses in tracts and other chants are clearly signalled in medieval manuscripts, although in different ways. There is generally a capital letter, sometimes in a contrasting ink colour, and this may appear with or without the letter v (often in majuscule), and/or a Roman numeral. These chants are early evidence for the division of psalms into verses in the Middle Ages. Most, but not all, eighth-mode tracts have verse divisions at the same place in all manuscripts. The three Easter Vigil canticles, which were not sung in the monastic office as often as the psalms, form the majority of the eighth-mode tracts with varying verse divisions. However, these differences have no effect on the selection of musical phrases, and musical analysis makes it possible to identify which verse outline was current when the chants developed, as the combination of the verse divisions with the text defined which phrases could be used. The differences in verse division, then, are purely scribal, and did not affect the musical outline. It is also possible on musical grounds to reconstruct verse divisions that have been entirely eliminated from the scribal tradition: *Qui confidunt* is the most striking example of this, as will be seen in Chapter 3.

A musical phrase is defined for the present purpose as a melodic outline ending with a cadence. Cadences may be identified as such because of the syntax of the text and also because they have standard melodic shapes. Cadences generally recur on several (if not many) occasions across the genre and they almost always end on g or f. The end of a musical phrase almost always coincides with the end of a text sense unit: a complete sentence, a relative clause, a prepositional clause, the subject, the predicate, the subject + verb, or the object.

Once the chants are broken up according to the syntax and the stereotyped cadence shapes, six phrase types emerge. Phrase ***A*** is used at the beginning of tracts and phrase ***E*** is used at the beginning of verses other than the first. Phrase ***B*** is used to end the first half-verse and phrase ***C*** is used to begin the second half-verse. Phrase ***D*** is used at the ends of verses except for the last one, where phrase ***F*** is used. Where the text does not divide into four sense units, one or more of the musical phrases is omitted. These phrases form the basis of the analysis in Chapter 3.

To identify six phrase types as the foundation of the genre suggests that the eighth-mode tracts are unsophisticated compositions, with each portion of text simply being attached to the phrase appropriate to the formal context. However, it is necessary only to compare, for example, *Beatus uir* with *Ad te leuaui* to see that the eighth-mode tracts are constructed in a manner which is much more complex than this.[38] Apart from phrase ***F***, each of the six phrase types may be divided into two or more subgroups. The subgroups of some phrases are related to each other by no more than their cadential patterns; the subgroups of others have essentially the same melodic movements, with variants determined by the number of syllables. However, phrases with the same letter name almost always appear in the same formal context. Numerical subscripts are used in the present study to differentiate between the subgroups (***B1, B2, B3***, etc.), beginning with the most usual versions; these are often the shortest and simplest. Chapter 3 includes an extensive examination of the textual and formal circumstances under which the different versions of these six phrase shapes appear.

This detailed study of the contexts in which the phrase types were used forms the background for an investigation of the melodic state of each tract. While some tracts fit closely with the formal scheme outlined in the earlier part of the analysis, others deviate from it, and sometimes the Old Roman and Gregorian traditions use different phrase shapes for a given text. Textual factors such as assonance, rhyme or syntax can generally be shown to account for apparent inconsistencies. Textual associations stimulate the use of certain melodic phrases, even when this clashes with what one would expect in the formal context.

Formulaic composition of this type has sometimes been referred to as 'centonate'. The term is avoided in this study, largely because it seems to imply a repertory of abstract and stereotyped formulae that are assembled in a patchwork manner to make a new composition. Use of the term with reference to formulaic compositions such as the eighth-mode tracts, where the formulae have such strong formal connotations, has been fiercely criticised.[39]

Previous Scholarship on the Eighth-Mode Tracts

Existing analyses of the eighth-mode tracts range from generalised accounts to exhaustive studies of the genre, but these have always been restricted to either the Gregorian or the Old Roman tradition. Those of Kainzbauer and Nowacki are two recent examples, but their consideration of only one tradition limits the conclusions that can be drawn from the

[38] An alphabetical index of the core repertory of eighth-mode tracts in *BEN5* and *ORC* may be found in Appendix 3.

[39] Treitler, L., '"Centonate" chant: Übles Flickwerk or *E pluribus unus*?', *JAMS* 28 (1975), 1–23.

analyses.[40] There are several occasions where the use of an unexpected version of a phrase or the provenance of an unusual melodic outline can only be explained when the two traditions are considered in parallel.

Eighth-mode tract analyses usually start with the identification of six basic phrases, and include a discussion of the similarity of tract verses to psalmodic recitation. Wagner's description of the tracts as 'psalmodieähnliche Variationen'[41] is a frequent starting point, and the terminology of psalmodic recitation is often used. For example, Apel identifies three elements in each eighth-mode tract verse: Intonation, Mediation, and Termination (which sometimes consists of two phrases).[42] This threefold structure is also identified by Cullin, who considers that the psalmodic recitation 's'articule en fait sur une *intonation* plus ou moins variable, une *corde de récitation* ponctuée d'une cadence de *médiante*, et la suite du récitatif terminée par la cadence finale. La cadence de *flexe* est ajoutée en fonction de la longeur du texte.'[43]

Both of these descriptions imply that the eighth-mode tract verses are usually tripartite, with an extra phrase added on when the length of the text allows. Both Apel and Cullin centre their analyses on the four Easter Vigil tracts, and most of their verses are indeed tripartite, ending with phrase ***C***. Phrase ***D***, Cullin's *flexe*, is used only once – in *Sicut ceruus*. However, the rest of the tradition gives a different impression of the relative importance of this phrase. Outside the Easter Vigil tracts, it is used at the ends of 23 of the 26 verses in the Gregorian tradition, and at the ends of 21 of the 24 verses in the Old Roman tradition (as the final verses of eighth-mode tracts always end with phrase ***F***, they are not included in these statistics). On some of these occasions one or more phrases are omitted because there is insufficient text to articulate a quadripartite verse structure, but phrase ***D*** is still retained. Phrase ***D***, ending the verse with a cadence on g rather than the f cadence of phrase ***C***, is more central to the standard verse structure than Apel's and Cullin's descriptions show.

Kainzbauer also takes the Easter Vigil tracts as the point of departure

---

[40] Kainzbauer, X., 'Der Tractus Tetrardus – eine centologische Untersuchung', *Beiträge zur Gregorianik* 11 (Regensburg, 1991), 1–132; Nowacki, E., 'Text Declamation as a Determinant of Melodic Form in the Old Roman Eighth-Mode Tracts', *EMH* 6 (Cambridge, 1986), 193–225.

[41] Wagner, P., *Einführung in die gregorianischen Melodien*, vol. 3: 'Gregorianische Formenlehre' (Leipzig, 1921), 353.

[42] Apel, W., *Gregorian Chant* (Bloomington, Ind., 1958), 318.

[43] The psalmodic recitation 'is articulated by a more or less variable intonation, a reciting tone punctuated by a mediant cadence, and then recitation ended by the final cadence. The flex cadence may be added, according to the length of the text.' (Cullin, O., 'L'Office de Pâques comme Miroir du Chant Grégorien: du Concept Liturgique à la Réalisation Musicale', *Analyse Musicale* (1990), 19–25; 20).

for his analysis, and this distorts his results in a similar manner. He uses the label **NO** to label the single phrase *C*, although he acknowledges that this is a single phrase that appears in a single formal slot. 'Der Grund, **N** und **O** trotzdem getrennt zu behandeln ist zweifach: 1. Legt die Vielfältigkeit der Varianten ein solches Vorgehen um der Übersichtlichkeit willen nahe, 2. Verwenden die OstervigilTR Cento **NO** als Zweiter Halbvers-Anfang *und* Ende, **N** ist als Anfang, **O** bildet das Zweiter Halbvers-Ende, wodurch **N** und **O** strukturell als je eigene Centones verwendet und ausgewiesen sind.'[44] Regarding Kainzbauer's first reason, it will be shown below that there are four versions of phrase *C* corresponding to different textual situations. It is not necessary separately to define the beginning and end of the phrase in order to give an accurate indication of the musical state. Kainzbauer's second reason for the **NO** labelling appears to be a desire to make the structure of the Easter Vigil tracts appear quadripartite. This actually distorts their tripartite outline, and makes the quadripartite structure of other eighth-mode tracts less transparent.

Analysis of a single, 'representative' tract also obscures the richness of the genre. Hucke has analysed a specimen eighth-mode tract, *De profundis*, in terms of psalmodic recitation.[45] This tract has certain idiosyncrasies not typical of the tradition as a whole: phrase ***E*** is only used once in this tract, at the beginning of the second verse, whereas in the rest of the genre it is widely used at the beginnings of verses. In Hucke's analysis, this phrase is treated merely as part of the 'recitation' that anticipates the 'mediation' (phrase ***B***), thus obscuring the importance of the phrase elsewhere in the tradition. Hucke labels phrase ***C*** as 'Intonation – Recitation – Flex',[46] although this lends a great deal of formal weight to a single phrase that only has recitation if the length of the text demands it. The 'Intonation' in the first verse of *De profundis* begins with a melodic figure that is only otherwise used at the beginning of the second half-verse in the third verse of the same tract. On this second occasion, the melodic figure is used to begin phrase ***D***. To analyse *De profundis* in isolation gives the impression that the second half of the verse begins in a uniform way throughout the repertory. In fact, this particular intonation is peculiar to this tract, and is stimulated by a special textual cue: both texts begin 'domine'.

These examples illustrate how it can be misleading to draw parallels

---

[44] 'The reason nevertheless to treat **N** and **O** separately is twofold. 1. The diversity of the variants suggests such an action for the sake of openness. 2. The Easter Vigil tracts use cento **NO** as the beginning *and* end of the second half-verse. **N** is the beginning and **O** forms the end of the second half-verse, so **N** and **O** are used and identified structurally as separate centos.' (Kainzbauer, X., op. cit., 31–2).

[45] 'Tract', *NG* 19, 108–10.

[46] This contrasts with Cullin's identification of phrase ***D*** as the *flexe*.

between eighth-mode tract structure and psalmodic recitation. Although it is possible that the origins of the genre lie in simple eighth-mode psalmodic recitation, by the time the genre was structured in the manner in which it appears in notated manuscripts, the chants were constructed of melodic phrases that are much more complicated than those of psalmodic recitation, each associated with a specific formal and textual context. The varying demands of the text can lead the structure far away from a psalmodic outline. McKinnon's article in the *New Grove Second Edition* gives a much more circumspect account than Hucke's earlier article.[47] McKinnon briefly acknowledges the presence of recurring phrases associated with particular formal contexts, and presents both the psalm-tone-model view and that which sees the formally specific phrases as 'a natural response to the need to mark off major breaks in the text'.[48] 'It is wholly reasonable to suppose that the chant's melodic characteristics were an essential part of the tract from the start, yet it is still possible to imagine that the psalm tone model might somehow have figured in the creation of the genre.'[49]

Apel identifies 'nine recurring G-phrases other than those for the opening and the close',[50] connecting the most common of these ($G_{1\text{-}3}$) with particular positions in the verse. 'The other G-phrases occur only a few times, which makes it difficult to say whether they were regarded as initial, mediant, or terminal formulae.'[51] This is not so, as will be made clear in Chapter 3. Comparison of the cadences of these phrases, the formal contexts in which they appear, the relationships of the melodic material with other phrases, and an understanding of the textual prompts, makes it possible to identify each of these G-phrases with a specific formal context.

Apel's analysis occurs in a general introduction to Gregorian chant; Hucke's and McKinnon's are relatively short dictionary articles. One would not expect any more than a broad overview of the genre in these contexts. A firm impression is given of the similarities between the eighth-mode tracts across the Gregorian repertory, and of the basic building blocks of the genre, but there is no subtle exploration of how the chants are constructed. The analyses of Kainzbauer, Nowacki, and Cullin are considerably more detailed.[52]

---

[47] *NG2*, vol. 25, 674–7.

[48] *WP*, 85.

[49] *NG2*, vol. 25, 676–7, referring to *WP*, 85.

[50] Apel, W., *Gregorian Chant,* op. cit., 321.

[51] Ibid., 322.

[52] Kainzbauer, 'Der Tractus Tetrardus', op. cit., 1–132; Nowacki, E., 'Text Declamation as a Determinant of Melodic Form in the Old Roman Eighth-Mode Tracts', *EMH* 6 (Cambridge, 1986), 193–225; Cullin, O., *Le Trait dans les Répertoires Vieux-Romain et Grégorien: un Témoin de la Psalmodie sans Refrain* (PhD, University of Paris, Sorbonne, 1990).

Kainzbauer's analysis of the Gregorian eighth-mode tracts shows the fundamental effect which the text, in particular the accentuation patterns and the lengths of the sense units, has had on the way in which the phrase patterns are used. The textual accents or stresses are also central to the composition of these chants: almost every melodic movement is associated exclusively with accented or with unaccented syllables. The consistency with which this technique is applied means that the melodic shapes may be used as a guide to the medieval manner of articulating these texts. The melodic movements associated with accents are marked with arrows in the catalogue of phrase shapes in Appendix 2, but the thoroughness of Kainzbauer's work makes further detailed exposition unnecessary. Similarly, in his analysis of the Old Roman tracts, Nowacki identifies the basic phrases and the varying versions in which they appear, and concludes that the text is of fundamental importance in the construction of the genre.

Cullin's doctoral thesis is mainly concerned with showing the common formal, modal and stylistic origins of the tracts and other genres of chant *sans refrain*. He also identifies connections between the Old Roman and Gregorian eighth-mode tracts. He asserts that, while the melodic material used is sometimes very different, there are Old Roman phrases equivalent to the Gregorian phrases that are used in parallel formal contexts, and there is sometimes a close melodic resemblance between the two traditions. Such connections are indeed to be found between the two traditions, but their full extent, and the implications of there being such connections, has not previously been explored.

The parallel nature of the eighth-mode tracts in the Gregorian and Old Roman traditions has not hitherto been investigated in detail. The analysis undertaken in Chapter 3 enables these chants to be used as evidence in assessing the nature of the oral tradition within which their common origin lies. Although the significance of such parallels in a single genre should not be exaggerated, this detailed analysis provides a valuable tool for the reassessment of the relationship between Gregorian and Old Roman chant.

Chapter 2
The Primary Evidence

Introduction

There is no single, authoritative version of an eighth-mode tract. Instead, different versions of the chants are found in manuscripts from different regions, different periods and different monastic traditions. It is therefore important to know which elements can and do vary between manuscripts and to appreciate the variants' significance before drawing conclusions about the fundamental characteristics of the genre or about the way it was understood by those who performed and notated it.

The analysis in Chapter 3 is based on the versions of the eighth-mode tracts in just two manuscripts; one in the Old Roman tradition (*ORC*), and one in the Gregorian tradition (*BEN5*).[1] The purpose of the present chapter is to identify how these two Graduals relate to the other manuscripts in their respective traditions, and to define the extent to which the melodic outlines of the chants vary in different manuscripts. The subsequent analysis is undertaken with a constant awareness of any conflicting evidence in other manuscripts. Great care is taken not to draw general conclusions from local characteristics and, where necessary, more than one manuscript is cited.

BEN5 and *ORC* have been chosen for their clarity and legibility, and because they use similar notational systems (Beneventan and Central Italian, respectively). *ORC* has been chosen to represent the Old Roman tradition because it is the oldest extant Old Roman Gradual, dated 1071.[2] *BEN5*, chosen primarily because of the notational similarities with *ORC* and because the two manuscripts are roughly contemporary, has versions of the eighth-mode tracts that are compatible with those found in sources from other areas of Western Europe: 'the connections between southern Italy and southern France have been well documented for musical variants and repertory'.[3]

---

[1] A table of the manuscripts cited in this study, their sigla, dates, and origins, may be found on pp. *xiii–xv*, above.

[2] Although *ORC* is liturgically incomplete, it includes all of the Feasts of the Lenten period, so that the repertory of tracts is as large as in the other Old Roman manuscripts.

[3] Gyug, R., *Missale Ragusinum: The Missal of Dubrovnik* (Toronto, 1990), 169. See also Stuart, N., 'Melodic "Corrections" in an Eleventh-Century Gradual (Paris, B.N., lat. 903)', *JPMMS* 2, (1979) 2–10; 2: 'on the basis of neumatic variants through the whole repertory, [Aquitanian and Beneventan manuscripts] are quite closely related to each other.'

It is unnecessary to provide a detailed description of the neume shapes and their interpretation here. For this, the reader is referred to the introductions to the facsimile editions of the two manuscripts.[4] The notation makes use of a primitive form of staff notation on lines, with the c-line coloured yellow (usually invisible in black and white photographs) and the f-line coloured red. The melodic interpretation of the point neumes, and of most compound neumes, is self-explanatory. Virgae (single notes) are found alone or at the beginning of neume groups, and are indicated by a short vertical line (for example, '(seruite) do(mino)' in *Iubilate* in *ORC*).[5] Longer vertical lines indicate two notes. These indicate two-note descending figures (clives) when preceded by a fine diagonal pen stroke leading to the top of the sign. This can occur also with notes a single step apart, which might otherwise be interpreted as virgae (for example, 'In(trate)' in *Iubilate* in *ORC*). Vertical lines indicate two-note ascending figures (pedes) when preceded by a hook on the left-hand side at the base of the vertical line, or when joined by a thin penstroke to the preceding (lower) note (for example, '(ser)ui(te)' in *Iubilate* in *ORC*). Vertical neume groups indicate descending figures unless the lowest note is written to the left of those following it, or the neume continues to the right from the top note (for example, '(In)tra(te)' in *Iubilate* in *ORC*). Liquescence is indicated by a horizontal (often ornate) line through the note. To assist in the interpretation of this notation, a transcription of a representative example of each phrase shape is included in the catalogue of phrase shapes in Appendix 2.

The Gregorian Tradition

The Manuscript Sample

The manuscript sample consists of many of the readily available manuscripts in facsimile, on microfilm, and in English libraries. Although this sample is fairly randomly chosen, some effort has been made to consider manuscripts from different times and regions, and in different notational styles. To identify one manuscript, or one group of manuscripts, as more authoritative than others is not the purpose of the present study. Instead, each group of selected manuscripts is illustrative of facets of chronological change and regional style. There is no attempt to give a complete picture of the transmission of Gregorian chant from the earliest

---

[4] Lütolf, M., *Das Graduale von Santa Cecilia in Trastevere* (Cologny-Genève, 1987), 24–31; *PM* 15, 71–161.

[5] For this, and for subsequent illustrations in this paragraph, see p. 335.

notated sources until some arbitrary cut-off point. The sample is necessarily incomplete because of the huge quantity of material available to the researcher in this field.

The earliest surviving Graduals, available in facsimile in *Paléographie Musicale*,[6] are central to this study because they represent the chronological strata as close as possible to the eighth-century Roman chant adopted in Francia. However, later neumed manuscripts are not discounted as they provide valuable witnesses to the minor details in which the chants increasingly varied in their written form. There is also detailed consideration of diastematic manuscripts from various areas of Western Europe. This is partly to ensure that the analysis, which focuses on melodic outline, has the broadest possible scope, but also because a critical assessment of the pitches found in the eighth-mode tracts across Europe in the eleventh and twelfth centuries is an essential backdrop to the interpretation of the earlier, unpitched, manuscripts. Further, pitched manuscripts are important for comparative study because the Old Roman tradition is notated exclusively in diastematic notation.

The lack of significant variants in the manuscript sample is striking.[7] In the earliest manuscripts, there are few variants of any kind. This is consistent with the Carolingian desire for uniformity: 'To err was in some sense to sin.'[8] Later neumed manuscripts have more variations in minor inflections, and the pitched manuscripts make manifest certain types of pitch variation that may have been present in the tradition for some time, but which are not shown by neumatic notations. The manuscript evidence supports the contention that as the tradition became more widely known in writing, and as notated versions of chants played a more active role in their transmission, local variations filtered in.

The earliest manuscripts The first group of manuscripts dates from the late ninth and early tenth centuries and contains only the core repertory of eighth-mode tracts. The St. Gall tradition is represented by *GAL1*, *GAL2*, and *MUR3*, and the Western Frankish tradition by *CHA1* and *LAN*.[9] These

---

[6] Hereinafter referred to as *PM*.

[7] For definitions of 'significant' and 'insignificant' melodic variants, see Hughes, D., 'Evidence for the Traditional View of the Transmission of Gregorian Chant', *JAMS* 40 (1987), 377–401.

[8] Ibid., 399.

[9] For descriptions of these manuscripts see:
GAL1: *PM* 2/2, 11–23; *GAL2*: *PM* 1, 71–95; *MUR3*: *PM* 4, 7–9; Lang O., (ed.), *Codex Einsiedeln 121: Kommentar* (Weinheim, 1991), especially Fischer, R., 'Das Graduale des Codex 121 der Stiftsbibliothek Einsiedeln', 71–95, and Joppich, G., 'Der rhetorische Komponente in der Notation des Codex 121 von Einsiedeln', 119–88; *CHA1*: *PM* 11, 23–131; *LAN*: *PM* 10, 17–40.

manuscripts are among the oldest surviving notated Graduals[10] and are widely available in facsimile in *PM*. The sample of early neumed sources used in this study is therefore representative of the surviving material.[11]

The original stimulus for the publication of the *PM* volumes was the search for the *Urtext* of Gregorian chant.[12] Although it now seems clear that no 'pure' and 'uncontaminated' written *Urtext* is recoverable, the intensive study of these early manuscripts means that the interpretation of the notation provides few problems, at least on a general level. There is little doubt about the melodic contours indicated by the neumes even though the exact pitches cannot always be reconstructed with certainty by reference to the later, pitched, manuscripts.

The melodic outlines of these early manuscripts are strikingly closely related, as will become clear below. They therefore provide a reference point for melodic outline, though not for pitch, in the examination of later, less unified, versions of the chants. The three St. Gall manuscripts even use identical neume shapes on many occasions. However, *CHA1* and *LAN*, which also have closely related melodic contours, use completely different notational styles: Breton and Messine respectively. Because the scripts and notations of the earliest surviving manuscripts are not directly related, it is clear that the ninth-century chant tradition was widely unified, either by the existence of a single neumed exemplar several decades before 900 (allowing time for the development of local notational styles), or by an effort of human will within an oral tradition. The strength of the evidence in favour of each of these hypotheses will be assessed in Chapter 4.

The later neumed manuscripts The sample of later neumed sources concentrates on manuscripts originating from the Eastern Frankish lands and northern Italy, where the arrival of pitched notation was late and scattered. The Bodleian Library is particularly rich in such manuscripts, which illustrate a shift away from a highly unified chant tradition to one where local trends are more clearly visible.

STM is a twelfth-century manuscript from a collegiate church of St.

---

[10] *GAL1* is in fact a Cantatorium, containing only the soloists' chants.

[11] Another complete Gradual, older than *GAL2*, survives in St. Gall. This is St. Gall 342, dated by Rankin to the early–tenth century. See Rankin, S., 'Ways of Telling Stories', in G. Boone (ed.), *Essays on Medieval Music in Honor of David G. Hughes*: *Isham Library Papers* 4 (Cambridge, Mass., 1995), 371–94; 376–86. For descriptions of other early Graduals, see Jeffery, P., 'The Oldest Sources of the *Graduale*: A Preliminary Checklist of MSS Copied before about 900', *JM* 2 (1983), 316–21.

[12] See Bergeron, K., *Decadent Enchantments: The Revival of Gregorian Chant at Solesmes* (Berkeley, 1998), especially Chapter 4.

Martin in Northern Italy.[13] Hiley uses the evidence of the German neumes in which it is notated, and also a rare Kyrie melody, to identify the manuscript as originating either from Aquileia or from Moggio, which is a little north of Aquileia.[14] Moggio is also represented by *MOG4*, which is from the monastery of St. Gall in Moggio, and dates from about 1216.[15] *PAS2* is a twelfth-century manuscript originating from the monastery of St. Paul in Carinthia.[16] Both *PAS2* and *MOG4* use adiastematic German neumes. *TYR*, a twelfth-century manuscript with St. Gall neumes, originates from Innichen, north west of Aquileia.[17]

As will be made clear below, these Eastern Frankish manuscripts do not reflect a melodic tradition as unified as that of the early group of manuscripts. Standard melodic shapes vary within each manuscript, not only in the neume shapes used and the interpretations these imply (for example, the pressus is used fairly interchangeably with the clivis within melismas), but also in the broader melodic outlines. By the twelfth century, therefore, the consistency and unity of the earlier tradition was either no longer highly prized, or was no longer possible in the Eastern Frankish lands.

The shift towards a less unified and less internally consistent written tradition appears to have begun as early as the eleventh century. *BRE* is an eleventh-century manuscript from the cathedral of Brescia, notated in adiastematic North Italian neumes.[18] Like the twelfth-century Eastern Frankish manuscripts, *BRE* has many internal inconsistencies. These occur in the melodic outline and also in the varying neume shapes used for standard melodic patterns.[19] But not all manuscripts are copied in this apparently casual manner: *LAV*, a Bolognese manuscript, dates from the second quarter of the eleventh century and shows a high degree of internal consistency, using stereotyped patterns of neumes for standard phrases.[20]

Three other unpitched manuscripts are considered here. The first is *CLU1*, the only surviving early medieval Gradual from the monastery of

---

[13] VD, 126; Flotzinger, R., *Choralhandschriften österreichischer Provenienz in der Bodleian Library, Oxford* (Vienna, 1991), 87–9; 88.

[14] *WP*, 419.

[15] VD, 91; *GR* II, 88; Flotzinger, op. cit., 49–66; 53.

[16] Flotzinger, op. cit., 9–34; 16. Earlier studies have identified the manuscript as originating more generally from Passau or Prague (VD, 124), or from the diocese of Salzburg (*GR* II, 88).

[17] VD, 96; Flotzinger, op. cit., 73–87; 78.

[18] VD, 95; *GR* II, 89. See also Barezzani, M., *La Notazione Neumatica di un Codice Bresciano (Secolo XI)* (Cremona, 1981), 14–19.

[19] For examples of some of the ways in which *BRE* differs from the mainstream melodic tradition, see Barezzani, op. cit., 109–13.

[20] *PM 18*, 9–40; *GR* II, 119–20.

Cluny itself.[21] Consideration of this manuscript provides a foundation for the examination of pitched manuscripts from north-west Europe that were affected to a greater or lesser extent by Cluniac reform. Ferreira asserts that 'most of the characteristic Cluniac variants in the Graduale are closely related to manuscripts from the Parisian area: early sources from Noyon and Saint-Denis, but also later sources from Paris (and Cambrai).'[22] In order further to assess this relationship, two other manuscripts from north-west Francia are considered here. *NOY4* is a late tenth-century manuscript from the Archdiocese of Reims. Although it probably comes from Corbie or Noyon, close to Laon, the melodic variants indicate that *NOY4* represents more closely the chant tradition of the Abbey of Saint-Denis, with which it appears to have been musically and culturally connected.[23] For this reason, *DEN1*, an eleventh-century manuscript from the Abbey of Saint-Denis, is also considered here.[24] The melodic outlines of the tracts in *NOY4* have many minor variants, and the manuscript has unexpected verse divisions in several places.

NOY4 does not have exactly the same tract repertory as the earlier manuscripts. This is due in part to an accident of manuscript survival: the Easter Vigil tracts are not included in the manuscript because there is a lacuna from Palm Sunday to the saints' days just before the feast of the Ascension. *NOY4* also has a unique version of *Beatus uir*, which bears no relation at all to the usual melodic shapes of eighth-mode tracts and is instead in the form of a second-mode tract. At first sight this seems like a complete anomaly. However, the tract with the same text sung on the same feast in *DEN1*, while indisputably an eighth-mode tract, has a different melody from that of the rest of the tradition. This suggests that *Beatus uir* was not firmly established as an eighth-mode tract within the chant tradition adopted in Francia, and supports the contention made in Chapter 7, below, that this tract is less ancient than the rest of the core repertory.

Pitched manuscripts It has already been mentioned that pitched notation came late to the Eastern Frankish lands. *KLO1* is the only pitched

[21] For descriptions of the manuscripts directly connected with Cluny, see Ferreira, M. P., *Music at Cluny: The Tradition of Gregorian Chant for the Proper of the Mass. Melodic Variants and Microtonal Nuances* (PhD, Princeton University, 1997), 45–72, and 58–61 for a description of *CLU1*. See also Hourlier, J., 'Remarques sur la Notation Clunisienne', *Revue Grégorienne* 30 (1961), 231–40, and Ferreira, M. P., 'The Cluny Gradual: its Notation and Melodic Character', in *CP: Eger*, 205–15.

[22] Ferreira, *Music at Cluny*, op. cit., 103.

[23] On the attribution of *NOY4*, see Walters Robertson, A., *The Service Books of the Royal Abbey of Saint-Denis* (Oxford, 1991), 425–34. See also *PM* 16, 15–47.

[24] Hesbert, R-J., 'Le Graduel de Saint-Denis', in *Monumenta Musica Sacrae* 5 (Paris, 1981); XI–XXXIII; *GR* II; 92.

manuscript from this region readily available for use in this study. It is a twelfth-century source with Messine Klosterneuburg notation on lines. It is from the monastery of Klosterneuburg, near Vienna.[25] A combination of the evidence of this isolated diastematic source with that of the four unpitched Eastern Frankish sources described above gives a broader picture of the nature of the chant tradition in this area in the twelfth century.

Two eleventh-century Aquitanian Graduals are considered in detail here, and a third has also been consulted. These manuscripts use a partially pitched notation, with carefully heighted neumes around dry point lines a fourth apart. As there are no clefs, it is not possible on the evidence of these manuscripts alone to determine where the semitones lie. If the dry point lines indicate g and c, for example, as in the eighth-mode tracts, there is a semitone below the upper line and another two notes below the lower one. If the lines indicate c and f, there are semitones below each of the lines.

ALB is from the monastery of St. Michel de Gaillac, a Benedictine foundation close to Albi, and dates from before 1079.[26] *YRX* is from the monastery of St. Yrieix, and dates from before 1060, when the monastery was secularised.[27] *TOU* is an eleventh-century Gradual from Toulouse.[28] The close relationship between these three manuscripts has long been recognised: 'C'est bien la même écriture, fine et régulière, la même notation à points superposés, et, dans l'ensemble, un dispositif analogue.'[29] *TOU* has not been considered in detail here because it would serve only to duplicate material.

Three Beneventan manuscripts have been consulted in the preparation of this study. *BEN5* is a twelfth-century diastematic Gradual from Benevento.[30] *BEN1* is a neumed Missal, possibly from Salerno, dating from around 1000, and with almost identical melodic contours to *BEN5*.[31] *RAG* is a thirteenth-century noted Missal from Ragusa (present-day Dubrovnik). 'The notation… is closely comparable in the appearance of the neumes and in the organisation of the staff to Ben 34 [*BEN5*].'[32] The Beneventan manuscripts are not only closely related to each other but, as was noted above, have very similar versions of the Mass Proper chants to the

---

[25] *PM* 19, 7*–42*; *GR* II, 53.
[26] *GR* II, 93–94.
[27] *PM* 13; 9–53, especially 9–16; *GR* II, 96.
[28] *GR* II, 64.
[29] *PM* 13; 43. The writer argues that the three were copied by Moissac scribes, or at least on the model of a common Moissac exemplar (52–3).
[30] Kelly, T. F., *The Beneventan Chant* (Cambridge, 1989), 300–1; *PM* 15, 9–70 and 162–175; *GR* II, 32.
[31] Kelly, op. cit., 300; *PM* 20, 9*–25*; *GR* II, 31.
[32] Gyug, R., *Missale Ragusinum: The Missal of Dubrovnik* (Toronto, 1990), 36. See also VD, 127.

Aquitanian manuscripts despite using a completely different notational system. The Beneventan and Aquitanian manuscripts are largely internally consistent, using standard patterns of note shapes for standard melodic phrases.

Another group of pitched manuscripts represents institutions directly or indirectly affected by Cluniac reforms.[33] Any investigation of chant transmission in the eleventh century must take into account the huge influence of the monastic reforms that had their source in the Benedictine monastery of Cluny.[34] *CLU1*, the neumed Gradual from the monastery of Cluny, forms a focus for the evaluation of this group of manuscripts, but the lack of pitched notation limits its use.

Cluniac traditions were adopted directly at Lewes, in East Sussex. This monastery is represented by *LEW*, a Gradual in square notation that dates from the second half of the thirteenth century.[35] Despite its late date, *LEW* has pitches that are almost always compatible with the neumatic outlines of *CLU1*.[36] This may give the impression that the central monastery at Cluny had a great influence on the pattern of the liturgy, and specifically of the musical observances, in reformed monastic houses. However, Cluniac reforms were adopted in different places in different ways. Some monasteries were constitutionally linked with Cluny, but others had more casual connections, and the nature of the connection affected the extent to which Cluny intervened in the affairs of the monastery.[37]

Cluniac reforms were widespread in Aquitaine and in Normandy, and were often instigated by powerful laymen. The career of William of Volpiano is well known. Details of his early monastic career in Northern Italy, his transferral to Cluny, his appointment to the abbacy of St. Bénigne in Dijon, and his subsequent career as a Cluniac reformer in Normandy at the invitation of Duke Richard II, have been well rehearsed, and need no further elaboration here.[38] *DIJ1* appears to have been copied at St. Bénigne

---

[33] To examine the chant styles of other reforming monasteries, such as Gorze and Hirsau, is beyond the scope of this study. Hiley (*WP*, 578) has pointed out that 'assessing such relationships with the aid of the Solesmes 'lieux variants' in proper-of-mass chants is... problematical, for the observed difference between eastern sources is so slight'.

[34] There are many accounts of this, including McKitterick, R., *The Frankish Kingdoms under the Carolingians 751–987* (London, 1983), 278–304; and Cowdrey, H. E. J., *The Cluniacs and the Gregorian Reform* (Oxford, 1970), 67–75.

[35] See Holder, S., 'The Noted Cluniac Breviary-Missal of Lewes: Fitzwilliam Museum Manuscript 369', *JPMMS* 8 (1985) 25–32. See also Ferreira, *Music at Cluny*, op. cit., 57; Leroquais, V., *Le Bréviare-Missel du Prieuré Clunisien de Lewes* (Paris, 1935).

[36] This has already been noted by Ferreira, op. cit., 8.

[37] Hunt, N. (ed.), *Cluniac Monasticism in the Central Middle Ages* (London, 1971), 2.

[38] See, for example, Browne, A. C., 'The a-p system of Letter Notation', *MD* 35 (1981), 5–54; Lawrence, C. H., *Medieval Monasticism* (New York, 1984), 101–2. See also Pognon, E., *L'An Mille: Oeuvres de Liutprand, Raoul Glaber, Adémar de Chabannes, Adalberon et*

in Dijon at the instigation of William of Volpiano, and perhaps even with his participation, in order to record the newly reformed chant of the Abbey.[39]

The influence of the Cluniac tradition, as filtered through Dijon, was immense, and Hiley has demonstrated that manuscripts from the monasteries reformed by William of Volpiano show very similar chant traditions to the one found in Dijon.[40] Manuscripts from such places as Mont-Saint Michel, Fécamp, St. Evroult, and Jumièges are therefore not considered further here. *ROG1* is a thirteenth-century Gradual from Rouen cathedral, a secular foundation.[41] Hiley has observed that although the alleluia series of *ROG1* and *DIJ1* are different, the two manuscripts have similar proper variants.[42] He has argued that a cantor at the cathedral before the copying of *ROG1* must have been trained in the Dijon singing style. This is borne out by the fact that the two manuscripts have almost identical versions of the eighth-mode tracts.

Bec was also reformed by Cluny and, like Dijon, became in its turn a centre for monastic reform. *BEC* is an important point of reference for the Bec singing tradition although, as it is a later, thirteenth-century, source,[43] alternative manuscripts have been considered here. *SAB* provides an example of a late twelfth-century manuscript closely modelled on Bec traditions: 'The most assiduous follower of Bec practice in Britain is St. Albans. And I take this to mean that St. Albans had its exemplars direct from the continent.'[44] The monastery of Meulan, south-east of Rouen, was also reformed by Bec. Comparison of *ROP*, a late twelfth-century Gradual from this monastery,[45] with *SAB* shows the unity of Bec-influenced practice. Despite having quite different notational styles (*SAB* is in square notation and *ROP* has Norman point neumes on lines) the melodies of the two manuscripts are closely allied.

Comparison of *CLU1* and *LEW* with *DIJ1* and *ROG1*, *ROP* and *SAB* shows that the Cluniac reforms as filtered through Bec and Dijon resulted

---

Helgaud (Paris, 1947), 91, a translation into French of Raoul Glaber's Life of William of Volpiano.

39 Hansen, F. E., *H159 Montpellier: Tonary of St. Bénigne of Dijon* (Copenhagen, 1974), 20*–1*.

40 Hiley, D., 'The Norman Chant Traditions – Normandy, Britain, Sicily', *PRMA* 107 (1980–1), 1–33.

41 Loriquet, H., Pothier, J. and Colette, A., *Le Graduel de l'Eglise Cathédrale de Rouen au XIIIe siècle*, 2 vols. (Rouen, 1907); *GR* II, 96.

42 Hiley, D., op. cit., 7.

43 Paris, B.N., Lat. 1105. See *GR* II, 97.

44 Hiley, D., op. cit., 9. See also VD, 104.

45 Hiley, D., op. cit., 14. Reproduced in facsimile in Thibaut, J., *Monuments de la Notation Ekphonetique et Neumatique de l'Eglise Latine* (St. Petersburg, 1912). For codicological information, see 54–68.

in closely related but distinct chant traditions. Cluniac-reformed chant is also clearly differentiated melodically from other Gregorian chant traditions.

IRI is a twelfth-century manuscript from a cathedral in Northern Ireland, notated in Anglo-Norman point neumes.[46] One might imagine a direct connection with *ROP*, which uses the same notational style. However, while *IRI* has a four-line staff with the b-flat/b-natural sign functioning as a clef, *ROP* has a three-line staff with the middle line labelled 'a'. Although the two manuscripts have similar neumes, *IRI* tends to have separate note shapes whereas *ROP* tends to have more continuous neumes. Further, the shape used for the clivis is quite different in the two manuscripts: in *IRI* it is arched in shape, but in *ROP* it is angular, consisting of a horizontal stroke followed by a vertical stroke down. The similarities of notational style in these two sources are superficial.

The melodic variants in *IRI*, while not identical with those found in any of the three centres of Cluniac reform considered here, are generally more closely aligned to the traditions of the Western Frankish manuscripts *DEN1* and *NOY4*, and perhaps to the traditions of Cluniac foundations, than to those of Benevento, Aquitaine, or Eastern Francia. Gwynn cites Norman, specifically Rouen, trading influences with Ireland, and remarks that the Codex Bigotianus[47] is a witness to links between Fécamp and Ireland in the eleventh century.[48] Cluniac customs are also known to have filtered to Ireland through Lorraine,[49] and the eleventh-century cathedral schools of northern Francia may also have provided a point of contact: 'I feel sure that Irish scholars began to frequent these centres soon after the turn of the [eleventh-twelfth] century.'[50] Given such cultural exchanges, it is unsurprising to find Anglo-Norman point neumes used to notate versions of the Mass Proper melodies influenced by Cluny, and more particularly by the Corbie-St. Denis sphere, in a twelfth-century Irish manuscript.

Manuscript Variants Not Considered in This Study

The present study focuses on melodic outline. For this reason, the manner in which a phrase is notated is generally only of interest in so far as it defines the intended melodic contour. The variants in neumed manuscripts tend to be interpretative, affecting repeated notes, nuances, liquescence, and other ornamental figures, and indicating the way a particular cantor might

[46] *GR* II, 89; VD, 90.
[47] Paris, B.N., Lat. 3182, an Irish Penitential.
[48] Gwynn, A., *The Irish Church in the Eleventh and Twelfth Centuries* (Dublin, 1992), 44.
[49] Ibid., 2.
[50] Ibid., 46.

perform the melody. Such manuscripts provide an abundance of evidence pertaining to the performance practice of these melodies in different regions at different times. However, the precise performance implications of the rhythmic and expressive signs remain contentious, and continue to be the subject of intensive investigation in the branch of scholarship that has become known as 'semiology'.[51] This means that a detailed exploration of the way in which the eighth-mode tracts' manuscript tradition can inform us about the performance practice of soloists' chants in the Middle Ages lies well beyond the scope of the present study.[52]

Spelling variations are not considered in this study, except for the very rare occasions when the use of a different word leads to a different melodic outline. 'Despite daily exposure to the psalter and the chants derived from it, inattentive scribes could still introduce unintentional variants without thereby creating a subsequent stemma.'[53] Bernard observes, in his description of the eighth-mode tracts, that the Frankish sources have the text variant 'celis' in *Ad te leuaui*, unlike the Roman Psalter, the Vulgate and the Old Roman Graduals, which have 'celo'. He identifies this as an ancient Merovingian text variant and claims that 'çela prouve que la réforme carolingienne et la romanisation du culte en Gaule franque n'ont pas fait table rase d'une liturgie gallicane moribonde.'[54] The variant 'celis' is indeed found in some Gallican Psalters,[55] but it is also the version of the widely known Psalterium Iuxta Hebraeos.[56] Most would hesitate to argue that the retention of a local grammatical variant in a text as well known as a psalm necessarily indicates its previous use in the same liturgical and musical context.

---

[51] As Treitler has pointed out, this is a different usage from that employed in linguistics. See Treitler, L., 'Paleography and Semiotics', in M. Huglo (ed.), *Musicologie Mediévale: Notations et Séquences. Actes de la Table Ronde du C. N. R. S. à l'Institut de Recherche et d'Histoire des Textes 1982* (Paris, 1987), 17–27. See also Huglo, M., 'Problematique de la Paléographie Musicale', in the same volume, 15–16. Periodicals such as *Études Grégoriennes* and *Beiträge zur Gregorianik*, and monographs such as Cardine, E., *Semiologia Gregoriana* (Rome, 1968; trans. R. Fowels: *Gregorian Semiology* (Solesmes, 1982)) demonstrate the directions of scholarship in this field.

[52] For a preliminary exploration of medieval performance practice, see McGee, T., *The Sound of Medieval Song: Ornamentation and Vocal Style according to the Treatises* (Oxford, 1998), especially Chapter 3.

[53] Dyer, J., 'Latin Psalters, Old Roman and Gregorian Chants', *Kirchenmusikalisches Jahrbuch* 68 (1984), 11–30; 18. See also Treitler, L., 'Observations on the Transmission of some Aquitanian Tropes', *Forum Musicologicum* 3 (Winterthur, 1982) 11–60; 12.

[54] Bernard, P., *Du Chant Romain au Chant Grégorien* (Paris, 1996), 176.

[55] See *Biblia Sacra Vulgata* (Stuttgart, 1994), 932.

[56] Ibid., 933.

The Melodic Variants in Iubilate

The broad survey above has done little more than hint at the relationships between manuscripts, and has not utilised the musical evidence. It is now necessary to give these general claims a firm foundation by making a detailed examination of the melodic variants found in the core repertory of eighth-mode tracts.

Although date, origin, and the evidence of regional notational styles are used where possible as a starting point for defining relationships between manuscripts, the main evidence used here to evaluate transmission patterns is that of melodic variants. An exhaustive survey of all melodic variants found in the eighth-mode tracts in the manuscript sample has been undertaken in the preparation of this study. However, it is unnecessary to reproduce this survey in full here. Examination of the variants found in a single chant, *Iubilate*, gives sufficient information about the manner in which the melodies vary in different manuscripts.[57]

For ease of reference, pitch, in the form of a-p letter notation, is ascribed to neumed manuscripts in the following descriptions where the pitched manuscripts are consistent.[58] At some points, the pitched manuscripts do not have a consistent tradition. If more than one pitched version is compatible with the neume patterns found in unpitched manuscripts, it is not possible to transcribe the neumes into pitches with any certainty. Some neumed manuscripts have neume patterns that are inconsistent with all of the pitched manuscripts; once again it is not possible to ascribe pitches to these outlines with any degree of certainty.

*1. 'Iubilate domino' [Phrase **A1**]* The early manuscripts, the Western Frankish manuscripts, and *LAV* have neume shapes that are entirely compatible with each other in this phrase, and in phrase ***A1*** across the repertory. The standard beginning of an eighth-mode tract was a point of great stability. The typical outline of this phrase is as follows:

g g ghih ghhg gkkl/hkkl h gfghhg
Iu-bi-la- te- do- mi-no

All pitched manuscripts have this outline, except that *KLO1* always has

[57] Appendix 1 contains each phrase of *Iubilate* in most of the sample manuscripts, and should be referred to for confirmation of the observations made below (see pp. 227–67, below). In *BEN1*, 18v has the end of Septuagesima and 19r begins with the offertory of Quinquagesima: as the tract for Quinquagesima, *Iubilate* falls in this lacuna. *RAG* also has a lacuna at this point. *BEN5* is therefore the only Beneventan manuscript used in the following discussion, although general characteristics are applicable to all three Beneventan manuscripts studied.

[58] An explanation of a-p letter notation may be found in the Preface (see p. *viii*, above).

ghkh instead of ghih in phrase *A1*. For *KLO1* to be internally consistent but to have a slightly different melodic outline to the rest of the pitched manuscripts is a pattern that will become familiar in the following discussion. The rise on 'do-' is the only point at which the pitches of the neumes in the adiastematic manuscripts cannot be reconstructed with certainty. Although most manuscripts have gkkl, three of the Cluniac manuscripts (*SAB, ROP* and *LEW*) have hkkl. This variant occurs on every occasion when phrase *A1* is used and is the first of many examples where the Cluniac manuscripts have different pitch outlines for standard melodic shapes, not only from other diastematic manuscripts, but also from each other, although the individual manuscripts are usually internally consistent. Although the Aquitanian manuscripts usually have gkkl in phrase *A1*, they have kkl in *Beatus uir 1*, *Commouisti 1*, and *Desiderium 1*, and *YRX* has hkkl in *Attende 1*.

PAS2 has only three rising notes (gkl?) at this point in almost all examples of phrase *A1*.[59] *MOG4* has a four-note rising figure on 'do-' (probably ghkl, if it follows the melodic outline of the other manuscripts), although it usually has the more customary gkkl/hkkl rise at this point.[60] The Eastern Frankish manuscripts often have insignificant and inconsistent variations in the melodic outline, often peculiar to a single manuscript. A further example in this phrase is the neumes used for the final syllable in *STM*. These are incompatible with the usual gfghhg outline and should perhaps be interpreted as gfhhg.

On '-te', *PAS2* has punctum, pressus, *MOG4* has punctum, virga, pressus, and *STM* has pes, pressus. In most neumed notations, there are two kinds of pressus: the pressus major has a hook on the left-hand side and indicates three notes, and the pressus minor has no hook on the left-hand side, is often joined to the preceding neume, and indicates two notes. The Eastern Frankish manuscripts do not distinguish between these two neumes, and appear to use the sign interchangeably with the clivis. There are several possible interpretations of this neume. It may be equivalent to the clivis, indicating two notes. It may indicate two notes, but with an interpretation distinct from that of the clivis (perhaps with a lengthened first note). It may indicate three notes, with the first pitch being reiterated. The inconsistency with which the Eastern Frankish scribes used this sign suggests that they were relatively indifferent to its precise interpretation. On this occasion, then, the melodic outline is g-h-g, but *PAS2* has ghg or ghhg, and *MOG4* and *STM* have ghhg or ghhhg.

On '-te' and '-no', *BRE* replaces the ghhg pattern with ghg. The

---

[59] gkkl? in *Attende 1*.

[60] In *Cantemus 1* and *Vinea 1* it has neumes compatible with ghikl, as does *TYR* in *Cantemus 1*.

tendency not to repeat notes is characteristic of this manuscript, not only in this phrase, but in many others as well.

*2. 'omnis terra' [phrase **B1**]* In this phrase, there are several places where the pitched manuscripts have different versions, all of which are compatible with the early manuscripts. The outline of the phrase is:
ik/kk hki i/k kkk lhhg hg ikh/kkh kggf/iggf
om- nis ter- ra

At the beginning of the phrase, the early manuscripts and the Northern Italian manuscripts have a two-note rise and the Aquitanian and Beneventan manuscripts have ik or iik while the other manuscripts in the sample have kk or virgae. The Aquitanian manuscripts also replace the usual k (or virga) on 'ter-' with i. The punctum in *GAL2* and the vertical placing of the tractulus in *LAN* suggest that they may also have i rather than k.

The final melisma of phrase ***B*** is notated in an ambiguous manner in the early manuscripts. Often, the trigon is used at the beginning of the cadence in unpitched manuscripts (on this occasion, *GAL1, GAL2, MUR3, CHA1, CLU1, NOY4, BRE, PAS2, STM* and *DIJ1)*.[61] This neume shape can be interpreted as kkh or ikh.[62] While the majority of pitched manuscripts begin the cadence kkh, *KLO1* usually has ikh.[63] Of the unpitched manuscripts that do not have a trigon on this occasion, *DEN1* has a torculus (ikh), *MOG4* has virga, clivis (kkh), and the neumes in *LAN* are heighted in a way that clearly indicates kkh. The general interpretation should probably be kkh, as only two (unrelated) manuscripts in the sample clearly have ikh. The high note before the final ggf shows more uncertainty: throughout the eighth-mode tract repertory, *IRI*, the Aquitanian manuscripts, and the Beneventan manuscripts have iggf; *KLO1, DIJ1, ROG1, ROP* and *SAB* have kggf; and *LEW* has iggf or *i*ggf. The neumes in the unpitched manuscripts are compatible with either of these.

The variants discussed so far are all connected with the pitches i and k, and Hughes has identified the ambiguity surrounding the semitone i/k as a common and 'insignificant' point of variance within the Gregorian tradition.[64] It is indeed common in the eighth-mode tracts and often serves (as here) to distinguish groups of manuscripts both chronologically and geographically: *KLO1* is independent, *IRI* is allied with the Aquitanian and

[61] *DIJ1* has no letter notation on this particular occasion. When there is letter notation, this trigon is consistently given the pitches kkh in phrase ***B***.

[62] See *WP*, 361.

[63] On two occasions kkh is used instead.

[64] Hughes, D., 'Evidence for the Traditional View of the Transmission of Gregorian Chant', *JAMS* 40 (1987), 377–401; 384–5.

Beneventan versions, and the Cluniac manuscripts form a group.

BRE demonstrates its usual tendency to replace two repeated notes with a single one (kk lhg instead of kkk lhhg at the beginning of the melisma). It also has an isolated variant: on '(om)nis', it has a punctum, a quilisma, two descending puncta and an apostrophe (hikihg?) instead of hki.

The Eastern Frankish manuscripts have several isolated variants. *PAS2* begins with a scandicus, possibly implying fhk, but certainly not the ik or kk found in most other manuscripts. *STM* and *KLO1* begin kkk. *MOG4, PAS2* and *STM* have a pes (hk?) instead of hki on '(om)nis'.[65] The melisma usually begins kkk but the second note is lower in *STM*. The usual ambiguity about repeated note figures is shown in these manuscripts on the following figure: *STM* has klhg, but *PAS2* and *MOG4* have a torculus for klh, and then a pressus, indicating hhg or hg. All three neumed Eastern Frankish manuscripts end with a pressus where the other manuscripts have a clivis or pressus minor. *CHA1* has a pressus major on this occasion although it usually has a clivis in such situations.

The torculus on '(om)nis' in *CLU1* is the 'special' torculus identified by Ferreira as indicating a microtonal nuance.[66] Ferreira has also identified a special form of the clivis, indicating a similar microtonal nuance. An example of this may be found in the third phrase of *Iubilate*, on '(serui)te'. At places where these shapes appear, most manuscripts have ki, but *LEW* almost always has kk. It seems almost certain that this microtonal nuance between i and k was part of the melodic tradition adopted in Lewes, but there was no way of showing it in the square notation of the source. Although *DIJ1* also has special signs for indicating microtonal nuances, they are not used in these contexts. The special sign in *CLU1*, and the use of kk in *LEW*, makes these two sources stand out from the rest of the tradition.

In this phrase, the Cluniac manuscripts are not entirely compatible with each other. On '-nis', as well as the distinctive special torculus in *CLU1* and hkk in *LEW* mentioned above, *ROG1* has hih while most manuscripts have hki.[67] *DIJ1* and *ROG1* replace the hg figure in the melisma with hghg. This is a variant characteristic of the two manuscripts, but which occasionally crops up in *BRE* and in the Eastern Frankish manuscripts (for example, in *STM* in this phrase).

IRI begins kki instead of the usual kk or ik. It has hkh on '-nis' where most manuscripts have hki. On 'ter-', *IRI* has kk instead of the usual k, and it has kk instead of kkk at the beginning of the following syllable. This is

---

65 *PAS2* also has this in *Laudate 2*, along with *MOG4*.

66 Ferreira, M. P., 'The Cluny Gradual: its Notation and Melodic Character', in *CP – Eger*, 205–15; 212–14.

67 In some phrases of this type it has hkih.

the kind of underlay variant that is characteristic of a scribal misreading rather than necessarily indicating a different performance practice. These three variants are unique to *IRI*.

3. *'seruite domino' [phrase **C4**]* The outline of the phrase is as follows:
f/g gfg/hfg ghki/ghkik k hik/hk ikhhg/ikhhhg/ikhg
ser- ui- te do-mi- no
The earliest manuscripts do not have completely equivalent neumes. *GAL2* begins with a clivis instead of a punctum. The phrase ends with ikh followed by a pressus minor (hg) in four of the five early manuscripts, but with a pressus major in *CHA1* (hhg). Most other manuscripts end hg. The Eastern Frankish manuscripts have a pressus (hg or hhg). *BRE*, as is usual in this manuscript, does not repeat the penultimate pitch, having ikhg instead of ikhhg or ikhhhg.

The neumes used on 'serui-' are consistent in all unpitched manuscripts, but the pitched manuscripts reveal an inconsistent tradition: most of the Cluniac manuscripts have g hfg, *IRI*, the Aquitanian manuscripts and the Beneventan manuscripts have f gfg, and *KLO1* has g gfg. These are not significant differences, but they broadly differentiate the three groups of pitched manuscripts.

The earliest manuscripts and the North Italian ones have neumes compatible with ghki on '-te', Although most of the other manuscripts have ghki, some have ghkik; this does not seem to be geographically or chronologically grouped (for example, *ALB* has ghkik and *YRX* has ghki). Deciding whether or not to avoid the repercussion of k (it appears on the following syllable 'do-'), making a smoother melodic line, was clearly not of great moment. *MOG4* has only three notes (gki?) and *PAS2* ends the figure with an apostrophe (ghkii?). The usual Eastern Frankish inconsistency is in evidence here.

The figure on '-mi-' is an example of a melodic figure used in phrases ***C, D, E*** and ***F***. On these occasions, while most manuscripts have hik, often with a quilisma, *DEN1, ROP* and *IRI* always have hk, *SAB* has hk except in the phrase ***E*** melisma, and *FITZ* and *ROG1* often have hk in the phrase ***D*** and phrase ***F*** melismas. There is a clear tendency in Cluniac pitched manuscripts to omit the intervening note i, and it may derive from the Western Frankish Saint-Denis tradition. *BRE* and the Eastern Frankish manuscripts are inconsistent in their treatment of this figure, sometimes having hk and sometimes having hik.[68]

[68] For a description of the interpretation of the quilisma, see *WP*, 358. In the eighth-mode tracts, the most common context for use of a quilisma is that of the semitone ik within the rise hik. It appears to have melodic as well as expressive significance.

*4. 'in letitia' [phrase **D1**]* At the beginning of the phrase, almost all manuscripts have three rising notes, a lower one, and a higher one, followed by either another lower note or a falling liquescence. On this occasion, *PAS2* has quilisma, virga, liquescent virga, missing out the first lower note. The rise at the beginning of phrase ***D1*** is a point of great variance in the pitched tradition, and many manuscripts are individually inconsistent at this point. *IRI*, the Aquitanian and Beneventan manuscripts have fgihih. *KLO1* has variously fgkhkh, fhkhk and fhkhih.[69] *ROG1* has variously fgihih, fhkhih, fgkhi, and fhkhk.[70] *SAB* has fgihih but fhihih in *De profundis 4* and fgihi in *De profundis 8*; *ROP* has fhkhkh but fgihih in *Laudate 4*. *LEW* uses the shapes fhkhih, fhkhkh, fhihih and fhihkh.[71] The uncertainty about the precise outline of this shape in the Cluniac tradition may be the reason why the scribe of *DIJ1* omits letter notation altogether for this figure in all relevant phrases. However, almost all manuscripts are leading towards k or a virga on the first accent ('le-' here). *LAN* and *LAV* have a pes, presumably indicating ik – this is a reminder that, despite their closeness, the melodies in the oldest manuscripts are not identical, although the variants can be very minor indeed.

The ***D1*** melisma begins ikkg in the Aquitanian manuscripts and the Beneventan manuscripts. The first note of the melisma in the early manuscripts and *LAV* is written lower than the next two, which suggests ikkg. The replacement of i with k in later manuscripts except those of Aquitaine and Benevento is seen yet again. The first three notes are of the same pitch in Eastern Frankish manuscripts, *NOY4, CLU1* and *BRE*, and *KLO1* has kkkg. *IRI* has kikg, and *DEN1* has neumes that are compatible with this. Cluniac manuscripts have kkkg,[72] kikg[73] or kikhg.[74]

The melisma continues kkhg higf hkhig in most of the pitched manuscripts, but *ROP* and *SAB* have ikhg h*i*gf hkhkg, and *KLO1* has ikhg hkgf hkhkg. There is a clearly defined Bec tradition, and *KLO1* is independent, as usual. On this occasion, as is common, *PAS2* has one (apparently random) extra note, and *BRE* has an extended version of the melisma, for which the pitches cannot be recovered. Most manuscripts have fg on the penultimate syllable but *CLU1*, *NOY4*, *DEN1*, *LEW* and *IRI* have

---

[69] fgkhkh in *Beatus uir 4*, *De profundis 4*, *Iubilate 8*, *Laudate 4*; fhkhk in *De profundis 7*; fhkhih in *Iubilate 4*.

[70] fgihih in *Iubilate 4*; fhkhih in *Beatus uir 4*, *De profundis 4*, *Iubilate 8*; fgkhi in *De profundis 8*; fhkhk in *Laudate 4*.

[71] fhkhih in *Iubilate 4*, *Beatus uir 4*; fhkhkh in *Iubilate 8*, *Laudate 4*; fhihih in *De profundis 4*; fhihkh in *De profundis 8*.

[72] *DIJ1*, *LEW* (but kikhg in *De profundis 8* and *De profundis 10*), *CLU1*; also *DEN1* and *NOY4*.

[73] *SAB* and *ROG1*.

[74] *ROP*, but kikg in *De profundis 8* and *De profundis 10*.

g. The final figure, ghhg, is replaced by ghg in *BRE*. The usual patterns are emerging: the Cluniac tradition is different from the rest and the pairs of manuscripts also have independent traditions; *BRE* does not repeat notes; and *KLO1* has independent pitches but is internally consistent.

*5. 'Intrate in conspectu eius' [phrase **E**]* The outline of the phrase is as follows:

g ghik recitation kki/ki/kk g hg hikih/hkih ikh hg/ghg
In-tra- te in con- spe- ctu e- ius

As has already been seen, where the earliest manuscripts have i, later manuscripts tend to have k, except for the Beneventan and Aquitanian sources. The most extensive body of evidence in this regard is the recitation in phrase ***E***. The earliest manuscripts all have a combination of puncta, pedes and virgae in these recitations, and comparison with later manuscripts suggests that the puncta indicate i, the virgae k, and the pedes ik. *CHA1, GAL1* and *MUR3* have puncta with pedes on accents and a virga on the last syllable of the recitation. *GAL2* has puncta with pedes but does not rise on the last syllable of the recitation. *LAN* has puncta with pedes on the accents and a quilisma (ik?) on the last syllable of the recitation. The Aquitanian and Beneventan manuscripts generally have i with ik on accents and k on the last syllable of the recitation (compatible with *CHA1, GAL1* and *MUR3*), although *YRX* is more varied.[75] In contrast, *NOY4, DEN1* and *NOV* recite with virgae (*KLO1* has k), and *IRI*, the Eastern Frankish manuscripts and the Cluniac manuscripts recite on k or virgae, or on k/virgae with ik/pedes on accented syllables.[76] *LAV* and *BRE* are less consistent. *BRE* usually has virgae with pedes on the main accents, but there are three exceptions to this.[77] Example **2.1** demonstrates some of the widely differing neume combinations used in the phrase ***E*** recitation in *LAV*. These two manuscripts may represent the moment of transition from a genre with higher recitation on i to one with higher recitation on k.

[75] k in *Cantemus 9*, *Laudate 5* and *Sicut 4*; k with ik on the accents in *Attende 4*, *Attende 9* and *Vinea 4*; ik i ik i k k k k k in *Cantemus 6. Qui regis 3* has i on the first syllable and then k in *YRX* and *TOU*.

[76] Except that *SAB* has kk instead of ik, and *IRI* and *ROP* have i on the last syllable.

[77] Punctum x4, pes, virga x5 in *Beatus uir 8*, punctum x2, virga x3 in *Cantemus 9*, and virga, pes, punctum in *Iubilate 5*.

Attende 4: i with ik on the accent and k ik on the last two syllables

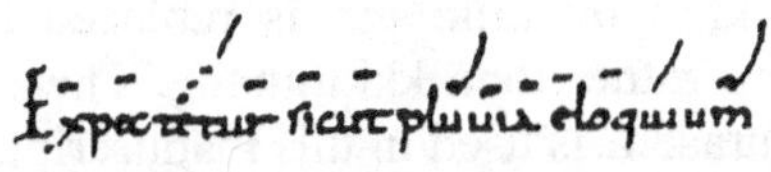

Attende 9: k with ik on the accent then i, with k ik on the last two syllables

Beatus uir 5: i with ik on the accent and ik on the last syllable

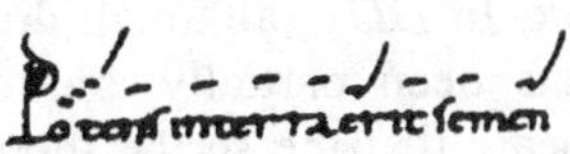

Cantemus 6: i with ik on the accents and k k k ik on the last four syllables

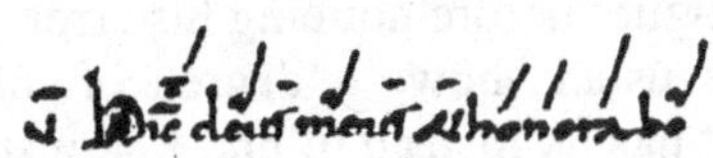

Attende 12: k with ik on the accents and on the last syllable

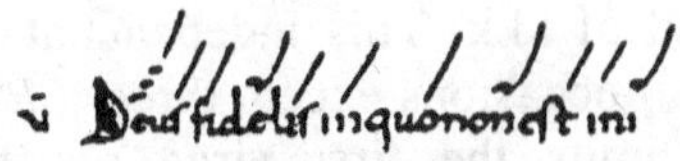

Example **2.1**

Apart from the recitation, the earliest manuscripts are entirely consistent with each other, with *LAV*, and also with the Western Frankish manuscripts in this phrase. *CLU1*, *DEN1*, *LEW* and *BRE* have ghg instead of hg on the final syllable, and *ROG1* omits ih in the melisma. Once again, *BRE* and the Eastern Frankish manuscripts have small variations: *BRE* has an extra virga on '-pec-', and a pes instead of g on '-tu'; and *PAS2* and *STM* have a quilisma and an oriscus (ghk?) instead of ghik on '(in)tra(te)'. The Eastern Frankish manuscripts have another minor variant: *MOG4, PAS2* and *STM* have a virga strata,[78] and *KLO1* has ki instead of kki on '-pec-'. The melisma provides a further example of the hik/hk figure: *DEN1, ROP, IRI* and *SAB* have hk, as do the three neumed Eastern Frankish manuscripts, while all other manuscripts have hik.

6. 'in exultatione' [phrase **C2***]* The early manuscripts are compatible with each other, except that *LAN* does not reiterate the pitch k between '-ti-' and '-o-', having hik instead of khik on the second of these syllables. It is possible to reconstruct most pitches in this phrase: the only pitched manuscript with an incompatible melodic outline is *KLO1*. It replaces the

[78] Interpreted as kk. See *WP*, 360–61.

pattern khik by ihik; igh is replaced by kgh, and the phrase cadences ikihihghg rather than kkkihihghg. These variants occur on every occasion when phrase ***C*** is used in this manuscript. The usual melodic outline is:

f fhk igh gfg/gfgh ghkik khik/khk kkkihihghg
in ex- ul- ta- ti- o- ne

The Cluniac manuscripts differ only in small details. *ROG1* begins the phrase on g rather than f. *IRI* repeats the penultimate note on about 2/3 occasions when phrase ***C*** is used. As usual, *SAB, ROP, DEN1* and *IRI* have hk instead of hik. In *DIJ1* (although this is not clear in the facsimile), the pes on '-ta-' has been partially erased, and the torculus is the neume intended. It appears that the scribe thought he had already copied the gfg figure in the previous torculus (really indicating igh), and started to write the ghkik figure before noticing his error.

BRE as usual shows a degree of independence from the rest of the tradition. It has hk instead of hik, f hk instead of f fhk at the beginning (also seen in *DEN1*), and an independent version of the melisma beginning with a pes instead of kkk. This independent version of the phrase ***C*** cadence appears on all occasions except three. *BRE* uses the usual shapes on two of these, and omits the first virga on the other. The Eastern Frankish manuscripts show the sort of casual deviation from the usual shapes that one might expect. *PAS2* begins f hik, if the quilisma + oriscus here indicates hik, as is usual. There is also a quilisma instead of the ghkik figure.

NOY4, IRI and *DEN1* have gfgh rather than gfg on '-ta-'. This is not an isolated variant. In phrase ***C***, the igh figure is sometimes followed by gfg and sometimes by gfgh. Kainzbauer's interpretation of the situation is based on there being certain patterns of notes associated exclusively with accented or with unaccented syllables in the eighth-mode tracts. The rise to k at the beginning of phrase ***C*** is always associated with an accented syllable. Accented syllables are followed either by one unaccented syllable (on the igh figure here) or by two unaccented syllables (on igh and gfg). Therefore, either the gfg figure falls on an accented syllable (and is therefore extended to gfgh) or the first note of the recitation falls on an accented syllable (and is therefore extended from g to gh). 'Daher sind an dieser Stelle nur die Neumenfolgen Porrectus und Pes [gfg gh], oder Viertonneume und Punctum [gfgh g] möglich.'[79]

The second of these cases – gfgh on an accented syllable followed by g on the first syllable of the recitation – indeed happens in all manuscripts in *Attende 8*, *Attende 11*, *Beatus uir 6*, *Beatus uir 9*, *Cantemus 3*, *Desiderium 3*, *Iubilate 10*, and *Vinea 8*. It also occurs in *Cantemus 5*, although *CHA1*

[79] Ibid., 33. The description of this figure may be found on pages 33–5.

has gfg ('Ch is hier wohl einfach als Fehler zu verstehen'), in *Vinea 6* (where it is *DIJ1* that errs, having gfg), and *Qui confidunt 5* (*BRE* has gfg).

However, Kainzbauer's interpretation does not seem to hold for all examples of phrase **C**. In *Vinea 3*, the earliest group of manuscripts has the 'correct' interpretation. Before gh on the accented first recitation syllable, *GAL1, GAL2* and *MUR3* (as well as *MOG4* and *TYR*) have gfg with an upward liquescence at the end, and *CHA1* and *LAN* (as well as *DIJ1* and *PAS2*) have gfg. According to Kainzbauer, the other manuscripts have misinterpreted this liquescence as indicating a full pitch: all diastematic manuscripts, *LAV, CLU1*, and *BRE* have gfgh followed by a pes on the accented first recitation syllable. *Sicut 3* has the same problem (gfg with gh on the accented first recitation syllable in four of the earliest manuscripts and *PAS2* but gfgh gh in *LAN* and all later manuscripts) as does *Sicut 10* (gfg with gh in all of the earliest manuscripts, *YRX, BRE, BEN5* and *PAS2*, but gfgh gh in all other later manuscripts). Further, although most manuscripts have gfg followed by an accented recitation syllable (gh) in *Sicut 6* and *Attende 3*, four of the pitched manuscripts (*IRI, SAB, ROG1* and *ROP*) have gfgh gh in *Sicut 6* and *IRI, SAB, ROP, CLU1, LEW, YRX, TOU, ALB*, and *BEN5* have gfgh gh in *Attende 3*. In fact, three manuscripts (*IRI, NOY4* and *DEN1*) tend to have gfgh regardless of the textual context.[80]

Can so many cantors and scribes have misunderstood the rules of articulating accented and unaccented syllables within the genre? In general, Kainzbauer's interpretation is valid when there is an accented syllable followed by recitation. However, when there is insufficient text for recitation, most manuscripts have gfg even though there is always an accent on these pitches (in *Beatus uir 3, Cantemus 8, De profundis 6, De profundis 11, Laudate 3, Qui seminant 6*, and *Iubilate 6*). Also, as has been demonstrated above, when there is an unaccented syllable followed by recitation, some manuscripts have gfg and some have gfgh. I suggest that there was a gradual shift, from using gfgh on an accented syllable and gfg both on unaccented syllables and also when there is no recitation, to using gfgh when there is recitation and gfg when there is none.

*7. 'scitote quod dominus' [phrase **C4**]* Most variants repeat tendencies that have already been identified. *CHA1* has f fhk instead of the usual f hk, and ends with a pressus major instead of a clivis or pressus minor. The Eastern Frankish manuscripts end with an undifferentiated pressus. As in the previous phrase, *ROG1* begins on g instead of on f. *KLO1* has kgh instead

---

[80] As *DEN1* has a lacuna until the later phrases of *Attende*, and only the first two phrases of *Sicut* are given as an incipit, it is not possible to ascertain whether the Saint-Denis tradition had gfgh in *Sicut* and *Attende* regardless of the textual context, as one might expect.

of igh, as usual. The hk/hik split is broadly as in 'seruite domino'; only *STM* changes, having hk on this occasion and hik on the previous one. *CLU1* uses the special torculus in the rise (usually gfghki), and *LEW* has gfghkk. *BRE*, avoiding repeated notes as usual, ends hg instead of hhg. Most manuscripts have gfghki but *MOG4* and *PAS2* have clivis, virga, pes (gfghk?), *KLO1* and *STM* have gfghkik, and *IRI* has gfghkik – further examples of small and mainly Eastern Frankish inconsistencies.

*8. 'ipse est deus' [phrase **D1**]* The opening pattern of phrase ***D1*** has been discussed above, as has the melisma. The syllables '-se est' usually have the pitches k k, but *BEN5* has ik k, *LAN* and *LAV* have pes, virga, and *CHA1* has virga followed by quilisma or oriscus.[81] These appear to be fairly random decorations of the recitation, and are not on accented syllables. The phrase ends ghhg but ghg in *BRE*, and with an extra virga before the final pressus in *MOG4* and *CHA1*. The first note of the melisma is omitted in *STM*, and *PAS2* has hihgf instead of the usual higf.

*9. 'Ipse fecit nos et non ipsi nos' [phrase **B5**]* As an extremely complicated (and unique) version of phrase ***B***, this phrase gives an impression of how well known less familiar melodic patterns were. Presentation of a list of variants is somewhat indigestible, but it does illustrate the fact that this unique phrase has more minor variants in it than more widely used phrases. The usual shape of the phrase is:

kkiki ig ikki/kkki/kiki ihg/ihh g hgf/hgg hgh/ghgh hkik hg
ip- se fe- cit nos et non ip- si
gfgkhlki hkih gkhg hghg kkh iggf/kggf
nos

The earliest manuscripts are consistent with each other. All three Western Frankish manuscripts have hghg rather than the hghghg figure seen in the earliest manuscripts. *NOY4* and *DEN1* have a low note before the opening kkiki, and also have a lower second note instead of kkki on 'fe-'.

BRE begins ikiki or possibly gkiki instead of the usual kkiki. Both *BRE* and *LAV* have ikki on 'fe-'. Both have a torculus rather than ihg or ihh on '-cit' (igh?). *BRE* has hg instead of hghghg and cadences ikhkhgf. Although the phrase ***B*** cadence has the usual shape in this manuscript on 24 occasions, it also appears with neumes which seem to indicate ikhkhgf,[82] ikhkggf,[83] kkhkhgf,[84] kkhkgf,[85] and ikhgf.[86]

[81] These signs are undifferentiated in *CHA1*. See *WP* 349; 350–51.

[82] In *Attende 2*, *Attende 7*, *Commouisti 6*, *De profundis 6* and *Iubilate 9*.

[83] In *Sepe 11*.

The Eastern Frankish manuscripts, as usual, have many minor variants. 'ip-' is usually kkiki but an extra oriscus is added at the end of the figure in *MOG4* and *STM* has an extra virga at the beginning and a pressus rather than a clivis at the end. '-se' is usually ig but kg in *KLO1*. 'fe-' is usually kkki or ikki but is different in all four Eastern Frankish manuscripts: iklk in *KLO1*; virga, pes (kik?) in *PAS2*; virga, torculus (kiki?) in *MOG4*; and pressus (kki?) in *STM*. '-cit' is usually ihg but clivis, virga with liquescence (ihh?) in *STM*. *STM* and *MOG4* end with a pressus instead of the usual clivis. *KLO1* has its own version of the cadence, ikhkggf, as usual.

The Aquitanian and Beneventan manuscripts follow the usual tendency to favour k over i, having ikki instead of kkki on 'fe-'. The next syllable is ihh or ihh liquescence rather than ihg. 'non' is usually ghgh but hgh in *ALB* and *YRX*, and *YRX* also has hghg instead of hghghg in the final melisma. *BEN5* has gihg where all other pitched manuscripts have gkhg.

The Cluniac manuscripts and *IRI* have many small variants: 'ip-' is gkkiki in *IRI*; 'fe-' is kiki in *IRI, SAB* and *ROP*; and '-cit' is ih in *ROG1*, ihh in *SAB* and *LEW*, ih liquescence in *IRI*, and ihhg in *ROP*; 'et' is usually hgg but hg in *LEW*, hggf in *ROP* and hg liq. in *IRI* and *SAB*; 'ip-' is usually hkik but hkhk in *LEW*; 'nos' usually begins gfgk but *SAB* has gfgi. This is usually followed by hl but by hkl in *ROG1*. The Cluniac manuscripts all have hghg instead of hghghg, and have their usual versions of the final cadence. *DIJ1* omits letter notation on 'et non ipsi', perhaps reflecting the uncertain pitch tradition seen in other Cluniac manuscripts.

There are more minor variants in this phrase than in most, and much of the uncertainty surrounds the oscillations between i and k, and liquescent syllables. As will be seen below, these are two of the most common types of variation which occur in the Mass Proper chants. Such clusters of variants are generally found in the phrases used less frequently in these chants.

*10. 'nos autem populus eius' [phrase **C1**]* All of the usual phrase ***C*** variants are found in this phrase, and need not be detailed once more. The Eastern Frankish manuscripts are very unstable within phrase ***C***. The rise after the recitation is normally ghkik: *PAS2* has ghkik, ghki,[87] ghk,[88] or a quilisma (probably hk);[89] *MOG4* has ghkik, ghki,[90] ghkk,[91] or ghik;[92] *STM*

---

[84] In *Ad te leuaui 10, Laudate 2, De profundis 2* and *Qui regis 3.*
[85] In *Qui regis 2, Qui regis 8.*
[86] In *De profundis.*
[87] In *De profundis 11, Desiderium 4* and *Sepe 8.*
[88] In *De profundis 6, Iubilate 10, Qui confidunt 5* and *Sicut 6.*
[89] In *Iubilate 6* and *Qui seminant 6.*
[90] In *Beatus uir 8, Cantemus 8, De profundis 6* and *Sicut 6.*
[91] In *Desiderium 9*

has ghkik, ghki,[93] or ghk;[94] and *TYR* has ghkik or ghk.[95] The following khik figure is also very varied in these manuscripts. The variant neumes found in *PAS2* may be used to illustrate this (Example **2.2**).

Commouisti 7: khikl?

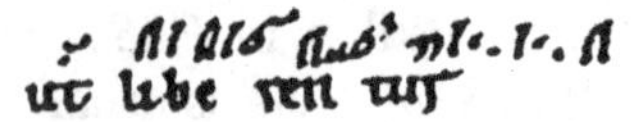

Beatus uir 7 (also *Beatus uir 11*,
Desiderium 3, *Iubilate 10*,
Qui confidunt 5: khikl?

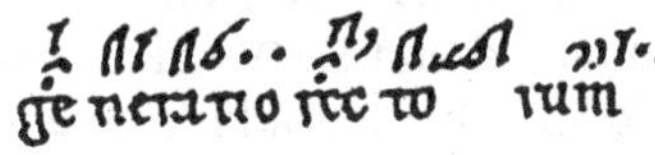

Qui confidunt 10: khiklk?

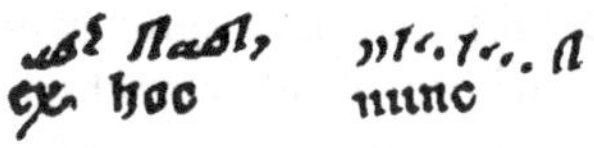

Laudate 3: khhiki?

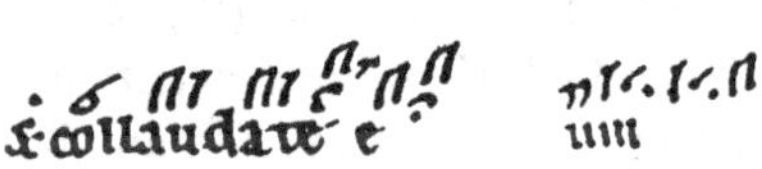

De profundis 11: khhikik?

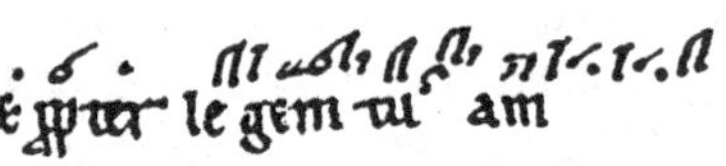

Example **2.2**

11. 'et oues pascue eius' [phrase F] The usual shape of the phrase is as follows:

gh gh g hghik/hghk ghgf fhk k
et o- ues pas- cu- e e-
kikhg gghggfg kkklkihhg hkihg ghg hikih khhg
ius

The early manuscripts are largely consistent with each other, although *LAN* has kkkk instead of kkk in the melisma. The final sign in *LAN* is not a neume but an 'etc.' indication. The three early manuscripts whose melismas reach sufficiently far (*GAL1*, *MUR3* and *CHA1*) have lkihhhg (with a pressus major) rather than lkihhg. *NOY4,* the Beneventan and the Aquitanian manuscripts are consistent with the early group, except that

[92] In *Ad te leuaui 9*
[93] In *Qui confidunt 5*
[94] In *Ad te leuaui 9*
[95] In *Ad te leuaui 9*

BEN5 (together with *BRE, ROG1* and *SAB*) begins with articulations familiar from the beginning of ***D2*** in *Qui seminant* and *Ad te leuaui* rather than with the hghik usually found at the beginning of ***D2*** and ***F***. This opening is found at the beginning of the final phrase in all manuscripts in *Commouisti* and *Qui seminant*, and in *BRE* in *Desiderium*. As both versions have a low recitation, then a rise to k and a fall to f before rising fhk, it is easy to see how they were alternative possibilities in both phrase ***D2*** and phrase ***F***.

In the recitation at the beginning, most manuscripts have gh gh g but *BRE* has pes, pes, virga (gh gh h?). Most manuscripts have a rise hghik on 'pas-', but hghk is a common variant at this point in phrase ***F***: on this occasion, *IRI* has hghk and *DEN1* and the Eastern Frankish neumed manuscripts have clivis, quilisma (hghk?). On '(pascu)e', most manuscripts have fhk, but *PAS2* has a quilisma. An extension of the rise to fhkl or fhikl is seen in about half of the manuscripts in the Easter Vigil tracts and *Beatus uir*.

In the melisma, the gghggfg figure appears as gggihgfg? in *STM*, and with a pressus rather than a clivis on the gf drop in *MOG4* and *PAS2*. Extra gs at this point are common in the Eastern Frankish manuscripts. The following kkk figure is commonly given as: kk in *MOG4*, *KLO1*, and *ROG1*; a lower punctum then three higher notes in *DEN1* (gkkk or hkkk?); a virga and three puncta in *CLU1* (hkkk or kkkk?); hkkk in *LEW* (although it has gkk in *Iubilate*); gkk in *IRI*; and g/h followed by a variable number of ks in *BRE*.

The lkihhg figure is usually lkih in *BRE* and sometimes in the Eastern Frankish manuscripts as well (*MOG4* has it here). *KLO1* and *IRI* usually have lkihg (and *STM* also has this in *Iubilate*) and although *ROG1* usually has the standard figure, on this occasion it has lkkihg in *ROG1*. This figure is followed in most manuscripts by hkihg, but this is usually missed out in *IRI* and *BRE* (also *ROG1* in *Iubilate*), and *STM* has a quilisma and two falling puncta in *Iubilate*. The following ghg figure is replaced by ghgf in *IRI* and *BRE* and by ghf in *ROG1*, *SAB* and *ROP*. The hikih figure is commonly replaced with hkih – here in *STM*, *SAB* and *LEW*. The final khhg figure is instead khg/ihg? in *BRE*, ihhg in *ROP*, ikhhg in *LEW*, and ikh then a pressus in *STM*. *DEN1* has an extra clivis, near the end of the melisma, the pitches of which cannot be recovered.

It is initially surprising to find so much variation in a standard phrase, used at the end of every eighth-mode tract. However, in many manuscripts the final phrases of eighth-mode tracts are not always notated fully (see Chapter 5 for a further exploration of this phenomenon). In *Iubilate*, this happens in *GAL2, LAN, CLU1, NOY4, PAS2, MOG4, ALB, DIJ1, IRI* and *ROG1*, and several of the variants cited above seem to be associated with these curtailments. Most of the other variants are of the kind already encountered: inconsistent variants in the Eastern Frankish manuscripts, and uncertainty surrounding rises to k, whether manuscripts repeat notes or not, and whether manuscripts have hk or hik.

Classification of Melodic Variants

In the above description, variants have simply been catalogued, without any consideration of their relative importance. This is because the purpose here is to show the way in which different manuscripts are grouped, and variants of all kinds help to build up the fullest possible picture. However, a body of evidence such as this provides further data in the classification of different types of variant already undertaken by several scholars.

Ferreira writes that notes of secondary importance are often discarded.[96] This is a familiar occurrence in the Eastern Frankish manuscripts and *BRE*. 'Memory works best with clear-cut tonal structures… this may be seen as the rationale behind the sliding of "abnormal" axial degrees to "standard" recitation tones.'[97] This is exactly the situation seen most strikingly in the phrase ***E*** recitation, but in other contexts in the eighth-mode tracts as well. Ferreira also writes that well known formulae tend to absorb more extended melodic passages. This does not occur in the eighth-mode tracts or, if it did, it occurred sufficiently before the surviving written documents to be unrecoverable. The rarity of this type of variant may be due to the formulaic nature of the eighth-mode tracts, where familiar melodic passages rarely vary anyway. Ferreira writes that some changes work towards melodic smoothness. In a pattern with two low notes and a subsequent higher one, the middle note will tend to slide upwards. An example of this may be found in phrase ***A*** where the later Cluniac manuscripts have hkkl instead of gkkl after the opening g. However, such patterns are not at all common in the eighth-mode tracts, whose contours appear to have been firmly established.

The fullest exposition of the different types of 'insignificant' variant remains that by Hughes.[98] His six types of variant may be summarised as follows:

1. Use of an ornamental neume instead of a normal one (for example, liquescence, quilisma or oriscus). This may be due to local preference, or may be due to an inability to find a written equivalent for a vocal nuance. Such variants are indeed widespread in the eighth-mode tracts.

[96] Ferreira, *Music at Cluny*, op. cit., 142–3.
[97] Ibid., 142.
[98] Hughes, 'Evidence for the Traditional View', op. cit., 383–5.

As they do not generally affect the melodic outline, they are not considered in detail in this study.

2. Variants in rhythmic notation. Either there was much divergence in local style and rhythm, or notators varied in their will or ability to fix it in writing. Because of these difficulties, and because questions of rhythm are not central to this study, I have not discussed such variants.
3. Variants in recitation passages. Not only are the variants in phrase ***E*** well defined, as described above, but the decoration of accented syllables with pedes in phrase ***C*** also varies from manuscript to manuscript.
4. Filling in of thirds. These appear to be due to local preferences, and may result from different interpretations of 'portato singing'; they probably result from the dropping or adding of a quilisma. This is characterised by the hk/hik figure, although the omission or addition of a 'transitional' note is found in other contexts as well.
5. Redistribution of notes among syllables. This only occurs occasionally in the eighth-mode tracts where, as has been shown by Kainzbauer, each melodic shape is exclusively associated with a given textual context.[99]
6. Variants involving e-f, and i-k. These pitches generated uncertainty. The use of the special torculus in *CLU1* is the most striking example of the difficulties in notating pitches in this area, but the many variants involving exchange of i and k also illustrate this type of variant.

'Significant' variants are extremely rare, and each one will be discussed in detail in Chapter 5. They generally entail a few manuscripts or a single manuscript having a completely different phrase, a completely different version of a phrase, or very different melodic patterns. All of the variants found in *Iubilate* are of the 'insignificant' variety, and the models of Ferreira and Hughes combine well to describe their types. Because most melodic shapes recur many times in the eighth-mode tracts, it is possible to use the insignificant variants within these phrases to build up a picture of the way in which manuscripts and groups of manuscripts are related to each other.

Conclusions

The melodic outlines in early manuscripts rarely vary from each other at all. The close relationship between them is illustrated most strikingly when they have a different melodic pattern from that of the later manuscripts. In

[99] This is a central theme of Kainzbauer, 'Der Tractus Tetrardus', op. cit.

QuiC2, most manuscripts begin kkkh, but *CHA1* has fhk and *GAL1, GAL2, MUR3* and *LAN* (and *NOY4* and *PAS2*) have fhki. There is clearly a more 'archaic' and a more 'modern' version of this phrase beginning.

The Eastern Frankish neumed manuscripts have many points of variance, and are not consistent in their treatment of standard phrases. This may be due to carelessness or to a lack of concern for consistency and unity. The internal inconsistencies suggest that the scribes were not trying to salvage unity out of a disintegrating tradition – there was no concern that the same melodic shapes should be notated in the same way (or even indicate the same melodic outline) on subsequent appearances. *KLO1* is similar in general characteristics to the late neumed sources from Eastern Francia but it is more internally consistent. The pitched notation also makes clear several idiosyncrasies. Some examples have been noted above, such as the phrase ***B*** cadence, the phrase ***D*** melisma, and several patterns within phrase ***C***. Also, in phrase ***B2***, the ilmkkh figure is always ilmikh in *KLO1*.

BRE is not internally consistent either. This is most striking at the places where most manuscripts have stereotyped neume shapes. For example, the ***D1*** melisma begins kikg, kkkg or ikkg in *BRE*. Treatment of the hk/hik figure is equally inconsistent. In phrase ***D*** and ***F***, *BRE* has hk, but in phrase ***C*** it has hik 22/30 times, and in phrase ***E*** it has hik on all but four occasions. Phrase ***F***, a phrase one might expect to be notated with well-defined and stereotyped neume shapes, highlights the characteristics of this source. The kkk figure appears as hkkkk,[100] hkkk,[101] hkk kkk, hkkkllk, hkk kkki, hikkk, kkk kk, kkk kkk, and hkk.[102] The next figure is usually lkihhg, but *BRE* also uses lkig,[103] lkihg,[104] and hiklkig.[105] The following hkihg figure is omitted in *BRE* except in *Qui confidunt 11* and *Ad te leuaui 11*. The eighth-mode tracts usually end ihhg or khhg. *BRE* also uses khg,[106] kkkihhg,[107] ikhhg,[108] ikhg,[109] and kkkih g.[110] Presenting strings of pitches in this manner is somewhat overwhelming, but it serves to illustrate the point that *BRE* notates standard, repeating phrases in inconsistent ways.

LAV is almost always consistent with the earliest manuscripts, and is a

---

[100] *Ad te leuaui 11*, *Laudate 8*, *Qui confidunt 11*, *Qui regis 7*, *Sepe 13*, and *Sicut 11*.

[101] *Sicut 11*, *Iubilate 11* and *Qui seminant 7*.

[102] *Desiderium 9*, *Attende 13*, *Vinea 9*, *De profundis 12*, *Beatus uir 10*, *Cantemus 10*, and *Commouisti 8*, respectively.

[103] In *Beatus uir 10*, *De profundis 12*, *Desiderium 9*, *Iubilate 11*, *Laudate 8*, *Qui confidunt 11*, *Qui regis 7*, and *Vinea 9*.

[104] In *Ad te leuaui 11*, *Attende 13*, *Cantemus 10*, *Qui seminant 7*, *Sepe 13*, and *Sicut 11*.

[105] In *Commouisti 8*.

[106] *Iubilate 11*.

[107] *Attende 13*.

[108] *Beatus uir 10*, *Cantemus 10*.

[109] *Commouisti 8*, *Qui confidunt 11*, *Qui seminant 7*.

[110] In *Sicut 11*. *LAV* and *BRE* have an extra g at the end for the syllable '-us'.

useful corrective to the impression, given by the other eleventh- and twelfth-century neumed manuscripts considered here, of a tradition where unity and consistency either were not a priority, or were no longer possible.

The Aquitanian and Beneventan Graduals are indeed closely related, as has long been recognised. However, as one might expect from the very different notational systems, they are not directly connected. An example of this is given by the setting of phrase *C* in *Beatus uir* (see Example **2.3** overleaf), where the Beneventan manuscripts have a localised method of setting the text to the phrase. This also occurs in *DEN1*. It seems more likely that this is coincidental than that there is a direct connection between the traditions of Benevento and St Denis, especially as they differ on so many other details.

In *Beatus uir 3*, the Beneventan manuscripts and *DEN1* take three syllables rather than one to rise fhk, leaving just one syllable to articulate igh gfghkik. In *Beatus uir 7*, they take three syllables instead of one to rise fhk which leaves sufficient syllables to articulate the rest of the phrase, but not enough for recitation. In *Beatus uir*, these manuscripts take three syllables instead of one to rise fhk, leaving only two syllables to articulate igh gfghkik. The textual stimuli for these variants will be discussed in detail in Chapter 5.

The division of the Cluniac manuscripts into pairs was made clear in the description above. The close relationship between *LEW* and *CLU1* is most strikingly illustrated by the parallel use of the special torculus in *CLU1* and kk in *LEW* when other manuscripts have ki. Oscillations around ghgf tend to have the same variant forms in these two manuscripts, and are an example of Hughes' fifth type of insignificant variant (the redistribution of notes among syllables). This is illustrated by the following table:

Phrase	Usual shape	*CLU1* and *LEW*
Sicut 7	ghgf f	gh gf
Commouisti 3	gf	ggf
Ad te leuaui 3 and 5	gf ghg	gf hg
Iubilate 4	fg	g
Desiderium 9, Sicut 11	ghgf f	gh gf

Beatus uir 3: *YRX* (representative of the mainstream)

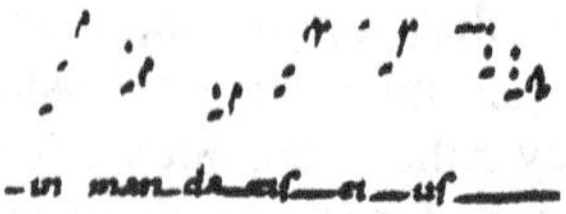

Beatus uir 3: *BEN5* (identical to *RAG* and *BEN1*)

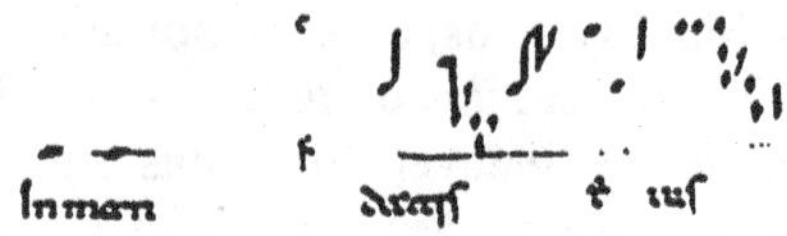

Beatus uir 3: *DEN1*

Beatus uir 7: *YRX*

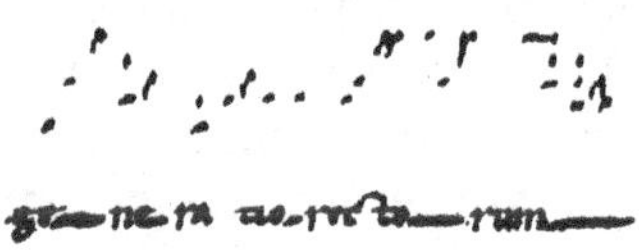

Beatus uir 7: *BEN5*

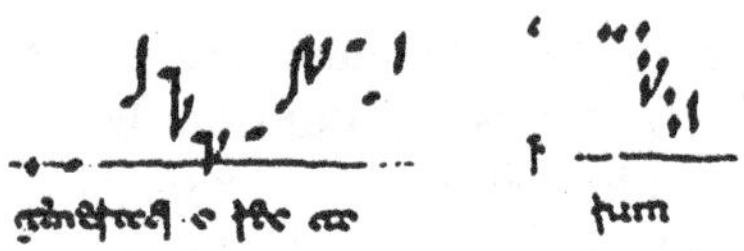

Beatus uir 7: *DEN1*

Beatus uir 11: *YRX*

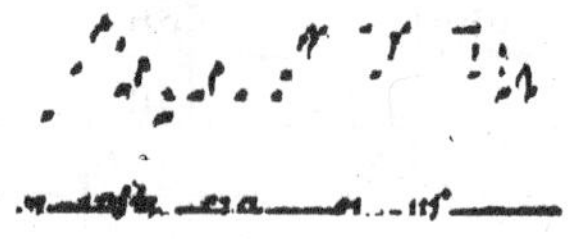

Beatus uir 11: *BEN5*

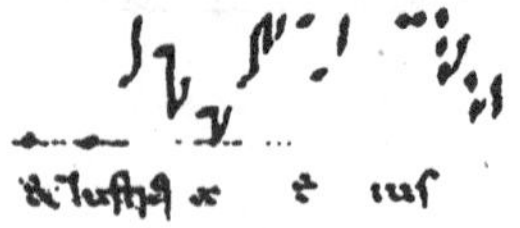

(*DEN1* has phrase ***B***)

Example **2.3**

DIJ1 and *ROG1* are also very closely related to each other. They both have hghg rather than hg in the phrase ***B*** melisma, a variant almost exclusive to these manuscripts. Similarities of process are seen even when there are variations from the usual shapes. Example **2.4** shows various examples of phrase ***B4***.

Ad te leuaui 10: *SAB* (representative of the mainstream)

Ad te leuaui 10: *DIJ1*

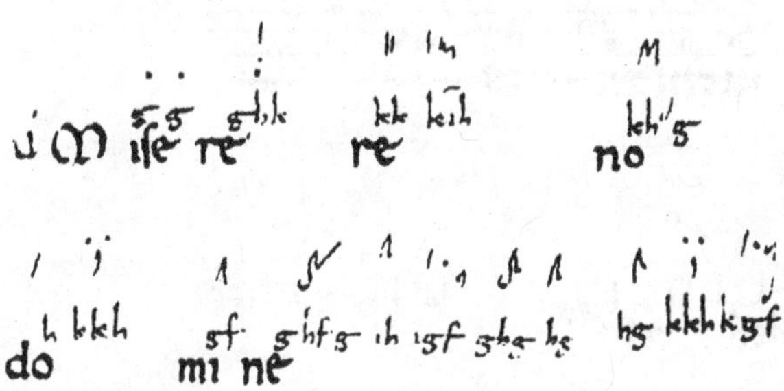

Ad te leuaui 10: *ROG1*

Desiderium 7: *ROG1* (usual shapes for phrase ***B$***)

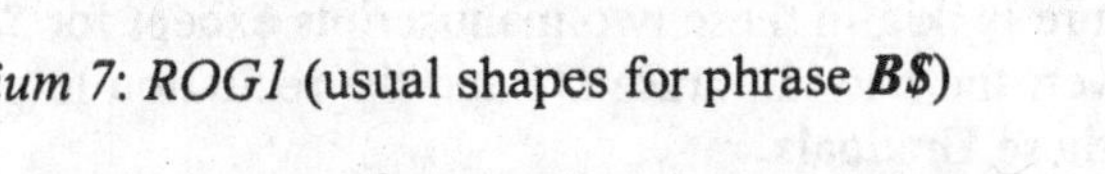

Example 2.4

Desiderium 7 in *ROG1* illustrates the usual outline of phrase ***B4***, and the version found in *ROG1* and *DIJ1* in *Ad te leuaui 10* is exactly equivalent. Both have the first main accent on the fifth syllable. The other manuscripts (represented here by *SAB*) have the kkkih figure (associated with an unaccented syllable) on 'no-' and treat 'do-' with the kh fall as the first main accent. There is therefore a different melodic outline.

However, there are some differences between *DIJ1* and *ROG1*.[111] For example, the ***B2*** rise is g gk in *DIJ1* and g hk in *ROG1*. This melodic shape is also adopted in *ROG1* at the beginning of *Beatus uir 9*, *Iubilate 6* and *Iubilate 7*, all examples of phrase ***C***, which one would expect to begin f hk. *De profundis 6* has very different melismas in the two manuscripts, as can be seen in Example **2.5**.

ROG1

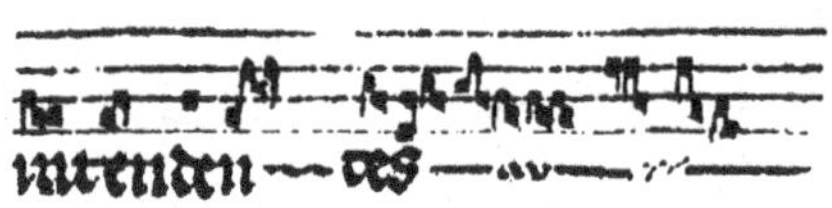

DIJ1

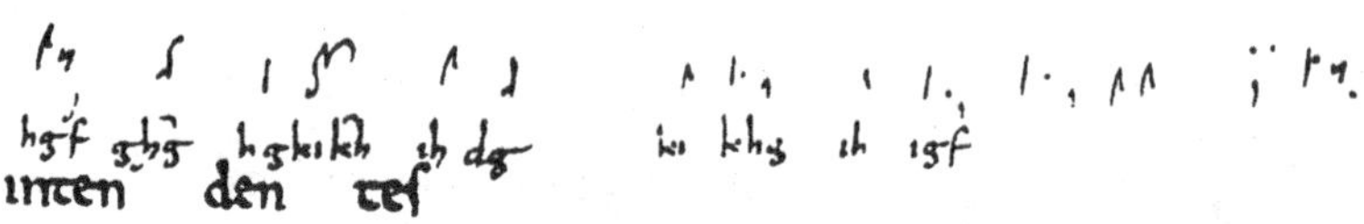

Example **2.5**

ROP and *SAB* are also very closely aligned. The ***D1*** melisma and the ***B2*** rise are strongly differentiated from the versions found in other manuscripts. There are many occasions when these two manuscripts have a small-scale variant that is peculiar to just these manuscripts. For example, in the ***D4*** melisma they have the same patterns of variants. The figure khfgh is usually kgfgh in these two manuscripts but kgfg in *Desiderium 4*, and the kkig figure is ikig in these two manuscripts except for *SAB* in *Ad te leuaui 2*. However, the rise in phrase ***D1*** and the recitation in phrase ***E*** are not identical in these Graduals.

The Western Frankish manuscripts are closely related, as suggested by Ferreira,[112] although there are places where one of the manuscripts differs from the other two in minor details, as the examination of variants in *Iubilate* demonstrated. *IRI* demonstrates an independent tradition, although it does have many features in common with the Western Frankish

[111] Some of these are notational. *ROG1* does not differentiate between i and *i* in these chants. There are several variants where *DIJ1* has *i* and *ROG1* has i or k.

[112] Ferreira, *Music at Cluny*, op. cit., 103.

manuscripts. The treatment of the khk/khik figure and of the phrase ***E*** recitation allies it with the Cluniac manuscripts, although it occasionally uses i rather than k like the Aquitanian and Beneventan manuscripts (for example, in the ***D1*** rise and the ***B*** cadence). Some important features are signs of independence in this source. For example: in phrase ***A2***, the figure hghfhkhk is hghfgihk in *IRI* alone; phrase ***E*** begins ghik but ghkk in just this manuscript.

The illustrative analysis above has confirmed the close relationship between the earliest manuscripts and *LAV*. Eleventh-century neumed manuscripts are generally less compatible with this earlier tradition. *KLO1* has a characteristically Eastern Frankish redaction, and is clearly melodically differentiated from other pitched sources. The Eastern Frankish neumed sources are remarkable for their inconsistent attitude to minor details. The Aquitanian and Beneventan manuscripts are closely related, and are often compatible with the earliest manuscripts. The Cluniac and Western Frankish manuscripts are more distantly related to these traditions, and are not always closely related to each other. This is important in the choice of which manuscript to use as the basis for the analysis. *DIJ1* has frequently been used as the pitch guide when transcriptions are being made from neumed sources. It was used by Solesmes from the outset, and is hence the basis of all its performing texts of the Mass Proper chants, including the *Graduale Romanum* (1974), itself used as the basis for the *Graduale Triplex* (1979), which many use to provide musical examples in scholarly discourse.[113] Perhaps the most extensive example is that of Hansen, who bases *The Grammar of Gregorian Tonality* on the pitches of *DIJ1*.[114] The stimulus for the use of *DIJ1* in such contexts appears to be a combination of several of the characteristics of the source. It is a Tonary, copied with the purpose of fixing the tradition, and acting as an authoritative reference manual. The neumes appear to lend an air of antiquity and authenticity to the manuscript, while the letters give precise pitch indications in a 'primitive' manner.[115] Although use of this manuscript as a reference for pitch causes no difficulties when chants are being discussed in general terms, any detailed musical analysis runs the risk of constructing a general narrative on the evidence of what has been demonstrated here to be a highly localised tradition.

---

[113] One example of this is Cullin, O., 'L'*Office de Pâques* Comme Miroir du Chant Grégorien: du Concept Liturgique à la Réalisation Musicale', *Analyse Musicale* (1990), 19–25.

[114] Hansen, F., *The Grammar of Gregorian Tonality* (Copenhagen, 1979).

[115] 'H159 is, if not the oldest, at least among the oldest unambiguously transcribable MSS, and it is at least the oldest MS which makes an unambiguous distinction between b and b flat.' Hansen, op. cit., 15.

This was one of the factors influencing the decision to use *BEN5* instead as the basis for the analysis in this study. Although there are some details in which this manuscript differs from the earliest manuscripts, most of the recurring points of variance in *BEN5* are compatible with the oldest manuscript tradition. It reflects eleventh- and twelfth-century chant traditions in both Aquitaine and Benevento, and although it differs from both Eastern Frankish and Cluniac versions of the chants, these are themselves so internally varied that it would be difficult to choose a 'representative' source for these regions. *BEN5* is not a 'better' or 'purer' manuscript than those from other regions, but it does reflect the chant tradition of the widest possible area. Because points of variance have been clearly identified and recognised, it is possible to make an analysis of the eighth-mode tracts in the Gregorian tradition without lending weight to melodic patterns that are representative of a localised practice, rather than of the wider tradition.

The Old Roman Tradition

The Old Roman tradition is represented by the three surviving Graduals. The earliest of these, and the one chosen as the basis for the analysis in this study, is *ORC*, which was copied for the church of St. Cecilia in Trastevere and is dated 1071.[116] *ORJ* is from St. John in the Lateran, and dates from the eleventh or twelfth century. *ORP* is from St. Peter's, and dates from the thirteenth century.[117] Old Roman notation belongs to the central Italian family of notations.[118] Although there does not appear to have been an extensive copying tradition before *ORC*, there was a local notational style from at least the early eleventh century.[119] As with the Gregorian tradition, a comparison of the versions of a single tract found in these manuscripts

[116] See Connolly, T., 'The *Graduale* of S. Cecilia in Trastevere and the Old Roman Tradition', *JAMS* 28 (1975), 413–58; Lütolf, M., *Das Graduale von Santa Cecilia in Trastevere* (Cologny-Genève, 1987).

[117] Huglo, M., 'Le Chant 'Vieux-Romain': Liste des Manuscrits et Témoins Indirects,' *Sacris Erudiri* 6 (1954), 96–124; 98–100.

[118] See Boe, J., 'Music Notation in Archivio San Pietro C 105 and in the Farfa Breviary, Chigi C. VI. 177', *Early Music History* 18 (1999), 1–45. Some of the distinctions between Beneventan and central Italian notation are detailed on pages 27–30. See also Boe, J., 'Chant Notation in Eleventh-Century Roman Manuscripts', in G. Boone (ed.), *Essays on Medieval Music in Honor of David G. Hughes: Isham Library Papers* 4 (Cambridge, Mass., 1995), 43–57; 44–5

[119] Before finding San Pietro C 105, Boe had tentatively concluded that 'there was no native Roman notation in general use before about 1020 at the earliest'. See Boe, 'Chant Notation in Eleventh-Century Roman Manuscripts', op. cit., and 'Music Notation in Archivio San Pietro C 105', op. cit.

gives a broad impression of the manner in which these chants varied from manuscript to manuscript.

The Melodic Variants in Iubilate

*1. 'Iubilate deo' [phrase **A1**]* The three manuscripts have the same melodic outline until the final cadence, where *ORC* has hfghihghg, *ORJ* has hfhihghg and *ORP* has hfghighg.

*2. 'omnis terra' [phrase **B1**]* *ORC* and *ORJ* have identical melodies. *ORP* begins g hk on 'omnis' instead of kih k..

*3. 'seruite domino' [phrase **C2**]* *ORC* has the cadence ikhihghg but *ORJ* and *ORP* have ikihihghg. On '-mi-', *ORJ* and *ORP* have two repercussed k's where *ORC* has a single horizontal penstroke. This is a common variant on k before a fall, and other examples of it will not be detailed exhaustively.

*4. 'in letitia' [phrase **D1**]* *ORC* and *ORJ* have identical melodies. *ORP* has ghihikih instead of ghihkih on the first syllable. In the melisma, the other two manuscripts have kkig and *ORP* has kkihg and *ORP* has hgf instead of hggf.

*5. 'In trate in conspectu eius' [phrase **E1**]* *ORC* and *ORJ* have identical melodies. *ORP* has ghkih instead of ghiki on 'tra-'.

*6. 'in exultatione' [phrase **B1**]* *ORC* and *ORJ* have identical melodies. *ORP* has hgf instead of ghgf on 'ex-'.

*7. 'scitote quod dominus' [phrase **C2**]* *ORC* and *ORJ* have identical melodies. *ORP* has the same variant cadence as on 'seruite domino', but this time *ORJ* has the same as *ORC*.

*8. 'ipse est deus' [phrase **D1**]* *ORC* and *ORJ* have almost identical melodies, but *ORC* has kig, *ORJ* has hkkig, and *ORP* has hkig near the beginning of the melisma. *ORP* also has hgf instead of hggf.

*9. 'Ipse fecit nos et non ipsi nos' [phrase **B5**]* *ORJ* and *ORC* have identical melodies. On '-cit', *ORP* has ihi instead of kihihih, and on 'nos' it has hgih instead of hghih. On 'et', it has gihgf instead of ghihgf.

*10. 'nos autem populus eius' [phrase **C1**]* *ORC* and *ORJ* have identical melodies. *ORP* has the same variant cadence as in 'seruite domino' and 'scitote quod dominus'.

*11. 'et oues pascue eius' [phrase **F**]* *ORC* and *ORJ* have almost identical melodies. On 'o-', *ORC* and *ORP* have hghkih and *ORJ* has hghkihg. *ORP* has ghi instead of ghih on the first syllable. It has kk instead of k on 'pas-'. Within the melisma, it has ghgf instead of ghg at the bottom of the descending pattern. On '-ius', it has hgf instead of hggf. At the end of the melisma, *ORP* falls to g where the other two manuscripts only fall to h.

In summary, the two earlier manuscripts are very closely related, both melodically and scribally. Not only do they almost always have the same melodies, but they often have the same neume shapes as well. *ORP* is less closely connected, chronologically, musically, and scribally. It tends to omit repeated notes, or intermediate notes within a melodic rise or fall. *ORP* differs from the other two manuscripts only in points of detail.

Melodic Variants in the Easter Vigil Tracts

The Old Roman manuscripts do not include chants in the local idiom for the canticles and processional tract of the Easter Vigil, instead using Gregorian forms of *Attende, Cantemus, Vinea* and *Sicut.* This has prompted widespread speculation about the age of these chants, about whether there once were Old Roman Easter Vigil tracts, now lost, and, if so, how they were characterised. These questions will be addressed in Chapter 7. Here, the Gregorian Easter Vigil tracts in the Old Roman Graduals are of interest because of the evidence they provide about the circumstances surrounding the copying of these manuscripts, and in particular *ORC*.

There are known connections between Montecassino and the church of St. Cecilia in Trastevere at the time of the copying of *ORC*. Desiderius, Abbot of Montecassino from 1058 to 1086, was also the Cardinal Priest at St. Cecilia in Trastevere until he became Pope in 1086.[120] 'It is not unreasonable, then, to see the influence of Desiderius and the Cassinese tradition behind the activity at S. Cecilia, though whether this can be extended to the changes in chanting is a difficult question. It may be pertinent to recall that Montecassino had recently been compelled to accept a change in its style of chanting.'[121] The connection between *ORC* and Benevento was recognised as early as 1954 by Huglo: 'Enfin, le graduel

---

[120] Cowdrey, H. E. J., *The Age of Abbot Desiderius: Montecassino, the Papacy and the Normans in the Eleventh and early Twelfth Centuries* (Oxford, 1983).

[121] Connolly, 'The *Graduale* of S. Cecilia in Trastevere', op. cit., 437–8. See also Lütolf, op. cit., 45–6.

compte 19 séquences et une vingtaine de tropes. Toutes ces pièces étrangères s'apparentent aux manuscrits bénéventains.'[122]

The Easter Vigil tracts provide evidence of just such a direct connection between the two centres (see 323, 327, 347 and 349 for copies of the chants). Despite the verse structures of these pieces varying widely in different manuscripts (see Chapter 3), they are almost identical in *ORC* and *BEN5*. *BEN5* has a verse division at *Vinea 6* where *ORC* does not,[123] and *ORC* has capital 'A' (but without a crossbar) followed by the complete word 'adiutor' at *Cantemus 5*. There is no musical reason for a new verse to begin here, although it does appear in several manuscripts.

ORC and *BEN5* have identical versions of almost all phrases. This is especially striking in the phrase ***E*** recitation, which often varies so widely between manuscripts.[124] In phrases ***D*** and ***F***, they replace the ghgf f figure with gh ggf. *ORC* and *BEN5* combine the two text phrases of *Sicut 4* and *Sicut 5* into a single musical phrase, using ***B*** while the other manuscripts have ***EB***.

However, the two manuscripts are not identical. The rise fhk is replaced by fhikl in *ORC* in *Sicut 7* and *Sicut 11*, but not in *BEN5*. The ***B1*** opening varies on only four occasions. In *Cantemus 2* and *Vinea 7 ORC* has g hk, and in *Cantemus 7* and *Sicut 7* it has gk k. In phrase ***C***, *ORC* has gfgh with no recitation in *Cantemus 3*, *Cantemus 8* and *Attende 6* while *BEN5* has the expected gfg. The most common variants occur when the two manuscripts have different numbers of repeated notes. For example, *ORC* has kkkh rather than kkh and kkk rather than kk in *Attende 2*, and ends the recitation pattern kk instead of k in *Attende 4*. The phrase ***C*** cadence is usually kkihihghg instead of kkkihihghg in *ORC*. Variants involving repeated notes occur commonly in the final phrase of these tracts:

BEN5	*ORC* *Cantemus 10*	*ORC* *Sicut 11*	*ORC* *Vinea 9*
ggghggfg	gghggfg	gggghggfg	
kkklhhg	kklhhg	kkkklhg	kkklhg

In *Attende 6*, *ORC* has 'gramina', and *BEN5* has 'gramen'. This grammatical variant is described more fully in Chapter 3, below, and has led to entirely different versions of phrase ***C*** being used.

---

[122] 'Le Chant 'Vieux-Romain': Liste des Manuscrits et Témoins Indirects,' *Sacris Erudiri* 6 (1954), 96–124 ; 99.

[123] *ORC* makes sense of the musical structure; *BEN5* highlights the fourfold repetition of phrases beginning 'et' in this text.

[124] The only difference is that in *Vinea 4*, *BEN5* has a pes on 'circum**d**edit' and *ORC* has one on 'cir**cum**dedit'.

It seems likely that the scribe of *ORC* learned these melodies in a specifically Beneventan version, probably provided by Abbot Desiderius, or by monks associated with him. The exemplar, while closely related to *BEN5*, was almost certainly a manuscript directly connected with Montecassino. In the absence of access to manuscripts from the monastery itself, it is not possible at this stage to ascertain whether a close exemplar for the Gregorian Easter Vigil tracts in *ORC* survives.[125]

The versions of the Easter Vigil tracts in *ORJ* and *ORP* are not as closely identified with Montecassino, as the table below illustrates:

	BEN5	*ORC*	*ORJ*	*ORP*
E melisma opening	klig	klig	klkg	klig
B opening	g gk	g gk usually	g hk usually	g hk usually
B cadence	kkhiggf	kkhiggf	kkhiggf	inconsistent
C cadence	kkkihihghg	kkihihghg usually	kkkihihghg (kkihihghg once; kkkkihihghg once)	kkihihghg usually; ikihihghg in *Cantemus 3*, *Vinea 3*
E recitation	i with ik	i with ik	k with hk	k with hk

ORP frequently eliminates the pitch repetitions found in the other manuscripts, as in the Old Roman eighth-mode tracts. It replaces the igh figure in phrase ***C*** with the Old Roman figure seen in the equivalent place in the Old Roman eighth-mode tracts: iihgh,[126] iihghi,[127] ihgh,[128] or ighi.[129] The figure khik which precedes the melisma in phrase ***C*** is similarly given the Old Roman shapes: kkhiki,[130] kkihiki,[131] kkihik, kkhik, khik, or it is omitted altogether.

In *Attende 11*, *ORP* has ghkik on 'iu-', and ghkik again on '-di-', where the other manuscripts have the rise. In *Vinea 8*, *ORP* has hghk on 'do-', and then ghki on 'sa-', where the other manuscripts rise. This may reflect the

[125] The idea that Roman scribes may have worked from Gregorian exemplars is most recently discussed by M-N. Colette in 'Grégorien et Vieux-Romain: Deux Méthodes Différentes de Collectage de Mélodies Traditionelles?', in J. Szendrei and D. Hiley (eds.), *Laborare Fratres in Unum: Festschrift László Dobszay* (Hildesheim and Zurich, 1995), 37–52, 39.

[126] *Cantemus 5* and *Vinea 8*; see *Qui seminant 6* in *ORP* for this shape.

[127] *Vinea 3*; see *Beatus uir 11* in *ORP* for this shape.

[128] *Cantemus 3*.

[129] *Attende 3*.

[130] See *Qui confidunt 6* in *ORP* for this shape.

[131] See *Iubilate 3*, *Iubilate 7*, and *Qui regis 5* in *ORP* for this shape.

Old Roman tendency towards repetition. Phrase ***D*** only occurs once in the four Easter Saturday tracts, and that is in *Sicut 7*. The melisma in *ORP* is different from that of the Gregorian version. The kihg fall is a familiar Old Roman phrase ***D*** shape, but this phrase ends with the Gregorian phrase ***C*** cadence (hkihihghg). *Sicut 8* has a different melisma altogether in *ORP*. It begins with phrase ***E*** material but ends hikhikhg. The internal repetition of the figure is typical of the Old Roman tradition. In *ORP*, the final phrase begins hghk twice but in the other two tracts it has hghkih, which is the usual opening of phrase ***F*** in the Old Roman tradition. Such borrowing from Old Roman shapes can be seen also in *ORP* (*Attende 10*, *Sicut 2*, *Sicut 5*, *Vinea 7*) and *ORJ* (*Cantemus 4*), where ***B2*** phrases with begin f hk, the Old Roman opening.

The small variants which may be found in many places in *ORJ* and *ORP* are well illustrated by Vi2 and At2:

usual shape	hki	khk	kkk	lhhg
ORP Attende 2	gki	k		lkg
ORP Vinea 2	gki	khk		lkg
ORJ Attende 2	gki	khk	kkk	lhhg
ORJ Vinea 2	gki	khk	kkk	lhhg

ORC has a direct connection with the Beneventan versions of the Easter Vigil tracts. *ORJ* is clearly differentiated from this (for example, in the phrase ***E*** recitation, in the phrase ***E*** melisma, and in the phrase ***B2*** opening), but is not melodically distant from *ORC*. In *ORP* many Old Roman elements have permeated the Gregorian versions of the Easter Vigil tracts.

Conclusions

ORP contains versions of the eighth-mode tracts that are distanced from *ORJ* and *ORC*, although the variants are consistently to do with small details rather than the broader melodic outline. To base an analysis on *ORP* would therefore give the least representative impression of the tradition and, what is more, it is a manuscript that greatly post-dates both the Gregorian manuscripts considered here and the other Old Roman manuscripts. The choice between using *ORC* and using *ORJ* as the basis for the analysis is not an urgent one, as the manuscripts date from a similar time, and have almost identical readings of the chants.[132] In choosing *ORC* and *BEN5* as the basis for the analysis, it is possible to get close to the meeting of the two traditions in eleventh-century Rome. It might be argued that the Old Roman tradition became infiltrated with Gregorian elements, especially considering the close relationship between the Beneventan Easter Vigil tracts and those found in *ORC*. To use a Beneventan manuscript to represent the Gregorian tradition meets this challenge head on. It will become clear in the analysis in Chapter 3 that although the two traditions are structurally closely related, they have very different dialects, and do not always have equivalent phrases. There was no synthesis of the Gregorian and Old Roman eighth-mode tracts in eleventh-century Rome. The two traditions were retained as separate and distinct entities.

132 The Gregorian Easter Vigil tracts are not as closely related in the two manuscripts, perhaps indicating – as one would expect – that they were not as well known as chants in the local melodic dialect.

Chapter 3
Analysis of the Eighth-Mode Tracts

Introduction

This chapter consists of a detailed analysis of the eighth-mode tracts. In the first part of the chapter, the subgroups within the six basic phrase types are identified, together with the formal or textual circumstances under which each is used. The different formal circumstances include different verses of tracts tending to have different versions of phrases, and different phrases being used when the verses divide into two, say, rather than four phrases. The textual circumstances include the number of syllables available, the number of accents, and the pattern of accented and unaccented syllables. Sometimes, particular words are associated with a particular version of a phrase. The second part of the chapter consists of an examination of each eighth-mode tract in turn, and an assessment of how close the melodic state of each is to the formal scheme outlined in the first part of the chapter. When tracts depart from the expected outlines, either in one tradition or in both, possible reasons for the departure are sought.

The analytical findings are complex, and the analysis is presented in an exhaustive manner. This is because the subsequent chapters of this study rely heavily on my understanding of the construction of the genre, and it is important that the reader should have access to my reasoning and to the evidence that forms the basis for it. Many characteristics of the chants combine as *aides-mémoires*. These include the association of certain phrases and certain versions of phrases with particular formal and textual circumstances, and the use of textual connections to cue an otherwise unexpected phrase type. There are also characteristics that do not seem to have been stabilised by mnemonics in the same way. These include the division of the text into verses and of the verses into phrases. Such *aides-mémoires* and less stable factors are presented in a linear fashion in the present chapter. They are then used as the foundation for an exploration in the rest of this study of how the eighth-mode tracts came to be transmitted so stably that the ninth-century Frankish and the eleventh-century Old Roman manuscripts have largely equivalent versions of the chants. They also form the basis for an investigation of how the tradition may have been understood by cantors once it was written down. They provide a new body of concrete evidence for a reappraisal of the relationship between the Old

Roman and Gregorian chant traditions, and their eighth-century Roman ancestor.

The eighth-mode tracts are a closely related group of chants. Their distinctive formal structure, as soloists' chants sung through directly without a refrain, is reflected in their musical structure. All of the eighth-mode tracts are made up of combinations of a small group of phrase shapes, each of which is associated with a particular formal context. As was shown in Chapter 1, above, phrase ***A*** is associated specifically with the beginnings of tracts and phrase ***E*** is used to begin verses other than the first verse. Phrase ***B*** is associated with the break at the half-verse, and phrase ***C*** is used to begin the second half of the verse. Phrase ***D*** appears last in verses apart from the final verse, which concludes with phrase ***F***. Each of the six basic phrase types may be divided into subgroups: some of these subgroups are closely related, but others share no more than the cadential figures at the end of the phrase.

These labels simply use the first six letters of the alphabet in the order in which phrases are normally encountered in the course of an eighth-mode tract. In itself, the label has no significance, but it is necessary to sing or read through only a few eighth-mode tracts to become accustomed to the characteristics of the phrase types associated with each formal context.

Those analysing the eighth-mode tracts have chosen various methods for labelling the phrase types. Apel labels the phrases as g_1, $g_2 \ldots g_n$.[1] As all phrases except phrase ***B*** cadence on g, to label the phrases according to the final note is less informative than to label the phrases according to their formal context. Cullin and Hucke use terminology associated with psalmodic recitation, such as 'intonation', 'mediation', or 'flex', to identify the different phrases and their formal contexts.[2] I have avoided such terminology because the textual context can lead the melodies far away from anything resembling a psalmodic outline. The difficulties associated with the adoption of this terminology in analyses of the eighth-mode tracts are exemplified by the fact that Cullin's *flexe* is equivalent to phrase ***D*** in the current study, whereas Hucke's 'flex' is equivalent to phrase ***C***. Kainzbauer and Nowacki both use letters of the alphabet, in a similar manner to that of the present study.[3] However, Kainzbauer's labels do not

[1] Apel, W., *Gregorian Chant* (Bloomington, Ind., 1958), 315–23.

[2] Cullin, O., *Le Trait dans les Répertoires Vieux-Romain et Grégorien: un Témoin de la Psalmodie sans Refrain* (PhD, University of Paris, Sorbonne, 1990); Hucke, H., 'Tract', *NG* 19, 108–10.

[3] Kainzbauer, X., 'Der Tractus Tetrardus – eine centologische Untersuchung', *Beiträge zur Gregorianik* 11 (Regensburg, 1991), 1–132; Nowacki, E., 'Text Declamation as a Determinant of Melodic Form in the Old Roman Eighth-Mode Tracts', *EMH* 6 (Cambridge, 1986), 193–225.

clearly show the equivalent formal contexts of the subgroups of the phrases. For example, the phrase types used at the ends of verses (***D1, D2*** etc in the present analysis) are labelled as **W**, **X**, **Y**, and **+R**. Objections to Kainzbauer's labelling of phrase ***C*** as **NO** were raised in Chapter 1. Nowacki's labelling does not always clearly show the differences between the subgroups of phrases.[4] For example, V–M is used to label indivisible first verse-halves when verse-opening elements are used before the phrase ***B*** cadence. Although this admirably indicates the formal function of the phrases, it does not differentiate between the very different phrase shapes found in, for example, *Iubilate 9* (p. 290–91), *De profundis 9* (p. 288–9) and *Commouisti 3* (p. 284 and 286).

The Old Roman and Gregorian chant traditions are treated in parallel throughout this analysis. Despite their different melodic dialects, the basic equivalence of the traditions is apparent within the eighth-mode tract repertory. The two traditions have six equivalent phrase types, equivalent subgroups within each phrase, and generally use equivalent phrases in a given context. When they do differ, it is almost always possible to identify the alternative formal and textual cues which have been followed. Musical examples accompanying the descriptions of each phrase type demonstrate the equivalence of the traditions. The melodic movements generally follow the same contours, with the same structurally important pitches. This is made clear in the short descriptions accompanying each comparative example, and the point will not be laboured in the body of the text. The analysis should be read in conjunction with Appendix 2 (pp. 269–323), in which the eighth-mode tract phrases are grouped according to phrase type.

The Six Phrase Shapes and their Subgroups

Phrase A

There are two types of phrase used for beginning an eighth-mode tract. The first begins and ends on g, using the upper range of eighth-mode pitches, and is generally used in phrases with up to seven syllables;[5] the second drops to the lower range of eighth-mode pitches, between d and g, and is found in phrases with eight or more syllables.

*Phrase **A1*** The phrases in group ***A1*** (271–2) are closely related to each other within each tradition. Any differences are directly stimulated by the textual outlines.

---

[4] Nowacki, op. cit., 217–19.

[5] Or two accented syllables, according to Kainzbauer, op. cit., 78.

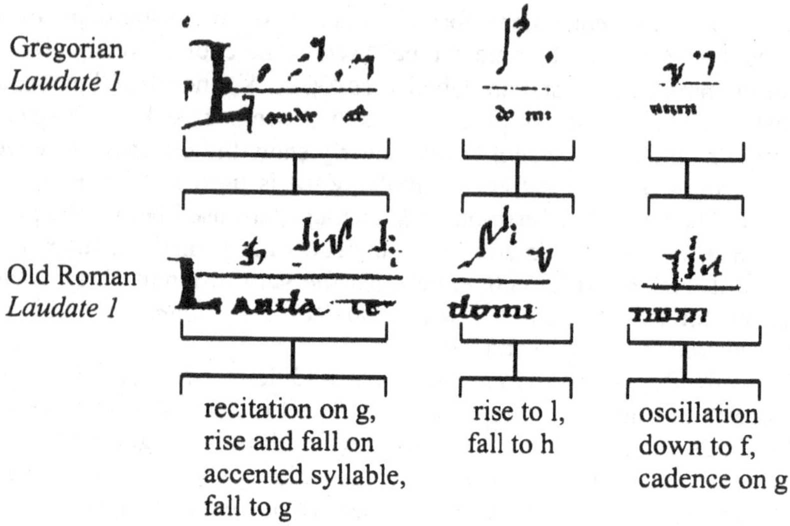

Example **3.1**

In both traditions, a series of invariable melodic patterns is associated with the end of the phrase, beginning with a rise on the last accent ('dóminum' in Example **3.1**). These patterns may be divided between one, two, or three syllables. At the beginning of the phrase, there is a pattern ending on g, (ghhg in the Gregorian tradition, hkihg in the Old Roman) usually at the end of the subject or the verb (one or two words). The next (and last) accented syllable is always associated with the rise to l. If there is another syllable after the pattern ending on g and before the rise, it is given the pitches fg (*Qui confidunt 1*, *Sicut 1*, *Beatus uir 1*, and *De profundis 1* in the Gregorian tradition, *Qui confidunt 1* and *De profundis 1* in the Old Roman).

'Sicut ceruus desiderat' uses this version of the phrase in the Gregorian tradition despite having eight syllables (phrase *A1* is usually associated with there being seven syllables or fewer).[6] The reason for this may be found by considering the liturgical context in which *Sicut* was used. It was sung at the end of the alternation of readings and canticle-tracts during the Easter Vigil, and was therefore the fourth eighth-mode tract sung in a row by the soloist.[7] The liturgical and associative considerations in favour of

[6] The four tracts associated with the Easter Vigil (*Cantemus, Attende, Vinea* and *Sicut*) are not found in Old Roman versions. The Old Roman manuscripts have Gregorian versions of these chants. See above, pp. 50–53.

[7] It was not sung during the procession to the baptismal font until the later Middle Ages. See McKinnon, J., 'The Gregorian Canticle-Tracts of the Old Roman Easter Vigil', in C-H.

starting *Sicut* in the same way as the three preceding canticle-tracts were sufficient to override the stimulus provided by its eight-syllable first phrase. Kainzbauer's assertion that phrase ***A1*** is used when there are only two accents provides an alternative explanation.[8]

Several phrases in group ***A1*** end with the word 'domino', 'dominum', or 'deo'. Such textual connections will have helped to keep the melodic movements stable before musical notation was widely used as a memory aid. 'Qui confidunt in domino' begins with this version of the phrase in both traditions. One might expect an opening phrase with eight syllables to use phrase ***A2***, but the textual stimulus to use ***A1*** is self-evident. Because there is more text than is usual in phrases in this group, there is an extra recitation note in both traditions, disturbing the usual conjunction of certain melodic patterns with accents: '(con)fi(dunt)' has the rise instead of 'cón(fidunt)'[9] In the Old Roman tradition, the usual hkihg figure at the end of the subject or verb is replaced in this phrase by a more extended melodic pattern, consisting of the six-note phrase ***D*** cadence with an extra hg oscillation (compare with p. 308). In the Old Roman tradition, the rise on 'do-' goes only to k, rather than to l, in all three manuscripts. There is no clear reason for this variation, although it was well established. It may simply be a more extended response than is found in the Gregorian tradition to there being an unaccented syllable between the first part of the phrase and the next text accent. The fact that the Old Roman version of *De profundis* has the same extended melodic pattern in the middle of the phrase and a parallel extra syllable supports this suggestion.

The syntax of the first phrase of *De profundis* is different from that of other phrases in the group. The phrase does not end with the usual cadence in either tradition. The Gregorian tradition uses phrase ***A2*** shapes on 'ad te' (seen, for example, on '(ocu)los' in *Ad te leuaui 1*: see p. 273), continuing seamlessly into phrase ***B5*** (p. 290). The Old Roman tradition omits the cadence, proceeding straight into ***B5*** on 'ad' (p. 291).

'Clamaui ad te' ('I have cried to you') carries the burden of the sense, while 'De profundis' is a prepositional phrase and 'domine' is a vocative, clarifying 'ad te'. 'De profundis' is too short to be given phrase ***A1***, and does not make sense on its own. The arrows in Appendix 2, indicating melodic movements associated with accented syllables, show clearly that ***A1*** always has at least two accents. 'De profúndis' has only one. One might expect there to be a break after 'De profundis clamaui', consisting of the

Mahling and R. Seiberts (eds.), *Festschrift Walter Wiora zum 90. Geburtstag* (Tutzing, 1997), 254–70

[8] Kainzbauer, op. cit., 78.

[9] Melodic figures usually associated with accented syllables are marked with arrows in Appendix 2.

prepositional phrase and the subject + verb, but the cantors have preferred to keep 'clamaui ad te', subject, verb, and prepositional phrase, as a single unit. It is not clear why a division of 'clamaui/ ad te' was so strenuously avoided, or why it was avoided in this way. To use ***A2*** for the full text of the first half-verse would side step any objection to dividing the text, and the use of the lower part of the eighth-mode range would be particularly apposite for the articulation of 'De profundis' ('out of the deep'). However, word painting of this nature is foreign to the aesthetic of formulaic chants like these. No eighth-mode tract begins with a twelve-syllable first phrase, and it may be that this text was simply too long to use as a single unit in this manner. The reasons for using phrase ***A1*** in this peculiar manner rather than dividing 'clamaui/ ad te', or using phrase ***A2*** remain obscure and serve as a warning that it is not always possible to deduce what the cues working on medieval cantors may have been in a given context.

A further phrase deviates from the standard melodic shapes. In the Old Roman tradition, *Qui regis 1* begins like the other phrases in the group, but 'isra-' has independent movement before the usual closing patterns on the final syllable. 'Israhel' is a Hebrew word, and has been treated as if the last syllable is accented, leaving two syllables to articulate between the hkihg figure at the end of the first part of the phrase and the rise to l associated with the following accent. The first of these syllables begins with ghihgf, a figure also used in the Old Roman tradition at the beginning of ***E2*** (see p. 317) and ***A2*** (at the beginning of *Ad te leuaui 7* on 'Ita', and *Sepe 3* on 'Dicat': see p. 274). The pitches of the second syllable are the opening pitches of the Old Roman phrase ***C1*** (see p. 295), although in their usual formal context they are never associated with a single syllable. The melodic movements attached to these two syllables outline g fg, but the specific figures used to achieve this have been drawn from eighth-mode tract commonplaces, in a process of centonisation.[10] *Sepe 3* has the text 'dicat nunc israhel'. In the Old Roman tradition, the textual connection with 'Qui regis israhel' has prompted the cantors to use exactly the same melodic patterns for the last word of these phrases, even though *Sepe 3* does not appear at the beginning of the tract.

In the Gregorian tradition, the textual connection with *Sepe 3* works in an inverse manner. The Gregorian *Sepe 3* ends with an abbreviated version of phrase ***B3*** on 'israhel' (p. 285). This is in an appropriate formal context, as it ends the first half of the second verse. In *Qui regis 1*, 'Qui regis' has the usual ***A1*** figures around g associated with the subject or verb, even though 'Qui regis' consists of both subject and verb within this relative clause, and 'israhel' is the object. Instead of continuing with phrase ***A1***

[10] This term is used in the current study only to refer to occasions where isolated melodic patterns are used out of their expected contexts, like a patchwork.

material, 'israhel' is given exactly the same phrase ***B*** material as is used in *Sepe 3* on the same word (p. 285), although the full phrase ***B*** cadence is avoided until the end of the half-verse at 'intende' (p. 290). The beginning of the melisma on '-hel' in *Qui regis 1* should undoubtedly belong with phrase ***B3*** in the Gregorian tradition (see pp. 284–5). This is the only version of phrase ***B*** to use this characteristic rise to l and fall to g, made very clear in *BEN5*, where the same neumes are used on each occasion. Instead of beginning fhki like the other ***B3*** melismas, *Sepe 3* and *Qui regis 1* have ghki klhhg in every pitched manuscript.[11] This is the figure seen at the beginning of the Old Roman ***A1*** melisma and also, of course, in the Old Roman versions of *Sepe 3* and *Qui regis 1* (p. 272). Around this strong textual cue, the two traditions have retained shared melodic features, despite using different phrase shapes. In the Old Roman tradition, *Qui regis 1* has the appropriate music for the formal context, whereas in the Gregorian tradition, *Sepe 3* has the appropriate music for the formal context.

'Beatus uir qui timet dominum' is difficult to parse. The verb 'to be' is assumed, and 'Beatus (est)' is the predicate, while 'uir qui timet dominum' is the subject, with a relative clause. The sentence translates as 'Happy is/ the man/ who fears the Lord'. The interpretation of 'Beatus uir' as the subject, 'the happy man', makes the sentence impossible to parse, as there is no verb. In the Old Roman tradition the tract begins with the usual, complete, phrase ***A1*** shapes attached to 'Beatus uir', and has phrase ***B2*** attached to the rest of the sentence (p. 281). This divides the relative clause from the rest of the sentence, a logical division. The Gregorian cantors instead interpreted the first phrase of this tract as 'Beatus uir qui timet/ dominum', with the usual phrase ***A*** cadence on '-met'. Instead of dividing the relative clause from the rest of the sentence, the subject + verb of the relative clause is divided from the object. This makes little sense of the text, leaving only three syllables to articulate a very short and syntactically incomplete phrase ***B*** (p. 277).[12]

The accents within the first phrase of *Beatus uir* are also unusually spaced, as has been shown at length by Kainzbauer.[13] Chants such as the eighth-mode tracts, where certain melodic movements are associated exclusively with accented or with unaccented syllables, provide evidence

[11] In *Qui regis 1*, most manuscripts have ghkklhg. Only *BEN5*, *KLO1*, *SAB* and *TYR* have ghkiklhhg. This is not a variant seen otherwise at the beginning of the ***B3*** melisma.

[12] One of the central themes of Haas's *Mündlicher Überlieferung und altrömische Choral: historische und analytische computergestützte Untersuchungen* (Bern, 1997) is that Old Roman chant shows a higher degree of Latin competency than Gregorian chant, and that Gregorian chant was developed in the North 'für Personen mit schlechtern Lateinkenntnissen' (stated most concisely on page 136).

[13] Kainzbauer, op. cit., 21–2.

about how Latin was accented in the middle ages. The first phrase of *Beatus uir* in the Gregorian tradition is an exception to this (Example **3.2**).

DIJ1 (this pattern seen also in *CHA1*, *CLU1*, *GAL1*, *GAL2*, *IRI*, *LAN*, *MUR3*, *PAS2*, *ROG1*)

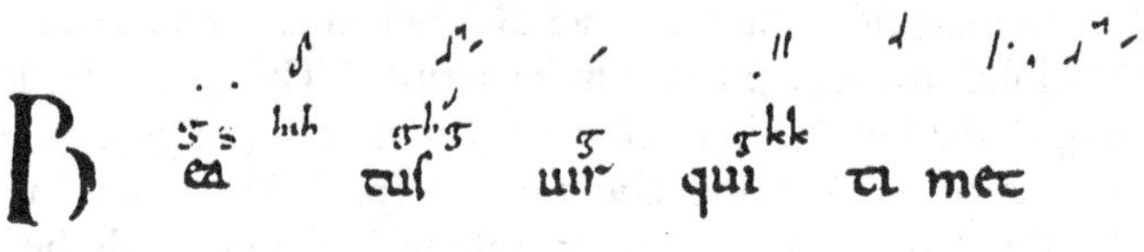

YRX (this pattern seen also in *ALB*, *LAV*, *TOU*)

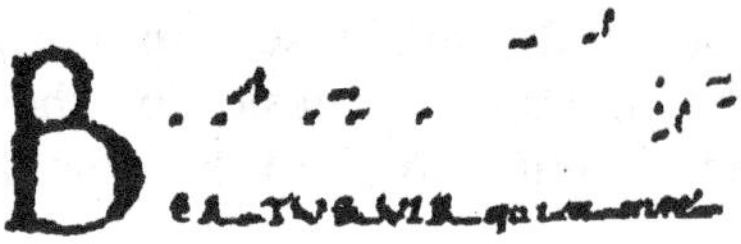

BRE

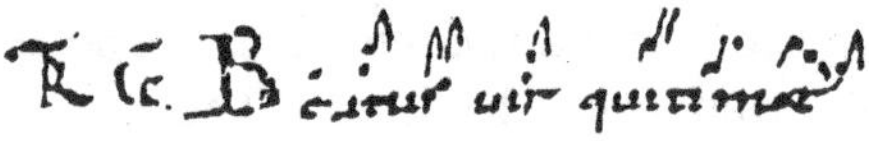

KLO1 (this pattern seen also in *BEN5*, *MOG4*, *RAG*)

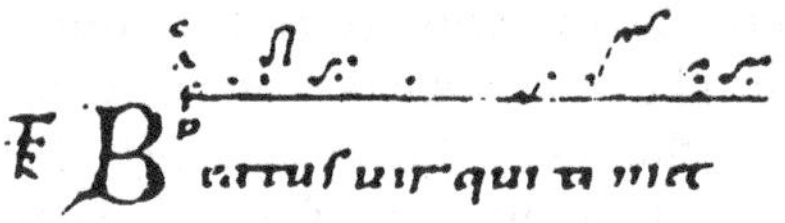

Example **3.2**

The gkkl figure usually associated with the accent is split in some manuscripts between ‘qui’ and ‘ti-’, and ‘uir’ is not treated as an accented syllable (*DIJ1* here). Some manuscripts split gkkl between the three syllables ‘uir qui ti-’, as if all are accented (*YRX* here). *BRE* treats ‘uir qui ti-’ as three accented syllables by using the decorated movements scandicus flexus (fghg?), pes virga (gkk?) and pes punctum (kll? ikl?). Some manuscripts treat ‘ti-’ as the accent, having fg gkkl on ‘qui ti-’ (*KLO1* here), which might be compared with *Qui confidunt 1*, *Sicut 1*, and *De profundis 1*, where the movement fg is attached to unaccented syllables.

Phrase A2 The second version of phrase *A* is completely different from the first except that three of the phrases have the same rise on the accented syllable immediately after the end of the predicate, followed by h, in both traditions. However, the phrase is extended because there are several more syllables to articulate. Phrases ***A1*** and ***A2*** both cadence on g.[14] Phrase ***A2*** is used to begin *Commouisti, Desiderium, Sepe, Ad te leuaui*, and *Qui seminant*, all of which have first phrases with eight syllables or more (pp. 273–6). The lower range of the eighth-mode is used, concentrating on f and dropping to d. This range is also characteristic of the second mode. These shapes, with their low range, are sometimes used to begin later eighth-mode tracts (see Chapter 6, below, for examples), and the opening of *Ad te levavi* and *Qui seminant* in the Gregorian tradition is also used to begin a later second-mode tract, *Tu es uas.*[15] Although the outlines of these first phrases are also used to begin other chants, the articulation is unrelated.[16] Despite their low range, these melodic shapes are not characteristic of second-mode tract beginnings.

The phrase shapes of group ***A2*** are interrelated, although they are not as uniform as group ***A1***. The first phrases of *Commouisti, Desiderium* and *Ad te leuaui* cadence in the same way (Example **3.3**).

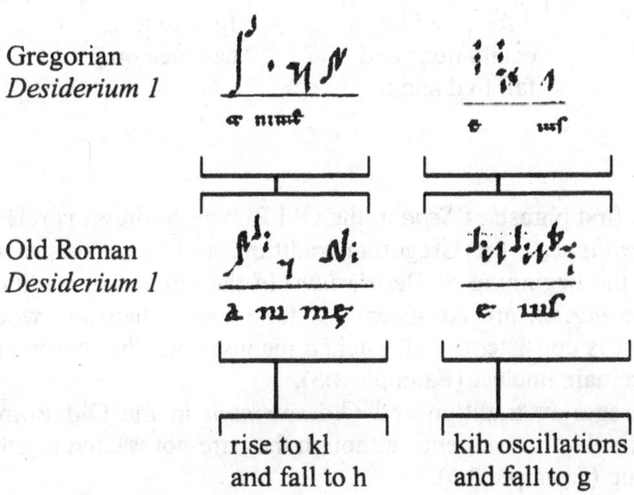

Example **3.3**

[14] Except for *Qui seminant 1* in the Old Roman tradition, which ends on h with a figure seen at the beginning of *Qui seminant 3* (***E3***) in all three manuscripts.

[15] This second-mode tract is identified as being a more recent composition by Cullin in the index of his doctoral dissertation, and also by W. Apel, op. cit., 313. It does not appear in any of the Old Roman manuscripts: see Cutter, P., *Musical Sources of the Old Roman Mass* (*Musicological Studies and Documents* 36) (Neuhausen-Stuttgart, 1979), 409–10.

[16] See Bryden, J., and Hughes, D., *An Index of Gregorian Chant. Volume II: Thematic Index* (Cambridge, Mass., 1969), 272 (*Ad te leuaui* and *Qui seminant*), 289 (*Commouisti*), 189 (*Desiderium*), 35 (*Sepe*).

Ad te leuaui, and *Qui seminant* start in the same way as each other in the Gregorian tradition, and *Sepe* and *Ad te leuaui* begin in the same way as each other in the Old Roman tradition (Example **3.4**).

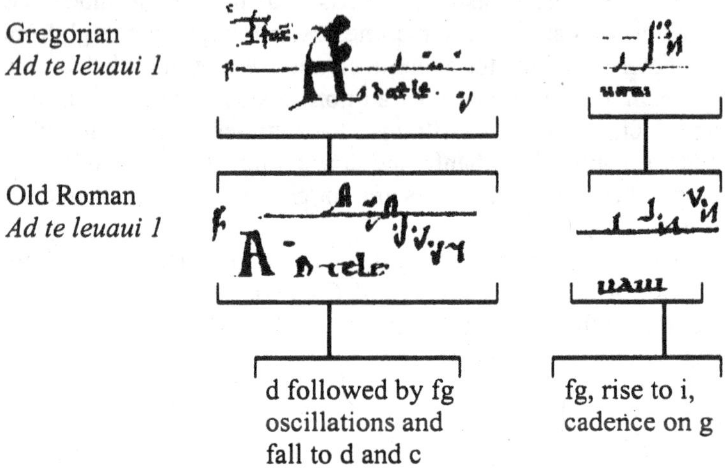

Example **3.4**

The end of the first phrase of *Sepe* in the Old Roman tradition is related to that of *Qui seminant* in the Gregorian tradition, and these shapes are closely related to the beginning of *Desiderium.* In the Gregorian tradition, the shapes on *Desiderium* are consistently a tone lower than one would expect. Although it is consistent in all pitched manuscripts, the reasons for the transposition remain unclear (Example **3.5**).

Sepe in the Gregorian tradition and *Qui seminant* in the Old Roman tradition have equivalent movements, although they are not related to other phrases in the group (Example **3.6**).

The beginning of *Commouisti* is not related to any other phrases, but the two traditions are related and, unusually, it is the Gregorian version that is more decorated (Example **3.7**).

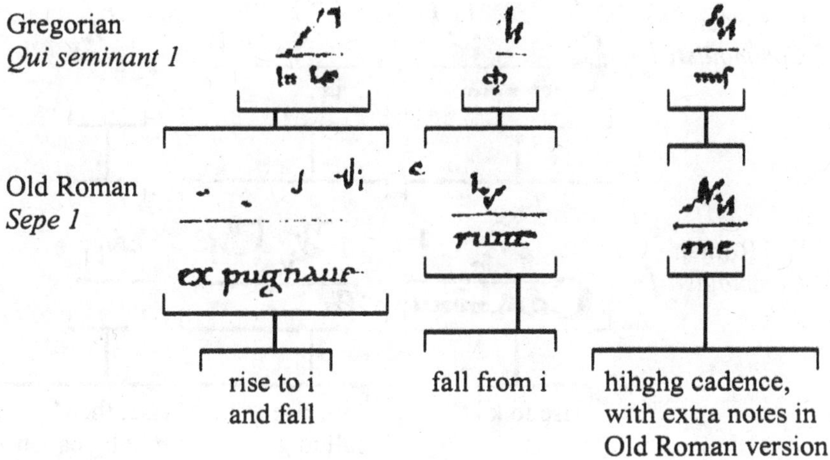

Example 3.5

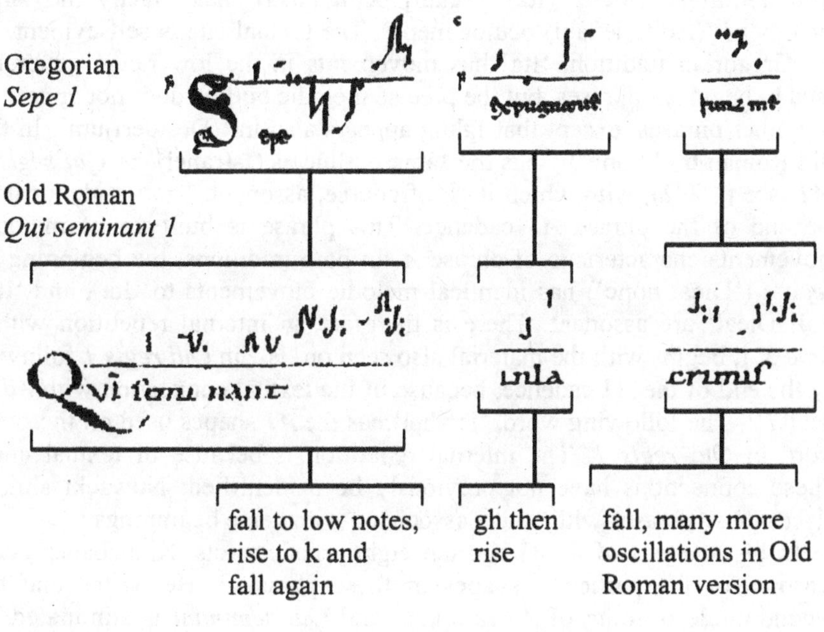

Example 3.6

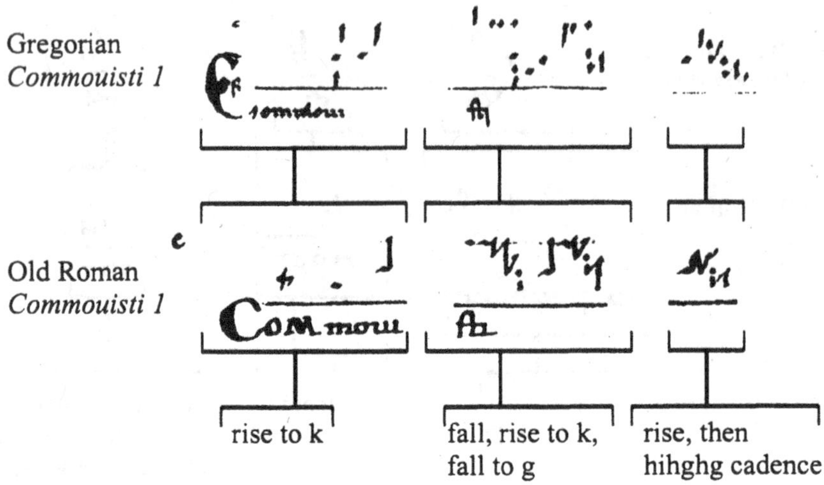

Example 3.7

The melodic patterns used to end *Commouisti, Desiderium* and *Ad te leuaui* are used in two other phrases. The first of these is *Ad te leuaui 7*, in both traditions, where '(Ita) [leuaui] oculi nostri' has exactly the same melody as '(Ad te leuaui) oculos meos'. The textual cue is self-evident. In the Gregorian tradition, 'Ita' has movements in the low range generally used to begin ***A2*** phrases, but the precise melodic outline does not appear in any other phrases, except that fghhg appears also in '(Desideri)um'. In the Old Roman tradition, 'I-' has the same outline as 'Is(rahel)' in *Qui regis 1* (***A1***: see p. 272), with which it is, of course, assonant. '-ta' is identical to the end of the phrase ***A1*** cadence. This phrase is built up of melodic movements characteristic of phrase ***A***. In both traditions, the beginning of *Sepe 3* ('Dicat nunc') has identical melodic movements to 'Ita', and 'Ita' and 'Dicat' are assonant. There is therefore an internal repetition within *Sepe 3*: it begins with the material also seen on 'is-' in *Qui regis 1* followed by the end of the ***A1*** cadence, because of the textual connection with *Ad te leuaui 7*. The following word, 'israhel' has the ***A1*** shapes used on the same word in *Qui regis 1*. The internal repetition is because of textual cues. These connections have not previously been identified: Nowacki simply places these phrases with others associated with verse beginnings.[17]

In his analysis of the Gregorian eighth-mode tracts, Kainzbauer gives reasons for the particular shapes of these phrases.[18] He writes that the second-mode opening of *Ad te leuaui* and *Qui seminant* is stimulated by

[17] Nowacki, op. cit., 211.
[18] Kainzbauer, op. cit., 78–84.

their sad texts, and that they later move to the 'inner joy' of the eighth mode at 'in gaudio' and 'in celis'.[19] However, *Ad te leuaui 1* rises to the upper range of eighth-mode pitches on 'oculos meos', with the gkkl figure and the cadence on g. Kainzbauer's explanation is even less convincing when the Old Roman tradition is considered as well as the Gregorian, as the Old Roman version of *Qui seminant* rises to the upper range of the eighth mode during the first phrase. It is clear that the meanings of the words are not affecting the course of a melody within a mode.

Kainzbauer also asserts that *Commouisti* starts on e, the keynote of deuterus, because that is the mode of mystical texts.[20] It is not necessary to address how one might define psalm texts as 'mystical' or 'non-mystical' as this tract starts on g in the Old Roman tradition, as well as in some Gregorian manuscripts.[21] The two-note opening on e is not an important melodic consideration, and it is inappropriate to draw conclusions from its use only in some manuscripts. The consideration of both the Old Roman and the Gregorian traditions, and of a wide sample of Gregorian manuscripts, is important in order to avoid constructing elaborate explanations for decorative or localised features that are not fundamental to the outlines of the melody.

It is not always possible to explain why phrases are constructed exactly as they are. The phrases in group ***A2*** are all related to each other, in one or both traditions, by the opening figures, the cadence, or both. The phrases are more expansive than those in the first group because of the length of text available; the compositional processes involved in choosing the varying melodic contours are probably irrecoverable. In the absence of concordances at the beginnings of other chants in the early Gregorian repertory, it may be impossible to reconstruct the provenance of these phrases and the circumstances prompting their use in these eighth-mode tracts (beyond the quantity of text).

*Phrase **B***

This phrase is associated with the caesura halfway through eighth-mode tract verses. All five subgroups within this phrase-type have the same cadence in each tradition: 'the frequency of [the cadence's] employment

---

[19] Ibid., 81.

[20] Ibid., 82.

[21] *SAB, ROG1, KLO1. IRI* starts on d. The pitches in *BEN5* are on top of the text, and cannot be defined with certainty, although they would presumably be closer to the f-staff if the pitch e was intended. It is, of course, not possible to define the pitch except as 'relatively low' in the neumed manuscripts.

has resulted in a particular version of it becoming habitual.'[22] The movements before the cadence, however, are clearly differentiated in the five subgroups, as will be made clear by a comparison of the descriptions of the melodic outlines of each subgroup (Examples **3.8** to **3.12**). The two traditions almost always use the same version of this phrase in a given context. ***B1*** and ***B2*** are generally used second in verses where the first half of the verse divides into two phrases. ***B3*** and ***B4*** are used when the first half of the verse consists of a single phrase. ***B5*** follows the first phrase in verses where this first phrase does not fully cadence.

Phrase ***B1*** The first version of phrase ***B*** (277–8) is used second in the first verse, when the first half-verse divides, unless there is an overriding textual or formal reason not to (Example **3.8**).

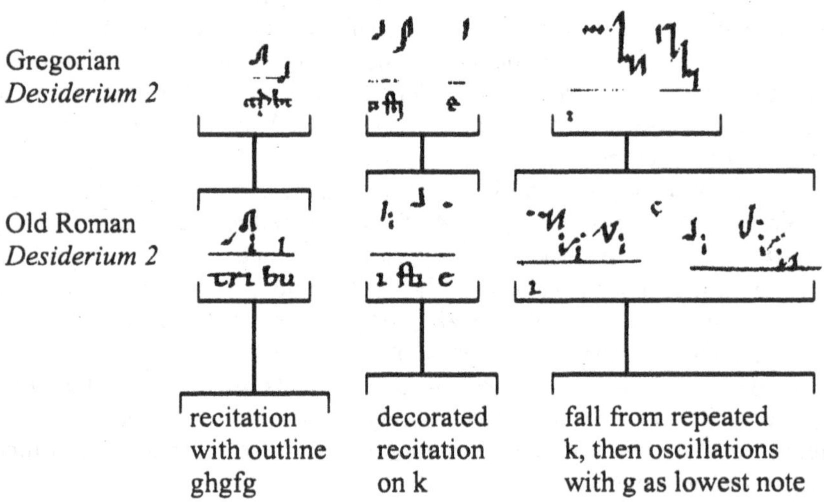

Example **3.8**

It is not used in the first verse of *Qui regis* in the Gregorian tradition because there is no cadence at the end of 'Qui regis israhel' (see 346), so ***B5*** is used to finish the verse-half (290). The first phrase of *De profundis* does not cadence fully in either tradition, for the textual reasons described above, so phrase ***B5*** (p. 290) is used instead of ***B1***. The second phrases of *Beatus uir* in the Old Roman tradition and *Cantemus* in the Gregorian tradition (there is no Old Roman version of this tract) use phrase ***B2***. In both traditions, the second phrase of *Qui confidunt* uses phrase ***B3***. The

---

[22] Nowacki, op. cit., 205.

reasons for the use of ***B2*** or ***B3*** in these contexts are discussed below, with reference to the individual tracts. In the Old Roman tradition, the second phrase of *Qui regis* (p. 306) begins with an f hik rise (reminiscent of phrase ***B2***), but the melisma is that of phrase ***D2*** and it has the ***A2*** cadence (seen for example on '(Commouis)ti' on p. 274). The return to ***A2*** material may be because of the syntax: 'intende' is the imperative verb phrase to which the relative clause 'Qui regis israhel' refers.

Phrase ***B1*** is used in all other first verses. It is also used in both traditions in the third verse of *Sepe*, possibly because the final word is assonant with the final word of the second phrase of *Desiderium* ('ei'/'michi'). The fourth verse of *Sepe* also uses phrase ***B1***, and the verse-half ends 'sibi' in the Gregorian tradition. The textual cue is the same as in the previous verse. However, in the Old Roman tradition, the text instead ends 'suas', and it is likely that the cue was associative since the same phrase had been used at the end of the previous verse.[23] Phrase ***B1*** is also used in the second verse of *Iubilate* in the Old Roman tradition, and the possible reasons for this will be discussed below.

In both traditions, phrase ***B1*** begins with a low recitation around g when there is sufficient text. The melodic movements are otherwise consistent in all phrases in this group in the Old Roman tradition, with an extra recitation note if necessary. In the Gregorian tradition, *Vinea 2*, *Attende 2* and *Beatus uir 2* have only three syllables. In most phrases, the last three syllables have hki k, and then the melisma, with the penultimate syllable being accented. *Vinea 2* and *Attende 2* are consistent with this, ornamenting their only accented syllable with the pitches khk. The text accent in *Beatus uir 2* is on the first of the three syllables, so that the usual association of particular melodic figures with accented syllables is lost. While most manuscripts have followed the formal cue of ending the verse half with phrase ***B1*** after a complete phrase ***A***, the Beneventan manuscripts follow the textual cue of *De profundis 2* ('domine'), and have ***B5*** for this phrase (see p. 290). This avoids the difficulties of accentuation, but implies that the phrase was not firmly fixed in the eighth-century tradition adopted in Francia.

Phrase ***B2*** The second version of phrase ***B*** (p. 279–83) is generally used second in verses other than the first (Example **3.9**).

[23] The text 'suas' appears in the Roman Psalter and 'suam' in the Gallican, but the origin of the variant 'sibi', found in all Gregorian manuscripts, is not known to me.

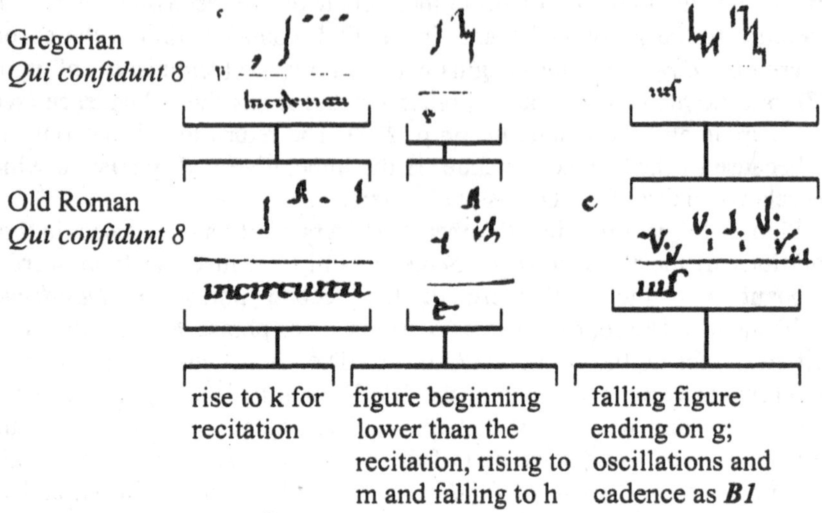

Example **3.9**

There are many textual connections between phrases in this group. Several texts end 'eius' or '-um'; in the Gregorian tradition, eight have the penultimate vowel 'e'. Because of textual cues, this phrase is used outside the expected formal context in the Gregorian tradition in the middle of a verse in *Attende* (*Attende 7*), at the beginning of the last verse in *Vinea*, and in the Old Roman tradition at the beginning of the second verse of *Qui regis*. A more detailed description of this will be given with reference to the individual tracts.

In both traditions, this phrase varies only in response to the number of syllables available for recitation, and in response to the accentuation. *Laudate 6* begins with the articulations around g usually associated with phrase ***B1*** (see pp. 277–8). This is because the first accent is on 'misericórdia'. Most phrases in group ***B2*** have an accented second syllable on which they rise to k. In order to rise to k on the first accent in *Laudate 6*, three syllables must first be articulated around g. Nowacki places *Laudate 6* with group ***B1***.[24] I consider that it belongs with group ***B2***: use of the ***B1*** opening is because of the accentuation and the melisma is the one associated with phrase ***B2*** rather than ***B1***.

In the Old Roman tradition, the melodic movements usually associated with the last two syllables, of which the first is accented, are joined to the final syllable in *Beatus uir 2* and *Qui regis 4*. The antepenultimate syllable

---

[24] Noawcki, op. cit., 207.

is accented, and the usual association of certain melodic movements with text accents has not been followed. The Old Roman version of *Beatus uir 6* begins with an accented syllable but the usual melodic shapes are followed, so the rise to k is not associated with an accent in this phrase. Two phrases in *Beatus uir* in the Old Roman tradition are not consistent with the way in which text and music are usually combined in group ***B2***. Once again, this tract appears to have been constructed with a less clear understanding than is found in the rest of the core repertory of the way in which text and music should be combined within this genre.

Nowacki writes that 'I am unable to discover any textual or contextual conditions that may have motivated the melodic differences between types 2 and 4 [that is, ***B1*** and ***B2***]; they appear to exhibit genuine melodic contrast'.[25] However, consideration of both the Old Roman and Gregorian traditions shows clearly that ***B1*** is generally associated with the first verse of a tract and ***B2*** is associated with other verses. Anomalies may generally be explained by textual cues.

Phrase ***B3*** When the first half-verse consists of a single sentence or clause, phrases ***B3*** and ***B4*** are used, with ***B4*** being used when this textual context occurs in the last verse of a tract. Apel refers to the beginnings of the ***B3*** phrases as 'free passages', except for the beginnings of *Commouisti 3* and *Commouisti 5*, which he identifies as 'c-phrases'.[26] *Commouisti 3* and *Commouisti 5* are indeed the core of a coherent group, in both traditions, but there is no cadence at the end of them, and I would hesitate to identify them as independent phrases.

In the Old Roman tradition, *Commouisti 3*, *Commouisti 5*, and *Qui regis 8* have an identical melisma at the end of the first or second word, followed by equivalent movements for the rest of the phrase (Example **3.10**; see also pp. 284–7). *Commouisti 3* has extra lki oscillations because it has more syllables to articulate. In the Gregorian tradition, *Qui regis 8* begins with shapes from the ***D3*** melisma (see p. 307) before joining the other two phrases for the rise to k. The hkigh figure seen towards the end of several phrases in the group, including *Qui regis 8*, may be found also towards the end of the ***D4*** melisma. It is not clear why *Qui regis 8* should adopt phrase ***D*** movements.

---

[25] Ibid., 209.
[26] Apel, op. cit., 321.

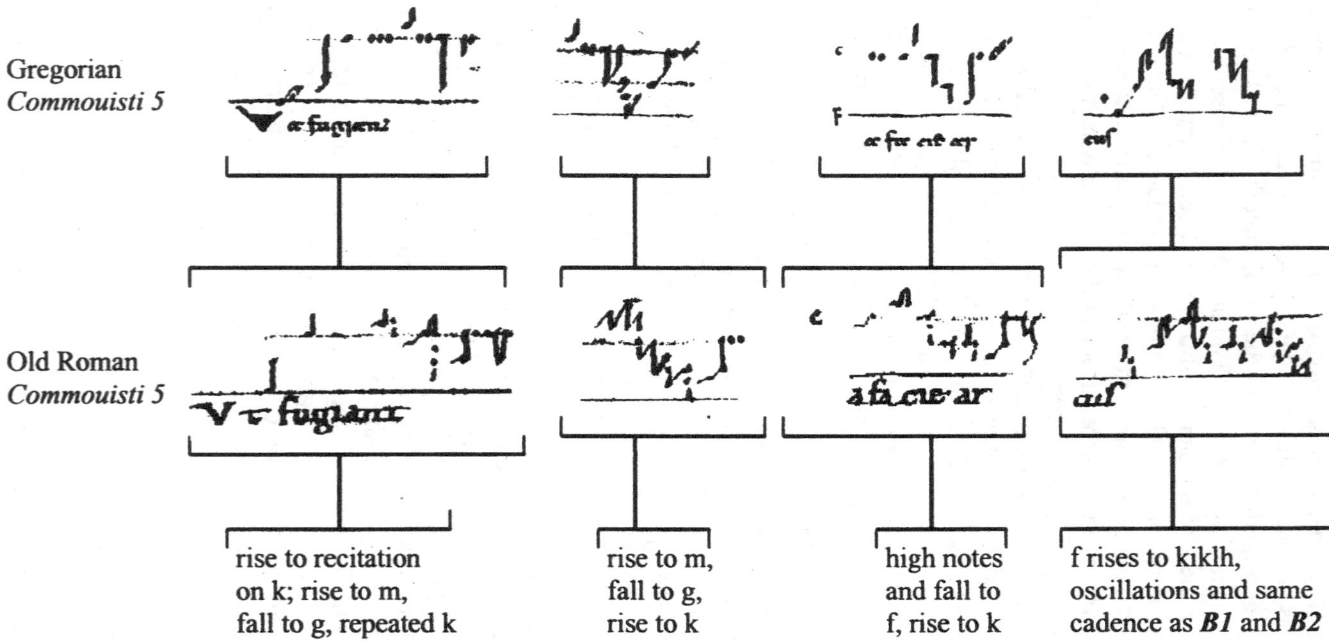
Gregorian
Commouisti 5
Old Roman
Commouisti 5
rise to recitation
on k; rise to m,
fall to g, repeated k
rise to m,
fall to g,
rise to k
high notes
and fall to
f, rise to k
f rises to kiklh,
oscillations and same
cadence as ***B1*** and ***B2***

Example **3.10**

Desiderium 6 belongs with this group in the Old Roman tradition. It begins with the opening articulations of phrase ***B1*** (see p. 278). This is not the expected phrase for this context, as it is not the second phrase in the tract, but the textual connection of 'in benedictione' with *Iubilate 6* ('in exultatione') will have functioned as a cue. Instead of continuing as a ***B1*** phrase, *Desiderium 6* has the extended internal melisma of ***B3*** on '(benedictio)ne'. The rest of the phrase does not follow the ***B3*** shapes: '-ce-' has kihkih, an Old Roman eighth-mode tract commonplace, and the klkihg figure familiar from its four repetitions within the ***D4*** melisma (see p. 310); '-dinis' has the ***D1*** movements seen at the end of *Beatus uir 8*, *Laudate 4* and *Iubilate 4*, but is not preceded by the ***D1*** melisma (see p. 303). *Desiderium 6* is the second phrase in the verse, but also the last. It has characteristics of both ***B*** and ***D*** phrases, but the reasons for the use of the ***B3*** melisma to connect the textually prompted ***B1*** opening and the formally appropriate phrase ***D*** ending remain obscure. Although this phrase clearly consists of ***B1-B3-D*** elements, and the beginning does not have implications of verse beginnings, Nowacki labels it as V–M.[27]

Qui confidunt 2 and *De profundis 11* are also attached to this group in both traditions. Like *Desiderium 6*, the Old Roman version of *Qui confidunt 2* begins with the opening of ***B1*** (see p. 278), followed by the lkilki figure seen also in *Commouisti 3*, and then hg before the melisma. The Gregorian phrase has equivalent movements on 'sicut mons', but is not built up of melodic fragments characteristic of the formal context in the same way. The ***B1*** opening is appropriate to the position of this phrase second in the tract, but as 'Qui confidunt in domino' ('He who trusts in the Lord') is a relative clause to 'sicut mons sion' ('[he shall be] like Mount Sion'), the use of ***B3***, associated with there being a single phrase in the verse-half, is appropriate. In both traditions, *De profundis 11* begins with the gd recitation seen also at the beginning of verses in *De profundis 9* (***B4***: see pp. 288–9), *Laudate 5* and *Desiderium 5* (***E1***: see pp. 313–15). In the Old Roman tradition, the figures on 'te' are familiar from the beginning of *Ad te leuaui 3* and *Qui seminant 3* (***E3***: see p. 319), and 'pro-' has a figure seen also at the beginning of ***E2*** (see p. 317). The figures on '-pitiatio' in the Old Roman tradition are only otherwise seen in *Ad te leuaui 5* (***E3***: see p. 319). These centonised movements, characteristic of Old Roman verse beginnings, are joined together here outside their usual context. The Gregorian version of *De profundis 11* is based on the Old Roman shapes rather than being built up of characteristic Gregorian verse opening movements. Nowacki places *De profundis 11* with group ***B1***.[28] It should be clear from this description, however, that the early part of the phrase is built

---

[27] Nowacki, op. cit., 217.
[28] Ibid., 207.

up of elements associated with verse beginnings. It should therefore be placed with group ***B3***.

The other Gregorian phrases attached to group ***B3*** do not begin verses. *Ad te leuaui 8* begins with the gk rise and recitation of ***B2*** (see pp. 279–80), as one would expect in this formal context. It does not continue with the ***B2*** shapes because 'ad dominum deum nostrum' is a prepositional phrase and makes no sense without 'Ita [leuaui] oculi nostri', so these two indivisible phrases make up the verse-half. *Qui regis 3* appears at the end of a verse. On 'qui deducis', it has a decorated recitation on g, a rise to k and khk. These shapes are reminiscent of phrase ***C*** (see pp. 292–4). This phrase uses ***B3*** because of the textual context: in *Qui regis*, the two other phrases beginning 'qui' appear at the beginnings of verses. The textual cue to treat this phrase also as a verse opening is clear. *Sepe 3* uses phrase ***B3*** as a continuation of the phrase ***A2*** shapes on 'dicat nunc', described above. As there is a single phrase in the half-verse, the formal context is appropriate. *Qui regis 1* uses this material because of the textual cue.

Commouisti 3, *Commouisti 5* and *Qui regis 8* are closely related throughout this phrase, in both traditions. Other phrases are related either for the internal melisma (*Desiderium 6* in the Old Roman tradition), or for the last few syllables. The melodic movements preceding these syllables derive mostly from verse openings, tract openings, and other versions of phrase ***B***.

Phrase ***B4*** The fourth version of phrase ***B*** (pp. 288–9) is used at the beginnings of the final verses of *Ad te leuaui, Desiderium* and *Qui seminant*, in both traditions (Example **3.11**).

It is also used at the beginning of the penultimate verse of *De profundis*. This phrase ends 'domine', as does the first phrase of the last verse of *Ad te leuaui*, and it would appear that this textual cue encouraged the cantors in both traditions to use this phrase out of its normal context. In both traditions, *De profundis 9* begins with the gd recitation seen also in *De profundis 11* (see pp. 284 and 287), *Laudate 5* and *Desiderium 5* (see pp. 314–15). The Old Roman phrases in group ***B4*** do not vary in melodic outline, although the underlay varies according to the textual context. In the Gregorian tradition, *De profundis 9* has an internal repetition (the patterns on '-seruaue-' are repeated on '-ris domin-') because it has more text than the other phrases in the group. The beginning of *Ad te leuaui 10* in the Gregorian tradition has a text underlay different from that of the other phrases in the group, found also in *Ad te leuaui 3* and *Ad te leuaui 5* (see p. 318), because the accent pattern is different from the other phrases in the group, and because there is the contextual cue that this shape is seen at the beginning of two other verses in the same tract.

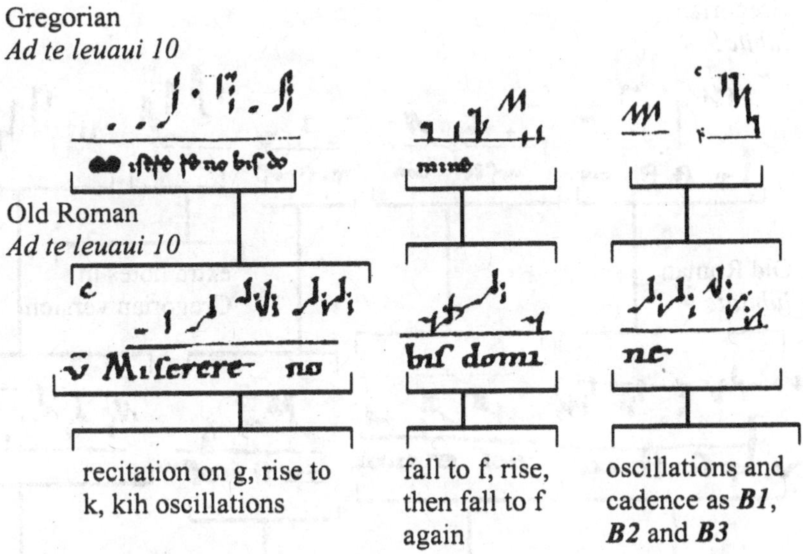

Example 3.11

In the Old Roman tradition, the shape of phrase ***B4*** is identical to that of two phrases in group ***E3*** (*Ad te leuaui 3* and *Qui seminant 3*: see p. 319) until the melisma. In the Gregorian tradition, it is the same as the opening in ***E3*** (*Qui seminant 3*: see p. 318), but not as far as the melisma. Nowacki groups together the beginnings of phrase ***B4*** and the beginnings of the two relevant phrases in ***E3***. However, I prefer to keep the two phrase types separate (while noting their common ground), because not all ***E3*** phrases have the same opening as the ***B4*** phrases, and because ***B4*** phrases end with the mid-verse cadence while ***E3*** phrases have verse-opening material only.

Phrase ***B5*** The last version of phrase ***B*** is used when the beginning of the verse does not have a fully articulated phrase (pp. 290–91). The three phrases in this group in the Old Roman tradition are closely related, but the five phrases in the Gregorian tradition are only closely related as a group for the melisma. ***B5*** is used second in the first two verses of *De profundis* in both traditions. In the first verse, this is because of the difficulties of breaking up the text of the first half-verse, and the second verse in the Old Roman tradition similarly has an abbreviated form of phrase ***E*** on the opening words (see p319).

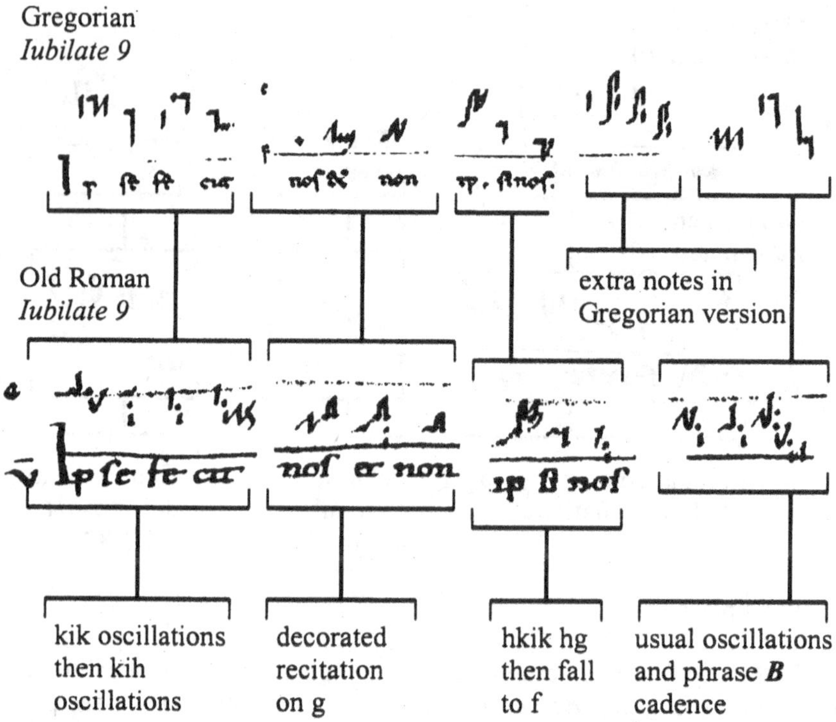

Example **3.12**

Iubilate 9 (Example **3.12**) begins a verse with familiar phrase ***E*** movements in the Old Roman tradition. The opening figure is that used to begin *De profundis 5* (***E3***: see p. 319). The following kih kih oscillations are characteristic of ***E1*** (see p. 315). The melodic material on '-cit nos' is closely related to the end of the first phrase of *De profundis* (***A1***: see p. 272). Verse openings in *De profundis* have been the model for this phrase. Nowacki places this phrase with the ***B4*** and ***E3*** beginnings.[29] However, the melodic shapes of *Iubilate 9* are very different to those of ***B4*** and ***E3***, and the identification of the centonised elements that make up the phrase is perhaps more satisfactory. It does not cadence but goes straight into ***B5*** at 'et non ipsi nos'. The Gregorian version of *Iubilate 9* is closely modelled on the Old Roman version.

In the Old Roman tradition, *De profundis 2* and *De profundis 6* have the same melodic movements as the end of *Iubilate 9* ('et non ipsi nos'). The second phrase of *De profundis* in the Gregorian tradition is very

[29] Ibid., 212.

abbreviated. The figures of 'ad te', attached in Appendix 2 to *De profundis 1* because they are phrase ***A*** movements (p. 271), are also related to the opening articulations of *De profundis 6* and *Qui confidunt 10*, and may thus be regarded as a pivot between the two phrase types. As was mentioned above, the Beneventan manuscripts have ***B5*** for *Beatus uir 2*, because of the textual cue of *De profundis 2*, and also, possibly, because of the difficulties associated with attaching this single three-syllable word to phrase ***B1*** material. The melodic movements of *De profundis 2* ('domine') and *Beatus uir 2* ('dominum') are identical in these manuscripts. The Gregorian version of *De profundis 6* begins with the articulations used in *Iubilate 9* on 'et non ipsi'. The dg figure at the beginning of the melisma in *De profundis 6* is also used in ***D5*** (see p. 311). The kikhg figure, familiar from ***D2*** (see pp. 304–305), is followed by ihigf, which is related to the next figure in ***D2***: kkhg higf.

The Gregorian tradition also uses ***B5*** for *Qui regis 2*. This begins with hg, the next pattern one would have expected to see in the abbreviated ***B3*** melisma at the end of the previous phrase (see p. 285). As with *De profundis 6*, the fhk rise and the kkkhg are familiar from ***D2*** (see pp. 304–305). Although the texts of *Qui regis 2* 'intende' and *De profundis 6* 'intendentes' are closely related, and both derive some of their material from phrase ***D2***, they are not constructed in the same way. The textual cue is of less relevance than the fact that these are both appropriate contexts for the use of ***B5***. In the Gregorian tradition, *Qui confidunt 10* has the same opening as *De profundis 6* and 'et non ipsi' in *Iubilate 9*, but has recitation on h for the extra text before the melisma. *Qui confidunt 10* is the fourth phrase in a verse consisting of six phrases. The opening figures of the phrase are reminiscent of the phrase ***C*** rise (see p. 293), and a link with the preceding, modified, phrase ***C*** (see p. 299) may have been intended: 'et dominus/ in circuitu populi sui'.

In summary, group ***B5*** is formed of closely related material in the Old Roman tradition but the Gregorian tradition is more disparate. *Iubilate 9* begins like the Old Roman phrase *Iubilate 9*, and then has the same articulations as the Gregorian *De profundis 6* and *Qui confidunt 10*. The beginnings of the melismas of these phrases are different. *De profundis 6* and *Qui regis 2* have ***D2*** figures around the beginning of the melisma. *De profundis 2* simply has ik hg before the melisma.

As this phrase only occurs five times in the Gregorian tradition, it is unsurprising that the melodic shapes were not standardised and well known. This is illustrated by the retention of the Old Roman shapes in the Gregorian version of *Iubilate 9*, rather than the use of a new phrase modelled on the equivalent Gregorian patterns. Also, as was seen in Chapter 2, above, the number of small variants in the outline of this phrase in different manuscripts shows that the phrase was not accurately remembered. The manuscript variants associated with the other occasions on which ***B5*** is used are similarly unstable. It is not necessary to describe this in exhaustive detail; *De profundis 6* will serve as an illustration (Example **3.13**).

In the Gregorian tradition, *De profundis 6* begins hgg, with liquescence. *ROG1* and *YRX* do not have the liquescence, *DEN1, IRI, KLO1* and *LEW* have only hg with liquescence, *DIJ1* has hgf, and *BRE* has a torculus (hgh?). On the following syllable, the early manuscripts, *DIJ1, LEW, ROG1* and *ROP* have ghg, with liquescence on the final note. The west Frankish manuscripts have ghg with no liquescence. The Beneventan manuscripts, the north Italian manuscripts and the East Frankish manuscripts have gh, some with liquescence, *YRX* has fg liquescence and *ALB* has h liquescence, as does *CHA1*. On '-den-', most manuscripts have hgkikh, with a liquescence on the final note. *LEW* has no liquescence, *SAB* has hgkiki, *KLO1* has hgkkkh, *NOY4* and *CHA1* appear to have hgkik, and *BRE* appears to have gkik. The melisma begins ihdg in the Aquitanian manuscripts, *BEN5,* and *DIJ1*, ihfg in *IRI*, ihfh in the other Cluniac manuscripts, and khfh in *KLO1*. The neumes in *BRE* are incompatible with all of these. This is followed by kikhg, but by nothing in *ROG1*, and the second high note is repeated in *STM* (kkih?). The following figure is ihigf in most pitched manuscripts, but ih in *ROG1*, kikhg in *KLO1*, ihihgf in *ROP*, and nothing in *STM*. The following khg figure appears as kkhg in *IRI*, ikhhg in *ROG1*, ?ikhg in *BRE*, ? kh in *STM*, and nothing in *SAB*. This is followed by hghghg or hghg (the manuscripts are fairly evenly divided), before the cadence, which has the usual variants.

It was shown in Chapter 2 that some manuscripts vary frequently from the rest of the tradition, and some of the variants found in this phrase are compatible with the usual idiosyncrasies of these manuscripts. In addition, the variants on the first syllable affect *LAN* and *YRX*. Those on the second syllable distance the Beneventan manuscripts, the Aquitanian manuscripts and *LAV* not only from the oldest manuscripts, but also from each other. Like *Iubilate 10*, this ***B5*** phrase was not accurately remembered in the Gregorian tradition. In contrast, there are no variants at all in the Old Roman manuscripts in this phrase, confirming that the Old Roman phrase ***B5*** shapes are not only closely related to each other, but were also well known.

Early manuscripts

GAL1

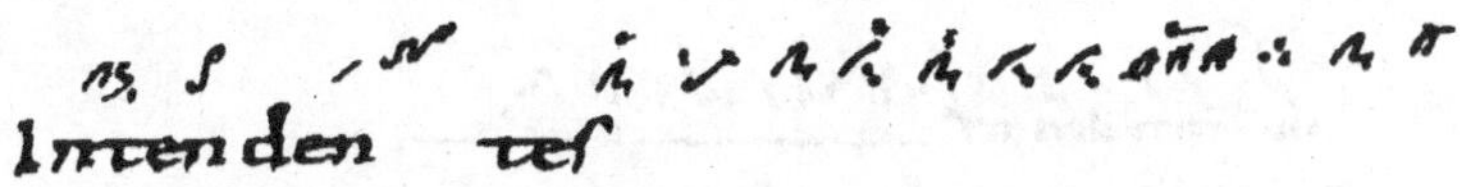

GAL2

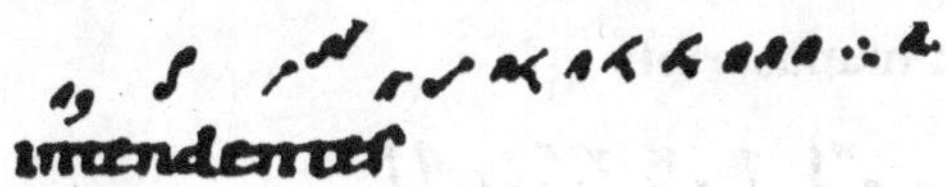

MUR3

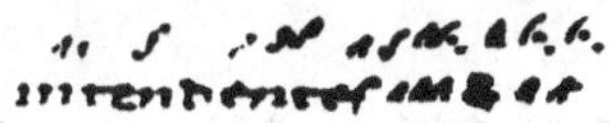

LAN

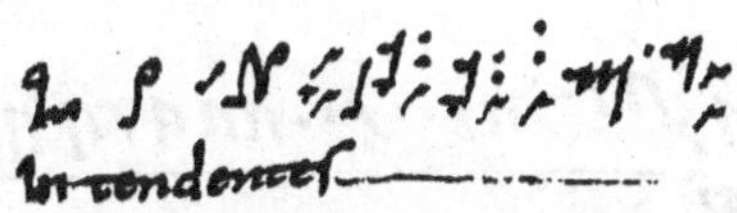

CHA1

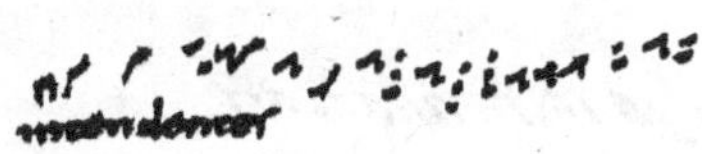

Western Frankish manuscripts

CLU1

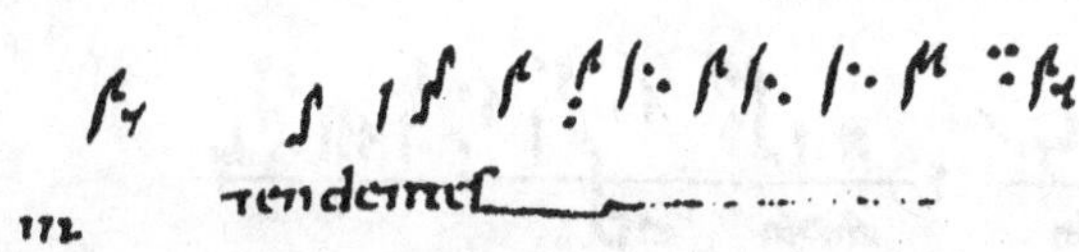

NOY4

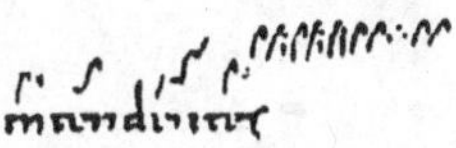

DEN1

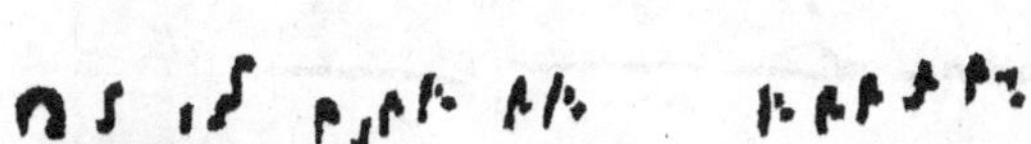

Northern Italian manuscripts

LAV

BRE

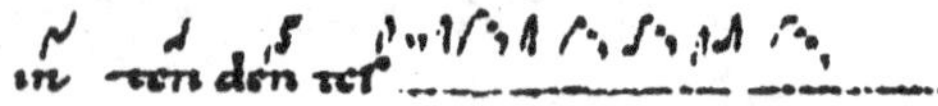

Eastern Frankish manuscripts

KLO1

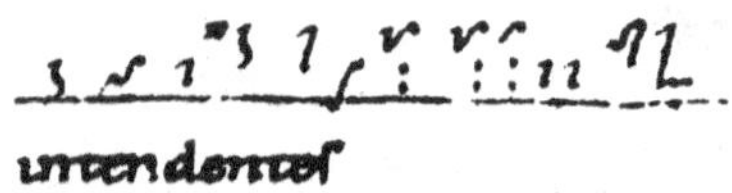

PAS2

MOG4

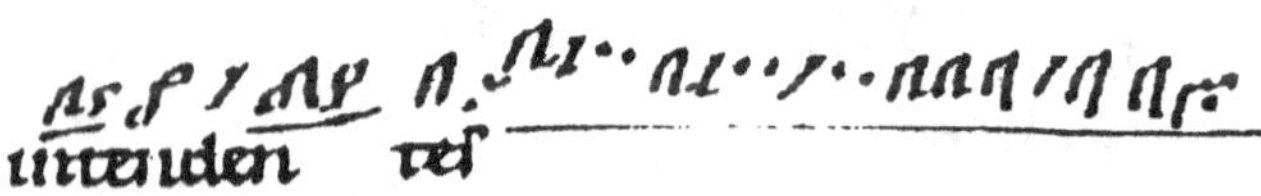

STM

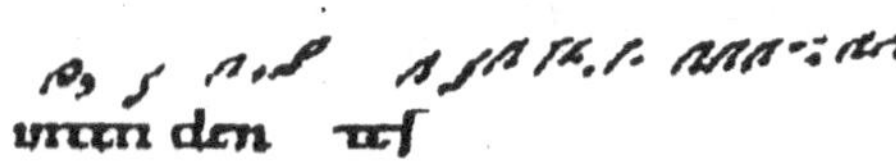

Beneventan manuscripts

BEN5

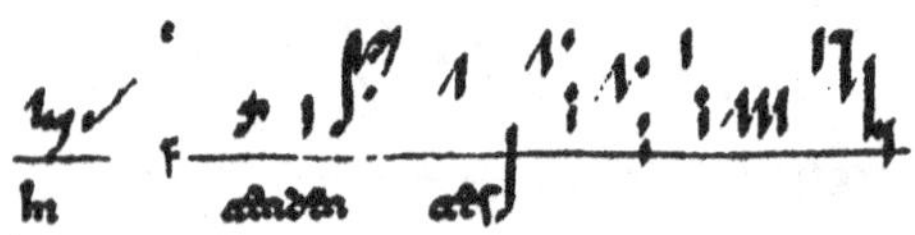

Aquitanian manuscripts

YRX

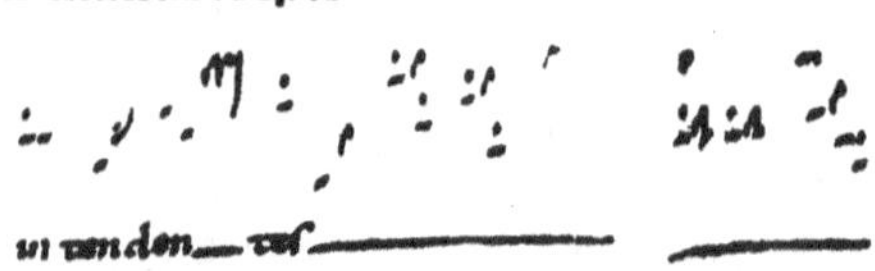

ALB

Cluniac manuscripts (pitched)

DIJ1

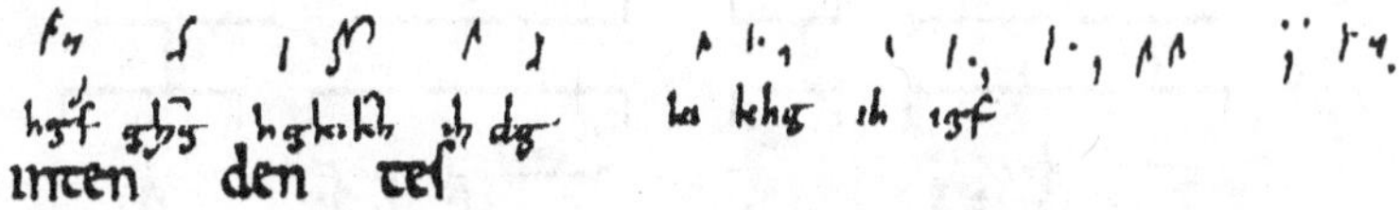

IRI

SAB

ROG1

Example **3.13**

Phrase ***C***

This phrase is associated with the beginning of the second half-verse, or with an indivisible second half-verse when the first half-verse consists of two phrases. Unlike phrase ***B***, which has clearly differentiated subgroups associated with different formal contexts, the different ways in which phrase ***C*** appears are dictated purely by the length of text available, and by the accentuation patterns within that text. There are four groups of phrases.

Group ***C1*** (pp. 292–5) has sufficient text to articulate the whole phrase, with a recitation passage in the middle (Example **3.14**). Group ***C2*** (pp. 296–8) has sufficient text to articulate all of the expected material, but does not have enough text for a recitation passage (six to eight syllables in the Gregorian tradition; five to eight in the Old Roman) (Example **3.15**).

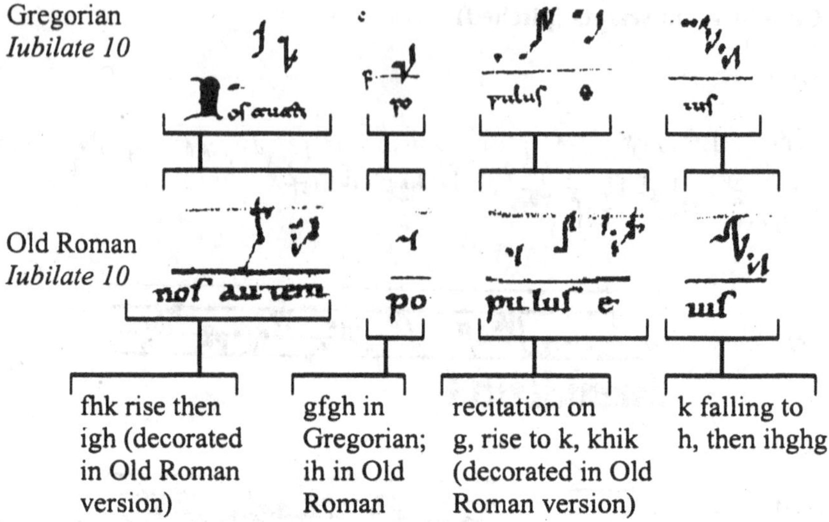

Example **3.14**

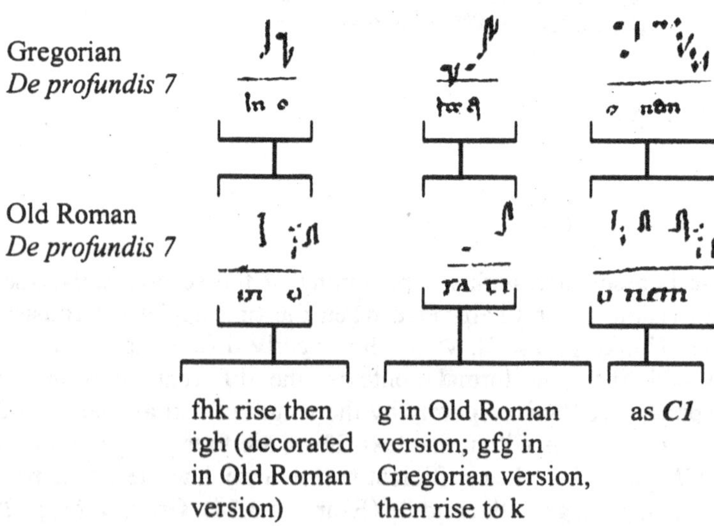

Example **3.15**

In the Gregorian tradition, use of ***C2*** rather than ***C1*** tends to be signalled by the use of gfg rather than gfgh after the igh figure.[30] In the Old Roman tradition, the phrases in ***C1*** have ih on the accent following the decorated igh figure, and rise ghki over two syllables. In ***C2***, the decorated igh figure is followed immediately by the same rise. The phrase shapes within these two groups are entirely consistent, allowing for the differences in numbers of recitation syllables in the Gregorian tradition, and for the differences in underlay in the Old Roman tradition, associated with the different numbers of syllables.

In group ***C3*** (pp. 299–300), there is insufficient text to articulate all the expected material in a straightforward manner. In the Old Roman tradition, the usual opening rise fhk has an inflection i on the end. This is followed by a single recitation note k when there are four syllables, and then the usual figures for the last two syllables. In the Gregorian tradition, *Qui confidunt 11* and *Desiderium 8* simply have the figures usually associated with the last three syllables of the phrase. *Commouisti 6* joins the figures gfg ghkik into gfghkik on a single syllable, articulating the first two and the last two syllables in the normal way. *Sepe 12* has many syllables, but, as in *Desiderium 3* 'et volunta-' (***C1***), the first main accent is on the fourth syllable. These phrases begin f f h hk and f f h k respectively. Although *Desiderium 3* has seven syllables left to articulate the rest of the phrase, which even leaves two for recitation, *Sepe 12* has only four syllables left to articulate the material usually associated with five syllables. As in *Commouisti 6*, the two figures gfg ghkik are joined into gfghkik on a single syllable. *Qui confidunt 9* has a variant form of this phrase in the Gregorian tradition, although it has the usual articulations in the Old Roman tradition. In this phrase, the usual shapes of phrase ***C*** are reduced to melodic patterns reminiscent of those generally associated with the last two syllables of the phrase. It is not clear why the phrase has been varied in this way, especially considering that the Old Roman tradition has the usual outlines.

The unusual accentuation patterns of *Desiderium 3* and *Sepe 12* have affected the opening patterns in the Gregorian tradition. This trend is widespread across phrase ***C***. In the Gregorian tradition, the rise is fhk when the first syllable is accented. When the second syllable is accented, the rise is f hk. The rise is f fhk on the three occasions involving 'exulta-/exalta-', which adds emphasis. When the first main accent is the third syllable, the rise is f f hk.[31]

Group ***C4*** (p. 301) consists of phrases with an antepenultimate accent but in the Old Roman tradition, this group does not exist, because such

[30] See pp. 34–5, above, for a full description of the uses of gfg and gfgh in this phrase.

[31] ***C4***: *Attende 6* 'sicut im-'; ***C1***: *Cantemus 3* 'honori-', *Attende 8* 'quia no-', *Sicut 6* 'quando ve-', *Vinea 6* 'et edi-'.

phrases are simply given an extra recitation note k before the material generally associated with the last two syllables. In the Gregorian tradition the antepenultimate accent has a great effect on the outline of the phrase. The khik figure is usually associated with the penultimate, accented syllable. Either the usual melodic patterns must be adjusted in these cases where the antepenultimate syllable is accented, or the usual connection of certain melodic patterns with accented or unaccented syllables must be ignored.

Iubilate 3, *Iubilate 7*, and *Laudate 7* have k hik ikhhg on the last three syllables.[32] This means that both the accent and the penultimate syllable are still associated with the khik figure. The altered cadence ikhhg is associated exclusively with these three phrases, all of which end 'domino/nus/num'. As in *Commouisti 6* and *Sepe 12* (***C3***), there is insufficient text in *Iubilate 7* and *Laudate 7* for the usual figures to be articulated, so gfg ghkik is joined together as gfghki or gfghkik. In all phrases in this group, ghkik and ghki are used fairly interchangeably, and individual manuscripts are not consistent between phrases. It is not necessary to give an exhaustive description of this, as the variant does not affect the melodic outline significantly. *Iubilate 3* does not have enough syllables to begin in the usual way, enunciating only f gfg before the rise.[33]

De profundis 3, *Sepe 3*, and *Attende 6* have the usual phrase ***C*** cadence. *De profundis 3* has the same abbreviated opening as *Iubilate 3*. *Sepe 4* begins fh hgh instead of fhk igh, and then has gfgh g ghkik, compatible with phrase ***C1***. In *De profundis 3*, the khik figure is split k khik between the accented syllable and the penultimate syllable. *IRI, LAN, LAV* and *NOY4* instead have g hkik khik, then the final melisma, ignoring the usual connection of certain melodic figures with accented syllables. In *Sepe 4* most manuscripts split the khik figure as k hik between the accented syllable and the penultimate syllable. *ROG1* and *BRE* have g ghkik khik followed by the final melisma, ignoring the accentuation.

Attende 6 begins in the same way as phrases in group ***C2***. It has the text 'sicut imber super gramen' in *BEN5, BRE, ORJ* and *YRX*, which permits a normal treatment of the phrase. The other manuscripts have 'sicut imber super gramina', which has an antepenultimate accent. Linguistically, these are equally correct: 'gramen' and 'gramina' are the singular and plural respectively of 'grass', and, as in English, the singular can be used to indicate more than one blade. The same variants are found as in other phrases with an antepenultimate accent. Most manuscripts have ghkik or

[32] The variants around these melodic patterns are not significant, and are described above (p. 30). In the present discussion, hik should be taken as meaning 'hk or hik, depending on the manuscript'. The pattern ikhhg also appears as ikhg and ikhhhg.

[33] The variants around this figure are described above (p. 30).

ghki followed by k hik or k khik before the final melisma. *LAV* and *SAB* instead have g ghkik khik before the final melisma.

Despite having 'gramen', *ORJ* rises ghki instead of ghkik, has just k on 'gra-' and the melodic patterns associated with the last two syllables on just the last syllable. These are the melodic patterns associated in other manuscripts with the text 'gramina'. This suggests that the exemplar for *ORJ* had the text 'gramina', and the melodic patterns usually linked with 'gramina' were retained. Although *ORJ* shares the text 'gramen' with *BEN5*, *BRE* and *YRX*, this seems to be a scribal slip, since the treatment of the phrase is quite different.

This is the only occasion in the eighth-mode tracts where a textual variant leads to a different melodic outline. The general stability of the texts may have been one of the factors that made a stable transmission possible. This will be explored further in Chapter 4.

The variations arising when the usual penultimate accent is replaced by an antepenultimate accent illustrate how important the matching of melodic patterns specifically to accented or unaccented syllables was as a mnemonic to the medieval cantors. The final melisma is altered in three phrases, all ending 'domin-'. More generally, some manuscripts split k hik, some instead have k khik, and some split the previous ghkik/ghki figure. Not all manuscripts are internally consistent in their treatment of these phrases.

The melodic shapes of phrase ***C*** do not vary because of the formal context, but in response to the textual context, either because of the number of syllables available, or because of the pattern of accented and unaccented syllables. In both traditions, the different subgroups are closely related throughout, unlike the subgroups of phrase ***B***. The distinction between the different subgroups of phrase ***C*** in the Old Roman tradition is less striking than in the Gregorian tradition. Nowacki does not differentiate between the subgroups identified here; as he was focusing only on the Old Roman tradition, this is perfectly defensible, and perhaps illustrates the melodic closeness of all phrases of type ***C*** more clearly than the present study.[34] However, the effect had by the lengths of the texts and their accentuation patterns on the Gregorian phrase shapes is sufficiently large that it is valuable to differentiate between four subgroups in this study.

*Phrase **D***

This phrase occurs at the ends of verses. Phrase ***D1*** is generally used in verses where there are two phrases in the second verse-half, that is, it is

[34] Nowacki, op. cit., 202–5.

usually preceded by phrase ***C***. Phrase ***D2*** is used when there is more text to articulate, and it has a more extended opening.[35] Phrase ***D3*** begins in the same way as phrase ***D2***, but the melisma is more extended. When phrase ***D2*** appears early in a tract, phrase ***D3*** is sometimes used in a subsequent verse as an ornamentation. Phrase ***D4*** is used at the ends of the first verses of three closely related tracts, and has a yet more extended melisma. Phrase ***D5*** is used only twice, and the formal and textual circumstances leading to its use will be described in more detail below.

Kainzbauer maintains that the placing of the 'Haupt-Akzent' and of the 'Sinnspitze' determine which of phrases ***D1***, ***D2*** and ***D4*** will be used. For example, he writes that 'Texte mit drei Akzenten, deren erster Haupt-Akzent und letzter Sinnspitze ist, verwenden cento W [***D4***].'[36] The 'main accent' and the 'high point of the sense' are not easily defined, and I prefer to differentiate between ***D1*** and ***D2*** according to the length of text available, and to consider ***D4*** as a special shape associated with three closely related tracts. Kainzbauer does not define ***D3*** as a separate group at all.[37] This is because the phrase shape is only used once in the Gregorian tradition. It is more widely used in the Old Roman tradition, and therefore demands a separate subgroup. The choice of ***D3*** rather than ***D2*** is for rhetorical reasons, rather than because of the distribution of accents.

Phrase ***D1*** In the first version of phrase ***D*** (Example **3.16**; pp. 302–303), the melodic movements are equivalent in all phrases except for *De profundis 10* in the Gregorian tradition. This phrase begins with the phrase ***C4*** opening seen in *De profundis 3* on the same word: 'domine' (see p. 301), continuing with phrase ***C*** outlines until the melisma. This is the only phrase in group ***D1*** not preceded by phrase ***C***, and there are clear textual and formal prompts to articulate the beginning of the text, unusually long for phrase ***D1***, with phrase ***C*** figures.

Phrase ***D2*** The second version of phrase ***D*** (Example **3.17**; pp. 304–306) is often used in bipartite verses, but is also used in the third verse of *Sepe* in both traditions, in the second verses of *Sicut* and *Beatus uir* in the Gregorian tradition, and in the third verse of *De profundis* in the Old Roman tradition. The melisma is the same as that found in ***D1*** (except for the first two notes in the Gregorian tradition) but the opening is different, allowing for the articulation of more syllables before the melisma. Most Old Roman phrases in this group are completely equivalent, with any

[35] Nowacki treats these phrases as equivalent within group K, even though they have different melodic shapes and appear in different textual contexts (ibid., 200–202).

[36] Kainzbauer, op. cit., 52.

[37] Ibid., 52.

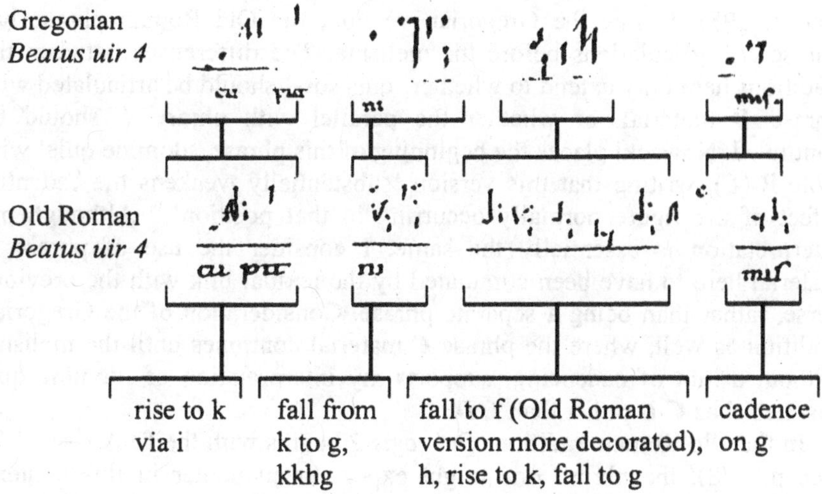

Example 3.16

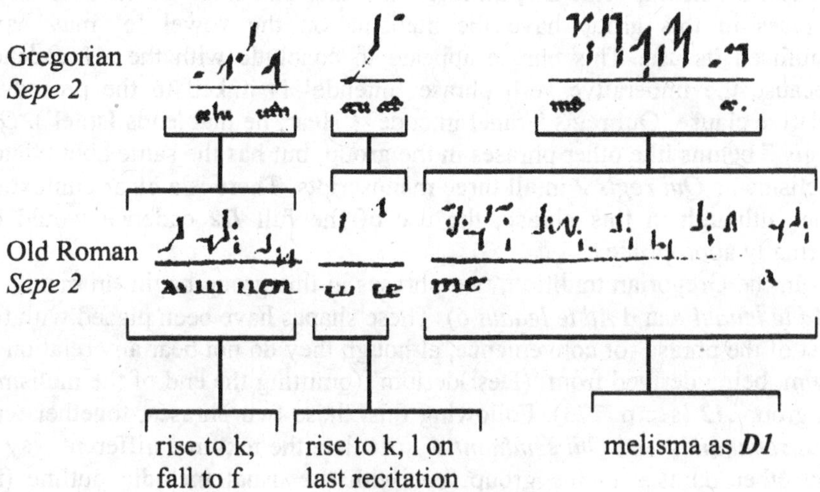

Example 3.17

differences being prompted by different numbers of syllables.

De profundis 10 belongs with group ***D2*** in the Old Roman tradition. As with the Gregorian phrase (***D1***: see p. 302), it begins with phrase ***C*** movements on 'domine', seen also in *De profundis 3* with the same text (see p. 298). Unlike the Gregorian version, the Old Roman phrase has phrase ***D2*** articulations before the melisma. The differences between the traditions here only extend to whether 'quis sus-' should be articulated with phrase ***D*** material, or whether the parallel with phrase ***C*** should be continued. Nowacki places the beginning of this phrase, 'domine quis' with table P (*C*), writing that this version 'substantially weakens the cadential effect of the figure normally occurring in that position'.[38] Although my interpretation is essentially the same, I consider the use of phrase ***C*** material here to have been stimulated by the textual link with the previous verse, rather than being a separate phrase. Consideration of the Gregorian tradition as well, where the phrase ***C*** material continues until the melisma without a hint of cadencing, supports my interpretation of 'domine quis sustinebit' as ***C-D*** rather than ***C D***.

In the Old Roman tradition, *Qui regis 2* begins with the f hik rise of ***B1*** (see p. 278), the phrase one might expect to encounter in this context, second in the tract. This is followed by most of the ***D2*** melisma, but the hggf figure functions as a pivot into the ***A1*** cadence in all three manuscripts (see p. 272). There is no clear reason why the ***D2*** melisma is used here instead of the expected ***B1***, although the fact that three of the four other phrases in this group have the melisma on the vowel 'e' may have stabilised its use. This phrase appears to conclude with the ***A1*** cadence because the imperative verb phrase 'intende' is linked to the preceding relative clause 'Qui regis israhel intende' ('Hear, he that leads Israel'). *Qui regis 7* begins like other phrases in the group, but has the same abbreviated melisma as *Qui regis 2* in all three manuscripts. There is a clear contextual cue, although in this phrase, the use of the full ***D2*** cadence would be formally appropriate.

In the Gregorian tradition, two phrases in this group begin 'in manibus' (*Ad te leuaui 4* and *Ad te leuaui 6*). These shapes have been placed with the rest of the phrase for convenience, although they do not bear any relation to them, being derived from '(Desi)derium' (omitting the end of the melisma) in group ***A2*** (see p. 273). Following this, these two phrases, together with *Qui seminant 2* and *Qui seminant 4*, articulate the text in a different way to the other phrases in the group, but with the usual melodic outline (hg followed by a rise to k, a fall to g, and then hgf). These phrases are part of a closely related group of verses, and this highlights their relationship. Kainzbauer writes that this phrase shape is used when there is a text with two accents, with the main accent first.[39] Other phrases with two accents belong with group ***D1***. Although the identification of main and subsidiary accents may prove problematic, this might have been one of the factors in

[38] Nowacki, op. cit., 202.
[39] Kainzbauer, op. cit., 51.

the choice of phrase shape.

*Phrase **D3*** The third version of phrase ***D*** (pp. 307–308) begins in the same way as ***D2***, but the melisma is more rhapsodic (Example **3.18**).[40]

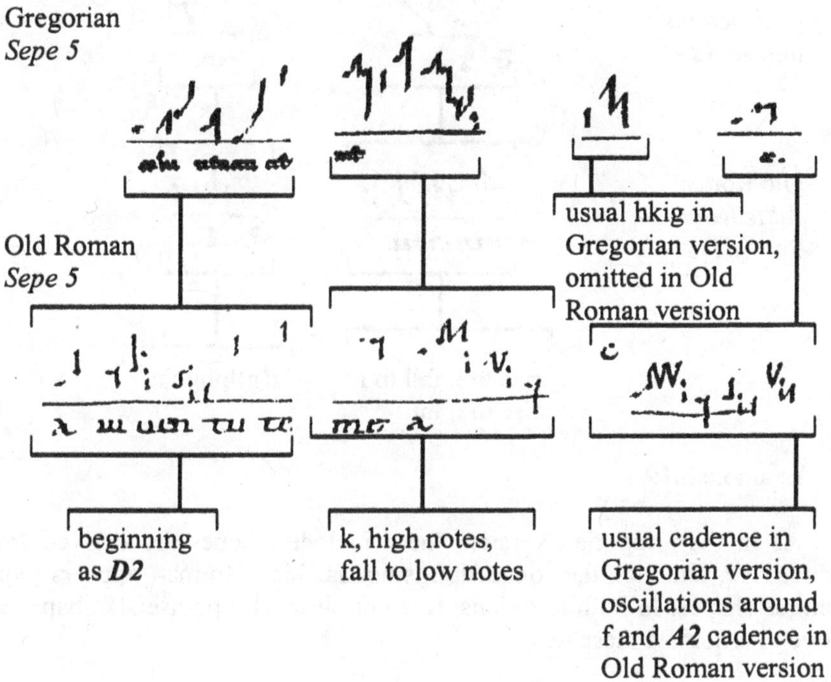

Example **3.18**

In *Sepe* and *Qui seminant* in the Old Roman tradition, this phrase is used in verses where the preceding verse ended with ***D2***. On these occasions, it may be seen as a rhetorical decoration, and this is certainly the case in the Gregorian tradition, where ***D3*** is used only on the repetition of 'a iuventute mea' in *Sepe*. In the Old Roman tradition, there is a textual cue to use this phrase also in *Ad te leuaui 6*: *Qui seminant 4* ends 'semina sua' and *Ad te leuaui 6* ends 'domine sue'. By extension, there is a cue to use the phrase in *Ad te leuaui 4*, whose text is closely related to that of *Ad te leuaui 6*. The phrase is used also in *Qui confidunt 6*. There is no clear reason why ***D3*** should be used here instead of ***D1/2***. The melodic outlines are the same in all of the phrases in this group, with extra recitation notes

[40] The omission of part of the Old Roman melisma in *Ad te leuaui 4* is due to a scribal error in *ORC*. The usual patterns may be found in the other Old Roman manuscripts.

when there are more syllables except for 'in manibus' in *Ad te leuaui 4* and *Ad te leuaui 6* (Example **3.19**).

Old Roman
Ad te leuaui 7
phrase *A2*

Old Roman
Ad te leuaui 6
Phrase ***D3***

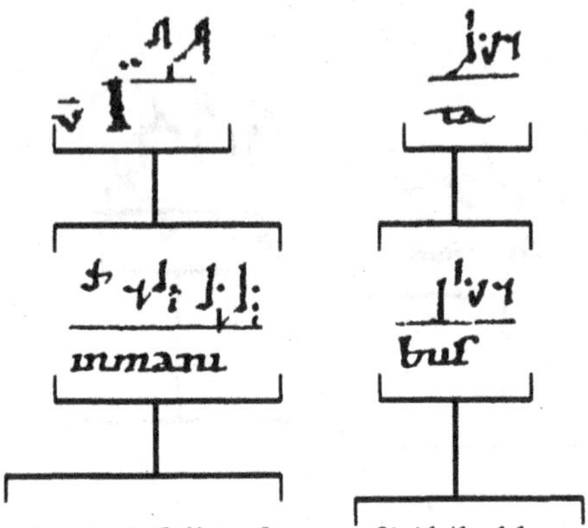

rise to i, fall to f, rise to i, fall

f(g)hihghhg

Example **3.19**

As in the Gregorian version, these melodic shapes are derived from phrase ***A2***, although the connection is not as close. 'In ma-' appears to use unique shapes. In both traditions, it is not clear why phrase ***A2*** shapes are used to articulate these texts.

Phrase ***D4*** The fourth version of phrase ***D*** (pp. 309–310) is associated with the last phrase of the first verse of *Desiderium*, *Ad te leuaui* and *Commouisti*, whose first verses are closely related throughout (Example **3.20**).

The beginning of the phrase is related to that of ***D2*** and ***D3***, although there is no rise to k/l before the melisma. The main feature of ***D4***, in both traditions, is the long and ornate melisma with much internal repetition.

In the Gregorian tradition, this phrase is also used at the end of the second verse of *Desiderium*. As in the Old Roman version of this phrase (***B3***: see p. 286), it begins with the ***B1*** articulations on 'in benedictio-'. At the rise fghk, usually close to the end of the melisma, this phrase has recitation on k to articulate the remaining syllables before the usual melodic patterns are used to end the phrase (with an extra ihg before fg ghhg). The decorations of this phrase occur in order to articulate the long text, and possibly also as a decoration of the phrase on its second occurrence in as many verses of *Desiderium*.

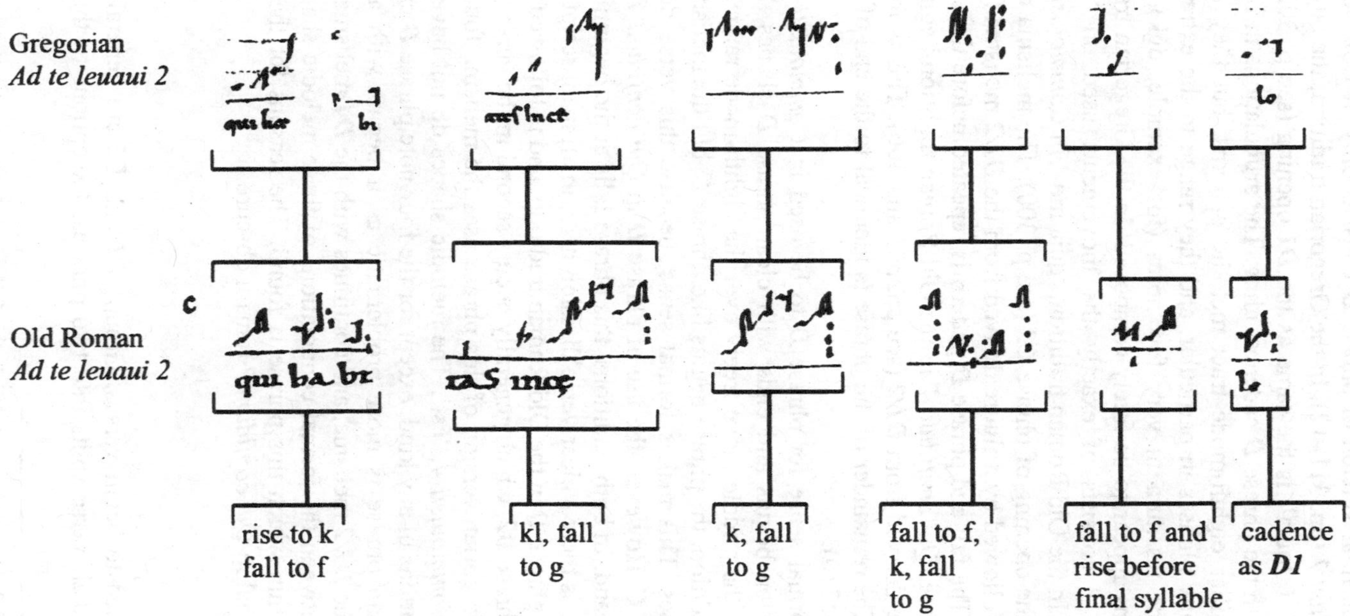
Gregorian
Ad te leuaui 2
Old Roman
Ad te leuaui 2
rise to k fall to f
kl, fall to g
k, fall to g
fall to f, k, fall to g
fall to f and rise before final syllable
cadence as D1

Example 3.20

Phrase ***D5*** The final version of phrase ***D*** consists only of *Commouisti 4* and *Qui confidunt 7* (pp. 311–12). In the Gregorian tradition, the beginning of *Commouisti 4*, 'quia', is the same as the ***D1*** opening (see p. 302). The phrase ends with the phrase ***D*** cadence, ghhg. The articulations in between consist of familiar eighth-mode tract melodic patterns, but they are not derived from any phrases in particular, and they range to the extremes of the eighth-mode tessitura in very few notes (for example, dgk). These melodic patterns appear to be freely composed. In the Gregorian tradition, *Qui confidunt 7* consists of exactly the movements used on 'est' in *Commouisti 4*. In the Old Roman tradition, 'quia mo-' in *Commouisti 4* has patterns from the opening of phrase ***C3*** (see p. 300). The melisma on 'est' has a fall gd[41] followed by a figure derived from the ***D1/2*** melisma (see pp. 303 and 306). The fall and phrase ***D*** pattern is repeated before the six-note phrase ***D*** cadence. *Qui confidunt 7* in the Old Roman tradition begins with the same figure derived from ***D1/2*** (see pp. 303 and 306). This is followed by glk ikihg. The remainder of the phrase is identical to the end of the ***D4*** melisma (see p. 310).

It makes formal sense for phrase ***D*** to be used in *Commouisti 4*. The Gregorian version begins and ends with clear phrase ***D*** shapes, but the articulations in the middle move freely over the eighth-mode range. In the Old Roman tradition, the phrase begins like phrase ***C***, but the melisma uses phrase ***D*** shapes. This makes formal sense, because this verse does not include phrase ***C***. However, the use of phrase ***D*** in *Qui confidunt 7* is less easy to understand. In both traditions, this phrase falls at the beginning of a verse. Not only is there a clear verse division here, in all manuscripts, but it is preceded by phrase ***D*** in the Old Roman tradition, and is followed in both traditions by phrase ***B2***, which generally occurs second in the verse (see pp. 344–5). The Gregorian version of this phrase uses the melisma found only otherwise on *Commouisti 4*, 'est'. The melodic shapes do not have strong formal connotations of any kind, except for the four-note phrase ***D*** cadence. The Old Roman phrase is more problematic as it begins with a figure derived from the ***D1/2*** melisma, and continues with the ***D4*** melisma. There is a conflict between the formal connotations of these melodic shapes and the context within which this phrase is found. The reasons for the use of phrase ***D*** material in *Qui confidunt 7* remain obscure.

Phrase ***E***

Phrase ***E*** is used to begin verses. Groups ***E1*** and ***E2*** are generally used when the first half-verse splits into two phrases. Exceptions to this occur

[41] None of the Old Roman manuscripts height this fall very accurately – it may be ge.

only in the Gregorian tradition. These are *Qui regis 4*, *Qui regis 6*, *Beatus uir 5*, *Beatus uir 9*, *Cantemus 9*, and *Attende 12*. Reasons for the use of ***E1/2*** instead of one of the phrase types generally associated with there being an indivisible verse-half will be discussed below, with reference to the individual tracts. The usual shape of the phrase is that seen in ***E1***. Group ***E2*** consists of phrases without sufficient syllables to articulate the phrase in the usual way. The phrases in group ***E3*** are generally found in verses where the first half-verse is not split.

*Phrase **E1*** In the Gregorian version of phrase ***E1*** (Example **3.21**; pp. 313–15), most phrases have the same melodic outline, with a varying number of recitation syllables, depending on the amount of text available.

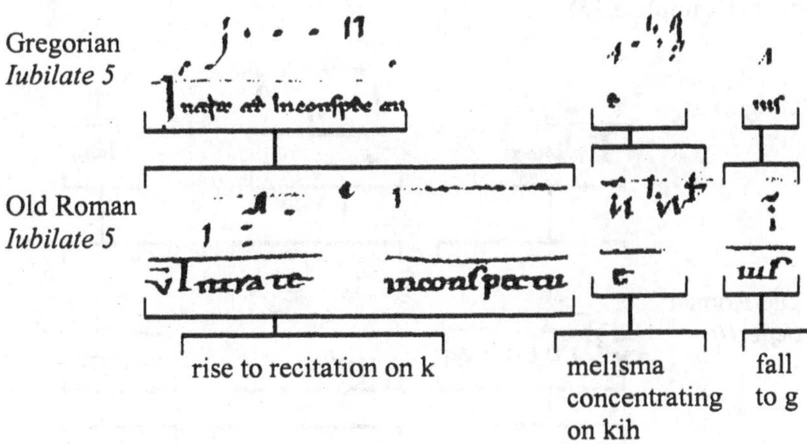

Example **3.21**

Most phrases have a penultimate accent, on which the melisma is placed, beginning klig (some manuscripts have klkig or klkg). *Attende 12* instead has an antepenultimate accent ('iníquitas'), and the klig figure is split as kl ig or kl kg between '-íqui-', with the melisma on the final syllable. *Iubilate 5*, *Laudate 5* and *Desiderium 5* have penultimate accents, but have kki g on the previous two syllables, with the rest of the melisma on the last accent. *De profundis 5* has kl ig on 'aúres', and the rest of the melisma on 'túe'. It is not clear why these phrases have joined text with music in a different way, but it is consistent across the Gregorian tradition. *Laudate 5* and *Desiderium 5* begin with a low gd recitation on 'Quoniam', and *Desiderium 5* has only enough text to rise g hk, without recitation.

In the Old Roman tradition, only four phrases belong with this group.

Laudate 5 and *Desiderium 5* begin with the gd recitation also seen in the Gregorian tradition. *Desiderium 5* and *Iubilate 5* rise in one way, and *Beatus uir 9* and *Laudate 5* rise in another. *Iubilate 5* and *Beatus uir 9* have recitation, and *Desiderium 5*, *Iubilate 5* and *Beatus uir 9* have the same melisma. *Laudate 5* instead has the movement around m used on the penultimate syllable in group ***B2*** (see pp. 281–2). The cadence is that seen in ***A2*** on, for example, '(Desideri)um'(see p. 275). The beginning and end of the phrase clearly suggest a verse beginning, but the reason for the use of a ***B2*** figure out of the usual formal context is unclear.

Phrase ***E2*** The second version of phrase ***E*** (pp. 316–17) is used in three phrases in the Gregorian tradition and in two phrases in the Old Roman tradition, when there is insufficient text to articulate the phrase in the usual manner (Example **3.22**).

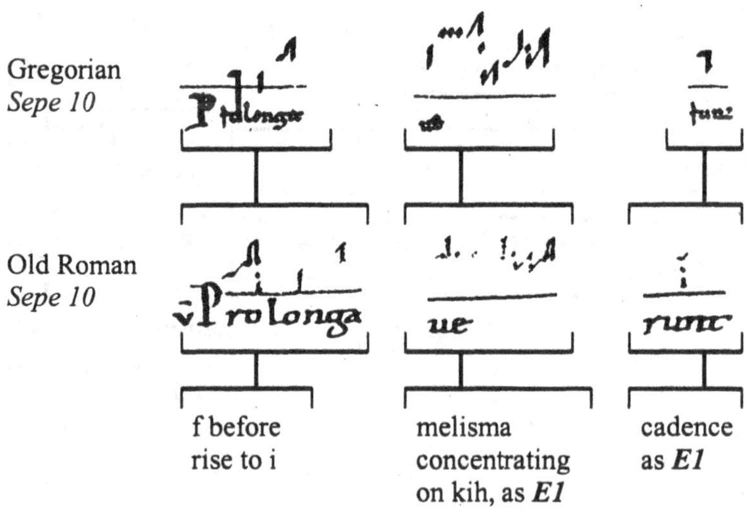

Example **3.22**

In the Gregorian tradition, *Sepe 10* and *Desiderium 5* begin with the gd recitation. All three phrases rise to k at the beginning of the melisma via hihi. In the Old Roman tradition, *Sepe 10* and *Desiderium 5* begin ghihgf, seen also in *Sepe 3* and *Ad te leuaui 7* (***A2***: see p. 274), before having the same melodic outline for the last three syllables as *Desiderium 5* (***E1***: see p. 315).

Phrase ***E3*** The last version of phrase ***E*** (pp. 318–19) is generally used when there is only one phrase in the first verse-half (Example **3.23**).

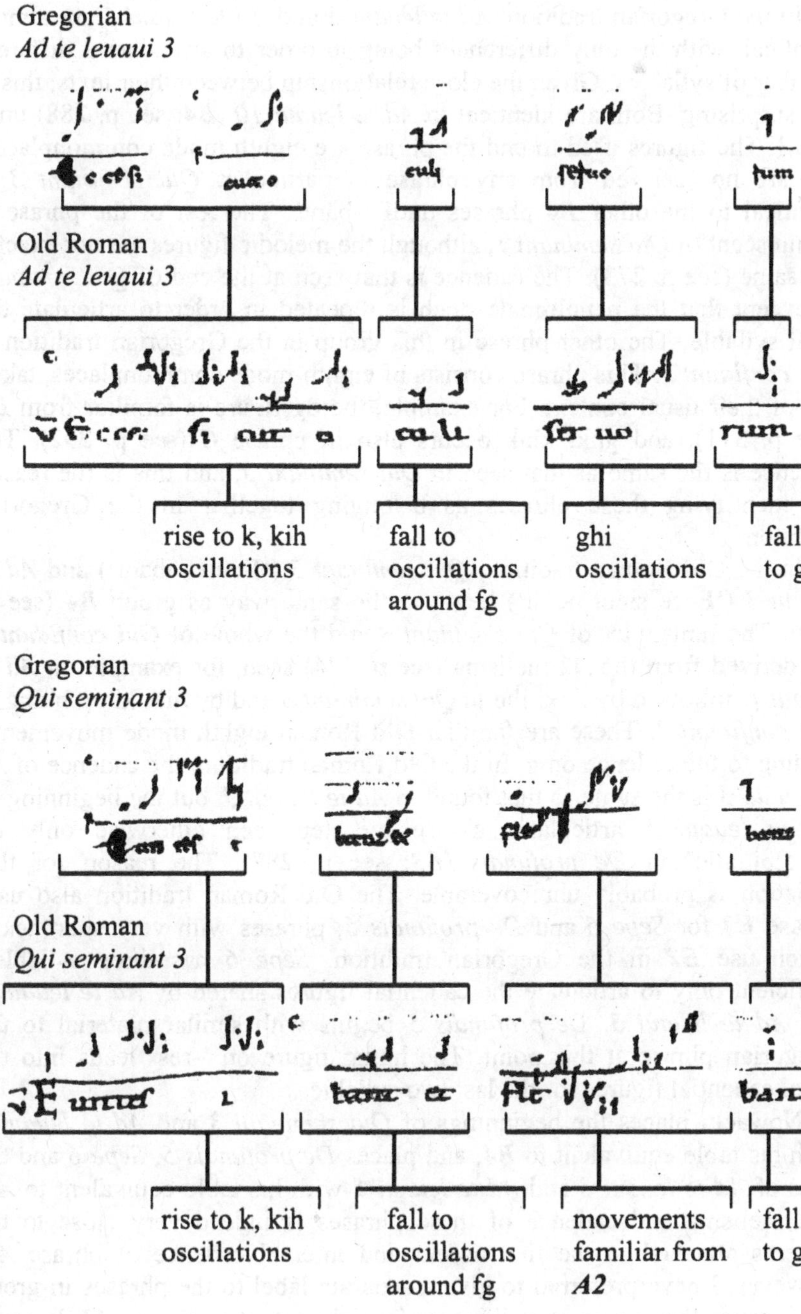
Gregorian
Ad te leuaui 3
Old Roman
Ad te leuaui 3
rise to k, kih oscillations
fall to oscillations around fg
ghi oscillations
fall to g
Gregorian
Qui seminant 3
Old Roman
Qui seminant 3
rise to k, kih oscillations
fall to oscillations around fg
movements familiar from A2
fall to g

Example 3.23

In the Gregorian tradition, *Ad te leuaui 3* and *Ad te leuaui 5* are almost identical, with the only differences being in order to articulate a different number of syllables. Given the close relationship between their texts, this is not surprising. Both are identical to *Ad te leuaui 10* (***B4***: see p. 288) until '-cu-'. The figures used to end the phrase are eighth-mode commonplaces, but are not derived from any phrase in particular. *Qui seminant 3* is identical to the other ***B4*** phrases until '-bant'. The rest of the phrase is reminiscent of *Qui seminant 1*, although the melodic figures are not exactly the same (see p. 273). The cadence is that seen at the end of *Qui seminant 1*, except that the penultimate pitch is repeated in order to articulate the final syllable. The other phrase in this group in the Gregorian tradition is *Qui confidunt 3*. This phrase consists of eighth-mode commonplaces, taken out of their usual context. For example, the dg figure is familiar from ***D5*** (see p. 311), and ghki khik occurs also in phrase ***C*** (see p. 292). The cadence is the same as that seen in *Qui seminant 3*, and this is the reason for identifying these phrases as belonging together in the Gregorian tradition.

In the Old Roman tradition, *Qui seminant 3* ('Euntes ibant') and *Ad te leuaui 3* ('Ecce sicut oculi') begin in the same way as group ***B4*** (see p. 289). The remainder of *Qui seminant 3* and the whole of *Qui confidunt 3* are derived from the ***A2*** melisma (see p. 274) seen, for example, in *Ad te leuaui 1*, followed by ihiki ihg in *Qui seminant 3* and by hiki kihig hkihg in *Qui confidunt 3*. These are familiar Old Roman eighth-mode movements, leading to the cadence on g. In the Old Roman tradition, the cadence of *Ad te leuaui 3* is the same as that found in *Ad te leuaui 5*, but the beginning of *Ad te leuaui 5* articulates a rise by step seen otherwise only on '(pro)pitiatio' in *De profundis* (***B3***: see p. 287). The reason for this variation is probably unrecoverable. The Old Roman tradition also uses phrase ***E3*** for *Sepe 6* and *De profundis 5*, phrases with very short texts, which use ***E2*** in the Gregorian tradition. *Sepe 6* has three syllables, sufficient only to articulate the cadential figures shared by *Ad te leuaui 3* and *Ad te leuaui 5*. *De profundis 5* begins with similar material to the Gregorian phrase at this point. The hkihg figure on '-res' leads into the usual cadential figures for the last two syllables.

Nowacki places the beginnings of *Qui seminant 3* and *Ad te leuaui 3* with his table equivalent to ***B4***, and places *De profundis 5*, *Sepe 6* and the ends of *Ad te leuaui 3* and *Ad te leuaui 5* with his table equivalent to ***A1***. The melisma and cadence of these phrases is indeed very close to the patterns attached to the first accent and internal cadence of phrase ***A1***. However, I have preferred to give a separate label to the phrases in group ***E3*** because they occur in a different formal context to phrase ***A1***, because they use only the opening material of phrase ***A1*** and they use it as a cadence, and because the Gregorian phrases have no equivalent parallel with phrase ***A1***.

Phrase F

Phrase ***F*** (pp. 320–23) is used to end eighth-mode tracts (Example **3.24**).

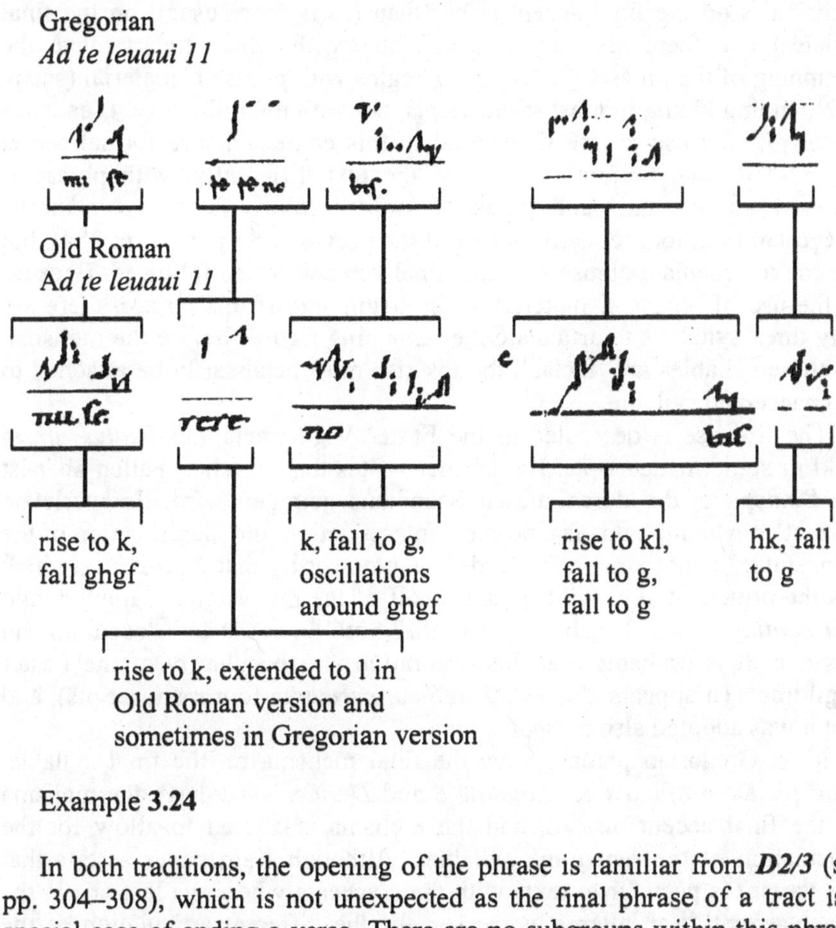

Example **3.24**

In both traditions, the opening of the phrase is familiar from ***D2/3*** (see pp. 304–308), which is not unexpected as the final phrase of a tract is a special case of ending a verse. There are no subgroups within this phrase. Differences in melodic outline are stimulated by different accentuation patterns, or by there being different numbers of syllables.

In the Gregorian tradition, the first main accent has the pattern hghik. This is followed by a combination of the pitches ghgf or ghf. These figures are used fairly interchangeably, and are attached to one or two syllables, depending on how many syllables there are between the first main accent (hghik) and the second (rise to k). *Commouisti 7*, *Iubilate 11*, and *Qui seminant 7* instead have low recitation before the variant ***D2*** opening seen in *Ad te leuaui 4*, *Ad te leuaui 6*, *Qui seminant 2* and *Qui seminant 4* (see p. 305), with the rise on the following (unaccented) syllable. There is no clear reason for this variant although it has clearly become the standard end-of-verse opening in *Qui seminant*. *De profundis 13* ignores the usual association of certain figures with accented syllables. This is because the melisma is on the final accent rather than (as is more usual) on the final syllable, and there are only five syllables with which to articulate the beginning of the phrase. *Qui regis 10* begins with phrase ***C*** material (see p. 292), ending kkkhg in most manuscripts, but with the full phrase ***C*** cadence in *BEN5*.[42] To use phrase ***C*** material in this context makes formal sense. The Old Roman tradition breaks up the text differently, with phrase ***C*** material on 'et ueni' and phrase ***F*** on 'ut saluos facias nos'. In the Gregorian tradition, 'et ueni' is part of the previous ***B3*** phrase (p. 284), but the cue to articulate phrase ***C*** in this final verse was also followed. Because of the use of phrase ***C*** material at the beginning of this phrase, there are only three syllables to articulate the remaining figures before the melisma. As these syllables are 'fácias', the fhk rise must necessarily be attached to an unaccented syllable.

The fhk rise is decorated in the Easter Vigil tracts and *Beatus uir* as fhikl in some manuscripts. Kainzbauer writes that 'in allen Fällen aber ist die Sinnspitze, die durch diesen Scandicus getragen wird, der vorletzte Akzent'.[43] Although this is a possible interpretation, the identification of the 'Sinnspitze' is not straightforward. It is noteworthy that *Beatus uir*, which has the ornamentation fhikl in about half of the manuscripts sampled, and *Qui confidunt*, which generally has fhk, both have the text 'seculum' on this rise. It is probable that this decoration is a peculiarity of the Easter Vigil tracts (it appears also in ***D2*** in *Sicut ceruus* in four manuscripts), and that it was adopted also in *Beatus uir*.

Most Gregorian phrases have the final melisma on the final syllable. *Sepe 13*, *De profundis 13*, *Laudate 8* and *Desiderium 9* have the melisma on the final accent instead, and the melisma is altered to allow for the articulation of the remaining syllables. Although Kainzbauer asserts that this variant is peculiar to texts with three accents where the last one is the 'Hauptakzent',[44] an alternative reason for the different articulation of the phrase may be found by examining the Old Roman tradition, where the melisma is usually associated with the final accent.

The Old Roman final phrases follow essentially the same patterns in all

---

[42] The phrase ***C*** cadence is used also in *ALB*, *ROG1*, *FITZ*, and *BRE*.

[43] Kainzbauer, op. cit., 41.

[44] Ibid., 46.

of the tracts, altered only in response to the number of syllables available. As in the Gregorian tradition, *De profundis 13* does not follow the usual connection of certain melodic movements with accented syllables. This occurs also in the Old Roman tradition in *Beatus uir 12* and *Qui confidunt 12*: there are only two accents in these texts, and phrase ***F*** usually has three accents. In *Qui seminant 7*, the melisma is on the last syllable rather than being on the last accent, possibly because of the rhyme with *Qui regis 10*: 'nos'/'(su)os' (Nowacki writes that it 'may be an error').[45] Because there are five syllables in *Qui seminant 7* with which to articulate the high recitation usually associated with two or three syllables, this phrase has the ***B2*** rise instead of the usual figures (see pp. 281–2).

The Old Roman melisma is on the last accent. The high point l is followed by a pattern falling from k to h, then k falling to h or g. In some phrases these intervals are filled in (for example, *Desiderium 9* has kih hikihg), but in others they are not (for example, *De profundis* has khkih). In *ORC*, the phrase endings vary, but they are all based around the same basic movements.[46]

Analysis of Each Eighth-Mode Tract

The analysis of the individual phrases, above, gives an abstract impression of how the genre functions. Each tract will now be considered in greater detail in order to achieve a fuller understanding of how the melodic and formal scheme outlined above is applied to each text.

Ad te leuaui

	Old Roman	Gregorian	Phrase no.
Ad te leuaui oculos meos	***A2***	***A2***	1
qui habitas in celis	***D4***	***D4***	2
Ecce sicut oculi seruorum	***E3***	***E3***	3
in manibus dominorum suorum	***A2'-D3***	***A2'-D2***	4
Et sicut oculi ancille	***E3***	***E3***	5
in manibus domine sue	***A2'-D3***	***A2'-D2***	6
Ita oculi nostri	***A2***	***A2***	7
ad dominum deum nostrum	***B2***	***B2-B3***	8

45 Nowacki, op. cit., 199.

46 The other Old Roman manuscripts consistently end ihkihg or ihkihhg.

donec misereatur nostri	***C1***	***C1***	9
Miserere nobis domine	***B4***	***B4***	10
miserere nobis	***F***	***F***	11

The first phrase belongs to the complicated group of tract openings because it has ten syllables. The remaining phrase in the first verse uses ***D4***, a phrase specifically associated with the first verses of *Ad te leuaui, Desiderium,* and *Commouisti*, the three tracts whose first phrases (***A2***) end in the same way.

The second and third verses are closely connected, both textually and musically. In the Gregorian tradition, the two verses have almost identical melodies throughout, altered only to allow for the different numbers of syllables. In the Old Roman tradition, *Ad te leuaui 5* has a different opening to *Ad te leuaui 3* (see p. 96, above), but the rest of the verses are almost identical. Nowacki interprets the texts of these verses as 'Ecce… manibus/ dominorum suorum' and 'Et sicut… manibus/ domine sue', having melodic material V K_1 in both verses.[47] Kainzbauer also links 'in manibus' with the preceding rather than the following text, but writes that the melodic patterns on 'in manibus' are an 'Überleitungsfloskel'. Within these verses, 'an keiner Stelle ist ein Halt sinnvoll'.[48] However, these ways of dividing the text both ignore the syntax, and it seems preferable to handle these verses on the basis of their textual structure. The subjects are 'oculi seruorum' and 'oculi ancille', with 'leuantur' implied in both cases. The rest of the text, 'in manibus dominorum suorum/domine sue', comprises the indirect object. Given the fact that *Ad te leuaui 3* and *Ad te leuaui 5* cadence quite satisfactorily, and given the syntax of the sentences, the interpretation ***E3 A2'-D2/3*** is the most accurate reflection of the textual and musical state.

One would expect ***E1*** to begin the following verse, with its divisible first verse-half, but the textual link 'oculi nostri/ oculos meos' with the first phrase of the tract has prompted the cantors, in both traditions, to use ***A2*** material at the beginning of this verse. The 'meos'/'nostri' link and the return to 'leuaui' (although it is only implied in the fourth verse) have overridden the 'oculi' link with other verses. This is followed by ***B2*** in the Old Roman tradition, as one would expect for the second phrase in the verse-half. The Gregorian tradition has ***B3***, partly because 'ad dominum deum nostrum' is a prepositional phrase that belongs with 'Ita [leuaui] oculi nostri', and partly to continue a parallel with the second verse of *Sepe*. In *Sepe 3*, 'Dicat nunc', which rhymes with 'Ita', is also given ***A2*** material

47 Nowacki, op. cit., 218.
48 Kainzbauer, op. cit., 99.

(see p. 273), but 'israhel' is given phrase ***B3*** material to conclude the verse-half (see p. 285), so the *Sepe* verse-half has ***A2-B3***. The *Ad te leuaui* verse-half has sufficient text to articulate fully both of these phrases. It has ***A2 B3***, although the second phrase begins like ***B2***. The formal cue to use ***B2*** and the associative and textual cues to use ***B3*** all appear to have been partly followed. Kainzbauer gives an alternative explanation: he maintains that the move to ***B3*** material is because of 'die individuelle Ausdeutung des Wortes "Deum"'.[49] This explanation is unconvincing because the usual stimulus for the use of ***B3*** is formal rather than textual. The second half of this verse uses phrase ***C*** as one would expect in a verse where the first half-verse was divided into two phrases.

The final verse begins with phrase ***B4***. This is the version one expects to encounter when the first verse-half of the last verse is made up of a single phrase. The final phrase proceeds as one would expect. Nowacki's table does not have a verse division here.[50] This is because he used *ORJ* as the basis of his analysis: the other two Old Roman manuscripts and the Gregorian manuscripts have a clear verse division at 'Miserere nobis domine', and it is also suggested by the musical state.

Apart from use of ***A2*** at the beginning of the fourth verse, prompted by textual parallels with the first phrase, and use of ***B3*** after this in the Gregorian tradition, prompted by the syntax and by parallels with *Sepe*, the tract is consistent with the scheme outlined above.

Attende[51]

	Gregorian	Phrase no.
Attende celum	***A1***	1
et loquar	***B1***	2
et audiat terra uerba ex ore meo	***C1***	3
Expectetur sicut pluuia eloquium meum	***E1***	4
et descendant sicut ros uerba mea	***B2***	5
sicut imber super gramina/gramen	***C4***	6
et sicut nix super fenum	***B2***	7
quia nomen domini inuocabo	***C1***	8
Date magnitudinem deo nostro	***E1***	9
deus uera opera eius	***B2***	10

---

[49] Ibid., 99.

[50] Nowacki, op. cit., 223.

[51] This tract does not appear in an Old Roman version.

et omnes uie eius iudicia	***C1***	11
Deus fidelis in quo non est iniquitas	***E1***	12
iustus et sanctus dominus	***F***	13

The psalms were regularly sung in the monastic office, so the verse divisions would have been firmly established by responsorial or antiphonal singing. One might expect the verse divisions of canticles to be less firmly established than those of psalms, because the canticles are less universally used throughout the liturgy.[52] This is indeed the case. Three of the tracts sung at the Easter Vigil are based on canticle rather than psalm texts, and different manuscripts have the verse divisions in different places. *Attende* is the first of these tracts to be considered; the others are *Cantemus* and *Vinea*. Although each of these chants is divided into verses in different ways in different manuscripts, the variants are clearly of no more than scribal significance: all manuscripts have the same musical phrases, even though this sometimes leads to unexpected phrases being used in the formal context. Given the stability of the association of each musical phrase with a specific formal context across the rest of the genre, it is clear that the cantors did not construct eighth-mode tracts with, say, phrase ***C*** at the beginning of a verse. Instead, the differing verse divisions are variants introduced by the text scribes. The stability of the verse divisions at the time the eighth-mode tracts were created formed a clear framework into which the appropriate phrases had to fit. The mnemonic power of this will be discussed further in Chapter 4.

All manuscripts divide for the second verse at 'Expectetur'. 'Date magnitudinem' is imperative rather than indicative, and this new mood has prompted a new verse in almost all the manuscripts. Five phrases are too many for a single verse, and there is a further division at 'Deus fidelis'.

The middle section is divided up in different ways. There are two pairs of 'sicut' phrases; the second pair has 'quia nomen domini inuocabo' joined on the end before the change of mood. One group of manuscripts does not divide these clauses. Their long middle verse is consistent with the verse divisions of the canticle as found in standard biblical texts.[53] A second group of manuscripts divides before the third 'sicut' clause ('sicut imber'), following the textual pairing, but making no musical sense.[54] A third group divides before the last of the four 'sicut' phrases, which does not follow the textual form but gives a musical rhyme to the chant: ***ABC, EBC, BC, EBC,***

---

[52] Similarly, the spelling tradition might be less firmly established, and even the actual words used.

[53] *ALB, KLO1, LAN, LAV, MOG4, MUR3, ROG1.*

[54] *BEN5, BRE, CHA1, GAL1, IRI, ORC, ORJ, ORP, PAS2, SAB.*

BF.[55] The different groups of manuscripts have prioritised different cues: textual, musical, and those of the biblical verse divisions. The tract outline following the structure of the canticle has been used as the basis for the analysis below and for the table above.

The first verse begins with the simple version of phrase ***A***, because of the number of syllables, followed by ***B1***, as one would expect in the first verse. There is only one phrase in the second verse-half, which is given phrase ***C***. The second verse has the expected versions of phrases ***E, B,*** and ***C*** followed by ***B2 C***. There is a strong textual cue for the repetition of ***B2***. It is also used earlier in the verse, beginning 'et' and having the vowel '-e-' on the penultimate syllable. The penultimate verse of *Attende* has the structure one would expect: ***E1 B2 C***. The last verse has phrase ***E1*** before the final phrase. One would expect ***B4*** or ***E3*** in a bipartite final verse. The reason for the unexpected use of a simple phrase here, which also occurs in the last verse of *Cantemus*, appears to be contextual. In all other verses of the four Easter Vigil tracts, ***E1*** is used to begin verses other than the first (except for one verse in *Vinea*).

The structure of the text of *Attende* means that simple versions of the phrases are used. ***B2*** is used in the middle of a verse because of a textual cue. The final verse begins ***E1***, possibly because of associative links with the other Easter Vigil tracts. Otherwise, this tract is consistent with the scheme outlined above.

Beatus uir

	Old Roman	Gregorian	Phrase no.
Beatus uir	***A1***	***A1***	1
qui timet	***B2***	***cont.***	2
dominum	***cont.***	***B1***	
in mandatis eius	***C2***	***C2***	3
cupit nimis	***D1***	***D1***	4
Potens in terra	***E2***	***E1***	5
erit semen eius	***B2***	***cont.***	6
generatio rectorum	***C2***	***C1***	7
benedicetur	***D1***	***D2***	8
Gloria et divitie	***E1***	***E1***	9
in domo eius	***B2***	***cont.***	10
et iusticia eius	***C1***	***C1***	11

55 *CLU1, TOU, TYR, YRX.*

manet	***cont.***	***F***	12
in seculum seculi	***F***	***cont.***	

The two traditions divide the text of the first half-verse into two phrases in different ways (see p. 61, above). The Old Roman manuscripts follow the usual phrase ***A1*** shapes with ***B2***, not usually associated with the first verse. There are several factors that will have prompted and stabilised the use of this version. The phrase ends with an antepenultimate accent, a stress pattern that never occurs in group ***B1***, and that occurs in ***B2*** in *Qui regis 4* in the Old Roman tradition, a phrase which also begins 'qui' and ends '-m'. Two other phrases in group ***B2*** also end '-um'. When such textual prompts are combined, the use of ***B2*** in the first verse of *Beatus uir* is unsurprising. As indicated above, the manner in which the Gregorian tradition divides the text is less satisfactory syntactically. Although ***B1*** is generally used, the normal association of certain melodic movements with accented syllables is not followed. The second half-verse consists of straightforward versions of ***C*** and ***D***.

The first half-verses of the second and third verses have the texts 'Potens in terra erit semen eius' (His descendants will be powerful in the land) and 'Gloria et divitie in domo eius' (Glory and wealth will be in his house). 'Potens in terra erit' is the predicate and 'semen eius' is the subject, but the verb 'to be' usually joins the two halves of a sentence and does not belong with either in particular, so that 'Potens in terra/ erit semen eius' also makes syntactical sense. The third verse beginning leaves the verb out, as is common in Latin: 'Gloria et divitie' is the subject and '(erit) in domo eius' is the predicate.

The Old Roman version divides subject and predicate into the two expected phrases: ***E1/2 B2***. The Gregorian tradition does not divide these texts, instead using ***E1*** with a long recitation passage. Verses with a single phrase in the first half-verse generally use ***E3, B3*** or ***B4***. It seems probable that the tract originally had four-part verses, as in the Old Roman tradition, but that the Frankish cantors substituted ***E1*** for ***E1/2 B2***. Kainzbauer writes that it would not be possible to divide the first of these phrases because 'erit' would be given the g-k rise of ***B2*** and this would attach too much weight to a relatively unimportant word.[56] He writes that the text at the beginning of the next verse is long enough to divide, 'müsste aber das Proparoxytonon "divitiae" auf die Kadenzfloskel von L1 legen'.[57] This objection is invalid: *Attende 12* also ends phrase ***E1*** with the accent pattern /--. The Old Roman cantors appear to have encountered no difficulties in

[56] Kainzbauer, op. cit., 95-96.
[57] Ibid., 96.

dividing the first half of each of these verses and this illustrates the value of considering more than one liturgical tradition in an analysis of this kind.

The second verse continues with phrase ***C***. The Old Roman tradition does not rise fhk until the third syllable, accenting 'generátio' and leaving insufficient text for recitation in the middle of the phrase. Most Gregorian manuscripts rise fhk on the first syllable 'ge(neratio)', although it is not accented, which leaves sufficient text for recitation (see Example **2.3**; p. 44). Two different versions of phrase ***C*** are therefore used. In the Old Roman tradition, the verse ends with ***D1***, like the first verse. In the Gregorian tradition, the second verse ends with ***D2***, which has a different articulation of the syllables before the melisma. The reasons for this are unclear, although it may be because the Frankish cantors mistakenly interpreted 'benedicétur' as 'bénedícetúr', therefore having two accents before the melisma – too many for the use of ***D1***.[58]

The second half of the last verse begins with phrase ***C***. The Old Roman tradition has the text 'et iusticia eius manet' (subject + verb), with 'in seculum seculi' (prepositional phrase) for the final phrase, but the Gregorian tradition has 'et iusticia eius' (subject) with 'manet in seculum seculi' (predicate) for the final phrase. Both of these make syntactical sense and it has not significantly affected the musical outline. In *ORC*, but not in *ORJ* or *ORP*, this tract ends with the six-note phrase ***D*** cadence instead of the usual cadence. This is probably a scribal error.

The first half-verse of each verse is treated differently in the two traditions, as is the end of the last verse. Several phrases ignore the usual alignment of text accent with certain melodic patterns (for example, *Beatus uir 2* in both traditions, *Beatus uir 6* in the Old Roman tradition, *Beatus uir 7* in the Gregorian tradition, *Beatus uir 12* in the Old Roman tradition). This tract was not well established in the mid-eighth-century tradition. A detailed investigation of the significance of this will be undertaken in Chapter 7.

Cantemus[59]

	Gregorian	Phrase no.
Cantemus domino	***A1***	1
gloriose enim	***B2***	2
honorificatus est equum et ascensorem	***C1***	3

[58] The Old Roman cantors also mistakenly interpreted the accentuation pattern as 'benedícetur' (see Nowacki, op. cit., 201).

[59] This tract does not appear in an Old Roman version.

proiecit in mare	***B2***	4
adiutor et protector factus est mihi in salutem	***C1***	5
Hic deus meus et honorabo eum	***E1***	6
deus patris mei	***B2***	7
et exaltabo eum	***C2***	8
Dominus conterens bella	***E1***	9
dominus nomen est illi	***F***	10

Like *Attende*, *Cantemus* is based on a canticle rather than a psalm text. The last two verse divisions are consistent in all manuscripts. This verse structure emphasises the textual connections between 'Hic deus meus et honorabo eum' and 'deus patris mei et exaltabo eum', although the music does not reflect them.[60] One group of manuscripts also divides at the phrase before, which fits with the canticle verse structure found in modern bibles, and the other does not, making sense of the musical structure.

This tract is very different from the scheme outlined above, but it is not necessarily a particularly poor example of the genre, or a later, corrupted composition. There is a contextual reason for the state of *Cantemus*. The melodic structure of *Cantemus* is identical to the second to fourth verses of *Attende*, apart from the fact that the first verse begins with ***A1***. These two tracts are sung in close proximity at the Easter Vigil.

In the first verse of *Cantemus*, ***B2*** is used for the second phrase instead of the expected ***B1***. The third phrase has the text 'honorificatus est equum et ascensorem'. This is not a single text unit. The sentence 'honorificatus est' ('he is honoured') is completely separate from 'equum et ascensorem/ proiecit in mare' ('the horse and its rider' (object)/ 'he has thrown into the sea' (subject + verb and prepositional phrase)). It is possible that the rhyme of 'ascensorem' with *Qui confidunt 5–6* (ending 'ierusalem') and *Beatus uir 7* (ending 'rectorum') prompted this unexpected division of the text into phrases. Kainzbauer has suggested that the division of 'equum et ascensorem /proiecit in mare' between the two phrases ***C*** and ***B2*** may have acted as a counter-balance to the impression given by use of phrase ***B2*** that there was a new verse within the five-phrase verse.[61] Similarly, phrase ***C*** is

[60] Kainzbauer maintains that the textual structure would have been shown more clearly by use of ***E*** for 'Hic deus meus', ***B*** for 'et honorabo eum', and ***C*** for 'deus patris mei et exaltabo eum', but that this would have meant obscuring the 'Sinnspitze' ('pátris'): as the second accent in phrase ***C***, 'pa-' would have had gfgh rather than a more prominent melodic figure. Arguably the sense would have been shown even more clearly if 'deus patris mei' had phrase ***C*** and 'et exaltabo eum' had phrase ***D***, but the same accentual objection may be raised. (op. cit., 92–3)

[61] Ibid., 92.

used on the 'adiutor' phrase to show clearly that there is no verse beginning at this point in the tract, even though 'Adiutor' marks the beginning of a new verse in the canticle.[62] Use of phrase ***C*** will have been stabilised by the '-em' rhyme with other phrases in the group.

The following verse has the expected versions of ***E, B*** and ***C***. The final verse has ***E1 F***, despite being bipartite. There is no clear textual reason for this.

The syntax has been ignored in the third and fourth phrases. The textual connections between the two halves of the penultimate verse are not reflected in the division of the text into musical phrases. The first and last verses use unexpected phrases, and 'Adiutor' is not treated as a verse beginning. These anomalies are most easily understood if this tract is viewed as a re-texting of the second to fourth verses of *Attende*.

Commouisti

	Old Roman	Gregorian	Phrase no.
Commouisti domine terram	***A2***	***A2***	1
et conturbasti eam	***D4***	***D4***	2
Sana contritiones eius	***B3***	***B3***	3
quia mota est	***C-D5***	***D5'***	4
Ut fugiant a facie arcus	***B3***	***B3***	5
ut liberentur	***C2***	***C3***	6
electi tui	***F***	***F***	7

The first phrase of this tract has nine syllables, which has prompted use of ***A2***. One might expect 'domine' to act as a stimulus to use ***A1***, with ***B1*** on 'terram', but 'Commouisti... terram' is the predicate and 'domine' is the subject, so the text unit is indivisible. The phrase is closely related in the two traditions, and based firmly in the eighth mode. The cadence is the same as that in the first phrase of *Desiderium* and *Ad te leuaui*. The single phrase left in the first verse uses ***D4***, associated with these three tracts.

The second verse begins with ***B3***, as one would expect with an indivisible verse-half. In the Old Roman tradition, the second (and last) phrase of the second verse (p. 312) begins like phrase ***C*** but continues with shapes derived from the ***D1/2*** and ***D4*** melismas (see p. 92, above). In the Gregorian tradition (p. 311), this phrase begins and ends like ***D1***. The rest of the phrase uses familiar eighth-mode movements, but it is not directly

[62] Ibid., 91.

derived from any phrase.

The third verse also begins with ***B3***. The following phrase ***C*** is abbreviated in both traditions. In the Old Roman tradition, the patterns usually associated with the first two syllables are joined onto a single syllable and abbreviated, and in the Gregorian tradition, the opening figures fhk igh are replaced by fghi hgh, and the next figures gfg ghkik are joined together on a single syllable.

This tract is entirely consistent with the scheme outlined above.

De profundis

	Old Roman	Gregorian	Phrase no.
De profundis clamaui	***A1-***	***A1-***	1
ad te domine	***B5***	***B5***	2
domine exaudi	***C2***	***C4***	3
uocem meam	***D1***	***D1***	4
Fiant aures tue	***E3***	***E1***	5
intendentes	***B5***	***B5***	6
in orationem	***C2***	***C2***	7
serui tui	***D1***	***D1***	8
Si iniquitates obseruaueris domine	***B4***	***B4***	9
domine quis sustinebit	***C-D2***	***C-D1***	10
Quia apud te propitiatio est	***B3***	***B3***	11
et propter legem tuam	***C2***	***C2***	12
sustinui te domine	***F***	***F***	13

As described above, the text of the first verse-half is not easily divisible into two phrases and this is reflected in the avoidance of the ***A1*** cadence and the use of ***B5***. In the Old Roman tradition, the rise on '-ma-' is also used on 'do-', which reinforces the unity of this first verse-half (see p. 337). In the Gregorian tradition, the following phrase ('domine exaudi') is treated as if the antepenultimate syllable is accented, and is therefore part of group ***C4***. As the last three syllables are used to articulate the cadential figures, there is insufficient text to use the figures generally associated with the beginning of the phrase. Instead, g gfg precedes the ghkik rise.[63] In the Old Roman tradition, this phrase is treated as a normal phrase ***C***. The verse concludes with phrase ***D1***.

[63] Pitched manuscripts have variously f gfg, g hfg, and g gfg.

The second verse begins with simple phrase ***E*** material in the Gregorian tradition. In the Old Roman tradition, the patterns for the first two syllables are closely related to the Gregorian treatment of the same phrase. The final pattern of the phrase, hkihg, is used on '-res' as a pivot back into the Old Roman ***E3*** material for the last two syllables. Use of this version of the phrase rather than the expected ***E1/2*** may have been prompted by the rhyme with *Ad te leuaui 5* '(ancill)e'. This is followed by ***B5***. In the Old Roman tradition, this makes formal sense, because the previous phrase used an abbreviated form of phrase ***E***. In the Gregorian tradition, there is no clear reason for the use of ***B5***. The verse concludes with simple versions of phrases ***C*** and ***D***.

The third and fourth verses begin with a characteristic gd recitation in both traditions, seen also in phrase ***E*** in *Desiderium 5* and *Laudate 5* (see pp. 314–15). Because of a textual cue (with 'miserere nobis domine' in *Ad te leuaui 10*), the third verse begins with ***B4***, even though this is usually associated with the final verse of tracts. This phrase has more syllables than other phrases in this group, so the melodic shapes of the middle section are repeated in both traditions. There is only one phrase in the second verse-half (pp. 302 and 306). It has the phrase ***C*** opening seen also in *De profundis 3* with exactly the same text (see pp. 298 and 301). In the Gregorian tradition, this opening pattern is peculiar to these two phrases. In the Gregorian tradition, this leads into ***D1*** material on 'sustinebit'. In the Old Roman tradition, 'quis sustinebit' instead uses ***D2***.

In both traditions, the final verse begins with the gd articulations seen at the beginning of the preceding verse. The Old Roman figures in the middle of the phrase are derived from phrase ***E***, and the Gregorian phrase is modelled on the Old Roman one. The verse ends ***CF***. In the Gregorian tradition, the final melisma is placed on the final accent rather than on the final syllable. The word 'domine' has great prominence throughout this tract, and the placing of the melisma on the accented 'dómine' serves to highlight this final use of the word.

In the Old Roman tradition, ***E3*** is used in the second verse, perhaps because of a rhyme. In both traditions, the third verse begins with ***B4*** because of the 'domine' prompt. 'Domine' causes the following phrase to begin with elements of phrase ***C*** because of the textual link with *De profundis 3*. The final melisma is on the last accent rather than on the last syllable, and the text is 'domine'. These departures from the scheme are all stimulated by textual considerations. It is not clear why the final verse begins with ***B3*** instead of ***B4*** material.

Desiderium

	Old Roman	Gregorian	Phrase no.
Desiderium anime eius	***A2***	***A2***	1
tribuisti ei	***B1***	***B1***	2
et uoluntate labiorum eius	***C1***	***C1***	3
non fraudasti eum	***D4***	***D4***	4
Quoniam preuenisti eum	***E1***	***E1***	5
in benedictione dulcedinis	***B3-D***	***B-D4***	6
Posuisti super caput eius	***B4***	***B4***	7
coronam	***C3***	***C3***	8
de lapide pretioso	***F***	***F***	9

In the Gregorian tradition, the first phrase begins like the end of the first phrase of *Qui seminant*, but one note lower. The reasons for this transposition are not clear. In the Old Roman tradition, the first phrase begins like the end of the first phrase of *Sepe*. The cadential section is the same as that of *Ad te leuaui* and *Commouisti* in both traditions. ***B1 C*** follows this, as one would expect. The last phrase of the verse uses ***D4***, which is not otherwise used at the end of a quadripartite verse. However, 'non fraudasti eum' strongly rhymes with *Commouisti 2* 'et conturbasti eam', and the first phrase of *Desiderium* ends in the same way as the first phrases of *Ad te leuaui* and *Commouisti*, the tracts which also end their first verse in this way.

The second verse begins with a gd recitation in both traditions at the beginning of ***E1***. This recitation is seen also in the second verse of *Laudate*, on the same word, 'quoniam'. The tract is not constructed as if there is only one phrase in the first half-verse. The other phrase in the verse begins with phrase ***B*** elements and ends with phrase ***D*** elements in both traditions, but the proportions of each are different in the two traditions (see pp. 73 and 90, above). Use of phrase ***B*** elements in the verse means that use of phrase ***E1*** rather than ***E3*** is formally appropriate.

The last verse has the expected phrases ***B4 C F***. All phrases in *Desiderium* are consistent with the scheme.

Iubilate

	Old Roman	Gregorian	Phrase no.
Iubilate domino/deo	***A1***	***A1***	1

omnis terra	***B1***	***B1***	2
seruite domino	***C2***	***C4***	3
in leticia	***D1***	***D1***	4
Intrate in conspectu eius	***E1***	***E1***	5
in exultatione	***B1***	***C2***	6
Scitote quod dominus	***C2***	***C4***	7
ipse est deus	***D1***	***D1***	8
Ipse fecit nos et non ipsi nos	***E-B5***	***(E)-B5***	9
nos autem populus eius	***C1***	***C1***	10
et oues pascue eius	***F***	***F***	11

Iubilate is the only tract, apart from the Easter Vigil tracts, where the verse divisions are inconsistent across the tradition. The Old Roman Graduals, as well as *LAV, CHA1, SAB* and *STM*, have divisions at 'Intrate' and 'Ipse fecit nos'. This follows the musical structure of the tract, and highlights the three imperative clauses which begin these three verses. However, this structure does not reflect the structure of the psalm, whose verse division is at 'Scitote'. Most Gregorian manuscripts divide in the same places as the Old Roman manuscripts, and at 'Scitote' as well. This is a scribal division and it is not reflected in the musical structure of the tract: phrase ***C*** is not associated with verse beginnings. *BRE, CHA, GAL1, GAL2, IRI,* and *MUR3* divide in all of these places, and also at 'Nos autem populus eius'. Some of the oldest manuscripts of the sample are among these. This does not reflect the musical or the psalmic structure, but it does emphasise the rhyme between the last two lines of text, both of which end 'eius', and it strongly separates the repetition of 'nos'.

One might expect the oldest manuscripts to show the verse structure of this chant most clearly. Three of the *AMS* sources have the text in full.[64] Verse divisions are indicated in Hesbert's edition by a full stop followed by a capital letter. Compiègne shares the verse divisions of the Old Roman manuscripts, Corbie has the four divisions of *BRE et al.*, and Monza divides at 'Intrate', 'Scitote', and 'nos autem', omitting the usual division at 'Ipse fecit nos'. The uncertainty displayed right across the manuscript tradition, including the earliest surviving non-notated Graduals, is prompted by a combination of the verse structure of the psalm, which demands a two-verse tract, and the textual cues from within the corpus that demand more than two verses. As with the Easter Vigil tracts, by the time these manuscripts were copied, the melodies of the chants were sufficiently firmly fixed that the different verse divisions are purely scribal and have no effect on the musical outline.

[64] Hesbert, R-J., *Antiphonale Missarum Sextuplex* (Brussels, 1935), item 36b.

The first verse of *Laudate* consists of two sentences. As the second word is 'dominum', it uses phrase ***A1***, dividing 'omnes gentes', an extension of the subject, from the rest of the sentence. The verbal parallel with 'Iubilate domino/deo omnis terra'[65] means that this tract also begins with ***A1 B1***, the expected material for the first half of the first verse, leaving two sentences to be articulated before the end of the psalm verse. This is too much material to fit into an eighth-mode tract half-verse, especially because there is a cue to attach 'seruite domino' to a particular version of phrase ***C*** which ends with the text 'domin-' (***C4***), also found in *Laudate*. This leaves only 'in letitia' for phrase ***D*** before the next sentence. The musical prompt to begin the second verse after this phrase is clear, despite the fact that the psalm does not divide.

The second verse begins with a normal ***E1***. This is followed by phrase ***C*** in the Gregorian tradition, prompted by the textual cue in *Qui seminant 6* ('cum exultatione'). The Old Roman tradition has ***B1***, which is generally used only in the first verses of tracts. Use of it here may have been stimulated by the partial assonance with 'iniquitates suas' in *Sepe*. Only one sentence has been articulated, although there is a psalm verse division before the next phrase. This division is ignored in the musical setting although most manuscripts have a verse division. Phrase ***C*** is used for the third phrase because of the cue that it ends 'dominus'. This word prompts use of ***C4*** in the Gregorian tradition. This leaves only 'ipse est deus' for the articulation of ***D2***. Again, there is a strong musical prompt to start the new verse here, even though it is not mirrored by the structure of the psalm.

The third verse begins with ***B5***. The Old Roman phrase borrows elements characteristic of verse beginnings from other phrases and the Gregorian version is modelled on the Old Roman version, rather than being constructed from characteristic Gregorian verse-opening figures. The tract ends with a straightforward ***CF***.[66]

In the Gregorian tradition, 'in exultatione' uses phrase ***C*** because of a textual cue. The rest of the tract is consistent with the scheme but the verse outlines of the tract do not coincide with those of the psalm because of textual cues within the genre.

Laudate

	Old Roman	Gregorian	Phrase no.
Laudate dominum	***A1***	***A1***	1

[65] 'Deo' is found in the Roman Psalter and the Old Roman chant. 'Dominum' is found in the Gallican Psalter and the Gregorian chant.

[66] A similar running commentary is given by Kainzbauer, op. cit., 106–7, although he does not mention the textual cues affecting 'Iubilate domino/deo' and 'omnis terra'.

omnes gentes	***B1***	***B1***	2
et conlaudate eum	***C2***	***C2***	3
omnes populi	***D1***	***D1***	4
Quoniam confirmata est super nos	***E1-B2-A2***	***E1***	5
misericordia eius	***B1-2***	***B1-2***	6
et ueritas domini	***C2***	***C4***	7
manet in eternum	***F***	***F***	8

The tract begins with ***A1*** because of the length of the text, and because of the cue of 'domin-'. This is followed by ***B1 C2 D1***, as one would expect.

The second verse begins with phrase ***E1*** in the Gregorian tradition, with the gd recitation on 'Quoniam' seen also in *Desiderium*. This recitation also begins the Old Roman phrase (p. 315), but after the rise to k, the syllable 'su-' uses the movement around high e generally associated with the penultimate syllable in ***B2*** (see pp. 281–2). There is a textual cue (the same figure is used on 'su(i)' in *Qui confidunt*). '-per nos' uses ghih hg, then the ***A2*** cadence (see pp. 274–5). The beginning and end of the phrase are firmly suggestive of verse beginnings, but the use of ***B2*** material in the middle of the phrase is unexpected. The textual cue may have stabilised use of the melodic pattern, but it is unlikely to have stimulated it, because the textual link only affects one syllable. This is followed by ***B2***, with the ***B1*** opening because of the accent pattern (see p. 70, above). The second verse-half uses ***CF***. The Gregorian tradition uses ***C4*** because of the word 'domini'.

Apart from the use of ***B2*** material in the first phrase of the second verse in the Old Roman tradition (perhaps to link the verb + prepositional phrase with the subject, 'misericordia eius'), *Laudate* is consistent with the scheme outlined above.

Qui confidunt

	Old Roman	Gregorian	Phrase no.
Qui confidunt in domino	***A1***	***A1***	1
sicut mons sion	***B1-B3***	***B3***	2
Non commouebitur	***E3***	***E3'***	3
in eternum	***B2***	***B2***	4
qui habitat	***C3***	***C1***	5
in ierusalem	***D3***	***cont.***	6
Montes	***D5***	***D5***	7
in circuitu eius	***B2***	***B2***	8
et dominus	***C3***	***C3'***	9

in circuitu populi sui	***B2***	***B5***	10
ex hoc nunc	***C3***	***C3***	11
et usque in seculum	***F***	***F***	12

Qui confidunt has two verses, the second of which begins at 'Montes'. When the musical structure is considered as well as the scribal verse divisions, it becomes clear that the cantors have acted as if there is an intermediate verse division at 'non commouebitur'. For this reason, the tract will be treated as if there are three verses.

The tract begins with ***A1*** because of the 'domin-' cue, despite it having eight syllables, which would generally act as a prompt to use ***A2***. The melodic outline is altered to accommodate the extra syllables (see p. 59, above). In the Old Roman tradition, the second phrase begins with the ***B1*** opening, as one would expect for the second phrase in the first verse-half, but it has the ***B3*** melisma. In the Gregorian tradition, some manuscripts begin with shapes which are very close to the Old Roman ones, as if this phrase was learned by rote in the Frankish tradition, and not adapted to the local dialect. Other manuscripts, all unpitched, have a rise followed by a one-note fall, which may indicate the pitches fhki. The figure fhki also begins the melisma, and, as there, is followed here by kl. The internal prompt is clear. ***B3*** is used because the relative clause, 'Qui confidunt in domino' makes no sense without 'sicut mons sion', and the two phrases constitute a single syntactical unit.

The third phrase marks the beginning of the second 'verse'. In the Old Roman tradition, it uses shapes characteristic of tract openings, but in the Gregorian tradition, the melodic patterns are more freely centonised, as was described above. There is no clear reason why unique material is used here in the Gregorian tradition, or why a more straightforward version of phrase ***E*** is not used in the Old Roman tradition. The following phrase uses ***B2***, usually associated with the second of four phrases in a middle verse. This is followed by phrase ***C1*** in the Gregorian tradition, and by ***C3 D3*** in the Old Roman tradition. The relative clause is perhaps divided in the Old Roman tradition in order to highlight the syntactical parallels with the main part of the sentence: both consist of subject + verb followed by a prepositional phrase beginning 'in'. The fact that the Gregorian phrase uses ***C1*** despite there being an antepenultimate accent, and despite the syntactical cue to split the phrase, suggests late variation from the original ***CD*** pattern rather than the Old Roman version being a variant. Unlike the choice of the phrase type appropriate for a given context, the division of the psalm verse into phrases appears to have been learned by rote, rather than by the application of rules. One would expect such elements, without clear cues for accurate recall, to be remembered less consistently than elements associated with mnemonic prompts. Examples of memory lapses connected to such rote-learned elements will be considered further in Chapter 4.

The complicated structure of this tract verse has elicited other scholarly interpretations. Nowacki identifies four textual elements: subject-predicate-predicate-subject. He writes that the cadences at the ends of these elements form 'a vivid chiastic pattern': G-F-F-G, and that the first verse is therefore arched in shape.[67] However, phrase ***B2*** has strong associations with being the second phrase in the verse, and ***E3*** contains material associated with verse openings, and it is for these reasons that I interpret the verse as being subdivided after the first sentence.

The next verse begins at 'Montes' in all manuscripts. As with the beginning of the previous 'verse', the Gregorian tradition has a freely composed phrase, ending with the four-note phrase ***D*** cadence. The Old Roman tradition has movements usually associated with phrase ***D***. There is no clear reason why this phrase should be freely composed in the Gregorian tradition and use melodic patterns inappropriate for the formal context in the Old Roman tradition. However, Kainzbauer maintains that ***C1*** is used to end the previous verse and phrase ***E*** is avoided on 'Montes' because the Frankish cantors wished to avoid having a strong verse beginning here: in the psalm, 'in ierusalem' is at the beginning of the second verse. The Old Roman version has phrase ***D*** ending the previous verse, which makes the argument less generally persuasive.

The second phrase in the verse is ***B2***, as one would expect. The following phrase ***C*** has a variant form in the Gregorian tradition, and is related to the melodic outlines usually associated with the last two syllables of a ***C*** phrase. This is followed by ***B5*** in the Gregorian tradition. The opening is reminiscent of phrase ***C***, providing a connection with the previous phrase. In the Old Roman tradition, the text link with *Qui confidunt 8* has prompted use of ***B2***, although this is not the most formally appropriate version of the phrase.[68] This is followed by straightforward versions of phrases ***C*** and ***F***.

The musical outline only makes sense within the constraints of the genre when a verse division is imagined at 'non commouebitur'. In the Gregorian tradition, three phrases in this tract are freely composed. The second phrase of the tract uses an unexpected version of phrase ***B*** in both traditions. The phrase at 'Montes' uses phrase ***D*** material in the Old Roman tradition despite beginning a verse. This tract is perhaps the least close to the scheme of all the eighth-mode tracts. This may be because of the unusual verse structure, and the difficulty that the cantors will have had in adopting this

---

[67] Nowacki, op. cit., 223.

[68] Nowacki writes that ***B2*** is used here because both *Qui confidunt 8* and *Qui confidunt 10* are predicates. He does not mention the textual link (ibid., 223–4).

text to the structure of an eighth-mode tract.

Qui regis israhel

	Old Roman	Gregorian	Phrase no.
Qui regis israhel	***A1***	***A1-B3***	1
intende	***B1-D2-A1***	***B5***	2
qui deducis uelut ovem ioseph	***C1***	***C-B3***	3
Qui sedes super cherubim	***B2***	***E1***	4
appare coram effraim	***C1***	***D2***	5
beniamin	***cont.***	***E2***	6
et manasse	***D2-A1***	***D2***	7
Excita potentiam tuam	***B3***	***D4-B3***	8
et ueni	***C3***	***cont.***	9
ut salvos facias nos	***F***	***C-F***	10

This tract begins with phrase ***A1***. In the Gregorian tradition, the textual prompt of *Sepe 3* ('israhel') has caused use of figures from ***B3*** instead of the usual ***A1*** conclusion. Because the phrase does not cadence properly, the verse-half continues with ***B5***. In the Old Roman tradition, both *Sepe 3* and *Qui regis 1* end with phrase ***A1*** shapes and 'intende' begins like the ***B1*** one would expect to see in this context, but continues with the ***D2*** melisma, perhaps because of a textual cue. The ***D2*** cadence is avoided, and the ***A1*** cadence is used, partly because this is not the end of the verse, and partly because 'intende' is the imperative verb phrase attached to the relative clause 'Qui regis israhel' (see p. 60, above). This is followed by phrase ***C*** in the Old Roman tradition, as one might expect. In the Gregorian tradition, 'qui deducis velut ouem ioseph' (p. 285) begins with a decorated recitation on g and a rise to k followed by hk. This is reminiscent of phrase ***C***. To begin the phrase with ***C*** material is unsurprising, but to continue with ***B3*** is initially surprising as the phrase ends rather than begins a verse. However, the other two phrases in the tract which begin 'Qui' both begin verses, and the cue to treat this as a verse opening is clear, although none of the Gregorian manuscripts have a verse division.

In the Old Roman tradition, there is one middle verse with the music ***B2 C1 D2***. There are textual similarities with *Beatus uir 2* which have prompted the unexpected use of ***B2*** at the beginning of the verse. Both begin 'qui' and end '-m'. 'appare coram effraim, beniamin et manasse' is the main sentence to which the relative 'Qui' clauses have been pointing. The Old Roman tradition uses phrase ***C*** to begin this, but separates the last item on the list. This begins in the same way as the other phrases in group ***D2***, but has the same abbreviation and phrase ***A1*** cadence as are found in *Qui regis 2*, possibly because of the internal associative prompt, and possibly also because of the parallel that, like 'intende', 'et manasse' only makes sense within the context of the words of the previous phrase.

The Gregorian tradition has two middle verses. The syntax of 'appare coram effraim beniamin et manasse' is completely ignored, and the second and third items of the list are each given new musical phrases. Each verse begins with a straightforward version of phrase ***E***, although one would expect ***E3*** in a verse-half that does not divide. It is probable that there was no verse division here originally, but that the rhyme 'beniamin'/'cherubim' prompted the cantors to use phrase ***E*** music for both of these phrases. Instead of ***E1 B2 C D2***, they used ***E1 B2 E2 D2***. It is a short step to use ***D2*** instead of ***B2*** for the second phrase as a further reinforcement of the rhyme, distorting the syntax, the musical outline, and the verse structure. As in *Qui confidunt*, this is an example where the divison of the text into phrases differs in the two traditions, with very different musical solutions as a consequence.

Nowacki cites a parallel between the two imperative verb phrases 'intende' and 'appare': 'The second verb phrase, *appare coram effraim beniamin et manasse* is taken to include its prepositional modifier. The reading imposed by the melody emphasises the implicit parallelism in the passage by arranging the two imperative verb phrases at the ends of their respective verses, thus giving them identical positions in the prosodic structure and enabling them to be declaimed with the same melodic inflection'.[69] However, 'intende' does not appear at the end of the verse. *ORJ* signals a new verse at 'qui deducis' but neither of the other two Old Roman manuscripts does, and all three Old Roman manuscripts clearly signal a new verse beginning at 'Qui sedes'. Further, 'intende' is not a full stop. It does not end with the phrase ***D*** cadence but is linked by the phrase ***A*** cadence with the previous phrase. Finally, the second imperative verb phrase is actually attached to phrase ***C***: it is the last part of the 'prepositional modifier' that has ***D2-A1***. The proliferation of relative clauses evidently gave both Frankish and Old Roman cantors some trouble: 'qui deducis velut ouem ioseph' is not directly attached to an imperative verb phrase, and it is not at all clear whether it should belong with the previous sentence or with the subsequent one. The Old Roman music suggests that 'qui deducis' was taken to belong with the previous sentence, as do the verse outlines of all manuscripts except *ORJ*. The Gregorian melody is muddled. The previous phrase, 'intende', has phrase ***B5***, which

[69] op. cit., 220.

has no associations of verse endings, and 'qui deducis' begins with phrase ***C*** material, which one would expect to appear in the second half of a verse. Both of these factors suggest that 'qui deducis' was interpreted as belonging with the previous sentence, but the use of phrase ***B3*** material at the end of the phrase instead suggests a verse beginning (perhaps implying that 'qui deducis' was interpreted as belonging with the following sentence).

In the Old Roman tradition, *Qui regis 8* has the ***B3*** outline seen also in *Commouisti 3* and *Commouisti 5* (p. 286). In the Gregorian tradition, *Qui regis 8* (p. 284) begins with ***D4*** shapes but continues with ***B3*** material. There is no clear reason why verse-ending material is used here. In the Old Roman tradition, 'et ueni' uses phrase ***C*** but, in the Gregorian tradition, it is part of *Qui regis 8*. The final phrase follows the expected patterns in the Old Roman tradition. In the Gregorian tradition, 'ut salvos' has phrase ***C*** material before the usual phrase ***F*** movements, altered because there is so little text available. Both traditions have ***B3***, ***C*** material and ***F*** in this final verse, but the combination of text and music is quite different. Here, the Gregorian cantors have misinterpreted the syntax: 'ut saluos facias nos' should be indivisible.

This tract is not close to the scheme outlined above. The first verse-half is treated in an unusual manner in the Gregorian tradition because of the textual connection with *Sepe 3*. In the Old Roman tradition, 'intende' uses ***D2*** material for no clear reason. The Gregorian tradition ends the verse with phrase ***B3***, perhaps because the text begins 'qui'. The second verse is split in the Gregorian tradition, and ***ED*** is repeated, possibly because of an internal rhyme. The Old Roman tradition has a single middle verse, starting with ***B2*** because of textual prompts. This verse ends with the same ***D2-A1*** material seen in the previous verse. The internal prompt has overridden the usual verse outlines. ***D4*** material is used within *Qui regis 8* in the Gregorian tradition for no apparent reason.

Qui seminant

	Old Roman	Gregorian	Phrase no.
Qui seminant in lacrimis	***A2***	***A2***	1
in gaudio metent	***D2***	***D2***	2
Euntes ibant et flebant	***E3***	***E3***	3
mittentes semina sua	***D3***	***D2***	4
Venientes autem uenient	***B4***	***B4***	5
cum exultatione	***C2***	***C2***	6

portantes manipulos suos	***F***	***F***	7

The first phrase of *Qui seminant* in the Gregorian tradition begins like the first phrase of *Ad te leuaui*. The melodic shapes on 'in lacrimis' are closely related to the beginning of *Desiderium*, but a note higher. In the equivalent parallel in the Old Roman tradition (*Sepe* and *Desiderium*), there is no transposition. The first phrase in the Old Roman tradition is independent in shape, but is related to the first phrase of *Sepe* in the Gregorian tradition. The second phrase of the first verse is ***D2***, often associated with the first verse of a tract.

The second verse begins with the complicated version of phrase ***E*** because the first verse-half does not divide (pp. 318–19). The opening uses melodic movements familiar from ***B4*** (see pp. 288–9). The melisma is derived from ***A2*** in both traditions (see pp. 273–76). The second phrase of the second verse uses exactly the same music as the previous verse in the Gregorian tradition. The Old Roman tradition decorates the phrase by using ***D3*** instead of ***D2***. There is a textual link between *Ad te leuaui 6* and *Qui seminant 4*, which are identical musically at this point in both traditions:
'-mine sue' (*Ad te leuaui 6*)
'-mina sua' (*Qui seminant 4*)

The third verse has the expected phrases ***B4 C F***. This tract is entirely consistent with the scheme outlined above.

Sepe

	Old Roman	Gregorian	Phrase no.
Sepe expugnauerunt me	***A2***	***A2***	1
a iuuentute mea	***D2***	***D2***	2
Dicat nunc israhel	***A2-A1***	***A2-B3***	3
sepe expugnauerunt me	***A2***	***C4***	4
a iuuentute mea	***D3***	***D3***	5
Et enim	***E3***	***E2***	6
non potuerunt michi	***B1***	***B1***	7
supra dorsum meum	***C2***	***C2***	8
fabricauerunt peccatores	***D2***	***D2***	9
Prolongauerunt	***E2***	***E2***	10
iniquitatem sibi/suas	***B1***	***B1***	11
dominus iustus concidet	***C1***	***C3***	12
ceruices peccatorum	***F***	***F***	13

In the Old Roman tradition, the openings of *Ad te leuaui* and *Sepe* are identical. The phrase ends in the same way as the beginning of *Desiderium*. In the Gregorian tradition, the first phrase of *Sepe* is unique, but it is related to the first phrase of *Qui seminant* in the Old Roman tradition. This is followed by ***D2***.

As was described above (see p. 66), the rhyme of 'Dicat' with *Ad te leuaui 7* ('Ita (oculi nostri)') has prompted use of ***A2*** material in both traditions. In the Old Roman tradition, 'israhel' uses ***A1*** material because of a textual link with *Qui regis 1*, but in the Gregorian tradition, the phrase continues with ***B3*** material, as one might expect, and *Qui regis 1* copies *Sepe 3*. In the Old Roman tradition, the repeat of 'sepe expugnauerunt me' uses phrase ***A2*** material again. The Gregorian tradition uses phrase ***C*** material for the repetition of 'sepe expugnauerunt me'. This does not follow the textual cue, but is less formally unexpected than the Old Roman version. The last phrase of the verse has the same text as the last phrase of the previous verse. The repetition is given rhetorical emphasis in both traditions by the use of the extended ***D3*** rather than ***D2***.

The third verse begins with a normal version of phrase ***E*** in the Gregorian tradition but with ***E3*** in the Old Roman tradition. The reasons for this are unclear. This is followed by phrase ***B1***. This may have been prompted by the textual connection with *Desiderium 2*: 'ei'/ 'michi'. The following phrase has an unusual version of phrase ***C*** in the Gregorian tradition. This is partly because it has only six syllables, and partly because the first main accent is not until the third syllable. Some pitched manuscripts begin with a decorated recitation g g hi on 'supra dor-' (missing out the opening figures), while others use the opening f f hk (missing out the middle figures). Some have f f hi, a mixture of the two. These different openings are followed in all manuscripts by the expected figures for the last three syllables. The third verse ends with ***D2*** once more, perhaps because the decorations of ***D3*** are specifically associated with a rhetorical context in this chant.

The last verse has the same pattern of ***E B1***. The first phrase in the Old Roman tradition uses ***E2***, found also in *Beatus uir 5* ('Potens in terra'). These two phrases have several identical syllable sounds, and an identical number of syllables, which may have prompted the use of the same melodic material. The second phrase ends 'sibi' in the Gregorian tradition and the rhyme with 'michi' (*Sepe 7*) and 'ei' (*Desiderium 2*) may have prompted the Frankish cantors to use ***B1*** in this phrase also. The cue is presumably associative in the Old Roman tradition where the text ends 'suas'. The third phrase is a usual ***C1*** in the Old Roman tradition. The last syllable rhymes with several other phrases in the group. However, it is the unusual ***C3*** in the Gregorian tradition, with two figures telescoped onto a single syllable, and an unusual opening. This is because 'iústus' is treated as the first main accent. Phrase ***F*** is straightforward.

The melodic material of the second verse is affected by textual and rhetorical prompts, particularly in the Old Roman tradition. This led the cantors to create an eighth-mode tract that does not follow the outline of the psalm verses. The psalm divides at 'dicat', 'supra dorsum' and 'dominus iustus'. However, in the tract, the textual cues in the second verse (the repetition of 'sepe expugnauerunt me a iuuentute mea' and therefore of phrase ***D*** material on 'a iuuentute mea') mean that the third verse begins at 'Etenim'. There is a single sentence before the next psalm verse. This is insufficient to articulate a tract verse, so the psalm verse division is ignored. Phrases ***C*** and ***D*** are articulated in the usual way, meaning that there is a new tract verse after the sentence 'supra dorsum meum fabricauerunt peccatores'. This means that, once again, there is only a single sentence before the next psalm verse, and the psalmic outline is ignored once more. Most manuscripts divide for the second verse at 'Dicat nunc israhel', but *NOY4* highlights the text repetition by having the verse division at 'Sepe expugnauerunt me'. After this, *NOY4* divides only at 'supra dorsum meum' (with the psalm). *DIJ1* splits the final verse of *Sepe expugnauerunt* at 'dominus iustus' (with the psalm), and *BRE* divides at both psalm divisions. The psalm verse structure has led the text scribes in *DIJ1*, *BRE* and *NOY4* to place the verse divisions in different places from the other manuscripts. However, by the time these manuscripts were copied, as with the Easter Vigil tracts and *Iubilate*, the melodies of these tracts were fixed in a written tradition and the verse divisions did not affect the musical outline.

Sicut[70]

	Gregorian	Phrase no.
Sicut ceruus desiderat	***A1***	1
ad fontes aquarum	***B2***	2
ita desiderat anima mea ad te deus	***C1***	3
Sitiuit anima mea	***E1***	4
ad deum uiuum	***B2***	5
quando ueniam et apparebo	***C1***	6
ante faciem dei mei	***D2***	7
Fuerunt michi lacrime mee	***E1***	8
panes die ac nocte	***B2***	9

[70] This tract does not appear in an Old Roman version.

dum dicitur michi per singulos dies	***C1***	10
ubi est deus tuus	***F***	11

Unlike the other Easter Vigil tracts, the verse divisions of *Sicut* are consistent between manuscripts, and this is probably because it is based on a psalm rather than on a canticle. The first phrase uses ***A1*** because of the liturgical connection with the other Easter Vigil tracts, despite having eight syllables. The verse continues with ***B2***. This phrase is used in the following verse in an expected formal context, and the closeness of the texts 'ad fontes aquarum' and 'ad deum uiuum' may have acted as a stimulus to use the same version of the phrase on both occasions. The first verse ends with phrase ***C***.

The second and third verses have straightforward quadripartite structures, using expected versions of each phrase. The final phrase of the second verse uses phrase ***D***. The rise fhk is decorated as fhikl in *MOG4*, *PAS2*, *TYR* and *KLO1*. This is a unique melodic shape in phrases in diagram ***D2***, which otherwise consistently have fhk or quilisma. This variant is related to phrase ***F*** where the tendency to decorate the fhk figure in the Easter Vigil tracts is pronounced in these manuscripts.

The first phrase uses ***A1*** despite having too many syllables, because of the liturgical context. The second phrase uses ***B2*** because of a textual prompt. The rest of the tract is consistent with the scheme outlined above.

Kainzbauer maintains that the first verse could have been divided into four parts, with phrase ***D1*** for 'ad te deus' to give consistently quadripartite verses, or that the second half of the second verse could have been given only phrase ***C***, making it tripartite like the canticle-tracts. He writes that the actual structure (***ABC EBCD***) constitutes a bridge between the canticles and the tracts.[71] This seems somewhat fanciful; there are possible textual reasons underlying the structure of these verses. The phrase 'ita desiderat anima mea ad te deus' would be difficult to split into two phrases because the prepositional phrase ('ad te deus') is divided by the subject ('anima mea') from the verb to which it refers ('desiderat'). It would be hard to maintain the connection between the verb and the prepositional phrase if the sentence was split into two phrases ('ita desiderat anima mea/ ad te deus'). There is no direct textual parallel with the beginning of the psalm, where 'desiderat' is followed immediately by the prepositional phrase 'ad fontes aquarum', or with the following verse, where 'apparebo' is followed immediately by 'ante faciem dei mei'. The use of a single phrase for 'ita desiderat anima mea ad te deus' may also have been stabilised by the rhyme with four phrases in group ***C1*** that end 'eius'. Kainzbauer maintains

[71] Kainzbauer, op. cit., 94–95.

that *Sicut* could have been constructed in a manner compatible with the other eighth-mode tracts if 'quando veniam et apparebo ante faciem dei mei' had been attached to a single phrase ***C***. This phrase would have nineteen syllables: phrase ***C*** never otherwise carries more than sixteen syllables. The phrase 'quando… apparebo' rhymes with *Attende 3* ('meo') and *Attende 8* ('inuocabo') in group ***C1***. These rhymes may have been a factor in the establishment of the phrase shape.

Vinea[72]

	Gregorian	Phrase no.
Vinea facta est	***A1***	1
dilecto	***B1***	2
in cornu in loco uberi	***C1***	3
Et maceriam circumdedit et circumfodit	***E1***	4
et plantauit uineam sorech	***B2***	5
et edificauit turrim in medio eius	***C1***	6
Et torcular fodit in ea	***B2***	7
uinea enim domini sabaoth	***C1***	8
domus israhel est	***F***	9

As with the other Easter Vigil canticles, different manuscripts place the verse divisions in different places. *GAL2* and *ORP* divide at 'et maceriam' and 'uinea enim'. The second of these divisions makes little sense musically, and was clearly not the original verse structure of the tract. Kainzbauer maintains that the centological structure is of two verses with the second verse beginning at 'Et maceriam'.[73] This is found only in *LAN* and *MUR3*. This hypothesis has the advantage that the two sources consistent with it are old. However, to have a six-phrase verse would be inconsistent with the rest of the genre. A large group of manuscripts divides at 'Et maceriam' and 'Et torcular'. This divides asymmetrically, before the last of the four 'et' phrases, but is logical musically.

Other manuscripts divide at various of the 'et' phrases; some divide with the canticle at 'uinea', and some do not. These divisions are scribal rather than being musically inspired. There are verse divisions at one or two of the 'et' phrases in any case and the word 'uinea' began the tract. Such patterns act as strong stimuli to have extra verse divisions in the manuscripts. The verse divisions that make musical sense (***ABC EBC***

[72] This tract does not appear in an Old Roman version.

[73] Kainzbauer, op. cit., 93.

BCF) are adopted in the following analysis.

The tract begins ***A1 B1 C1***, as one would expect. The second verse is similarly straightforward. The last verse has ***B2 C F***. The use of phrase ***B2*** for the first verse-half is stimulated by the use of ***B2*** in the previous verse in its normal formal context with the same 'et' beginning. A similar parallel occurs in *Attende 5* and *Attende 7*.

Vinea only differs from the scheme in that it has ***B2*** for the first verse-half of the final verse, and this is due to a textual cue.

Conclusions

The eighth-mode tracts are constructed from a small group of standard melodic shapes, each associated with a specific formal and textual context. Although the Old Roman tradition is generally more decorated than the Gregorian, the outlines of the phrases tend to be the same. The textual context is critical to the construction of a tract. On one level, every phrase has melodic movements specific to accented or unaccented syllables. On a more fundamental level, sentences and clauses are almost always divided into logical syntactical units to make musical phrases. Sometimes the division is between subject and predicate, sometimes relative clauses or prepositional phrases are given separate musical phrases, and sometimes the subject and the verb are joined together and the object is given a separate phrase. Sometimes a clause or sentence is joined to a single phrase. It is not always possible to identify why one way of dividing the psalmic text into tract phrases has been chosen instead of another. Textual cues permeate both traditions, often prompting use of phrases outside their usual formal context. These cues do not always function in the same way in both traditions. The reasons for at least some of the differences in formal structure between the traditions may lie in a different interpretation of how the formal outline and melodic patterns might best be manipulated in the articulation of a given text.

The detailed analysis of the fifteen eighth-mode tracts of the core repertory shows that they are largely consistent with the scheme outlined earlier in the chapter. Deviations from this scheme, in one or both traditions, are usually stimulated by textual cues, and occasionally because of associative links. On the basis of the analysis above, it is possible to identify three groups of eighth-mode tracts.

The four tracts sung at the Easter Vigil form a close-knit musical group. They appear only in Gregorian versions, even in the Old Roman Graduals. Three of these tracts have canticle texts and are sometimes described as canticles, sometimes as tracts.[74] The term canticle-tract indicates not only their textual origin, which distinguishes them from the rest of the corpus, but also their musical and formal characteristics. They are sung in a dramatic context, immediately following readings of the Vigil. Although *Sicut* has a different textual origin from the other three, it is sung in the same liturgical context and, for the soloist, these four chants would be consecutive.[75]

The three Easter Vigil canticle-tracts have a different textual structure from that of other eighth-mode tracts. The verses tend to be tripartite rather than the quadripartite and bipartite structures usually seen in psalmody. Because of this, the canticle-tracts never use phrase ***D***, which is generally used fourth in a verse, or second in a bipartite verse in one of its complicated forms. *Sicut*, the psalm-based tract, falls instead into a quadripartite structure, and in the second verse there is enough text to articulate the four phrases ***EBCD***. Apart from this difference, which is prompted by the format of the text, the four Easter Vigil tracts are constructed in the same way.

On two occasions (in *Attende* and in *Vinea*), ***B2*** is used because of the stimulus of 'et', as described above. *Cantemus* is modelled on *Attende* rather than being constructed in the usual manner. The Easter Vigil tracts have the fhikl decoration in the final phrase and in phrase ***D*** in *Sicut*, further identifying them as a group. This group of tracts is used in a different liturgical context to the other eighth-mode tracts. This in itself has not affected their melodic outline. The textual structure, combined with associative and verbal prompts, has determined the melodic shapes used.

The second group of eighth-mode tracts consists of *Beatus uir, De profundis, Iubilate,* and *Laudate*. In most verses, each verse-half consists of one sentence, and these are usually split into two phrases, so ***A1, E1, E2, B1, B2*** and ***D1*** are used. Notable exceptions to this are the third and fourth verses of *De profundis* and the third verse of *Iubilate*, where the first verse-halves have been treated as indivisible units, and complicated versions of phrase ***B*** have been used. This group of tracts tends to use ***D1***; this is not the version of the phrase used in *Sicut*.

There are close connections between tracts in this group, which were described above. For example, the Old Roman version of *Iubilate 9* is closely modelled on verse beginnings in *De profundis*; 'domin-' leads to an idiosyncratic phrase ***C*** ending in *Iubilate* and *Laudate*; the first two phrases of *Iubilate* and *Laudate* have parallel texts and music.

[74] *AMS*, 97-98.

[75] 'Until the later middle ages, [*Sicut*] was not... chanted during the procession to the baptismal font, as is regularly reported in the musicological literature' (McKinnon, *The Advent Project*, op. cit., 293).

In some tracts, the sentences and clauses have been treated as indivisible units, leading to there being bipartite verses. This particularly affects *Ad te leuaui, Sepe, Commouisti, Qui seminant,* and *Desiderium*. However, not all verses in these tracts are constructed in this way. In the third verse of *Ad te leuaui* there are two phrases in the first half-verse. 'Ita [leuaui] oculi nostri' is the main part of the sentence, and 'ad dominum deum nostrum' is a prepositional phrase. In the first verse of *Desiderium*, there are four phrases. 'Desiderium anime eius' is the object and 'tribuisti ei' is the subject + verb. The second half-verse begins 'et voluntate labiorum eius'. This is the indirect object belonging to the next phrase 'non fraudasti ẹum'. Even though these clauses are divided into two phrases, the text of the first phrase is still sufficiently long for ***A2*** to be used. In the last verse of *Commouisti*, the subject + verb and object are divided between two musical phrases. In the last verse of *Qui seminant*, 'Venientes autem uenient' is the subject + verb, 'cum exultatione' is a prepositional phrase, and 'portantes manipulos suos' is an extension of the subject followed by the object. It would not be possible to divide this sentence into musical phrases in a way that did not divide the different parts of the subject. In the last verse of *Desiderium*, 'Posuisti super caput eius', the subject + verb and preposition, is given one phrase, while the object ('coronam') and the prepositional phrase ('de lapide pretioso') are divided into two musical phrases. The first verse in *Sepe* consists of a single sentence, but there is enough text within 'Sepe expugnauerunt me' to articulate ***A2***. The second verse is so affected by textual cues that it is not appropriate to draw conclusions about tract structure from it. The last two verses of this tract are quadripartite, with each sentence being divided into two parts. In the penultimate verse, 'etenim' ('but') is given a separate phrase from the body of the sentence 'non potuerunt michi'. In the second sentence, 'supra dorsum meum', the prepositional phrase, is given a separate musical phrase from the main part of the sentence, 'fabricaverunt peccatores'. In the last verse, each sentence is divided into verb + subject and object. It is clear from these examples that although these tracts tend to have bipartite verses, there are still occasions where they divide sentences according to the syntax in order to have more than one musical phrase in a verse-half.

The long text for the first phrases of these tracts means that ***A2*** is used rather than ***A1*** in this third group of tracts. There are many connections between tracts in this group. For example, the second and third verses in *Ad te leuaui* are paralleled by the second verse of *Qui seminant*; the first verses in *Ad te leuaui, Desiderium* and *Commouisti* have parallel structures, as do the last verses in *Ad te leuaui, Desiderium* and *Qui seminant*.

Two tracts have verse structures which do not fall into any of the three categories described above. In *Qui regis*, this is because of the multitude of textual cues, which prevent the tract from following the usual scheme closely. In *Qui confidunt*, the uncertainty surrounding the verse structure is reflected in the use of unusual phrase shapes, and of phrases in unexpected places.

Textual links may be found between tracts in the same group, but also occur between tracts in different groups. A few examples may be given to illustrate this. 'Israhel' in *Qui regis* affects use of the same word in the Old Roman version of *Sepe*. 'Domin-' near the beginning of the tract cues the use of phrase ***A1***, whichever group the chant belongs to. 'In exultatione' in *Iubilate* uses phrase ***B*** in the Old Roman tradition, but the Gregorian tradition uses phrase ***C***, cued by 'cum exultatione' in *Qui seminant*.

Broadly speaking, four types of verse structure occur in the eighth-mode tracts. The first of these is when the verse splits into three roughly equal portions. This usually occurs in the canticle texts, and tripartite verses consisting of ***ABC*** or ***EBC*** are characteristic of this group of tracts. The second type of verse structure occurs when a verse consists of two sentences or clauses, and each of these are split, leading to ***ABCD, EBCD, EBCF,*** with ***A1, E1, E2, B1, B2, D1, D2, C*** and ***F*** being used. This mostly occurs in *Laudate, Iubilate, Beatus uir*, and *De profundis*, but also occurs in tracts in the third group. The third type of verse occurs when the two sentences are treated as single units. In this situation, ***A2, E3, B3, B4, D2, D3*** and ***D4*** are used. Although this is most commonly found in the third group of tracts, it occurs also in *Iubilate* and *De profundis*.

The Easter Vigil tracts are clearly differentiated from other eighth-mode tracts because of their tripartite verse structure. The second and third groups of tracts are distinct because different methods of breaking up the text to fit it to the music have been preferred. The overlap between the processes of these two groups suggests that these techniques are not separate, favoured in different places or times, but were different, equally valid, ways of constructing chants within the genre. The textual and musical connections between the groups, and the fact that *Qui regis* and *Qui confidunt* are indisputably eighth-mode tracts despite not belonging to any of these groups, confirms that the eighth-mode tracts were constructed within the constraints of a single genre.

Chapter 4
Methods of Transmission of the Early Chant Tradition

Introduction

It was demonstrated in Chapter 2 that the eighth-mode tracts do not generally vary significantly within traditions. It was demonstrated in Chapter 3 that the Old Roman and Gregorian traditions have largely equivalent versions of these chants, despite their different melodic dialects. These findings suggest that the eighth-century Roman versions of the eighth-mode tracts were extremely stable in their structure, and that this stability was retained over the years until it is confirmed by the earliest extant written sources. An alternative interpretation would hinge on continuing musical contacts between Rome and Francia and alteration of one or other of the traditions to reach closer conformity. Continuing centralised Frankish attempts to learn Roman chant after the time of Charlemagne would presumably have been remarked upon, as would the shocking converse of Roman cantors turning to Frankish authority. Further, although the eighth-mode tracts demonstrate great continuity between the two traditions, the connections in other genres are not generally as close. It seems more likely that certain genres, such as eighth-mode tracts, have characteristics that lend themselves to stable transmission than that there were continuing Franco-Roman musical contacts in only a few select genres. This chapter explores the possible reasons for the continuing stability of the eighth-mode tracts in the two traditions.

As was indicated in Chapter 1, unity in religion was an essential component of political stability in the Carolingian theocracy and uniformity of worship was a tangible expression of this unity. Liturgical chant was portrayed by the Carolingians as the result of a single act of divine inspiration. To sing the Mass Propers in a form believed to be that in which the Holy Spirit had given it to Gregory the Great was a proclamation of religious orthodoxy.[1] There are clear doctrinal and political reasons for the importance of maintaining the liturgy in a form as close as possible to that in which it was performed in Rome.

---

[1]Treitler, L., 'Homer and Gregory: The Transmission of Epic Poetry and Plainchant', *MQ* 60 (1974), 333–72; 334–40.

McKinnon, among others, has asserted that textual and liturgical concordances between the Old Roman and Gregorian traditions may be used to establish some of the characteristics of their eighth-century Roman ancestor, and he has concluded that 'the overwhelming majority of the two repertories are a perfect match'.[2] This is certainly true for the eighth-mode tracts: the same core repertory of chants, with almost identical texts, is used for the same feasts in both traditions, from the unnotated Frankish manuscripts of the ninth century to the Old Roman Graduals of the eleventh century. The fact that the earliest extant notated Graduals from Francia have almost completely equivalent melodic outlines for the Mass Proper chants suggests that the maintenance of musical unity was as successful as the maintenance of unity in liturgical texts and their placing.

The uniformity of the liturgy within Francia and the stability of the music of the Mass Proper chants in the earliest sources are well known. However, the reasons for this stability remain contentious. While some maintain that the tradition was fixed in writing towards the end of the eighth century, others claim that the tradition was maintained orally until the end of the ninth century. If the tradition was not fixed by an authoritative written version, either the Carolingian cantors were capable of prodigious feats of memory, or certain characteristics of the chants made them conducive to accurate recall by expert singers. These possibilities will be examined in detail.

Transmission Aided by an Early Neumed Exemplar

In a series of articles, Kenneth Levy has argued that Frankish chant was notated long before the earliest extant notated Graduals, and that there were neumed archetypes of the Mass Proper chants by about 800.[3] This theory rests on a series of seven indices. In his third index, Levy cites Aurelian of Réôme's references to acute and circumflex accents in the mid-ninth-century *Musica disciplina* as evidence that neumatic signs were known by about 840.[4] Hiley has pointed out that 'the passages read more easily if we assume that the vocal inflexion, but not a written representation of it, is

[2] 'Vaticana Latina 5319: Witness to the Mid-Eighth-Century Roman Proper of the Mass', in *CP: Sopron*, 403–11; 406.

[3] Levy, K., 'Charlemagne's Archetype of Gregorian Chant', *JAMS* 40 (1987), 1–30; 'On the Origin of Neumes', *EMH* 7 (1987), 59–90; 'The Two Carolingian Archetypes of Gregorian Chant', in *IMS 1987*, 501–4; 'Gregorian Chant and Oral Transmission', in G. Boone (ed.), *Essays on Medieval Music in Honor of David G. Hughes: Isham Library Papers* 4 (Cambridge, Mass., 1995), 277–86.

[4] Levy, 'Charlemagne's Archetype', op. cit., 9–10.

meant'.[5] Musical notation was certainly developing around this time, and Aurelian's *De musica* uses neumes in two musical examples in Chapter 19, but it does not necessarily follow that the Mass Proper was regularly notated in its entirety. In his response to Levy's article, Treitler reminds readers of the passage in *Musica disciplina* where Aurelian, quoting Isodore of Seville (*Etymologiae*, book 3, Chapter 15), writes that music, 'unless it is impressed on the memory, is not retained'.[6] Levy asserts in his fourth index that Charlemagne's instruction in the *Admonitio generalis*, exhorting all clergy to teach the boys psalmi, nota, and cantus, is evidence of late eighth-century notation.[7] Hiley has shown that the passage instructs that the boys should be taught to write, but not specifically that they should be taught musical notation. *Nota* means 'sign', and a gloss connects it with *notarius*, the secretary.[8]

Several of Levy's indices rest on the fact that, despite the political isolation of different regions, the chant tradition is very unified. In his second index, Levy refers to the East/West split of the Frankish Empire, formalised at the Treaty of Verdun (843), and notes that there are few discrepancies in the Mass Proper chants to reflect this political upheaval.[9] This is certainly an indication that the tradition was very stable, but it does not necessarily follow that this stability was achieved in written form.

Levy's third and fourth indices concern the adoption of Gregorian chant in Benevento by the end of the eighth century. This is not in dispute, and the evidence has been clearly evaluated by Kelly.[10] Although the Beneventan melodies are close to the Frankish mainstream, certain features of the tradition are localised. Levy interprets this as indicating that a neumed version of the Gregorian tradition was adopted in Benevento and that the area was then liturgically isolated. As with the second index, stable adoption of a tradition is not necessarily synonymous with its written adoption. Further, the independence of various features of Beneventan chant practice does not necessarily signal cultural isolation. The repertory of non-standard eighth-mode tracts, discussed in Chapter 6, below, includes chants found in both Aquitaine and Benevento and, on one occasion, a version of a tract found in Benevento (*In columbe*) is preserved in an Aquitanian manuscript (*ALB*) as an alternative. These non-standard tracts appear in tenth- and eleventh-century manuscripts, and it would appear that there were direct connections between these regions, at least in the early

[5] *WP*, 364.
[6] Treitler, L., 'Communication', *JAMS* 41 (1988), 566–75; 573.
[7] Levy, 'Charlemagne's Archetype', op. cit., 10–11.
[8] *WP*, 363.
[9] Levy, 'Charlemagne's Archetype', op. cit., 8.
[10] Kelly, T., *The Beneventan Chant* (Cambridge, 1989); 19–22.

part of this period. The close relationship between Aquitanian and Beneventan versions of the Mass Proper chants, already noted in Chapter 2, may be attributable not to a neumed exemplar, but to continuing cultural contacts.

Levy's first index of an early date for the neumation of the Mass Proper chants rests on the distinctive characteristics of the neumes in the earliest notated Graduals from different regions, dating from c. 900.[11] He cites the work of the 'école Cardine' in support of the view that a common neumatic archetype lies behind these regional styles, and asserts that at least half a century should be allowed for the development from this archetype of the regional notational characteristics. Because the notations used are highly sophisticated, it is clear that they do not represent the first experiments in notation in their respective regions. The work of the semiologists may indeed indicate that the notational styles had a common origin, but it does not necessarily follow that the entire Mass Proper had previously been notated, or that there was a neumed exemplar. Others have suggested that the development of notation was localised. 'If notation came into use first in one region, then in another, but without being circulated from the Carolingian court, it is quite likely that a cantor from one still illiterate region might travel to another where a notation was known, and then bring back the idea of notation without being committed to any particular style or form.'[12]

Levy's final index refers to the rare chant, *Factus est repente*.[13] His contention that it fell out of use in northern Europe some time after Gregorian chant was taken to Benevento is logical. However, the identification of an isolated northern manuscript containing the chant does not constitute a proof that the whole tradition, or even just this chant, was taken to Benevento in notated form. Despite Levy's claims of equivalence between the northern and Beneventan versions of this chant, there are melodic variants between them. Further, the neumations are not visually identical, but use equivalent shapes in the local style, as comparison of the first phrase of the chant in Levy's figures 1 and 2 demonstrates.[14]

One of the chief objections to Levy's hypothesis is that there are no preserved examples either of early ninth-century neumed archetypes, or of early copies of them. Levy argues that as later notations emerged the early ones became obsolete, so the books were not kept. This is not borne out by

---

[11] Levy, 'Charlemagne's Archetype', op. cit., 7.

[12] Hughes, D., 'The Implications of Variants for Chant Transmission', in P. Cahn and A-K. Heimer (eds.), *De Musica et Cantu: Helmut Hucke zum 60. Geburtstag* (Hildesheim, 1993), 65–74; 72.

[13] Levy, 'Charlemagne's Archetype', op. cit., 11–25.

[14] Ibid., 16 and 18.

the preservation of unnotated ninth- and tenth-century Graduals, or by the keeping of neumatic sources as diastematic notations developed. Innovations do not invariably displace earlier techniques. If there had been a neumed archetype, one might expect it to have been preserved with the same sort of reverence as Charlemagne's *Admonitio generalis* and other documents of the Carolingian reformers.[15] Although one might argue that musical notation would not have been accorded the same status as verbal documentation, liturgical chants have biblical texts, and Gregory the Great was believed to have composed the melodies. These factors will have lent quasi-canonical status to the books in which the Mass Proper chants appear.

In order further to assess the strength of Levy's argument, it is valuable to identify the extant early examples of musical notation, and to establish their uses. It is then possible to decide whether the forms and functions of these notations suggest a culture in which notation of the Mass Proper chants might have been practised. The earliest extant examples of notated chant tend to be of isolated pieces, unusual in some way.[16] The earliest manuscripts containing Mass Proper notation have been identified by Jeffery, and appear to have been written for the use of the celebrant. 'If it is indeed correct that many or most of the earliest Graduals are actually components of primitive "Missals", then the great majority of surviving non-fragmentary sources are Missals of some sort – books intended for use by the celebrating priest and not by the choir… Hardly any of the surviving sources were practical copies intended to serve the singers who actually performed the chants.'[17] Primitive gestural notations, then, developed as aids for members of the clergy who were not necessarily gifted musicians, and who may have required written assistance to maintain the uniformity demanded by the Carolingian reformers. If they wished to sing or recite within a private Mass the parts of the Mass usually performed by Schola or Cantor, their lack of specialist training may have made written assistance essential.

Musical notation appears to have developed as an aid to theoretical writing, divorced from practical use, within the intellectual culture of Carolingian monasteries. The Carolingian educational programme aimed to re-establish schooling through the ancient curriculum of the seven liberal arts.[18] *Musica* was one of these arts, but the academic discipline of *Musica*

[15] McKitterick, R., *The Frankish Church and the Carolingian Reforms 789–895* (London, 1977), especially Chapters 1 and 2.

[16] Jammers, E., *Tafeln zur Neumenschrift* (Tutzing, 1965), 26ff.

[17] Jeffery, P., 'The Oldest Sources of the *Graduale*: A Preliminary Checklist of MSS Copied before about 900', *JM* 2 (1983), 316–21; 317.

[18] McKitterick, R., 'The Foundations of the Carolingian Renaissance', in R. McKitterick (ed.), *The Frankish Kingdoms under the Carolingians 751–987* (London, 1983), 140–68.

had fallen out of use since late Antiquity. One of the concerns of the newly developing discipline was to find connections between the abstract music theory of the ancients and the living tradition of liturgical chant. Pitch-specific notation, using Boethian letters or daseian signs, was used in the second half of the ninth century to provide concrete illustrations for the *Ars musica* treatises. Such notations are not necessarily useful for showing the pitches of melismas; nor do they show musical expression.

Because there were few treatises on ancient music theory available to the Carolingians, and because those that were available were very difficult to understand, especially with regard to contemporary music-making, the ninth-century music treatises relied heavily on the model of the *Ars grammatica*.[19] There are direct parallels between the prosodic accents of grammar, as well as the terms used to describe them, and 'the conceptual matrix of ninth-century musical notation'.[20] According to Atkinson, glosses on Donatus' *Ars maior* define the prosodic accents in terms of movements up and down, rather than in terms of higher and lower pitches.[21] This is consistent with Palaeofrankish notation, a graphic notation in which, for example, a single stroke / indicates two notes, and ∧ indicates three. The sources containing Palaeofrankish notation identified by Hourlier and Huglo mostly originate from the Carolingian heartland of north-east France, also the intellectual centre of the Carolingian educational reforms.[22] Most extant examples of this notation are concerned with peripheral chants; many examples are fragmentary, or consist of marginal additions to manuscripts. Hourlier and Huglo identified none of the manuscripts containing Palaeofrankish notation as dating from before the late ninth century. Levy, however, maintains that there were two neumed archetypes of chant by about 800; the first of these, in Palaeofrankish notation, was replaced around 800 by a gestural notation where the signs above would indicate one and two pitches respectively.[23] However, Atkinson's theory connecting Palaeofrankish notation with the intellectual culture of the Carolingian monasteries in the mid ninth century weakens the argument

---

19 Bower, C., 'The Grammatical Model of Musical Understanding in the Middle Ages', in P. Gallacher and H. Damico (eds.), *Hermeneutics and Medieval Culture* (Albany, NY, 1989), 133–45.

20 Atkinson, C. M., 'De Accentibus Toni Oritur Nota Quae Dicitur Neuma: Prosodic Accents, the Accent Theory, and the Paleofrankish Script', in G. Boone (ed.), *Essays on Medieval Music in Honor of David G. Hughes: Isham Library Papers 4* (Cambridge, Mass., 1995), 17–42; 42.

21 Ibid. Described also in an (unpublished) paper entitled 'Glosses on Music and Grammar and the Advent of Music Writing in the West', presented at the 1997 *IMS* meeting in London.

22 Hourlier, J. and Huglo, M., 'Notation Paléofranque', *EG* 2 (1957), 212–19.

23 Levy, 'Gregorian Chant and Oral Transmission', op. cit., 280.

that there was a late eighth century Palaeofrankish archetype of Gregorian chant.

The extant evidence suggests that notation developed in the ninth century in various contexts and in various forms, according to the function for which it was required. Gestural notations appear to have developed as memory aids for non-specialist singers, to help promote and maintain liturgical uniformity in the Frankish Church. The graphic Palaeofrankish notation appears to have developed within ninth-century Carolingian monastic culture, and was largely used to notate unusual chants. More pitch-specific notations, not used in liturgical books, were used to provide short musical examples in treatises. The extant evidence does not point to the existence of a late eighth-century neumed exemplar of the entire Mass Proper.

The principal evidence that a lost notated archetype from the late eighth or early ninth century was the model for the early Carolingian cantors is the stability of the early Graduals themselves.[24] However, there may be alternative explanations for this stability. It is possible that the tradition changed a great deal when it was written down, but 'it is worth noting that however far back one wishes to place it, there must have been... a time in which some sort of chant was sung without the aid of notations... Either (1) what we have now is an accurate reproduction of the music transmitted orally, in which case the oral transmission was equal to its task; or (2) it is not an accurate reproduction. If the lack of accuracy is serious – if, that is, the notated chant is a fundamentally new repertoire – one would expect rather more to have been made of the change than we in fact find.'[25]

The Role of Memory in Early Liturgical Chant Transmission

The question of whether or not there was an early neumed exemplar is not, and may never be, finally resolved. However, wherever the beginnings of music notation are placed chronologically by scholars, the liturgical chant tradition was carried entirely by memory before that time. This is only one reason why the examination of the role of memory is fundamental to any study of the transmission of medieval chant. Further, intimate and expert knowledge of the repertory is required in order to make the neumed chants readable. The function of the early notations was 'nicht als Vorlage für den Gesang, sondern als Archivsstücke anzusehen, als Richtschnur und Nachschlagebuch für Vortrag und Unterricht, an dem man nachprüfen

[24] Planchart, A. E., 'Old Wine in New Bottles', in P. Cahn and A-K. Heimer (eds.), *De Musica et Cantu: Helmut Hucke zum 60. Geburtstag* (Hildesheim, 1993), 41–64; 42–3.

[25] Hughes, 'The Implications of Variants for Chant Transmission', op. cit., 66 (footnote 5).

konnte, ob man sich noch in der Tradition befand'.[26] 'In the early stage of neuming the full melodic substances were thought secure enough in professional memories for the pitch-levels to be slighted by the notation. The real seat of melodic transmission then lay in memory, and for so long as staffless neumes continued as the basic medium of written transmission, memory continued as the guarantor of full melodic substance.'[27] The writing down of the Mass Proper chants was an *aide-mémoire,* and early notated manuscripts functioned as reference tools in the maintenance of stability, but they did not replace the necessity for highly trained cantors to learn the whole repertory. Whether the Frankish versions of the Mass Proper chants were written down in the ninth century or not, the role of memory in stabilising the tradition was central.[28]

The first, and widely influential, studies of the role of memory in the transmission of medieval chant were undertaken by Leo Treitler. [29] In a scholarly climate where the search for the written *Urtext* of Gregorian chant was still continuing, and where attempts were still being made to construct stemmas showing the scribal relationships between the earliest manuscripts, Treitler found similarities between the structures of certain categories of chant and genres known to be oral. It was suggested by Wolf as early as 1795 that Homeric epic had been carried orally rather than in written form.[30] The much later comparisons by Milman Parry and Albert Lord of Homeric epic with the oral tradition of epic poetry in early twentieth-century Serbia gave a contemporary body of evidence with which to re-examine the way in which Homeric epic is structured.[31] The traditional view of Homer had been based on the concept of the Work, the result of a single creative impulse. Parry and Lord claimed that Homeric epic, like Serbian epic poetry, was composed and transmitted orally, constructed around the building blocks of formulas and themes. While an oral origin of

---

26 Hucke, H., 'Der Übergang von mündlicher zu schriftlicher Musiküberlieferung im Mittelalter', in *IMS 1977*, 180–91; 190.

27 Levy, 'Gregorian Chant and Oral Transmission', op. cit., 280.

28 The importance of a highly trained memory was central until much later than the eleventh century in some areas. Szendrei has written about the isolation of manuscripts connected with Klosterneuburg as examples of staff notation in middle Europe, and has identified areas where German neumes were in practical use into the fifteenth century. See 'The Introduction of Staff Notation into Middle Europe', *Studia Musicologica Academiae Scientiarum Hungaricae* 28 (Budapest, 1986), 303–19; especially 314–17.

29 Treitler, 'Homer and Gregory', op. cit.; '"Centonate" Chant: Übles Flickwerk or *E Pluribus Unus*?', *JAMS* 28 (1975), 1–23; 'Transmission and the Study of Music History', in *IMS 1977*, 202–11.

30 See Treitler, '"Centonate" Chant', op. cit., 1.

31 See, for example, Lord, A., *The Singer of Tales* (Cambridge, Mass., 1964); *Epic Singers and Oral Tradition* (Cornell, 1991).

Western liturgical chant had been proposed as early as 1950 by Cardine,[32] it was not until Treitler developed a theory based on that of Parry and Lord that the whole issue of chant origins could be released from the straitjacket of written transmission.

The wholesale adoption of the analytical methods of Parry and Lord in chant scholarship is not appropriate, as Levy has pointed out.[33] Homeric epics are many thousands of lines long; the Serbian epic poems studied by Parry and Lord are similarly gargantuan. In such lengthy compositions, verbatim recall is not a priority; the poems are rather 'recomposed' in performance based on a highly trained knowledge of the structures, rhythms, formulas and themes of the genre.[34] Liturgical chants are built on a much smaller scale, and comparisons with epic poetry are not necessarily apposite. Furthermore, the most common types of Mass Proper chants are not formulaic, like the second-mode tracts studied by Treitler, but are 'idiomelic' – that is, each has a distinctive melody. Treitler's writings do not explain how such 'idiomelic' chants would have been 'recomposed' in performance.

While Treitler's theories were an invaluable corrective to the widely held assumption that medieval liturgical chants were fixed works of art, others have objected that if the Mass Proper chants were recomposed within each performance, one might expect much more variation between written sources than is in fact found. One of the difficulties here may be semantic. 'Recompose' has unfortunate connotations of reworking, and this does not seem to be compatible with the closeness of the Mass Proper chants in the early written sources. However, 'recompose' may also be synonymous with 'reconstitute' or 'remember'. In this study, the term 'remember' is used to mean an active process of recall, where chants are re-membered, or re-embodied by drawing on a combination of rote learning and an abstract knowledge of how the genre is structured.

The memory burden of the Mass and Office chants was a large one: Haas calculates it as being around eighty hours of music. In 'On Gregorian Orality', Levy asks: 'were the memories of church singers without the support of musical notations capable of managing the amounts of melodic substance that this implies?'[35] However, Haas warns against making inappropriate comparisons between the memory burden of the Mass and

[32] Cardine, E., 'L'Edition Critique du Graduel: Nécessité, Avantages, Méthode', in *Congresso Internazionale di Musica Sacra* (Rome, 1950), 187–91.

[33] Levy, K., 'On Gregorian Orality', *JAMS* 43 (1990), 186–92.

[34] See Hunt, 'Lengthy Verbatim Recall (LVM) and the Mythical Gift of Tape-Recorder Memory', in K. Lagerspetz and P. Niemi (eds.), *Psychology in the 1990s* (Amsterdam, 1984), 425–40.

[35] Levy, 'On Gregorian Orality', op. cit., 219–20.

Office chants and that involved in remembering the entire corpus of Wagnerian opera. Instead, he poses a different series of questions with which one can assess the memory burden associated with memorisation: '*Was* soll auswending reproduziert werden, was genau meint *auswendig* und welche *Technikender memorierung* werden angewandt?'[36] This study attempts to address these questions by identifying the characteristics of the eighth-mode tracts that may have functioned as mnemonics. In addressing Haas's second question, it should be recalled that accuracy was highly valued by the Carolingians. Memorisation was normal within medieval culture, and the sanctity of the liturgical texts, as well as the supposed authorship of Gregory the Great, will also have affected the tunes attached to them.[37]

It is possible that the melodies of the Mass Proper chants were learned entirely *ad verba* – that is, by rote. The closeness of the early written sources has led Levy to describe the tradition, especially of the 'idiomelic' chants, as 'concretized'.[38] However, rote learning is an inflexible means of remembering, and it makes it almost impossible to continue when a memory lapse occurs. In the Middle Ages, writers on memory and memory training instead advocate memory *ad res* – that is, an active and trained mental process where recall is structured, and the use of mnemonics is widespread.[39] The paramount importance of memory in the Middle Ages is well documented, as are the techniques used for developing memory.[40]

In order to discover how the Mass Proper repertory was memorised so well, it may be valuable to explore the role of mnemonics in chant. However, contemporary commentators pay little if any attention to the processes involved in the memorisation of music. The academic discipline of *Musica* was largely abstract, describing such matters as the divisions of the monochord. Passages of more practical relevance in treatises concern matters such as the choice of the correct psalm tones for introit verses, but they do not give guidance about how these may be remembered. By the time of the first music treatises grounded in practical music-making, notably the twelfth-century *De musica* of John Cotton,[41] chant performance was supported by a widespread and usually diastematic written tradition.

---

36 Haas, M., *Mündicher Überlieferung und altrömische Choral* (Bern, 1997), 38

37 Hughes, D., 'Evidence for the Traditional View of the Transmission of Gregorian Chant', *JAMS* 40 (1987), 377–401; 400.

38 Levy, 'On Gregorian Orality', op. cit., 215–16.

39 See Yates, F., *The Art of Memory* (London, 1966), and Carruthers, M., *The Book of Memory* (Cambridge, 1993).

40 See Carruthers, op. cit., esp. 1–15, and Chapter 3.

41 Babb, W., Palisca, C. and Planchart, A., *Hucbald, Guido and John on Music* (New Haven and London, 1978), 101–87. See also Atkinson, C., 'From 'Vitium' to 'Tonus acquisitus': On the Evolution of the Notational Matrix of Medieval Chant', in *CP: Tihany,* 181–98.

Theorists do not mention how music should be learned and remembered. This should not, in fact, be surprising: 'while child and adult speakers may use rules governing several hierarchical levels simultaneously, they usually do not know those rules consciously. While every speaker of a given language follows the rules, typically only linguists can state them, and even linguists find it far from trivial to describe all the regularities that are normally followed.'[42] 'The rules formulated by scholars are followed, but they cannot be stated by the native speakers. This is true for the music as well as the words that accompany it.'[43] Such twentieth-century conjecture is borne out by the medieval evidence: 'In Alcuin's dialogue with Charlemagne (ninth century), the king asks his magister, Alcuin, if there are any specific precepts for *memoria*, which is the noblest aspect of rhetoric. There are none, replies Alcuin, except disciplined exercise in memorizing, practice in writing, and the discipline of cogitation or mental composition.'[44]

In order to examine how the chant repertory was stabilised, one must use the internal evidence of the chants themselves. However, this exposes a further methodological problem. 'Any conjectures about oral tradition... are based on the received Carolingian music text, and that is not only written, but it has in its fabric marks of considerable editorial intervention.'[45] According to Levy, such editorial intervention is made manifest in the tailoring of chants to the eight mode system and the alteration of chromatic chants to make them consistent with diatonic notation. It is also apparent in the homogenisation of ornate melismas, in the attachment of particular words to particular music, in the adaptation of a pre-existing musical model to a new text, and in sensitivity to text accent and syllable count. 'All these are indications of written editorial activity.'[46]

To examine the chants in their written form in the hope of encountering characteristics that helped to keep them stable before the advent of notation appears to be a fruitless task. However, closer examination of Levy's written-editorial characteristics reveals that they are not all clearly connected with early scribal processes, nor with neumatic notation. Sensitivity to text accent and syllable count may be as characteristic of an oral tradition as a written one: the metre of the text and the number of syllables to be articulated form a framework for the way in which the melody can be expressed. Rather than being necessarily written-editorial, this can act as a powerful mnemonic. The attachment of particular words to

[42] Rubin, D., 'Cognitive Processes and Oral Traditions', in *IMS 1977*, 173–80; 176.
[43] Rubin, D., *Memory in Oral Traditions* (Oxford, 1995), 136.
[44] Carruthers, op. cit., 144.
[45] Levy, 'Gregorian Chant and Oral Transmission', op cit., 282–3.
[46] Ibid., 283.

particular melodies, perhaps out of the usual formal context, may similarly function as a mnemonic. The homogenisation of melismas may be a written standardisation, but may also indicate that the repetition of familiar material within an oral tradition became stereotyped. These factors are not clearly indicative of written-editorial intervention, as Levy supposes, and an alternative interpretation of such evidence will be offered below.

The adaptation of a musical model to a new text without sensitivity to the original relationship of words and music may certainly indicate that it was a copying exercise rather than carefully organised composition in the genre. In the eighth-mode tracts, however, the only such examples are isolated and do not appear in early manuscripts.[47] The alteration of the eighth-mode tracts to fit the tonal constraints of the eight mode system, and the eradication of chromatic elements, seem to have been primary concerns only when pitched notation developed in the eleventh century, and do not affect the early written tradition. Such issues will be discussed in more detail in Chapter 5, below.

Undoubtedly the development of notation changed the manner in which these chants were remembered and disseminated. While the development of neumatic notation does not appear to have fundamentally affected the way chant was archived and kept stable, acting as an extension to the cantors' memories rather than replacing their expertise,[48] a significant change did take place in the eleventh century. By this time, the corpus of Gregorian chant was largely fixed in writing, and, increasingly, in pitch-specific notation. Pitch is indicated in very different ways in different centres, which shows not only that its notation developed independently in different places, but also that the representation of pitch was a widespread concern.

Systems of letter notation originated in theoretical treatises as early as the ninth century and, in the eleventh century, the system based on the letters a-p became one of the two alphabetical notations associated with use of the monochord. This seems to have inspired the use of the notation for the chant repertory, mostly for rare or new pieces.[49] The a-p notation is commonly used in Norman sources, most famously and most extensively in *DIJ1*, and appears to have been closely associated with William of

[47] A single exception to this might be *Cantemus*, whose structure parallels that of *Attende*. However, because of the liturgical closeness of these chants, I think it possible that the parallels arose within an oral tradition, and were retained because of textual and associative cues. See pp. 106–7, above, for a fuller description of the construction of this chant.

[48] Carruthers, op. cit., 16: 'In none of the evidence I have discovered is the act of writing itself regarded as a supplanter of memory'. See also Chapter 1 more generally. See also Treitler, L., 'The "Unwritten" and "Written transmission" of Medieval Chant and the Start-Up of Musical Notation', *JM* X (1992), 131–91; 135.

[49] Browne, A. C., 'The a-p System of Letter Notation', *MD* 35 (1981), 5–54.

Volpiano.[50] The other such notation, that associated with Guido of Arezzo and his Italian contemporaries, was invented in about 1025. It also is based on a system of letters, from a-g, reduplicated at the octaves A-G, a-g, aa-gg. The staff is a way of harnessing this nomenclature to the already existing idea of relative 'height'. It is perhaps because this notation combines pitch-specific letter notation with a readily readable graphic representation of the melody that it has enjoyed universal currency in the West over subsequent centuries. Eleventh-century Aquitanian manuscripts have a related system, in which the neumes are accurately, or relatively accurately heighted, and the lines scratched into the parchment to act as guides for the text scribes are used by the music scribes to anchor two pitches, usually a fourth apart. These lines are not always clearly visible, especially in facsimiles. Because there are no clefs, and b flat and b natural are not always distinguished,[51] it is not always possible to tell from the notation where the tones and semitones should lie. Because of this, it was essential that performers using the notation should have prior knowledge of the melodies.

The development of these new notational systems meant that it was possible to sing liturgical music at sight (except within the Aquitanian system). This was a great innovation, and was recognised as such at the time.[52] Intimate knowledge of the repertory and a highly trained memory were no longer necessary in order to reproduce the annual cycle of chants or to perform new compositions. The use of written Graduals, at least by the cantors, in rehearsal or performance seems to have become much more central to the liturgy, as it expanded with ancillary chants such as tropes and sequences. It is arguable that the manner in which the tradition was maintained changed dramatically when pitched notations developed.

Reasons for the Stability of the Eighth-Mode Tracts

In order to identify the characteristics of the eighth-mode tracts that may have aided memory before the development of pitched notation, it is first necessary to establish that verbatim recall is possible within a complex oral genre. A striking general comparison may be made with children's rhymes. In rhymes used for counting out (selection of 'it'), for keeping time while skipping, or for regulating clapping and other games, deviations from the

---

[50] Corbin, Solange, 'Valeur et Sens de la Notation Alphabétique, à Jumièges et en Normandie', *Jumièges Congrès Scientifique du XIIIe Centenaire* (Rouen, 1955), 913–24.

[51] But see Colette, M-N., 'La Notation du Demi-Ton dans le Manuscrit Paris, B. N. Lat. 1139 et dans Quelques Manuscrits du Sud de la France', in C. Leonardi and E. Menesto (eds.), *La Tradizione dei Tropi Liturgici* (Spoleto, 1990), 297–311.

[52] Babb *et al.*, op. cit., 49–51.

expected course are frequently regarded as cheating. The rhymes are constructed in such a way that those being chanted by small children in today's playgrounds are virtually identical to those recorded in Victorian anthologies.[53] The example of children's rhymes is not only apposite, but also deeply familiar. We are easily convinced that this genre is carried orally, and that it is maintained stably by normal children without exceptional memory skills. The combination of melody, narrative, rhythm, rhyme, alliteration, assonance, and often gesture, actually makes it difficult for the performer to introduce deviations from the usual route. A theory of remembering, in which cues and constraints such as these act upon the performer, causing him to sing things which fit within the genre, has been constructed by the cognitive psychologist David Rubin.[54] His work informs the subsequent discussion.

It is not appropriate in a study of this nature to draw wide-ranging conclusions about the characteristics within the tradition of liturgical chant that helped medieval cantors to keep it stable. It is possible, however, to use the body of evidence provided by the analysis of the eighth-mode tracts in Chapter 3, to present a model of the construction of this group of chants. Indeed, Levy has singled out the eighth-mode tracts as a genre where the internal structure is such that the cantors did not necessarily memorise the individual chants, but may have memorised the way in which the genre worked as a whole.[55] It is possible to assess how the construction of the eighth-mode tracts might have led to the stability seen within and between traditions.

The Gregorian eighth-mode tracts are a musical genre whose texts would have been very familiar to the performer. It is of great importance to reproduce the authoritative version of each chant, and the lengths of the pieces are short enough to make this accuracy feasible. The contrast with epic poetry is stark: the poems are long, verbatim recall is not important, and music does not have a primary function. Instead of basing this study on organisational characteristics identified with regard to another genre, it is more appropriate to identify the organisational characteristics peculiar to this group of chants.[56]

---

[53] Opie, I. and Opie, P., *Children's Games* (Oxford, 1969). See also Rubin, D., *Memory in Oral Traditions* (Oxford, 1995), 227.

[54] Rubin, op. cit.

[55] Levy, 'On Gregorian Orality', op. cit., 217.

[56] This is a charge that has been levelled at Treitler by Levy. However, after summarising Treitler's contribution, and exploring the nature of its indebtedness to Parry and Lord, Haas writes that Treitler's theory of chant transmission is based on the metaphor of Homeric epic rather than positing a direct parallel (op. cit., 25–34). This has been widely misunderstood by subsequent critics.

Texts

The invariable bases of the eighth-mode tracts are their texts. As mentioned above, the same texts are used in all manuscripts and in both traditions. There are spelling variants and occasional substitution of words (for example, 'magnificentiam' for 'magnitudinem' in *Attende*), but these rarely occur in places where they would affect the melodic flow.[57] These psalmic texts were very well known: not only was it the Psalter from which children learned to read and write, but novice monks were expected to know their Psalter by heart and to be able to supply any verse that was requested. Holding the verses for a particular eighth-mode tract in the memory, and manipulating the music to fit with the text, would have seemed an entirely natural task to a trained monastic singer.

Verse Divisions

The structure of the eighth-mode tracts is based around the verse, which usually coincides with the verse divisions of other sources containing these psalm texts. Although the numbering of biblical verses had not developed in this period, and the placing of commata and colata in biblical manuscripts is somewhat inconsistent, the verse divisions of the psalms were essential for the correct singing of the psalms within the monastic office, and were on the whole well established. Most Graduals agree completely about where new verses begin in tracts and other chants containing more than one biblical verse.

As was mentioned in Chapter 3, the Easter Vigil canticles have very varied verse placing in the manuscripts, as one might expect for these texts which would have been sung less regularly in the monastic office than the psalms.[58] *Iubilate* and *Sepe* also have varied verse divisions in different manuscripts because the chants (for reasons outlined above – see pp. 111–12 and 121) do not follow the verse outlines of their psalms. Some scribes followed, or partially followed, the familiar psalm divisions. However, in each case, one way of dividing the canticle text into verses was clearly accepted at the time when the chants developed, because only one version of each chant makes formal sense. By the time the manuscripts were copied, it was no longer crucial to performance that the cantor should be cued to begin verses in the correct place, and the different verse divisions are purely scribal; they have no effect on the music.

Two manuscripts exhibit variants of verse-division in other eighth-mode

---

[57] A single exception is 'gramen'/'gramina' in *Attende 6*. See pp. 84–5, above.

[58] *Cantemus* is sung regularly at Lauds. *Attende* is also sung at Lauds, but with a different version of the text. *Vinea* is not used in this context.

tracts.[59] In *Ad te leuaui, LAN* has no verse division where all other manuscripts place the final verse. This seems to be simply a scribal omission. *NOY4* joins the last two verses of *Desiderium* into a single verse, following the verse divisions of the psalm. In *Qui regis* in the Gregorian tradition there is one more verse division than in the Old Roman tradition because of a textual cue. It is signalled not only by a capital letter or V in the manuscripts, but also by the use of phrase ***E*** material. The stimulus for the use of phrase ***E*** material and an extra verse appears to have been the verbal connection between 'beniamin' in the extra verse and 'cherubim' at the beginning of the previous verse.

Apart from these examples, some of which affect only a few manuscripts, and only one of which affects the melodic phrases used, the division of the texts into tract verses was almost entirely stable within the oral tradition. This provided a framework into which the appropriate phrases had to fit, and will have been a powerful memory aid.

Phrase Divisions

In order to decide which phrases were appropriate in a given tract, the singer would need to be aware of the text of the whole verse, if not of the whole tract, and of how this text should be broken up into phrases. It is not usually possible to identify why, for example, some verses consisting of two sentences are divided into four phrases, and why some are divided only into two. It seems likely that this element of construction was learned by rote, and this contention is supported by the fact that sentences can be divided up in different ways, as was shown in Chapter 3, and by the fact that the two traditions occasionally have different solutions. Characteristics learned by rote are more easily forgotten than those cued by memorial prompts.

The text of the second 'verse' of *Qui confidunt* is divided into three phrases ***E3 B2 C1*** in the Gregorian tradition, but the relative clause, 'qui habitat in Ierusalem' is divided as ***C3 D3*** in the Old Roman tradition (see pp. 113–15, above). Once this variation had occurred, the phrases used were firmly established by textual and associative cues. To have phrase ***C*** ending with the text 'in Ierusalem' (as in the Gregorian tradition) is paralleled by the ends of *De profundis 7* ('in orationem'), *Cantemus 3* ('et

[59] The verse divisions in the *AMS* sources are shown in Hesbert's 1935 edition by a capital letter preceded by a full stop. These manuscripts are unexpectedly inconsistent about the placing of verse divisions, but in the absence of the opportunity to examine the manuscripts themselves in order to determine whether these are original to the sources, or whether they are copying errors of Hesbert, I would hesitate to draw any conclusions from this.

ascensorem'), and *Cantemus 5* ('in salutem'). The Old Roman division of 'qui habitat/ in Ierusalem' parallels the division of 'commouebitur/ in eternum' earlier in the verse. It is not possible to identify why this variant occured, but it is easy to see why each version was maintained so stably.

As was mentioned above, the middle verse of *Qui regis* is split into two verses in the Gregorian tradition, but is retained as a single verse in the Old Roman tradition. The Gregorian tradition splits the list of three names into three phrases: 'appare coram effraim/ beniamin/ et manasse'. The Old Roman tradition gives a new phrase only to 'et manasse'. The Old Roman tradition uses the phrases one might expect in a tripartite verse with an indivisible first verse-half, except that the first phrase uses ***B2*** rather than ***B3*** because of textual cues. The Gregorian cantors appear to have been stimulated by the verbal parallel 'cherubim'/'beniamin' to use the same phrase ***E*** music at each occurrence, and therefore to have an extra verse (see pp. 116–18, above). The Old Roman tradition largely follows the expected outline, but the Gregorian tradition instead follows internal textual and associative cues, leading to an unexpected verse outline. Once again, it is possible to identify how the different solutions were stably remembered.

In the final verse of *Qui regis*, the two traditions have a different combination of text and music. The Old Roman tradition has 'Excita potentiam tuam/ et veni/ ut salvos facias nos' with the music ***B3 C F***. The Gregorian tradition has 'Excita potentiam tuam et veni/ ut salvos/ facias nos' with the music ***B3*** followed by elements of ***C*** and then ***F*** (see p. 118, above). The misinterpretation of the syntax in the Gregorian tradition has not overturned the cantors' knowledge of the melodic elements to be articulated within this verse.

Beatus vir also has a different interpretation of the syntax at the end of the final verse in the two traditions (see p. 105, above), but on this occasion the different interpretation of the syntax makes no significant difference to the melodic outline. In the Old Roman tradition, the subject + predicate groups at the beginning of the second and third verses (see pp. 104-105, above) are split into two phrases, with the word 'eius' at the end of ***B2*** stabilising use of this, expected, phrase because of the textual parallels with other phrases using ***B2***. In the Gregorian tradition, the subject and predicate are joined into a single phrase ***E1***. This is not the version of the phrase one would expect in this formal context, and the reasons for its use are uncertain. In the first verse, the Old Roman version divides the relative clause 'qui timet dominum' from the rest of the sentence, making syntactical sense, but in the Gregorian tradition, the relative clause is instead divided (see p. 61, above). This does not follow the sense of the text. The significant variants seen in this chant in the Beneventan manuscripts and, most strikingly, in *DEN1* and *NOY4* (see Chapter 5), indicate that the chant was not stably remembered within the Gregorian tradition. The possibility that it was a later composition than the rest of the core repertory is considered in detail in Chapter 7.

It is clear from these examples that the cantors generally remembered how the texts of the psalms should be broken up to create these chants, and that different solutions only arose in the two traditions when each solution would be kept stable by textual or associative cues. The only exception to this is *Beatus vir*, possibly a later chant, in which the rationale behind the Gregorian version remains unclear.

The Overall Pattern of the Chant

In order to perform an eighth-mode tract, the singer would need first to recall the overall pattern of the piece – that is, the structural pitches and perhaps also the stereotyped melodic patterns. Dobszay has identified tonal skeletons common not only to chants in different traditions, but also to Eastern European folksongs. He has argued that such structures must be alive in the mind of the singer, consciously or subconsciously, and suggests that a singer might silently recall the foundation of the piece before starting the performance in order to anchor the pitches and patterns required.[60] In the intonation formulae, medieval theorists provide examples of what were thought to be the essential elements of each mode.[61] These formulae tend to be combinations of the modal outline with standard melodic shapes. Performers might have planned the performance before starting by recalling one of the characteristic eighth-mode intonation formulae, or they might have made a more detailed preparation by remembering how the text should be broken up into verses and phrases, and how text and music should be combined. 'Oral performance' – that is, without the aid of written music – does not imply unprepared public renditions.

The Phrase Types

As was described in detail in Chapter 3, the six phrases, each with a fixed cadence shape and final pitch, are each associated with a particular formal context, and provide a basic framework around which the eighth-mode tracts are constructed. Within each phrase type there are subgroups for more specific formal contexts within the verse or within the tract. Once one of these phrase shapes is begun, the rest is almost always inevitable, within

---

[60] This was described in an (unpublished) paper at the 1997 *IMS* meeting in London.
[61] Described in more detail in Chapter 5, below.

local practice.[62] The narrow context within which each of these phrases appears has been described in exhaustive detail in Chapter 3 above. These are the fundamental building blocks of the genre. Variations from the formal scheme are usually dictated by the verbal context.

Accent Patterns

Within each phrase, certain melodic patterns are specifically associated either with accented or with unaccented syllables, as is shown in Appendix 2 by the arrows above the patterns associated with accented syllables. Kainzbauer has comprehensively demonstrated how the textual context, and in particular the stress patterns, influenced the text-music alignment of the eighth-mode tracts.[63] When these expectations are impossible to fulfil, the solutions of the manuscripts are varied and sometimes garbled. An example of this is provided by phrase ***C4***, whose texts have an antepenultimate instead of the usual penultimate accent (see pp. 83–5, above). The figures usually associated with the last two syllables (/-) have to be fitted around three syllables (/--). Some manuscripts split k hik; some have k khik; some split the previous figure g hkik. The figure ghkik is sometimes abbreviated to ghki, but manuscripts are not internally consistent. The patterns of accented and unaccented syllables in the texts rarely influence the choice of which phrase to use, but are fundamental in deciding how the given phrase will be fitted to the text.

Textual Cues

It will already be clear from the identification of differences between the traditions and of deviations from the expected formal outline that the words themselves affect which phrase shapes are used, frequently overturning the formal expectations. Examples of direct textual cues, assonance and rhyme affecting the phrases used in the eighth-mode tracts permeate the descriptions of the individual chants in Chapter 3. A few striking examples will serve here to illustrate the point.

The beginning of the fourth verse of *Ad te leuaui* has the text 'Ita oculi nostri' (*Ad te leuaui 7*). Because of the verbal parallel with the beginning of the tract, 'Ad te leuaui oculos meos', ***A2*** material is used in both traditions (for descriptions of this verse and its network of associations, see pp. 66, 100–101 and 120, above). In the second verse of *Sepe*, 'Dicat nunc israhel'

[62] Exceptions occur when textual cues demand use of elements of more than one phrase with one portion of text.

[63] Kainzbauer, X., 'Der Tractus Tetrardus – eine centologische Untersuchung', *Beiträge zur Gregorianik* 11 (Regensburg, 1991), 1–132.

also begins with ***A2*** material in both traditions because of the assonance ('dicat'/'ita') with *Ad te leuaui 7*. 'Israhel' uses ***B3*** material in the Gregorian tradition, as one would expect for a single phrase in the first verse-half, and the identical text in *Qui regis 1* also uses ***B3*** material (but without the full cadence).

The Gregorian version of *Ad te leuaui 8* then follows the associative cue of the second verse of *Sepe* and concludes with ***B3*** material. It is possibly also following the syntactical cue that 'ad dominum deum nostrum' (*Ad te leuaui 8*) is a prepositional phrase associated with the previous clause. It has the ***B2*** opening, as one would expect for the second phrase in the verse half, but concludes with ***B3*** material. The parallel verses thus have the musical material ***A2-B3*** in *Sepe*, verse 2 and ***A2 B3*** in *Ad te leuaui*, verse 4.

Conversely, in the Old Roman tradition, *Qui regis 1* has ***A1*** material throughout, and the end of *Sepe 3* follows this textual cue. There is, then, no associative cue to have ***B3*** in the fourth verse of *Ad te leuaui*, and the Old Roman tradition instead has ***B2*** for *Ad te leuaui 8*, following the usual formal scheme.

The rest of the second verse of *Sepe* in the Gregorian tradition has ***C D***. The Old Roman tradition does not have the formally expected phrases, but follows another textual cue. The second half of the verse repeats the text of the first verse: 'sepe expugnauerunt me/ a iuuentute mea'. In the Old Roman tradition, ***A2*** is reused for the repetition of the text 'sepe expugnauerunt me'.

The stem 'domin-' plays a crucial cueing role in various contexts in the eighth-mode tracts. It prompts use of ***A1*** in several tracts, including the beginning of *Qui confidunt in domino*, even though it has eight syllables (see p. 59, above). 'Domino/ni/nus' ends phrase ***C*** in *Iubilate 3*, *Iubilate 7* and *Laudate 7*, and these phrases have a unique cadence shape. The word 'domine' has a central role in *De profundis* (see pp. 108–9, above) 'Domine' begins the second half of the first verse (***C***). In both traditions, the same opening is used at the beginning of the second half-verse of the third verse, even though the phrases are subsequently unrelated. The word 'domine' ends the previous phrase in both verses, and on both occasions has the phrase ***B*** cadence. This is formally expected, but also highlights the parallel. The first phrase of the third verse uses ***B4*** rather than the formally expected ***B3*** because the same word ends the first phrase of the final verse in *Ad te leuaui*. The tract ends with the word 'domine', and in the Gregorian tradition, the melisma is on the accent rather than, as usual, on the final syllable.

Other examples of textual cues stimulating use of the same music include: the gd recitation on 'quoniam' in *Laudate 5* and *Desiderium 5*; the use of ***B2*** in *Attende* and *Vinea* out of the expected context because the phrase begins 'et'; ***D4*** being used at the end of the first verse of *Desiderium*, even though it is usually associated with bi-partite verses, because of the textual connection with *Commouisti 2* ('non fraudasti eum'/'et conturbasti eam'); and the use of phrase ***C*** in the Gregorian version of *Iubilate 6*, because of the textual connection with *Qui seminant 6* ('cum exultatione'/'in exultatione').

Textual cues do not always take precedence. For example, in *De profundis*, 'sustinui te' does not use the melody found in the previous verse with the text 'sustinebit'. 'Sustinui te domine' is the last line of text of the tract, and the singer would have been cued to use phrase ***F*** rather than repeating phrase ***D***. In the first verse of *Commouisti*, one might expect the text 'Commouisti domine terram' to cue use of ***A1***. However, 'Commouisti... terram' is the predicate and 'domine' is the subject, so the text unit is indivisible, and ***A2*** is used, as one would expect with a nine-syllable first phrase.

Rhetorical Cues

Deviation from the expected phrase shapes for the sake of musical expression appears to be foreign to the aesthetic of the eighth-mode tracts. However, rhetorical cues do occasionally function. The ***D3*** melisma is more extended than the ***D2*** melisma, and ***D3*** tends to be used in verses which follow verses ending with ***D2***. This occurs in *Sepe* in both traditions, where the text 'a iuuentute mea' ends both the first and the second verses. The extension of the melisma, both in the tessitura and also in the number of notes, by using ***D3*** in the second verse, is a striking rhetorical gesture.

Combining Cues and Constraints

The effects of textual, formal, and associative prompts may readily be identified in the pieces themselves. However, the recall of these chants will not have relied on such cues alone. It is characteristic of oral genres that verbatim recall or rote learning is combined with the constraints and cues. The two modes of remembering cannot easily be disentangled. The role of different groups of singers is important. Hucke has identified different melodic styles in the chants sung by the cantor, by the *schola*, and by the monastic community. The different types of music presumably lend themselves to the level of exactitude necessary for the contexts in which they appear. 'Es ist auffällig, dass die Stücke für die Schola sich weithin vielfältiger, weniger normiert, individueller ausformuliert präsentieren als die Kantorenstücke.'[64] Chants sung by certain groups of people would be memorised by rote; others would require specialised knowledge of the construction of the genre in question.

Once one combines the underlying form, the melody shapes associated with particular formal contexts, the standard melodic patterns, the way of matching text with music, the stimuli of rhymes or the same words, the rhythm of stressed and unstressed syllables, associative cues, and rhetorical cues, it begins to be possible to comprehend how a group of chants that were transmitted so widely without notation remained so well defined. There are so many memory prompts that there is actually little creative choice.

It has been asserted by Rubin that within an oral genre, any variants will be consistent within the constraints of that genre. Within each tradition, almost all variants are insignificant, as was established in Chapter 2. However, it is necessary to consider whether the few significant variants are incompatible with the constraints and cues of the genre. Several significant variants between manuscripts may be found in *Beatus uir*. These will be considered in more detail in Chapter 5, below. Here, it suffices to say that none of the variants within Gregorian manuscripts is inconsistent with the scheme outlined above, and they sometimes bring the chant closer to that scheme than the mainstream version. The other significant variants within the Gregorian tradition, also described in Chapter 5, are all the result of copying errors, and are not compatible with the construction of the genre. There are no significant variants in the Old Roman tradition.

The Old Roman tradition remained purely oral for much longer than the Gregorian. While some have maintained that the Old Roman tradition was improvisatory until quite soon before it was written down, and that the differences between the two traditions are caused by changes in the Old Roman tradition,[65] others have asserted that one would expect a greater reliance on standard formulas, and more reliance on textual cues in the Old Roman tradition, because these are less burdensome on the memory than remembering many different phrases.[66] It must first be pointed out that the two traditions have exactly equivalent subgroups of phrases. If there was a greater reliance on standard formulae in the Old Roman tradition than in the Gregorian tradition, one might expect some of these subgroups to have

[64] Hucke, 'Der Übergang von mündlicher zu schriftlicher Musiküberlieferung im Mittelalter', op. cit., 184.

[65] Lipphardt, W., 'Gregor der Grosse und sein Anteil am römischen Antiphonar', in H. Anglès, *Congresso Internazionale die Musica Sacra, Rome, 1950* (Tournai, 1952), 248–54.

[66] See Cutter, P., 'Oral transmission of the Old Roman responsories?', *MQ* 62 (1976), 182–94; and 'The Old Roman Chant Tradition: Oral or Written?', *JAMS* 20 (1967), 167–81.

been amalgamated.

The two traditions differ in several places. Some of the differences are stimulated by different attitudes towards the breaking up of the text into phrases, as described above. However, the ensuing differences do not indicate that the cantors of one tradition were more expert in matching text to music within the genre than the other, except in *Beatus uir*. Some accentuation patterns are interpreted differently in the two traditions, sometimes leading to differing versions of phrases (for example *Beatus uir* 7, where the Old Roman tradition uses ***C2*** and the Gregorian tradition uses ***C1*** because of a misinterpretation of where the accent falls in 'generátio'), but these are isolated and once again do not indicate a fundamental difference between the processes of transmission used in each tradition.

On several occasions, the two traditions follow different cues. On eight occasions, the Old Roman tradition follows a textual cue while the Gregorian tradition follows the expected formal one.[67] On five occasions, the Old Roman tradition follows the expected formal pattern while the Gregorian tradition follows a textual or associative cue.[68] If the Old Roman tradition had followed textual cues and the Gregorian tradition had preferred to follow formal cues on a significant number of occasions, one might conclude that the Old Roman tradition was more influenced by the text than the Gregorian tradition, as Cutter has suggested.[69] However, a sample of this size, with a ratio 8:5 of emphasis on different types of cues, is not statistically significant.

The variants between the two traditions do not demonstrate that they are fundamentally different in process. Text, form, and rhetoric all influence how the chants are constructed, and sometimes they make conflicting demands. While the tradition was still entirely oral, the Old Roman and the Gregorian traditions responded to these conflicting demands in different ways, and the independence of their solutions is evident in the manuscript culture.

Conclusions

The evidence does not suggest that there was a late eighth- or early ninth-century neumed archetype of the Mass Proper chants. Instead, it would appear that the tradition was carried by memory. Whether or not there was a neumed archetype at this early stage, memory played a vital role in

[67] *Beatus uir 2*, *De profundis 5*, *Desiderium 6*, *Qui confidunt 10*, *Qui regis 1*, *Qui regis 4*, *Sepe 3* (twice).

[68] *Ad te leuaui 8*, *Iubilate 6*, *Qui regis 3*, *Qui regis 5* and *Qui regis 6*.

[69] Cutter, 'Oral transmission', op. cit. and 'The Old Roman Chant Tradition', op. cit.

keeping the tradition stable until the development of pitched notation. Instead of asserting merely that people in the Middle Ages were used to memorisation, or that the chants were so familiar to expert singers that they remembered them accurately, a detailed model has been constructed here of the characteristics of the eighth-mode tracts that would have stabilised the oral transmission.

The Old Roman and Gregorian eighth-mode tracts bear all the hallmarks of having originated, not only orally, but also within the same oral tradition. Differences between the traditions are almost always consistent within the constraints of the genre, and seem to have arisen soon after (or perhaps as) the Roman chant was adopted in Francia. Stability was so crucial in the Carolingian Church that variants within the Frankish tradition rarely arose. The closeness of the manuscript sources is now not so very surprising. With so many prompts, and with unity being a priority, it is conceivable that this tradition was maintained with a high degree of stability, and that it could be notated independently in different places in almost identical versions. If we can accept that trained memories are capable of maintaining complex genres with a high degree of unity, then there is no longer any need to posit an early ninth-century written exemplar, at least for the eighth-mode tracts.

Chapter 5

The Medieval Understanding of the Eighth-Mode Tracts I: Characteristics of the Notated Sources and Theoretical Writing

Introduction

In the preceding chapter, it was demonstrated that memory played a vital role in the transmission of the chant tradition at least until pitched notation developed in the eleventh century. This chapter addresses the question of how the core repertory of eighth-mode tracts was understood by cantors once the tradition was widely supported by writing. Various kinds of information within medieval sources may be used in exploring this question. The way in which the eighth-mode tracts are notated in the manuscripts may contain information about how they were understood by those writing them down. For example, some variants may indicate clearly that the manuscript is the result of a copying exercise, and that the scribe did not understand the structure of the genre he was copying. Alternatively, the notational treatment of phrases of the same type may indicate that the scribe was aware of their musical and formal equivalence.

The chant repertory was introduced to Francia independently of theoretical writing, but affected, and was affected by, the development of the eighth-mode system. The way in which these chants are considered by theorists and the effect of musical theory on the melodies provide further insight into the medieval understanding of the genre, and into the relationship between theory and practice.

Direct evidence about how well the chants were understood by those performing them is at first sight elusive. Variant readings of the tracts in different manuscripts may provide evidence of a continuing understanding of the way in which the genre worked, although there is no way of telling whether this evidence is contemporary with the manuscript in question, or whether it is a written residue of earlier practice. However, some eighth-mode tracts appear to have been composed after the development of notation and the spread of medieval musical theory. The extent to which these eighth-mode tracts were composed in a manner consistent with the core repertory is a reliable indication of the knowledge the composers had of the construction of the genre. These 'more recent' eighth-mode tracts will be considered in Chapter 6.

The Medieval Understanding of the Genre: The Notation of the Core Repertory

While literary texts could be copied by monastic scribes without any deep understanding of what they were copying, the circumstances surrounding the writing of musical manuscripts are rather different. The ability to notate music was a distinct technical skill, almost certainly not possessed by all scribes. The 'copying' of a manuscript containing notation for liturgical chant appears, at least in the tenth century, to have been based on a combination of reading an exemplar and using the scribe's own memory of the shape of a piece.[1] Hughes asserts that because most variants appear to be the result of mishearing rather than misreading, those providing the musical notation for liturgical manuscripts were probably cantors themselves.[2] Less highly trained scribes may have been dictated to by authoritative singers. Although this seems unlikely to have occurred within a busy scriptorium, the question of who was holding the quill does not affect the combination of reading and remembering involved in the copying process. The variants found in manuscripts in this study support the contention that the writing of tenth- and perhaps eleventh-century manuscripts relied on a combination of remembering and copying.

The largest group of examples demonstrating that some scribes or cantors remembered the structure of a tract in a different form from others may be found in *Beatus uir*. *DEN1* has a different melodic outline in several places (Example **5.1**).

[1] Hughes, D., 'Evidence for the Traditional View of the Transmission of Gregorian Chant', *JAMS* 40 (1987), 377–401; 400–401. Treitler has argued that manuscripts containing tropes were written by the singers as a memorial aid, rather than being slavishly copied. See Treitler, L., 'Observations on the Transmission of some Aquitanian Tropes', *Forum Musicologicum* 3 (Winterthur, 1982) 11–60; 15.

[2] See also Fassler, M., 'The Office of the Cantor in Early Western Monastic Rules and Customaries: A Preliminary Investigation', *EMH* 5 (1985), 29–51.

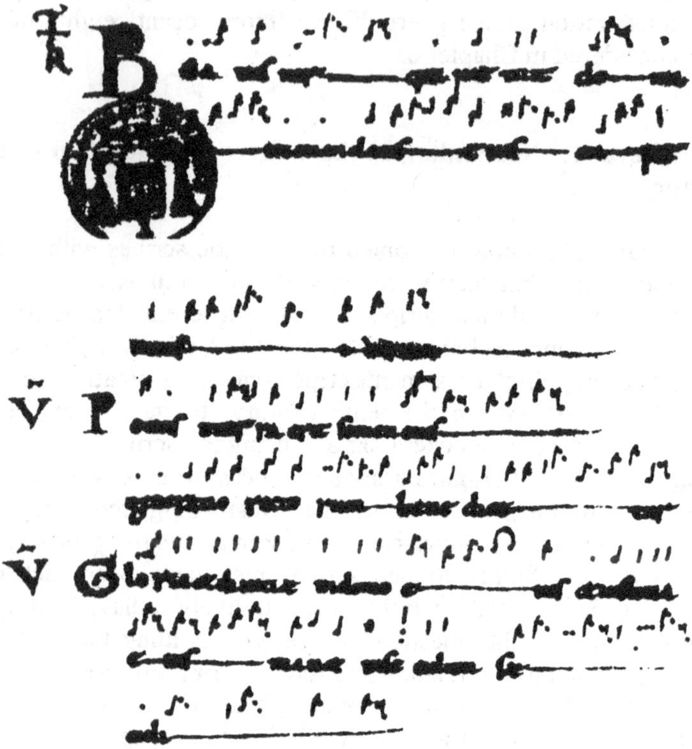

Example **5.1**

In the first verse, this manuscript has ***A1*** for 'Beatus uir' and ***B2*** for 'qui metuit dominum'. This is exactly the solution found in the Old Roman manuscripts. *DEN1* differs from the other Gregorian manuscripts, where the relative clause is divided: 'Beatus uir qui timet/ dominum' (see p. 61, above).[3] The use of ***B2*** instead of the ***B1*** usually associated with the first verses of tracts may have been stimulated in *DEN1* by the rhyme of 'dominum' with *Sicut 2* ('ad fontes aquarum'), *Sicut 5* ('ad deum uiuum'), *Attende 7* ('et sicut nix super fenum'), and *Qui confidunt 4* ('in eternum').

The second verse of *Beatus uir* usually begins with phrase ***E1*** in the Gregorian tradition. The neumes on 'Potens in terra' in *DEN1* are not compatible with any other phrase. Although they cannot be reconstructed with any degree of certainty, the pitches implied appear to be kk g h hggfg hg. These are shapes characteristic of the eighth mode, but they are not

[3] For the usual outline of this chant in the Gregorian tradition, see *DIJ1* in Appendix 4 (pp. 365–6). *BEN5* has an idiosyncratic version (p. 330).

specifically connected with any eighth-mode tract phrases. The following portion of text, 'erit semen eius', has the usual phrase ***B2*** shapes. *Qui confidunt 8*, *Attende 10* and *Laudate 6* also end phrase ***B2*** with the word 'eius'. *DEN1* ends the second verse with ***D1*** rather than the ***D2*** seen in other Gregorian manuscripts. This is compatible with the previous verse in the same tract, and also with the group of three tracts closely connected with *Beatus uir* (*De profundis, Laudate* and *Iubilate*). The first phrase of this verse is not compatible with any other phrases, but the rest of the verse makes sense within the constraints of the genre, and uses the same phrases as the Old Roman tradition.

The final verse of *Beatus uir* in *DEN1* begins with phrase ***E1***, as in the rest of the Gregorian tradition. However, while other Gregorian manuscripts follow this with phrase ***C***, *DEN1* has phrase ***B2*** on 'et iusticia eius'. The textual cue of 'eius' is clear, and this is also the phrase that one would expect to encounter after ***E1***.

It is not possible to tell whether these differences arose through contact with the tradition later codified in the Old Roman manuscripts, or whether a northern French cantor arrived independently at a similar solution. These variants may have arisen at the time *DEN1* was written, indicating that the structure of the genre was still alive in the mind of the singer, or they may be what remains in written form of the way it had been known in earlier times. Either way, these variants show that *Beatus uir* was not as melodically stable as most tracts when it was adopted in Francia.[4] The nature of the variants demonstrates that at some time between the adoption of *Beatus uir* in Francia and the writing of *DEN1*, the memorial prompts of textual connections and an abstract understanding of the construction of the genre could still affect the structure of this chant.

A further type of variant occurs in *Beatus uir*. As was mentioned in Chapter 2, the Beneventan manuscripts have an interpretation of the text accents in phrase ***C*** different from that of the mainstream Gregorian tradition (see Example **2.3**, p. 44). In *Beatus uir 3*, they rise on 'in man<u>dá</u>-' instead of on 'in'. In *Beatus uir 7*, they rise on 'gene<u>rá</u>-' instead of on 'ge-'. In *Beatus uir 10*, they rise on 'et ius<u>tí</u>-' instead of on 'et'. This is a correct interpretation of the accentuation of the text, shared also by the Old Roman manuscripts. In *Beatus uir 3* and *Beatus uir 10*, rising on the third instead of the first syllable means that there are insufficient syllables remaining to articulate the phrase properly, and ***C3*** is used, with the gfgh and ghkik figures joined onto a single syllable. In *Beatus uir 7*, the variant means that there is enough text remaining to articulate the phrase, but not enough for recitation, so ***C2*** is used instead of ***C1***. *DEN1* has exactly the same as the

4 For a discussion of the possibility that *Beatus uir* was composed later than the other tracts in the core repertory, see Chapter 7.

Beneventan manuscripts in *Beatus uir 3* and *Beatus uir 7* (in *Beatus uir 10* it uses phrase ***B*** instead of phrase ***C***). Because these manuscripts use phrase ***C*** in a manner consistent with the genre, the variants are connected with singers who understood how the music should be manipulated given the textual context. It is not possible to tell whether this variant occurred at the time of copying these manuscripts, but it does indicate that at some time after the spread of the Gregorian tradition, cantors still understood the manner in which the genre was constructed, at least on the level of how the phrase should be manipulated to fit the text associated with it.

In *Sicut*, the two phrases 'sitiuit anima mea/ ad deum uiuum', usually given the music ***E1 B2***, are instead joined together as a single phrase ***E1*** in *BRE* (Example **5.2**).

Usual melodic outline
YRX

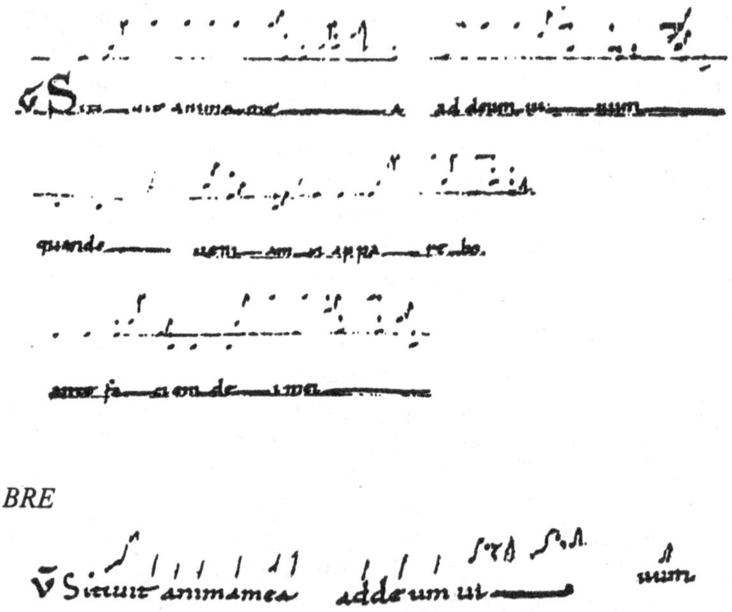

BRE

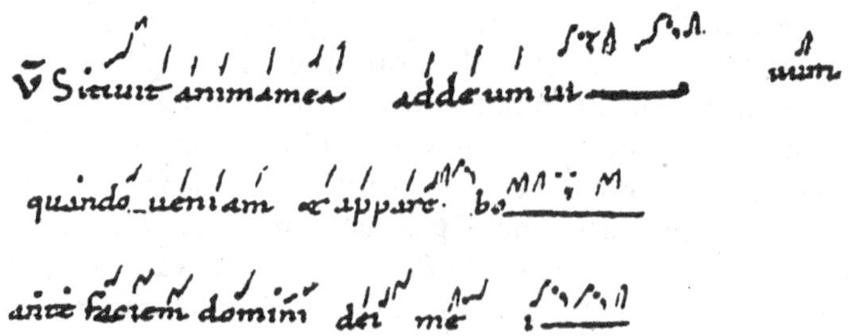

Example **5.2**

This manuscript continues with ***B2*** and ***C*** for the remainder of the verse. This change has a fundamental effect on the structure of the verse, moving the half-verse caesura at the end of phrase ***B*** to the end of 'quando ueniam et apparebo', and avoiding use of phrase ***D*** in the tract. Phrase ***D*** is not used in the Easter Vigil tracts at all in *BRE*, making these a homogenous musical group. This is not simply a scribal slip, but demonstrates a local understanding of the construction of this verse, where the sentence is attached to a single phrase, and the verse continues in the tripartite manner found also in the Easter Vigil canticles. This variant is consistent with the structure of the genre.

In the penultimate phrase of *Sepe*, most manuscripts have gfgh ghkik on the accented syllable 'con-', leaving the usual figures to be attached to the final two syllables. In *TYR* the gfgh ghkik figure is split between the two syllables 'conci-', as is more usual in phrase ***C***, but this leaves no syllable for the articulation of khik before the final melisma and it is omitted (Example 5.3).

Usual outline
GAL1

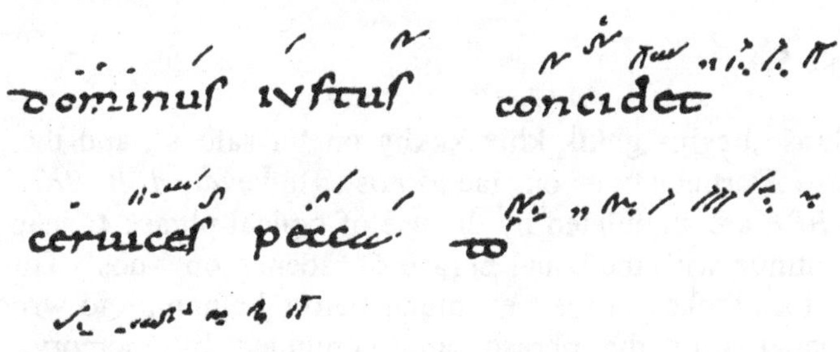

TYR

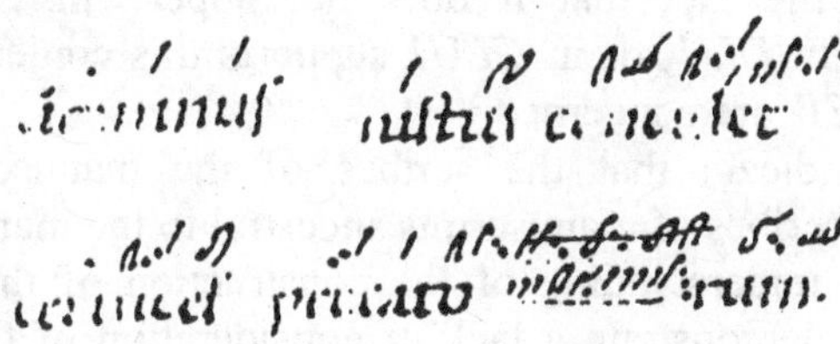

Example 5.3

Such minor carelessness is scarcely worthy of mention. However, when copying the following phrase, the scribe was careless once more. Phrase ***F*** begins in exactly the same way as phrase ***D2***, and the scribe of *TYR* erroneously wrote the ***D2*** melisma on '-to-'. This is crossed out with dark ink and the correct melisma is written in below. It is clear from these examples, and particularly from the second one, that the scribe of *TYR* glanced only intermittently at his exemplar to remind himself of the beginning of the phrase, and then wrote the rest of the phrase from his memory.

The final phrase of *Qui regis* is third in a verse, and has the text 'ut saluos facias nos' (Example **5.4**).

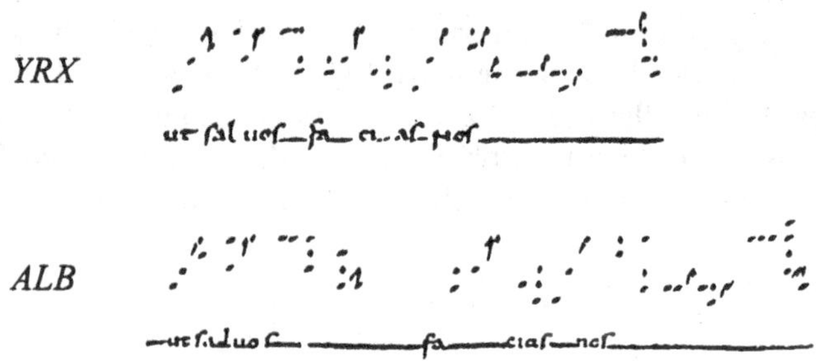

Example **5.4**

The phrase begins ghkik khik kkkhg on 'ut saluos', and then has the usual phrase ***F*** articulations on 'facias nos'. However, *ALB, BEN5, ROG1, LEW* and *BRE* are stimulated by the use of typical phrase ***C*** shapes on 'ut sal-' to continue with the usual phrase ***C*** cadence on '-uos'. This implies that the scribes looked at their exemplar before beginning to write out the melodic patterns of the phrase, and continued by memory. As was mentioned in Chapter 4, once a phrase is begun, the rest is generally inevitable. It is possible that this variant arose at the time of the copying of these manuscripts, and the fact that it does not appear in the other Aquitanian manuscripts, in *DIJ1*, or in *CLU1* supports this conjecture, as far as *ALB, ROG1* and *LEW* are concerned.[5]

These variants all indicate that the scribes of the manuscripts in question, or possibly the scribes of manuscripts ancestral to the manuscripts in question, had a clear understanding of the construction of the genre. However, some variants demonstrate a lack of consideration of the usual outlines of the genre. In *ORC* and *BEN5*, the first two phrases of the second verse in *Sicut*, 'sitiuit anima mea/ ad deum uiuum', are joined into a single phrase beginning with the rise ghik of phrase ***E***, followed by a long

[5] *BEN1* does not have *Qui regis*, there being a lacuna at this point, so it is not possible to tell in this study whether this was an established Beneventan variant.

recitation passage and the phrase ***B*** cadence (Example **5.5**).

ORC

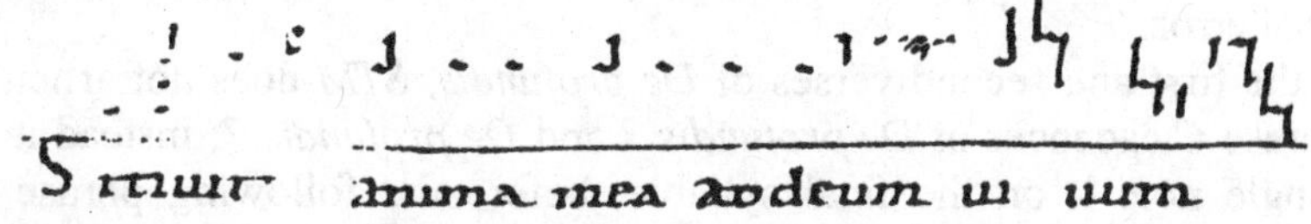

BEN5

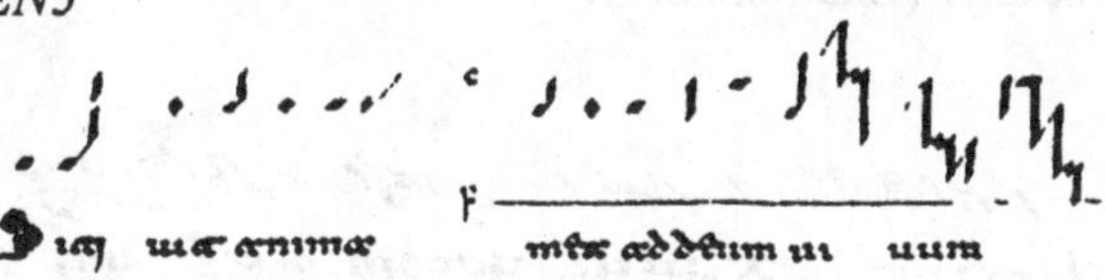

Example **5.5**

This hybrid musical phrase suggests that this probably occurred outside the context of performance. A cantor who decided in performance that this text should be attached to only one musical phrase would presumably continue with the ***E*** phrase with which he had started the verse, as is the case in the same phrase in *BRE* (see Example **5.2**, above). A similar scribal error occurs in *ROG1*. In *Attende*, most manuscripts have ***B2 C*** for 'deus uera opera eius/ et omnes uie eius iudicia'. The scribe of *ROG1* appears to have been distracted by the word 'eius' occurring twice in close proximity, and the text 'eius et omnes uie', together with the end of phrase ***B*** and the beginning of phrase ***C*** usually associated with it, is simply omitted (Example **5.6**).

normal melodic outline (*SAB*)

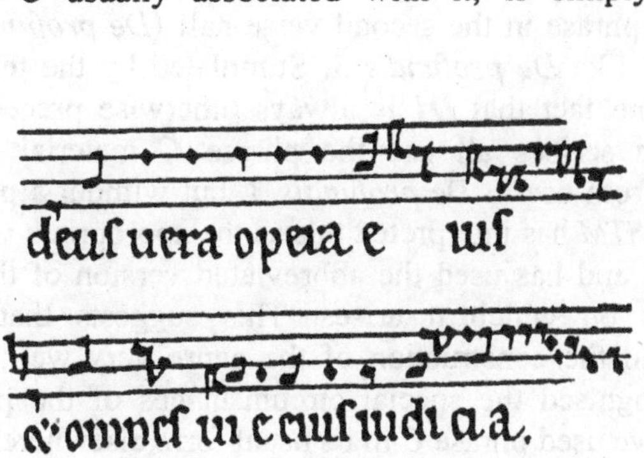

ROG1

Example **5.6**

The abrupt shift from the recitation on k associated with phrase ***B*** to the recitation on g associated with phrase ***C*** is alien to the genre. This is clearly a scribal error.

In the first and second verses of *De profundis, STM* does not articulate the phrase ***C*** cadences of *De profundis 3* and *De profundis 7*; instead it has the single note k on the final syllable, before the following phrase ***D1*** begins in the normal manner (Example **5.7**).

De profundis 3

De profundis 7

De profundis 10

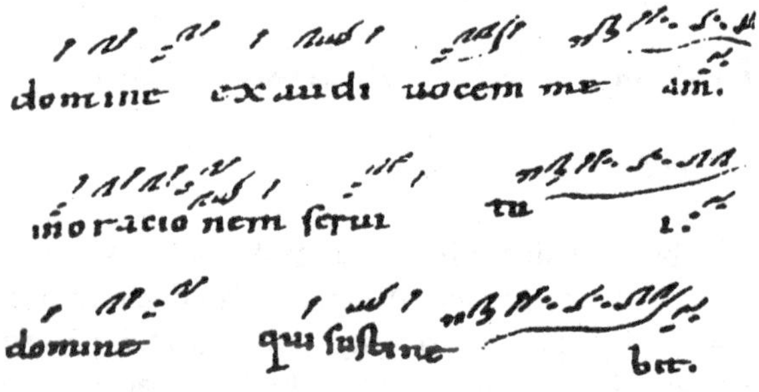

Example **5.7**

One would not expect this variant to arise within performance, because once phrase ***C*** was begun, it would generally be completed. There is an internal cue for this change. In the penultimate verse of this tract, there is only one phrase in the second verse-half (*De profundis 10*), and it begins 'domine', like *De profundis 3*. Stimulated by the textual connection, and also by the fact that ***D1*** is always otherwise preceded by phrase ***C***, the Gregorian scribes all use the phrase ***C*** material on 'domine' already familiar from use in *De profundis 3*, but without a phrase ***C*** cadence. The scribe of *STM* has interpreted this as the appropriate version of phrase ***C*** for this tract, and has used the abbreviated version of the phrase on all three occasions on which it arises. This suggests that the scribe did not understand the construction of the genre very well; if he had, he would have recognised the special circumstances of the penultimate verse and would have used phrase ***C*** in its usual form elsewhere.

The examples given above show that scribes sometimes copied as a mechanical exercise, making mistakes incompatible with the structure of the genre. However, they show also that the copying of these chants sometimes occurred as a combination of copying from an exemplar and remembering. On the many occasions where the melody appears in the usual version, it is not easy to tell whether the primary impulse was remembering or copying. Although melodic variants do provide evidence about the way in which these chants were understood in the early Middle Ages, it has been established only in a very few cases that the scribes were using their own memory of the pieces while making the copy. In almost all of these cases, the evidence only exists because the scribe's memory failed him in some way.

The importance of musical proficiency and an understanding of the rules of plainchant are recurrent themes in medieval theoretical writing.[6] It seems probable, at least before pitched notations became widespread, that musicians had some understanding of the structure of the eighth-mode tracts to reinforce *ad verba* memory and notational cues.[7] One possible piece of evidence about the understanding the medieval scribes had of eighth-mode tract structure is that there are no further mistakes similar to that found in *TYR*, where the scribe carelessly wrote the wrong version of a phrase after a standard opening. No other scribes mistake when the ***D2/3*** articulation should proceed into the phrase ***D*** melisma, and when it should be proceed into the phrase ***F*** melisma. There are other examples of such care being taken. The three ***C*** phrases ending 'domin-' have ikhhg instead of the usual cadence. No scribes write the normal phrase ***C*** cadence in this context. The repetition of 'a iuuentute mea' in *Sepe* is consistently decorated as ***D3*** even though this version of the phrase is never otherwise used in the Gregorian tradition. No scribe, stimulated by the use of the same text with ***D2*** in the previous verse, forgot to extend the melisma in the second verse. These are striking examples of the consistency of the tradition: more generally, the Gregorian scribes use the same versions of phrases as each other almost all of the time. This evidence is inconclusive. It may indicate that the tradition was well known by cantor-notators, but it may also indicate that there was a unified written tradition of the tracts, and that this was carefully followed.

There is some evidence that scribes recognised standard phrases as such. The first example of this is that many manuscripts use standard neume patterns for standard phrase shapes. Some phrases in group ***E1*** in *LAN* may be shown as an example of this (Example **5.8**).[8]

---

[6] McGee, T., *The Sound of Medieval Song: Ornamentation and Vocal Style According to the Treatises* (Oxford, 1998), 20–21.

[7] Treitler has claimed that Aquitanian trope sources provide evidence that the music was known as a structure in the mind of the singer. See Treitler, 'Observations on the Transmission of some Aquitanian Tropes', op. cit., 49.

[8] M. Barezzani gives a description of the neume shapes characteristic of certain melodic figures in *BRE* in *La Notazione Neumatica di un Codice Bresciano (Secolo XI)* (Cremona, 1981), 109–13.

Attende 9

Beatus uir 5

Qui regis 4

Sicut 8

Vinea 4

Attende 12

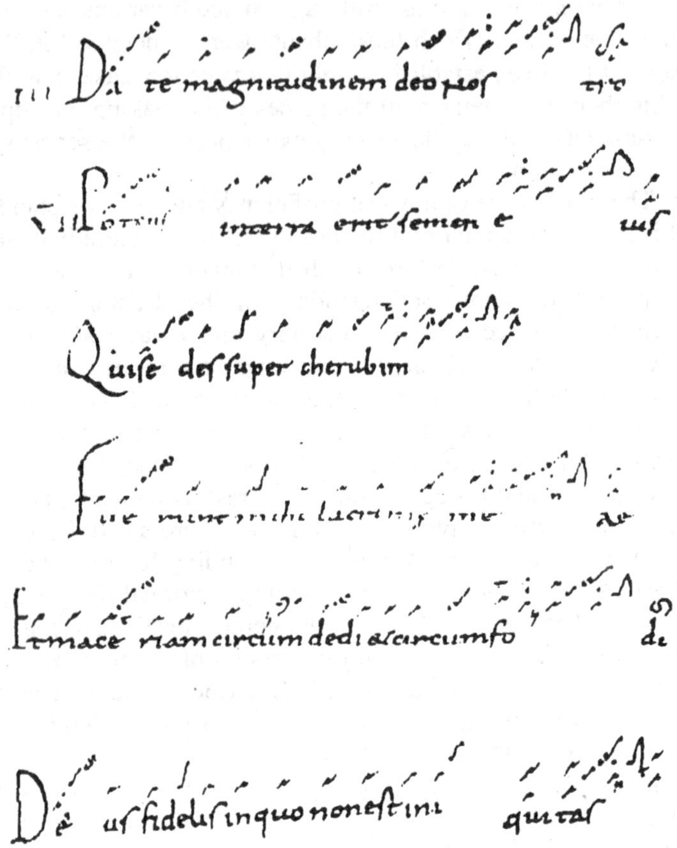

Example **5.8**

A more extreme example is that scribes in certain manuscripts conclude the final melisma early.[9] Although this usually occurs simply because insufficient space has been left by the text scribe before the beginning of the next chant, there are a few cases where the melisma is not completed, despite there being sufficient space remaining. In *DIJ1*, the final melisma in *Beatus vir* is not written out in full (see p. 366, below). As it is the sixth eighth-mode tract in a row in this source, to write the final melisma once more may have seemed superfluous.

Most manuscripts do not have the eighth-mode tracts copied in a group in the manner of *DIJ1*; instead, these chants are scattered through the

[9] The abbreviation of the final melisma of a chant was a widespread practice in medieval manuscripts.

source in their appropriate liturgical contexts. The final melisma tends to be abbreviated in the Easter Vigil tracts, where four eighth-mode tracts are copied in close proximity. In *LAN*, the final melismas of *Attende* and *Vinea* are not completed, although there would have been room for the whole melisma if the scribe had written above the rubrics for the following piece, as he did with the following tract, *Sicut*. Similarly, in *YRX*, three of the Easter Vigil tracts do not have complete final melismas, despite there being unutilised space over the rubrics of the chants following *Cantemus* and *Attende*, and a little space left after *Sicut*. In *PAS2*, there is about an inch of free space left after the final melisma in *Vinea*, but the scribe has written no more notes than in the previous tract, *Cantemus*, where the melisma ends early due to lack of space. In *ROG1*, the end of the final melisma in *Sicut* is omitted, despite there being space remaining on the page.

GAL2 is the only manuscript apart from *DIJ1* where the final melisma is curtailed in tracts other than the Easter Vigil tracts, even when there is ample space remaining. This occurs in *Beatus uir, Commouisti, Iubilate* and *Qui regis*. The fact that *Qui regis* is the first eighth-mode tract in the manuscript, and that the other three tracts are used towards the beginning of the Lenten season, is a firm indication that these chants were very well known. Once the beginning of the final melisma had been articulated, the rest would be remembered, and need not be notated in full.

On one occasion, the omission of the end of the final melisma is for a reason other than lack of space, or because it was assumed that the melisma would be known by the reader. In *Sicut ceruus* in *MUR3*, the scribe appears to have left insufficient space for the final words of the text before the new line where the next chant begins (see Example **5.9**, overleaf).

The alleluia has to be squeezed onto this page to permit the next opening to be dedicated entirely to illuminations announcing Easter. Some space was left free at the end of a previous line in order that the final verse of the tract would begin on a new line of the page. As there is insufficient room for the last words of the tract to be included on the final line assigned to it, the scribe has returned to this space, and filled it with the text '-es ubi deus tuus', together with the appropriate music. The scribe omitted 'est' after 'ubi', and it has been added in the margin. This appears to have occurred because of a lack of forward planning by the scribe, and to have been dictated by the layout of the manuscript, rather than because the scribe remembered the text incorrectly.

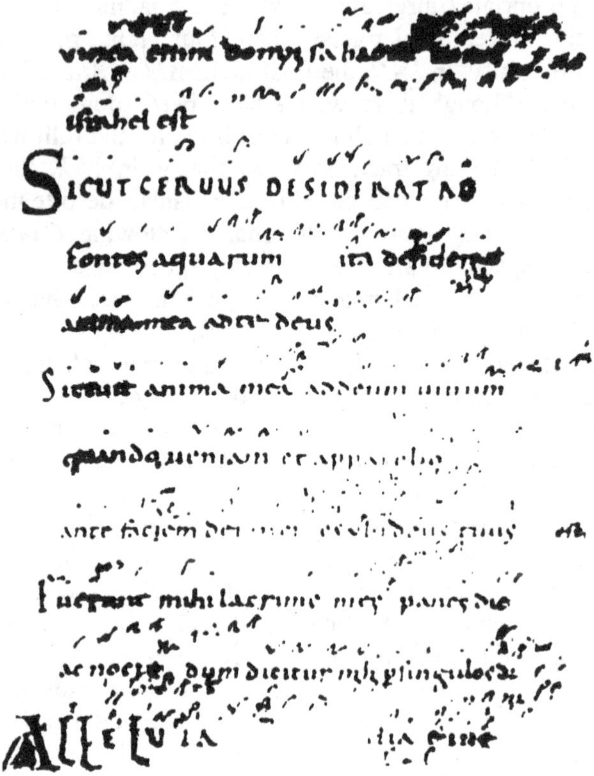

Example **5.9**

The final melisma is not the only melisma to be abbreviated. In a few manuscripts, the ***D2*** melisma is not fully articulated.[10] On most occasions, this is because insufficient space has been left to articulate the whole melisma. However, in *ROG1*, the *Sicut 7* melisma ends after kikhg, and the *Beatus uir 7* melisma ends after kikhg kkhg, even though there is plenty of space remaining (Example **5.10**). The same circumstance arises in *GAL2*, where the *Beatus uir* melisma ends after kikhg kkhg, despite there being plenty of room.

[10] *MOG4, ROG1, GAL2, TYR, YRX* and *PAS2.*

Beatus uir 7

Example **5.10**

The examples above demonstrate that the final melisma of the tracts and the ***D2*** melisma were recognised as standard patterns by some scribes. However, it is possible to demonstrate more widely that the equivalence of the same patterns in different tracts was recognised by at least one medieval scribe. The notation of the eighth-mode tracts in *DIJ1* is particularly informative about the way in which these chants were understood, partly because, unlike liturgical sources, the eighth-mode tracts are copied together as a group, but also because of the notational peculiarities of the manuscript.[11] *DIJ1* is notated both with neumes and a-p letter notation. Space was left for both notations, and it is generally agreed that both were fundamental to the design of the manuscript. However, not every phrase is fully notated with letters as well as neumes. It was unnecessary fully to notate standard phrase shapes on their third or fourth occurrence in a few folios. One might expect there to be progressively less notation through this group of tracts but this is not entirely the case, as the following table makes clear:

Tracts in the order of a mixed Gradual	Tracts in the order of the Dijon Tonary	% of neumes notated with letters
9	*Ad te leuaui*	95
2	*Nunc dimittis*	100
6	*Commouisti*	94
10	*Sepe*	86
1	*Qui regis*	100
5	*De profundis*	21
4	*Beatus uir*	4
7	*Iubilate*	33
3	*Desiderium*	93
11	*Cantemus*	57
12	*Vinea*	0
8	*Laudate*	0

[11] A full fascimile of the relevant folios in *DIJ1* may be found in Appendix 4.

Qui regis and *Nunc dimittis* would be the first eighth-mode tracts to be notated in a mixed Gradual and are completely notated with both letters and neumes in *DIJ1*. *Desiderium* would be the third eighth-mode tract to appear and it is completely notated except for the letters at the end of the final melisma, which had been notated eight times already on the previous five openings. However, the fourth tract in the liturgical order, *Beatus uir*, has very little letter notation. In *DIJ1*, there are factors other than the liturgical order affecting the extent to which the chants are notated with both letters and neumes.

The first tract in *DIJ1*, *Ad te leuaui*, is completely notated except for two occurrences of the ***D2*** melisma. The letter scribe begins the melisma kikhg, but the following letters kkgf ghgf are not consistent with the usual shape of the melisma found elsewhere in the tradition (usually kkhg higf). It may be that the exemplar had the wrong pitches here, or that the Dijon scribe went wrong. In either case, the scribe was then uncertain about how to finish the melisma. It is probable that his exemplar, if it also had letter notation, would not have articulated the shapes of this melisma fully. *Ad te leuaui* is the ninth tract one would expect to find in a mixed Gradual, and phrase ***D2*** would already have appeared twice in *Qui regis*, twice in *Nunc dimittis*, once in *Beatus uir* and twice in *Qui seminant* (although this tract does not appear in *DIJ1*).

The third tract in *DIJ1*, *Commouisti*, is completely notated except for the letters of the final melisma, which has already been fully articulated twice in the manuscript. The fourth tract, *Sepe*, is completely notated except for the final melisma and the ***D2*** melisma, which has been fully notated once in *Sepe*, once in *Nunc dimittis*, and twice (incompletely and 'incorrectly') in *Ad te leuaui*. These tracts are mostly notated fully with both letter notation and neumes because they are the first of the eighth-mode tracts to be notated in this source. *Qui regis* and *Nunc dimittis*, which also appear in this early group, are fully notated, probably because they appear early in the liturgical year, and would have been fully notated in the exemplar.

The following tracts are not as fully notated. *De profundis* appears to have been very well known to the scribe, perhaps because of its secondary function within the Mass for the Dead. The first phrase is only notated to the gkkl rise, even though the following melodic patterns are peculiar to this tract, and the pitches cannot be supplied from elsewhere in the repertory. Within this phrase, gf*i*hg is supplied, to anchor the pitch before the well-known phrase ***B*** cadence. The beginning of the following phrase, which follows an outline peculiar to two phrases in this tract, both beginning 'domine', is not fully notated.

The next phrase is ***D1***. Although this is the first occasion on which the phrase is used in the Tonary, the pitches of the opening articulation are not specified here. Neither are they supplied in any other tracts that use the melodic shape, including *Beatus uir*, which would appear before *De profundis* in a liturgically ordered source. The reason for this is not that the pitches were so well known that it was not considered necessary to supply them. On the contrary, the Cluniac manuscripts have varying pitch outlines in this context, and individual manuscripts are not internally consistent, as was demonstrated in Chapter 2 above. It is probable that the uncertainty surrounding the choice of pitches for this rise prevented the scribe from fully notating the melodic pattern.

The unusual kl g on 'aures' in the following phrase is supplied, followed by complete notation for the rest of the phrase, and for the following phrase, which has unique shapes. The beginning of the ***D1*** melisma at the end of the verse is also given letters, even though it was not given pitched notation in the previous verse, where it appeared for the first time in the manuscript. The unusual opening articulations of both of the following verses are supplied. The lack of letter notation for phrases not previously notated but common in the repertory, and the addition of letter notation from 'fiant' at points where the shapes are unusual, indicate that this piece was extremely familiar to those involved in copying *DIJ1*. They felt no need at any stage in the copying and correcting process to supply these irrecoverable pitches.[12]

The following tract, *Beatus uir*, has letter notation only for the beginning of the first verse, to identify the starting pitches. The rest of the tract is not notated with letters. The following tract, *Iubilate*, is treated in exactly the same way until the beginning of the new folio, where 'sci-' is anchored with an f, and the unique phrase, 'Ipse fecit nos et non ipsi nos', is almost entirely lettered.

This is followed by *Desiderium*, which is almost fully notated with letters, either because of its position in the exemplar, or because it uses several unusual phrase shapes. *Cantemus* follows on the same folio and has a great deal of notation, despite appearing late in the group, consisting largely of phrases that have already been notated fully, and being among the last eighth-mode tracts in the liturgical year, sung at the Easter Vigil. Having started with *Desiderium,* the letter scribe appears to have continued to fill in the pitches on this page, omitting the letter notation at the cadence points. The final phrase concludes on a new folio, and has no letters at all. There are no letters in either of the remaining tracts. The letter scribe may have been distracted by another task, or it may have been a conscious omission since all of the phrases in these tracts have been used before in the

[12] On corrections in *DIJ1*, see Hansen, F., *H159 Montpellier: Tonary of St. Bénigne of Dijon* (Copenhagen, 1974), 25* and 28*–33*.

Tonary.

The scribe of the eighth-mode tracts in *DIJ1*, therefore, was not mechanically copying an exemplar. He was aware of the standard melody shapes, and tended not to copy them out with letter notation as well as neumes when they had already appeared several times. Some melodic patterns were so well known to the scribe that letter notation is never supplied (for example, in *De profundis 1* and *De profundis 3*), or were so uncertain that he did not wish to commit himself to a particular interpretation (for example, the beginning of ***D1***). *DIJ1* is of particular use in exploring the extent to which standard phrases were recognised as equivalent, both because of the peculiarities of its notation and because the tracts were copied as a group, presumably in a short space of time.

The Medieval Understanding of the Genre: Theory, the Eighth Mode, and the Eighth-Mode Tracts

The eighth-mode tracts were composed as a melodic group, but not as a group of 'eighth-mode' chants. Their composition predated the adoption in the West by the late-eighth century of the eight-mode system, derived from the Byzantine system of *echoi* or melody types. The Saint-Riquier Tonary, which dates from this time, includes the earliest evidence that all Mass Proper chants in the Gregorian repertory were expected to belong to a system of eight tones, and these tones appear to have been understood as melody types. This Tonary contains text incipits of Mass Proper chants, organised according to mode. Unfortunately the descriptions of modes six to eight do not survive.[13] The earliest extant Carolingian music treatises date from the ninth century, and Aurelian of Réôme's description of the eight tones in his *Musica disciplina* concentrates on the psalm tones and the conjunction of the antiphon with an appropriate psalm verse.[14] He also writes that the offertories belong to the eight-tone system. These do not have any *differentiae*, and the linking of each of these chants with a tone does not appear to have served any practical function. The earliest practical source using the eight modes as a system for organising antiphons is the

[13] Huglo, M., *Les Tonaires: Inventaire, Analyse, Comparaison* (Paris, 1971), 25–6.

[14] *WP*, 456-458. This is generally cited as the earliest surviving Carolingian musical treatise, but opinion is still divided on when it was written. Recent work by Jane Bellingham (*The Development of Musical Thought in the Medieval West from Late Antiquity to the Mid-Ninth Century* (DPhil thesis, University of Oxford, 1998)) supports Gushee's date of c840 ('The *Musica Disciplina* of Aurelian of Réôme, a Critical Text and Commentary' (PhD, Yale University, 1963)).

ninth-century Metz Tonary.[15] It was not until the latter part of the ninth century that the eight tones were defined according to pitch content. Boethius' term for the different scale types, *modus*, gradually came into use instead of *tonus* to describe different classes of Gregorian chant, leaving the term *tonus* free to describe the interval of a whole tone.[16]

Rather than being composed within eight melody types in the Byzantine manner, Western chants appear to have been composed within melody types associated with particular genres, and were later assigned to the eight modes.[17] The matching of chants to modes led to some striking anomalies. Eva Rungwald has identified a group of antiphons composed within the same melody type that are divided between two different modes, the first and the third.[18] Much parchment was devoted to the problems of assigning chants to modes, and representing them diastematically.[19] That the eight-mode system was a recent theoretical construct was recognised by medieval writers, for whom the description of four modes extended to eight (to differentiate between chants with different tessituras) is a commonplace.[20]

Because the eighth-mode tracts are sung *in directum*, there was no need to define their mode in order to assign an appropriate psalm tone for a verse. However, they may have been assigned to the eighth mode early on, in order to anchor where the semitones and tones lie. As the eighth-mode tracts were not composed as eighth-mode chants, the relationship between these chants and modal theory is of particular interest. One would not expect the abstract ninth-century Carolingian discipline of music theory to prescribe rules for the composition of specific types of chants,[21] but one

[15] Lipphardt, W., 'Der karolingische Tonar von Metz', *Liturgiewissenschaftliche Quellen und Forschungen* 43 (Münster-Westfalen, 1965).

[16] *WP*, 459–460. In *De musica* (c1100), John Cotton reverted to the previous usage of *tonus*, and *modus* was used about a century later in the theoretical description of rhythm. See Atkinson, C., 'Johannes Afflighemensis as a Historian of Mode', in J. Szendrei and D. Hiley (eds.), *Laborare Fratres in Unum: Festschrift László Dobszay* (Hildesheim and Zurich, 1995), 1–10.

[17] There are several theories about the 'tonal' system within which Western chant was constructed. J. Claire, in 'Les Répertoires Liturgiques Latins avant l'Octoéchos. I. L'Office Férial Romano-Franc', *EG* 15 (1975), posits a system based on three 'cordes-mères', which developed into the melodic state of the written sources. F. Hansen has put forward a construction based on pentatonic scales in *The Grammar of Gregorian Tonality* (Copenhagen, 1979). More recently, E. Nowacki has hypothesised that the structure of the Old Roman repertory might be based on the interval of a third (in *CP: Visegrad 1998*, forthcoming).

[18] *CP: Visegrad 1998*, forthcoming.

[19] See Atkinson, C, 'From 'Vitium' to 'Tonus acquisitus': on the Evolution of the Notational Matrix of Medieval Chant', in *CP: Tihany*, 181–97.

[20] See Atkinson, 'Johannes Afflighemensis as a Historian of Mode', op. cit.

[21] 'Chapters 15 and 16 [of Guido d'Arezzo's *Micrologus*, c1030] constitute the first theory of melodic writing in the West.' Palisca, introduction to Guido's *Micrologus* in Babb, W.,

might expect to find descriptions of the characteristics of different types of chant. There are general references by medieval theorists to the eighth-mode tracts, usually in the context of liturgical discussion, but there do not appear to be specific references to their modal assignment and melodic character.[22]

There was, however, an awareness of the modal context of these chants, as may be seen in the earliest Graduals. *CHA1*, for example, has modal indications (VIII) next to each verse of the eighth-mode tracts, showing that they were known as eighth-mode chants by the late ninth century. The eighth-mode tracts do not appear in any of the early tonaries discussed by Huglo in *Les Tonaires,*[23] other than *DIJ1* in which they are labelled simply as 'Tetrardus'.

Once theorists began to describe the modes in terms of octave species, the eighth-mode was consistently assigned the range from c to l with the final on g,[24] and the tenor of simple eighth-mode psalm tones was identified as k.[25] These observations accurately describe the structural notes of the eighth-mode tracts, but are not specifically connected with them in the treatises. There is other evidence suggesting that g was the final and that k was considered to be the secondary tone of the mode. Medieval theorists describe and give examples of three kinds of intonation formulae, and Bailey suggests that these might have been used as internal vocal preludes by the singers.[26] Two of these types of formulae will be discussed below. Here it suffices to mention the 'noeane' formulae, which served to identify the character of the modes. These formulae were included in the earliest Tonaries and were an integral part of the eight-mode system as it developed. They have a g-k-g outline (Example **5.11**).[27]

Palisca, C. and Planchart, A., *Hucbald, Guido and John on Music* (New Haven Conn., 1978), 54. See also 71–4.

22 I have searched the *TML* database, without any success.

23 Huglo, M., *Les Tonaires: Inventaire, Analyse, Comparaison* (Paris, 1971).

24 For example, in Hucbald's *De Musica*. Gerbert, *Scriptores* (Sankt-Blasien, 1784), 121; Babb *et al.*, op. cit., 44.

25 For example, Johannes [Affligemensis] *De Musica*, ed. J. Smits van Waesberghe (Rome, 1950) = *CSM* 1, 82–3; Babb *et al*, op. cit., 118.

26 Bailey, T., *The Intonation Formulas of Western Chant* (Toronto, 1974), 16.

27 'Both NOEANE and Echemata made it easier for the singers to have fixed in their ears the position of the half-tone steps of the scale.' (Raasted, J., 'The "Laetantis Adverbia" of Aurelian's Greek Informant', in *Aspects de la Musique Liturgique au Moyen Age: Actes des Colloques de Royaument de 1986, 1987 et 1988*, ed. C. Meyer (Paris, 1991), 56–66; 58). See also Huglo, M., 'Les Formules d'Intonations "Noeane Noeagis" en Orient et en Occident', in the same volume; 44–53.

Bailey, *The Intonation Formulas of Western Chant*, 57

1.
2.
3.
4.
5.
6.
7.
8.
9.
10.
11.

Example 5.11

In the early Graduals, the recitation in phrase ***E*** of the eighth-mode tracts is on i, but by the later sources it had risen to k, which is compatible with this theoretical definition of the eighth mode.[28] The rise of the upper important note to k altered various other melodic patterns too, such as the ik/kk beginning of phrase ***B1***. The early manuscripts recite on i, mostly with ik or k on the last syllable (except *GAL2*, which remains on i). By the late tenth century, the theoretical consideration appears to have taken effect in the Saint-Denis/Noyon sphere, where recitation is on k. Later manuscripts from all areas except Aquitaine and Benevento have recitation on k. Use of i rather than k in the Aquitanian and Beneventan eighth-mode tracts may be a local inflection, or it may be a vestige of an older tradition.[29] Despite reciting on k, *ROP* and *IRI* have i on the last syllable, indicating perhaps the enduring attraction of the rising inflection at the end of the recitation passage. *LAV* and *BRE* are inconsistent, having a mixture of recitation on i, recitation on k, or recitation on one and then the other in the same phrase. The scribe of *LAV* in particular appears carefully to have written down the way in which an individual performed these phrases, without applying a consistent rule (see Example **2.1**, p. 33). *LAV* illustrates the conflict between theory and practice at the beginning of the eleventh century.

We have other evidence that certain manuscripts were compiled with an awareness of the conflicts between the practical repertory and music theory, and it is possible to identify 'correction' in some Graduals to bring them into line with contemporary modal theory. Stuart has shown that the compilers of *YRX* reformed the versions of several chants to 'conform to certain developments in musical theory of the eleventh century'.[30] He identifies *YRX*, and to a lesser extent, *BEN5* and *TOU*, as being affected by such reforms, but his examples show that *ALB* and *DIJ1* do not make such theoretically inspired revisions. Within the eighth-mode tracts, the versions

[28] The recitation on three notes g, i, and k within the eighth-mode tracts is taken as proof of the 'évolution modale' by Jean Claire and his followers. For example: 'Une modalité archaïque basée sur trois cordes-mères seulement a existé et reste visible dans les pièces les plus anciennes de l'*Office pascal*, c'est-à-dire les cantiques' (Cullin, O., 'L'*Office de Pâques* Comme Miroir du Chant Grégorien: du Concept Liturgique à la Réalisation Musicale', *Analyse Musicale* (1990), 19–25; 20–21). Kainzbauer, not in the French 'school', identified this change and cited it as evidence of corruption in later manuscript sources in 'Der Tractus Tetrardus – eine centologische Untersuchung', *Beiträge zur Gregorianik* 11 (Regensburg, 1991) 1-132; 23–8.

[29] In a study of two Easter processional antiphons, C. Roederer has hypothesised that recitation on i instead of k in chants on g is a local Aquitanian characteristic. However, in the examples she cites, i/k is a secondary reciting tone, the primary one being l. (Roederer, C., 'Can we Identify an Aquitanian Chant Style?', *JAMS* 27 (1974), 75–99; 95–6).

[30] Stuart, N., 'Melodic "Corrections" in an Eleventh Century Gradual (Paris, B. N., lat. 903)', *JPMMS* 2, (1979) 2–10; 3.

of the chants in the three Aquitanian sources and the Beneventan sources are extremely close. The lack of differentiation between *ALB* and these other manuscripts suggests that it was not necessary to revise the eighth-mode tracts to conform with musical theory.

Many chants are quite different in the Old Roman and Gregorian traditions, and attempts to compare them in the manner undertaken in this study would be fruitless. However, the traditions were related at the time when the Roman chant was adopted in Francia. Although there is no direct evidence, it is possible that some differences were caused by Gregorian revisions to make the chants fit the eight-mode system. 'L'uniformisation de l'octoéchos aura été un élément de fusion musicale pour donner un nouveau répertoire'.[31] Old Roman chant is not always characterised by the mode it is in, but Gregorian chant is.[32] The fact that the eighth-mode tracts are closely related in the two traditions might reflect the small amount of revision required to make these chants compatible with contemporary music theory.

The melodic movements of eighth-mode tracts are very close to those regarded by medieval theorists as representative of the mode. 'Noeane' formulae were often followed by 'neumas'. Bailey's examples of these contain turns of phrase characteristic of the eighth-mode tracts (see Example **5.12**, overleaf). The stepwise rise g-k can be seen in phrase ***E***. The high note l is generally approached by way of k – as, for example, in phrase ***A***. The cadence pattern is reminiscent of phrase ***C***.

The eighth-mode neumas as a whole are reminiscent of the final melisma of the eighth-mode tracts (see Example **5.13**).

Neumas

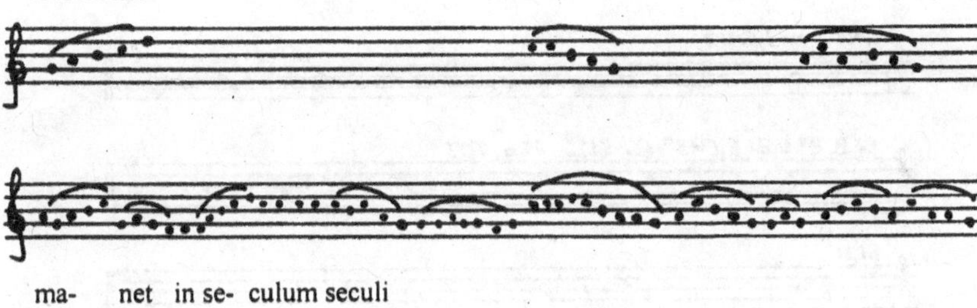

Beatus uir

Example **5.13**

[31] Claire, op. cit., 128.

[32] Stäblein, B., 'Die Gesänge des altrömischen Graduale Vat. La. 5319: Einführung', in *Monumenta Monodica Medii Aevi* 2 (1970), 38.

Bailey, *The Intonation Formulas of Western Chant*, 77

Example 5.12

A third type of formula used a text which incorporated the number of the mode concerned, for example, 'Primum querite regnum dei' for the first. Different compilers use different musical phrases in their formulae, which are said by medieval commentators to embody the essential characteristics of the mode. They also were often followed by 'neumas'. Bailey suggests that such patterns are often close to antiphon melodies. The formulae for mode eight given by Bailey (see Example **5.14**) outline f-k-g and do not appear to be close to the tracts, except for the fhk pattern.

Bailey, *The Intonation Formulas of Western Chant*, 90

Example **5.14**

However, in *De Musica*, John Cotton gives an 'Octo sunt beatitudines' pattern similar to the melismas of the eighth-mode tracts as well as showing the usual range of the eighth-mode tracts and the importance of g and k (see Example **5.15**).

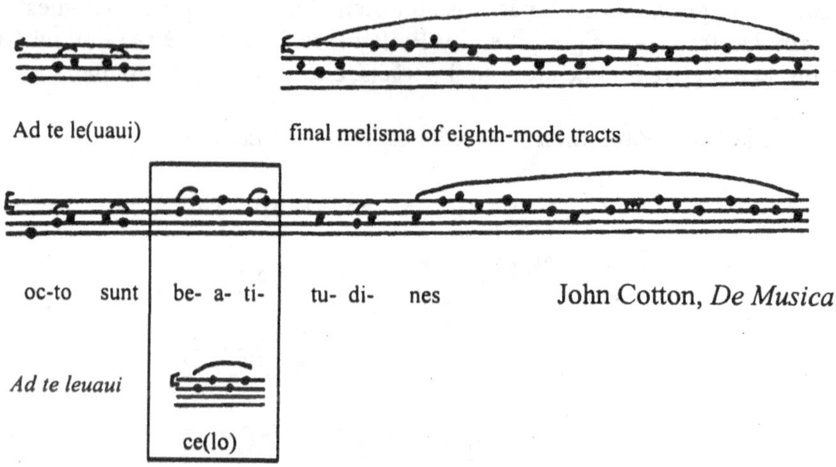

Example **5.15**

John Cotton may have used an eighth-mode tract as his model for showing the characteristic melody patterns of the mode.[33]

Conclusions

The standard phrases were known and treated as such by scribes, who notated them with consistent patterns of neumes and sometimes omitted the ends of the familiar ***D2*** and ***F*** melismas. The scribe of *DIJ1* omitted the letter notation of many phrases when these had already been fully notated in the manuscript. Some significant variants in isolated manuscripts demonstrate a continuing understanding of the construction of the genre, while some are purely scribal slips. Knowledge of the structure of the eighth-mode tracts appears to have been part of the cantor's art, even after neumatic notation had developed.

The fact that the eighth-mode tracts were eighth-mode chants was known by scribes, theorists, and presumably also cantors, at least from the ninth century. Their melodic shapes are so typical of the eighth mode that

[33] *CSM* 1, 86. Variants are given on page 89.

one type of intonation formula is remarkably close to the final phrase of the eighth-mode tracts, and John Cotton appears to have used an eighth-mode tract as his model when devising an 'Octo sunt beatitudines' formula. The rise from i to k within the phrase ***E*** recitation may be a response to developments in modal theory. The isolation of this change, and the close relationship between the Gregorian and Old Roman repertories may indicate that these chants needed little revision in order to conform to the theoretical concept of the eighth mode, as it developed from the ninth century onwards.

Chapter 6
The Medieval Understanding of the Eighth-Mode Tracts II: Tract Composition in the Tenth and Eleventh Centuries

Introduction

In the previous chapter, a greater knowledge of the medieval understanding of the eighth-mode tracts was gained by examining both medieval theory and the way in which the core repertory is notated in the written sources. This chapter examines a third kind of evidence: some manuscripts, dating from the tenth century and later, contain eighth-mode tracts other than those in the core repertory.[1] The manner in which these eighth-mode tracts are constructed is a reliable indication of the way in which their composers understood the genre.[2]

Non-standard eighth-mode tracts appear only in manuscripts from certain areas, chiefly Aquitaine, Benevento, and Italy.[3] Some chants appear only in one of these regions; some are common to two or more. The geographical connections between Benevento and Italy are self-evident. That non-standard tracts appear in Aquitanian manuscripts is also unsurprising, given the geographical proximity of Aquitaine and Benevento, and the ease of communication by sea. As was described in Chapter 2, manuscripts from these two regions also have very similar

[1] There is an extensive index of such eighth-mode tracts, including the manuscripts in which they can be found, in Cullin, O, *Le Trait dans les Répertoires Vieux Romain et Grégorien: Un Témoin de la Psalmodie sans Refrain* (PhD, University of Paris, Sorbonne, 1990), vol. III, 417ff. This index is not wholly correct. For example, although *IRI* is included in this index, *Nunc Dimittis* is not identified as appearing in the source. *Quomodo in me*, the continuation of *Aue Maria* in *LAV*, is not identified at all. There may be similar errors in the descriptions of manuscripts I have not seen. However, as Cullin had access to the extensive microfilm archive at Solesmes, the sample may be assumed to be representative.

[2] Non-standard second-mode tracts also appear in manuscripts dating from the tenth century and later. Cullin's index indicates that these are found in manuscripts originating from all over Western Europe. Detailed consideration of these chants is beyond the scope of this study.

[3] In this chapter, 'Italy' will consistently be used to refer to Northern and Central Italy.

variants in Mass Proper chants. One chant, *Nunc dimittis*, appears also in a group of manuscripts from Normandy, Ireland and England. The possible circumstances under which this chant was adopted in Northern Europe will be discussed in more detail below.

It has not been possible, within the limitations of this study, to investigate more than a handful of the manuscripts in which the non-standard eighth-mode tracts are found; nor has it been possible to study all of the non-standard tracts identified by Cullin.[4] Aquitaine is represented here by *ALB, TOU* and *YRX*.[5] Benevento is represented by *BEN1, BEN5* and *RAG*.[6] Italy is represented only by *BRE* and *LAV*.[7] Although these two

---

[4] I have not been able to study *Aue uirgo*, which appears in *BEN7*, *Aduiua nos*, which appears in *BEN3* and without music in *LAV*, *Clamauerunt*, which appears in *VEC1, VEC2,* and *VEC3*, or *O Judea*, which appears in *NOR*.

[5] Cullin has identified several other Aquitanian manuscripts containing non-standard eighth-mode tracts. These are: *NAR* (Paris, BN lat. 780, an eleventh- or twelfth-century Gradual from Narbonne; *GR* IV, 94), *AKI2* (Madrid, Palacio Nacional 429, a late twelfth-century Missal, copied from an Aquitanian manuscript for use in Castille; *GR* IV, 67), *MIL1* (Madrid, Acad. de la Hist. 51, an eleventh- or twelfth-century Gradual from St. Millan in Aquitaine; *GR* IV, 67), and *MIL2* (Madrid, Acad. de la Hist. 18, an early twelfth-century Gradual from St. Millan in Aquitaine; *GR* IV, 66).

[6] Cullin has identified several other Beneventan manuscripts containing non-standard eighth-mode tracts. These are: *PLO* (Montecassino, NN540, a eleventh- or twelfth-century Missal written at Montecassino, and used at Plombariola; *GR* IV, 74), *BEN6* (Benevento, Bibl. Cap. V. 19-20, a twelfth-century combined Breviary and Missal from Benevento; *GR* IV, 32), *BEN7* (Benevento, Bibl. Cap. VI.35, a early twelfth-century Gradual from Benevento; *GR* IV, 32), *CAS1* (Rome, Bibl. Vat. lat. 6082, an early twelfth-century Missal from Montecassino; *GR* IV, 125), *CAS2* (Montecassino, NN546, a twelfth- or thirteenth-century Gradual from Montecassino; *GR* IV, 74), and *BEN3* (Benevento, Bibl. Cap.VI.39, a late eleventh-century Gradual from Benevento, which lacks the folios before Easter Monday and has many other lacunae, and is therefore not rich in eighth-mode tracts; *GR* IV, 33).

[7] Cullin has identified several other manuscripts from Northern and Central Italy containing non-standard eighth-mode tracts. These are: *NOR* (Rome, Bibl. Vallicell. C.52, a eleventh- or twelfth-century Gradual from Norcia; *GR* IV, 123; see also Sironi, M., *Il Graduale Ms. Vallicelliana C52: Studio storico-liturgico e musicologico* (Tesi diploma, U. Degli studi di Pavia (Scuola di Paleografia e filologia musicale), 1992-93)), *ITN1* (Rome, Bibl. Vat. Rossi 231, a twelfth-century Gradual from Northern Italy; *GR* IV, 128), *IVR1* (Ivrea, Bibl. Cap. 60, a mid-eleventh century Gradual from Pavia; *GR* IV, 54), *MON4* (Monza, Bibl. Cap. c. 13/76, an eleventh-century Gradual from Monza; *GR* IV, 76), *MON1* (Monza, Bibl. Cap. c. 12/75, an early eleventh-century Gradual from Monza; *GR* IV, 76), *VEC1* (Vercelli, Bibl. Cap. 161, a late eleventh-century Gradual from Vercelli; *GR* IV, 149), *VEC2* (Vercelli, Bibl. Cap. 146, an early twelfth-century Gradual from Vercelli; *GR* IV, 149), *VEC3* (Vercelli, Bibl. Cap. 162, a twelfth-century Gradual from Vercelli; *GR* IV, 149), *COM2* (Verceilli, Bibl. Cap. 186, an eleventh- or twelfth-century Gradual from Como, *GR* IV, 149-150), *LUC1* (Lucca, Bibl. Cap. 606, an early eleventh-century Missal from Lucca; *GR* IV, 65), *VER1-VER2* (Verona, Bibl. Cap. CV, an eleventh- or twelfth-century Missal from Verona; *GR* IV, 151), *SUB* (Rome, Bibl. Vat. Lat. 4770, a tenth or eleventh-century Missal, perhaps from Subiaco), *BOB3* (Turin, Bibl. Naz. F.IV.18, a

manuscripts are notated with neumes rather than pitched notation, it is almost always possible to reconstruct the melodies of their non-standard eighth-mode tracts by comparing the neumes with those used in each of the standard phrases of the core repertory.[8]

Before analysing these chants in order to decide how the genre was understood by their composers, it is necessary first to ascertain when they were composed. The fact that these eighth-mode tracts do not appear in the early unnotated manuscripts published in *AMS* indicates that they were not included in the repertory of Roman chant adopted in Francia in the eighth century. This is supported by the fact that the few early Sacramentaries containing chant cues do not include any of these chants,[9] and also by the fact that they do not appear in any of the early notated Graduals.

The Old Roman manuscripts provide final confirmation that these chants were not part of the eighth-century Roman tradition. Only *ORC* contains any eighth-mode tracts apart from those in the core repertory, and the texts of these three chants, *Effuderunt, Adducentur*, and *Nunc dimittis*, are also used to provide the texts for Gregorian eighth-mode tracts found in Beneventan manuscripts. It takes only a cursory inspection of the facsimiles of these tracts given in Appendix 5 (pp. 385–7), and the accompanying tables, to show that these tracts are not composed in a manner compatible with the construction of the core repertory. They are clearly in the Old Roman style, but phrases are often centonised from familiar melodic patterns taken out of their usual formal contexts. It is not necessary to describe all of these tracts in exhaustive detail; *Adducentur* will serve as an example.

'Adducentur' has the opening material of ***A2*** seen also in *Ad te leuaui*, although fg on '-ua-' is replaced by gh at the beginning of '-tur', and the cadence is ghihghg rather than ihihghg. Instead of having the usual material for the rest of the phrase, 'regi uirgines' begins with the rise to l which is characteristic of the final accent in ***A1***. The following figure, hkihgh, is an eighth-mode commonplace; 'uir-' has the rise to l once more; and '-gines' has the end of the phrase ***B*** cadence, although these figures are not usually split between two syllables. The following phrase, 'proxime eius' begins with the hghkihg articulation generally used to begin phrase ***D***, and '-me' repeats the ***A2*** cadence seen at the end of '(Adducen)tur'. The following

twelfth-century Gradual from Bobbio; *GR* IV, 146), and *FOR* (Modena, Bibl. Cap. O. I. 7, an eleventh- or twelfth-century Gradual from Forlimpopuli; *GR* IV, 72).

[8] A similar reconstruction has been undertaken of *Adnunciatum est*, a second-mode tract that appears in *BRE*. See Barezzani, M., *La Notazione Neumatica di un Codice Bresciano (Secolo XI)* (Cremona, 1981), 121–75.

[9] None of the text incipits appears in Deshusses, J. and Darragon, B., *Concordances et Tableaux pour l'Etude des Grands Sacramentaires* (Fribourg, 1982).

word, 'eius', has the low melisma familiar from ***A2***, followed by the closing figures of phrase ***D***. The final phrase in the verse, 'afferentur tibi', begins with the ***B2*** rise. The material on '-rentur' is reminiscent of the fall in the ***B3*** internal melisma, omitting hgf. The patterns at the beginning of 'ti-' are also used in the ***B3*** internal melisma, but the hkihihkih figure is seen in the ***E3*** melisma, and the following patterns are derived from the phrase ***F*** melisma. The hihg hihg figures at the beginning of '-bi' are familiar from the beginning of the phrase ***F*** melisma. The patterns that usually follow have already been used on 'ti-' and are omitted here, but the rest of the phrase ***F*** melisma is given in full. The second verse of *Adducentur* begins with a g-l rise reminiscent of that seen in Ad5 (***E3***) followed by patterns from the ***B3*** melisma, taken out of their usual order. A high recitation familiar from the middle of ***B3*** is followed by material from phrase ***C2***, omitting the first pitch f. The usual rise hki is replaced by hghk; the following figure is omitted, but the usual phrase ***C*** cadence is used. The final phrase begins with the ***B2*** rise followed once again by material related to the ***B3*** fall, although lklm is not the usual way of approaching this material. The syllables 'in tem-' have the usual opening of phrase ***F***, but '-plum' has the phrase ***C*** cadence, and although 'regis domino' continues with phrase ***F*** material, much of the melisma is missing.

Adducentur is built up of melodic patterns familiar from the core repertory of eighth-mode tracts, with a particular emphasis on the internal ***B3*** melisma and phrase ***F***, but the melodic patterns are used out of their usual formal contexts. The melodies of *Nunc dimittis* and *Effuderunt* have been similarly centonised with little reference to the construction of other chants in the genre. Further, textual connections with familiar tracts in the core repertory have not been followed. For example, in *Effuderunt*, the texts 'in circuitu' and 'hierusalem' do not use the material found in *Qui confidunt* with the same texts. In *Adducentur*, 'in leticia' does not use the material found in *Iubilate* with the same text, and although 'et exultatione' does use phrase ***C*** material, it is not the same as that found in *Qui seminant* with the same text. In *Nunc dimittis*, 'omnium populorum' does not use the ***D1*** shapes found at 'omnes populi' in *Laudate*, even though both occur at the end of a verse, and 'oculi mei' does not use the ***A2*** material found in *Ad te leuaui* with the text 'oculos meos'.

These tracts appear to have been composed by people who did not know the repertory sufficiently well to respond to clearly defined textual cues, and who did not understand, or who did not wish to follow, the formal and melodic principles on which the core repertory of eighth-mode tracts is constructed. The idea that a cantor might consciously write an eighth-mode tract incompatible with what he understood to be the construction of the genre appears to be foreign to medieval ecclesiastical culture, where stability and continuity were held in such high regard. It is possible that the Old Roman repertory was learned by rote in the eleventh century, which might account for the ignorance displayed by the composer(s) of the construction of the genre. However, it seems unlikely that a cantor trained in the oral Old Roman tradition would compose eighth-mode tracts without instinctively responding to textual cues and thereby displaying knowledge of other chants in the repertory.

Because these chants do not appear in *ORJ* or *ORP*, it would appear that they were not widely known in the Old Roman tradition. It has already been suggested that Montecassinese monks were directly involved in the writing of *ORC*.[10] This is supported by the known historical connections between Montecassino and the church of St. Cecilia in Trastevere, by the close melodic relationship between the Easter Vigil tracts found in *ORC* and those in Beneventan manuscripts, and by the fact that *ORC*, unlike the other two Old Roman manuscripts, contains about thirty Gregorian alleluia verses.[11] It seems probable that when the Feasts of Holy Innocents, St. Agatha, and the Purification were reached by those notating the tradition, the Montecassinese overseers discovered that, unlike their local Beneventan tradition, the Roman liturgy did not include tracts for these occasions. The Montecassinese monks therefore dictated new chants with the texts they knew to be appropriate for the occasions, but in the Old Roman melodic idiom. Although purely hypothetical, this scenario explains the composers' apparent lack of understanding of the formal outlines of the genre. Non-standard eighth-mode tracts were not an integral part of the Roman liturgy.

The Texts of the Non-Standard Eighth-Mode Tracts

The non-standard eighth-mode tracts based on psalmic texts do not derive their texts from the Psalter in the same manner as the core repertory of eighth-mode tracts. The texts of the other non-standard eighth-mode tracts are either derived from parts of the Bible not usually associated with eighth-mode tracts, or they are not biblical at all.

Apart from the three Easter Vigil canticle-tracts, all eighth-mode tracts in the core repertory are composed on psalm texts. The texts are almost always drawn from consecutive verses, starting at the beginning of the psalm, and it has been argued that this is an indication of the relative

---

[10] See pp. 50–51, above.

[11] Huglo, M., 'Le Chant 'Vieux-Romain': Liste des Manuscrits et Témoins Indirects,' *Sacris Erudiri*, VI (1954), 96–124 ; 99, and Connolly, T., 'The *Graduale* of S. Cecilia in Trastevere and the Old Roman Tradition', *JAMS* (1975), 413–58; 414.

antiquity of the chants.[12] Six of the non-standard eighth-mode tracts also have psalmic texts, but these are not drawn from consecutive verses starting at the beginnings of psalms, as the table below indicates.

Tract	Textual origin	Liturgical context	Regions in which the tract is found
Adducentur	Psalm 44: 15–16	St. Agatha, 21/1	It/Ben
Effuderunt	Psalm 78: 3, 10b	Holy Innocents 28/12	It/Ben/Aqu
Conuertere	Psalm 114: 7–9	Mass for the Dead	It
Posuisti	Psalm 20: 4–5	St. Vincent, 22/1	It/Ben
Sancti et iusti	Psalm 32: 1, 12	Faustina and Giovita 16/2	It

The texts of some non-standard eighth-mode tracts derive from books of the Bible not usually associated with the provision of texts for chants. The text of *Iustorum anime* comes from Wisdom 3: 1. *Nunc dimittis* is based on the canticle text that forms part of the biblical narrative of the Purification (Luke 2: 29–32), the Feast to which it is attached. Unlike the Easter Vigil canticles, which are sung in a dramatic context, this chant is sung within the usual liturgical context of the Mass. *Aue Maria* is based on elements of the narrative of the Annunciation, found in Luke 1: 28, 42, and is attached to that Feast. *LAV* has a continuation of this tract, *Quomodo in me*, the text of which derives from Luke 1: 34–5, 38. The beginning of the text of *Venite* is part of the parable of the sheep and the goats (Matthew 25: 34), the beginning of the second verse is derived from 1 Corinthians 2: 9, and the text at the beginning of the last verse is derived from 1 Peter 5: 4.

The texts of some non-standard eighth-mode tracts are not derived from the Bible at all. *In columbe,* sung at the Feast of the Translation of St. Benedict's relics from Montecassino to Fleury, is freely adapted from the *Dialogues* of St. Gregory, noted by Gyug.[13] In *LAV*, the text continues after the end of the tract, and space has been left between the words as if the scribe expected music to be added. This text is derived from later in the *Dialogues*.[14] This is a similar technique to that found in the same

[12] Cullin, O., 'Pour une Reévaluation des Formes Littéraires de la Psalmodie sans Refrain: Canticum et Tractus', *Modus* 3 (Lisbon, 1989–92), 41–8; 41.

[13] Gyug, R., *Missale Ragusinum: The Missal of Dubrovnik* (Toronto, 1990), 171.

[14] De Vogüé, A. (ed.), *Grégoire le Grand: Dialogues*, 3 vols. (Paris, 1978), vol. 2, 236–8: lines 15–26. Passages in bold form the tract text; passages in brackets are in the tract text, but not in the *Dialogues*. 'Cumque uir Domini Benedictus, adhuc quiescentibus fratribus, instans uigiliis, nocturnae orationis tempora praeuenisset, ad fenestram stans et omnipotentem Dominum deprecans, subito **intempesta noctis hora** respiciens, **uidit** fusam [sanctus benedictus fusam desuper] **lucem,** desuper **cunctas noctis tenebras exfugasse** tantoque splendore clarascere, ut diem uinceret lux illa, quae inter tenebras

manuscript on the Feast of the Annunciation, four days later. On both occasions, the texts added to the end of the tracts may be found later in the narratives of the Feasts. The text of *Benedicamus patrem*, found only in *BEN5*, is a special doxology used at the end of the Canticle of Daniel on Good Friday and Holy Saturday in the Milanese rite.[15] If it had also been used in the Beneventan rite, this might explain the retention of the text in a Beneventan manuscript. However, I have been unable to trace uses of this text in either the Gregorian or the Beneventan traditions. *Absolue domine*, attached to Masses for the Dead in many Italian manuscripts, is a prayer.

The Liturgical Contexts of the Non-Standard Eighth-Mode Tracts

In the core repertory, eighth-mode tracts are sung on the four Ember Saturdays of the liturgical year, and on some Sundays and some Saints days during Lent. The date of Easter varies by a factor of five weeks, between 22 March and 25 April and the moveable Feasts associated with Easter vary by the same factor. Medieval scribes notated tracts instead of alleluias from Septuagesima, which can be as early as 18 January or as late as 1 March. There was some uncertainty concerning whether Saints days at the extremes of this period, which are only occasionally in Lent, should be assigned tracts or alleluias. Some manuscripts give one or both of these types of chants, or even more than one of each, while others do not attach either tracts or alleluias to these liturgically ambiguous Feasts.

Four Saints days to which non-standard eighth-mode tracts are attached fall in the early part of the Lenten period:

Tract	Liturgical context	Regions in which the tract is found	Textual origin
Effuderunt	Fabian and Sebastian, 20/1	*ALB* only	psalm
Adducentur	St. Agatha, 21/1	Ben/It	psalm
Posuisti	St. Vincent, 22/1	Ben/It	psalm
Nunc dimittis	Purification, 2/2	Ben/It/Aqu/ Northern	relevant canticle: Luke 2

It is not necessary to make an exhaustive survey of the chants found on

radiasset. **Mira** autem ualde **res in hac speculatione secuta est**, quia, sicut post ipse narrauit, omnis etiam [nam totus] **mundus**, uelut sub uno solis radio collectus, **ante oculos eius adductus est**.'

[15] See Bailey, T., *The Ambrosian Cantus* (Ottawa, 1987), 46–7.

these Feasts, but some examples will serve to illustrate the situation. On the Feast of Saints Fabian and Sebastian, *LAN, YRX* and *CHA1* have an alleluia, *Sancti tui domine*, and *KLO1* has an alleluia, *Fulgebunt*. On the Feast of St. Vincent, *LAN* and *YRX* have an alleluia, *Beatus uir qui timet*, but *KLO1* has no alleluia or tract. On the Feast of St. Agatha, *YRX* has an alleluia, *Specie tua*, but *KLO1* and *LAN* have no alleluia or tract. On the Feast of the Purification, *CHA1* has no alleluia or tract, *KLO1* has the second-mode tract *Audi filia*, and *LAN* has an alleluia, *Adducentur*.[16]

Two Feasts fall at the end of the Lenten period and their celebration would often have been eclipsed by Holy Week and by other Paschaltide ceremonies:

Tract	Liturgical context	Regions in which the tract is found	Textual origin
In columbe	Translation of St. Benedict, 21/3	Ben/It/Aqu	St. Gregory's *Dialogues*
Aue Maria	Annunciation, 25/3	Ben/It	Luke 1

As with the Feasts at the beginning of Lent, different manuscripts have different chants for these Feasts. For example, on the Translation of St. Benedict, *BEN1* and *TOU* have the eighth-mode tract *Desiderium,* and *SAB* and *ROP* have the second-mode tract *Domine non secundum*. *LAN* and *KLO1* do not have this Feast at all. On the Feast of the Annunciation, *LAN* has no alleluia or tract, *KLO1* has the eighth-mode tract *De profundis*, and *YRX* has a second-mode version of *Aue Maria.*

Three other Feasts of the Sanctorale have eighth-mode tracts attached to them. The first of these is the Mass of Holy Innocents on 28 December, to which *Effuderunt* is attached in many manuscripts from Aquitaine, Benevento, and Italy, and to which *Iustorum anime* is attached in *BRE*. 'The Gregorian Feast of the Holy Innocents does not fall in the prohibited period [i.e., in Lent], and the appearance of a Tract is a late anomaly not found in the earliest Gregorian books, and dates from a time when the

[16] The ambiguity surrounding the liturgy for this Feast is reflected in the diverse names given to it. See Moreton, M. B., *The Eighth-Century Gelasian Sacramentary: A Study in Tradition* (Oxford, 1976), 122–3. In Rome, Vat. Reg. 316 (the 'Old Gelasian' Sacramentary) the rubric is *Orationes in Purificatione Sanctae Mariae.* In the eighth-century Gelasian Sacramentaries it is referred to as the Feast of St. Simeon. In the 'Hadrianum' Sacramentary (an early type of Gregorian Sacramentary), the Feast is referred to as *Ypopanti*, which is Greek for 'meeting' and refers to the meeting of Simeon and Anna with Mary and Jesus. The Feast is also referred to as Candlemas.

"sorrowful" nature of the Tract seemed appropriate to the occasion.'[17] A description of the Feast as penitential is given by Amalarius of Metz in *De ecclesiasticis officiis*.[18] Ulrich of Zell wrote in the 1079–80 Cluniac *Consuetudines* that no alleluia should be sung on the Feast of Holy Innocents. '[It] might be that a second gradual was to be sung instead of an alleluia, such as occurred in the Paris liturgy.'[19] *Effuderunt* is identified as 'Tractus de innocentibus' in Regino of Prüm's Tonary, written in about 901, when he was in Trier.[20] This Feast was regarded as a penitential memorial of the Slaughter of the Innocents in the Middle Ages, and the use of a tract or second gradual rather than an alleluia is clearly indicated by contemporary commentators. This appears to be the only Feast for which the use of a non-standard eighth-mode tract is prescribed outside musical sources.

An eighth-mode tract is also attached to the Brescian Feast of Faustina and Giovita, two local Saints. [21] As the Feast falls on 16 February, well within the Lenten period, one would expect a tract to be assigned to it in any manuscript including the Feast. However, the celebration of this Feast is very localised.[22] The third Feast of the Sanctorale to which a new eighth-mode tract is attached is the Transfiguration on 6 August. Only *BEN5* attaches an eighth-mode tract, *Benedicamus*, to this Feast, in the midst of a particularly lavish celebration including two alleluias and a sequence as well as the tract.

One other non-standard eighth-mode tract occurs in Lent. In Aquitanian manuscripts, *Venite* is attached to Feria II after the first Sunday of Quadragesima; on this day most manuscripts have a simple ferial Mass without a tract. Non-standard eighth-mode tracts are also attached to the

---

[17] Bailey, T., *The Ambrosian Cantus* (Ottawa, 1987), 13, fn 4. See also Dudley, M., '*Natalis Innocentium*: The Holy Innocents in Liturgy and Drama', *Studies in Church History* (Ecclesiastical History Society: Oxford, 1994), 233–42; 236–7.

[18] Hanssens, J. (ed.), *Amalarii Episcopi Opera Liturgica Omnia,* 3 vols. (Vatican City, 1948–50), vol. 2; 193 and 519–25 (cited by Dudley, op. cit., 237).

[19] Hiley, D., 'Cluny, Sequences and Tropes', in C. Leonardi and E. Menesto (eds.), *La Tradizione dei Tropi Liturgici* (Spoleto, 1990), 125–38; 131.

[20] see *WP*, 328 and 458–9. This tract does not appear to have been part of the repertory in the Trier region: only the fifteen eighth-mode tracts of the core repertory appear in the Echternach Sacramentary. See *Echternacher Sakramentar und Antiphonar: Vollständige Facsimile-Ausgabe in Originalformat der Handscrift 1946... aus dem Besitz der Hessischen Landes- und Hochschulbibliothek Darmstadt, Codices Selecti* 74 (Graz, 1982).

[21] See Barezzani, *La Notazione Neumatica*, op. cit., 25–6.

[22] The tract appears in *BRE* and in *VEC1-VEC2*, a manuscript from Vercelli, which is quite close to Brescia. It also appears in *ERA1* (Munich, BR, 14083, an eleventh-century Sequentiary-Cantatorium from Ratisbon [Regensburg]; see *GR* II, 80), but I have not been able to ascertain whether or not the liturgical context is the same in this manuscript. These saints are also culted (very rarely) in Francia.

Rites for the Dead. *De profundis* is most commonly prescribed for the Mass for the Dead, but *Conuertere* appears in *LAV* and *NUR*, *Aduiua nos* appears in *LAV* and *BEN3*, and *Absolue domine* appears in many Italian manuscripts.

Non-standard eighth-mode tracts are thus attached to Feasts whose Mass Proper chants were not firmly fixed in the mid-eighth-century Roman liturgy, mostly because they fall at the extremes of Lent. In itself, this does not constitute decisive evidence that these chants were composed later than the core repertory; they might have been composed at the same time, but adopted only in certain centres. However, combined with the absence of evidence that any of these chants existed before the late ninth or early tenth century, the lack of genuinely Old Roman concordances, and the fact that the texts of these chants are clearly differentiated from those of the core repertory, the marginal nature of the Feasts to which they are attached makes it clear that they are later compositions. These 'new' eighth-mode tracts are therefore an ideal body of evidence to use in the exploration of how the genre was understood by cantors after the spread of the authoritative 'Roman' chant in Western Europe.

The Melodies of the Non-Standard Eighth-Mode Tracts

Introduction

Adducentur, Aue Maria, In columbe, and Posuisti These tracts appear mostly in Beneventan manuscripts from the tenth or eleventh century onwards.[23] One version of *Nunc dimittis* appears only in Beneventan manuscripts from the tenth century onwards, and *Benedicamus patrem* appears only in *BEN5*. *Absolue, Conuertere, Iustorum anime*, and *Sancti et iusti* appear in Italian manuscripts from the eleventh century onwards. *Effuderunt* was composed in Benevento, Italy or Aquitaine by the tenth century, and the mainstream version of *Nunc dimittis* appears in Italian, Aquitanian and Northern manuscripts from the eleventh century onwards. *Venite benedicti* and *In columbe* appear in Aquitanian manuscripts from the eleventh century onwards. The appearance of these chants only in manuscripts from the tenth or eleventh century at the earliest suggests that they were not composed much before this time. However, *Effuderunt* is mentioned as early as 901 (see p. 186), and the accidents of manuscript survival mean that these tracts may have been composed well before their earliest appearance in an extant source. No attempt is made here to

[23] Facsimiles of the individual chants may be found in Appendix 5.

reconstruct a compositional chronology of these chants.

Some new eighth-mode tracts appear in manuscripts from only one region. It is assumed here that they were composed in that region, partly because minor differences in compositional procedure between the regions may be identified. Through identification of these differences, the possible origins of chants that appear in more than one region may be deduced. However, the chief interest here is in the compositional procedures found in all regions, and in the relationship between these procedures and the construction of the core repertory.

The Beneventan/Italian In columbe Two of the new eighth-mode tracts are contrafacts – that is, re-textings of previously existing eighth-mode tract melodies. A version of *In columbe* found in Beneventan and some Italian manuscripts from the eleventh century onwards is simply a re-texting of the tract *Commouisti*, as is illustrated by the table below.[24] The tract also appears in *ALB*, attached to the second Mass on the Feast of the Translation of St. Benedict, and this is clear evidence that there was direct contact between Italy or Benevento and Aquitaine.

Tract text	Phrase	Tract text	Phrase
Commouisti domine terram	***A2***	In columbe specie uidit	***A2***
et conturbasti eam	***D4***	beatus benedictus	***D4***
Sana contritiones eius	***B3***	Celsa omnipotens ethera	***B3***
quia mota est	***D5***	et animam sancte	***D5***
Ut fugiant a facie arcus	***B3***	Scholastice mox nunciat illud	***B3***
ut liberentur	***C3***	fratribus deo	***C4***
electi tui	***F***	gratias egit	***F***

At first sight, it appears to have been the fortuitous similarity of the lengths of the texts that made it possible to join the new text to the existing melody without making any changes. However, even the most cursory examination reveals that the adaptation has taken place with little or no regard for the sense of the text. For example, 'In columbe specie uidit beatus benedictus' is divided against the sense of the text, as is 'deo gratias egit', and 'sancte scholastice' is split, not only between two musical phrases, but also between two verses.

The Italian or Beneventan version of *In columbe* is no more than a

[24] This appears in *BEN5*, *PLO*, *CAS1*, *CAS2*, *BEN6* and *BEN7* from Benevento, and in *LAV*, *FOR* and *SUB* from Italy. In the manuscripts I have seen, *In columbe* appears as part of the second or third Mass attached to the Feast of the Translation of St. Benedict.

clumsily executed re-texting of a pre-existing tract. To make a contrafact in this manner is completely alien to oral processes of composition and transmission, as has been observed by Levy.[25] However, such a literal transcription, ignoring the sense and the structure of the new text, does not occur in any other new eighth-mode tract.

Aquitanian Tracts

The Aquitanian In columbe The second contrafact is also on the text *In columbe*, and appears in Aquitanian manuscripts.[26] However, unlike the Italian or Beneventan version, the adaptation has been undertaken not only with an understanding of the syntax of the text, but also with an understanding of how the model chant melody should be altered to fit the new text in an appropriate manner.

Tract text	Phrase	Tract text	Phrase
Qui confidunt in dómino	***A1***	In columbe spécie	***A1***
sícut mons síon	***B3***	uídit beátus	***B3***
non commouebitur	***E3***	benedictus	***E3-C***
in eternum	***B2***		
qui habitat in Ierúsalem	***C1***	celsa omnipotens éthera[27]	***C1***
Montes	***D5***	Et animam	***D5***
in circuitu eius	***B2***	sancte scholastice	***B2***
et dominus	***C'***		
in circuitu populi sui	***B4***		
éx hoc núnc	***C3***	móx ut núnciat ire fratribus[28]	***C1***
et usque in seculum	***F***	deo gratias egit[29]	***F***

In columbe has less text than the model, *Qui confidunt*, so it does not use all of the melodic phrases available. The accent patterns of these two texts are often similar (marked ´ in the table above), and this may have determined which phrases would be omitted. The third phrase ends with the ***E3*** cadence in *Qui confidunt*, but with the phrase ***C*** cadence in *In columbe*. As was described in Chapter 3, it appears that *Qui confidunt* was

[25] Levy, K., 'Gregorian Chant and Oral Transmission', in G. Boone (ed.), *Essays on Medieval Music in Honor of David G. Hughes: Isham Library Papers* 4 (Cambridge, Mass., 1995), 277-86; 283.

[26] *ALB* and *YRX*.

[27] 'hetera' in *ALB*.

[28] 'mox nunciat illud fratribus' in *ALB*.

[29] 'deo gratias' in *ALB*.

constructed with an extra verse division at 'non commouebitur' although this is not reflected in the written versions of the chant (see pp. 114–15). The 'second' verse consists of ***E3***, which suggests a verse beginning; ***B2***, which is generally used second in verses other than the first; and ***C***, which one would expect third in the verse. In contrast, the first verse of *In columbe* consists of only four elements, spread over the phrases which constitute the first two 'verses' in *Qui confidunt*. The use of phrase ***E*** in the middle of this verse would be inappropriate, and this is perhaps why the phrase ***C*** cadence has been substituted. Phrase ***C*** is used to conclude the verse, as in *Qui confidunt*. *Qui confidunt 5–6* is the only phrase in group ***C1*** where there is an antepenultimate accent. Instead of using ***C4*** shapes, '-rúsalem' has the shapes normally associated with the last three syllables, and the usual connection of certain melodic movements with text accents is ignored. The equivalent word in *In columbe*, 'éthera', also has an antepenultimate accent, and also uses the normal melodic shapes for the last three syllables.

The second phrase of the next verse uses phrase ***B2*** in both tracts, but 'sancte scholástice' has an antepenultimate accent whereas all the other phrases in group ***B2*** have a penultimate accent. The ilmkkh figure is split between '-lásti-', as ilmkk h, retaining the association of the figure with the penultimate syllable and also with the last accent of the phrase. The next two phrases in *Qui confidunt* are omitted in *In columbe* because of the lack of text available. The textual parallel between 'móx ut núnc(iat)' and 'éx hoc núnc' may have stabilised the use of phrase ***C*** although the penultimate phrase in *Qui confidunt* uses ***C3***, because there is very little text, and *In columbe* has sufficient text to articulate the usual ***C1***. Once again, the antepenultimate accent is ignored.

The composer of the Aquitanian version of *In columbe* adapted the model in a knowledgeable way, unlike the mechanical joining of text and music in the Beneventan or Italian version. He adapted a three-verse to a two-verse structure by altering the cadence of the third phrase and omitting the fourth phrase, which is strongly identified as the second phrase in a verse. He altered one phrase ('sancte scholastice') to fit a different accentuation pattern, and another ('mox ut nunciat ire fratribus') to give the appropriate version of phrase ***C*** for the number of syllables. Although ***C1*** is used instead of ***C4*** on the two occasions where phrase ***C*** ends with an antepenultimate accent, this occurs also in the model, *Qui confidunt*.

Venite One other new eighth-mode tract appears only in Aquitanian manuscripts. *Venite benedicti* appears in *YRX* and *ALB*.[30]

[30] It also appears in *NAR*, *AKI2* and *TOU*.

Tract text	Phrase
Venite benedicti	***A1***
patris mei	***B1***
percipite regnum	***C3***
quod uobis preparatum est	'Phrase before ***D***'
ab origine mundi	***D2***
Quem[31] nec oculus uidit nec auris audiuit	***E1***
nec in cor hominis ascendit	'Phrase before ***D***'/ ***C1***
hoc quod preparatum est uobis	***D2***
Percipietis immarcescibiles[32] eterne	***B3-E1***
glorie coronas[33]	'Phrase before ***D***'/ beginning of ***F***
et fulgebitis sicut sol in seculorum secula/ in regno meo	continuation of ***F***

The first phrase has seven syllables and therefore uses ***A1***. The second phrase uses ***B1***, as one would expect for the second phrase in the tract, with the opening articulations usually associated with there being four syllables. In the third phrase, the gfgh and ghkik figures are joined together, as one would expect in phrase ***C*** with insufficient syllables to articulate the figures in the usual way. The verse ends with ***D2***.

All of these phrases follow the structures found in the core repertory of eighth-mode tracts. However, to have a five-part first verse in an eighth-mode tract only otherwise occurs in *Qui confidunt*. The beginning of the fourth phrase of the verse is newly composed, but the cadence in *ALB* and *YRX* is familiar from ***E3***. *TOU* starts the phrase with the gh recitation seen *ALB* and *YRX*, but follows this with g hih gh ggf. These are patterns seen elsewhere in eighth-mode chants, but they constitute a decorated recitation on g rather than an independent phrase.

The second verse of *Venite* has three phrases. The first phrase uses ***E1***, although the first half-verse is not divided into two phrases. *YRX* continues with ***C1 D2***, which are the phrases one would expect for the second half-verse. Instead of ***C1***, *ALB* uses the same 'phrase before ***D***' seen in the previous verse. One manuscript has picked up on a localised and internal cue, while the other uses the more standard phrase. The final verse begins with a hybrid phrase. It begins like the final verse of *Qui regis*, with the ***B3*** melisma followed by recitation on k. However, instead of continuing into the phrase ***B*** cadence, 'eterne' has the ***E1*** melisma. This is followed by the

[31] 'Que' in *YRX*.
[32] 'immarcescibilem' in *YRX*.
[33] 'coronam' in *YRX*.

final phrase in *YRX*, but *ALB* uses the 'phrase before ***D***' instead of the opening articulations of the final phrase.

Conclusions Aquitanian composers of new eighth-mode tracts appear to have had a clear awareness of how text and melody should fit together within the genre, and this is particularly apparent in *In columbe*, where the model chant is sensitively adapted to the new verbal context. The composers generally used phrases appropriate to the formal context, in the version one would expect given the textual circumstances. There are some exceptions. In *In columbe*, ***C1*** is used with an antepenultimate accent, as in the model, *Qui confidunt*. In *In columbe* and *Venite*, hybrid phrases are used. In *In columbe*, this appears to be in order to avoid use of the ***E3*** cadence in the middle of a verse. In *Venite*, the phrase at the beginning of the final verse uses material generally associated with two different phrases, both appropriate for the beginning of a verse, although the ***E1*** cadence is used despite there being only one phrase in the verse-half. Phrase ***E1*** is also used when there is only one phrase in the verse-half in the second verse of *Venite*. This is seen in several other new eighth-mode tracts. In *Venite*, one phrase is newly invented. This phrase falls outside the usual syntax of the eighth-mode tracts and was not well known; different melodic shapes are used in *TOU*, and while it does not recur in *YRX*, it is used in all three verses in *ALB*.

Beneventan Tracts

Adducentur This chant appears in *BEN1*, *BEN5*, and in *RAG*.[34]

Tract text	Phrase
Adducentur regi uirgines	***A2***
proxime eius	***B5***
offerentur tibi	***D4***
In leticia	***D5***
et exultatione	***C2***
adducentur in templum regi domino	***F***

The chant begins with the version of ***A2*** found also in *Desiderium*. When tracts begin with phrase ***A2***, the first verse often ends with ***D4***, as here. However, the second phrase uses the version of ***B5*** found in *De profundis 6* even though the first phrase of the verse is complete. This is not a formal context in which ***B5*** is found in the core repertory. The second

[34] also *NOR, PLO, CAS1, CAS2.*

verse begins with ***D5***, used also at the beginning of the second verse of *Qui confidunt*. The second phrase, 'et exultatione', is linked textually with *Qui seminant 6* and *Iubilate 6*, and uses the same version of phrase ***C***. This tract uses an unexpected version of phrase ***B***, but is otherwise consistent with the construction of the core repertory. The textual cue in the penultimate phrase is responded to.

Benedicamus patrem This chant appears only in *BEN5*.

Tract text	Phrase
Benedicamus patrem	***A1***
et filium	***B1***
et sanctum	***C3***
spiritum	***D1***
Laudamus et superexaltemus	***E1***
eum	***C3***
in secula	***D2***
Benedicta sit sancta trinitas	***E1-3***
in secula	***C3***
seculorum amen	***F***

The text of the first verse is 'Benedicamus patrem et filium et sanctum spiritum'. The composer of the tract has given a new phrase to each item in the list, and has split 'et sanctum spiritum' between two musical phrases. This is not compatible with the usual way of dividing up a sentence into syntactical units. The verse is quadripartite rather than articulating the sense of the text in the usual way. The first two phrases use the normal simple versions of phrases for the beginning of a tract, although this tract uses the version of ***B1*** usually associated with there being three syllables, with kk on the extra syllable. The last two phrases use the expected phrases for the formal context, but in abbreviated forms because there is so little text available. It would have made more sense of the text to have phrase ***C4*** for the whole of 'et sanctum spiritum'.

The second verse begins with ***E1***, despite being the only phrase in the first verse-half. The text has not been divided before the object and prepositional phrase, giving a very long first phrase ('Laudamus et superexaltemus/ eum/ in secula'). As with the preceding verse, the musical phrases after the first one have so little text that the usual phrase shapes cannot necessarily be articulated. Although the final phrase of the verse has the usual ***D2*** shapes, there are only two syllables for the articulation of phrase ***C***. The first syllable has the pitches gh gf ghki khik, which is a composite of the usual phrase ***C*** shapes fhk i**gh gfg ghkik khik**, with the repeated notes usually associated with new syllables being omitted on this single syllable.

The third verse begins with phrase ***E*** but the end of the cadential melisma ikh hg is replaced by iki hihgh hg, which is similar to the cadence shape seen in ***E3***. As in the previous verses, the first phrase has the bulk of the available text attached to it. The second phrase begins ghgfg, which is a joining together of pitches from the middle of phrase ***C***, as in the previous verse. The following three syllables have the usual patterns for the end of phrase ***C***. The text for the final phrase is part of the same text unit as the previous phrase, 'in secula seculorum/ amen'. The text of *Benedicamus* is broken up into phrases according to completely different principles than are found in the core repertory, perhaps because the text of this doxology is completely unsuited to adaptation to the formal structure of an eighth-mode tract. The manner in which the standard phrases are adapted to the text available is not always compatible with that found in the core repertory, especially phrase ***C*** in the second and third verses.

Nunc dimittis An eighth-mode tract with this text appears in manuscripts from various regions, but the Beneventan version of the chant is different, both textually and musically, from that found elsewhere. The variant text, 'nunc dimittis domine seruum tuum' instead of 'nunc dimittis seruum tuum domine', is found in liturgical manuscripts right across Europe as the text for an antiphon and for the processional chant for the Feast of the Purification, but it has not been possible to confirm that this is an Old Latin variant.[35] The Beneventan version of *Nunc dimittis* appears in *BEN1* and *BEN5*.[36]

---

[35] *ORC* shares this textual variant, further supporting the contention that there was a direct link between the Old Roman version of this tract and Benevento. 'Nunc dimittis domine seruum tuum' appears in an antiphon (Lucca, Bibl. Cap., 601 [*PM* 9 (Solesmes, 1906), 350]; Worcester, Cathedral Library, F.160 [*PM* 12 (Solesmes, 1922), 272]; Oxford, Bod. Lib., Lat. Liturg. c.34 [Milanese Winter Gradual] and London, BL, Add. 34209 [Milanese Gradual]), in a great responsory (Worcester, Cathedral Library, F.160 [op. cit., 270]), and in the pre-Mass processions in London, BL, Add. 11862 (eleventh- or twelfth-century, Cologne), London, BL, Add. 38723 (thirteenth-century, Paris), *MUR3, NOY4, LAV, YRX* and *KLO1*.

The Vulgate word order, 'Nunc dimittis seruum tuum domine' is found in Jülicher, A. (ed.), *Italia: das Neue Testament in Altlateinischer Überlieferung* 3 vols. (second edition: Berlin, 1970–76); *Old Latin Biblical Texts* 7 vols. (Oxford, 1883–1923); and Scrivener, F. (ed.), *Bezae Codex Cantabrigiensis* [fifth-century Greek and Latin Gospels] (Cambridge, 1899). The Vulgate word order is also shared by various Psalters that include canticles (for example, London, BL, Arundel 155, an eleventh-century Roman Psalter altered to Gallican, and London, BL, Add. 37517, a tenth-century English Psalter).

[36] Also *PLO, BEN6, BEN1, CAS1*, and *CAS2*.

Tract text	Phrase
Nunc dimittis domine	***A1***
seruum tuum	***B1***
secundum uerbum tuum in pace	***C1***
Quia uiderunt oculi mei	***E1***
salutare tuum	***D2***
Quod parasti ante faciem omnium populorum	***B4-C***
Lumen ad reuelationem gentium	***E1***
et gloriam plebis tue israhel	***F***

The textual variant means that the first phrase consists of seven syllables, with 'domine' as the final word. This is a strong prompt to use ***A1***, which is followed here, as usual, by ***B1***. This is used in the version generally associated with there being three syllables, with k on the extra syllable. Tripartite verses usually end with phrase ***C***, as here. The melodic outline found here is completely different from that of the mainstream version, described below. The second verse begins with phrase ***E1***, even though this is not usually associated with bipartite verses; this is followed by ***D2***. The third verse consists of a single phrase. This begins with the opening articulations of ***B4***. The recitation on g is extended, and continues into the melodic shapes associated with the last three syllables in phrase ***C***, perhaps inspired by the rhyme with 'rectorum' (*Beatus uir 7*). The final verse begins with ***E1***, although one might have expected use of ***E3, B3,*** or ***B4*** at the beginning of a bipartite final verse. This tract twice uses ***E1*** in a bipartite verse, and the third verse consists of a single phrase. The second phrase uses an unexpected version of ***B1***.

Posuisti This chant appears in *BEN1* and *BEN5* as well as in other manuscripts, mainly from Benevento.[37]

Tract text	Phrase
Posuisti domine	***A1***
super caput eius	***B1***
coronam	***C3***
de lapide pretioso	***D2***
Vitam petiit et tribuisti ei	***E1-D4***
Longitudinem dierum	***E1***

[37] *NOR, PLO, CAS1, CAS2, BEN6, BEN7.*

in seculum seculi	***F***

The first phrase uses ***A1***, because it has seven syllables, and also because of the 'domine' cue. The second phrase uses ***B1***, but in the version usually associated with there being four syllables, with k kkk on the extra syllables. The third phrase, 'coronam', uses phrase ***C*** in exactly the same way as *Desiderium 8* ('coronam'). The following phrase in *Desiderium* ('de lapide pretioso') has the same text as the next phrase in *Posuisti*. *Desiderium 9* is the last phrase of the tract and therefore uses phrase ***F***. By using ***D2***, which has the same opening articulation as the final phrase, the composer of *Posuisti* has maintained the connection with *Desiderium*. The second verse of *Posuisti* consists of a single phrase. This begins with the phrase ***E*** intonation and recitation, and ends with the ***D4*** melisma. There is a textual connection with phrases in the core repertory that use this melisma: 'tribuisti ei'/ 'conturbasti eam' (*Commouisti 2*)/ 'fraudasti eum' (*Desiderium 4*). The third verse begins with ***E1***, despite being the only phrase in the verse-half. As in *Nunc dimittis*, ***E1*** is used in a bipartite verse, the second phrase uses an unexpected version of phrase ***B1***, and one verse consists of a single phrase. The general outline is compatible with that of tracts in the core repertory, and the textual connections with *Desiderium* have been followed.

Aue Maria (1) This chant appears in *BEN1* and *BEN5*. It appears in a different version in *LAV*, considered below. It appears also in *VEC*, but all other manuscripts in which it appears are Beneventan, suggesting strongly that it was a Beneventan composition.[38]

Tract text	Phrase
Aue Maria gratia plena	***A2***
dominus tecum	***D4***
Benedicta tu inter mulieres	***B4-D2***
Et benedictus	***C3***
fructus uentris tui	***F***

The tract begins with the phrases one would expect to see in a bipartite first verse. The second verse consists of a single phrase. It begins with ***B4*** material. On 'tu', there is an abrupt shift to a double articulation of the hghik ghggf figure associated with the beginning of ***D2***. The phrase goes straight into the ***D2*** melisma, omitting the middle of the phrase. The last

[38] *PLO, BEN6, BEN7, CAS1* and *CAS*.

verse begins with phrase ***C***, although this is not usually associated with the beginning of a verse. As in *Nunc dimittis* and *Posuisti*, one verse consists of a single phrase. The only phrase used out of the expected context is the penultimate phrase.

Conclusions Several compositional characteristics are common to this group of tracts. *Benedicamus domino, Nunc dimittis* and *Posuisti* all use ***B1*** in a version inappropriate for the number of syllables, with extra reciting notes on k. This occurs also in the Italian tract, *Conuertere*. In *Nunc dimittis, Aue Maria,* and *Posuisti,* there are verses consisting of a single phrase. All of these outline the elements one would expect to encounter in a full verse: *Nunc dimittis* has ***B4-C***; *Aue Maria* has ***B4-D2***; and *Posuisti* has ***E-D4***. ***E1*** appears alone in the first verse-half twice in *Nunc dimittis,* once in *Benedicamus domino*, and once in *Posuisti*, but also once in the Aquitanian tract, *Venite*, once in the version of *Aue Maria* found in *LAV*, and once in *Iustorum anime*. The widespread nature of this characteristic suggests that the association of ***E1*** with there being two phrases in the first verse-half was forgotten soon after the tradition was adopted in Francia. There are only two occasions when a phrase is used in a completely inappropriate context. In *Aue Maria*, phrase ***C*** is used to begin a verse, and in *Adducentur*, ***B5*** is used in the first verse although the first phrase is complete. The text of *Benedicamus* is unsuitable for adaptation to an eighth-mode tract, and it is broken up in a manner not encountered in the core repertory.

Italian Tracts

Aue Maria (2) Both Beneventan and Italian manuscripts have an eighth-mode tract with this text, but the version of the tract found in *LAV* is completely different from that found in the Beneventan manuscripts. As I have not been able to study *VEC*, the other Italian manuscript containing this chant, it has not been possible to ascertain whether or not this version was local to Bologna.

Tract text	Phrase
Aue Maria gratia plena	***A2***
dominus tecum	***D4***
Benedicta tu	***B4-B2***
inter mulieres	***D2***
Et benedictus	***C4***

fructus uentris tui	***F***
Quomodo in me fiet hoc	***E1- unique***
quia uirum non cognosco	***C1***
Spiritus sanctus superueniet in te	***B4***
et uirtus altissimi obumbrauit tibi	***D2 opening, then unique***
Ecce ancilla domini	***E1***
fiat mihi secundum uerbum tuum	***F***

The first and third verses are identical to those found in the Beneventan version. The second verse also begins with the ***B4*** opening on 'benedicta' but, unlike the Beneventan manuscripts, the single-phrase verse is avoided by use of the ***B2*** cadence on 'tu'. This is not a version of the cadence usually associated with a bipartite verse. It is followed by ***D2***, as in the Beneventan version. The avoidance of the single-phrase verse in *LAV* suggests that it is a characteristic of Beneventan composition.

In *LAV*, this tract is followed immediately by another eighth-mode tract, beginning 'Quomodo in me'. However, instead of beginning with phrase ***A***, the phrase appears to rise ghik followed by recitation on k. This is followed by neumes compatible with hkihg ghg gf, seen in phrase ***F***. These shapes are also seen on the second neume group on '(tu)or(um)' in *Effuderunt* in this manuscript. 'Fiet hoc' has a low recitation and a four-note figure, but it is not possible to identify the pitches with any certainty (fghg? ghih?). The second verse begins ***B4***, perhaps because of the assonance of 'in te' with *Ad te leuaui 10* '(do)mine'. The next phrase has the usual ***D2*** opening, with the rise fhk ornamented as fhikl. The melodic patterns after this are not compatible with the phrase shapes usually found in eighth-mode tracts. One interpretation might be that the neumes indicate hkig gh hghfgh gh ghkk kk, followed by the beginning of the ***D2*** melisma, but it is not possible to establish this with any degree of certainty. The final verse begins with ***E1***, even though it is a bipartite verse. Although the composer of *Quomodo in me* was clearly conversant with the melodic shapes associated with the eighth-mode tracts, the usual structures were not followed. To use the melodic patterns in the manner seen in the core repertory was either not a priority, or was no longer possible.

Absolue domine In direct contrast to *Quomodo in me*, *Absolue domine*, which also appears in *LAV*, uses compositional techniques that are completely consistent with those employed in the core repertory.[39]

[39] Also in *IVR, MON1, LUC1, VEC1, VEC2, VEC3, NOR*, and *BOB3*.

Tract text	Phrase
Absolue domine	***A1***
animas eorum	***B2***
ab omni uinculo delictorum	***C1***
Et gratia tua illis succurente	***B2***
mereantur euadere iudicium ultionis	***C1***
Et lucis eterne	***B2***
beatitudines perfrui	***F***

The use of ***A1*** in the first phrase is prompted both by the number of syllables and also by the word 'domine'. The second phrase uses ***B2***, perhaps prompted by the rhyme of 'eorum' with 'uiuum' and 'aquarum' in *Sicut*, and with 'eternum' in *Qui confidunt*. The last phrase of the verse uses ***C1***. The second and third verses begin with ***B2*** despite appearing in bipartite verses, perhaps prompted by the textual link with the two phrases in *Attende* and the two phrases in *Vinea* that also begin 'et' and use this phrase, even though it is not always formally appropriate. There may have been a further textual prompt to use ***B2*** for 'Et lucis eterne'; the connection between 'eterne' and 'eternum' in *Qui confidunt* is self-evident.

Sancti et iusti This chant appears in *BRE*.[40]

Tract text	Phrase
Sancti et iusti	***A2***
in domino gaudete	***D4***
Vos elegit deus	***E1***
in hereditatem sibi	***B1***
Ut oretis pro populo eius	***E3***
in loco isto	***F***

This eighth-mode is composed in a manner compatible with the techniques found in the core repertory. The first verse uses ***A2 D4***. These are the phrases one would expect in a bipartite first verse. The second verse consists of ***E1 B1***. The use of ***B1*** second and last in the verse is initially surprising, but there is a textual cue. The melody attached to 'iniquitatem sibi' in *Sepe* is exactly the same as that used here, and the similarities between the texts are self-evident. The third verse begins with ***E3***, as one would expect in a bipartite final verse.

[40] Also in *ERA2* and *VER1-VER2*.

Conuertere This eighth-mode tract appears in *LAV*.[41]

Tract text	Phrase
Conuertere anima eius	***A1***
in requiem tuam	***B1***
quia dominus	***C4***
bene fecit tibi	***D2***
Quia eripuit anima eius de morte	***E1***
oculos eius/meos	***E'***
a lacrimis	***C4***
pedes eius a lapsu	***D2***
Placebo domino	***E1***
in regione uiuorum	***B1-F***

The chant begins with phrase ***A1*** despite having nine syllables, and the second phrase uses the version of ***B1*** usually associated with there being three syllables, with recitation on k for the extra syllables. This technique is otherwise seen in Beneventan tracts. The third phrase begins with an ascent, possibly from g to k. The figures usually associated with the last two syllables of phrase ***C*** are split between the three syllables of 'dominus' because of the antepenultimate accent. The solution is similar to that found in other ***C4*** phrases but, on this occasion, the special cadential shape associated with words beginning 'domin-' is not found. The final phrase of the verse uses a normal ***D2***.

The first phrase of the second verse is a normal phrase ***E1***. The second phrase has only the text 'oculos eius'. In *LAV*, the correction 'meos' is written above. One might expect a connection with the melody attached to the same text in *Ad te leuaui*, which uses the complicated form of phrase ***A***. However, the melodic shapes instead suggest an abbreviated form of phrase ***E***. A low recitation (on gh and g?) is followed by neumes compatible with hghik kih instead of hghikih, and the ikh figure that usually follows in the phrase ***E*** melisma is omitted. *Iubilate 5*, *Beatus uir 9*, and *Beatus uir 5* end 'eius', and this may have provided a textual stimulus to use phrase ***E***. However, several phrases in group ***B2*** also end with the word 'eius'. It is not clear why phrase ***B2*** was not used here. The third phrase has four syllables with an antepenultimate accent, and uses the same abbreviated form of phrase ***C*** as was used in the previous verse. As with the previous verse, the final phrase is a straightforward phrase ***D2***. The first phrase of the last verse uses phrase ***E1*** although the extra repeated notes at the

[41] Also in *NOR*.

beginning of the melisma are usually seen in ***E2***. Phrase ***E1*** is usually followed by ***B***, and the usual opening figures of the final phrase are replaced by ***B1*** articulations, seen also on 'misericordi-' in La6, which has very similar vowels. A rise (ghki i?) leads straight into the final melisma.

Iustorum anime This tract appears in *BRE*.[42]

Tract text	Phrase
Iustorum anime	***A1***
in manu dei sunt	***C-B1***
et non tanget illos tormentum malicie	***C1***
Visi sunt oculi insipientium mori	***E1***
illi autem sunt in pace	***F***

The first phrase uses phrase ***A*** as there are six syllables. The second phrase has material consistent with the phrase ***C*** rise g ghki k, and 'dei sunt' has a variant version of ***B1*** similar to that seen in the same manuscript in *Vinea 2*, 'dilecto'. The usual shape is hki khk kkklhhg, but *BRE* has neumes compatible with hkh k hklhg in *Vinea 2* and k hk hklhg in this phrase. This is followed by hg and the usual phrase ***B*** cadence. The following phrase has a normal ***C1*** except that there is an antepenultimate accent and the usual joining of certain melodic patterns to accented syllables is ignored. The next verse begins with a normal ***E1***, even though there are only two phrases in the verse, and ends with phrase ***F***.

Conclusions *Absolue domine* and *Sancti et iusti* are constructed in a manner compatible with the construction of the core repertory. The composers' intimate knowledge of the core repertory of eighth-mode tracts is demonstrated by their reactions to textual cues. The version of *Aue Maria* found in *LAV* avoids the single-phrase verse, but is otherwise identical to the Beneventan version. However, the other eighth-mode tracts found in *LAV* and *BRE* are less close to the construction of the core repertory. ***E1*** is used alone in a verse-half, as in the Beneventan tracts. *Conuertere* has an unexpected version of phrase ***A*** and a version of phrase ***B1*** not usually associated with the number of syllables available. Although ***C4*** is used for the two phrases with antepenultimate accents, the textual cue of 'domin-' is not followed. In *Iustorum anime*, ***C1*** is used although there is an antepenultimate accent. There are three composite phrases, none of which outlines the expected material for the formal context: ***B4-B2*** at the beginning of a bipartite verse in *Aue Maria*; ***C-B1*** in the first verse of

[42] Also in *IVR1, MON1, MON4, VEC1, FOR, VEC2,* and *VEC3.*

Iustorum anime; and ***B1-F*** in the final verse of *Conuertere*. In *LAV*, an abbreviated version of phrase ***E*** is used out of the expected context in *Conuertere*, and unique material is used on two occasions in *Quomodo in me*. Although *Aue Maria, Iustorum anime* and *Conuertere* display a basic knowledge of the construction of the genre and of the phrase shapes to be used, they show less concern than *Absolue domine* or *Sancti et iusti* for the subtleties of joining text and music, and for the exact formal contexts in which phrases and melodic patterns are usually found in the genre.

Effuderunt

This tract is attached to the Feast of Holy Innocents in *YRX*,[43] in *BEN1* and *BEN5*,[44] and in *LAV*.[45] It appears on the Feast of Saints Fabian and Sebastian in *ALB*.

Tract text	Phrase
Effuderunt sanguinem sanctorum	***A2/ A2-E3***
uelut aquam in circuitu ierusalem	***D4***
Et non erat qui sepeliret	***E-D4-B3-D3-E-C***
Vindica domine sanguinem sanctorum	***B4***
tuorum	***unique***
qui effusus est super terram	***F***

The first phrase uses the version of ***A2*** found also in *Desiderium*. In the Aquitanian manuscripts, the cadence is that used in *Ad te leuaui 3*, with the text '(ser)vorum' (***E3***), and the textual connection is clear. The second phrase uses ***D4***, associated with first verses beginning ***A2***. Because there is more text in this phrase than usual in ***D4***, the recitation on g followed by hghik is repeated. The ***A2 D4*** pattern is found also in the Beneventan tracts *Adducentur* and *Aue Maria*, and in the Italian tract *Sancti et iusti*, although it is not common in the core repertory.

The second verse consists of a single phrase, in which fragments of eighth-mode tract phrases are combined, without making formal sense. It begins with the usual phrase ***E*** opening from g up to c. This is followed by a portion of the ***D4*** melisma used in the previous verse, and then by a fragment of the ***B3*** melisma. The syllable 'li-' has kklk, seen in the ***D3*** melisma, followed by the beginning of the phrase ***E1*** melisma, followed by kkhihf. The syllable '-ret' begins ghi hik, and the cadence pattern ihihghg

[43] It also appears in *NAR*.

[44] It also appears in *PLO, BEN6, CAS1* and *CAS2*.

[45] It also appears in *IVR1, LUC1, FOR, COM2* and *ITN1*.

is reminiscent of that seen in phrase ***C***. This verse consists of melodic patterns characteristic of the eighth-mode tracts, mostly used out of the usual context. Despite being composed of such disparate elements, this phrase appears in the same version in all the manuscripts that I have seen. Verses consisting of a single phrase occur also in three Beneventan tracts, although, on these occasions, the outline of the phrase follows the formal outline one might expect to see in a verse. On three occasions in Italian tracts, phrases are built up of eighth-mode movements taken out of context, and unique material is used twice in *Quomodo in me*.

The third verse of *Effuderunt* begins with ***B4***. Only *ALB* has the full melisma. All other manuscripts have the abbreviated version of the melisma seen in *BEN5* (see pp. 376–7). The following word, 'tuorum', is given a separate phrase rather than being attached to the rest of the text. This word is articulated in a different way in each region, with only the final cadence being the same in Italy, Benevento and Aquitaine, and this is derived from the end of the previous verse. The beginning and end of the phrase in the Aquitanian and Beneventan sources are equivalent, but the melismatic patterns in the Beneventan sources are replaced by kih in the Aquitanian manuscripts. In the absence of pitched, or even accurately heighted Italian manuscripts, *LAV* is untranscribable before the final cadence. In this manuscript, the opening shapes of the phrase appear to be attached to the previous syllable, '-rum', after the phrase ***B*** cadence. The version of *Effuderunt* found in a fragment from Chieti[46] further illustrates the instability of this phrase. The writing of the manuscript is Beneventan, but the notation is central Italian, perhaps indicating that the Beneventan and Italian traditions merged into one another at the limits of the Beneventan-influenced territory.[47] As in *LAV*, it is not possible to transcribe 'tuorum', and it is in yet another different version. It ends with the phrase ***B*** cadence, and the melismatic shapes before that are reminiscent of ***B5***. Freely composed phrases of this type are characteristic of new Italian tracts, and a freely composed phrase also occurs in the Aquitanian tract, *Venite*.

This tract, as well as *Quomodo in me, Iustorum anime, Absolue* and *Benedicamus* has the final melisma on the last accent rather than the last syllable. This characteristic is too isolated to give a firm idea of the origins of the chant, but the centonised nature of the single-phrase second verse and the unique phrase on 'tuorum' suggest that *Effuderunt* may be Italian in origin.

---

[46] See *PM* 14, Plate XLV.

[47] 'L'explication de ce curieux accomplement est chose aisée si l'on observe que Chieti se trouve exactement à la limite de la zone Bénéventaine. Il n'est donc pas étonnant qu'aient pu concourir à la transcription du manuscrit deux scribes, dont l'un était accoutumé à la minuscule bénéventaine, l'autre à la notation de l'Italie Centrale' (*PM* 14, 251).

Effuderunt was clearly not well known in the eleventh century. In the Aquitanian manuscripts, the first phrase ends in a different way from that of the Italian and Beneventan manuscripts, and a textual cue appears to have been followed. The phrase on 'tuorum' appears in completely different versions in the three regions, and the version in the Chieti fragment is different once again. However, the consistent manner in which the single-phrase verse appears in all manuscripts containing this chant indicates that there was indeed a single version of this tract in circulation. The fact that a centonised phrase could appear so consistently indicates strongly that the tract circulated in written form. If a chant such as this was transmitted only with the aid of memory, unique phrases like 'tuorum' would presumably have been standardised to fit with the genre, and centonised phrases would be more likely to use the complete phrase with whose material they began.

Nunc Dimittis – The Mainstream Version

This tract appears in *LAV*, *BRE* and *NOV2*,[48] in *ALB*, *TOU* and *YRX*,[49] and in *IRI*, *SAR3*,[50] *ROG1* and *DIJ1*. Three groups of manuscripts are clearly differentiated by melodic variants, but these groups are not compatible with the geographical origins of the manuscripts.

Tract text	Phrase
Nunc dimittis seruum tuum domine	***A2'***
secundum uerbum tuum in pace	***D2***
Quia uiderunt oculi mei	***E1***
salutare tuum	***B1/ D2***
Quod parasti	***E2***
ante faciem omnium populorum	***D3***
Lumen	***A2***
ad reuelationem gentium	***B1/D2/ part of B4***
et gloriam	***A2***
plebis tue israhel	***F***

[48] Also *IVR1*, *MON1* and *MON4*. *NOV2* dates from c1050-1100 and is from 'Abbeys of St. Peter, Breme-Novalese (Lombardy)' (VD, 105). It is in eleventh-century North Italian diastematic notation with some Notker letters (see *GR* II, 88). Although this is a Tropary-Sequentiary, it contains many pieces from the Mass Proper, including two eighth-mode tracts, *Nunc dimittis* and *Beatus uir*.

[49] Also *MIL1* and *MIL2*.

[50] Oxford, Bod. Lib., Rawl. Lit. d.3, a late thirteenth-century Gradual from England. It is missing the Temporale before Easter Sunday, and is therefore of limited interest in a study of the tracts. The Sanctorale is extant and begins on f. 75v.

The first phrase of the mainstream version of *Nunc dimittis* begins with a rise defg, and then follows the opening articulations of *Sepe* with the cadence found on '-ui' in *Ad te leuaui*. It combines the opening parts of two phrases rather than using the usual ***A2*** cadence. This is followed by ***D2***. The second verse begins with ***E1***, although this is not usually associated with bipartite verses. This is followed by 'salutare tuum', which appears in two distinct versions (see Appendix 5). The Northern and Italian manuscripts have ***B1***, out of the usual context. The Aquitanian sources (*ALB, TOU* and *YRX*) use ***D2***. The same phrase was used in the previous verse at the words 'secundum uerbum tuum in pace'. This has acted as a textual prompt, as well as making formal sense. *NOV2* begins the phrase like the Aquitanian manuscripts, but misses out the pitches hkhig before the final syllable. In the previous verse, these pitches were attached to the syllable 'in'. There is no syllable to attach them to here, which may be why they have been omitted.

The third verse also begins with a version of phrase ***E*** not usually associated with bipartite verses. This is followed by ***D3***. The fourth verse begins with the ***A2*** material also used to begin verses in *Sepe* ('Dicat nunc') and *Ad te leuaui* ('Ita'). Although 'Lumen' is not directly linked textually to these parallel phrases, it is of a similar length. The second phrase of the last verse appears in three distinct versions, which fall into three groups of manuscripts (see pp. 380–81). The Northern manuscripts and *BRE* use ***D2***, although this phrase occurs in the middle of the verse. The Aquitanian manuscripts and *NOV2* instead have the opening articulations of ***B4***, usually associated with the beginning of the final verse of a tract. This is equally inappropriate for the second phrase of the verse. *LAV* has ***B1***, although this is usually associated with the first rather than the last verse of a tract. None of the manuscripts has material appropriate for the formal context.

There is sufficient similarity between the versions of *Nunc dimittis* found in the three groups of sources for it to be clear that it was not independently composed in each of these regions. However, local variants have emerged, and highlight the fact that the new eighth-mode tracts were not firmly established. This is particularly apparent in the Italian manuscripts. *NOV2* is allied with the Aquitanian manuscripts, *BRE* is allied with the Northern manuscripts, and *LAV* is independent.

It is not possible, on musical grounds, to decide where *Nunc dimittis* originated. The chant could have travelled to northern centres from either Aquitaine or Italy, and not necessarily from the region in which it originated. There were many connections between Aquitaine and Cluny. 'Abbots Odo, Aymard, Maiol and Odilo all came from southern families, and the south-west expansion of the Cluniac Order (especially during the tenth century) provided regular contacts and personal exchanges with Aquitaine.'[51] However, although the tract appears in the Cluniac sources *DIJ1* and *ROG1*, it does not appear in *CLU1, LEW, SAB,* or *ROP*, and was therefore not general to the Cluniac liturgical tradition. This suggests that the route of transmission might instead have been via Italy, as does the fact that the version of the chant found in Northern manuscripts is very closely related to that found in *BRE*.

As a child, William of Volpiano was placed in the monastery of Lucedio near Vercelli in Northern Italy. He travelled to Cluny after meeting Mayeul, one of Cluny's great abbots. In 989, William was sent to bring Benedictine reform to the Abbey of St. Bénigne in Dijon. As Abbot of St. Bénigne, he worked to extend the Benedictine revival in his homeland of North Italy, founding among other houses the Piedmontese Abbey of Fruttuaria. This became the central house from which Cluniac reform was worked in Lombardy, and the reform was aided by the close ties between Cluny and the Northern Italian nobility. In the Cluniac Martyrologies there are many names of Italian nobles who had presented churches to Cluny, including some from the Brescia region.[52] It seems probable that *Nunc dimittis* was known in the Northern Italian monastery in which William of Volpiano started his career, and that he introduced the chant to Dijon: it was at his instigation, and perhaps even under his supervision, that *DIJ1* was copied.[53] The influence of William of Volpiano in Normandy and across the Channel is well attested, although no direct link between Dijon and *IRI* or *SAR3* is known.

Conclusions

The textual origins of these chants, their localised and late appearances, and the marginal character of the liturgical occasions with which they are associated combine to suggest that they were locally composed after the spread of the Roman liturgy in the late eighth century. Their melodic construction is therefore a vital piece of evidence in the consideration of how the genre was understood by medieval cantors.

---

[51] Ferreira, M-P., *Music at Cluny: The Tradition of Gregorian Chant for the Proper of the Mass. Melodic Variants and Microtonal Nuances* (PhD, Princeton University, 1997), 20.

[52] For example, the Martinengas, who were counts of Bergamo and landed proprietors in the region of Como, Bergamo and Brescia. See Schwarzmaier, H., 'The Monastery of St. Benedict, Polirone, and its Cluniac Associations', in N. Hunt, (ed.), *Cluniac Monasticism in the Central Middle Ages* (London, 1971), 123–42; 139–40.

[53] That chants may have been transmitted to Normandy from Italy via Dijon has already been recognised by Hiley. See 'The Norman Chant Traditions - Normandy, Britain, Sicily', *PRMA* 107 (1980–81), 1–33; 4.

Apart from the Italian or Beneventan version of *In columbe*, the new eighth-mode tracts are all composed in a manner which is, to varying degrees, consistent with the structure of the core repertory. In general, the expected phrase shapes are used in the appropriate formal contexts, and are altered to fit the number of syllables available in the usual manner. Several new eighth-mode tracts follow textual cues, making the connection with the core repertory very clear.

However, several verses in Beneventan tracts consist of a hybrid phrase, combining the elements one would expect to encounter in a verse. Hybrid phrases also occur in Italian tracts, although single-phrase verses are avoided, and these phrases do not make formal sense. *Effuderunt* has a single-phrase verse consisting of apparently randomly selected eighth-mode patterns. In Aquitaine, the hybrid ***E3-C*** is used to avoid the ***E3*** cadence in the middle of a verse, and ***B4-E1*** is used at the beginning of a verse. In the mainstream version of *Nunc dimittis*, the beginning of ***A2*** is not followed by the expected cadence, but by the beginning of a different version of ***A2***. ***E1*** is used in an abbreviated version and out of the expected formal context on one occasion in an Italian tract. Within an oral genre, once a phrase is begun, the rest is inevitable, unless there is a strong textual cue. The combination of elements of more than one phrase in the manner encountered in the new eighth-mode tracts from all three regions is therefore evidence that these chants were composed with the aid of an abstract knowledge of the genre, through the medium of writing. A newly composed phrase appears in *Venite, Effuderunt*, and on three occasions in Italian tracts. Within an oral genre, unique phrases are very rare, and these also suggest a culture where written versions of the chants were used as an *aide-mémoire*.

Composers of new eighth-mode tracts do not always use the expected phrase for the formal context, and they do not always display an awareness of the nuances governing how the phrases should be manipulated for a given text. Standard phrases are used out of the expected context without any apparent textual stimuli twice in Beneventan tracts, once in an Italian tract, and also in the mainstream version of *Nunc dimittis*. This suggests that the finer details of the construction of an eighth-mode tract were no longer important, or were no longer remembered. This is borne out by: the treatment of ***B1***, which appears in a version inappropriate for the number of syllables in Beneventan and Italian tracts; the use of ***C1*** despite there being a penultimate accent in two Aquitanian phrases and in the Italian tract, *Iustorum anime*; the use of ***C4*** ending with the word 'domine' in *Conuertere*, but without responding to the textual cue by using the special cadence; the use of ***E1*** alone in the verse-half in manuscripts from all regions.

As common sense would suggest, an understanding of the construction of the genre was not lost as soon as Roman chant was widely adopted in Western Europe. The melodic shapes of the eighth-mode tracts, and the formal and textual context with which each phrase-type is associated, were known in the tenth and eleventh centuries, but the widespread use of notation meant that it was no longer necessary to construct chants within the highly memorable framework of the oral genre. Once the mnemonic of a written version was widely available, it was not necessary to remember the finer details of how text and music should be fitted together. The composers of these tracts took advantage of the new tool of writing to construct chants with unique phrases, centonised phrases, and phrases out of their expected contexts. These compositional techniques were not possible or were not appropriate within an oral genre where stability and orthodoxy were of paramount importance.

Chapter 7
Questions of Chronology

Introduction

The eighth-mode tracts are generally regarded as being very old. For example, in 1921, Wagner asserted that 'seine Melodik ist altertümlich'.[1] Because of this, and because they are such a closely related group of chants, many scholars have identified compositional layers within the corpus in an attempt to understand the development of Western chant before the time of written sources. Some base their conclusions on the antiquity of the Feasts to which the tracts are attached, or other facets of liturgical history; some base their conclusions on the musical and stylistic features of the chants themselves; some combine the two types of evidence. In this chapter, both musical and historical features are used to evaluate such hypothetical chronologies.

The core repertory of eighth-mode tracts was well established by the middle of the eighth century, when Roman chant was adopted in Francia. This repertory was liturgically stable. From the unnotated Frankish manuscripts of the eighth and ninth centuries to the Old Roman Graduals of the eleventh and twelfth centuries, the same core repertory of eighth-mode tracts is used for the same Feasts in both traditions, with the same texts.[2] Although the melodic dialect of the two traditions is very different, the close structural relationship between the Old Roman and Gregorian eighth-mode tracts confirms their common, Roman, origin.

Because of the close textual, liturgical, and musical relationship between the eighth-mode tracts in the two traditions, and because the importance of orthodoxy to the Carolingians is so well documented, it is probable that these chants appear in the earliest manuscripts in a form that is structurally close to that adopted by the Franks. However, when chants in the two traditions differ in structure, it is not usually possible to ascertain which version was the earlier. Because of this, any consideration of a possible compositional chronology using the states of the melodies as evidence must take account of both traditions.

It is probable that the ancestors of the eighth-mode tracts, before the

---

[1] Wagner, P., *Einführung in die Gregorianischen Melodien,* vol. 3: 'Gregorianische Formenlehre' (Leipzig, 1921), 353.

[2] Apart from the tracts attached to the Easter Vigil, to be discussed below.

eighth-century adoption of Roman chant in Francia, had characteristics still evident in these chants. The practice of non-responsorial psalmody being sung by a soloist between the readings of the Mass is very old,[3] and the melodic patterns of the eighth-mode tracts, with their recitation patterns, their clearly articulated and standardised cadences, and their clear verse structure, are indeed reminiscent of simple psalmody. This has been recognised by those analysing the chants, and the terminology of psalmodic recitation has often been used (see pp. 11–12). However, although the roots of the eighth-mode tracts certainly lie in psalmodic recitation, the analytical reduction of these chants to a psalmodic outline obscures rather than illuminates the essential characteristics of the genre. As was demonstrated in Chapter 3, the demands of the text can lead the melodic structure far away from the psalmodic basis, and the reduction of the six phrase types with all of their subgroups to 'intonation', 'mediation', and 'flex' obscures the often stark differences between the subgroups of phrases. As the association of the subgroups with different formal contexts appears to have been fundamental in keeping the tradition stable before it was notated, these subgroups are integral to the genre as we have it and cannot meaningfully be stripped away to uncover an earlier layer, closer to simple psalmody. This investigation of the pre-written history of the eighth-mode tracts is therefore based on the genre as we have it, not on a hypothetical reconstruction of earlier melodies.

The Melodies of the Core Repertory of Eighth-Mode Tracts

As was described in Chapter 3, the eighth-mode tracts can be divided into groups with distinct formal characteristics and melodic outlines. These groups favour different versions of the six basic phrases, and sometimes have different verse structures (see pp. 124–7). One group of eighth-mode tracts tends to have melodic phrases attached to whole sentences or clauses, and therefore bipartite verses; another tends to divide each sentence into two according to the syntax, leading to a quadripartite structure. However, there is such an overlap between the verse outlines found in these two groups that it would be difficult to argue that the different ways of breaking up the text predominated at different times. The melodic outlines of the Easter Vigil canticle-tracts are defined by their tripartite verses, and cannot be used to differentiate them chronologically from other tracts.

It is possible that the more complicated phrase shapes associated with longer sections of text, and usually occurring in bipartite verses, are more

[3] Bailey, T., *The Ambrosian Cantus* (Ottawa, 1987), 7–8; McKinnon, J., *The Advent Project: The Later-Seventh-Century Creation of the Mass Proper* (Berkeley, 2000), 283.

recent than the simple, shorter phrase shapes. However, musical simplicity does not necessarily indicate antiquity. Further, within the oral genre taken to Francia in the mid eighth century, each phrase type was associated with a particular textual and formal context, suggesting that a degree of conscious organisation had taken place at some stage. Even if the different phrase shapes did emerge at different times, inferences about the relative ages of chants including certain phrase shapes cannot be drawn, because the association of phrase shapes with certain verbal and formal contexts may have been newly organised in the oral tradition of the eighth century.

McKinnon has found extensive evidence of compositional planning in the annual cycle of proper chants, and he has traced this, the Advent Project, to the Roman *schola cantorum* in the late seventh century.[4] 'Its aim was to bring to fulfillment the uniquely Roman concept of the *circulum anni*, that is, to move away from the earlier practice of selecting psalms, responses and antiphons on an *ad hoc* basis at each service, and to provide a proper set of chants for each day of the rapidly expanding church year.'[5] In the chants affected by such revisions, 'earlier material was no doubt preserved, but much of it would have required reworking to match the style of the newer compositions within the various genres'.[6]

More Recent Eighth-Mode Tracts

In Chapter 6, it was possible to identify the non-standard eighth-mode tracts as being more recent than the rest of the corpus, not only on textual, liturgical and historical grounds, but also because they are usually constructed in a slightly different manner from the core repertory. If the melodic construction of any tracts in the core repertory can be distinguished from the rest in a similar manner, it may be possible to identify them as having been composed more recently.

Beatus uir The Old Roman version of *Beatus uir* has three quadripartite verses. The expected versions of the phrases are used, except that the second phrase of the tract uses ***B2*** rather than ***B1*** because of a textual cue.

---

[4] Several articles paved the way for *The Advent Project*, op. cit. These include: 'The Eighth-Century Frankish-Roman Communion Cycle', *JAMS* (1992), 179–227; and 'Properization: The Roman Mass', in *CP: Eger*, 15–22.

[5] McKinnon, 'The Eighth-Century Frankish-Roman Communion Cycle', op. cit., 196. On the Roman *schola* and its liturgical activities, see Tomasello, A., 'Ritual, Tradition, and Polyphony at the Court of Rome', *JM* 4 (1985), 447–71. See also Dyer, J., 'The Schola Cantorum and its Roman Milieu in the Early Middle Ages', in P. Cahn and A-K. Heimer (eds.), *De Musica et de Cantu: Helmut Hucke zum 60. Geburtstag* (Hildesheim, 1993), 19–40.

[6] McKinnon, 'The Eighth-Century Frankish-Roman Communion Cycle', op. cit., 197.

The Gregorian version is less close to the usual structures of the genre (see pp. 104–5). At the beginning, most manuscripts have 'Beatus uir qui timet/dominum', splitting the prepositional phrase 'qui timet dominum' rather than dividing 'Beatus uir' between the two parts of phrase *A1*. 'Dominum' uses phrase ***B1***, but the usual association of certain melodic movements with text accents is ignored. The Beneventan manuscripts instead have ***B5*** for 'dominum' even though the first phrase is complete, following the textual connection with *De profundis 2* ('domine'). In the second and third verses, most Gregorian manuscripts have the first subject + predicate pair with phrase ***E1***, although this is not generally used when there is a single phrase in the verse-half. This occurs also in several of the new eighth-mode tracts, described in Chapter 6. ***D2*** ends the second verse, although this phrase is not otherwise used in the tracts to which *Beatus uir* is closely related. The last phrase has a decorated rise fhikl in some manuscripts. This is seen also in the Easter Vigil canticle-tracts and in several of the new eighth-mode tracts, in at least some manuscripts, but it is not associated with other tracts in the core repertory.

Several significant variants occur in this tract within the Gregorian tradition. As was shown in Chapter 5 (see pp. 153–5), *DEN1* has almost the same outline as the Old Roman version of the tract, except that it uses ***E1*** for the first subject + predicate in the final verse, like the other Gregorian manuscripts. The unique use of ***B2*** instead of ***C1*** for the penultimate phrase in this manuscript is prompted by a clear textual cue. *NOY4*, the other manuscript from the Saint-Denis/ Noyon sphere has a unique second-mode version of *Beatus uir*. In this tract, the Beneventan manuscripts and *DEN1* have a different conjunction of text and music from other manuscripts on all occasions when phrase ***C*** is used, following the accent patterns of the text (see pp. 155–6). The instability of *Beatus uir* in the Gregorian tradition, and the fact that the mainstream Gregorian version deviates from the usual outlines of the genre, suggests that this tract was not well established in the eighth-century Roman tradition taken to Francia. This is supported by liturgical factors. The cult of St. Gregory was not established until the eighth century, when it spread very rapidly and very widely.[7] 'St. Gregory does not appear early. The first signs of cult discernible are during the eighth century in the Hadrianum, the standard Gospel-Lists, and the Gradual; and ecclesiologically under Leo III (795–816).'[8] *Beatus uir*, the

[7] Described by Hiley at the Medieval and Renaissance Music Conference in York in July 1998, in a paper entitled 'The English Antiphons in the Historia Sancti Gregorii'.

[8] Frere, W. H., *Studies in Early Roman Liturgy*, 1 (Alcuin Club Collection, 28, Oxford, 1930), 97. 'Et super corpus beati Gregorii confessoris atque pontificis facit vestem albam olosiricam cum tabulis de chrisoclabo et cruce' (Life of Leo III in Duchesne, L., *Liber Pontificalis* (Paris, 1888-92), ii. 10,18).

tract associated with this Feast, was probably composed after the establishment of the rest of the genre, and possibly separately in Rome and Francia.

Qui regis One other eighth-mode tract in the core repertory does not appear to have been well established in the eighth-century Roman tradition. The Old Roman and Gregorian versions of *Qui regis* are quite different (see pp. 116–18). The Old Roman version follows a scheme compatible with the usual outlines of the core repertory, except that the second phrase consists of ***B1-D2-A2*** material. The Gregorian tradition has two middle verses instead of one. This does not follow the outline of the psalm or the sense of the text, and the music used is ***E1 D2 E2 D2***, although ***E1/2*** is not usually associated with there being only one phrase in the verse-half. The use of the second ***E*** phrase may have been a response to the textual connection between 'cherubim' and 'beniamin', and the use of ***D2*** for 'appare coram effraim' may have arisen as a parallel to this. In the last verse, the Gregorian tradition begins with ***D4-B3***. It is not clear why phrase ***D*** material is used at the beginning of a verse.

All other Ember Saturdays use the tract *Laudate*, and *Qui regis* appears to have replaced *Laudate* on the Ember Saturday of Advent at a late date. McKinnon sees the use of a text specifically connected with Advent in this chant as indicating that it was composed at the time of the Advent Project, when the proper texts of the December Ember Days acquired Advent content. All four graduals attached to these days have texts with Advent overtones, and two are derived from the same psalm as *Qui regis*.[9] Bernard instead suggests that *Qui regis* is a Frankish composition and that the Roman cantors later adopted the text but gave it a melody in the Roman idiom. 'Deux indices le suggèrent; tout en étant bien romaine, sa mélodie simplifie un peu le timbre des traits en *DO*, ce qui est habituellement une marque d'emprunt, l'emprunter simplifiant et normalisant les mélodies qu'il emprunte. D'autre part, le graduel *Excita*, tiré du psaume 79 comme le trait *Qui regis*, n'a pas le même verset à Rome et dans le chant grégorien: quand Rome adopta le trait *Qui regis*, on changea le verset du graduel *Excita*, pour éviter la redite. Rome lui a donné un verset *Fiat manus tua* tandis que le grégorien a gardé le verset *Qui regis*. La création de ce trait en Gaule explique ce problème de verset.'[10] It is possible that the Roman cantors altered the adopted Frankish chant to be more consistent with the usual structure of the genre. However, given the interest of the Roman cantors in Advent texts at the time of the Advent Project, it seems more likely that *Qui regis* was composed in Rome according to the usual

[9] McKinnon, *The Advent Project,* op. cit., 290–91.
[10] Bernard, P., *Du Chant Romain au Chant Grégorien* (Paris, 1995), 215.

constraints and cues of the genre, and that in Francia 'a particularly bad performance was not recognised as such and became the basis for the officially sanctioned version'.[11]

The Liturgical Contexts in which Eighth-Mode Tracts are Found

The Feasts to which the eighth-mode tracts are attached were established at different times. The Feast of St. Valentine (*Desiderium*) was established in Rome in the mid-fourth century. The six-week Lenten Fast, during which *Ad te leuaui, Qui confidunt* and *Sepe* were sung, was established by 384. The Vigil at the end of this Fast is equally ancient, reflecting liturgical structures characteristic of the early Church before the fourth-century rise of monasticism.[12] There is evidence that the readings were followed by their respective canticles from an early date.[13] Quinquagesima (*Iubilate*) and Sexagesima (*Commouisti*) were introduced in the sixth century. St. Gregory rededicated the previously Arian church of St. Agatha in about 590, and presumably established her Feast (*Qui seminant*). The Ember Saturdays (*Qui regis* and *Laudate*) were established by the seventh century. Septuagesima (*De profundis*) was established in the mid-seventh century.[14]

The eras in which these Feasts were established have been combined with the textual characteristics of the chants to establish chronological strata within which the chants originated, by Cullin and, most recently, by Bernard, who derives much of his material from Cullin's work.[15] Cullin maintains that different groups of tracts can be delineated 'par différentes strates discernable par leur situation liturgique, mais aussi par leur qualité littéraire'.[16]

Cullin takes as his starting point the work of Jean Claire, who believes that the most archaic music may be found in the most ancient Offices, such

---

[11] Nowacki, E., 'Text Declamation as a Determinant of Medlodic Form in the Old Roman Eighth-Mode Tracts', *EMH* 6 (Cambridge, 1986), 193–225; 220.

[12] The Easter Vigil dates from as early as the second century and had acquired its 'classic' shape by the fourth century. See Talley, T., *The Origins of the Liturgical Year* (New York, 1986), 31–3; and McKinnon, *The Advent Project*, op. cit., 293.

[13] Schneider, H., 'Die altlateinischen biblischen Cantica', *Texte und Arbeiten* 29–30 (Beuron, 1938), 184; McKinnon, *The Advent Project*, op. cit., 293.

[14] On the establishment of Feasts of the Temporale, see Vogel, C., *Medieval Liturgy: an Introduction to the Sources*, rev. and trans. W. Storey and N. Rasmussen (Washington DC, 1986), 310–11. On the establishment of the relevant Feasts of the Sanctorale, see Frere, *Studies in Early Roman Liturgy*, op. cit., 94–7.

[15] Bernard, op. cit., 179ff.

[16] Cullin, O., 'Pour une Réevaluation des Formes Littéraires de la Psalmodie sans Refrain: Canticum et Tractus', *Modus* 3 (1989–92), 41–7; 43.

as the Ferial Office.[17] The combination of elements of Mass and Office in the Easter Vigil is used by Cullin to support an argument that the Easter Vigil canticle-tracts are the oldest of the core repertory.[18] If, as Claire asserts, the ancient Offices contain traces of the oldest layer of chant, then the Easter Vigil canticles, as chants in a celebration that has its roots in an ancient Office, must be the oldest eighth-mode tracts. 'Nous sommes ici aux origines du chant liturgique de l'Antiquité tardive: il est issu des lectures, comme par scissiparité. Cette forme liturgico-musicale, la plus ancienne qui nous reste, est une *lectio cum cantico*'.[19] Cullin asserts that Jean Claire's theory of a modality based on three *cordes-mères* 'a existé et reste visible dans les pièces les plus anciennes de l'office paschal c'est-à-dire les cantiques'.[20] The canticles are 'psalmodie ornée très régulière, comprenant un *incipit* (qui n'appartient qu'au premier verset), et une cadence finale (qui n'appartient qu'au dernier); puis trois teneurs successives: *si*, avant la flexe; *do* avant la médiante; et *sol* avant la terminaison, ce qui représente le même 'plan tonal' que le verset de répons du 8e mode'.[21] The Easter Vigil canticle-tracts appear 'avec les mélodies des traits du 8e mode sous sa forme la plus archaïque, la plus proche de la psalmodie, sans aucune ornementation originale'.[22] However, the eighth-mode tracts were transmitted as a single genre of which the Easter Vigil tracts were an integral part, at least in eighth-century Francia.[23] The Easter Vigil canticle-tracts have a certain melodic structure because of their texts, not because they maintained an autonomy that reflects the most ancient state of developed *psalmodie sans refrain.*

Cullin's second stratum consists of *Sicut* and the three tracts of the six-week Lenten Fast (*Ad te leuaui, Qui confidunt, Sepe*). That the texts of these three tracts are used within the Roman Mass Proper only as eighth-mode tracts is cited by Bernard as an indication of their antiquity. *Sicut* 'ne s'agit plus de *lectio cum cantico*: ce psaume n'est ni la continuation lyrique d'une lecture, ni la réponse à une lecture: c'est seulement un chant de

[17] Claire, J., 'Les Répertoires Liturgiques Latins avant l'Octoéchos. I. L'Office Férial Romano-Franc', *EG* 15 (1975), 5–192; 11.

[18] In the early period, the Easter Vigil was an extension of the evening Office. It developed before the distinction of Mass and Office. See Taft, R., *The Liturgy of the Hours in East and West* (Collegeville, Minnesota, 1986), 189.

[19] Bernard, op. cit., 107. See also Cullin, 'L'*Office de Pâques* Comme Miroir du Chant Grégorien: Du Concept Liturgique à la Réalisation Musicale', *Analyse Musicale* (1990), 19–25.

[20] Cullin, 'L'*Office de Pâques*' op. cit., 21.

[21] Claire, J., 'Le Répertoire Grégorien de l'Office. Structure Musical et Formes' in *Le Chant Grégorien, Patrimonie Artistique de l'Europe: Les Actes du Colloque International de Musicologie* (Louvain, 1980), 27–46, 39.

[22] Claire, 'Les Répertoires Liturgiques Latins avant l'Octoéchos', op .cit., 135.

[23] On the probable eighth-century Frankish origin of these chants, see below, pp. 221–4

procession, une sorte d'introït du baptême. C'est par conséquent une pièce moins antique que les précédentes; elle est cependant pourvue d'une mélodie pratiquement semblable à celle des trois *cantica.*'[24] However, *Sicut* was sung at the end of the series of readings and canticles during the period in question, and not as a processional chant.[25] To separate this tract from the canticle-tracts on the grounds of its liturgical context is meaningless.

Bernard's third chronological stratum consists of *De profundis*, attached to Septuagesima, and *Qui seminant*, the tract of the ancient Sanctorale. *Qui seminant* is identified as a relatively recent tract despite the age of the Feast to which it is attached because Psalm 125 is here displaced from its expected place on the third Friday of Lent, and because the text is not taken from the beginning of the psalm. Cullin, however, classes these three tracts with the previous group.

The other tracts are classed separately, despite the fact that the dates of origin of their Feasts are intertwined with those for which chronological strata are posited. The explanation in the case of *Iubilate* is that the text is used in other places within the chant repertory. *Commovisti,* whose Feast was also established in the sixth century, is also identified as a late composition because 'ce trait est une pièce que présente dèja des marques d'évolution'[26]. The melodic outline is indeed more complicated than the tracts identified as older, although this is not necessarily an indication of its lesser antiquity.

Although different strata are identified by Cullin and Bernard on liturgical and textual grounds, it is not clear whether they refer only to these texts being used for *in directum* psalmody on these liturgical occasions, or whether they refer also to the melodies.[27] If these strata have significance only for the texts, then they have little relevance in a study of the music. If the assumption is made that strata identified on textual and liturgical grounds may be used in tracing compositional development, serious methodological flaws emerge. Although the texts of the eighth-mode tracts appear in manuscripts from around 800 onwards, and the melodies appear in manuscripts from the late ninth century, we have no direct evidence of the existence of these chants in anything resembling their current form before this time. Common sense militates against speculating about the

[24] Bernard, op. cit., 123.

[25] McKinnon, *The Advent Project*, op. cit., 293; and 'The Gregorian Canticle-Tracts of the Old Roman Easter Vigil', in C-H. Mahling and R. Seiberts (eds.) *Festschrift Walter Wiora zum 90. Geburtstag* (Tutzing, 1997), 254–70; 258.

[26] Bernard, op. cit., 198.

[27] McKinnon's chapter on tracts in *The Advent Project*, op. cit. (280–97) traces the origins of the Feasts and the times of probable entry of the relevant texts into the liturgy, but cautions 'it must be borne in mind... that not the tracts as such but their predecessors are involved, full psalms sung *in directum*' (284).

state of the genre very much before the written sources.[28] This is compounded by the likelihood of extensive revisions in the Roman chant repertory after the dates when these Feasts were established, but before the chant was adopted in Francia. The Advent Project took place in the late-seventh century, according to McKinnon, and it is probable that the eighth-mode tracts were revised and fixed by the Roman *schola* at this time. Because of this, it may be methodologically inadvisable to combine the internal musical and textual evidence with the external historical evidence of the origins of the relevant Feasts in order to construct compositional strata.

The Easter Vigil Canticle-Tracts

The transmission of the Easter Vigil tracts, which is rather different from that of the rest of the eighth-mode tracts, has prompted speculations that these tracts are either very much older than the rest of the corpus, or that they are very much younger. They appear in Gregorian, specifically Beneventan, versions in the Old Roman manuscripts, as was shown in Chapter 2 (see pp. 50–53). None of these four tracts survives in an Old Roman version.

Performance of these canticles was clearly central to the Roman Easter Vigil: the *Ordines Romani* indicate that the reader of the Lesson would stay in the pulpit and sing the canticle as a continuation of the reading. For example, an early ninth-century copy of Ordo XXIV has the instruction 'Et ascendit lector in ambonem... expletas lectiones cum canticis earum.'[29] Other Ordines have similar rubrics.[30] These appear to be lector rather than cantor chants and there is no evidence that these chants took the form of eighth-mode tracts in Rome.[31] One possibility is that they were responsorial settings of the kind represented by *Vinea domini*, which appears in *NOR*,[32] and also in *OJA2*.[33] This chant is given as an alternative to the usual

---

[28] As may be seen in the refutation of the composition strata identified by Chavasse. See McKinnon, J., 'Antoine Chavasse and the Dating of Early Chant', *PMM* 1 (1992), 123–48.

[29] Andrieu, M., *Les Ordines Romani du Haut Moyen-Age,* III (Louvain, 1931-61), 295.

[30] Ibid., 'Ordo XXIII'; 272, 'Ordo XXVIII (Appendix)'; 412, and 'Ordo XXXB'; 472.

[31] On the distinction between the two, see McKinnon, J., 'Lector Chant versus Schola Chant: A Question of Historical Plausibility', in J. Szendrei and D. Hiley (eds.), *Laborare Fratres in Unum: Festschrift Laszlo Dobszay* (Hildesheim and Zurich, 1995), 201–11.

[32] Huglo, M., 'Notes Historiques à Propos du Second Décret sur la Vigile Paschale: Les Cantiques de la Vigile Pascale', *Revue Grégorienne* (1952), 121–36; 130–32.

[33] Pistoia, Bibl. Cap. C. 119, an early twelfth-century Gradual from central Italy. See *GR*II, 115. Cited in Huglo, M., 'Le Chant 'Vieux-Romain': Liste des Manuscrits et Témoins Indirects', *Sacris Erudiri* 6 (1954), 96–124 ; 100.

Gregorian version, in the manner of the Old Beneventan chants preserved in Gregorian manuscripts. Rather than being an *in directum* chant, it is responsorial, with the text 'domus israhel' used as a refrain. An unnotated Missal from the same church also preserves the text, as well as that of *Cantemus domino*, in a similar layout. Huglo identified 'le style très particulier du chant-vieux romain' in this piece by comparing it with the Lectionary of St. Cecilia in Trastevere[34] '[qui] donne la mélodie du Cantique de Jonas et de la prière d'Azarius, chants à comparer au style musical vieux-romain'.[35] Although only one Ordo (XXVIII) has a rubric specifically indicating use of this canticle, and it has only the word 'Vinea',[36] the variant 'Vinea domini' is found in several manuscripts of the Gelasian sacramentary, an originally Roman collection.[37] Others have dismissed this chant as a local variant, and it is true that it may have been a local composition modelled on the Beneventan Easter Vigil canticles: *NOR* also contains several new eighth-mode tracts originating from Benevento, and there was certainly contact with the region.[38]

Another possibility is that the canticles were not sung to composed chants in Rome. The eighth-century Sárospatac leaf found by Jeffery has Old Roman texts including those for the Masses around Easter.[39] The rites for Easter Saturday were not included in the manuscript in its original state and the Mass, but not the Vigil, was added in the margin. The omission of the Easter Vigil canticle texts from this leaf has been interpreted by both McKinnon and Boe as an indication that the Old Roman Easter Vigil did not include elaborate composed canticles.[40] McKinnon instead suggests that the canticles 'were chanted by the lector, even if somewhat more lyrically than the preceding portion of the reading, and... [the canticles] were recited in their entirety'.[41] Further supporting the suggestion that the Old Roman Easter Vigil did not include canticle-tracts is the fact that the *Ordines*

---

[34] This Sacramentary is held in the Fitzwilliam Museum in Cambridge. Huglo, 'Notes Historiques', op. cit., 132; fn 2.

[35] Huglo, 'Le Chant 'Vieux-Romain'', op. cit., 100–101.

[36] Andrieu, op. cit., 413.

[37] Mohlberg, L. C., Eizenhöfer, L. and Siffrin, P. (eds.), 'Liber Sacramentorum Romanae Aeclesiae Ordinis Anni Circuli (Sacramentarium Gelasianum)', *Rerum Ecclesiasticarum Documenta* 4 (Rome, 1960), 71.

[38] P. Bernard has suggested that the Old Roman Easter Vigil canticles may have been in the style of the Beneventan equivalents. Bernard, op. cit., 110.

[39] Described in a paper read at the American Musicological Society meeting in Chicago in 1991

[40] Boe, J., 'Chant notation in Eleventh-Century Roman Manuscripts', in G. Boone (ed.), *Essays on Medieval Music in Honor of David G. Hughes: Isham Library Papers* 4 (Cambridge, Mass., 1995), 43–57; McKinnnon, *The Advent Project*, op. cit., 292–5.

[41] McKinnon, *The Advent Project*, 293. The canticle-tracts use only portions of the canticle texts.

Romani never cite the canticle-tracts, although they cite every other fore-mass chant of Holy Week and every other Easter Vigil chant.[42]

As has been made clear by McKinnon and Boe, the possibility that the Roman liturgy included canticle-tracts in the local melodic dialect which were replaced by Gregorian versions in the eleventh-century Roman manuscripts is remote. The suggestion of Jean Claire and his followers that these chants represent the most ancient state of the eighth-mode tracts must be approached with circumspection.

If the canticle-tracts are indeed Frankish compositions, it is necessary to consider once more their relationship with the rest of the core repertory. McKinnon repeats Hucke's assertion that 'the melodies were evidently composed at a later stage in conjunction with the tracts of the eighth mode, especially with *Laudate*, but according to different rules'.[43] To group *Laudate* with the Easter Vigil tracts is tempting because it also is sung on Easter Saturday, at the Mass which follows the Vigil.[44] However, *Laudate* is used on two other Ember Saturdays in the Church year, and is sung within the context of the normal Eucharistic Fore-mass, a different liturgical context from that of the Vigil tracts. It also has a psalmic, quadripartite text, uses phrase ***D1*** rather than the ***D2*** seen in *Sicut*, has fhk rather than fhikl in the final melisma, and has the last syllable of the piece on the final accent rather than on the final syllable.[45] It is true that *Cantemus* may be regarded as a retexting of *Attende* rather than as an independent chant.[46] It is also true that the Easter Vigil tracts are a close-knit group within the genre, as was demonstrated in Chapter 3. This is unsurprising given their liturgical and, presumably, compositional proximity. But the wider identification of the Easter Vigil tracts as having been composed according to different principles from the rest of the tradition does not withstand close inspection. The eighth-mode tracts function as a genre, with many connections between chants, including the Easter Vigil tracts. The Easter Vigil tracts are consistent with the behaviour of the genre as a whole rather than being modelled on a single chant.

One further factor may affect the tentative conclusions reached here

[42] Ibid., 294.

[43] Hucke, H., *NG*, vol. 18, 108–10; McKinnon, *The Advent Project*, op. cit., 294

[44] Apel claims that these five tracts are the 'central group', but does not attach chronological significance to the grouping (Apel, W., *Gregorian Chant* (Bloomington, Ind., 1958), 318).

[45] In 'Der Übergang von mündlicher zu schriftlicher Musiküberlieferung im Mittelalter', in *IMS 1977*, 180–91; 187, Hucke wrote 'Die Cantica der Osternacht stellen eine sondergruppe innerhalb der Tractus des 8. Tons dar. Sie sind nicht nach den gleichen Regeln wie die anderen Tractus geformt, sondern einer einzigen, am Tractus „De profundis" abgezogenen Melodie parodiert'. Similar liturgical and musical objections may be raised to this parallel.

[46] See pp. 105–7.

about the relative youth of the canticle-tracts. Bailey identifies the Easter Vigil chants as 'stand[ing] closer to the early Roman tradition that must be the common ancestor of the Gregorian, the Old-Beneventan, the Old-Roman and the Ambrosian versions that we know. It is interesting to note that, of the tracts and cantus that share texts, only those of Holy Saturday have the same liturgical assignment.'[47] To discover whether this close relationship may indeed be found, it will be necessary to undertake a comparison of the Ambrosian cantus with the Gregorian and Old Roman eighth-mode tracts. Only then will it be possible to determine whether they are constructed on the same structural principles, and, if so, whether the Easter Vigil tracts are indeed more closely related between the traditions than other chants.[48] This may be the key to discovering whether these four chants are older than, younger than, or contemporary with, the rest of the genre. Such an analysis is beyond the scope of the present study.

Conclusions

The Easter Vigil canticle-tracts appear to be eighth-century Frankish creations and provide further evidence that the Frankish cantors of that time understood the rules and melodic outlines of this particular genre very well indeed. But for the rest of the core repertory, the search for a compositional chronology has not proved conclusive. Only two eighth-mode tracts of the core repertory stand apart. *Qui regis* and *Beatus uir* were less firmly established than the other eighth-mode tracts adopted in Francia in the eighth century, and they were probably composed during that century, perhaps separately in Rome and Francia. The remaining eighth-mode tracts of the core repertory existed in something akin to their present state by the beginning of the eighth century, a time when the Papal *schola* in Rome appears to have been undertaking other revisions of the repertory. The careful and coherent structure of the genre means that it is likely that the eighth-mode tracts were codified as a group at this time. The origins of the eighth-mode tracts in the form in which we have them may only pre-date their adoption in Francia by a couple of decades. We cannot reach beyond that time for a historically valid model of the construction of the repertory. The state of the melodies is defined by the constraints and cues of the oral genre, which kept the chants stable. Any chronological clues contained within the musical framework of the eighth-mode tracts will have been subsumed in the eighth century by the structure of the genre as we have it.

[47] Bailey, op. cit., 48.

[48] Ibid., 136–40. See also Bailey, T., 'Ambrosian Chant in Southern Italy', *JPMMS* 6 (1983), 1–7; 5.

Chapter 8
Conclusions

Introduction

In 1985, Nowacki warned against using comparison of isolated pairs of chants in more than one tradition in order to define their relationship: 'the substance of musical composition is found, rather, in the structures that many examples jointly embody. Comparative work in medieval music must recognize this reality by extending its reach to all the examples in each given dialect in order to make the most well-informed analytical generalizations.'[1] The current study has responded to this call by making a comprehensive analysis of the eighth-mode tracts, considered in parallel in the Old Roman and Gregorian traditions. This analysis has revealed not only that the eighth-mode tracts in the two traditions are closely related, but also that they are structurally and musically equivalent. The forms and structures common to the eighth-mode tracts in both traditions may therefore be identified with those of the Roman ancestors to these chants that were adopted in Francia in the eighth century. It has been recognised by chant scholars for some time that the two traditions had a common, Roman, origin. This study confirms that view, at least as far as this group of chants is concerned, with incontrovertible musical evidence.

The Oral Tradition and its Characteristics

The forms and structures of the eighth-mode tracts are used to examine how these chants may have been transmitted before the development of pitched notation. It is generally accepted that memory played a vital role in maintaining the stability of liturgical chants at this time, but the current study has given a new focus to the definition of the Old Roman and Gregorian traditions as 'oral'. It has been possible to construct a model of how the formal, melodic and textual characteristics of the chants helped to keep the genre stable, and the consideration of both traditions has highlighted the means by which such stability was achieved. For example,

[1] Nowacki, E., 'The Gregorian Office Antiphons and the Comparative Method', *JM* 4 (1985), 243–75; 275.

structural differences between the traditions usually arise when one tradition has responded to a textual cue, and the other has responded to a conflicting formal cue. Perhaps the clearest example of this is provided by the second verse of *Sepe*, described in detail in Chapter 3. The Old Roman tradition follows three textual cues in a row, having a verse consisting of ***A2-A1 A2 D3***, whereas the Gregorian tradition follows only the first of these textual cues, having a verse that follows the expected outlines of an eighth-mode tract verse: ***A2-B3 C1 D3***.

One of the fiercest criticisms of theories of oral transmission has been that the models of 'recomposition' are not borne out by the consistency of the manuscript tradition. The close relationship between early Gregorian manuscripts suggests that there was an officially sanctioned version of each chant, and some have argued that such accuracy is feasible only within the context of there having been a written exemplar. However, the state of the eighth-mode tracts in the Old Roman tradition demonstrates that consistent and coherent transmission of this group of chants was possible within a culture where the arrival of musical notation was late. Further, the description in this study of how the various cues and constraints may have combined with rote learning to keep the tradition stable shows that, for this group of chants at least, it is not necessary to conclude that the stability of the tradition would only have been possible if there was a neumed exemplar. As medieval commentators suggest, *ad verba* memory would have worked in tandem with *ad res* memory, and subconscious memory prompts will have aided the process of recall. Each phrase is so closely constrained within the genre that significant variants rarely arise. The Easter Vigil canticle-tracts, apparently composed in eighth-century Francia (see pp. 217–20), support the contention that the structure of the genre was well understood by the Frankish cantors. While they form a particularly closely related group of eighth-mode tracts, they are clearly constructed within the same set of cues and constraints as the other eighth-mode tracts in the core repertory.

If there was indeed a single, officially sanctioned version, constructed in such a way that accurate oral transmission was feasible, then one would expect to encounter significant variants on the occasions when the official version deviates from the structures of the genre that usually help to keep it stable. And in the case of *Beatus uir*, this is exactly what happens, as has been described above. Such major variations from the usual version are not easily explained within the context of a fixed neumed exemplar, but may simply be the result of different cantors following different cues within the same oral tradition.

It should be acknowledged that detailed consideration of a much larger group of chants is required before firm conclusions may be drawn about whether or not the Franks aided their adoption of the Roman chant with a neumed exemplar. Close analysis of other groups of chants may reveal that they could not have been so accurately transmitted without the aid of writing.

The Evidence of the Written Sources

A common criticism of theories claiming that chant was orally transmitted is that the primary evidence is necessarily written. Levy has claimed that writing fundamentally changed the structure of the chants. Hughes has written instead that if the tradition had changed significantly when it was written down, one would expect rather more to have been made of the change than in fact was. This study has engaged with this question by examining the way in which the chants were understood once they were written down. I have studied the way in which they were notated, the way in which they were regarded by theorists, and the processes of composition seen in the group of new eighth-mode tracts.

Close study of the manuscripts reveals that standard phrases were known and recognised as such. The way in which the manuscripts are notated suggests that in the tenth century, written exemplars were employed as *aide mémoires* for text underlay and phrase structure, but that whole phrases were written down as remembered rather than being copied by rote. Study of the 'new' eighth-mode tracts confirms what the notational characteristics of the manuscripts suggests; that the basic shapes and the formal contexts with which they were associated were well known, but the nuances of text-music alignment were no longer required to stabilise the chants, and were ignored or forgotten. This is in direct contradiction to Levy's claim that careful text-music alignment is the result of a written, not an oral, process. Phrases are also used out of their expected formal contexts within the new eighth-mode tracts, again because the mnemonic function of phrase shapes being specifically associated with certain contexts was no longer urgent in the tenth century. New techniques of composition, specifically associated with the technology of writing, also arise. Some verses consist of a single centonised phrase, a circumstance that would be highly unlikely to arise within an oral context. The way in which the completely new phrases in *Effuderunt* and *Venite* differ so greatly from manuscript to manuscript shows that memory was still playing an important role even at this late stage: transmission was not purely a copying process. Phrase shapes not usually associated with the genre were not transmitted as consistently as the usual patterns.

Theoretical writing does not explicitly define what constitutes an eighth-mode tract, or how one should be remembered. However, the intonation formulae provide a contemporary model for the deeper levels of construction of the genre. The closeness between the intonation formulae and the eighth-mode tracts hints at the answer to another question. The close relationship between the eighth-mode tracts in the two traditions is not mirrored by many other groups of chants. Although changes undoubtedly took place in both traditions between the adoption of the Roman chant in Francia and the notation of each tradition, it is possible that at least some of the changes to Frankish chant were conscious alterations in order to conform to the emerging eight-mode system. It may be that the eighth-mode tracts were so close to the theoretical definition of the eighth-mode as it emerged that it was not necessary to alter them to conform with the theory. This hypothesis is supported by the closeness of the eighth-mode tract outlines to intonation formulae, but also by the close relationship between the eighth-mode tracts and the *Octo sunt beatitudines* melody in John Cotton's *De Musica*, one of the first truly practical music treatises. This is as yet an untested hypothesis, and it remains to be seen whether other chants that are very similar in the two traditions are equally consistent with Carolingian modal theory.

The Relationship between Old Roman and Gregorian Chant

To study a group of chants in both the Old Roman and the Gregorian traditions is not new. Hucke was the first to make a parallel analysis of a group of chants in both traditions, and his findings have been echoed by many since. Scholars have continued to find close connections between the structures of the two traditions, that the Old Roman tradition is generally more decorated than the Gregorian, and that it tends to repeat patterns and to move by step. However, this is the first study of the two traditions where sufficiently little material is considered, and where the chants studied are sufficiently closely related that it is possible to identify how the eighth-century Roman ancestors of the chants in question were structured and kept stable.

Marie-Noël Colette has found some instances where the two traditions are not only closely related, but have 'la même mélodie, différement écrite'.[2] Some of these are occasions where the scribe of the Old Roman melody has written out note-for-note figures that were notated with

[2] Colette, M-N., 'Grégorien et Vieux-Romain: Deux Méthodes Differentes de Collectage de Mélodies Traditionelles?', in J. Szendrei and D. Hiley (eds.), *Laborare Fratres in Unum: Festschrift Laszlo Dobszay* (Hildesheim and Zurich, 1995), 37–52; 39.

ornamental neumes in the early Gregorian manuscripts, and she concludes that 'il arrive en effet que le romain ait recopié une version notée grégorienne'.[3] The close relationship between the eighth-mode tracts in the two traditions, and the fact that they follow the same melodic contours means that these chants were a fertile ground for Colette to find examples. The hihg/hg figure in the phrase ***B*** melisma is cited: 'les formules se trouvent identiques, d'après les critères ornementaux que nous avons démontrés'. Colette's interpretation is that the Old Roman scribes copied out Gregorian melodies with local ornamentation. However, the analysis undertaken in this study indicates that the dialects are distinct, although Roman scribes were undoubtedly aware of Gregorian chant. The Easter Vigil canticles are of course notated in Gregorian versions in *ORC* and *ORJ* without characteristic Old Roman features being added. *ORP*, a thirteenth-century manuscript, does introduce some of these ornaments.[4]

Other detailed studies of the eighth-mode tracts have been made. These have provided an invaluable starting point for my own investigations. However, the two traditions have not been treated in parallel in a detailed manner before, and certain features of the construction of the chants, including some of the features that point most clearly to their common oral origin, only became apparent when the two traditions were considered in parallel.

A limitation of this study is that only two chant traditions have been considered. The work of Bailey on the Ambrosian cantus, and the consideration by Cullin of *in directum* chants in, for example, the Mozarabic rite, suggests that there may be connections between the eighth-mode tracts and chants that are used in the same liturgical context in other traditions. The question of the relative age of the Easter Vigil tracts cannot conclusively be resolved by studying only the Gregorian and the Old Roman traditions. Consideration of the equivalent *in directum* chants in other melodic traditions, especially the Ambrosian, may provide an answer, and this study has given a firm analytical basis from which such investigations may be made.

Only a very small group of chants has been considered in the current study. This has made it possible to look in great detail at how these chants are structured, but it means that it is not possible to draw wide-ranging conclusions about the relationship between the two traditions. Other genres of chants are clearly not as closely related in the two traditions, and for these types of chants, completely different techniques of analysis may be required to discover the common ground. Completely different, but also

---

[3] Ibid., 39.
[4] See pp. 52–3, above.

fruitful, analytical methods have been developed by Nowacki in his work on the antiphons, by Maloy in her work on the offertories, and by van Deusen in her study of the graduals. As well as not being so closely related in the two traditions, most genres of chant are not formulaic, and do not lend themselves to the kind of analysis undertaken here. It is possible that solo chants, schola chants, and congregational chants were transmitted in completely different ways, and that music of the Eucharist and the music of the monastic Office differ in transmission process. But the success of this analysis in demonstrating the parallel oral modes of organisation in the eighth-mode tracts in the two traditions suggests that it may be fruitful to look for oral modes of organisation and memory prompts in other groups of chants. This is certainly apposite for other formulaic genres, such as the great responsories, the second-mode graduals and the second-mode tracts, but it may also have applications in the consideration of idiomelic chants. It is important that analytical methods should be sufficiently flexible that they may be defined by the genre one is analysing rather than being a pre-existing set of rules. Nowacki's syntactical analysis of the antiphons has uncovered the underlying grammar of this group of chants. This style of analysis would not have revealed the structures of the eighth-mode tracts, and Nowacki did not apply it to his work on the Old Roman eighth-mode tracts. The analysis of monophony is initially challenging for Western musicologists trained in the 'classical' tradition, but the need to develop new analytical methods is a tremendous opportunity to experiment in order to find the analytical techniques best suited for the task in hand. It is hoped that the comparative analysis undertaken here will be added to the analytical arsenal of chant scholars.

Now that it has been established that claims of 'orality' may be put on a rigorous footing with close musical analysis, and that it is through study of more than one tradition that such structures become apparent, it is necessary for other genres of chants to be subjected to detailed comparative work. The analytical techniques developed here may be of use in the study of other genres of formulaic chants, but others must be applied to idiomelic chants. Only when a more varied selection of chants has been considered will it be possible to come to wide-ranging conclusions about the relationship between the Old Roman and Gregorian traditions, about their relationship with eighth-century Roman chant, and about how these repertories were kept stable between the eighth century and the development of pitched notation.

Appendix 1
The Versions of *Iubilate* in the Manuscript Sample

1. 'Iubilate domino'

Early manuscripts

GAL1

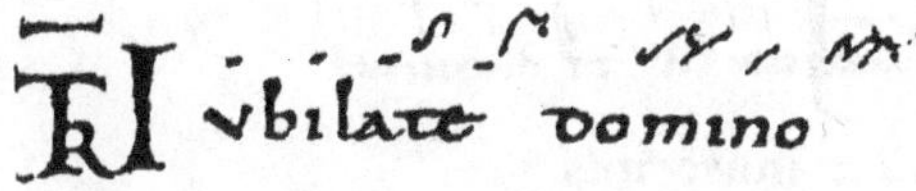

GAL2

MUR3

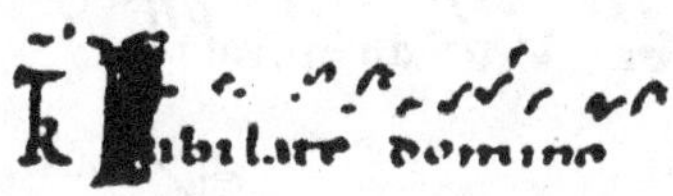

LAN

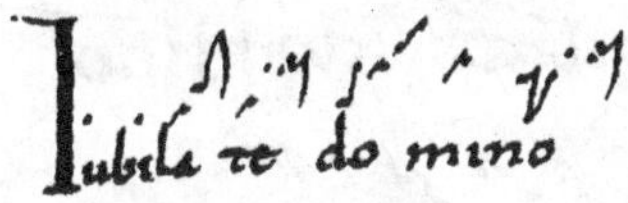

CHA1

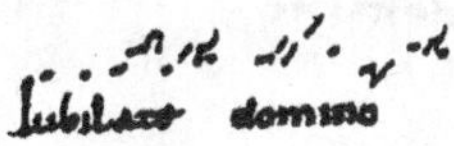

Western Frankish manuscripts

CLU1

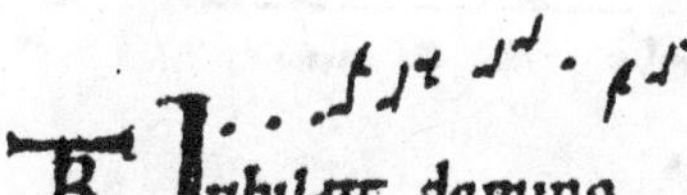

NOY4

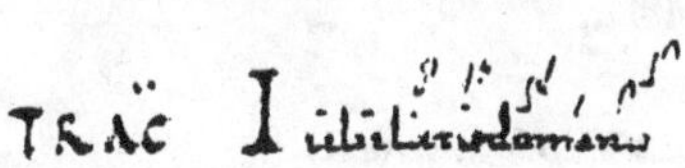

DEN1

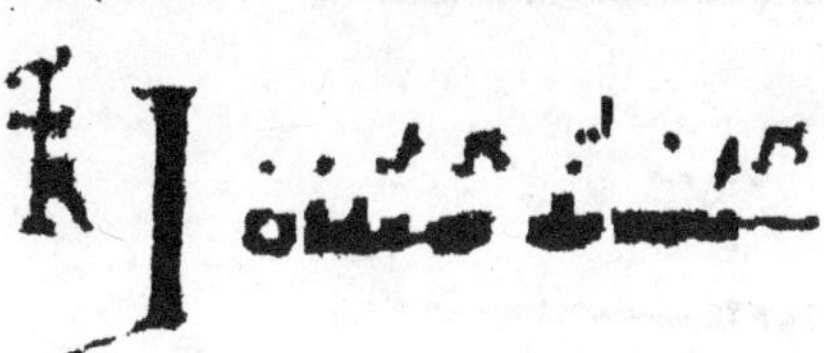

Northern Italian manuscripts

LAV

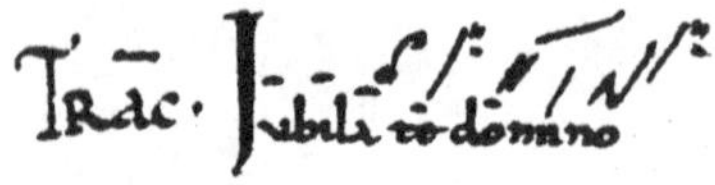

BRE

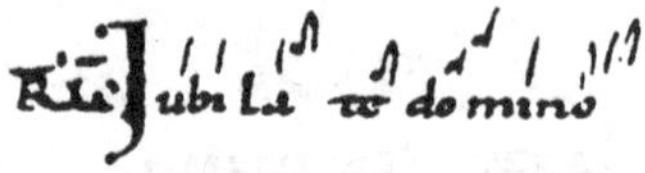

Eastern Frankish manuscripts

KLO1

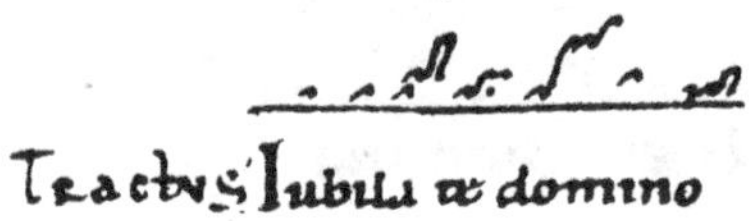

PAS2

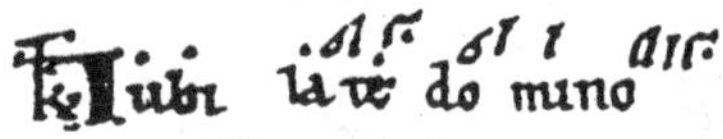

MOG4

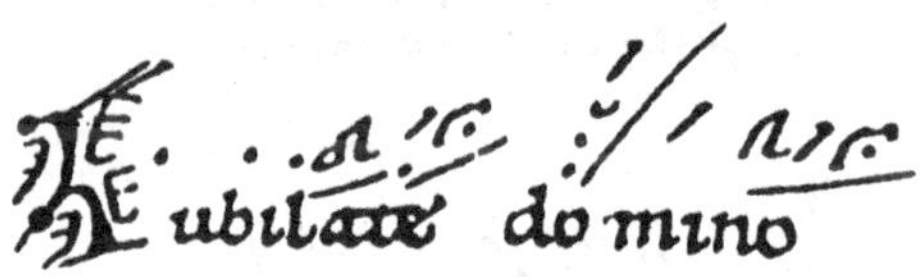

STM

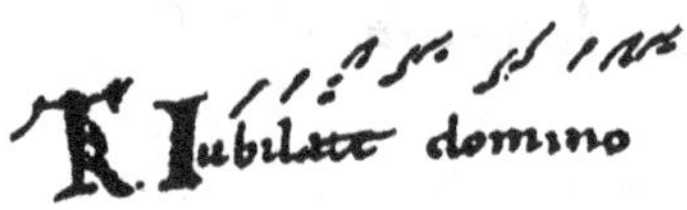

Beneventan manuscripts

BEN5

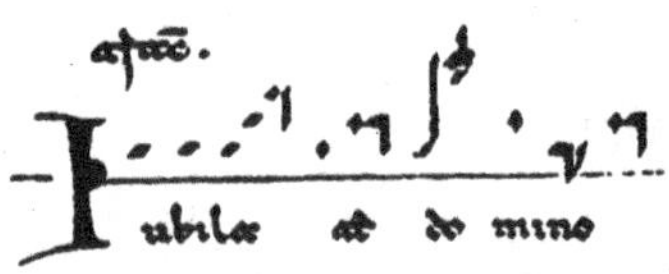

Aquitanian manuscripts

YRX

ALB

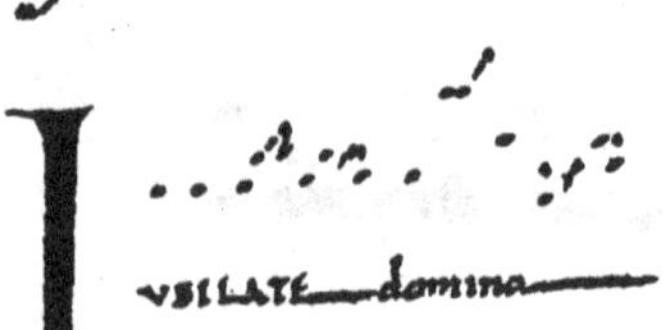

Cluniac manuscripts (pitched)

DIJ1

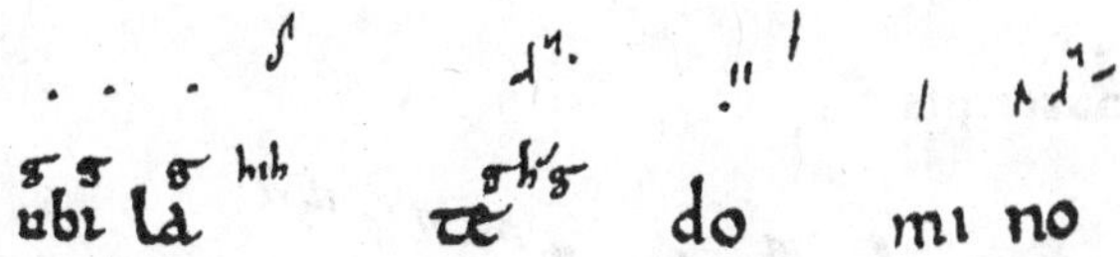

IRI

SAB

ROG1

2. 'omnis terra'

Early manuscripts

GAL1

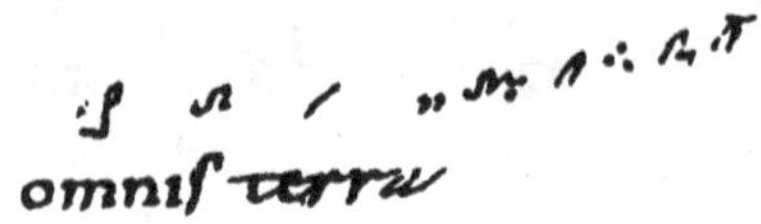

GAL2

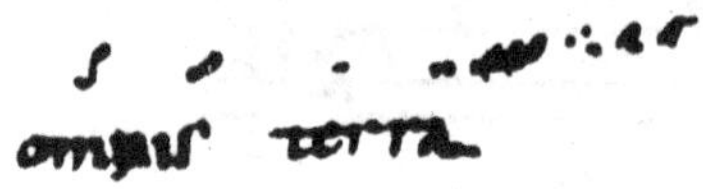

MUR3

LAN

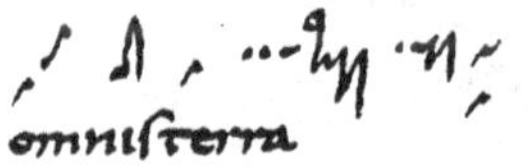

CHA1

Western Frankish manuscripts

CLU1

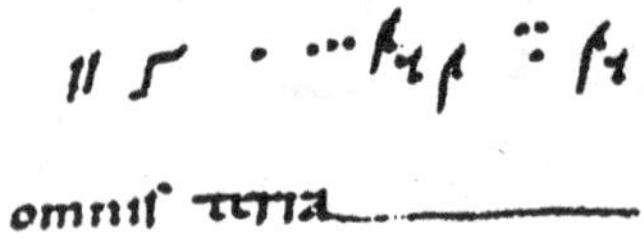

NOY4

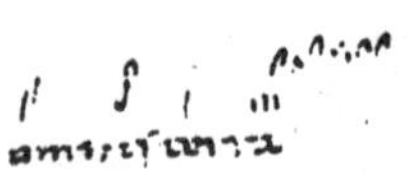

DEN1

Northern Italian manuscripts

LAV

BRE

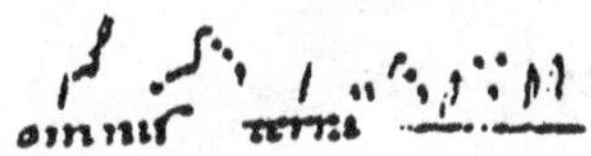

Eastern Frankish manuscripts

KLO1

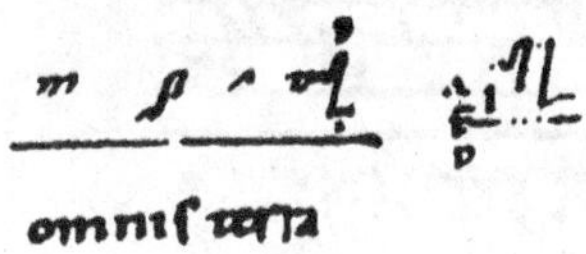

PAS2

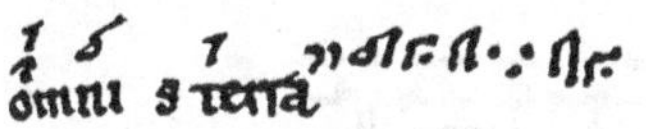

MOG4

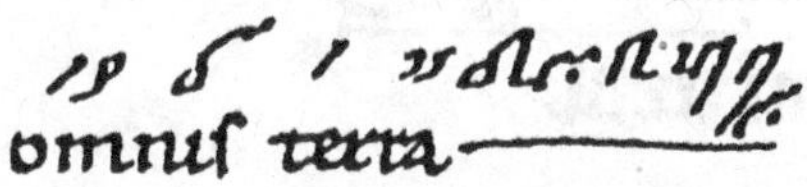

STM

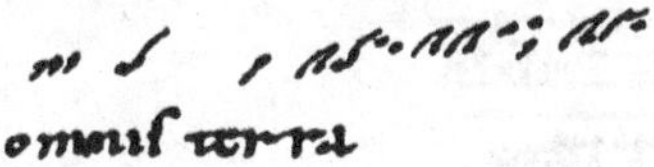

Beneventan manuscripts

BEN5

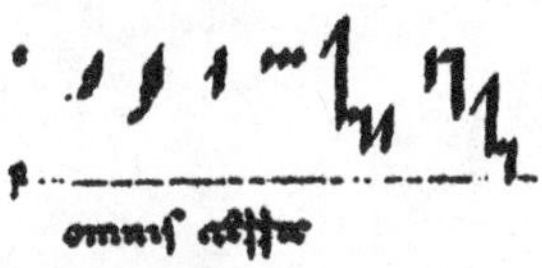

Aquitanian manuscripts

YRX

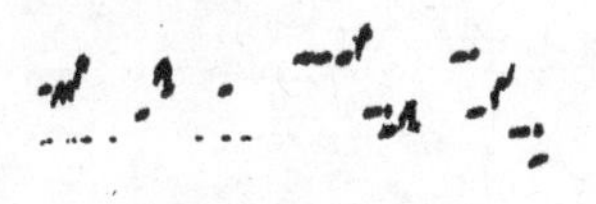

ALB

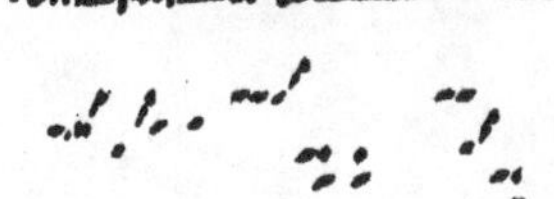

Cluniac manuscripts (pitched)

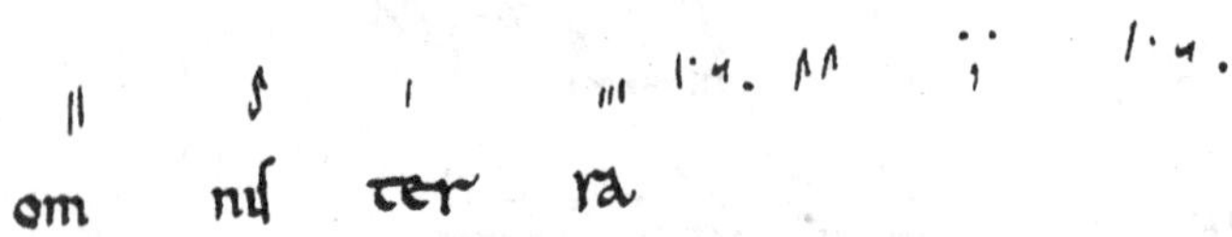

DIJ1

IRI

SAB

ROG1

3. 'seruite domino'

Early manuscripts

GAL1

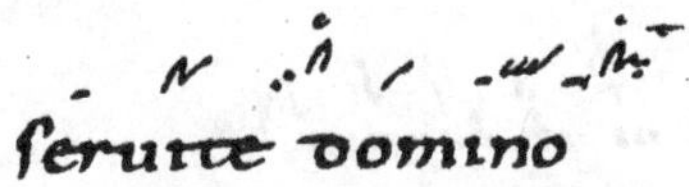

GAL2

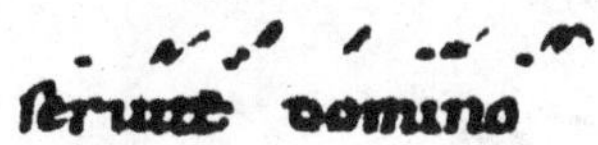

MUR3

LAN

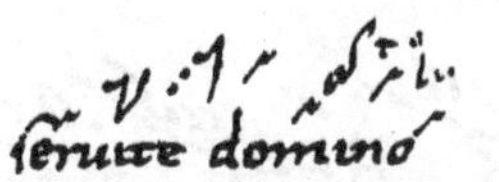

CHA1

Western Frankish manuscripts

CLU1

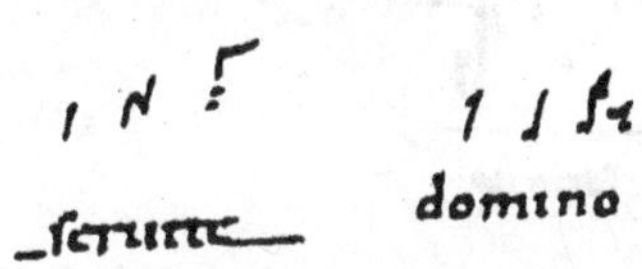

NOY4

DEN1

Northern Italian manuscripts

LAV

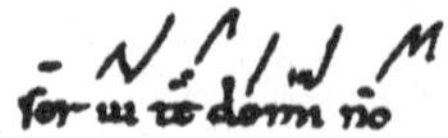

BRE

Eastern Frankish manuscripts

KLO1

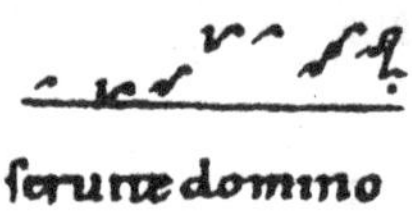

PAS2

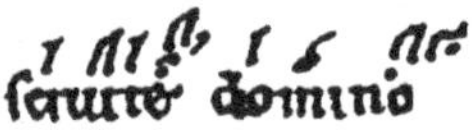

MOG4

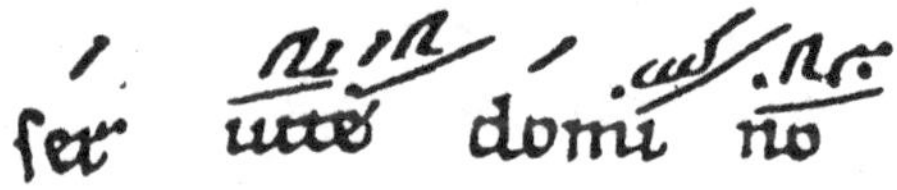

STM

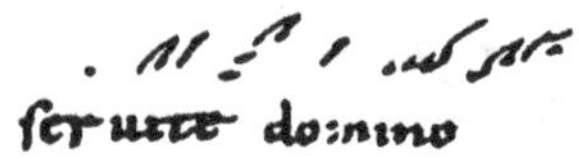

Beneventan manuscripts

BEN5

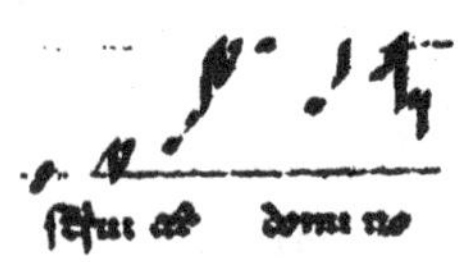

Aquitanian manuscripts

YRX

ALB

Cluniac manuscripts (pitched)

DIJ1

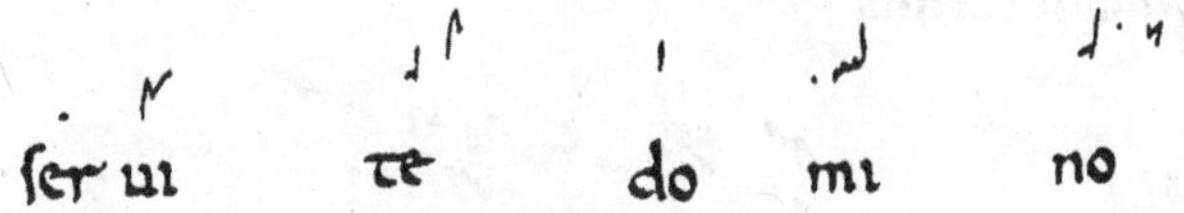

IRI

SAB

ROG1

4. 'in letitia'

Early manuscripts

GAL1

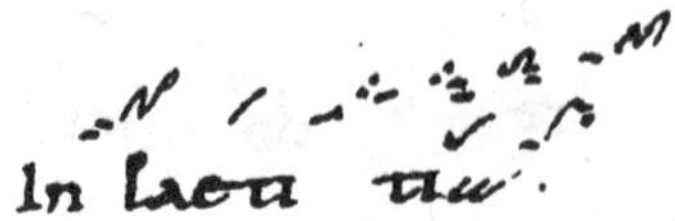

GAL2

MUR3

LAN

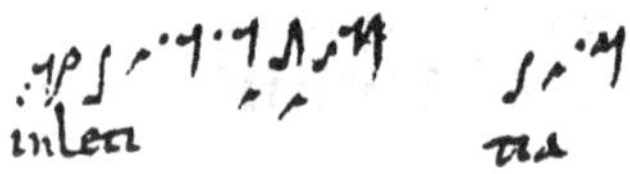

CHA1

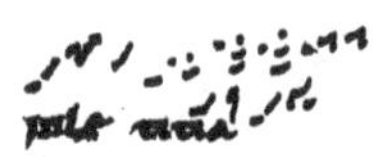

Western Frankish manuscripts

CLU1

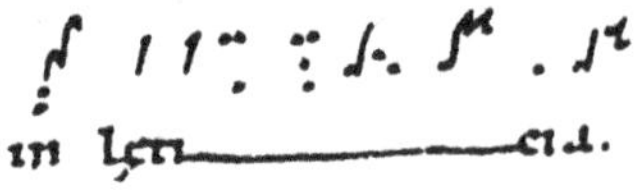

NOY4

DEN1

Northern Italian manuscripts

LAV

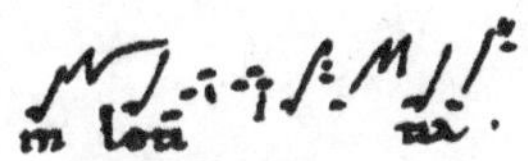

BRE

Eastern Frankish manuscripts

KLO1

PAS2

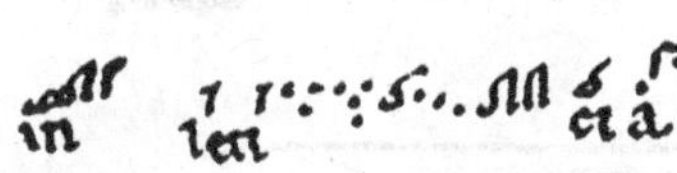

MOG4

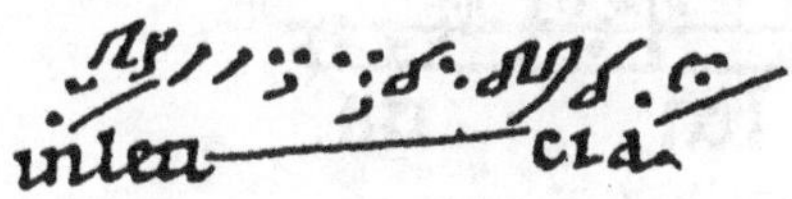

STM

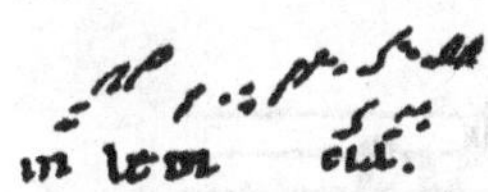

Beneventan manuscripts

BEN5

Aquitanian manuscripts

YRX

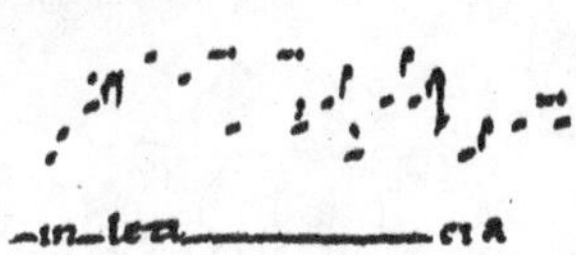

ALB

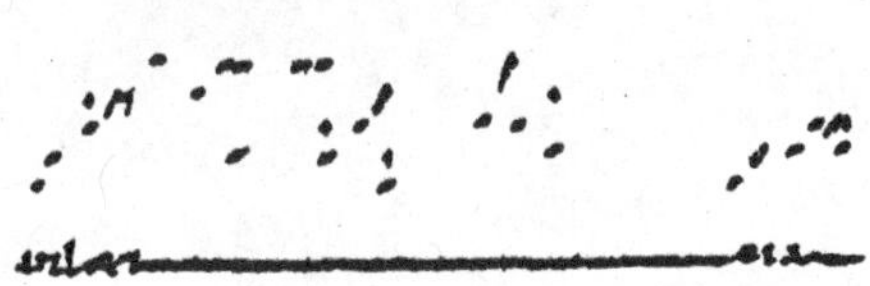

Cluniac manuscripts (pitched)

DIJ1

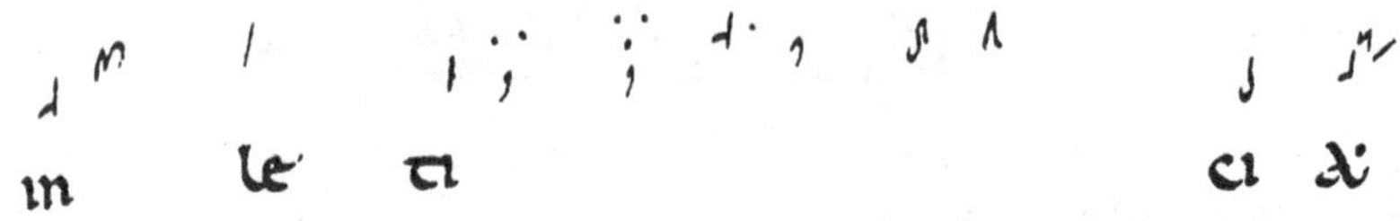

IRI

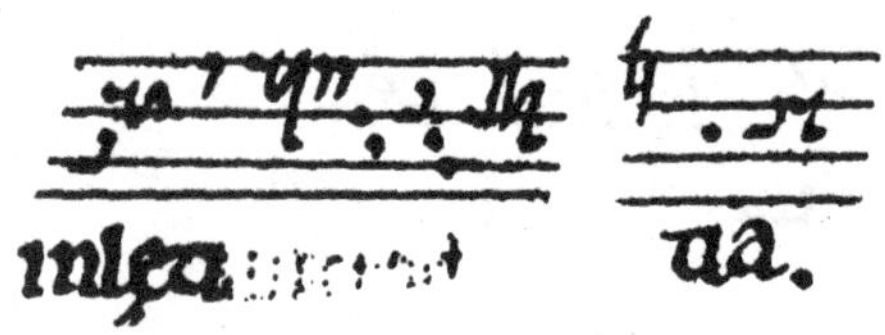

SAB

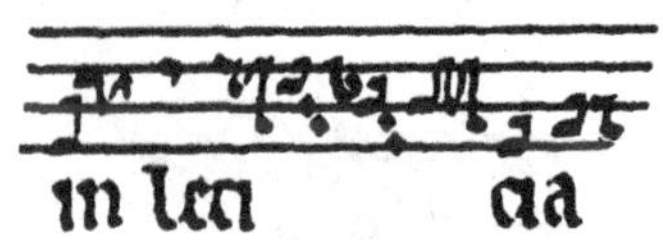

ROG1

5. 'Intrate in conspectu eius'

Early manuscripts

GAL1

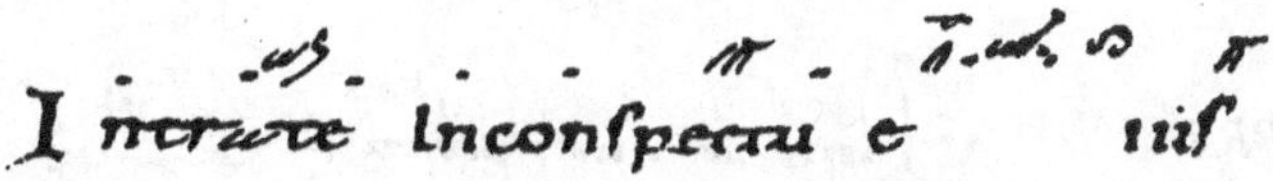

GAL2

MUR3

LAN

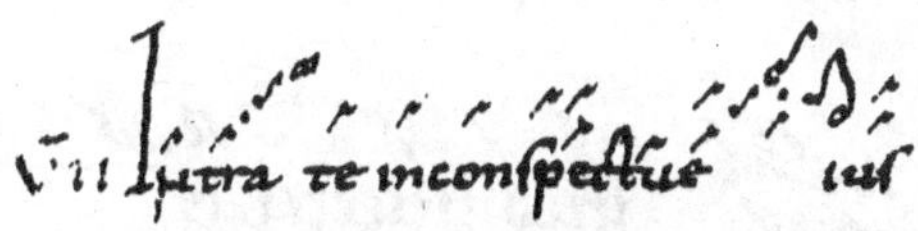

CHA1

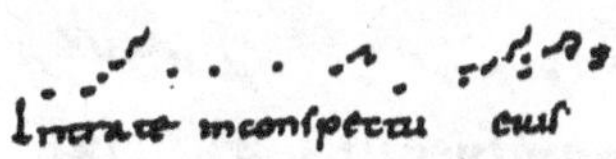

Western Frankish manuscripts

CLU1

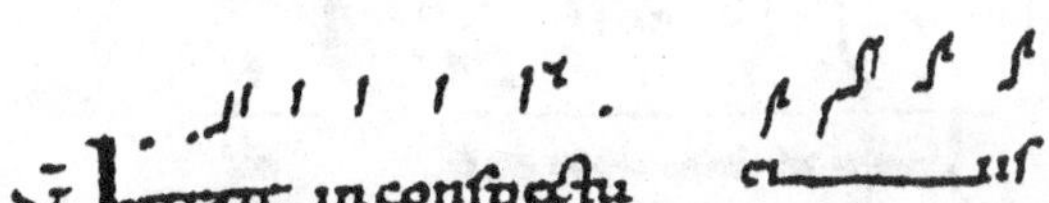

NOY4

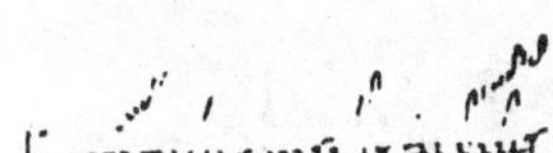

DEN1

Northern Italian manuscripts

LAV

BRE

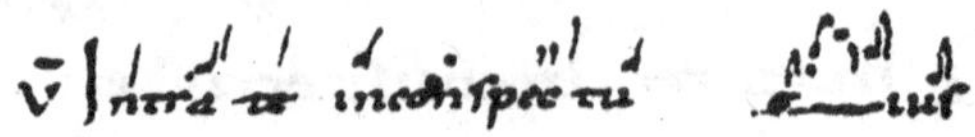

Eastern Frankish manuscripts

KLO1

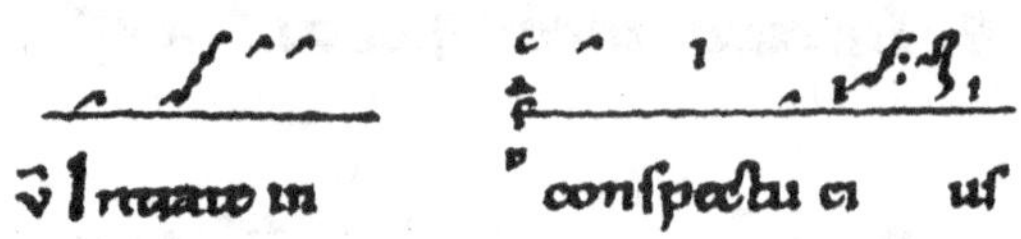

PAS2

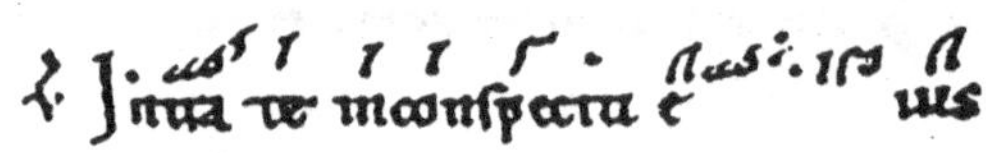

MOG4

STM

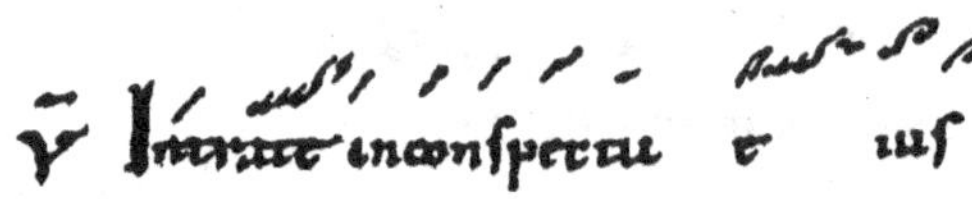

Beneventan manuscripts

BEN5

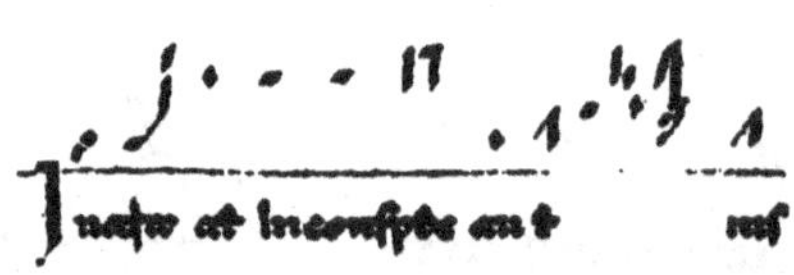

Aquitanian manuscripts

YRX

ALB

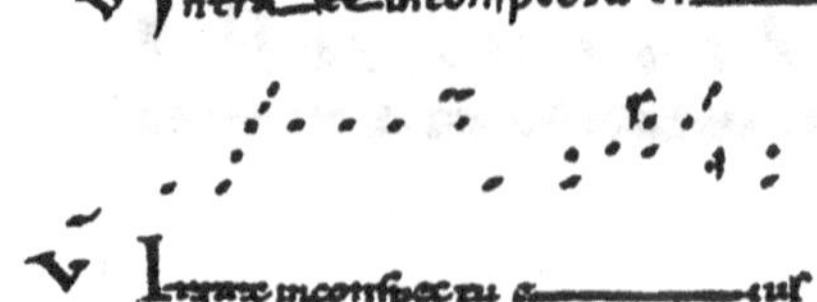

Cluniac manuscripts (pitched)

DIJ1

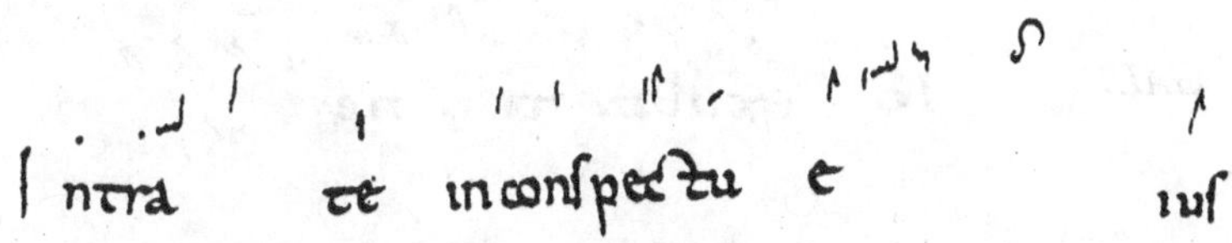

IRI

SAB

ROG1

6. 'In exultatione'

Early manuscripts

GAL1

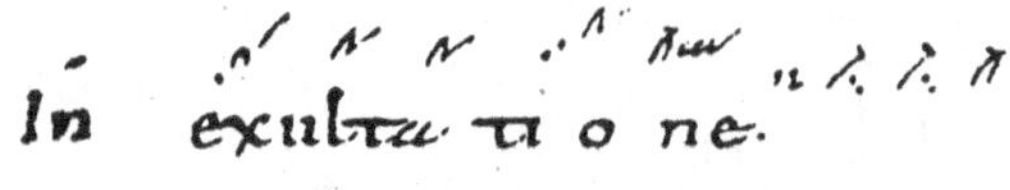

GAL2

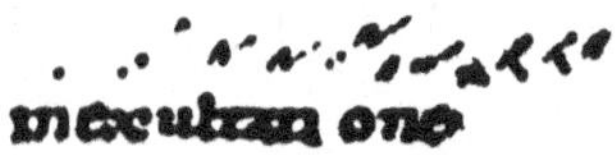

MUR3

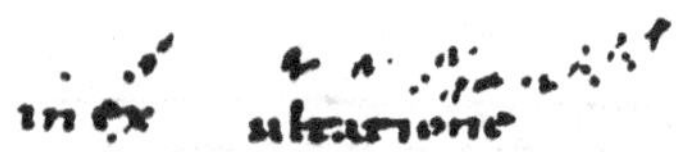

LAN

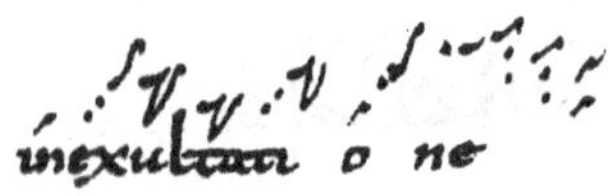

CHA1

Western Frankish manuscripts

CLU1

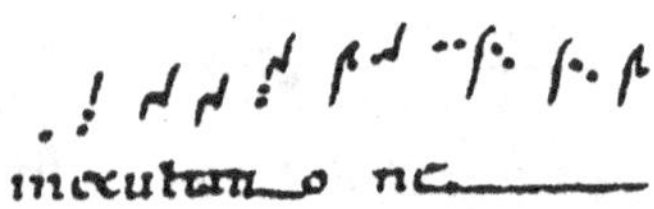

NOY4

DEN1

Northern Italian manuscripts

LAV

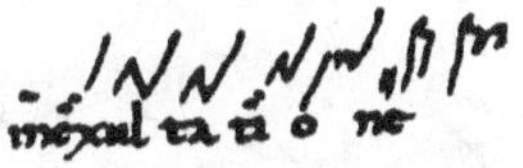

BRE

Eastern Frankish manuscripts

KLO1

PAS2

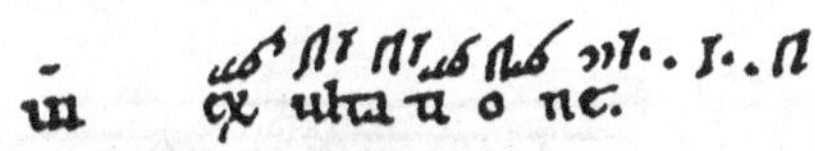

MOG4

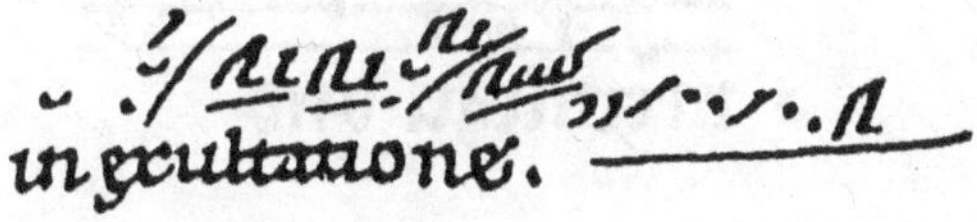

STM

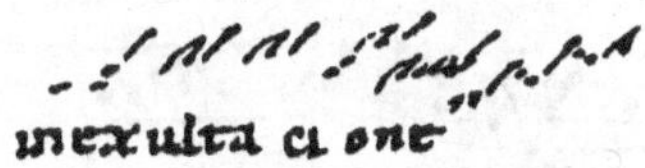

Beneventan manuscripts

BEN5

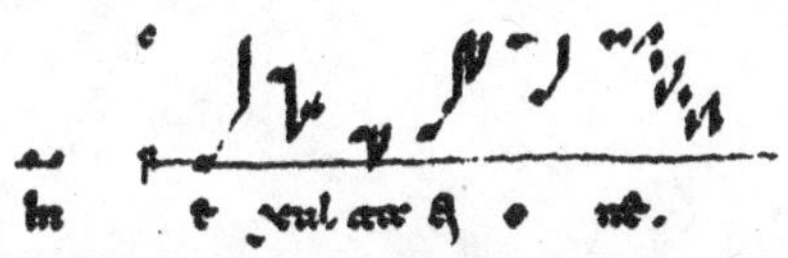

Aquitanian manuscripts

YRX

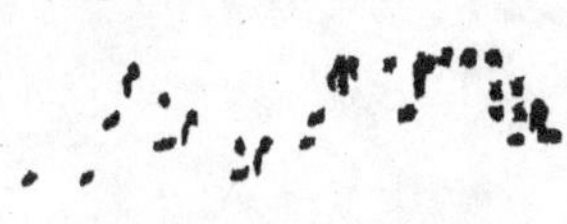

ALB

Cluniac manuscripts (pitched)

DIJ1

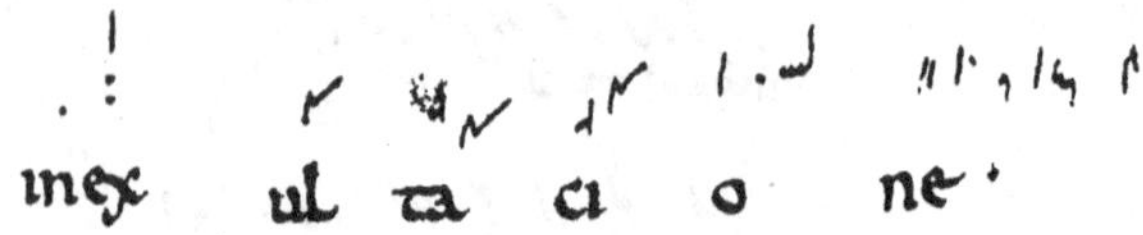

IRI

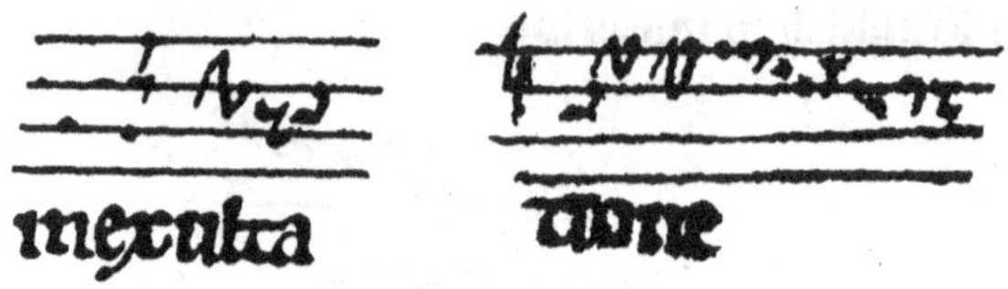

SAB

ROG1

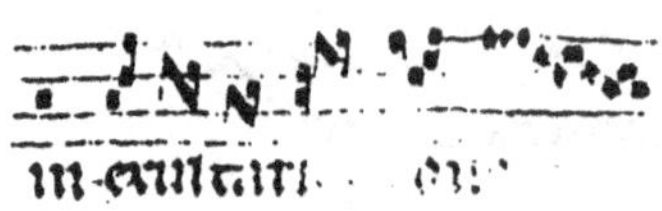

7. 'Scitote quod dominus'

Early manuscripts

GAL1

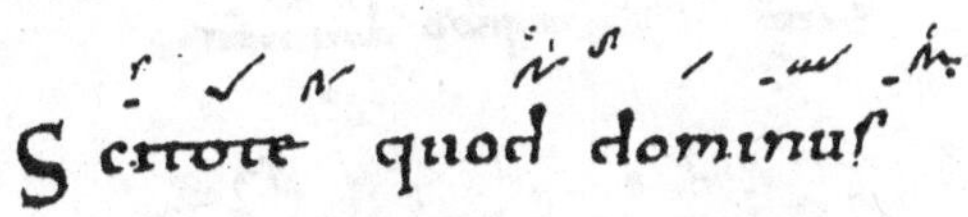

GAL2

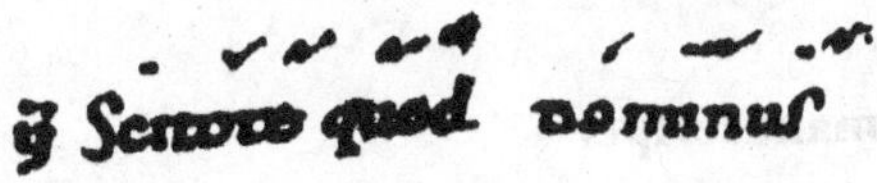

MUR3

LAN

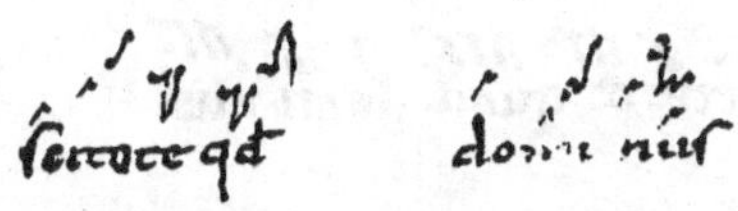

CHA1

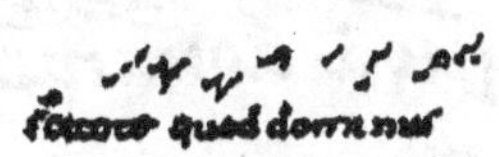

Western Frankish manuscripts

CLU1

NOY4

DEN1

Northern Italian manuscripts

LAV

BRE

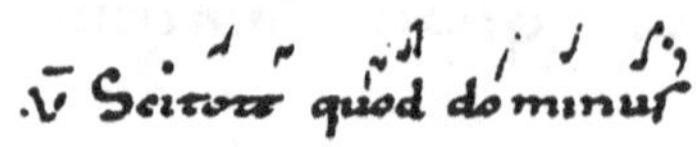

Eastern Frankish manuscripts

KLO1

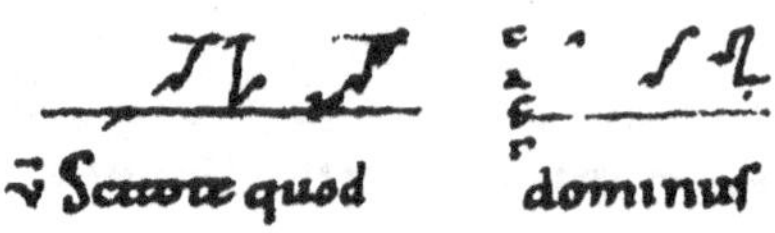

PAS2

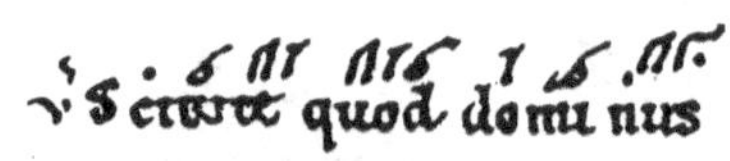

MOG4

STM

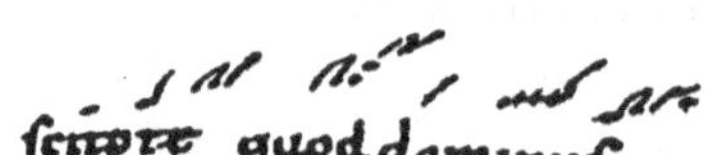

Beneventan manuscripts

BEN5

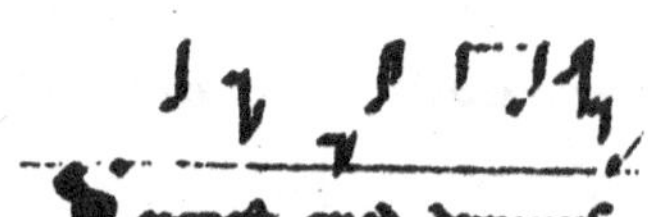

Aquitanian manuscripts

YRX

ALB

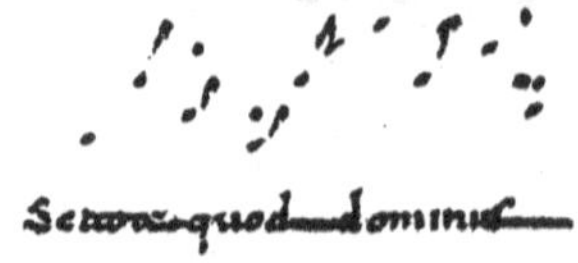

Cluniac manuscripts (pitched)

DIJ1

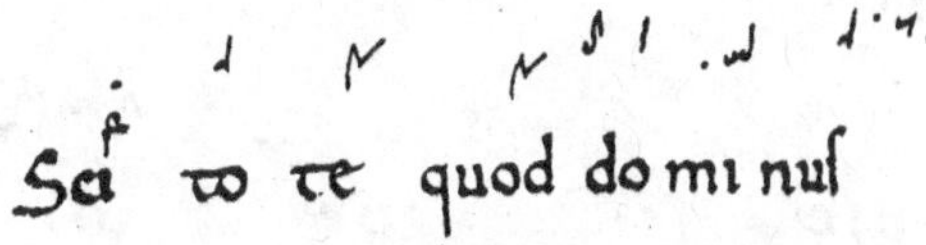

IRI

SAB

ROG1

8. 'ipse est deus'

Early manuscripts

GAL1

GAL2

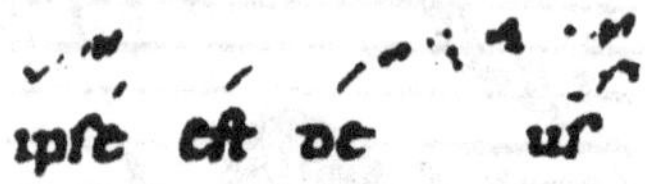

MUR3

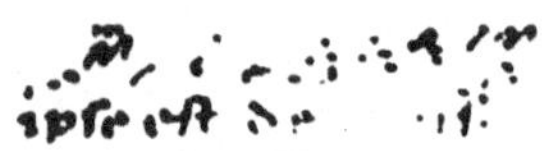

LAN

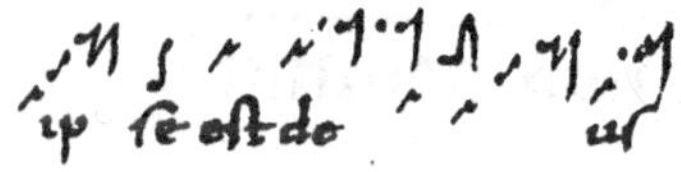

CHA1

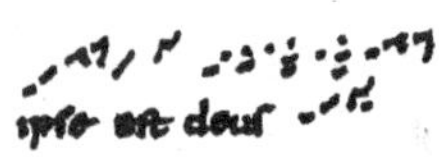

Western Frankish manuscripts

CLU1

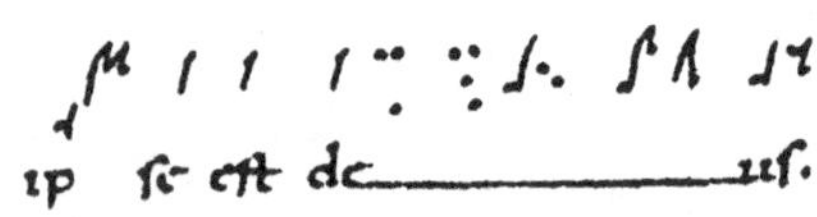

NOY4

DEN1

Northern Italian manuscripts

LAV

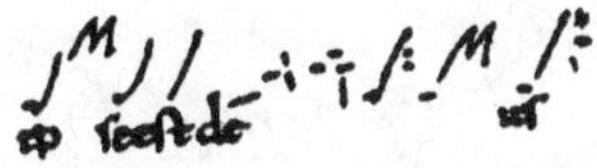

BRE

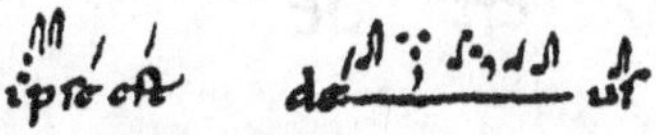

Eastern Frankish manuscripts

KLO1

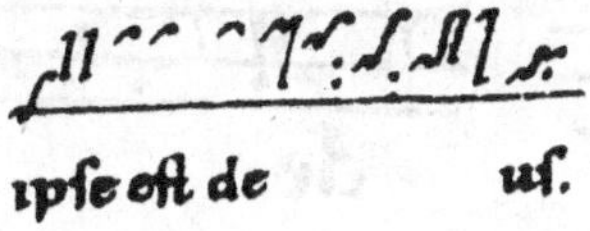

PAS2

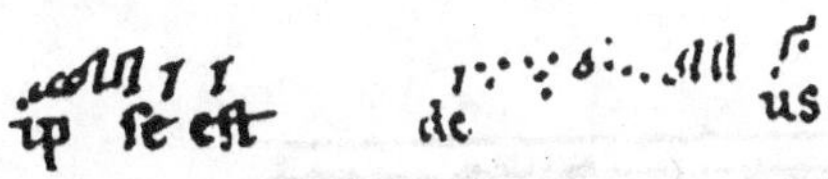

MOG4

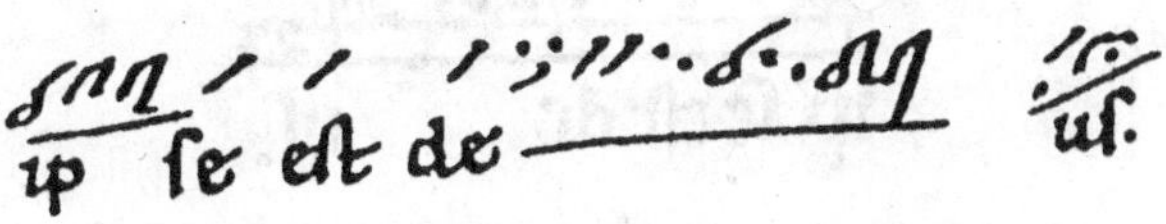

STM

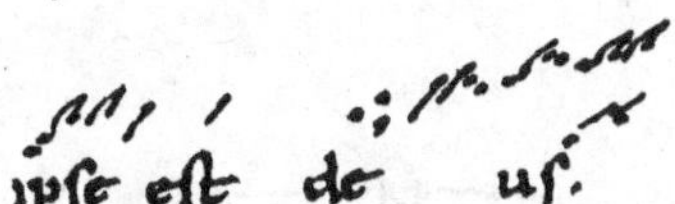

Beneventan manuscripts

BEN5

Aquitanian manuscripts

YRX

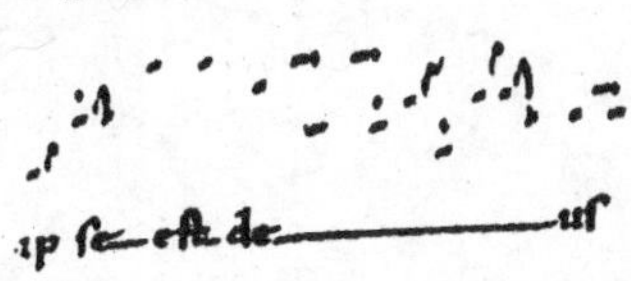

ALB

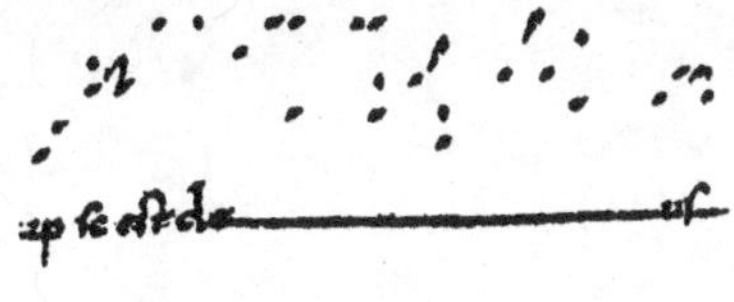

Cluniac manuscripts (pitched)

DIJ1

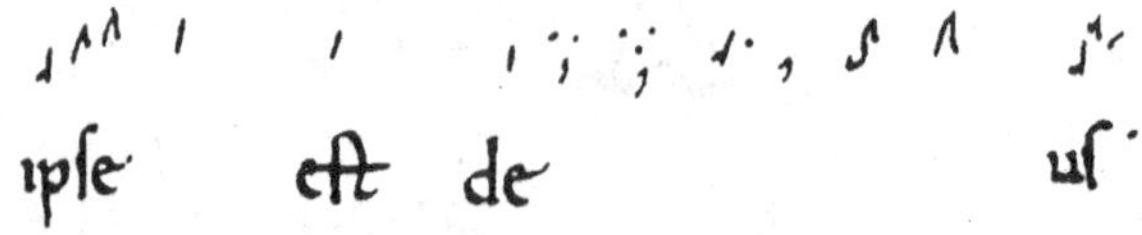

IRI

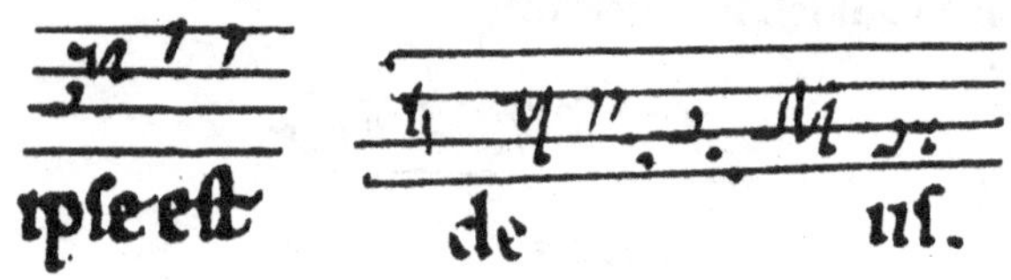

SAB

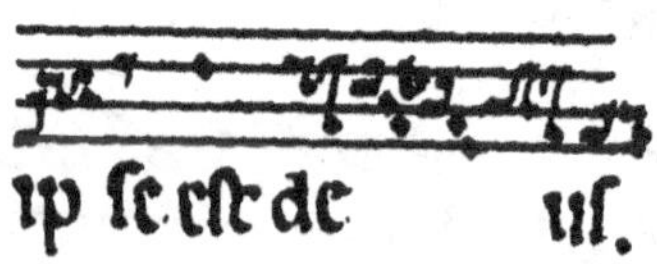

ROG1

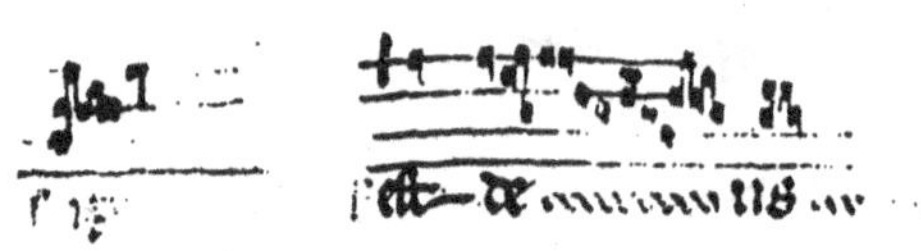

9. 'Ipse fecit nos et non ipsi nos'

Early manuscripts

GAL1

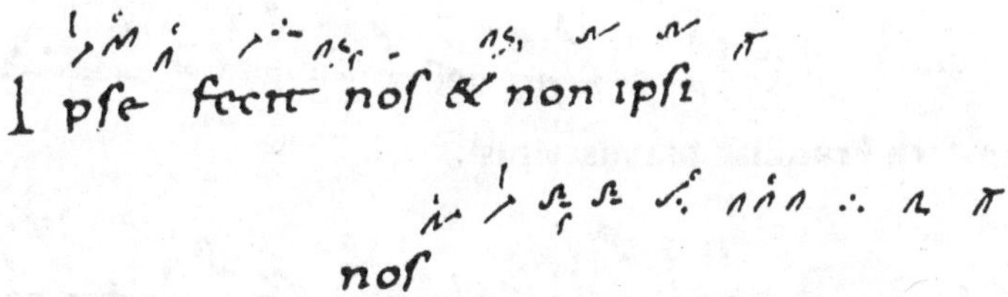

GAL2

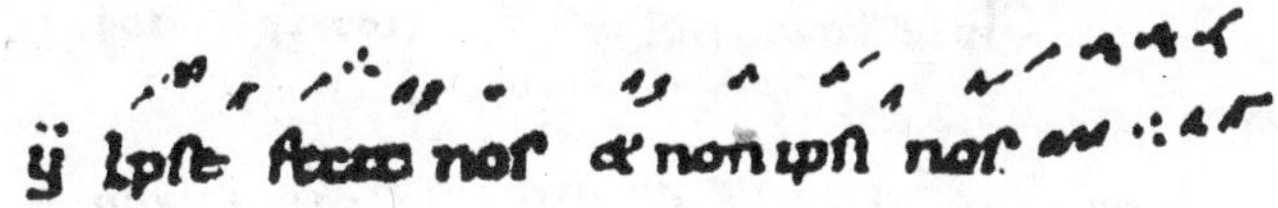

MUR3

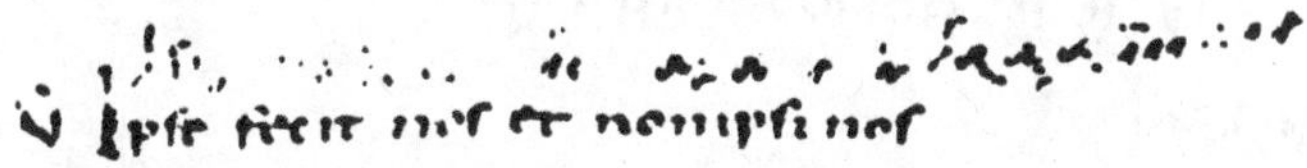

LAN

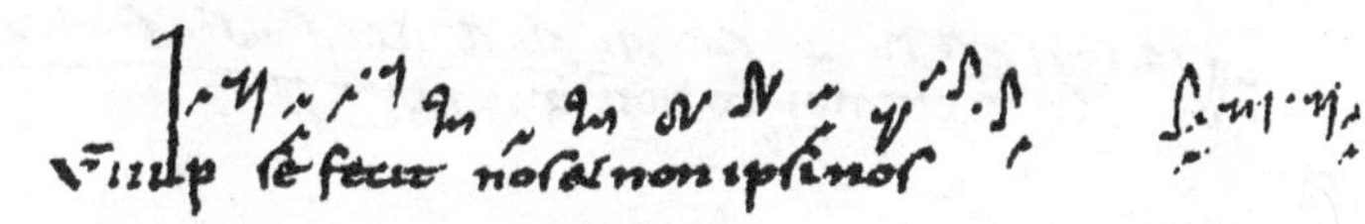

CHA1

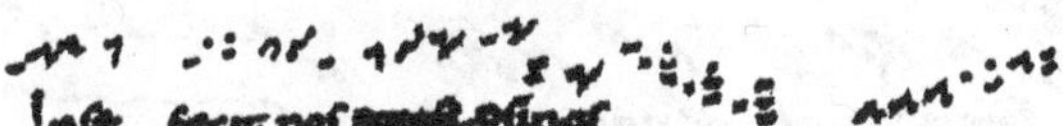

Western Frankish manuscripts

CLU1

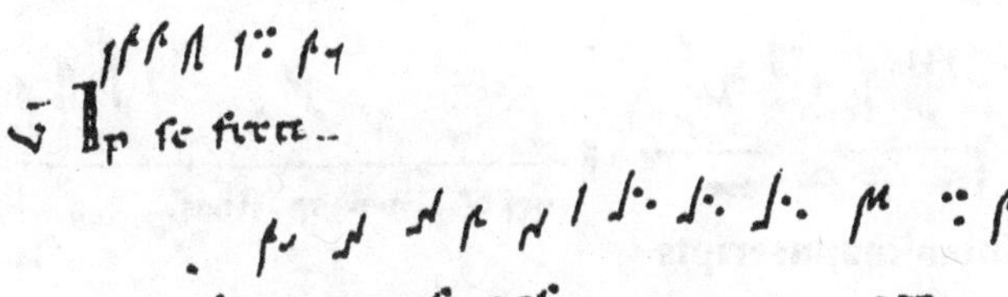

NOY4

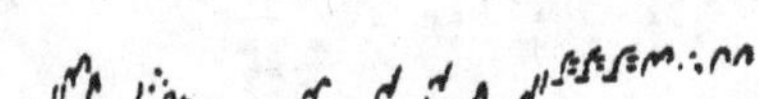

DEN1

Northern Italian manuscripts

LAV

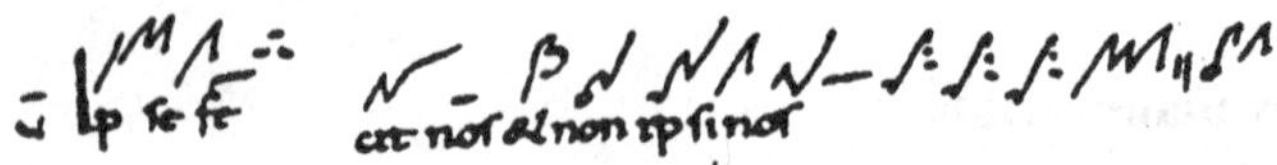

BRE

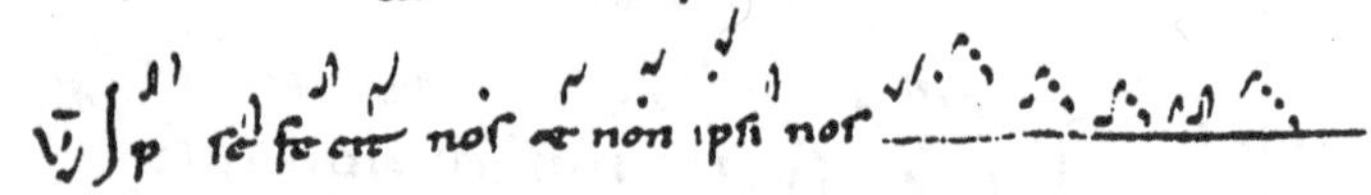

Eastern Frankish manuscripts

KLO1

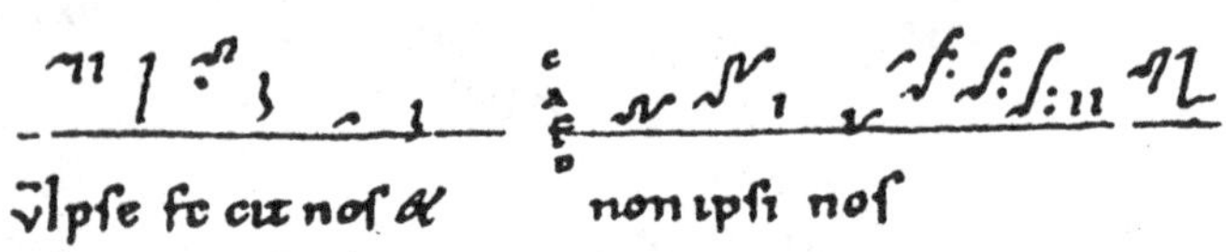

PAS2

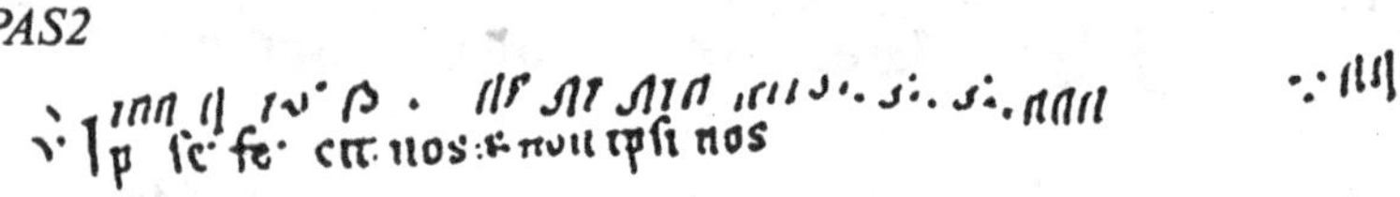

MOG4

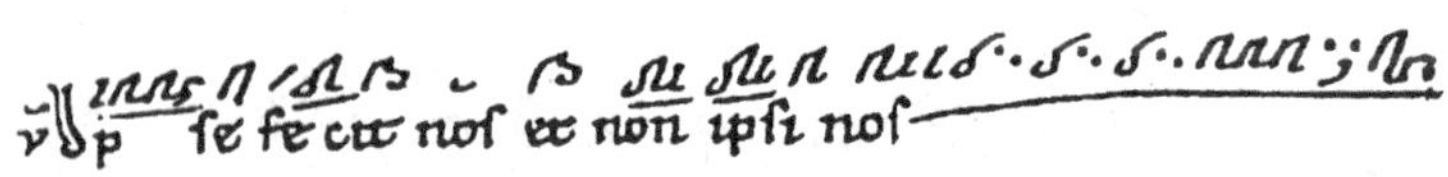

STM

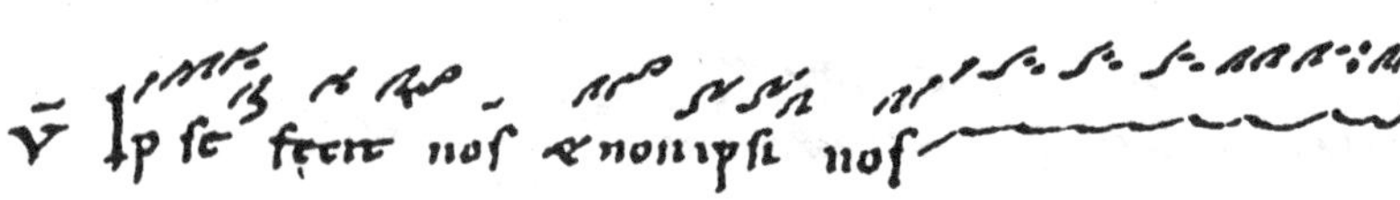

Beneventan manuscripts

BEN5

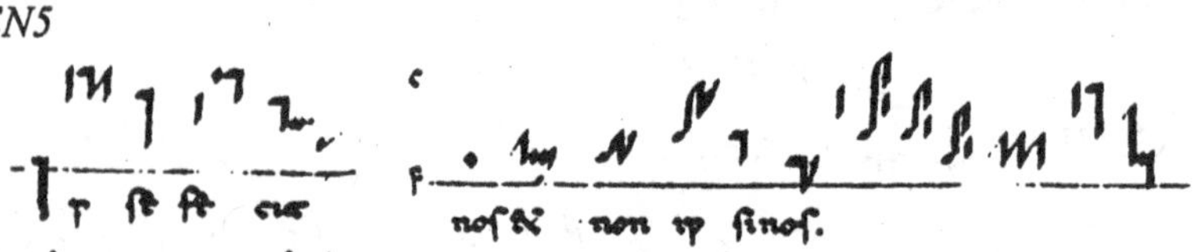

Aquitanian manuscripts

YRX

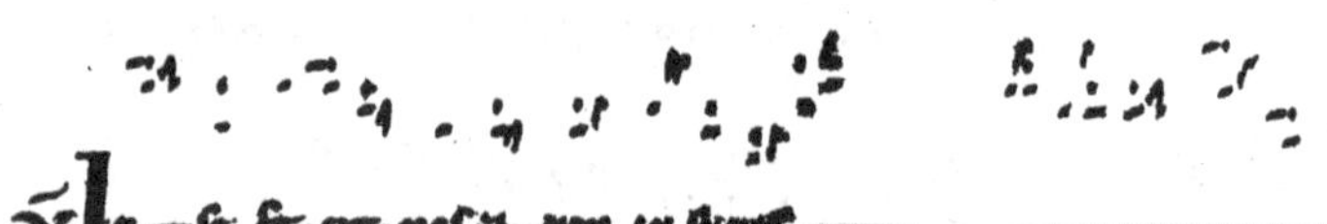

ALB

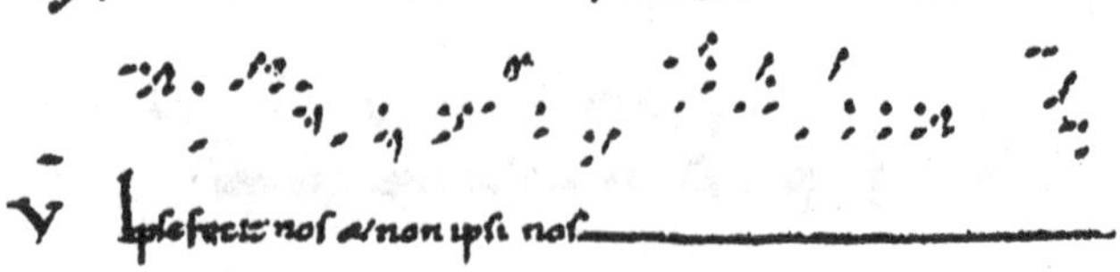

Cluniac manuscripts (pitched)

DIJ1

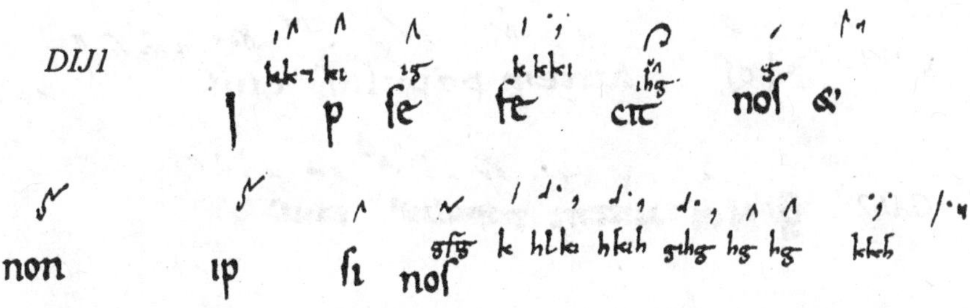

IRI

SAB

ROG1

10. ' nos autem populus eius'

Early manuscripts

GAL1 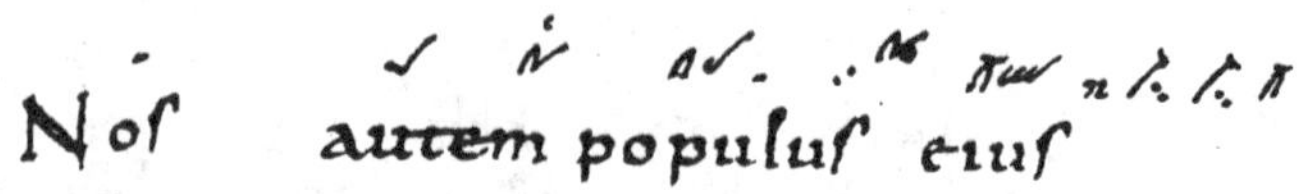

GAL2 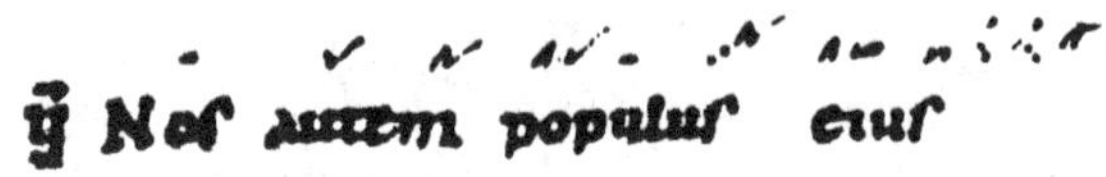

MUR3 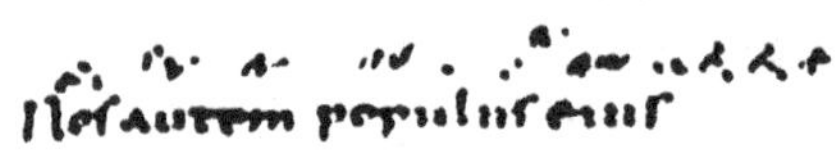

LAN 

CHA1 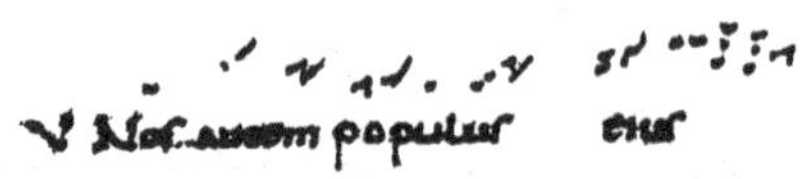

Western Frankish manuscripts

CLU1 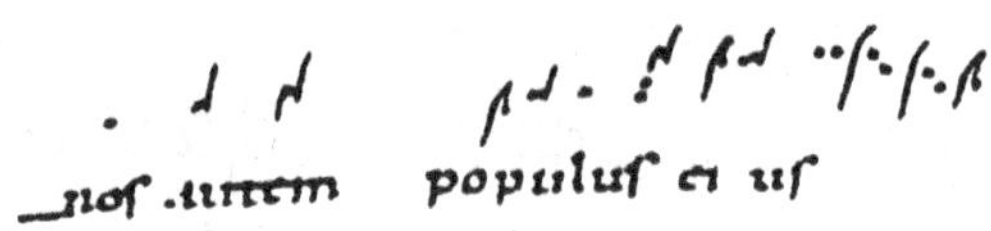

NOY4 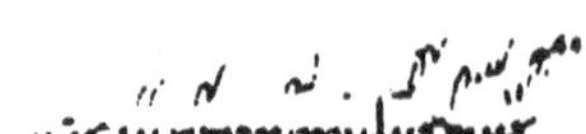

DEN1 

Northern Italian manuscripts

LAV

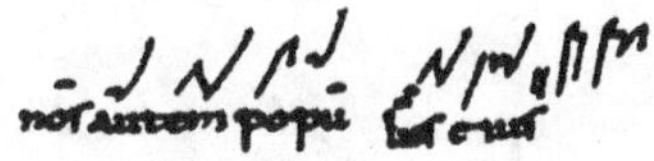

BRE

Eastern Frankish manuscripts

KLO1

PAS2

MOG4

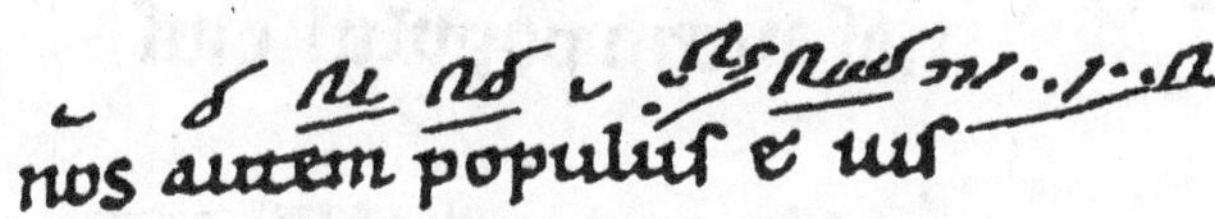

STM

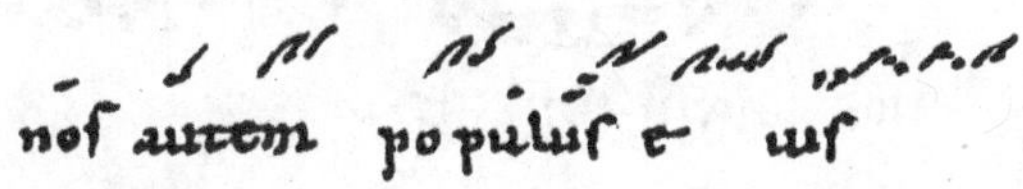

Beneventan manuscripts

BEN5

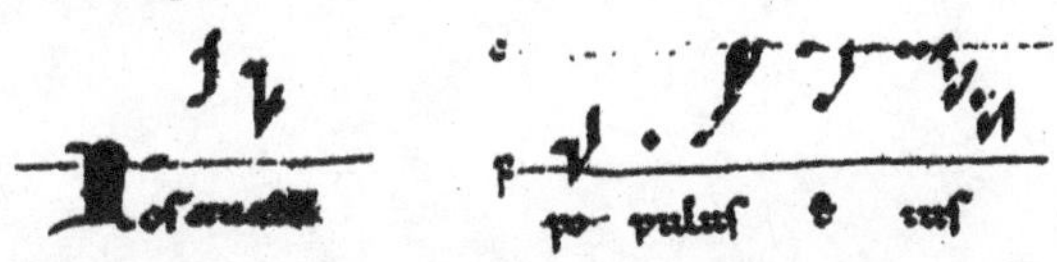

Aquitanian manuscripts

YRX

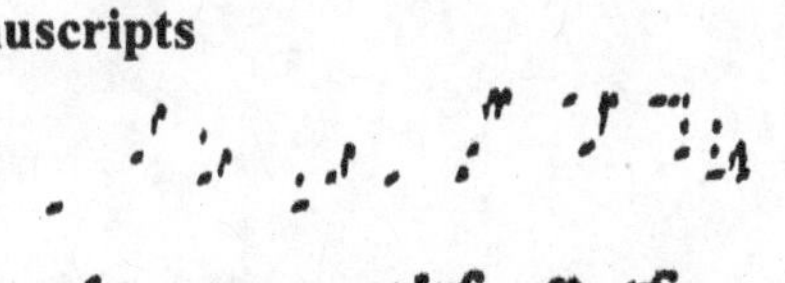

ALB

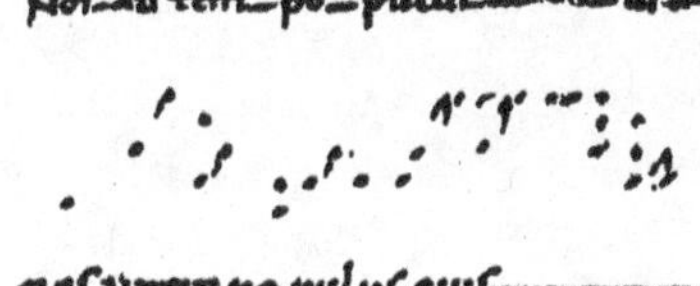

Cluniac manuscripts (pitched)

DIJ1

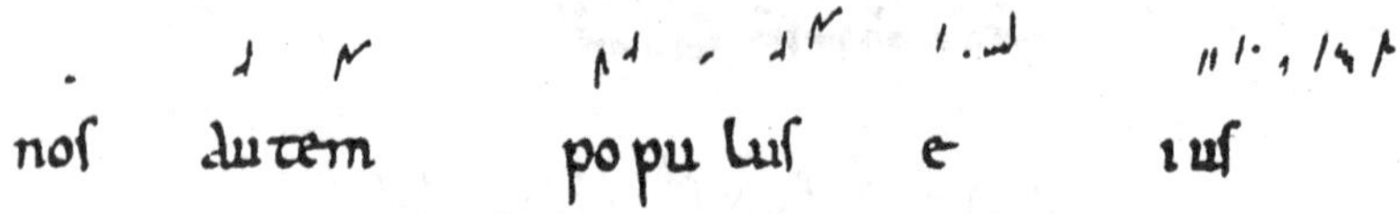

IRI

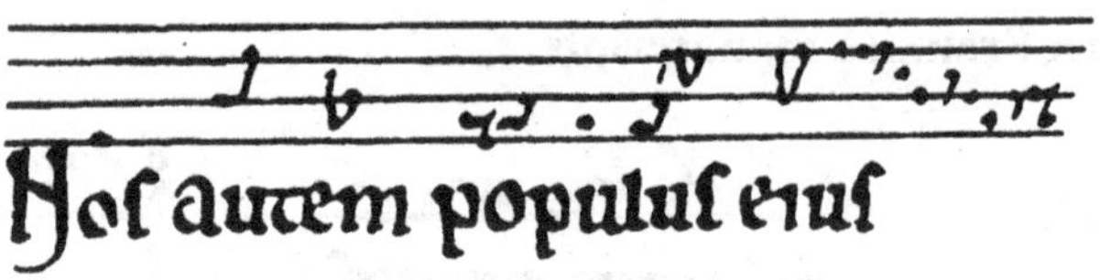

SAB

ROG1

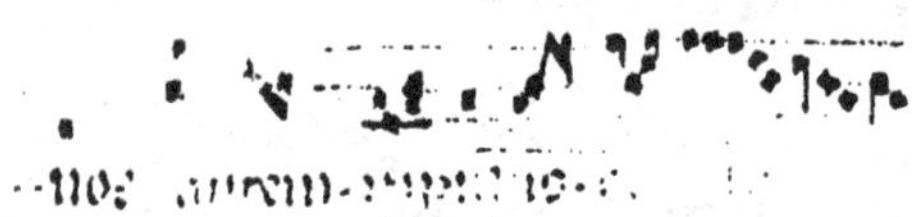

11. 'et oues pascue eius'

Early manuscripts

GAL1 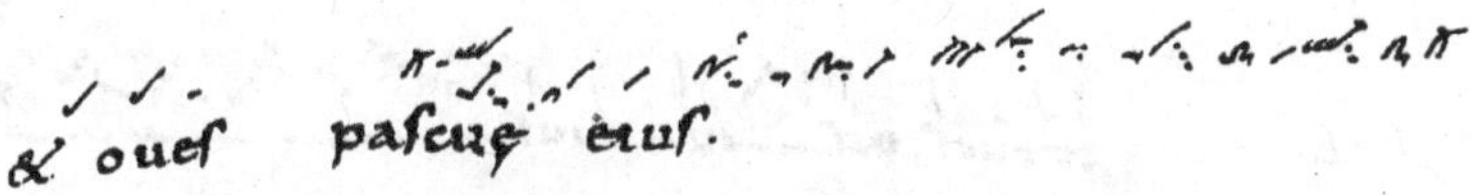

GAL2 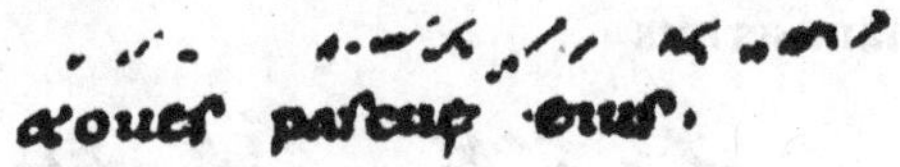

MUR3 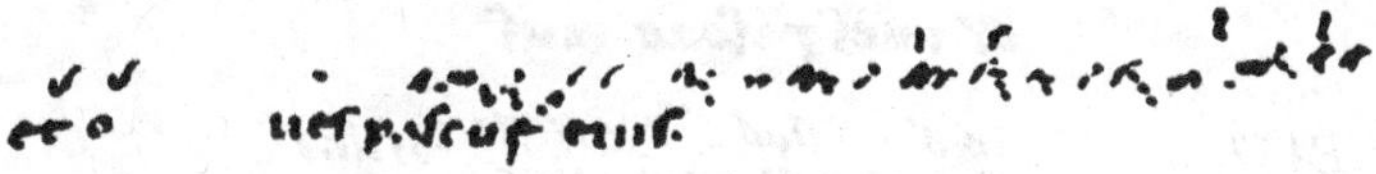

LAN 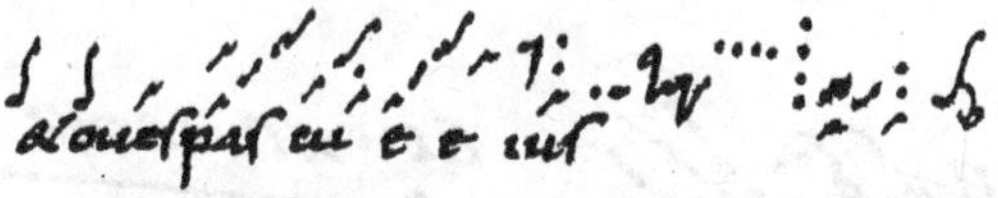

CHA1 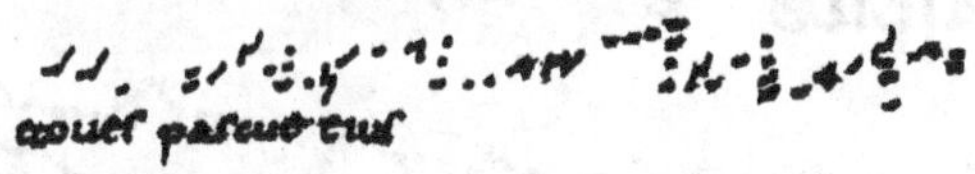

Western Frankish manuscripts

CLU1 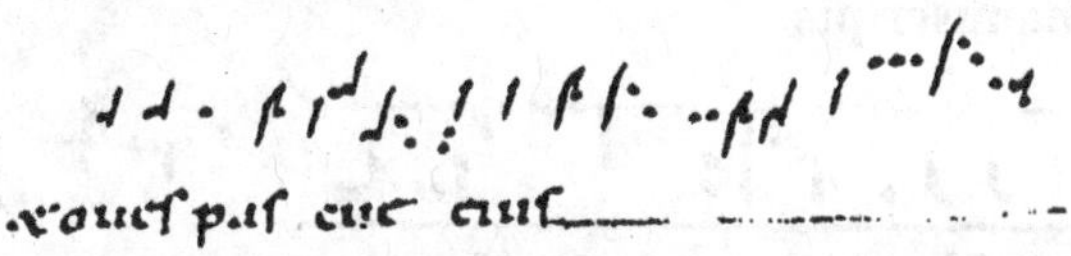

NOY4 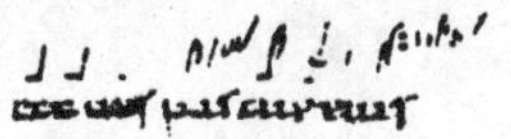

DEN1

Northern Italian manuscripts

LAV

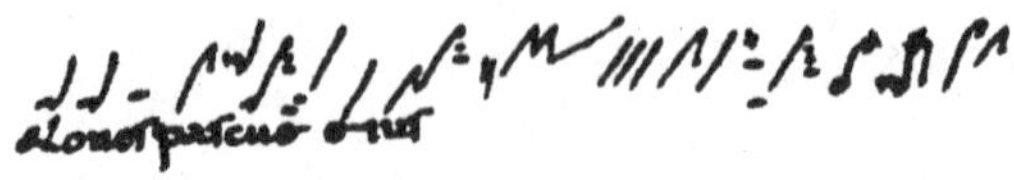

BRE

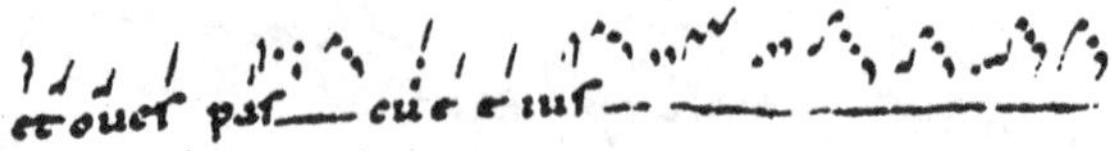

Eastern Frankish manuscripts

KLO1

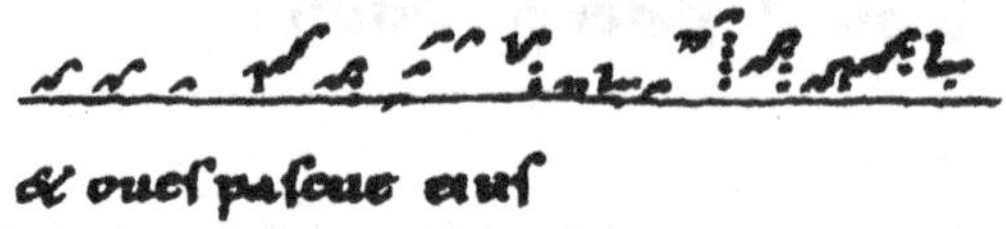

PAS2

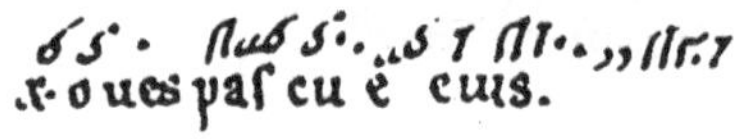

MOG4

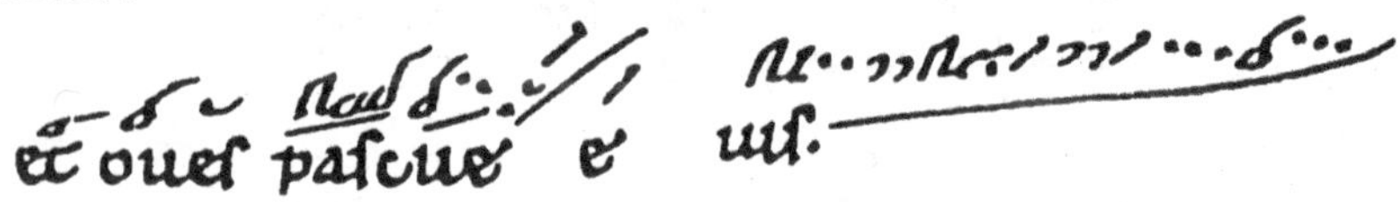

STM

Beneventan manuscripts

BEN5

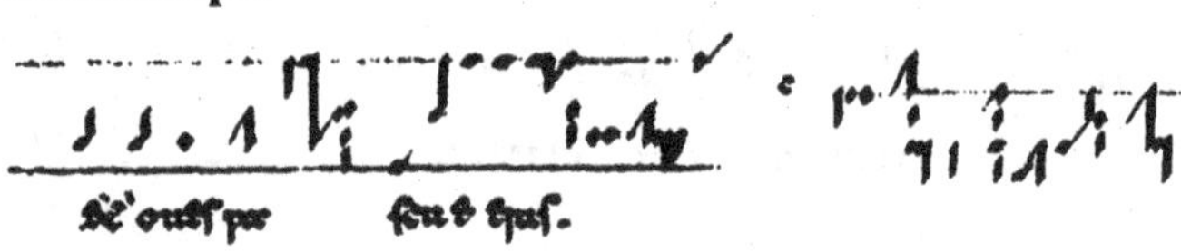

Aquitanian manuscripts

YRX

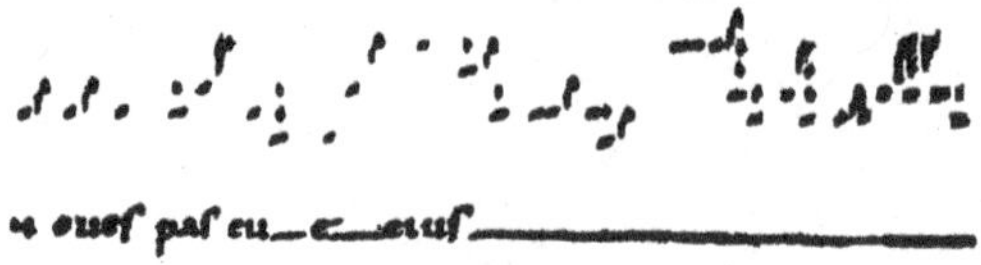

ALB

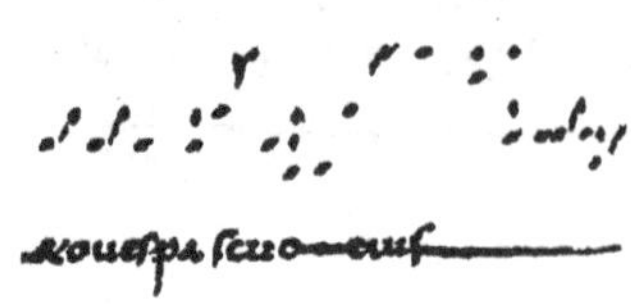

Cluniac manuscripts (pitched)

DIJ1

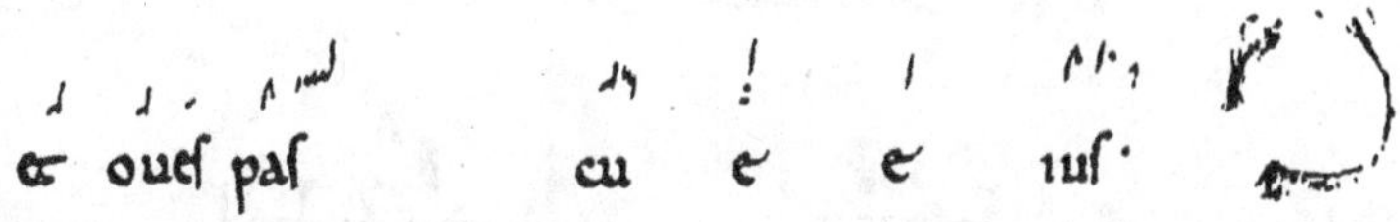

IRI

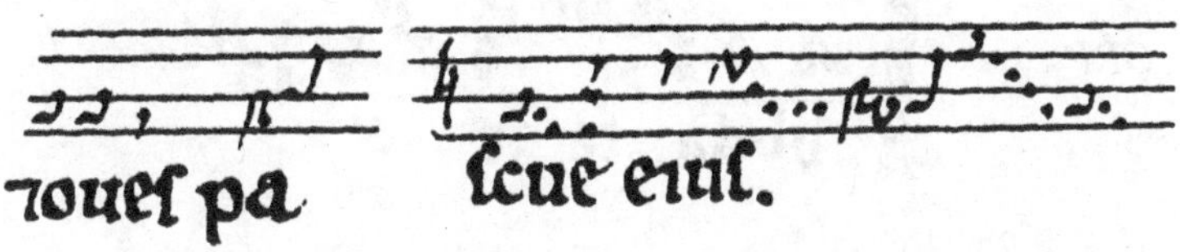

SAB

ROG1

1. 'Iubilate deo'

ORC

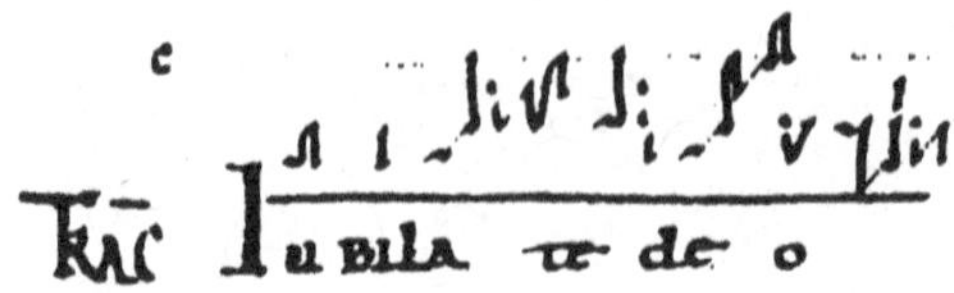

ORJ

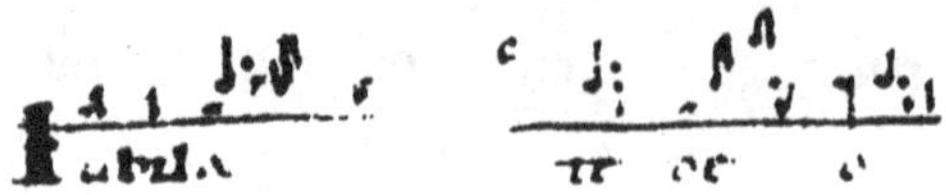

ORP

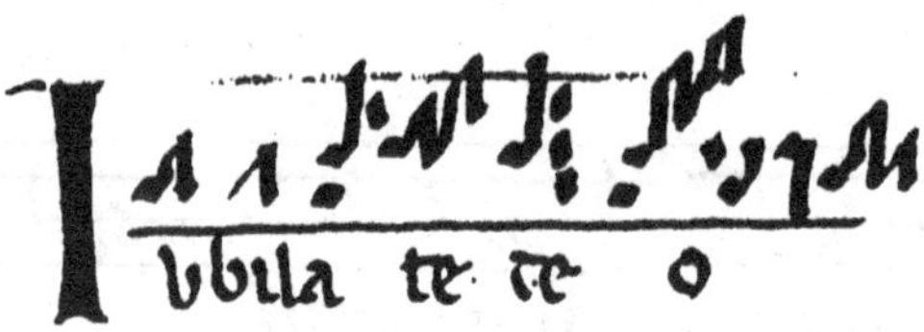

2. 'omnis terra'

ORC

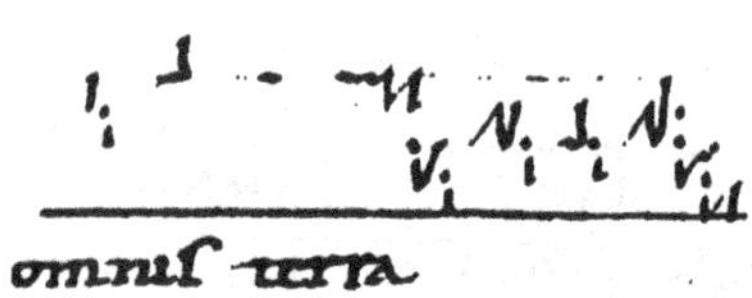

ORJ

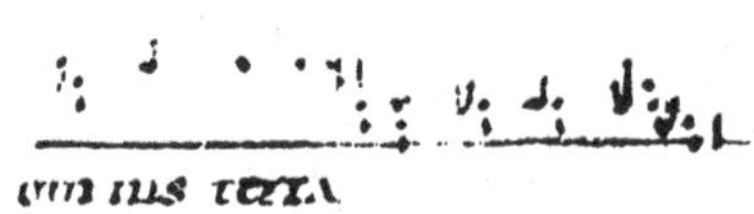

ORP

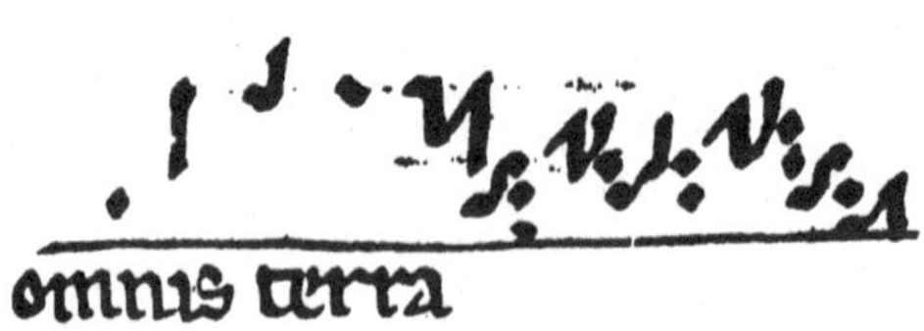

3. 'seruite domino'

ORC

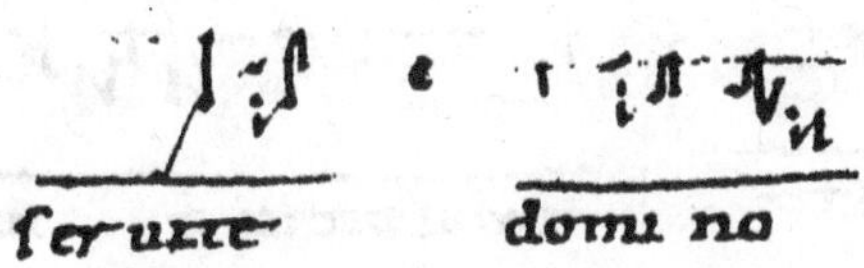

ORJ

ORP

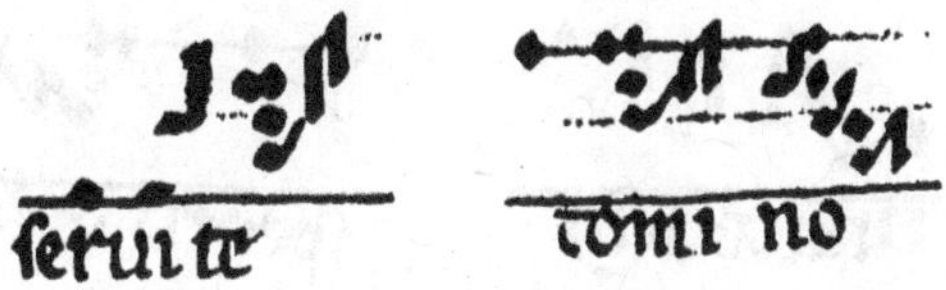

4. 'in letitia'

ORC

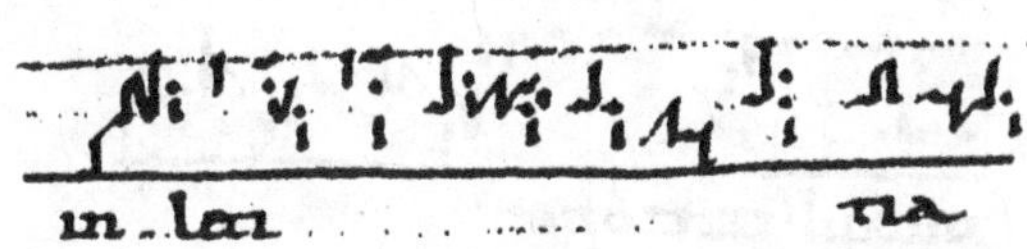

ORJ

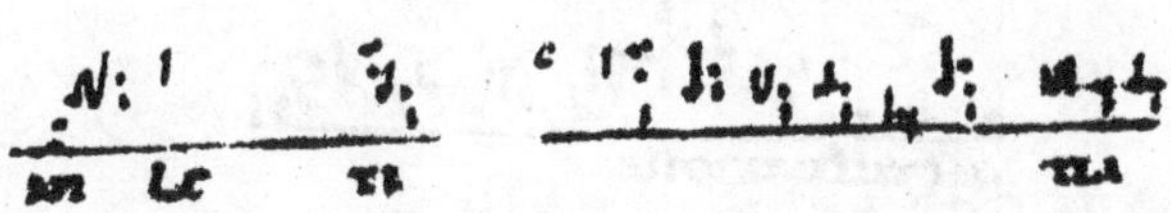

ORP

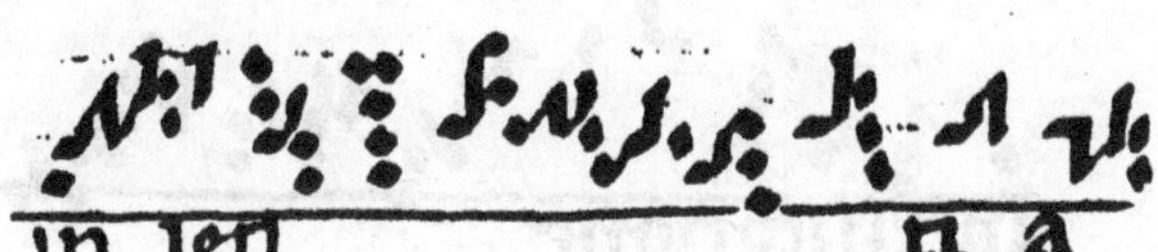

5. 'Intrate in conspectu eius'

ORC

ORJ

ORP

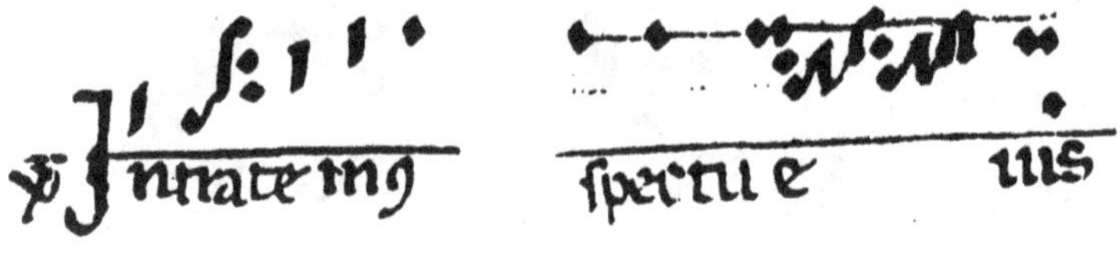

6. 'in exultatione'

ORC

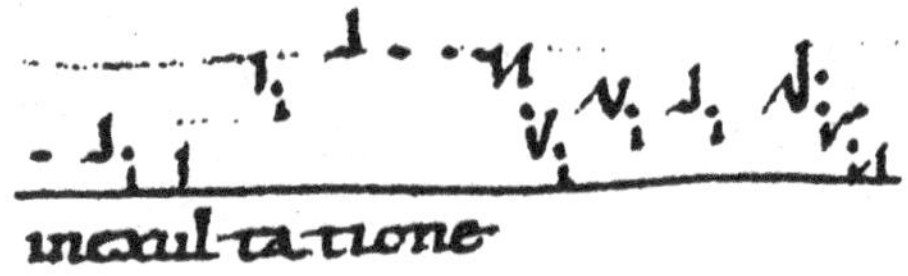

ORJ

ORP

7. 'Scitote quod dominus'

ORC

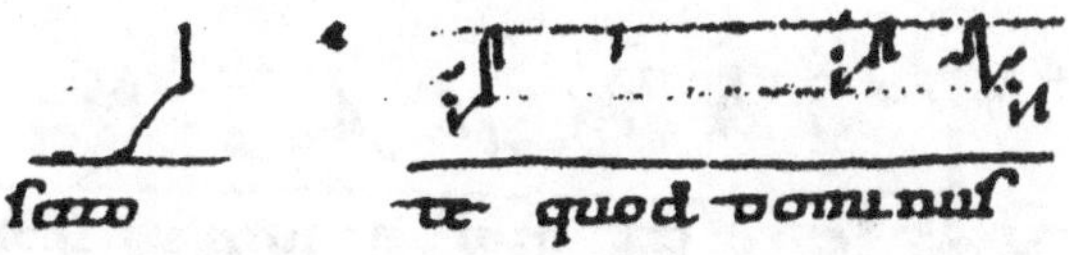

ORJ

ORP

8. 'ipse est deus'

ORC

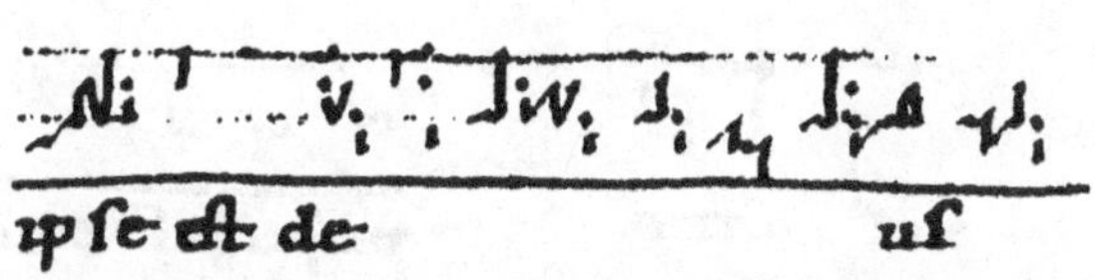

ORJ

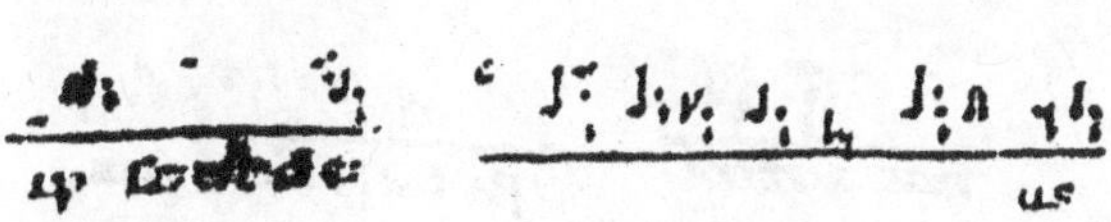

ORP

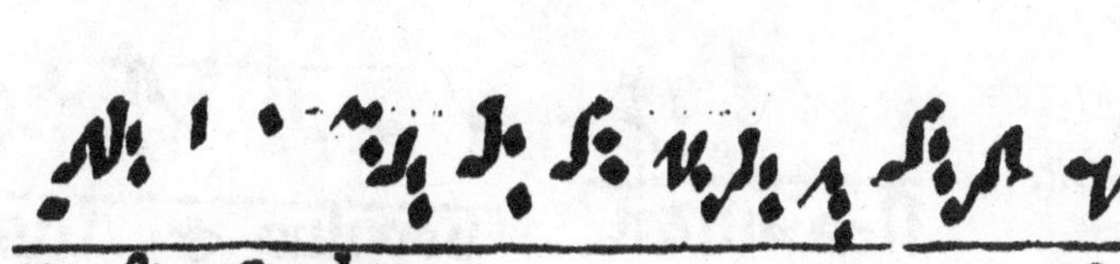

9. 'Ipse fecit nos et non ipsi nos'

ORC

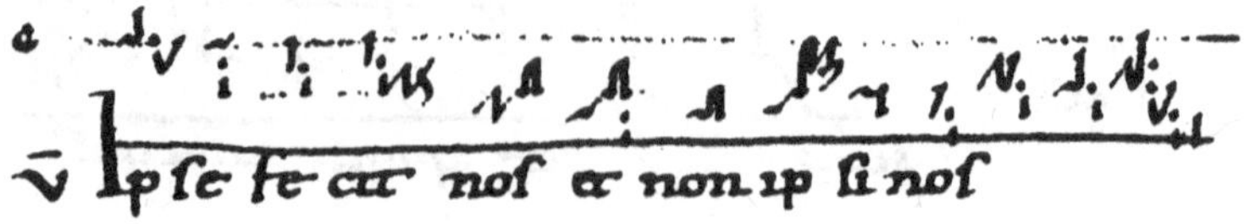

ORJ

ORP

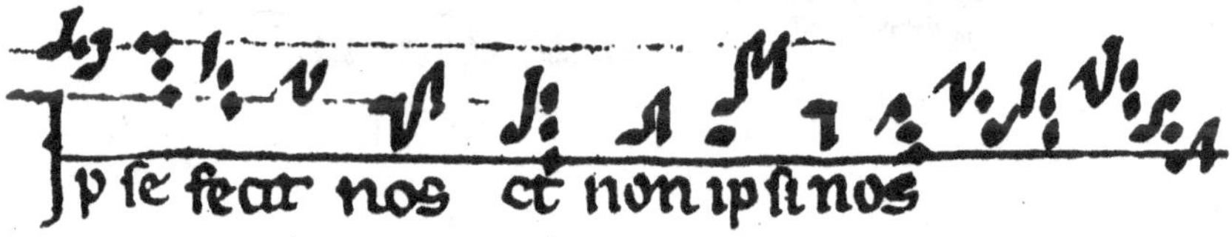

10. 'nos autem populus eius'

ORC

ORJ

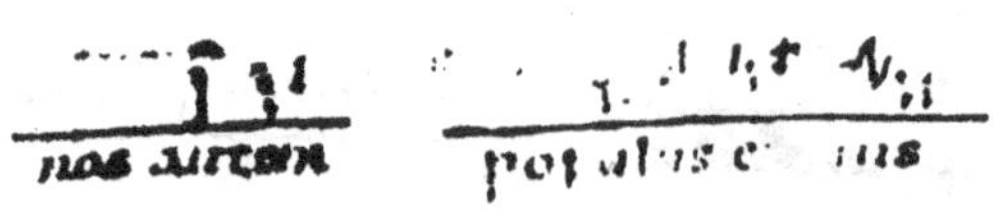

ORP

11. 'et oues pascue eius'

ORC

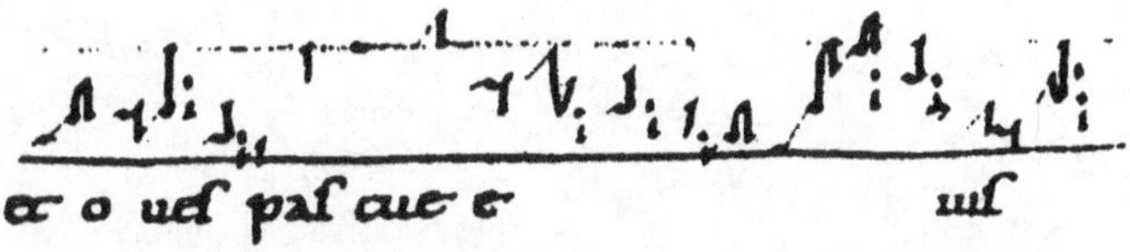

ORJ

ORP

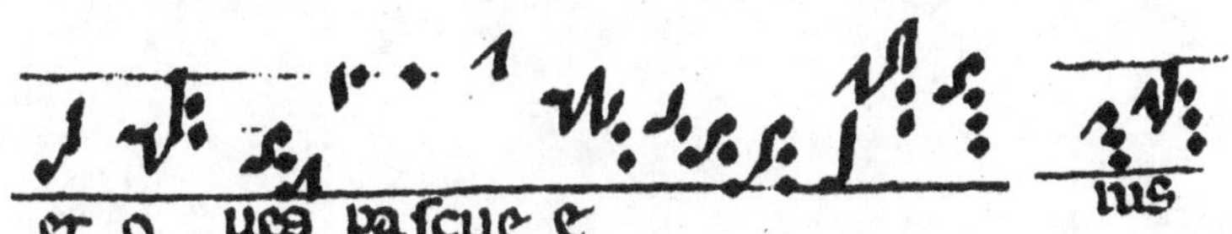

Appendix 2

The Phrase Types and their Subgroups in the Old Roman and Gregorian Traditions

Phrase *A1* (Gregorian)

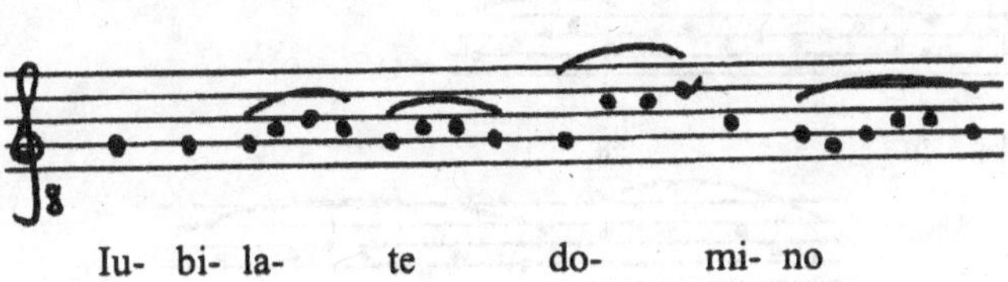

Phrase *A1* (Old Roman)

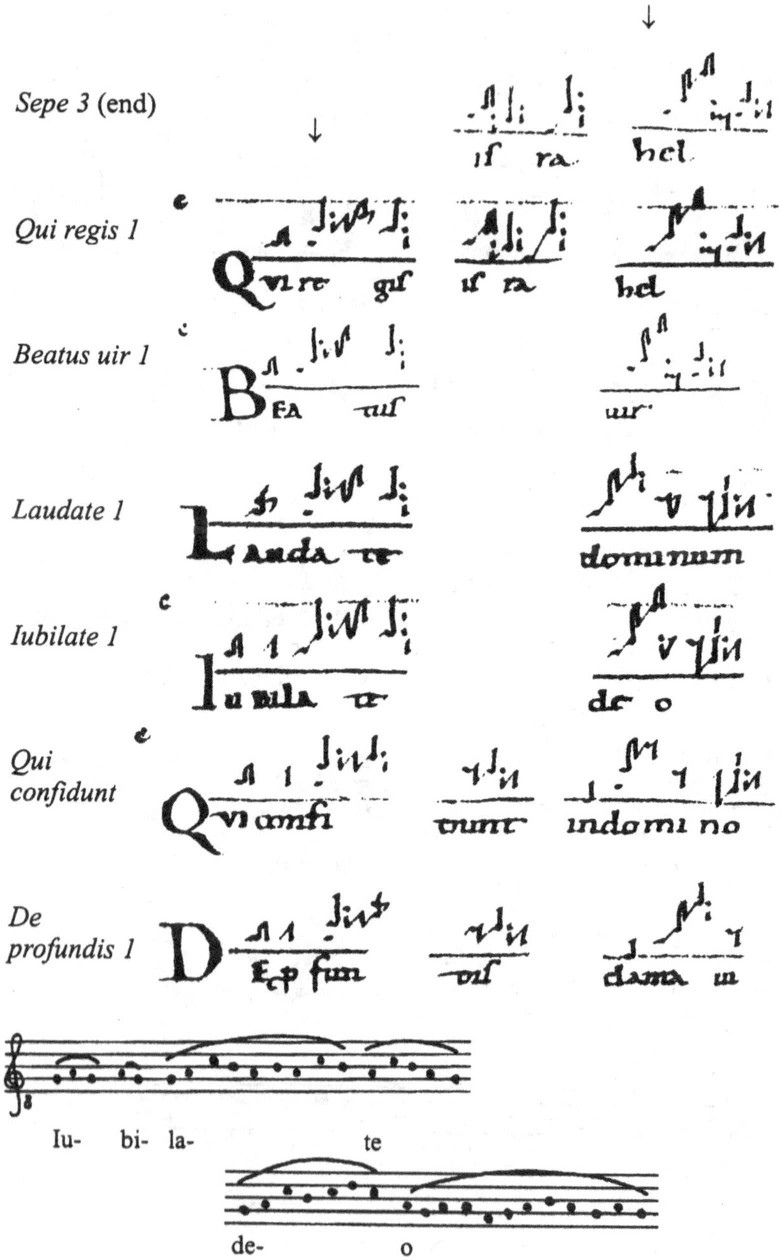

Phrase *A2* (Gregorian)

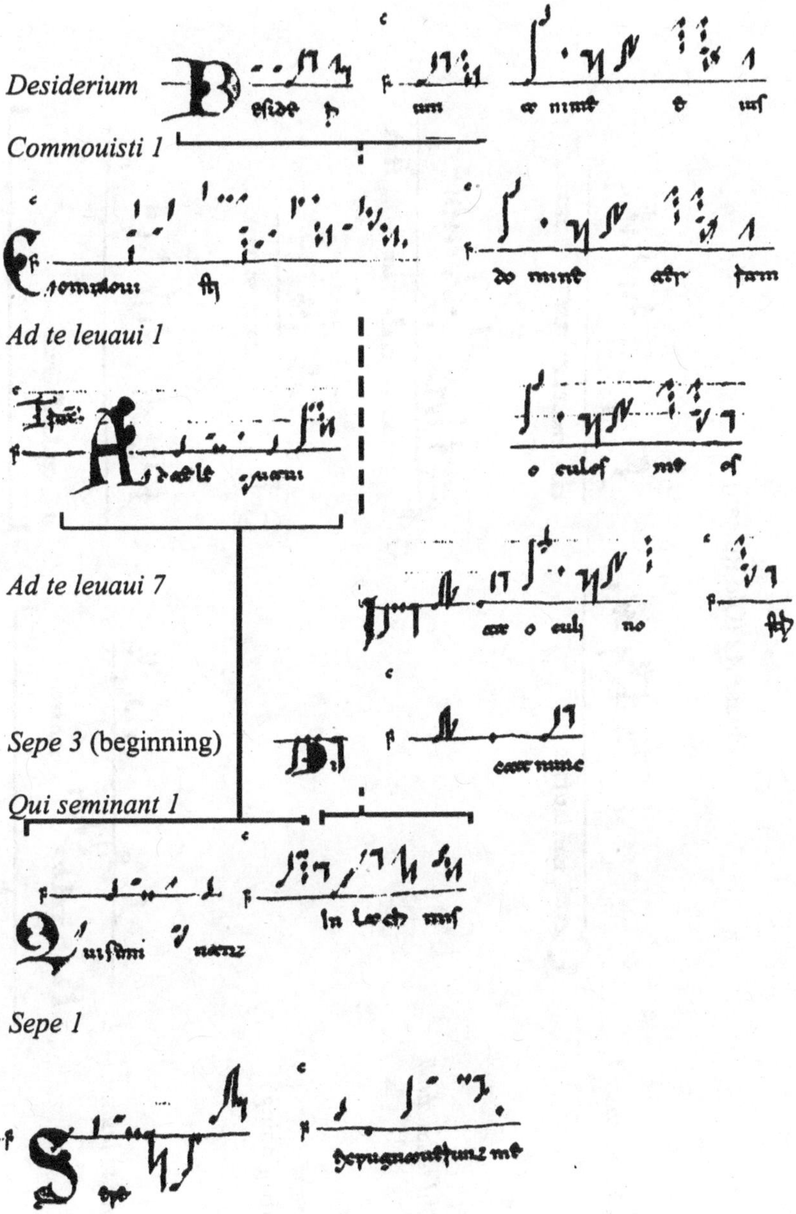

Phrase *A2* (Old Roman)

Commouisti 1

Ad te leuaui 7

Sepe 3 (beginning)

Ad te leuaui 1

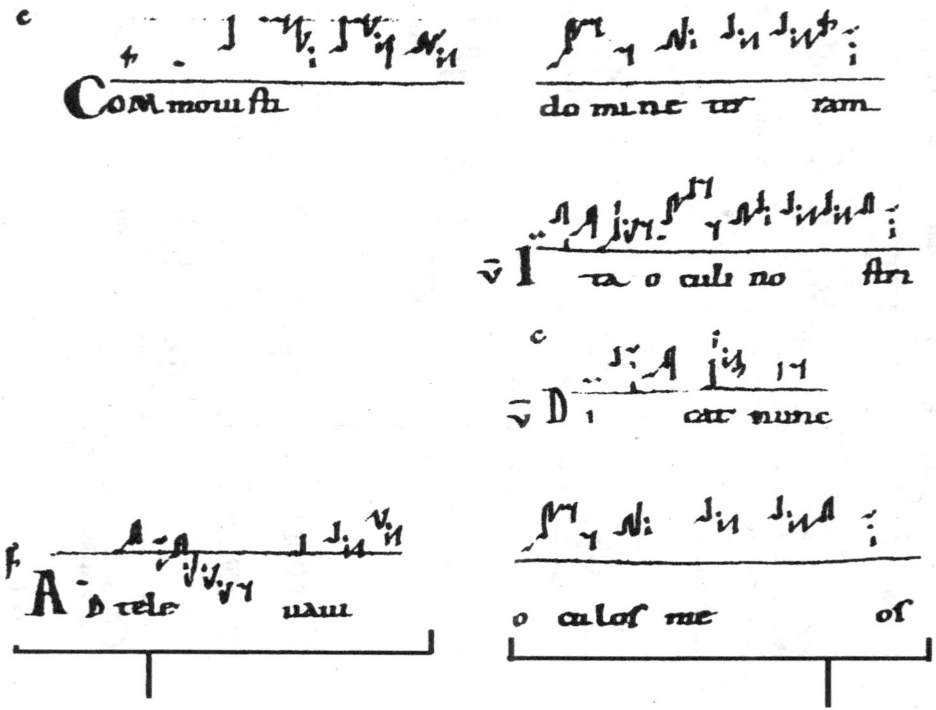

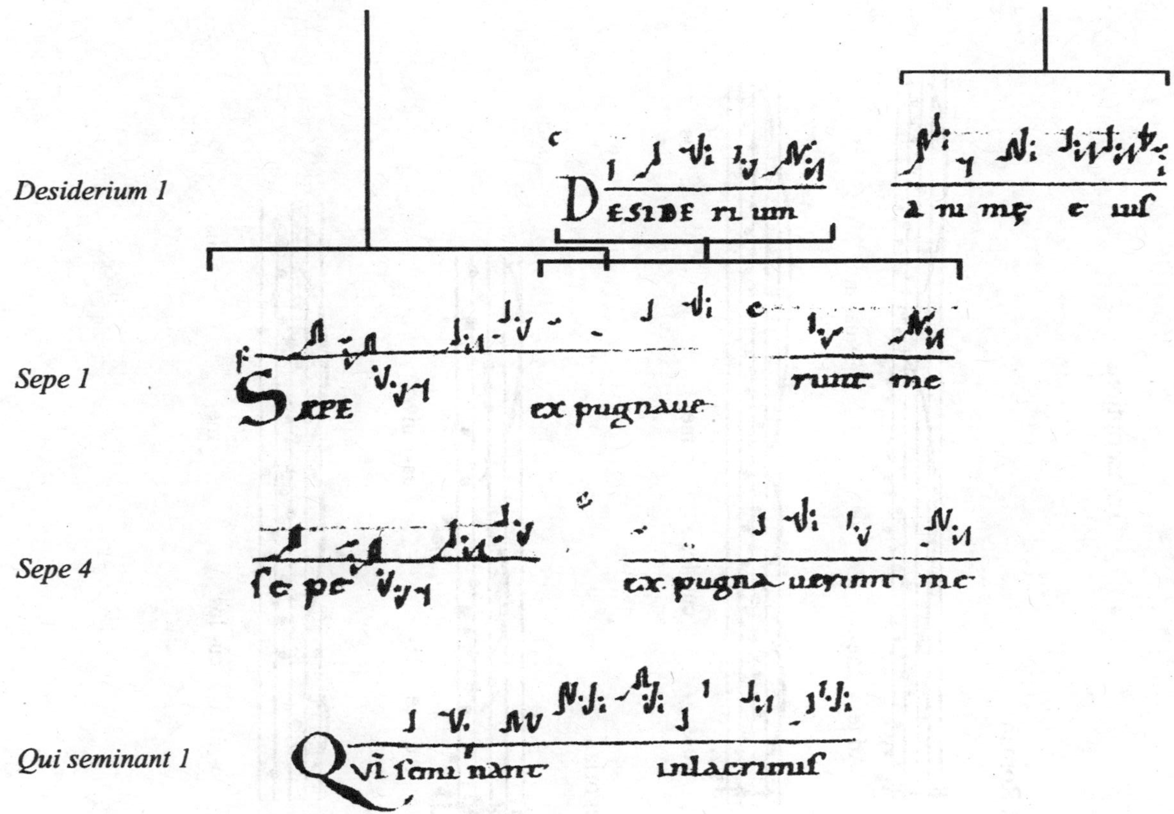
Desiderium 1
Sepe 1
Sepe 4
Qui seminant 1

Phrase *A2* (Gregorian and Old Roman)

Transcriptions

Old Roman

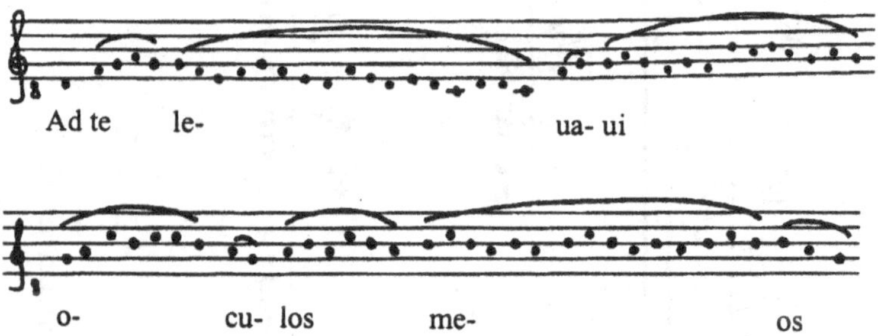

Gregorian

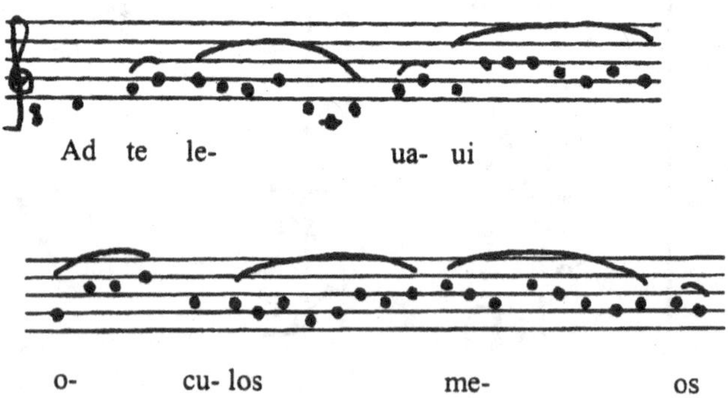

Phrase *B1* (Gregorian)

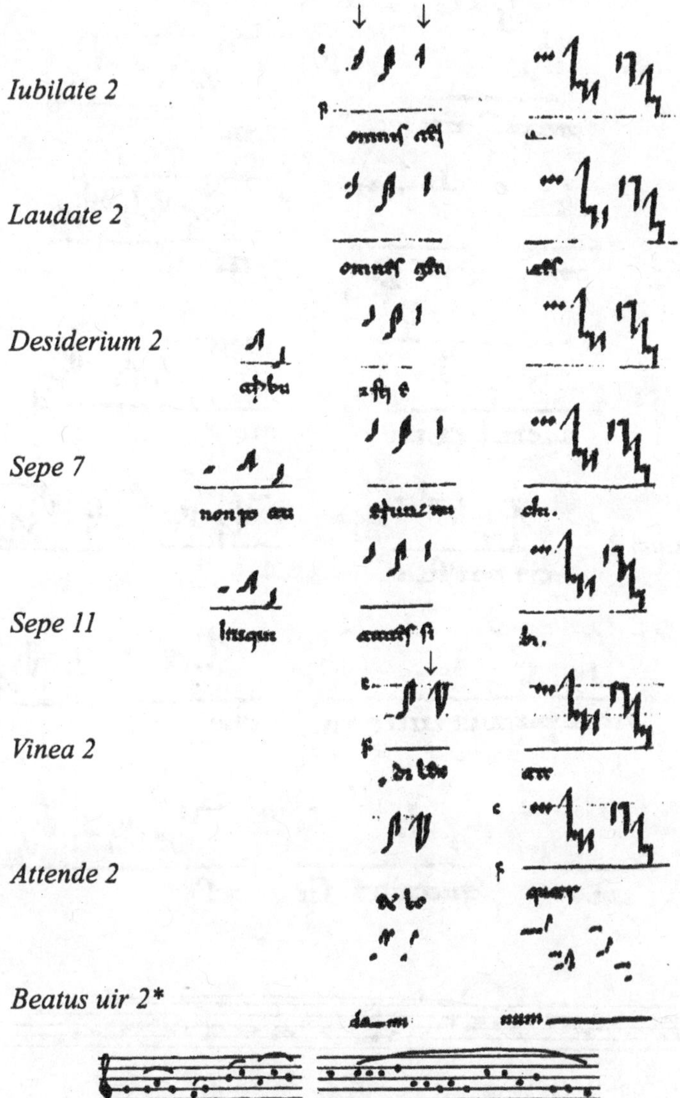

*The Beneventan manuscripts have ***B5*** instead of ***B1*** for this phrase, prompted by the textual connection with De profundis 2, 'domine'. *YRX* has therefore been used to provide this example.

Phrase *B1* (Old Roman)

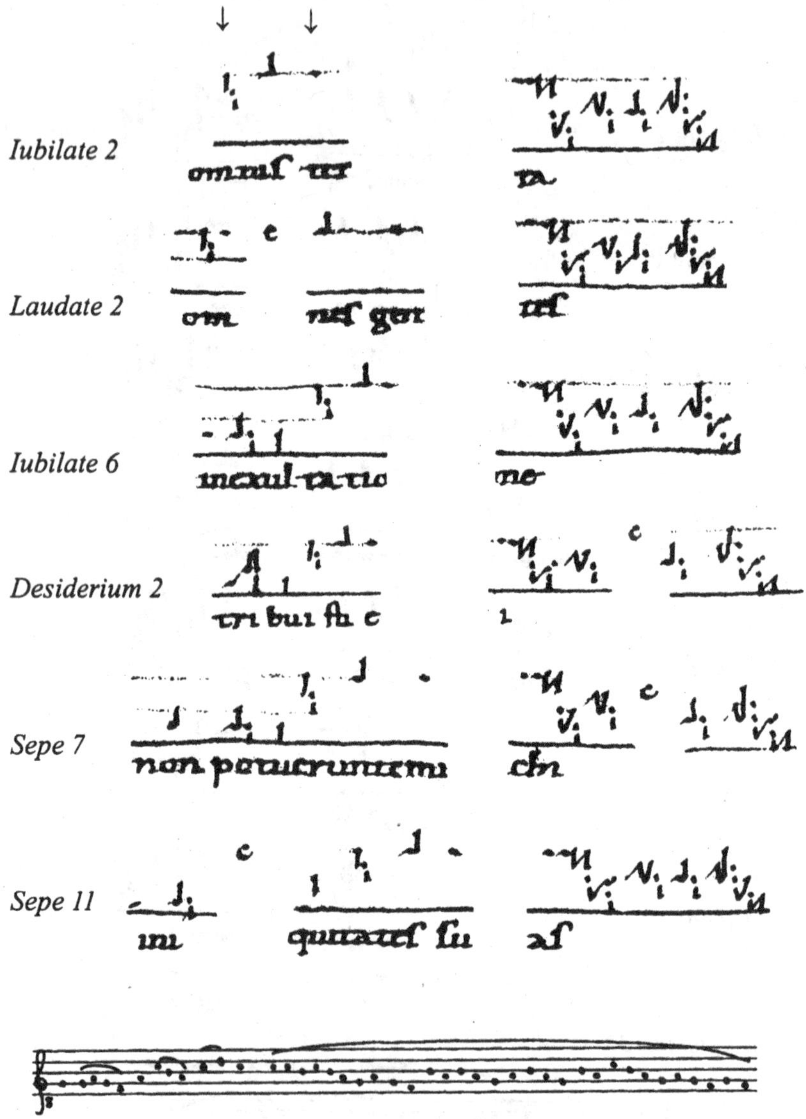

Phrase *B2* (Gregorian)

Cantemus 2

Cantemus 4

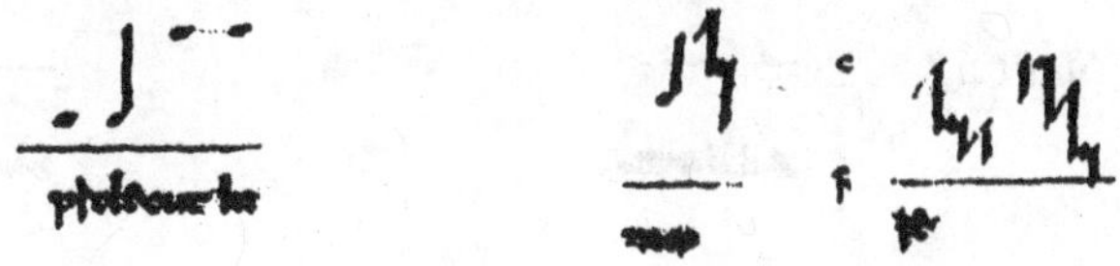

Cantemus 7

Vinea 5

Vinea 7

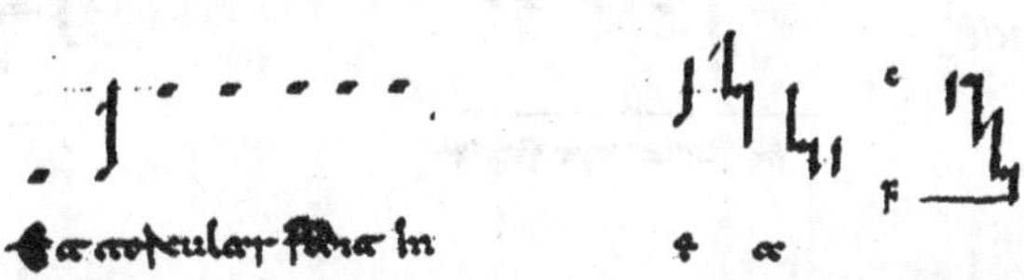

Qui confidunt 4

Qui confidunt 8

Phrase *B2* (Gregorian) *cont.*

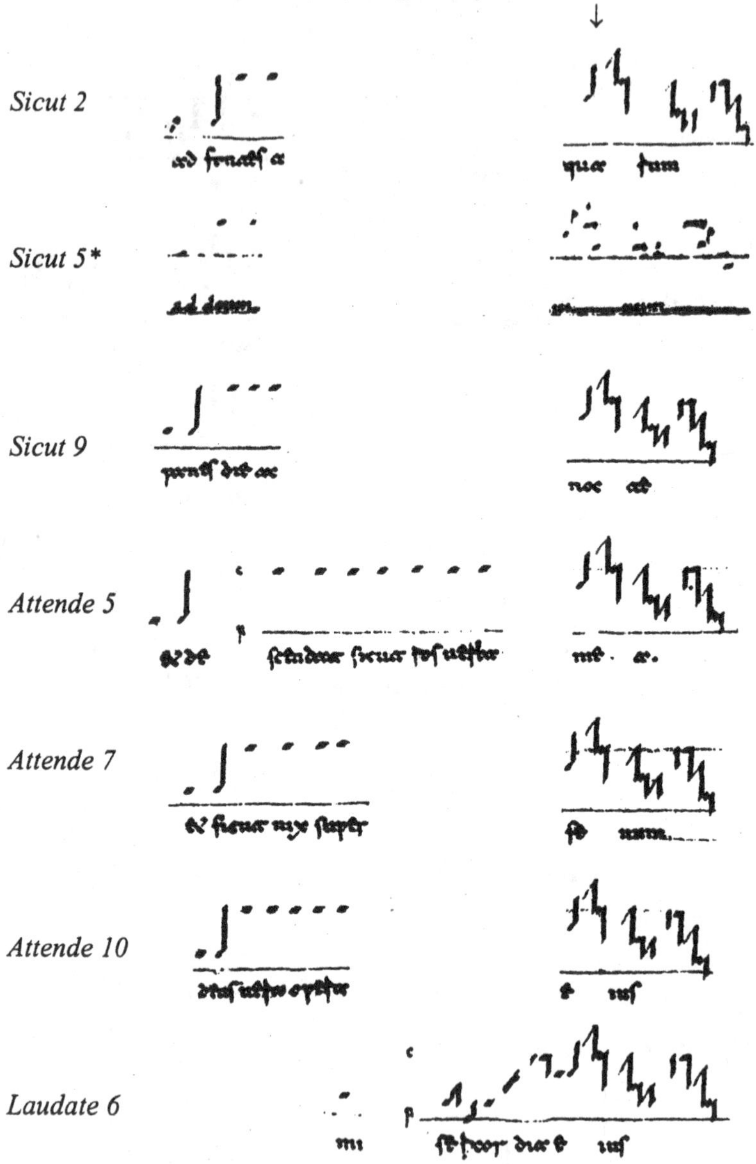

* The Beneventan manuscripts have a single phrase ***B2*** for the first two phrases of this verse (usually ***E1 B2***). *YRX* has therefore been used to provide this example

Phrase *B2* (Old Roman)

↓ ↓

Ad te leuaui 8

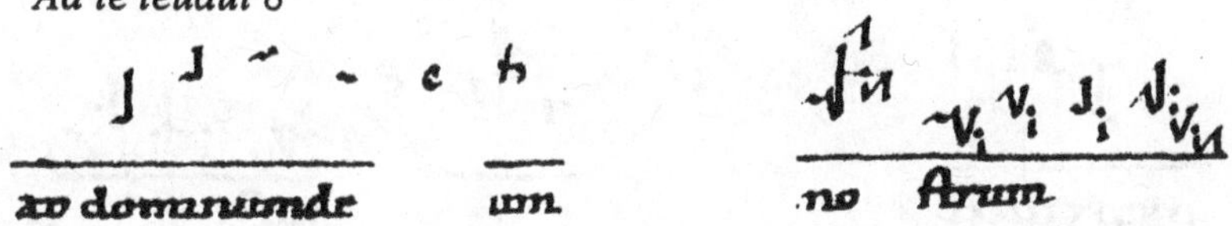

Qui regis 4

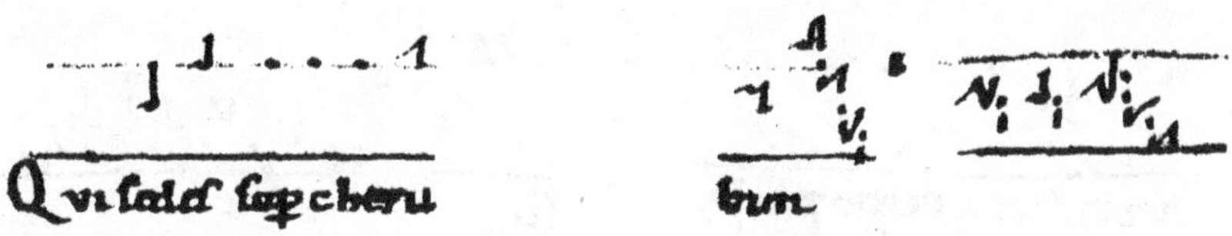

Beatus uir 2

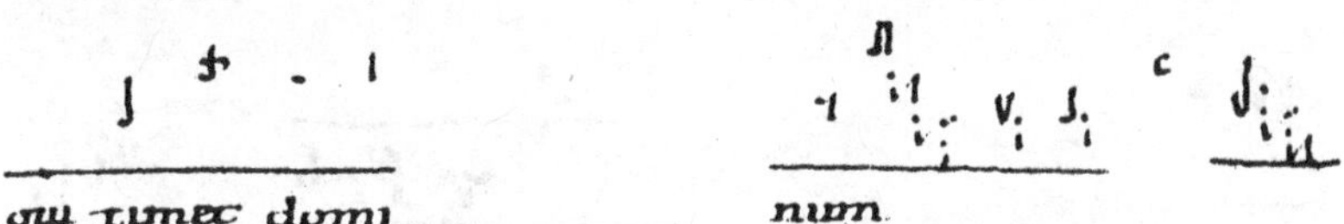

Beatus uir 6

Beatus uir 10

Phrase *B2* (Old Roman) *cont.*

Qui confidunt 8

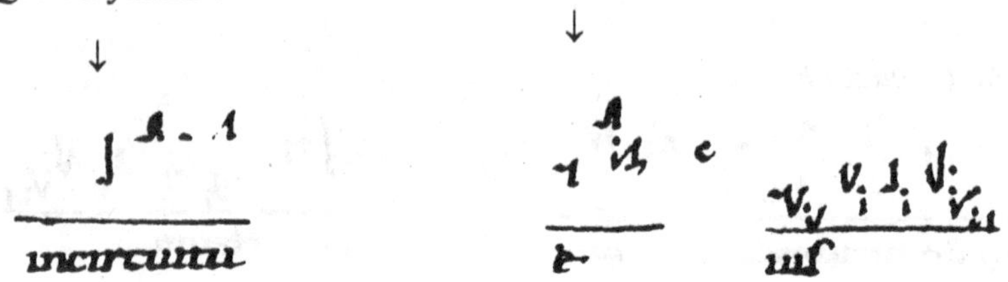

Qui confidunt 10

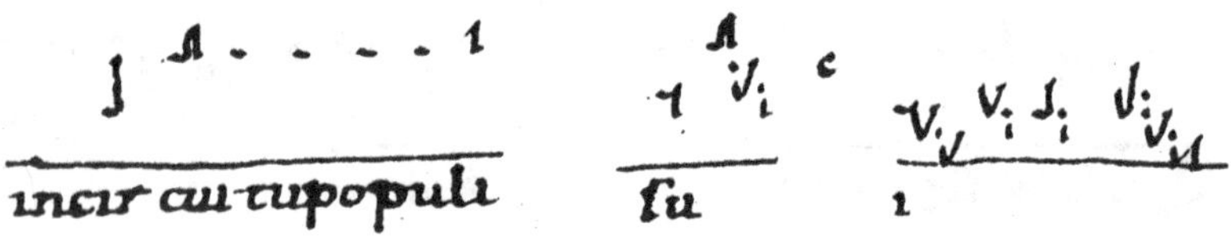

Qui confidunt 4

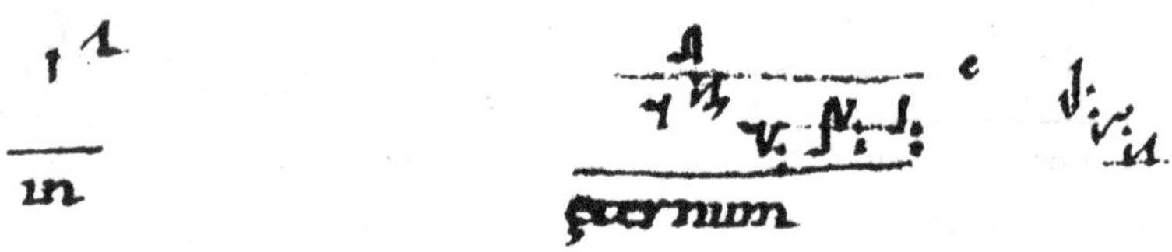

Laudate 6

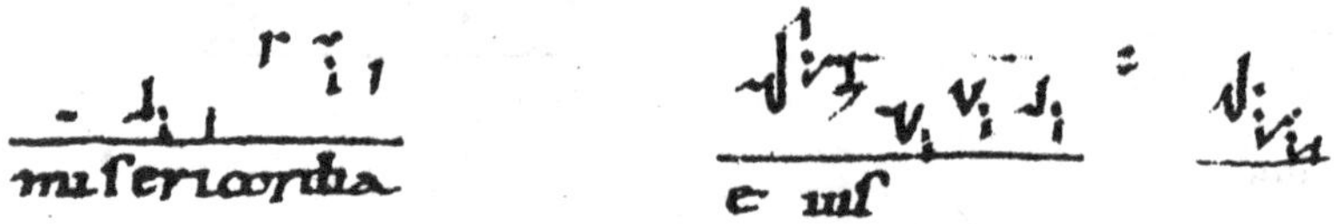

Phrase *B2* (Gregorian and Old Roman)

Transcriptions

Old Roman

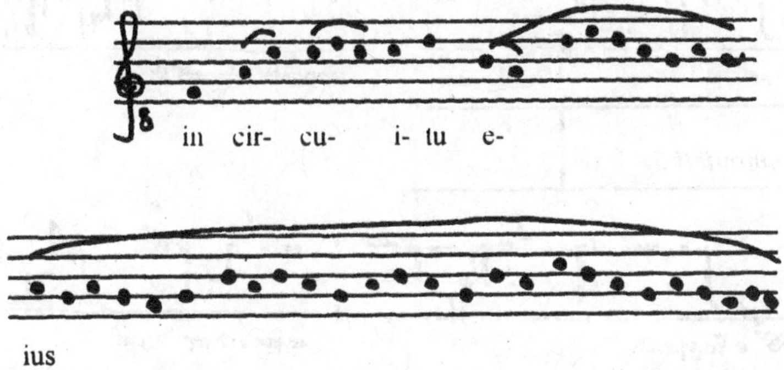

Gregorian

Phrase *B3* (Gregorian)

Commouisti 3

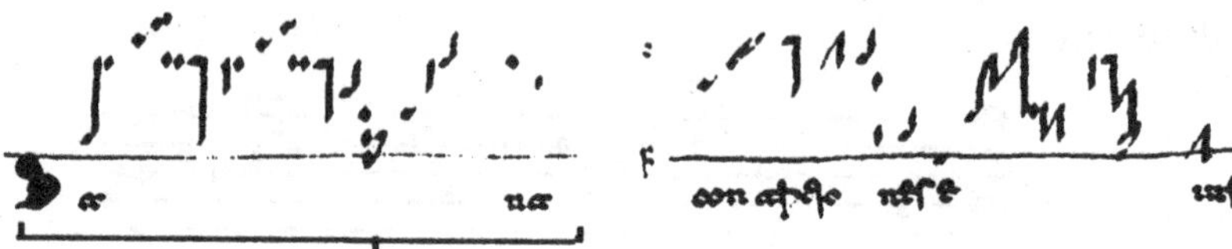

Commouisti 5

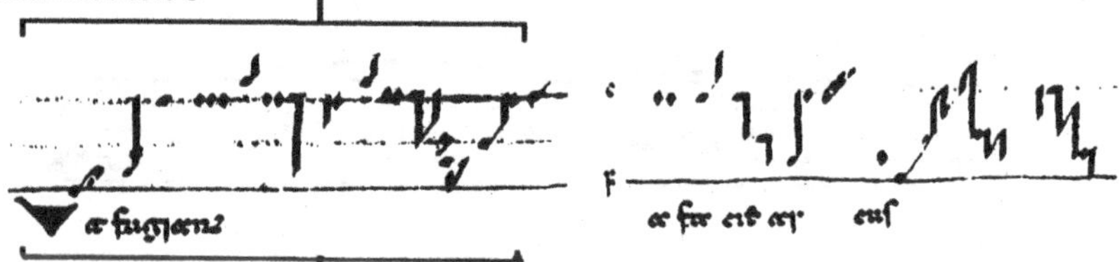

Qui regis 8

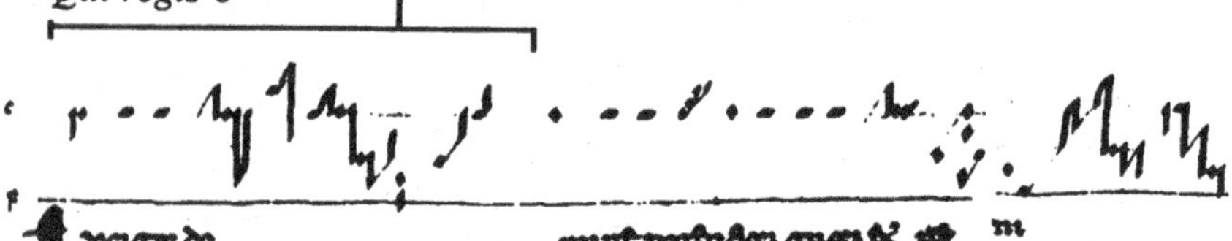

Ad te leuaui 8

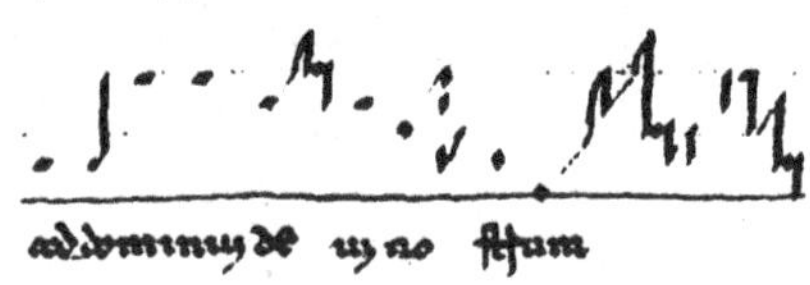

Qui confidunt 2

De profundis 11

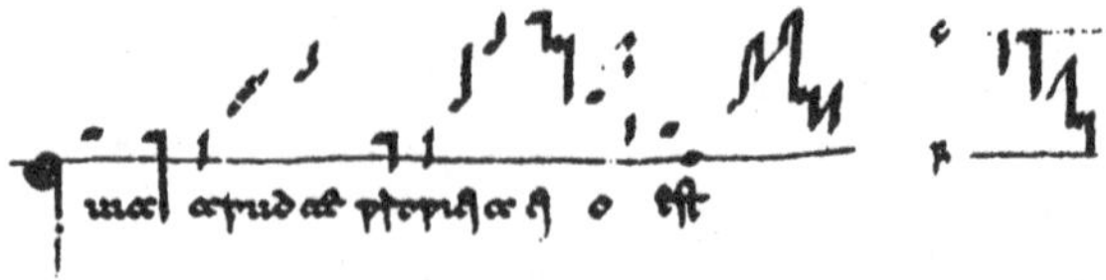

Phrase *B3* (Gregorian) *cont.*

Qui regis 3

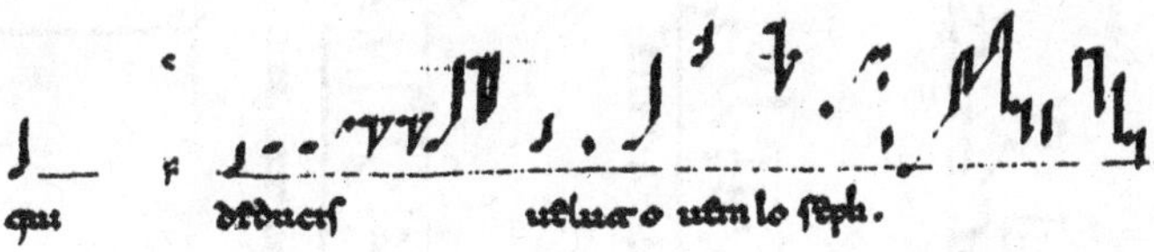

Sepe 3 (end)

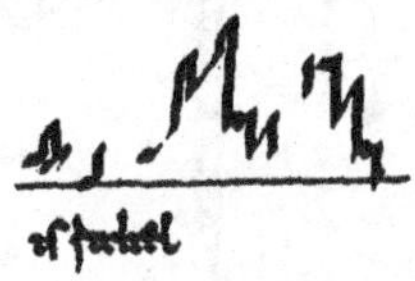

Qui regis 1 (end)

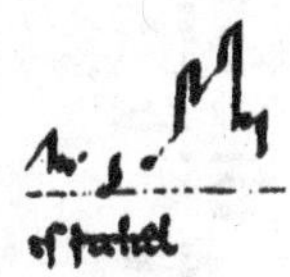

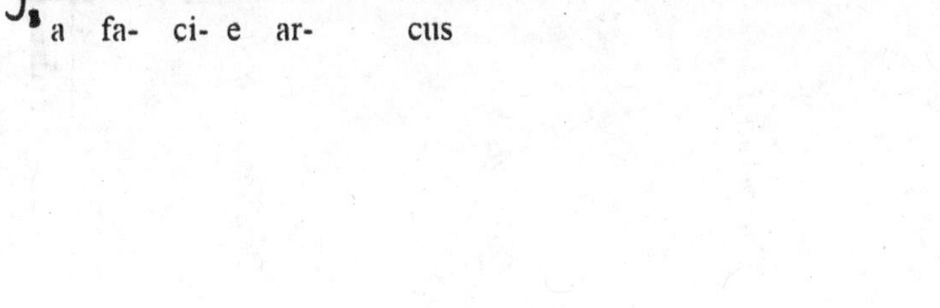

Phrase ***B3*** (Old Roman)

Commouisti 3

Commouisti 5

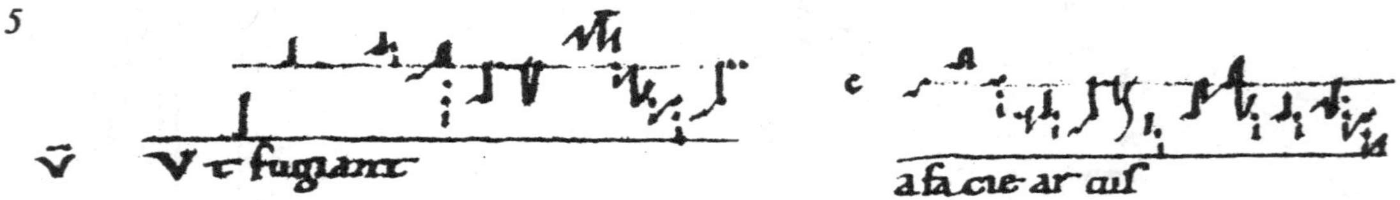

Qui regis 8

Desiderium 6

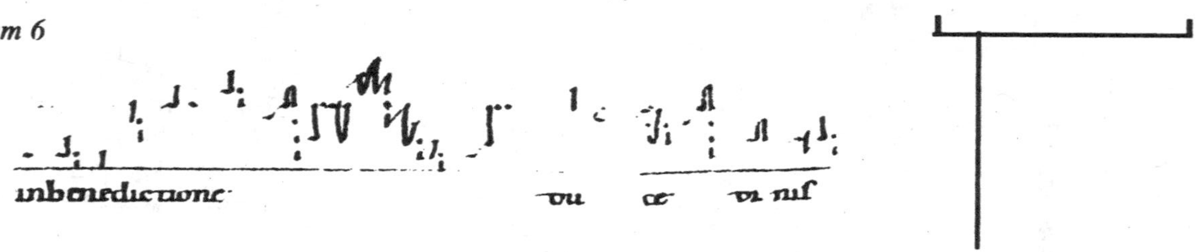

Qui confidunt 2

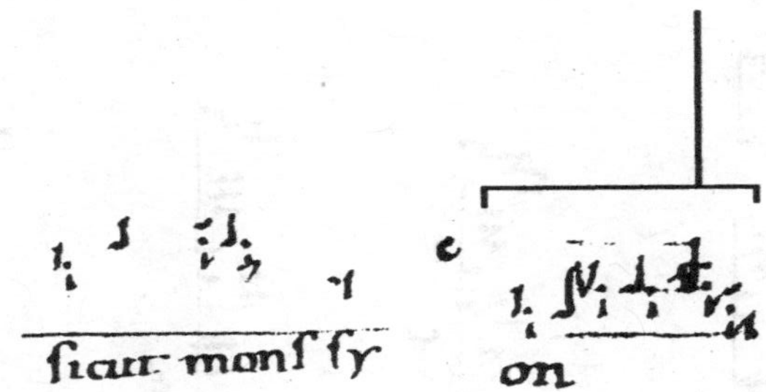

De profundis 11

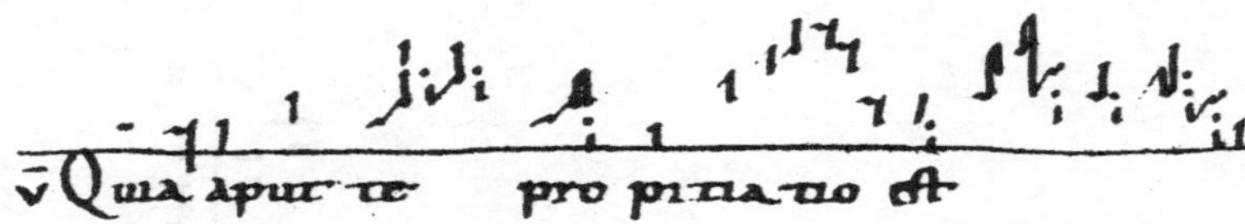

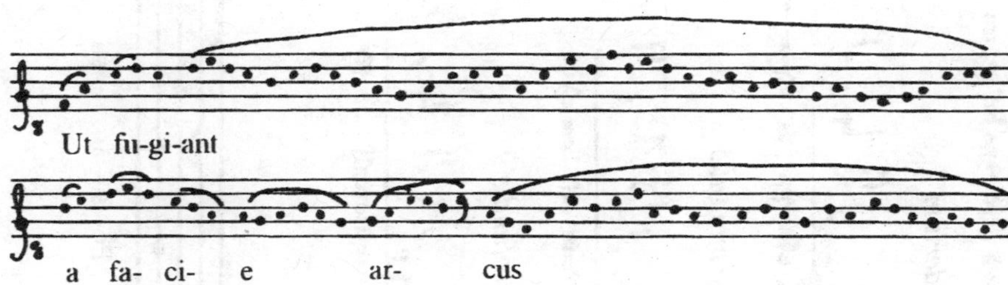

Phrase *B4* (Gregorian)

Ad te leuaui 10

Desiderium 7

Qui seminant 5

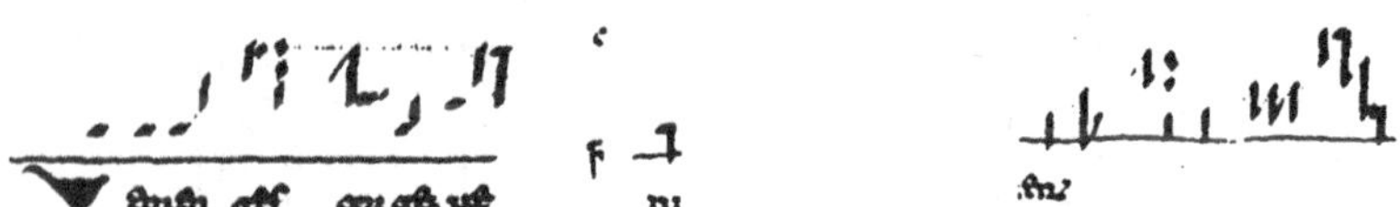

De profundis 9

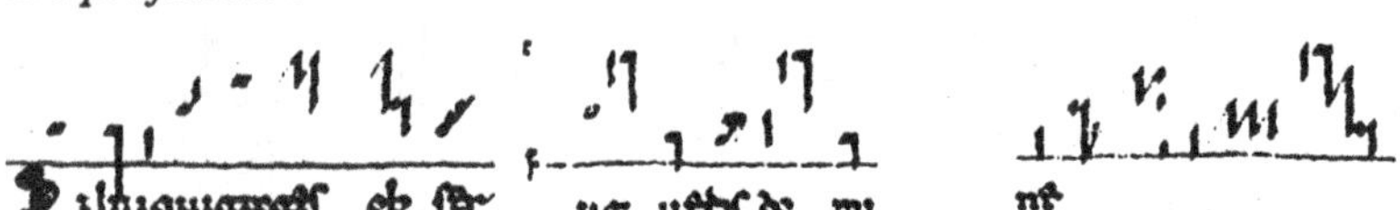

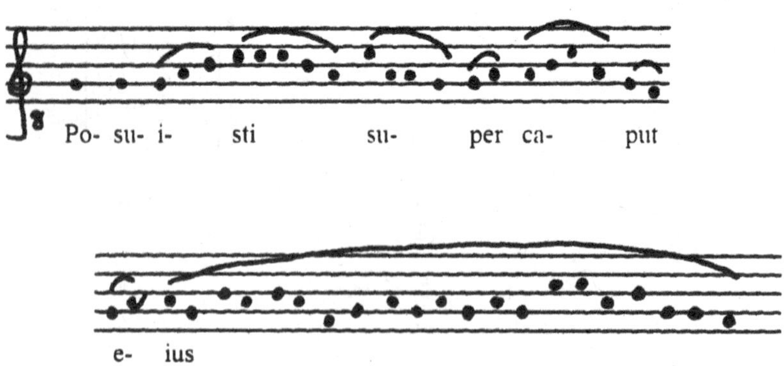

Phrase *B4* (Old Roman)

Ad te leuaui 10

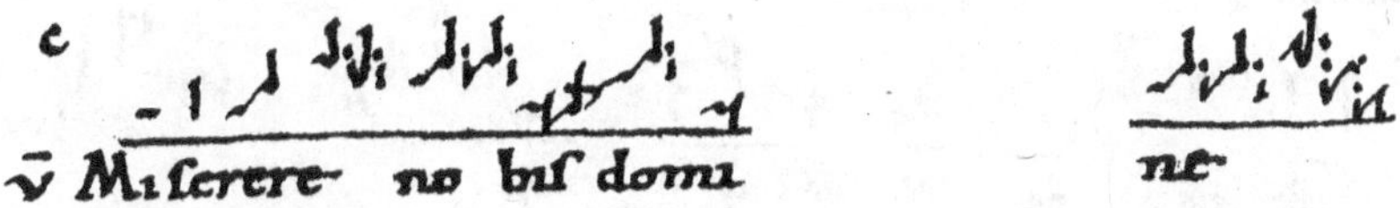

Desiderium 7

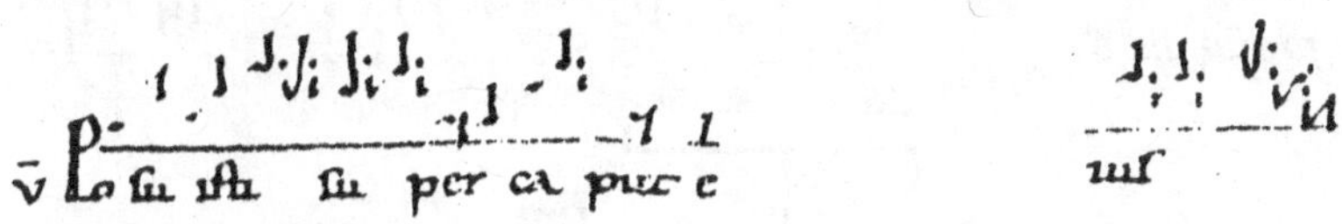

Qui seminant 5

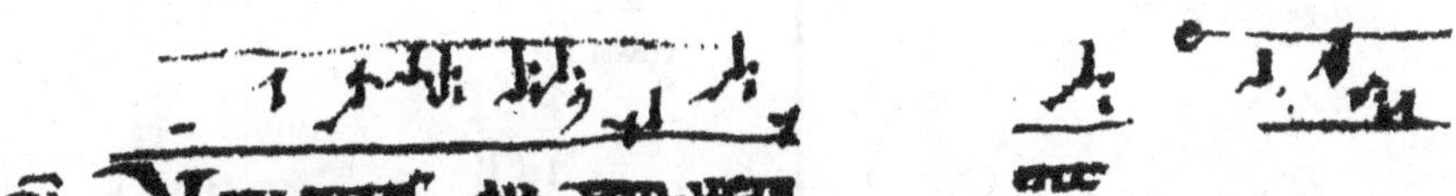

De profundis 9

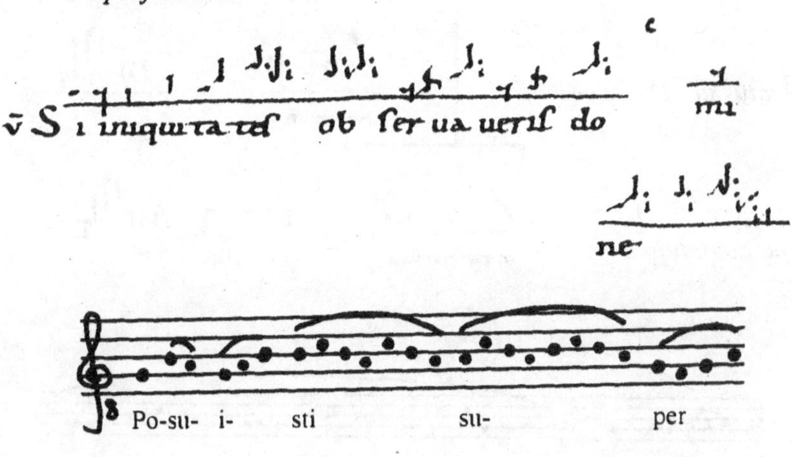

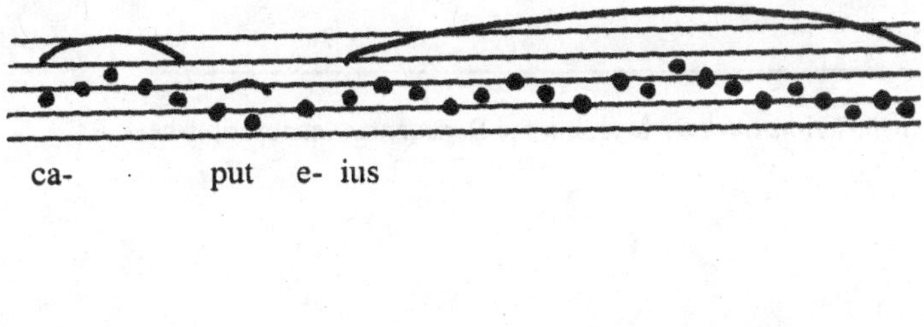

Phrase *B5* (Gregorian)

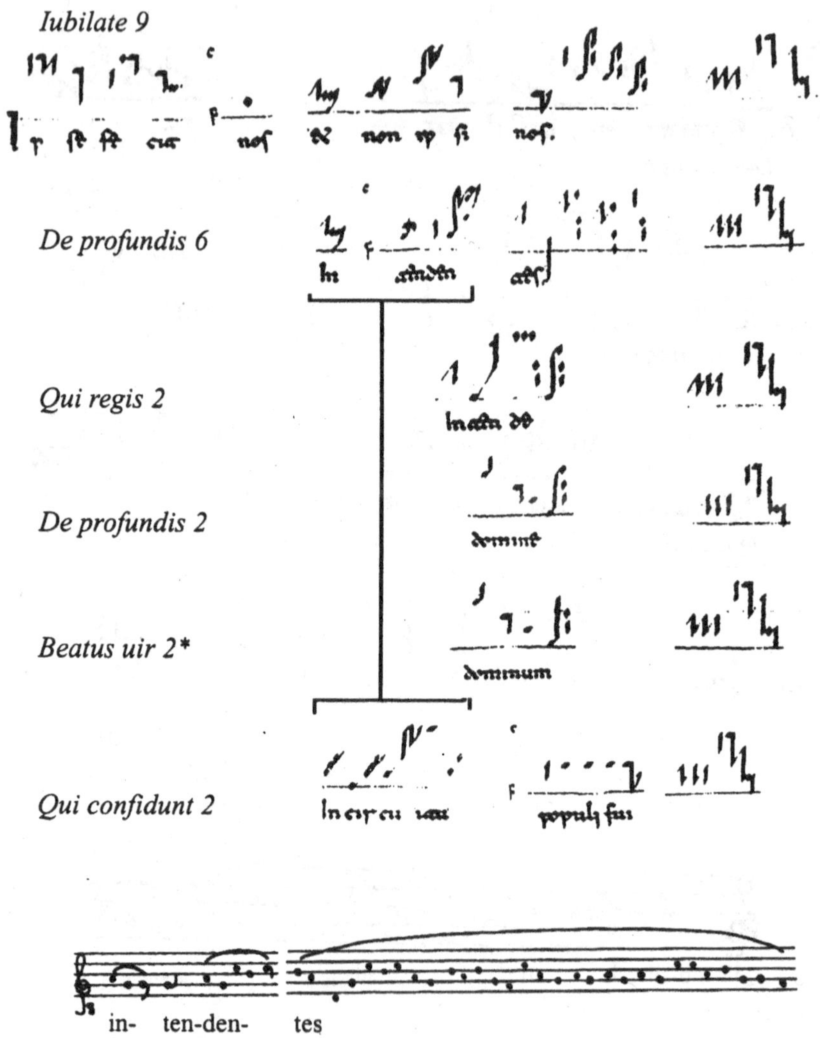

* Most manuscripts have ***B1*** here, but the Beneventan manuscripts have ***B5***

Phrase *B5* (Old Roman)

Iubilate 9

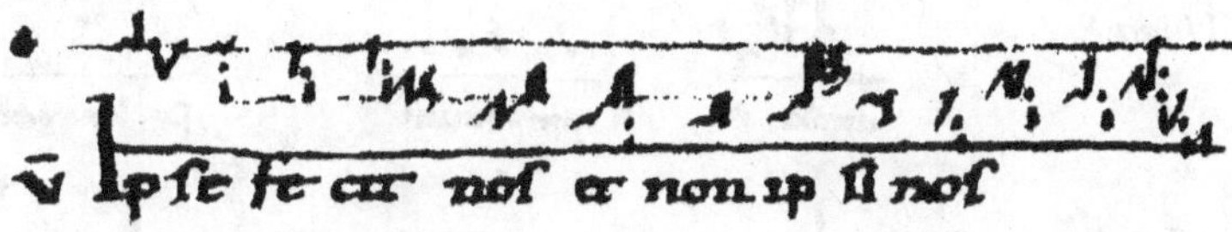

De profundis 2

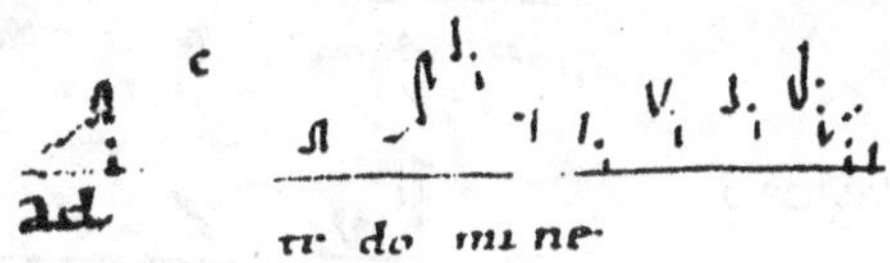

De profundis 6

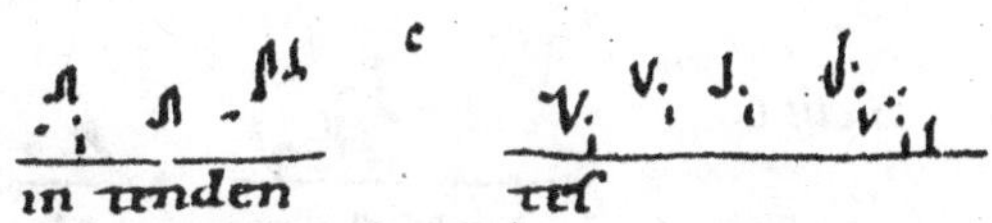

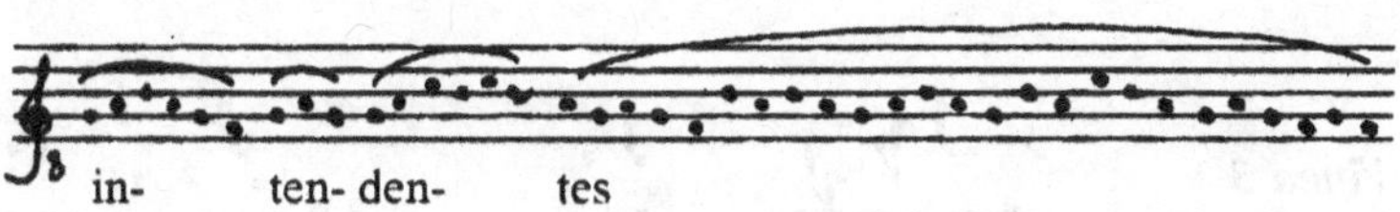

Phrase *C1* (Gregorian)

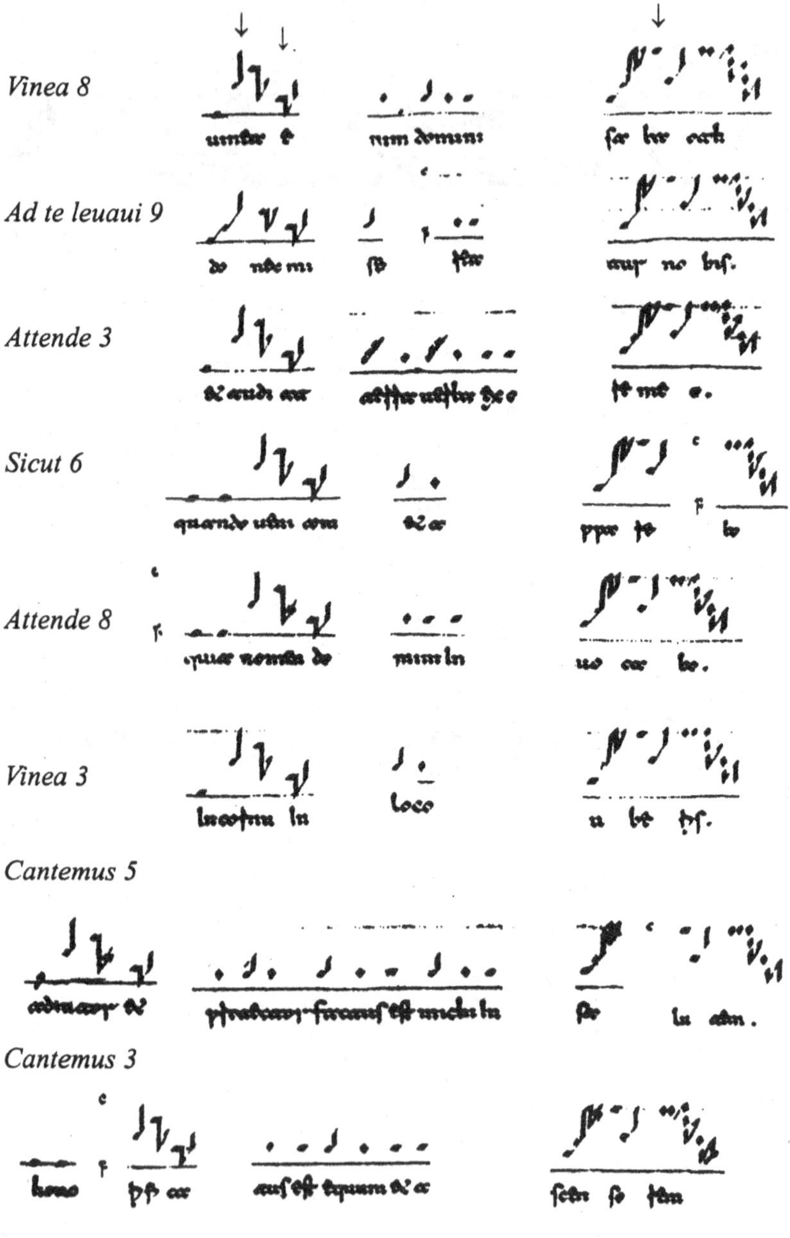

Phrase *C1* (Gregorian) *cont.*

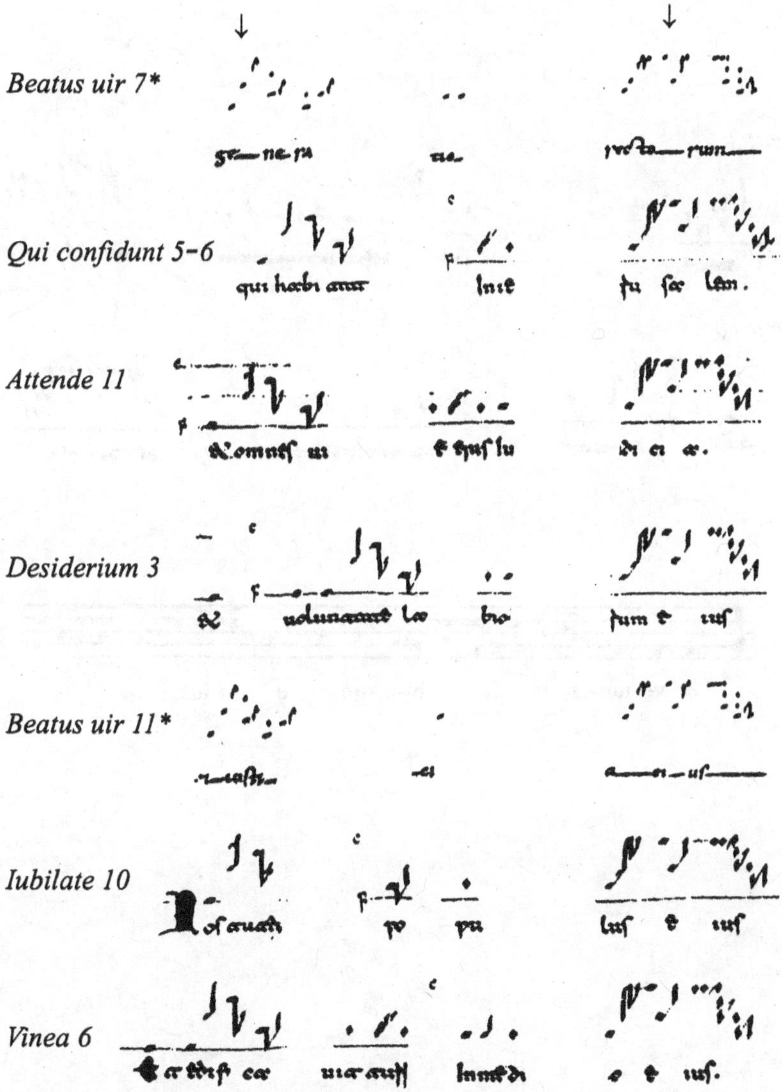

*The Beneventan manuscripts have a different version of phrase *C* to the rest of the tradition in *Beatus uir 7* and *Beatus uir 11*. *YRX* has therefore been used to provide these examples.

Phrase *C1* (Gregorian) *cont.*

Sicut 3

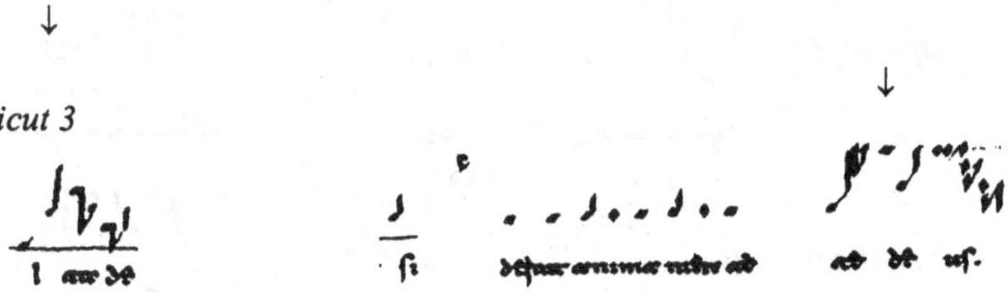

Sicut 10

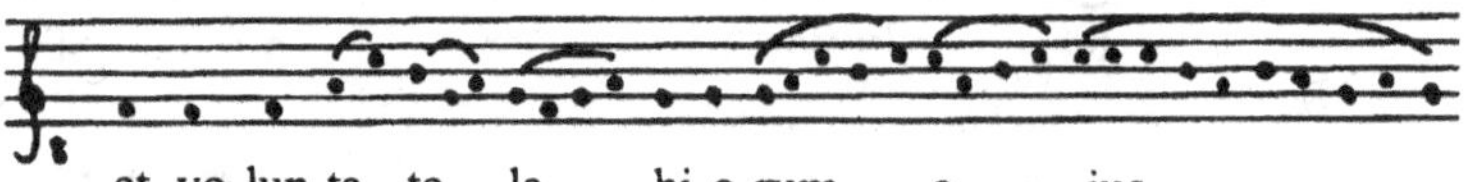

Phrase *C1* (Old Roman)

Phrase *C2* (Gregorian)

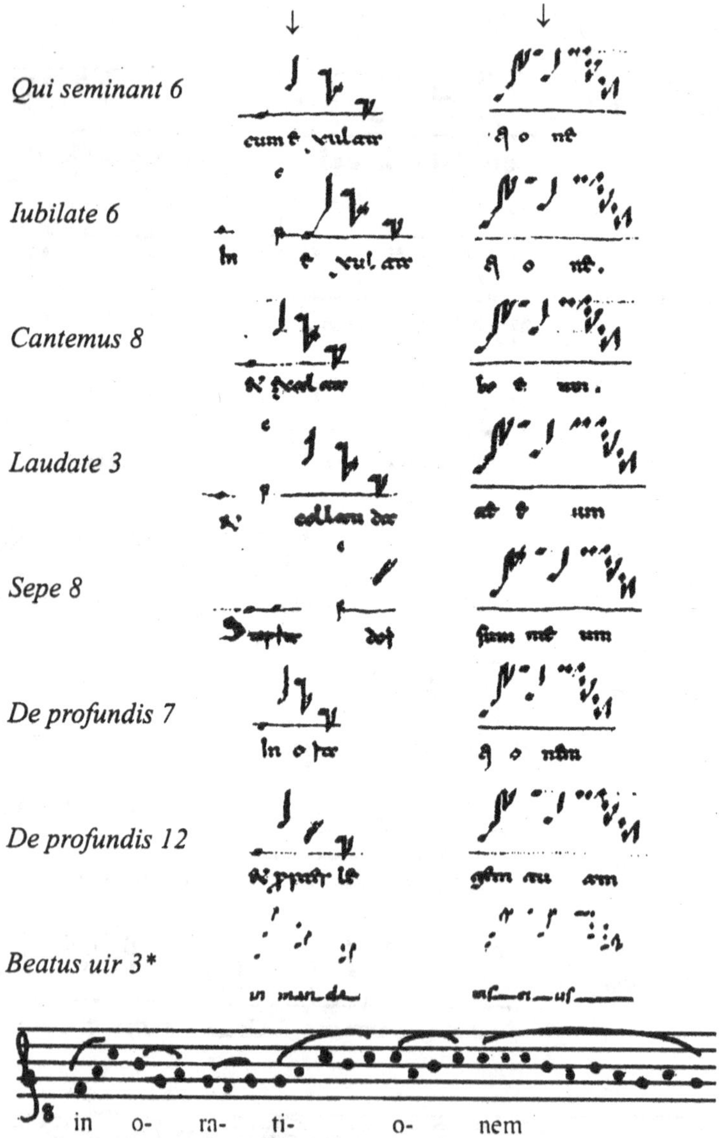

* The Beneventan manuscripts have a different version of phrase *C* to the rest of the tradition. *YRX* has therefore been used to provide this example.

Phrase *C2* (Old Roman)

Iubilate 3

Laudate 7

Iubilate 7

Beatus uir 3

Commouisti 7

Qui seminant 6

De profundis 7

De profundis 12

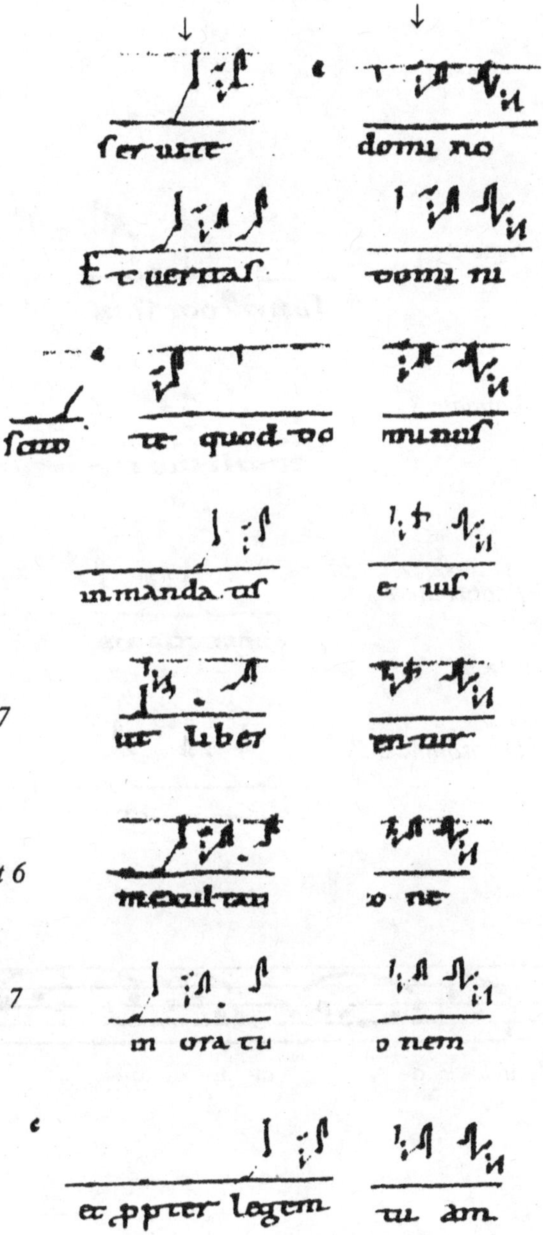

Phrase *C2* (Old Roman) *cont.*

Sepe 8

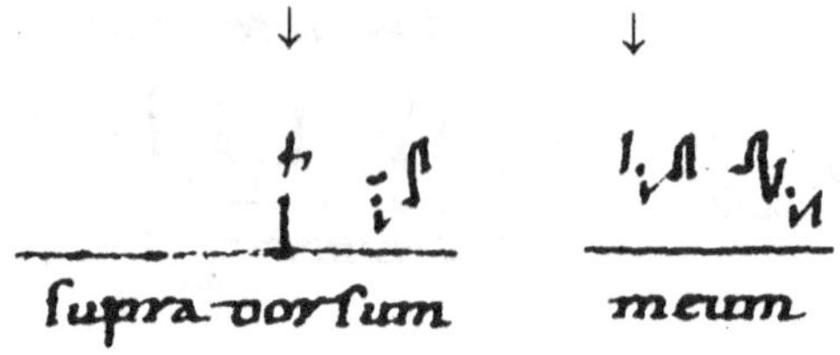

Laudate 3

Beatus uir 7

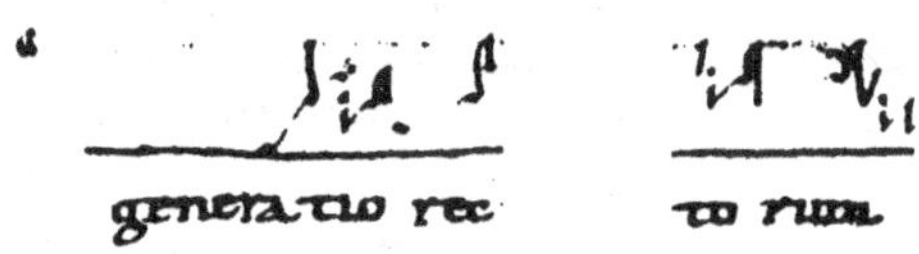

De profundis 3

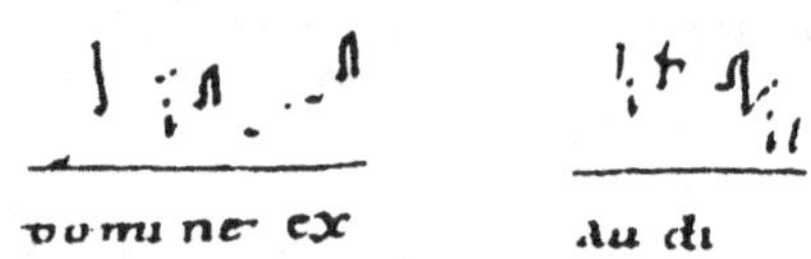

Phrase *C3* (Gregorian)

Qui confidunt 11

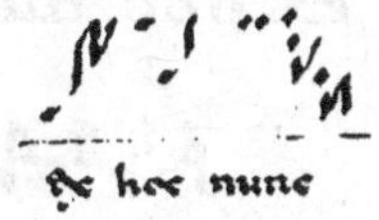

Desiderium 8

Commouisti 6

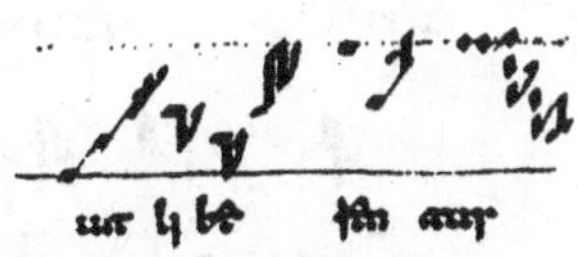

Sepe 12

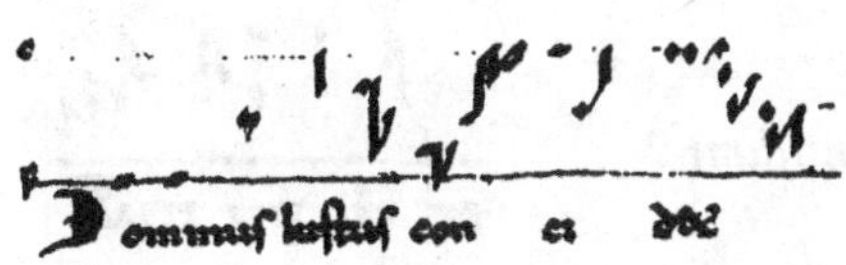

Qui confidunt 9

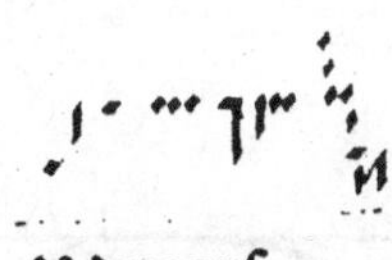

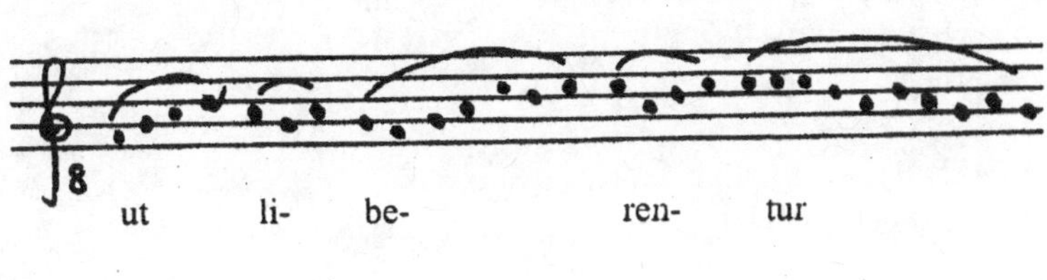

Phrase *C3* (Old Roman)

Qui confidunt 11

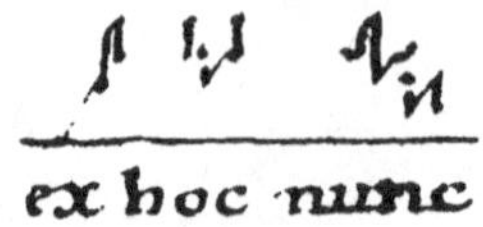

Qui regis 9

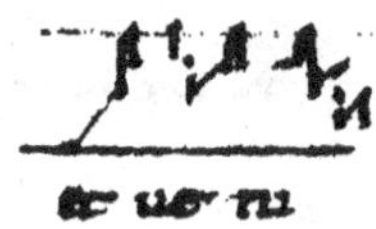

Desiderium 8

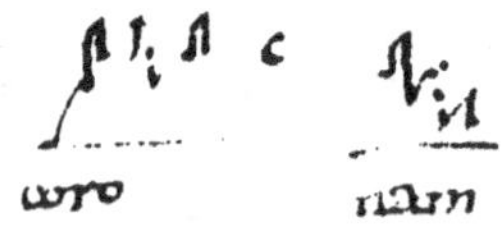

Qui confidunt 5

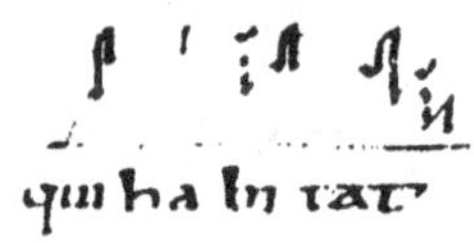

Qui confidunt 9

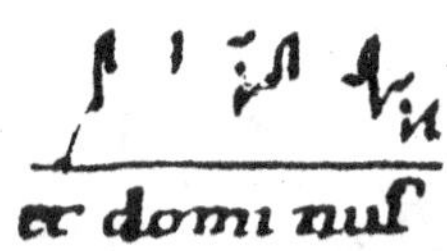

Phrase *C4* (Gregorian)

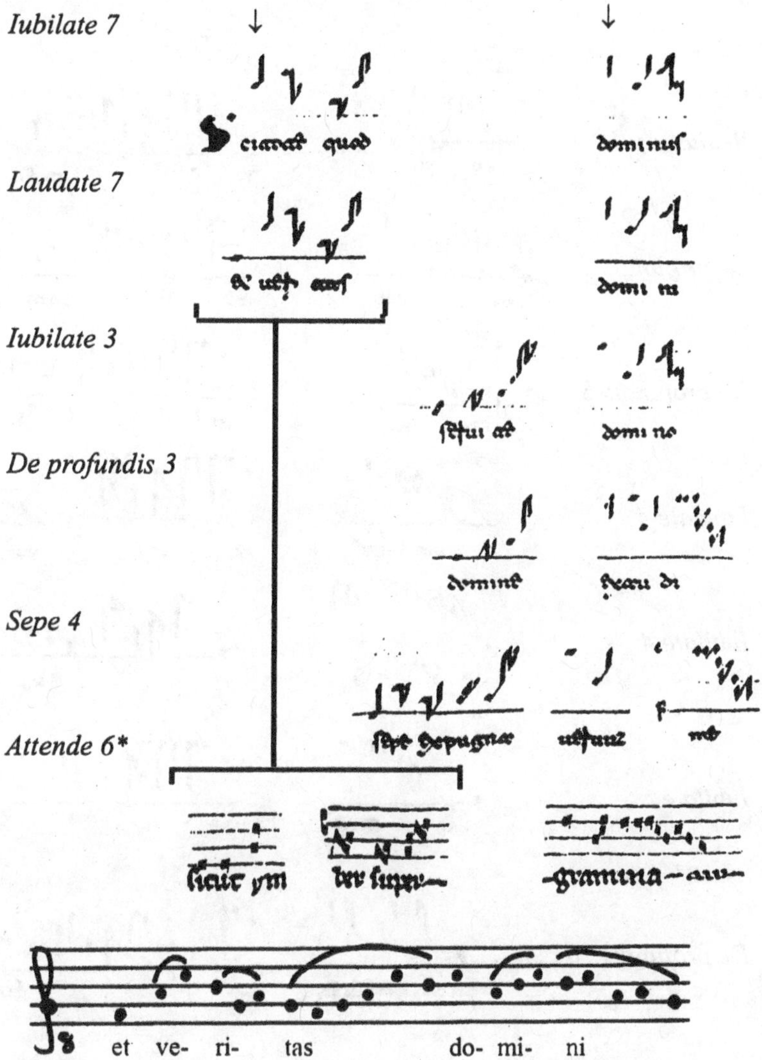

---

* *BEN5* and *YRX* are among the four manuscripts in the sample with the text 'gramen' instead of 'gramina'. *ROG1* has therefore been used to provide this example.

Phrase *D1* (Gregorian)

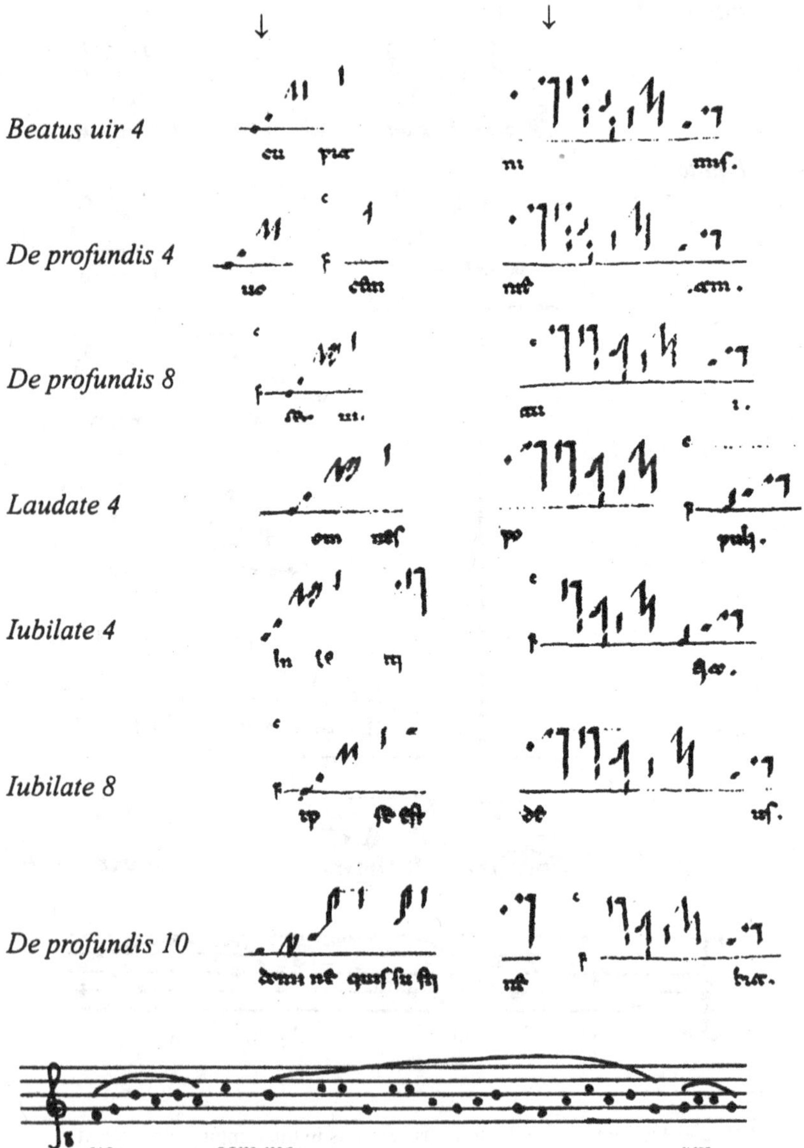

Phrase *D1* (Old Roman)

Beatus uir 4

Beatus uir 8

De profundis 4

De profundis 8

Laudate 4

Iubilate 4

Iubilate 8

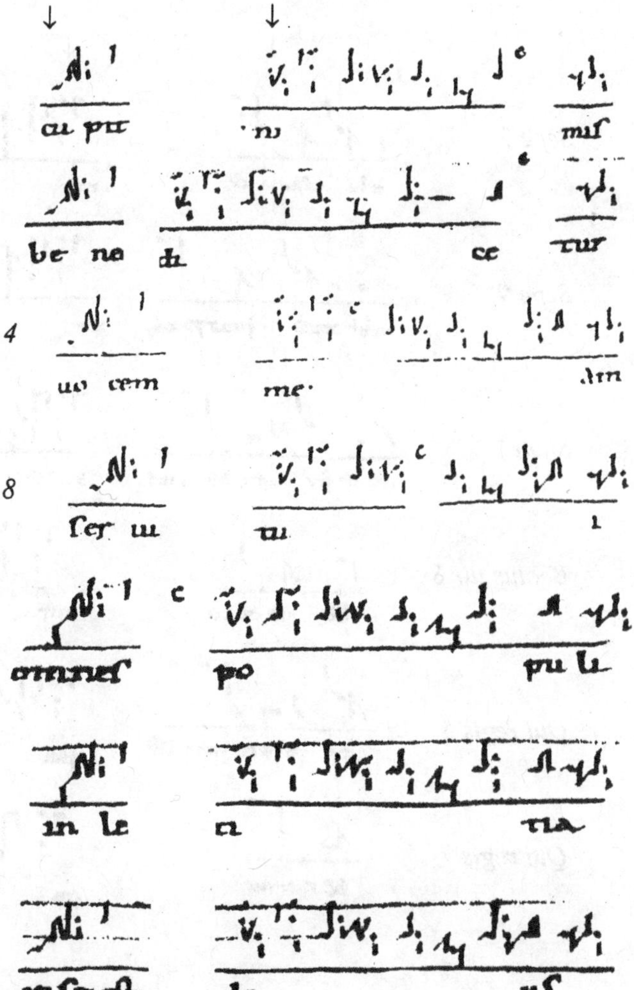

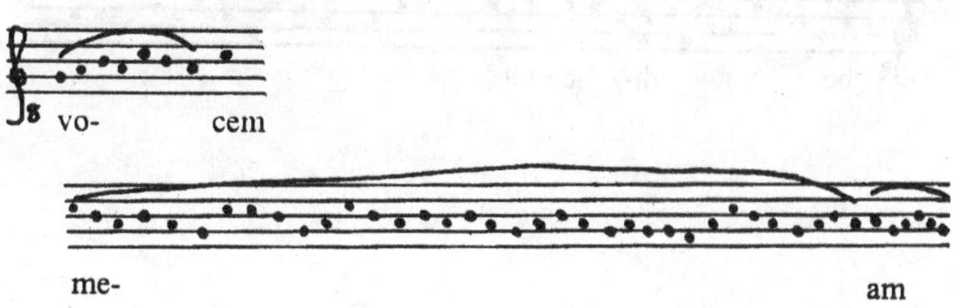

Phrase *D2* (Gregorian)

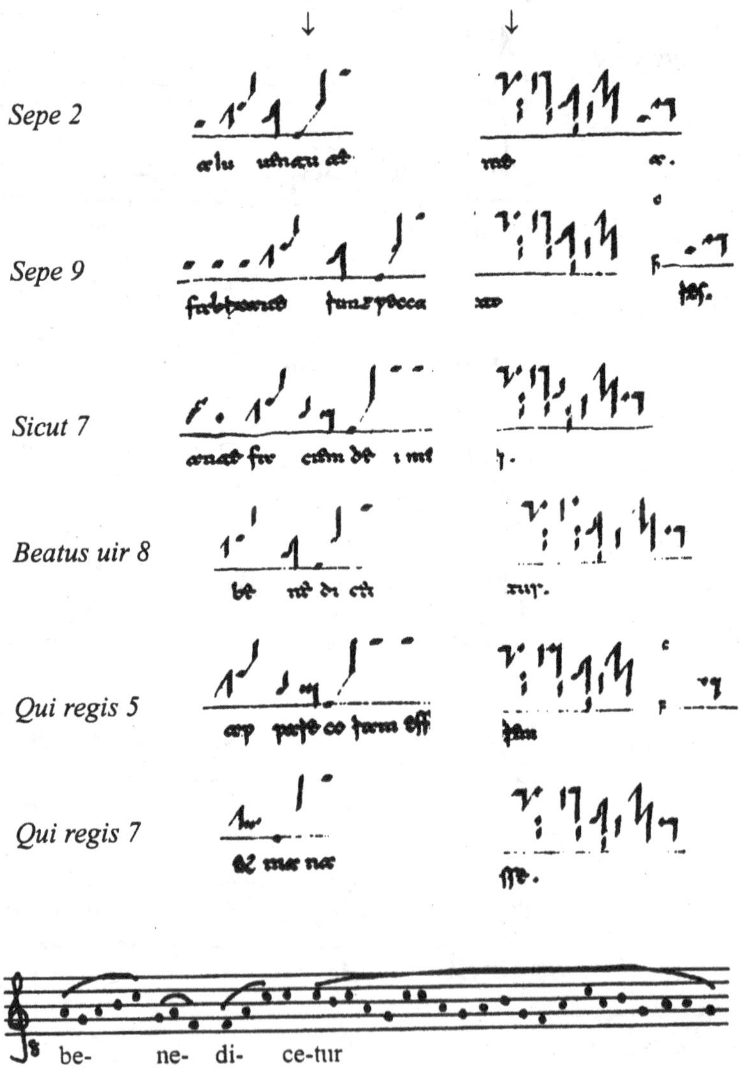

Phrase *D2* (Gregorian) *cont.*

Qui seminant 2

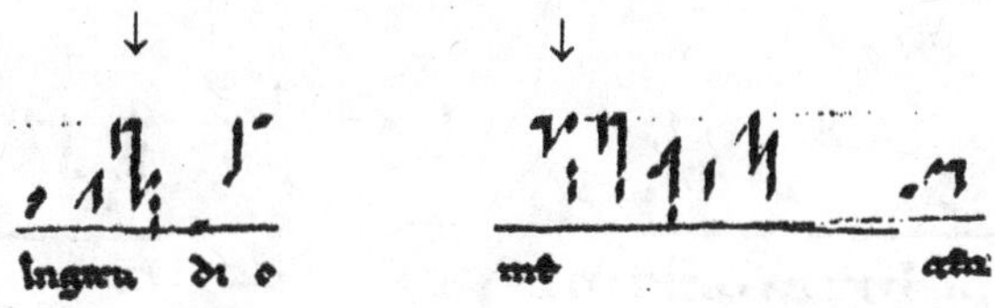

Qui seminant 4

Ad te leuaui 4

Ad te leuaui 6

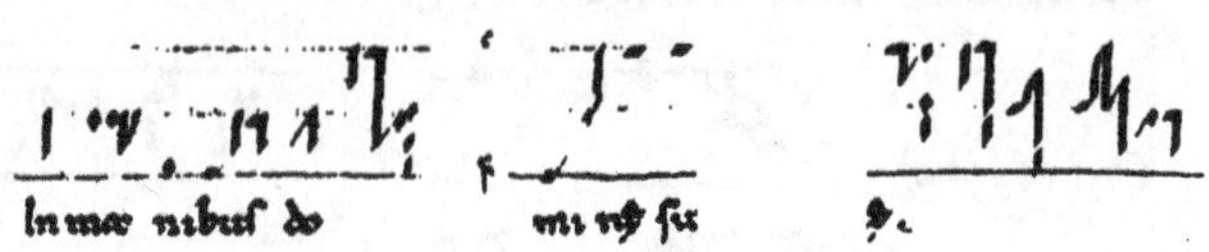

Phrase *D2* (Old Roman)

Phrase *D3* (Gregorian)

Sepe 5

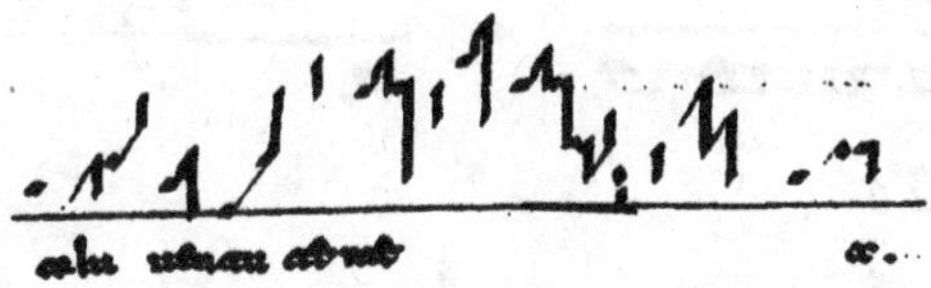

Phrase *D3* (Old Roman)

Sepe 5

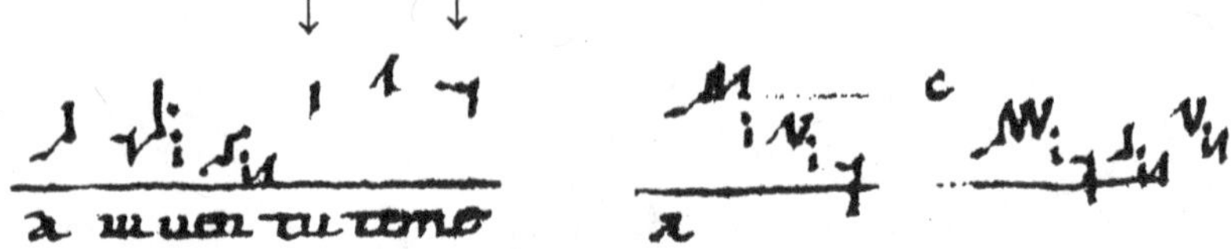

Qui confidunt 6

Qui seminant 4

Ad te leuaui 4

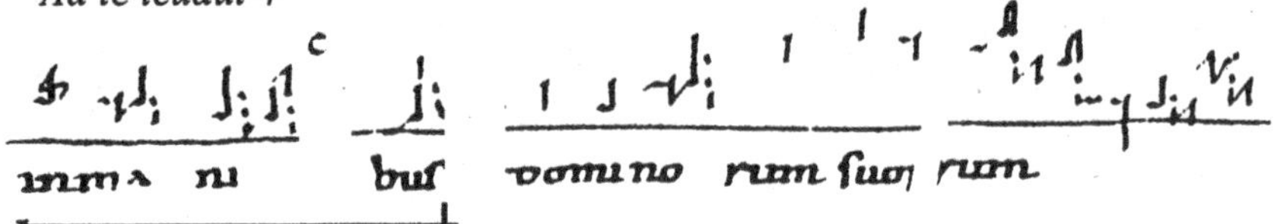

Ad te leuaui 6

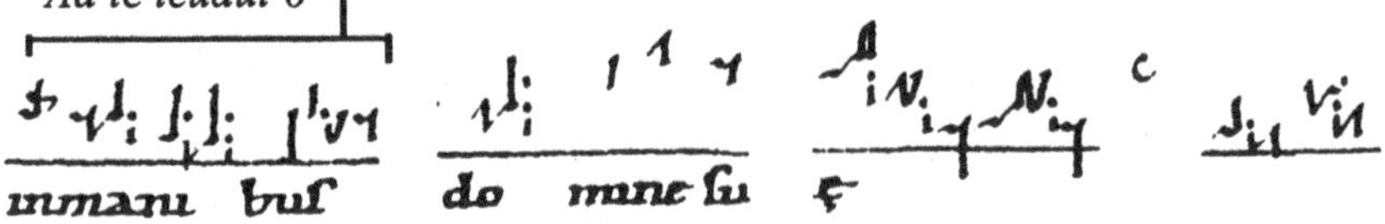

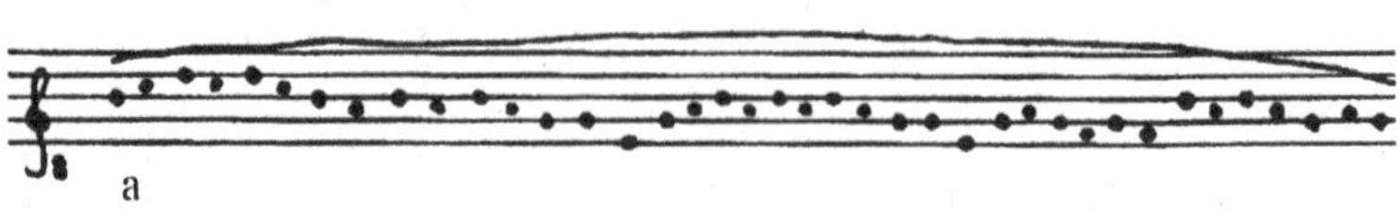

Phrase *D4* (Gregorian)

Ad te leuaui 2

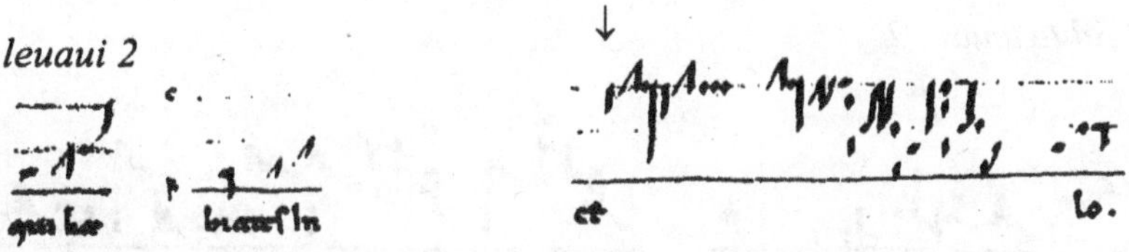

Commouisti 2

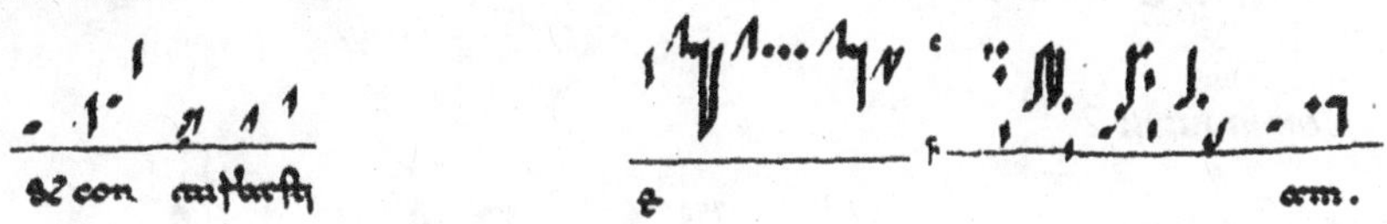

Desiderium 4

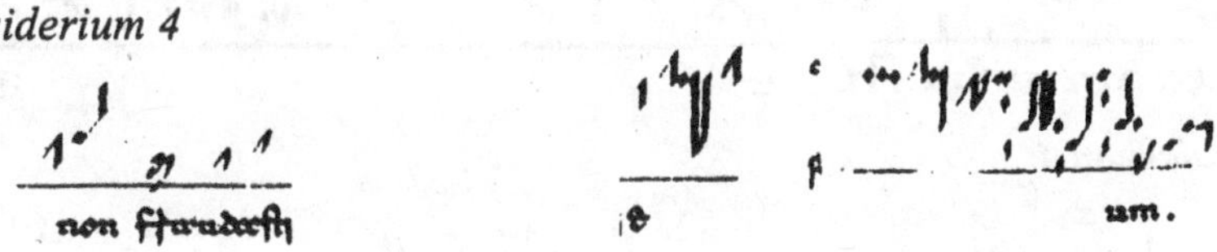

Desiderium 6

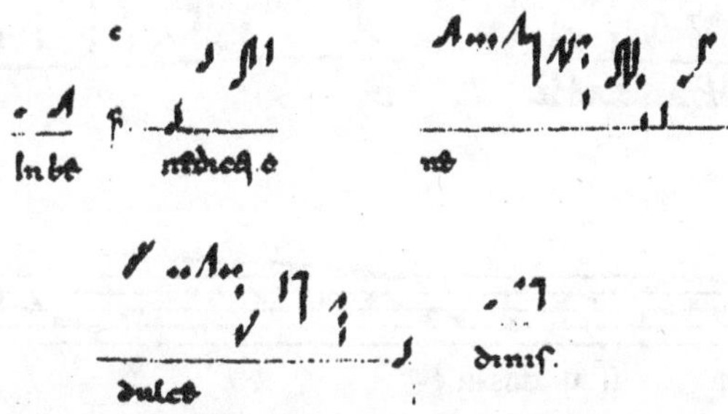

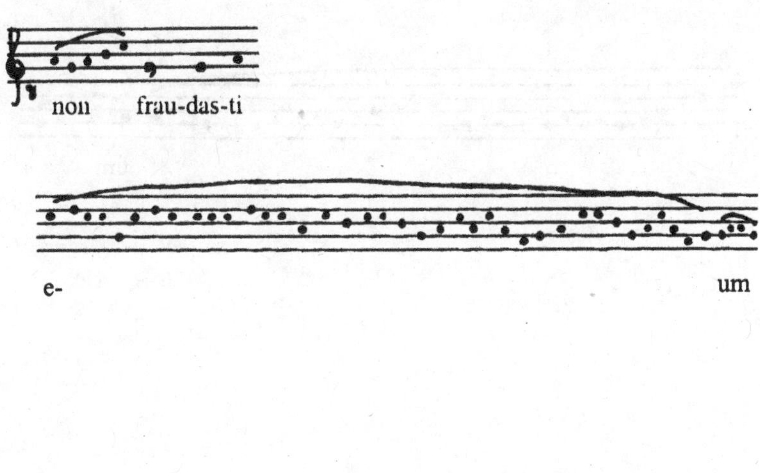

Phrase *D4* (Old Roman)

Ad te leuaui 2

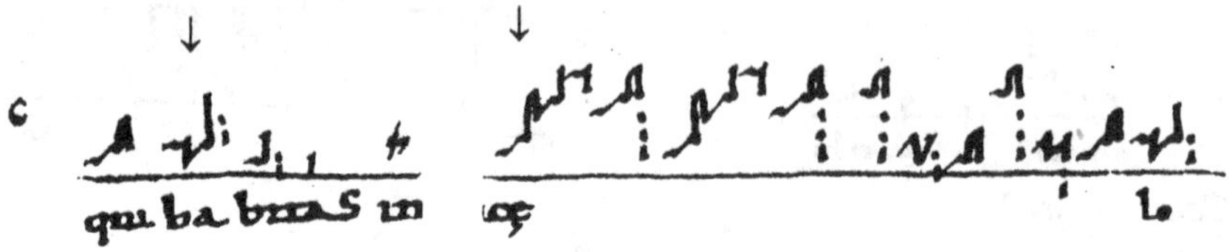

Commouisti 2

Desiderium 4

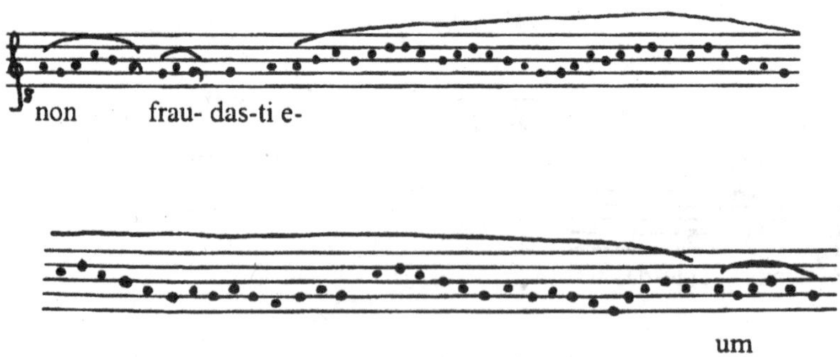

Phrase *D5* (Gregorian)

Commouisti 4

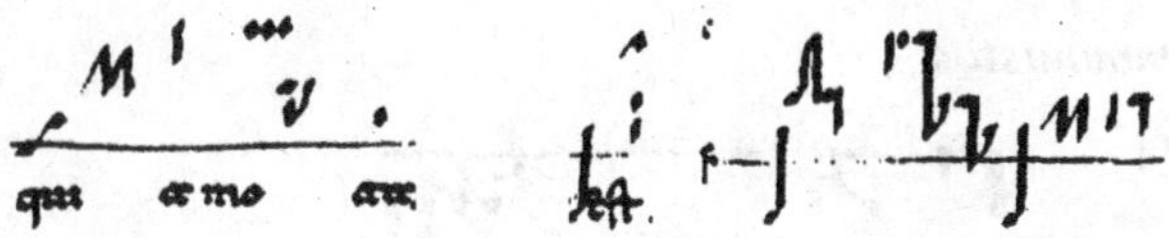

Qui confidunt 7

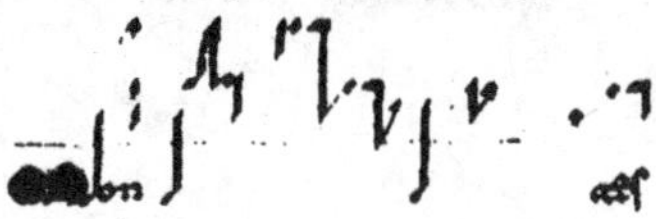

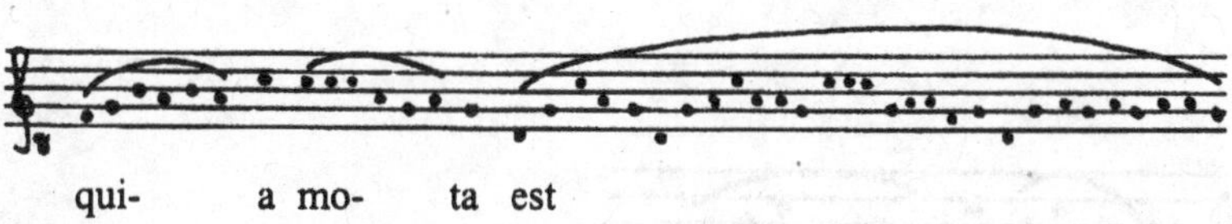

Phrase *D5* (Old Roman)

Commouisti 4

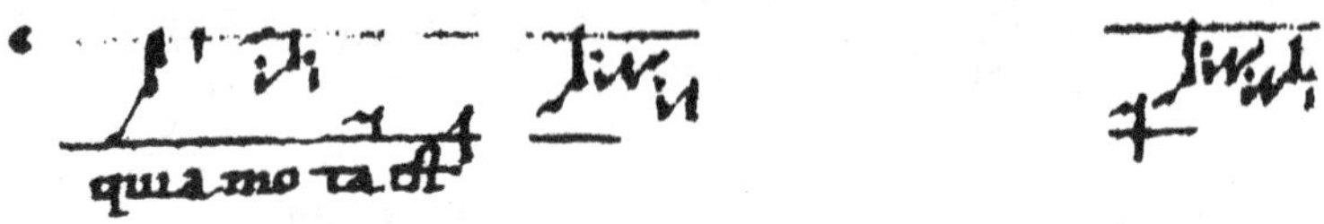

Qui confidunt 7

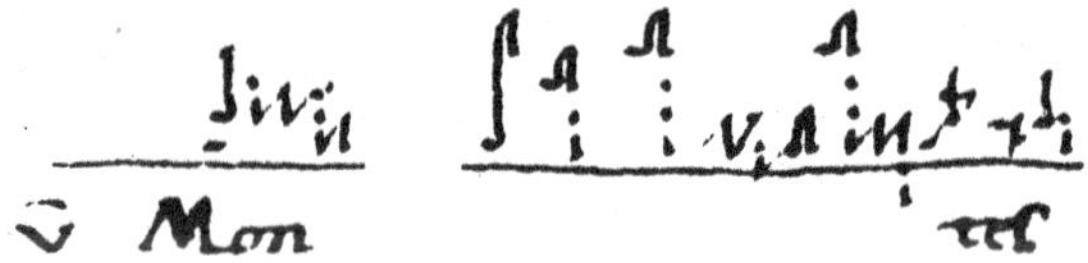

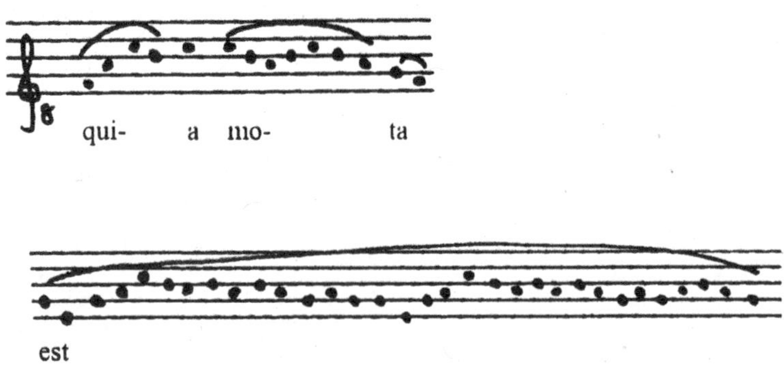

Phrase *E1* (Gregorian)

De profundis 5

Iubilate 5

Qui regis 4

Cantemus 6

Sicut 8

Attende 9

Vinea 4

Attende 4

Attende 12

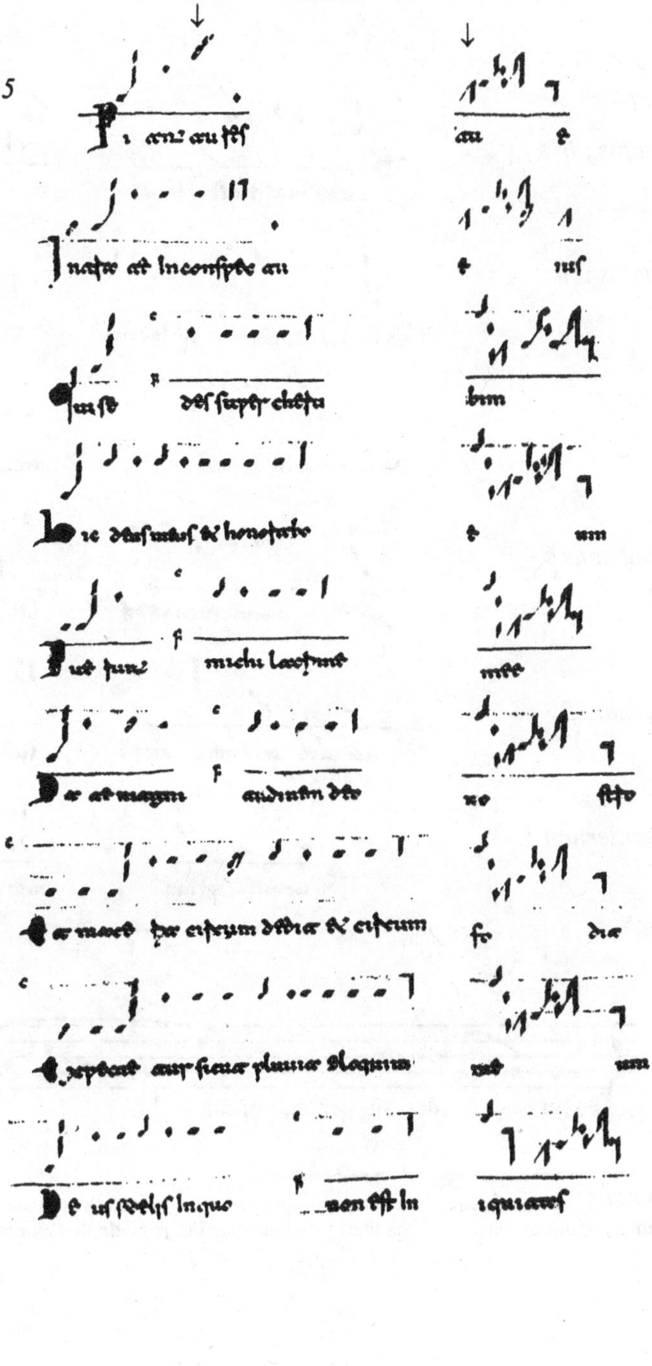

Phrase *E1* (Gregorian) *cont.*

Beatus uir 5

Beatus uir 9

*Sicut 4**

Cantemus 9

Laudate 5

Desiderium 5

* *BEN5* has the phrase ***E*** recitation, but moves straight into the phrase ***B*** cadence on 'ad deum uiuum'. *YRX* has therefore been used to provide this example.

Phrase *E1* (Old Roman)

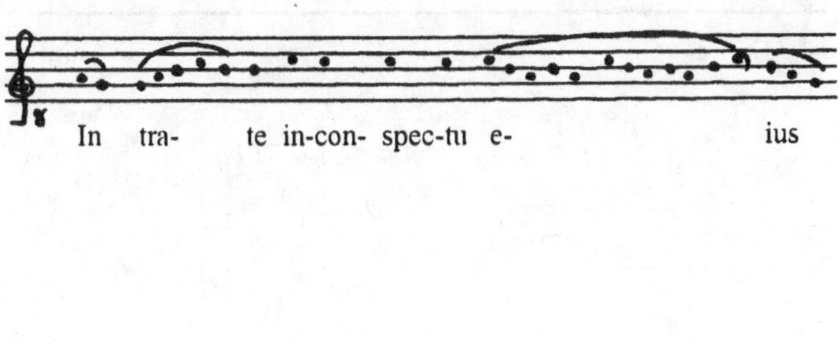

Phrase *E2* (Gregorian)

Sepe 10

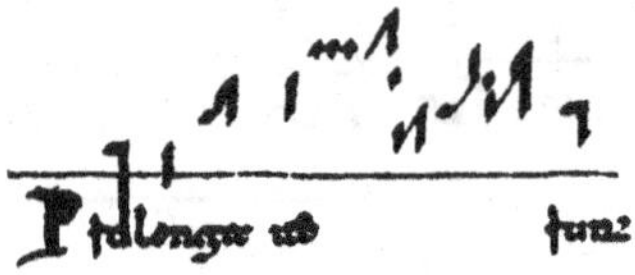

Sepe 6

Qui regis 6

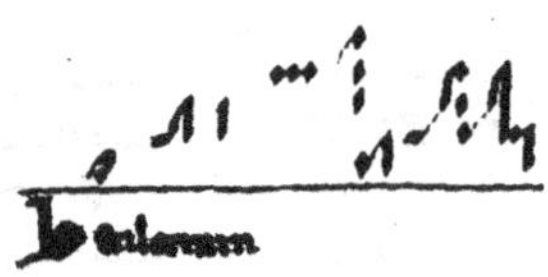

Phrase *E2* (Old Roman)

Sepe 10

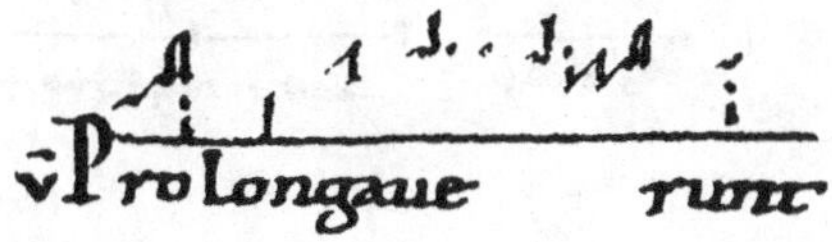

Beatus uir 5

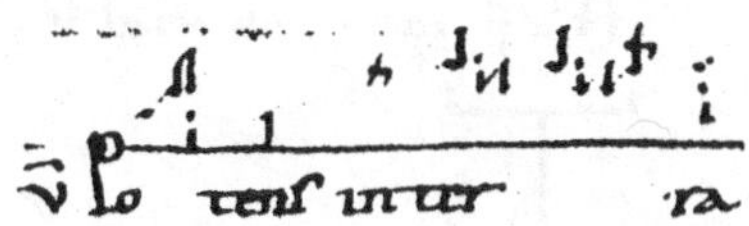

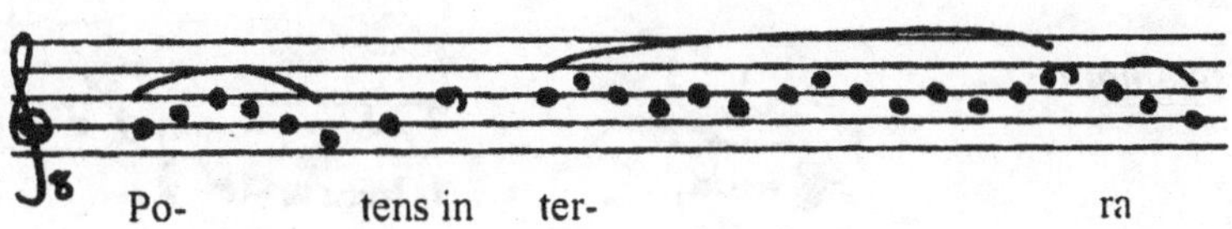

Phrase *E3* (Gregorian)

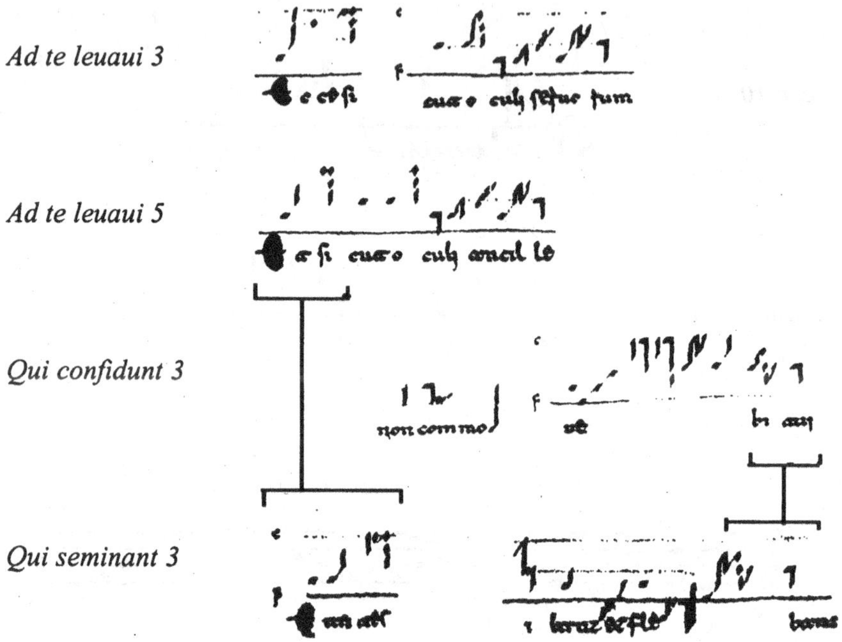

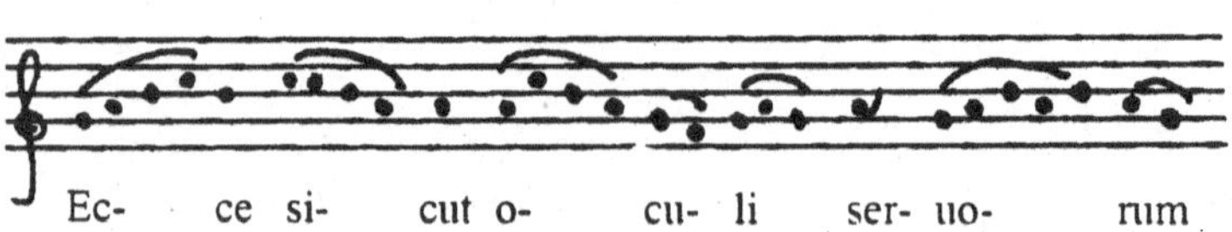

Phrase *E3* (Old Roman)

Qui confidunt 3

Qui seminant 3

Ad te leuaui 3

Ad te leuaui 5

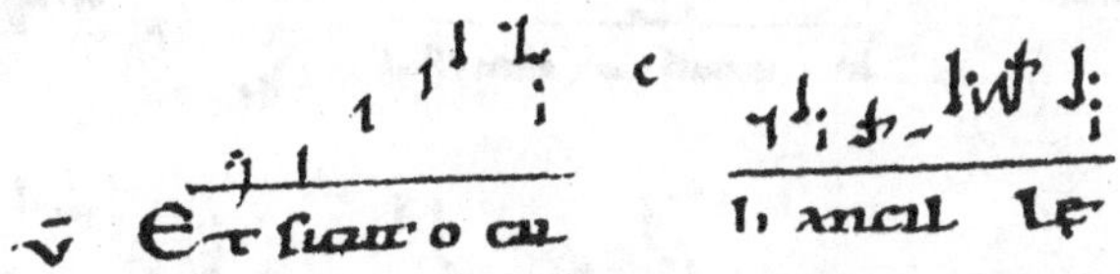

Sepe 6

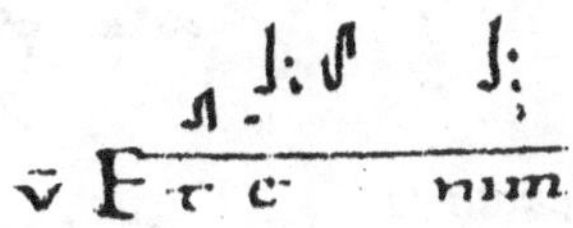

De profundis 5

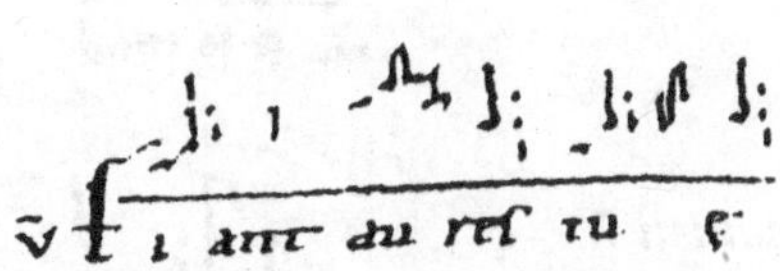

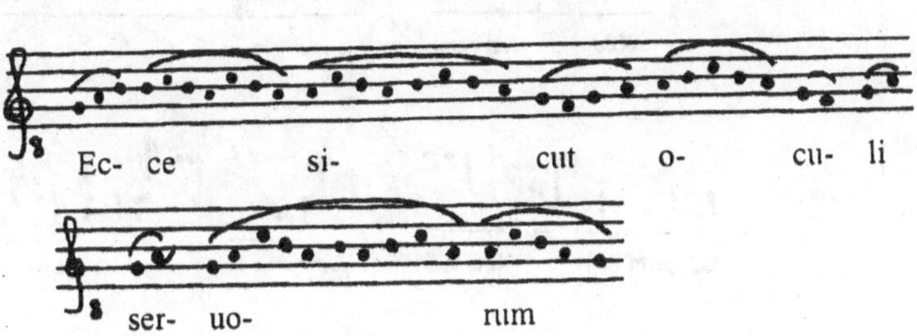

Phrase *F* (Gregorian)

Vinea 9

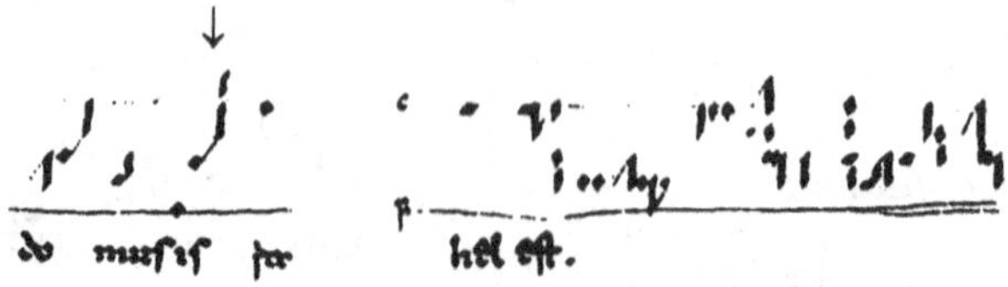

Attende 13

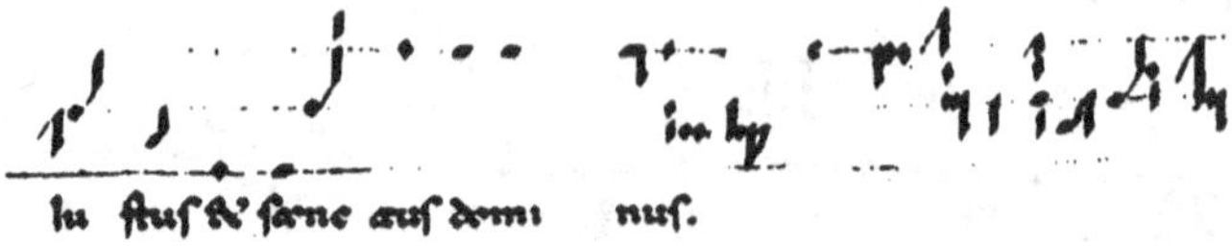

Sicut 11

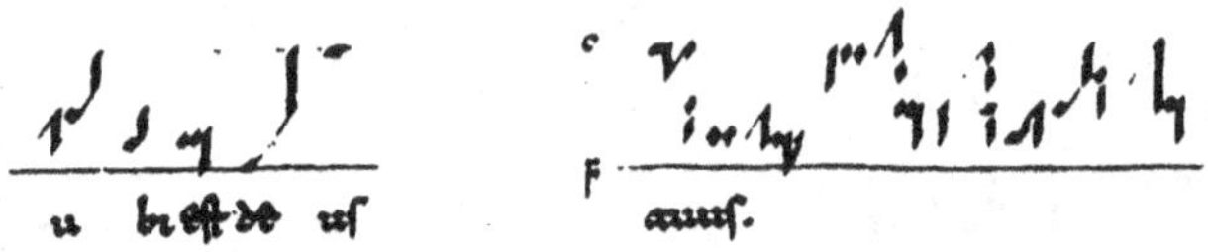

Cantemus 10

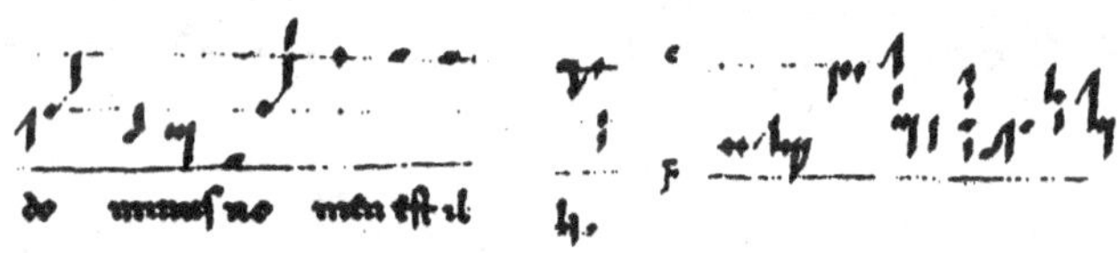

Desiderium 9

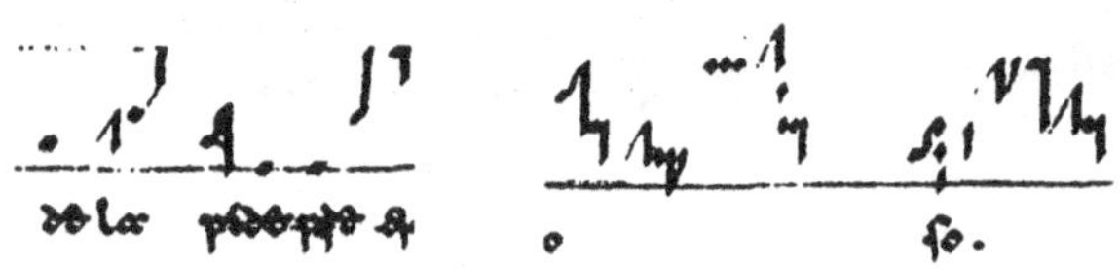

Ad te leuaui 11

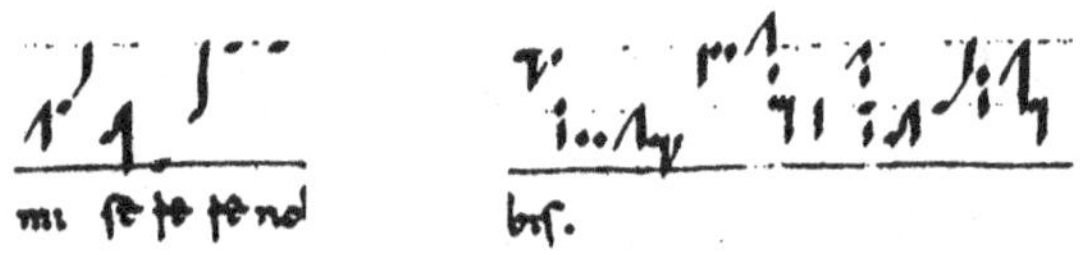

Commouisti 7

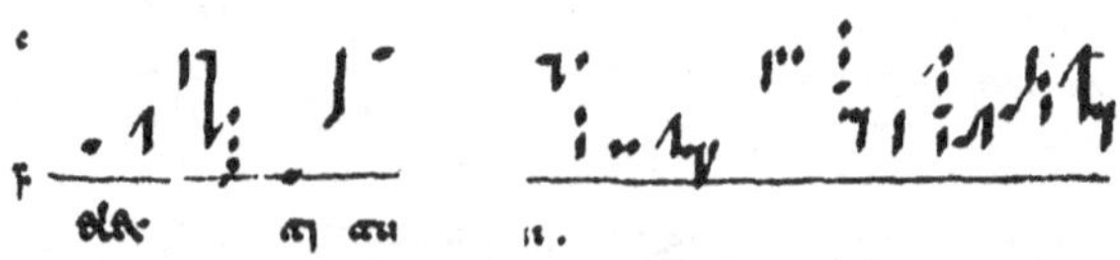

Iubilate 11

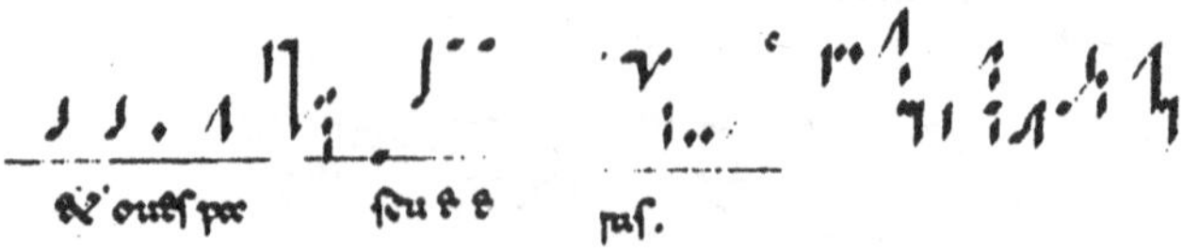

Phrase *F* (Gregorian) *cont.*

Qui seminant 7

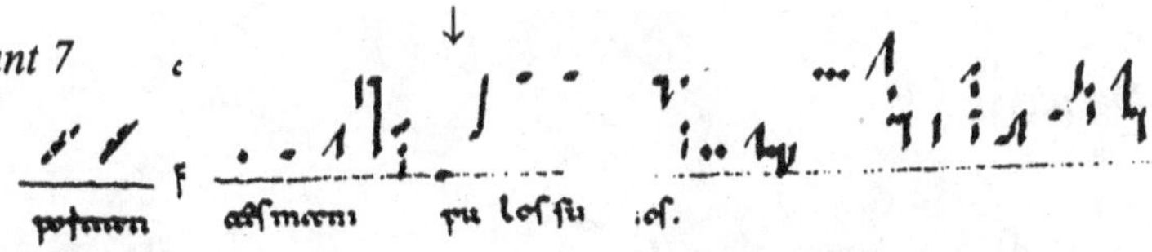

Qui regis 10

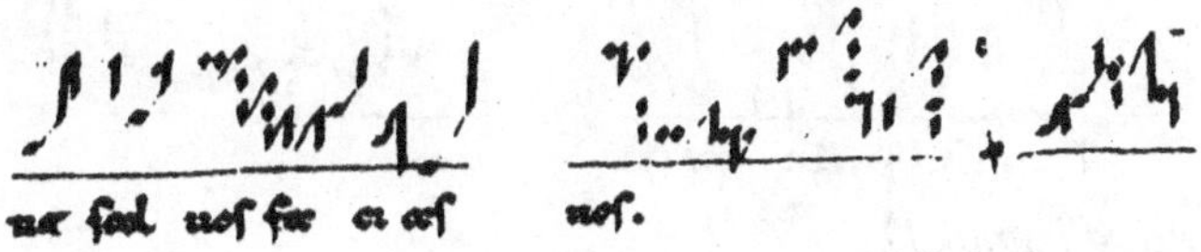

Qui confidunt 12

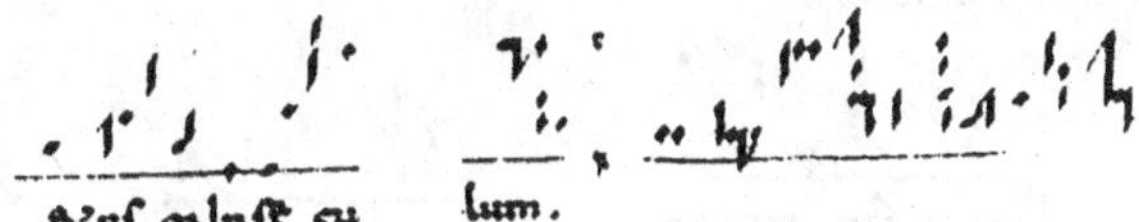

Beatus uir 12

De profundis 13

Sepe 13

Laudate 8

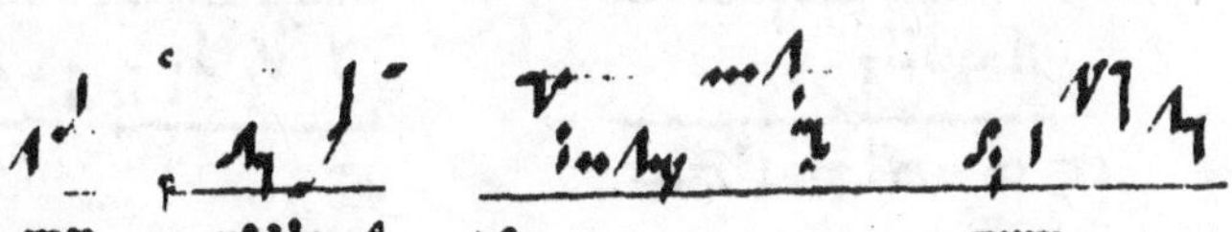

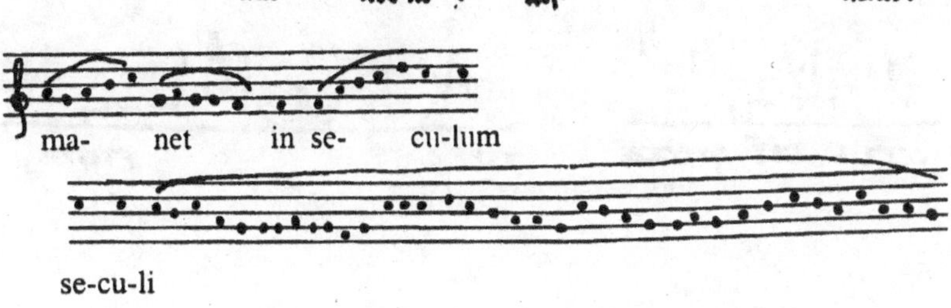

Phrase *F* (Old Roman)

Desiderium 9

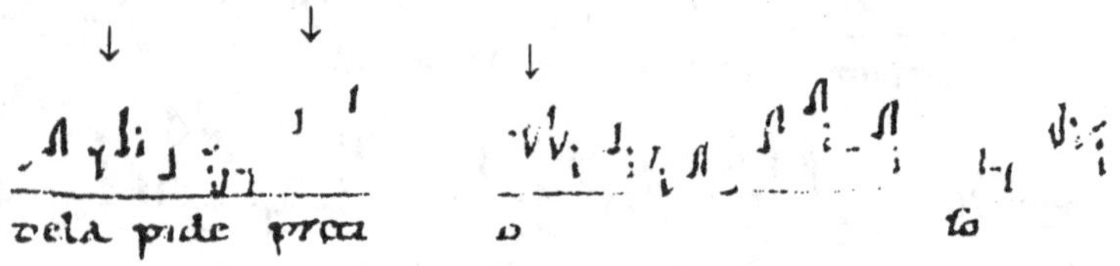

Ad te leuaui 11

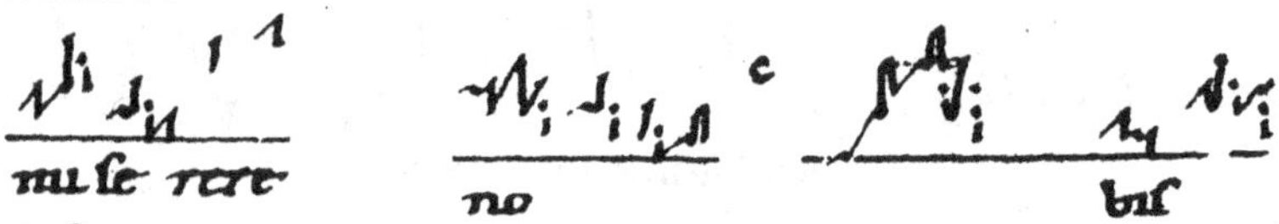

Laudate 8

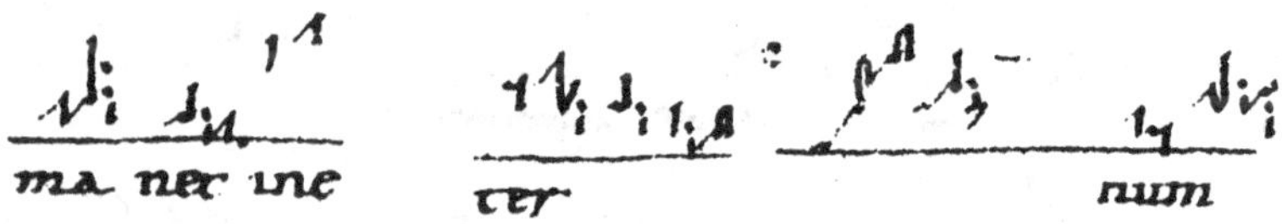

Commouisti 7

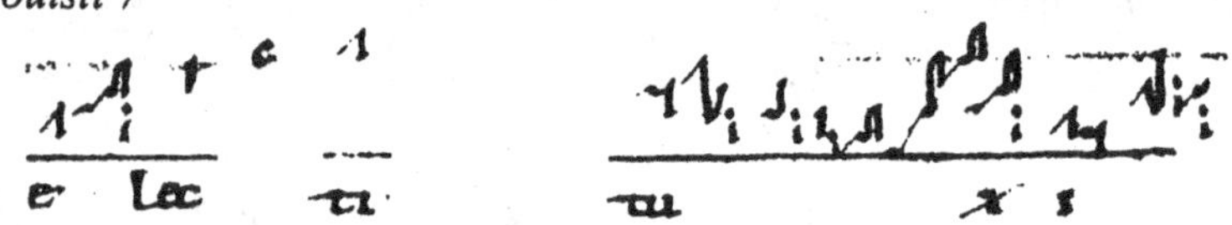

Iubilate 11

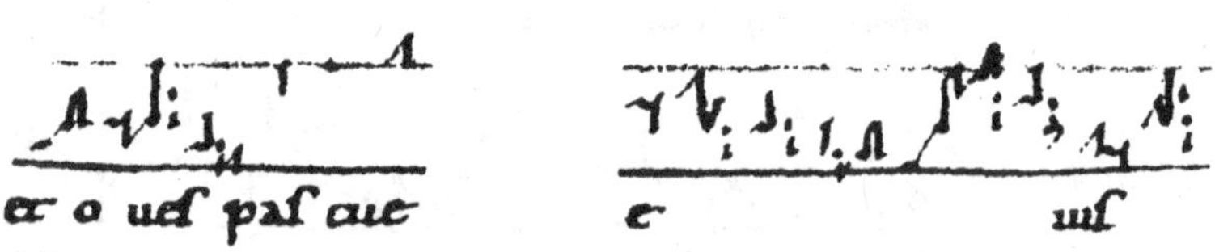

Sepe 13

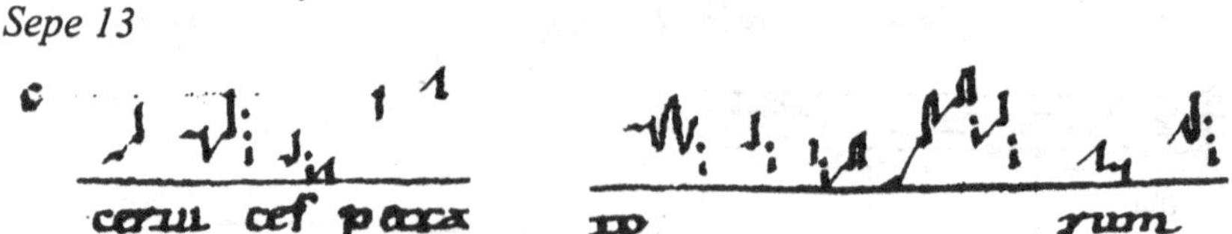

Phrase *F* (Old Roman) *cont.*

Qui seminant 7

Qui regis 10

Qui confidunt 12

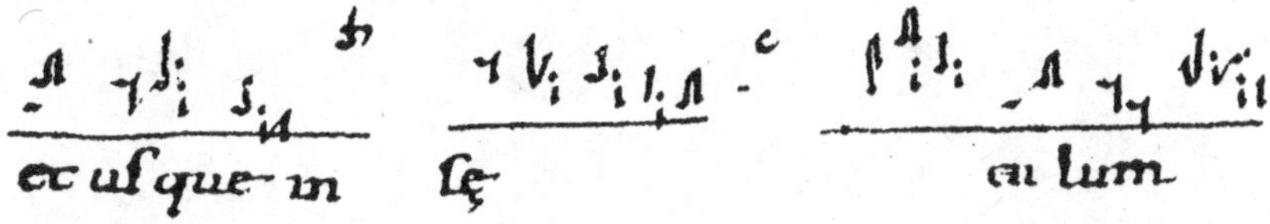

Beatus uir 12

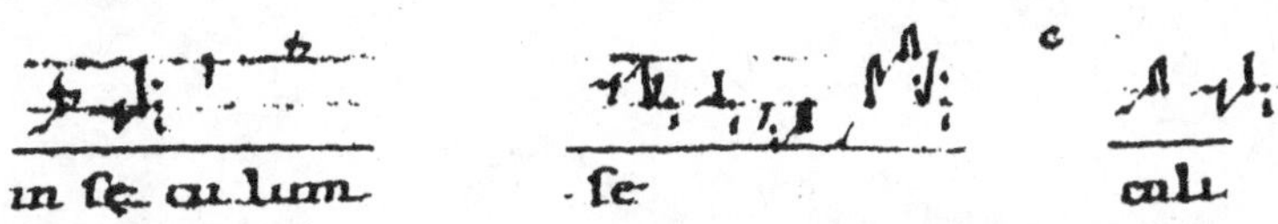

De profundis 13

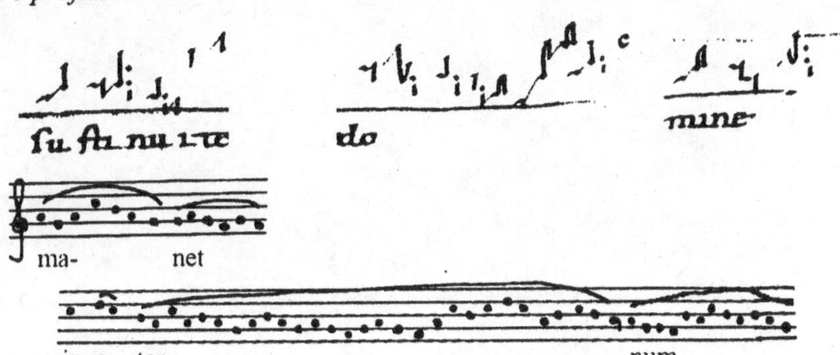

Appendix 3
The Core Repertory of Eighth-Mode Tracts in *BEN5* and *ORC*

Ad te leuaui

Gregorian

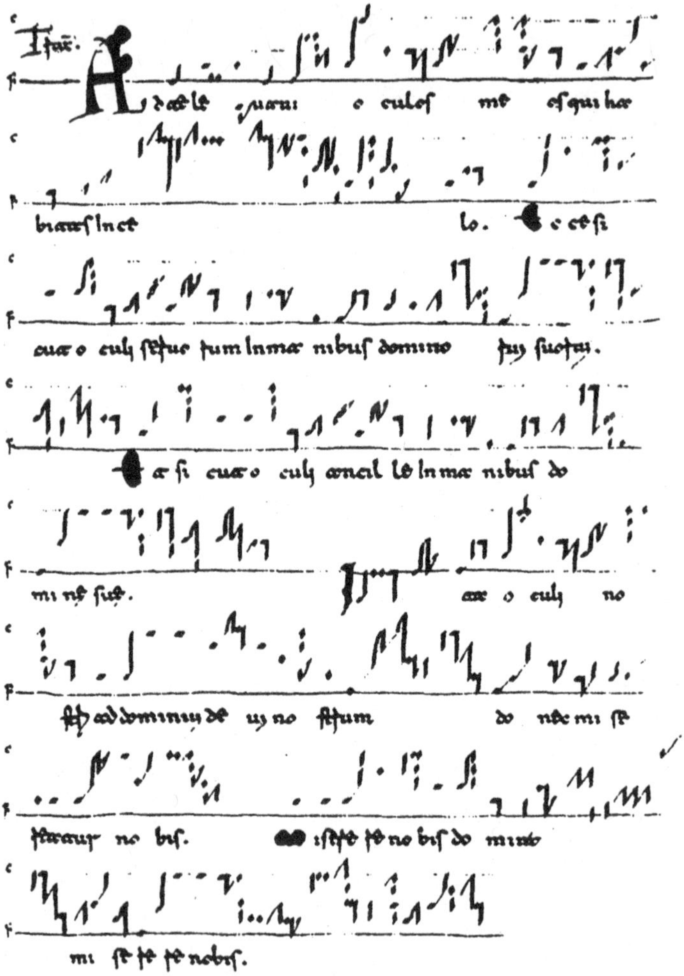

Ad te leuaui

Old Roman

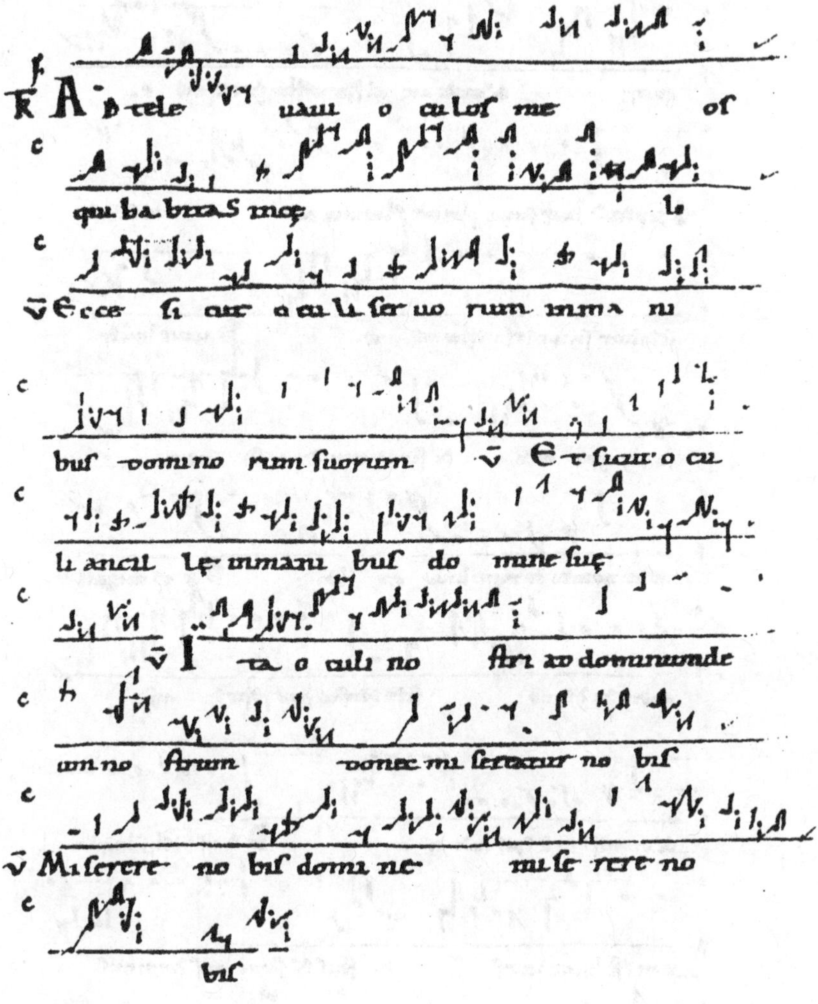

Attende

Gregorian

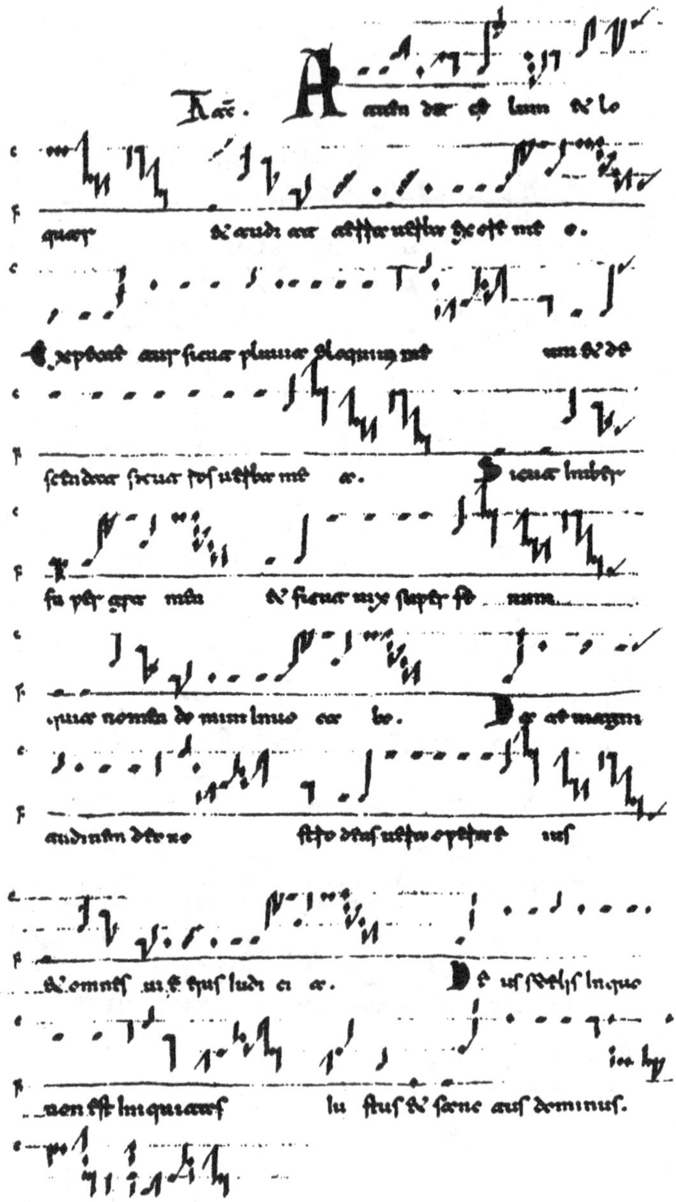

Attende

Old Roman

Beatus uir

Gregorian

Beatus uir

Old Roman

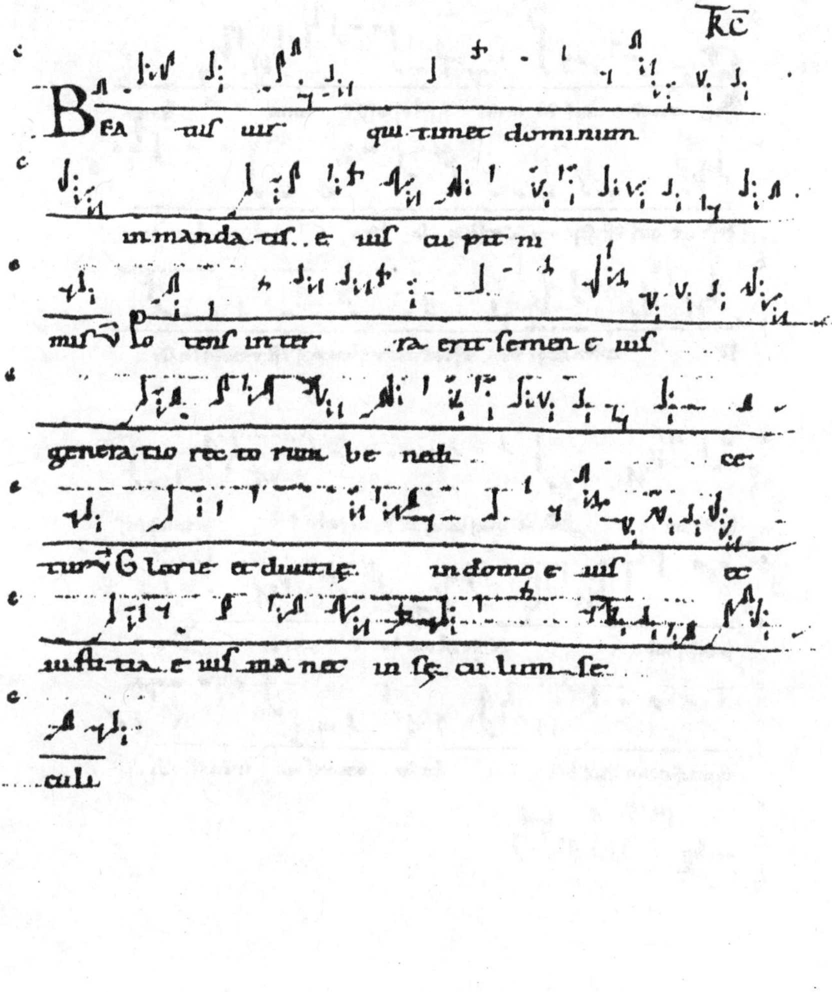

Cantemus

Gregorian

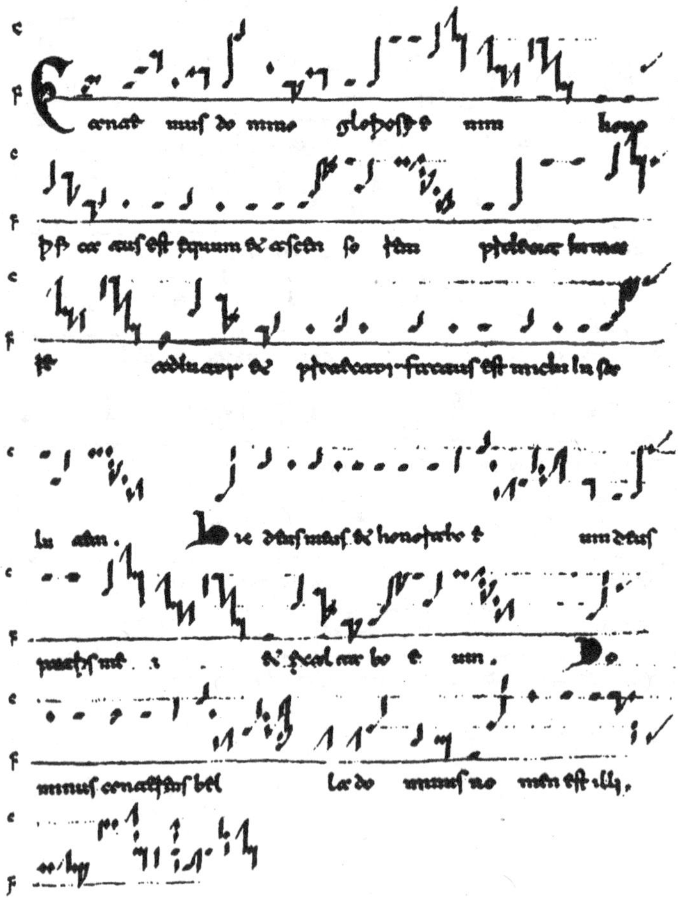

Cantemus

Old Roman

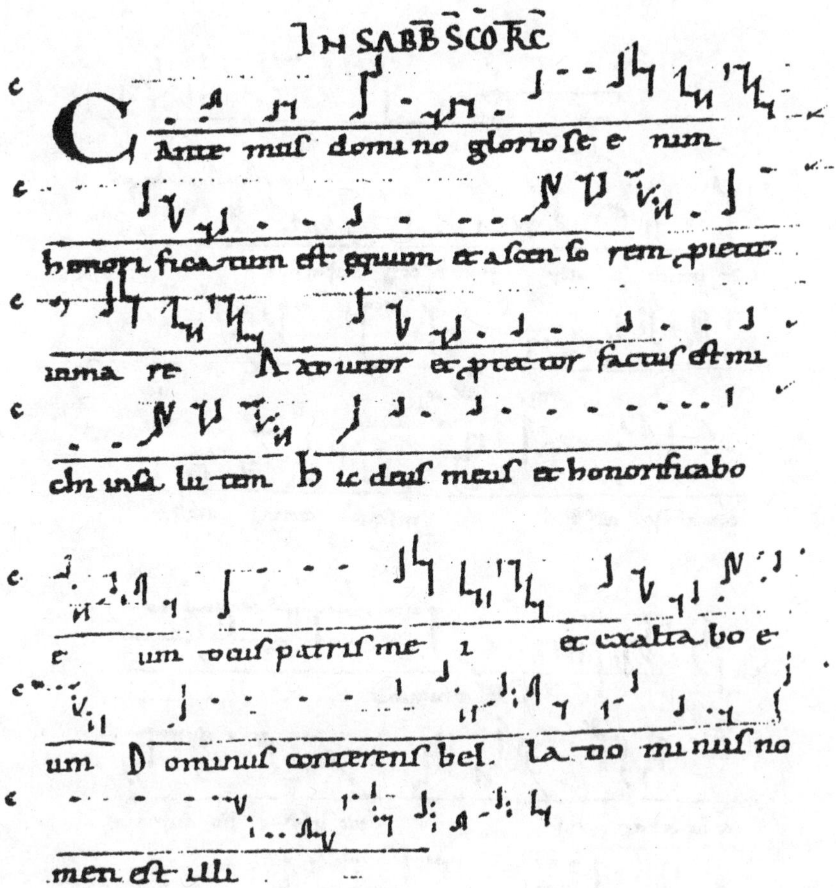

Commouisti
Gregorian

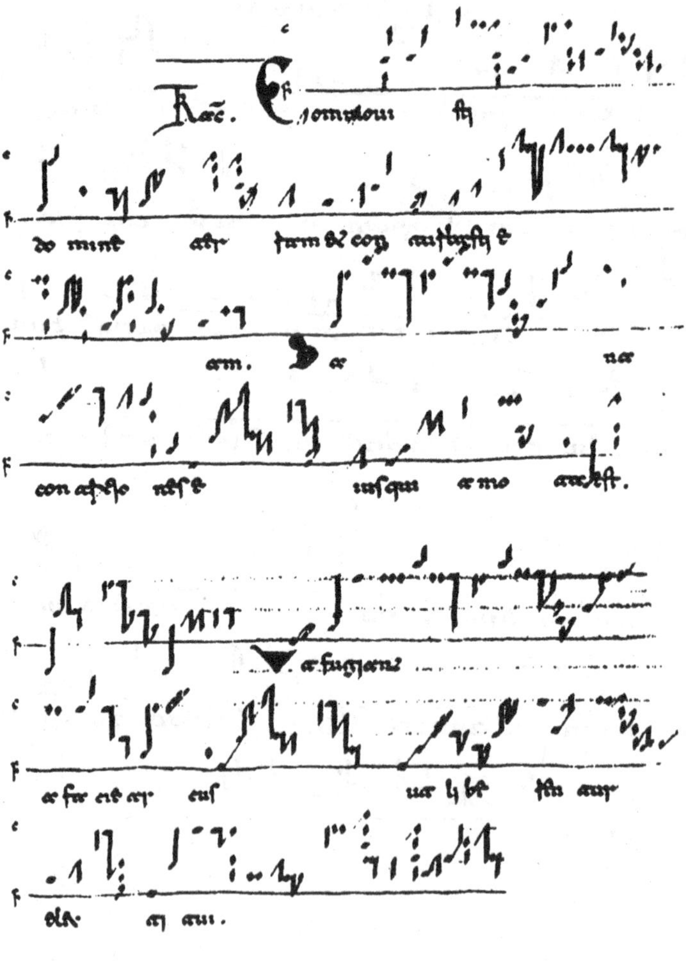

Commouisti
Old Roman

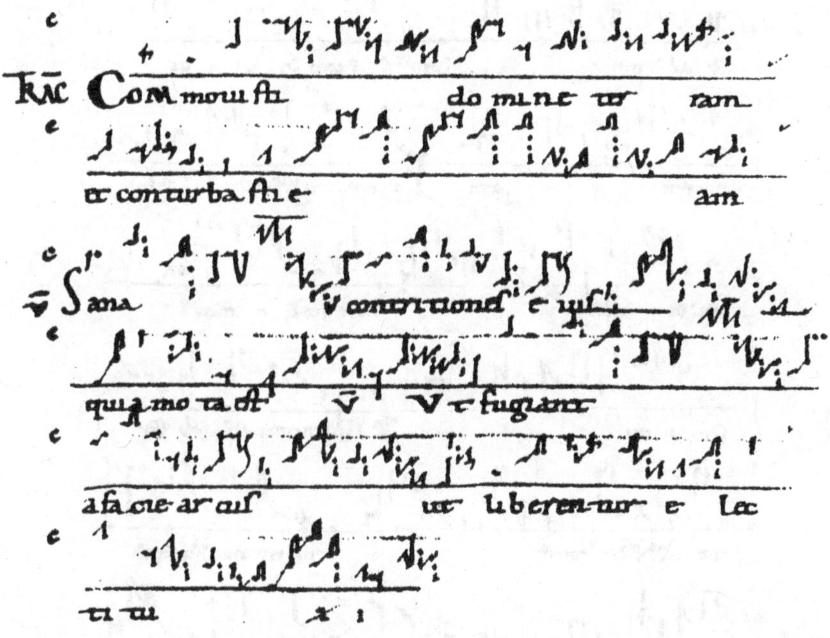

De profundis
Gregorian

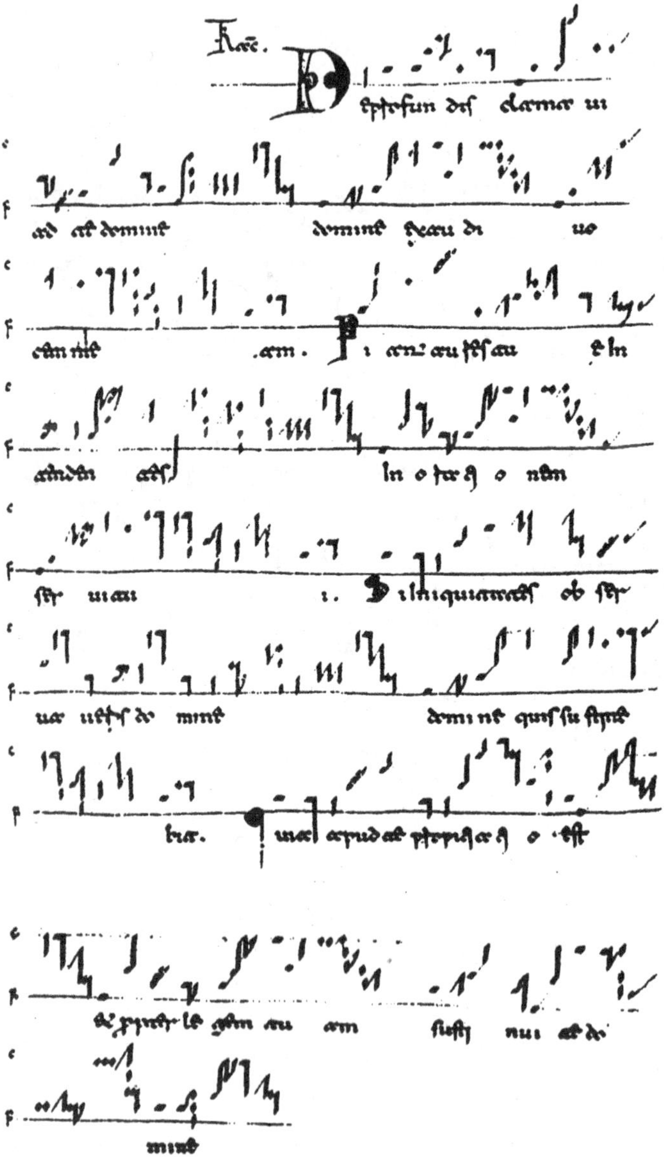

De profundis
Old Roman

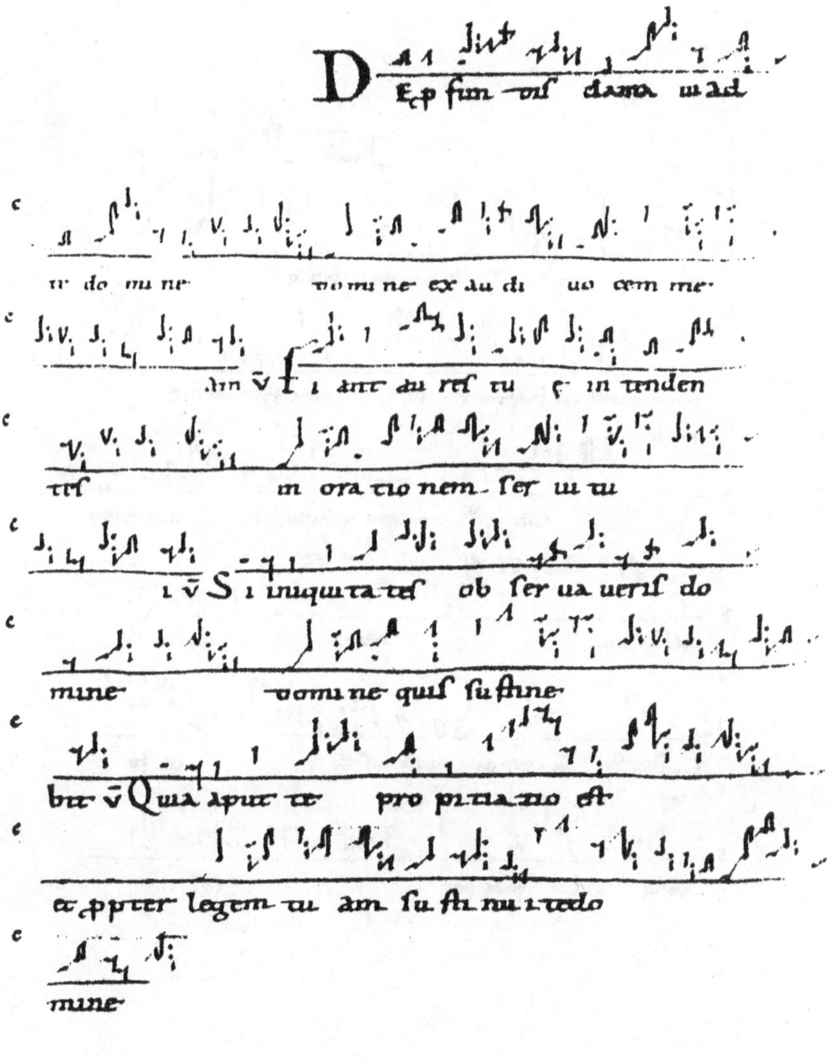

Desiderium

Gregorian

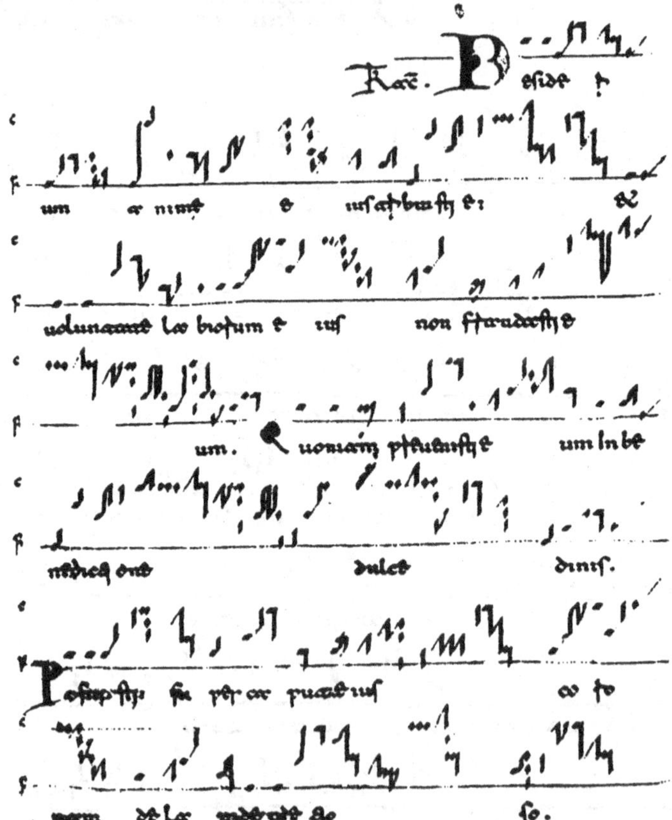

Desiderium

Old Roman

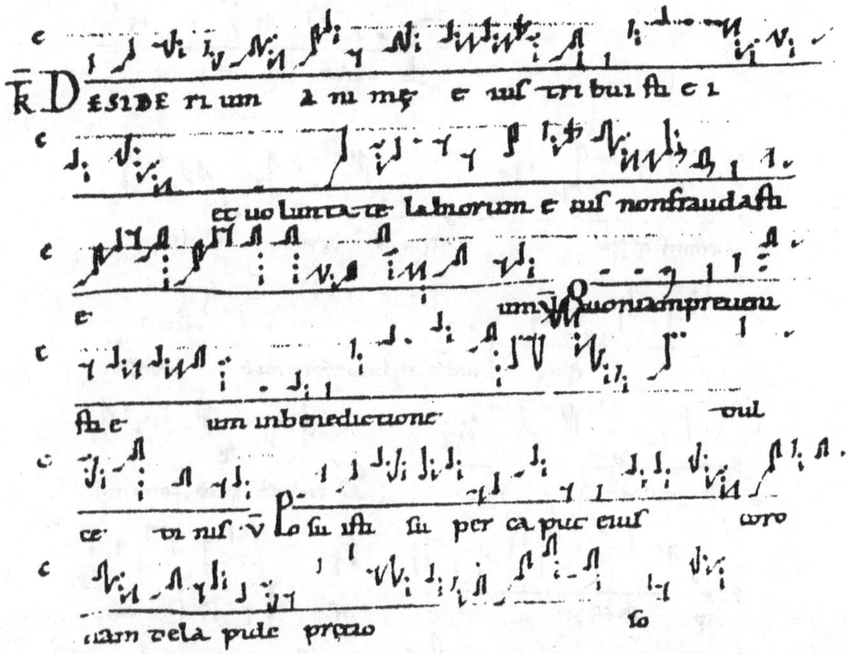

Iubilate

Gregorian

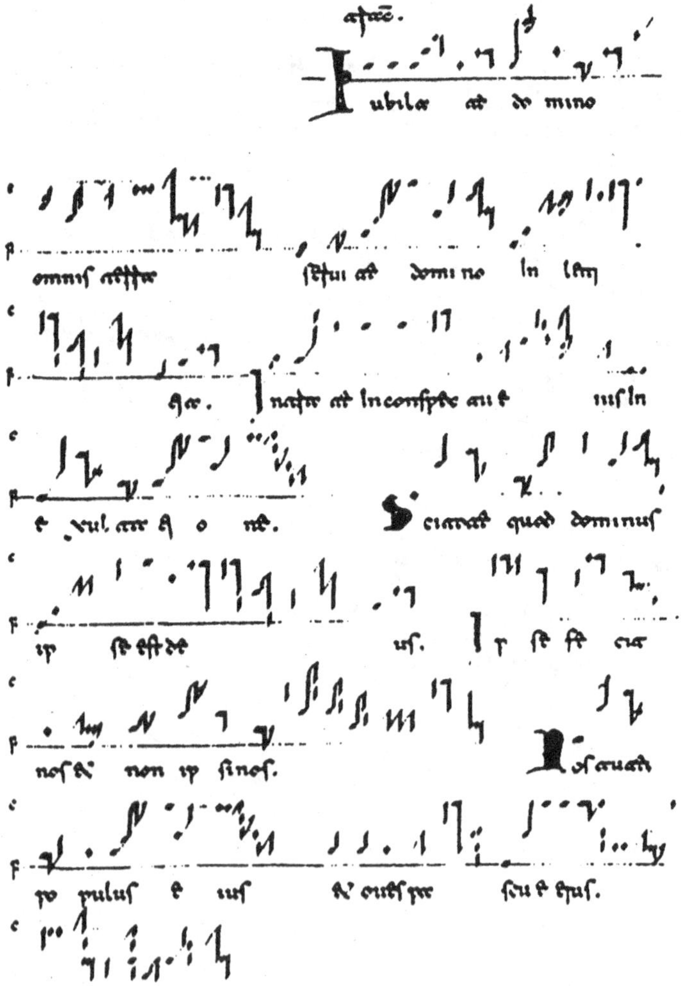

Iubilate
Old Roman

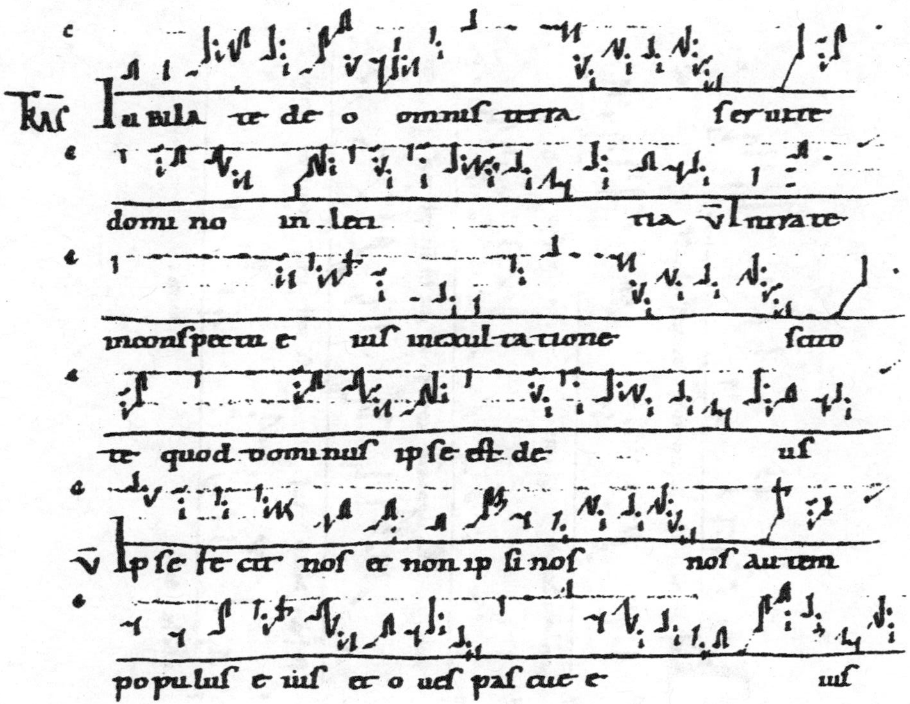

Laudate
Gregorian

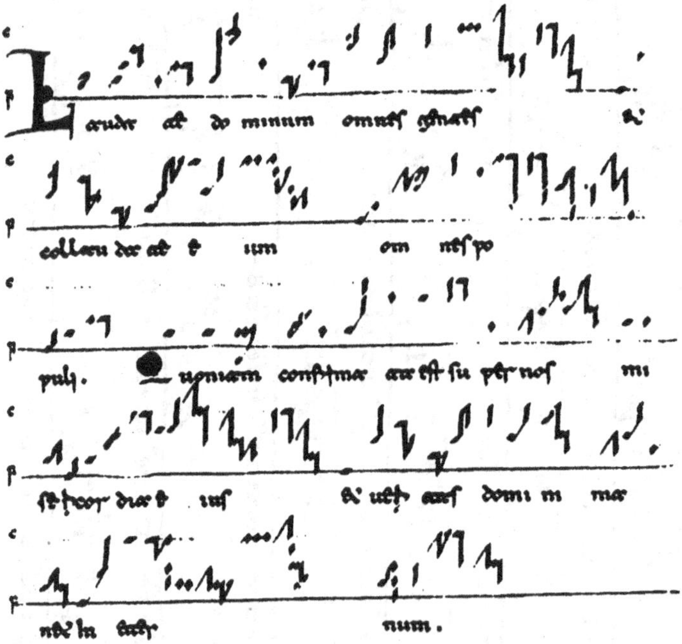

Laudate
Old Roman

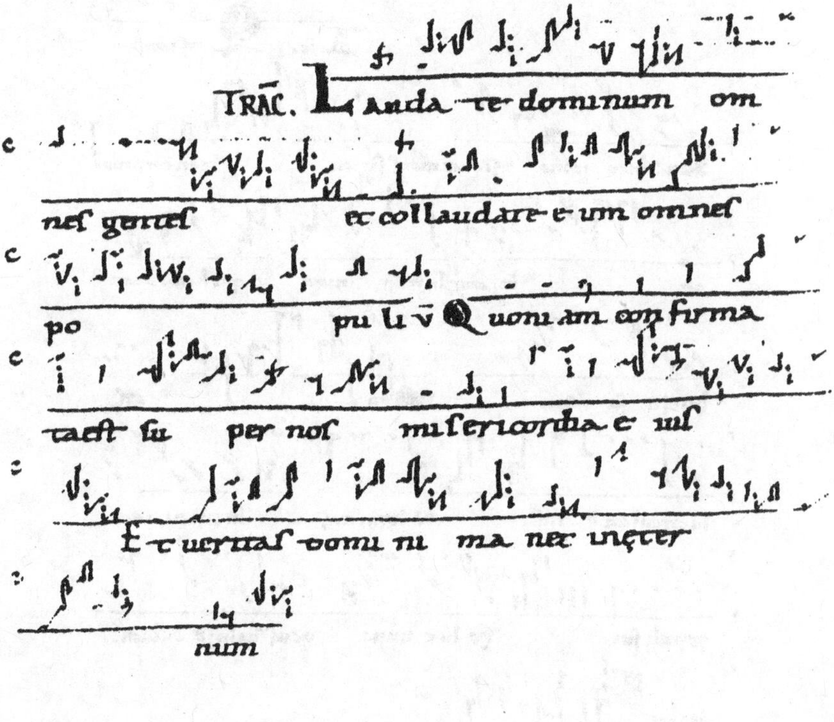

Qui confidunt

Gregorian

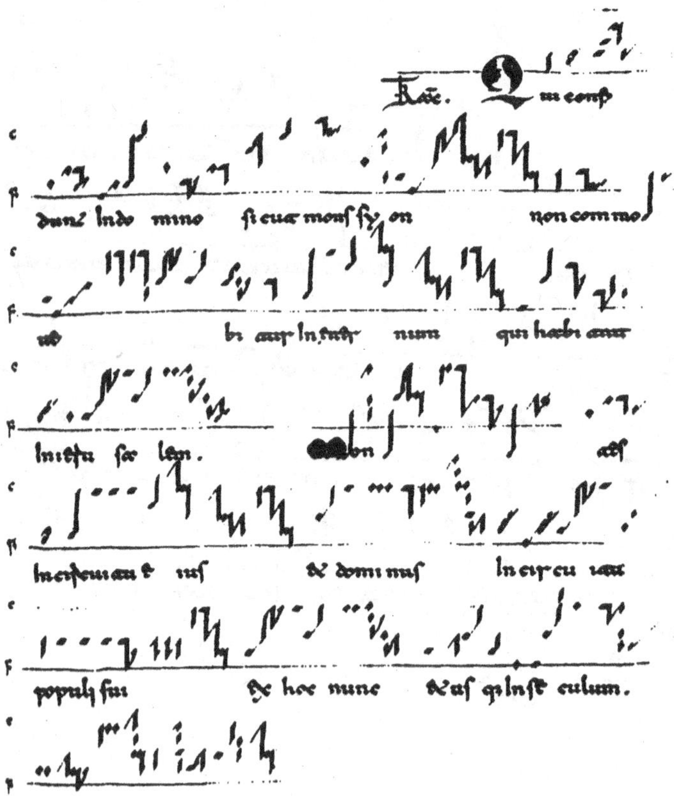

Qui confidunt

Old Roman

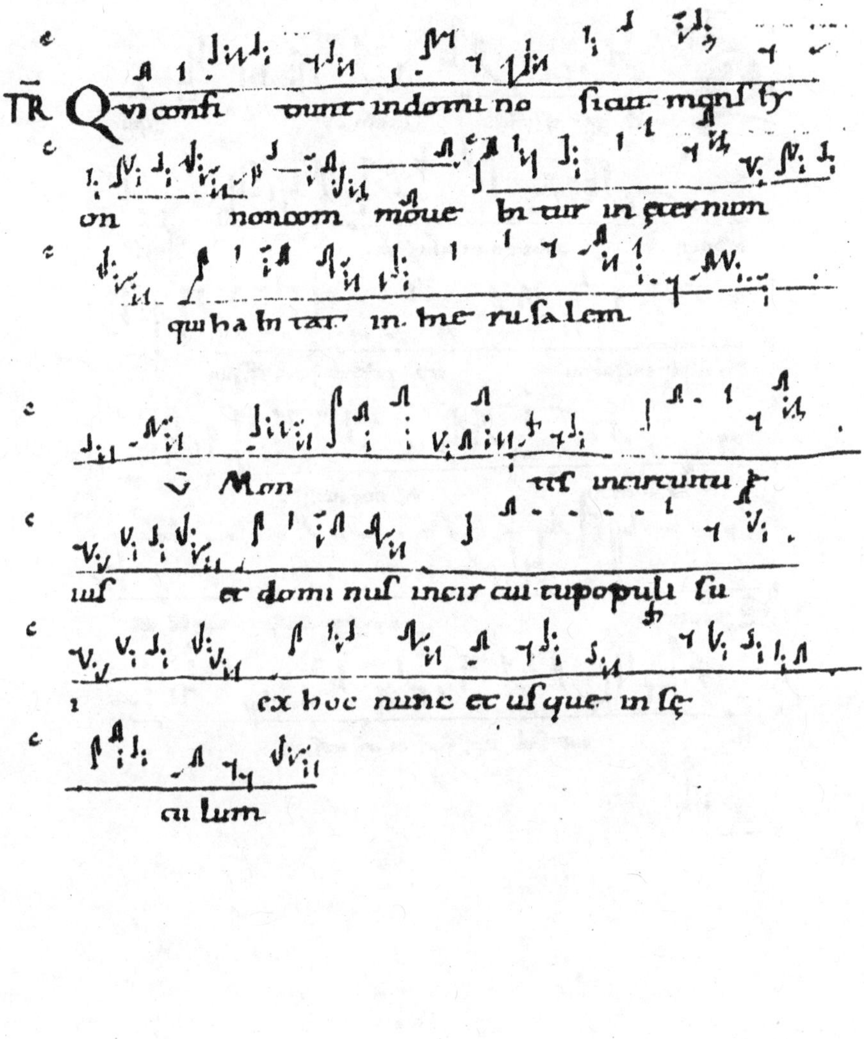

Qui regis

Gregorian

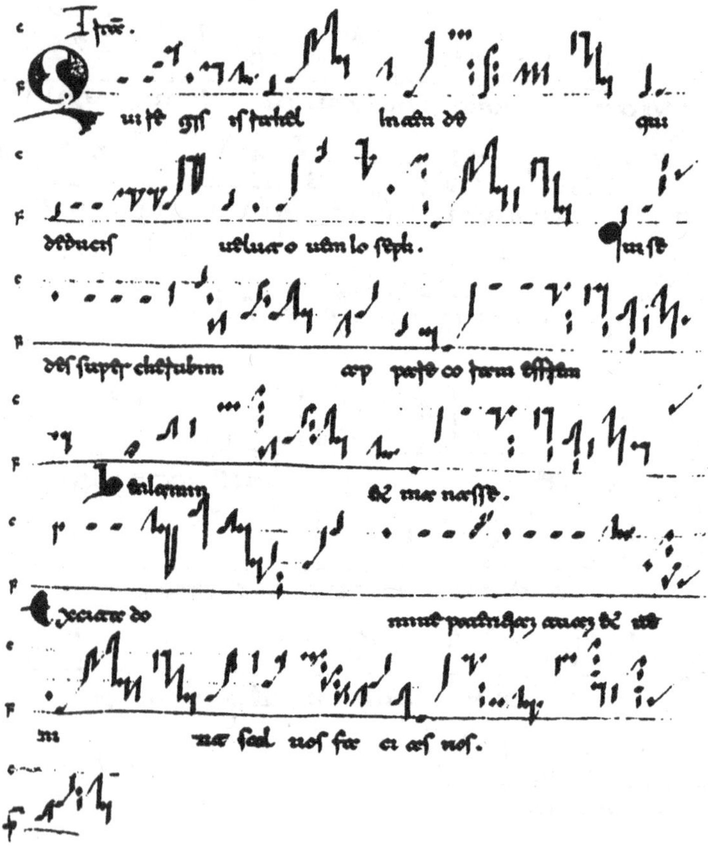

Qui regis

Old Roman

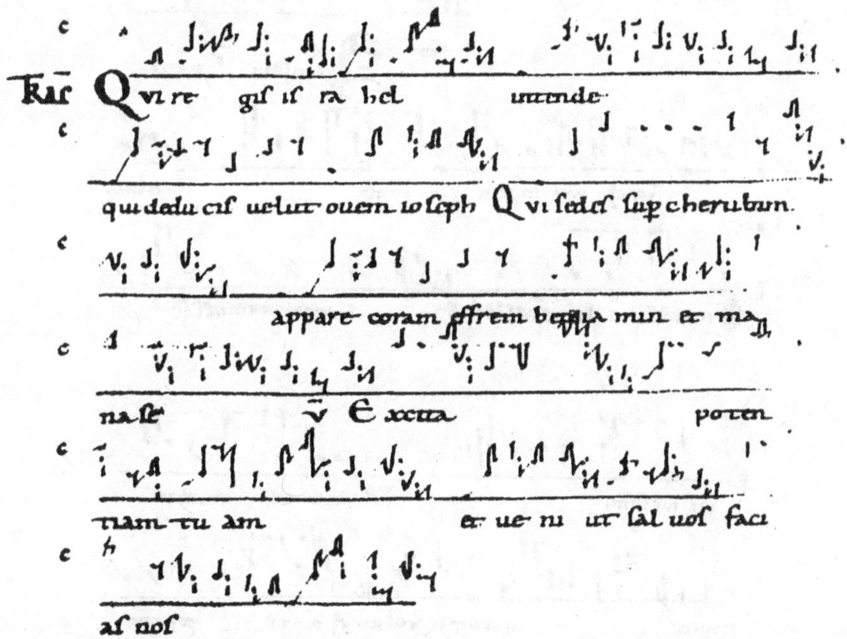

Qui seminant

Gregorian

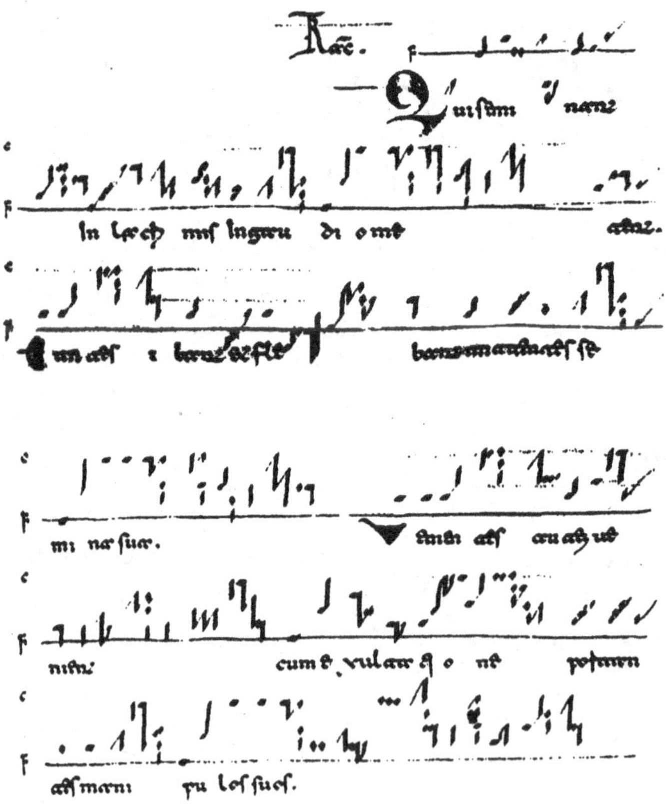

Qui seminant

Old Roman

Sepe

Gregorian

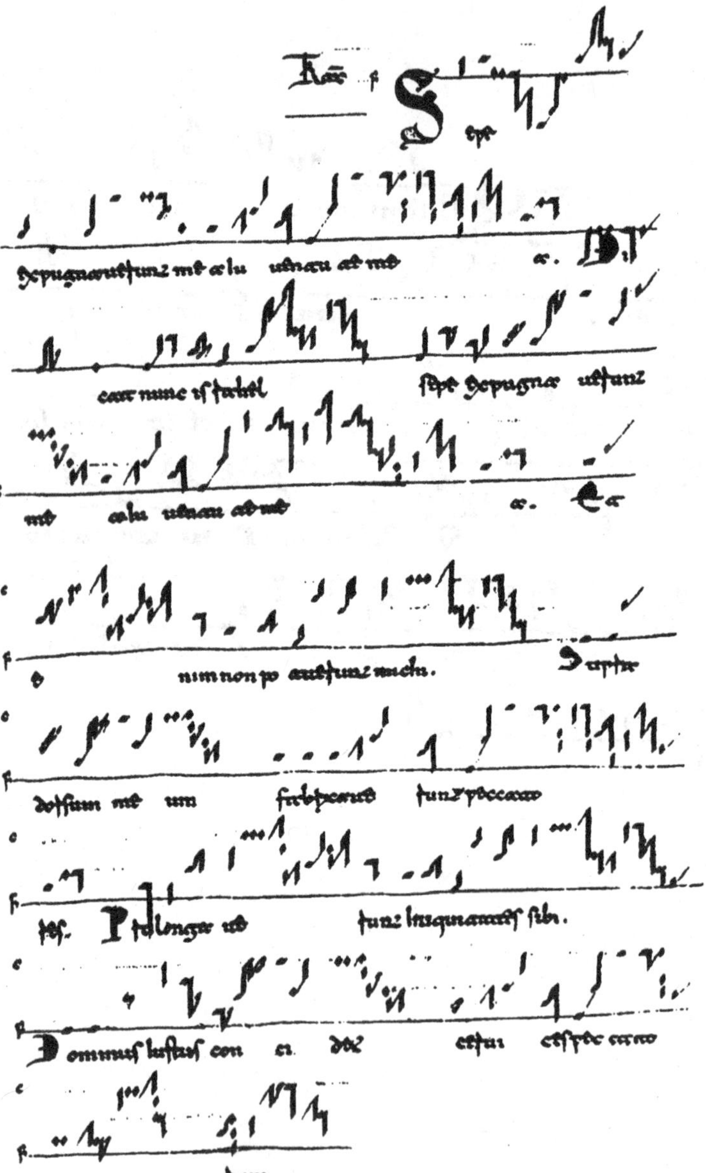

Sepe

Old Roman

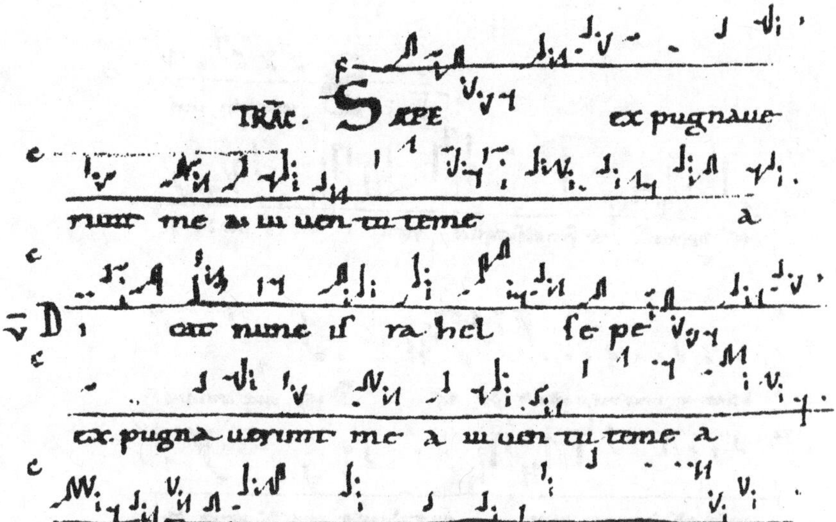

Sicut

Gregorian

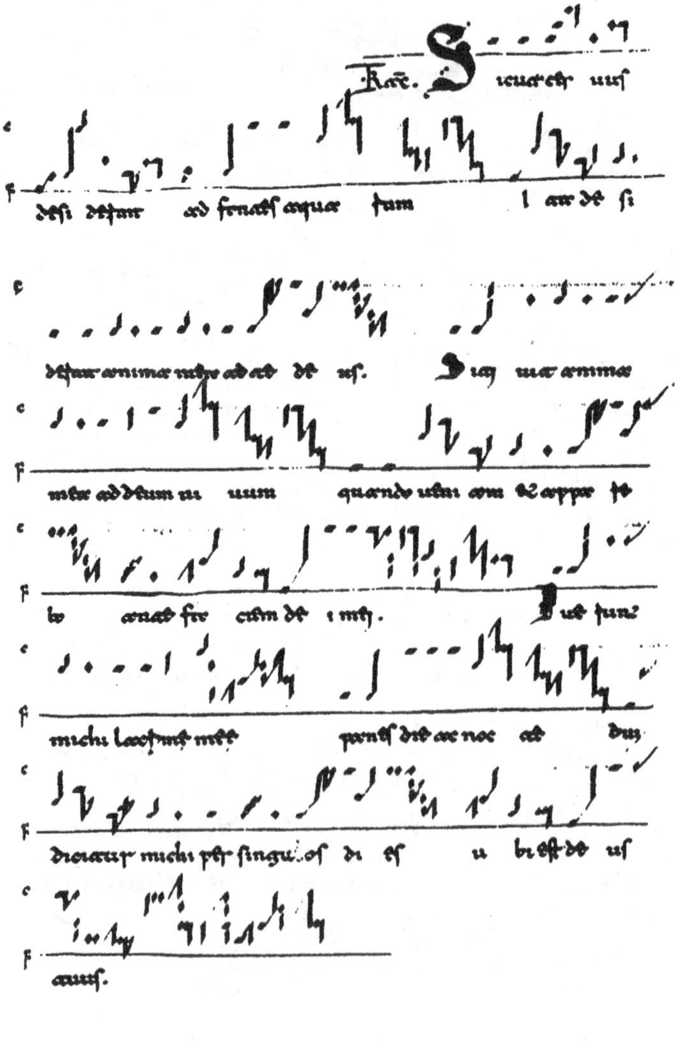

Sicut
Old Roman

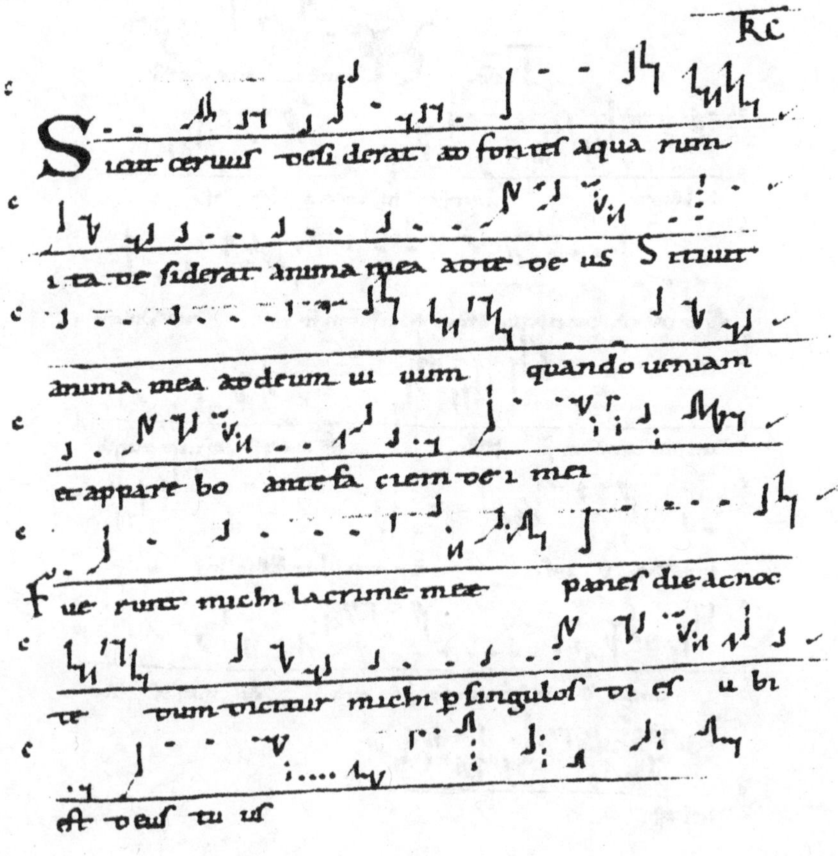

Vinea

Gregorian

Vinea
Old Roman

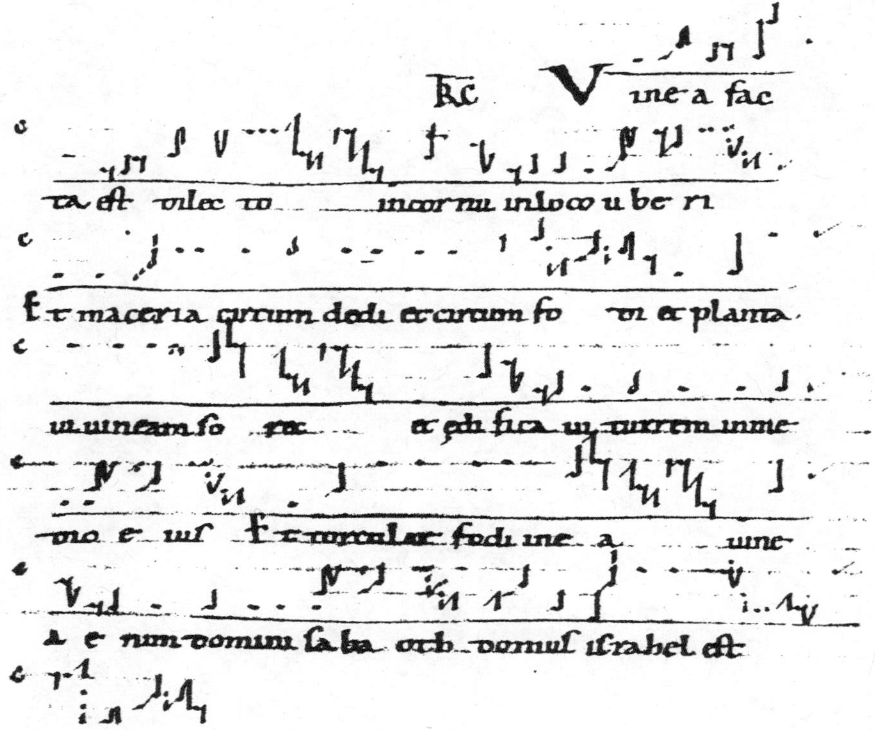

Appendix 4

The Eighth-Mode Tracts in *DIJ1*

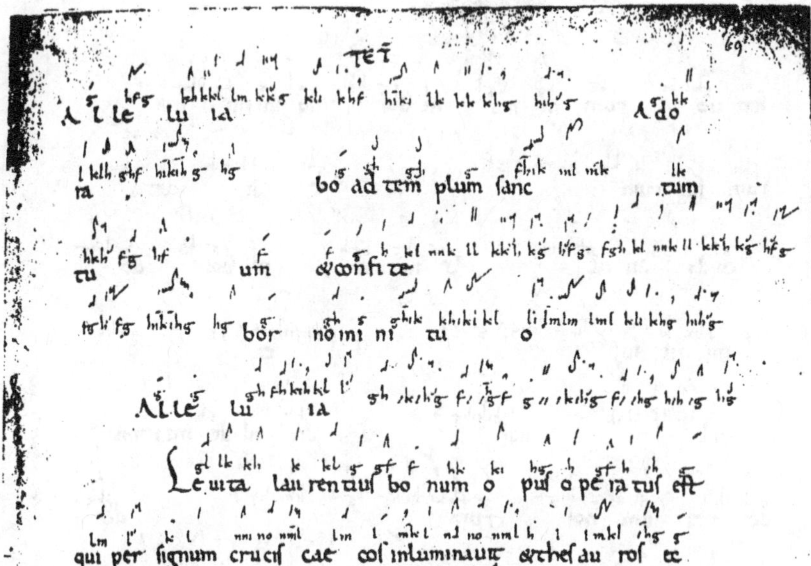

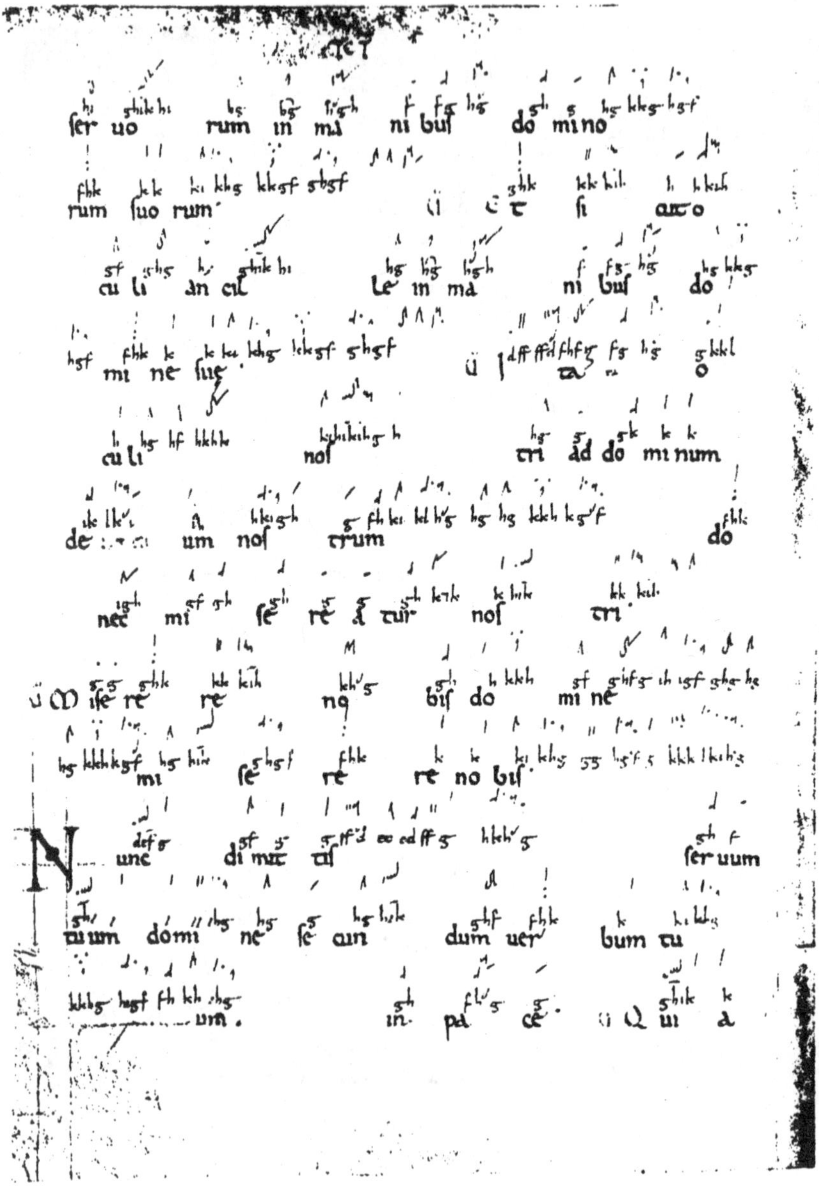
ser uo rum in ma ni bus do mino
rum suo rum
cu li an cil le in ma ni bus do
mi ne sue
cu li nos tri ad do mi num
de um nos trum do
nec mi se re a tur nos tri
Mi se re re no bis do mi ne
mi se re re re no bis
Nunc di mit tis ser uum
tu um domi ne se cun dum uer bum tu
um in pa ce Qui a

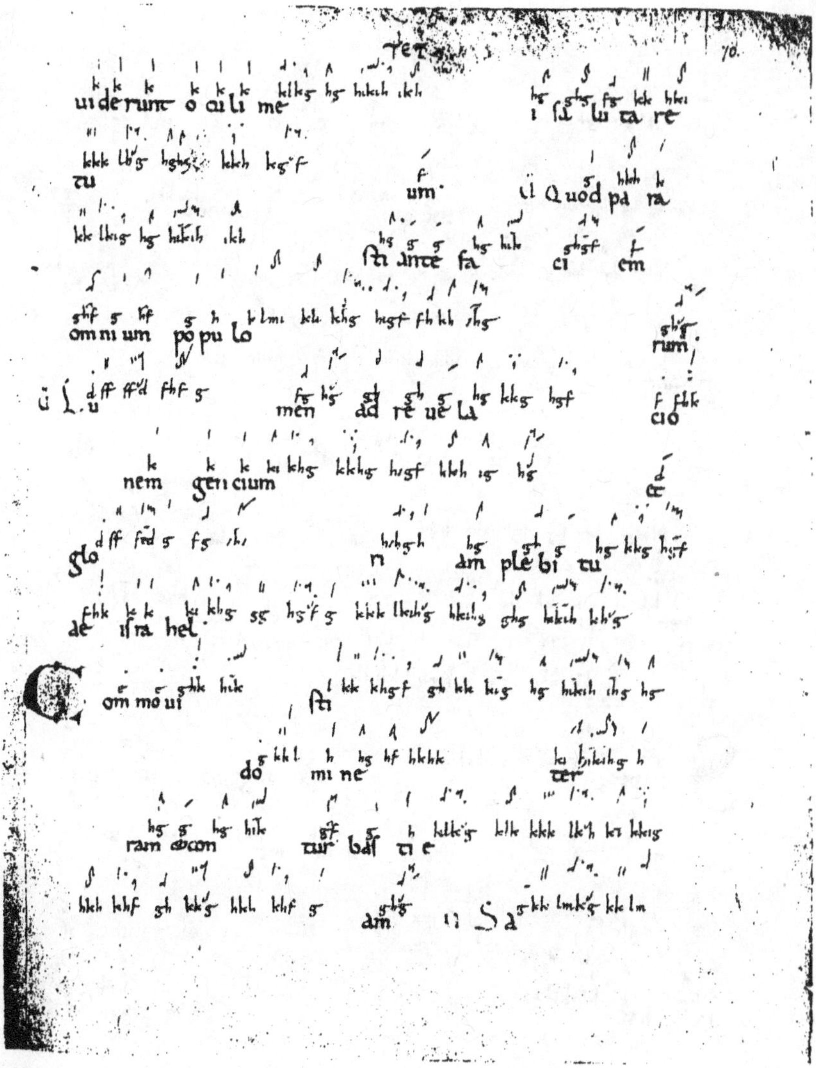

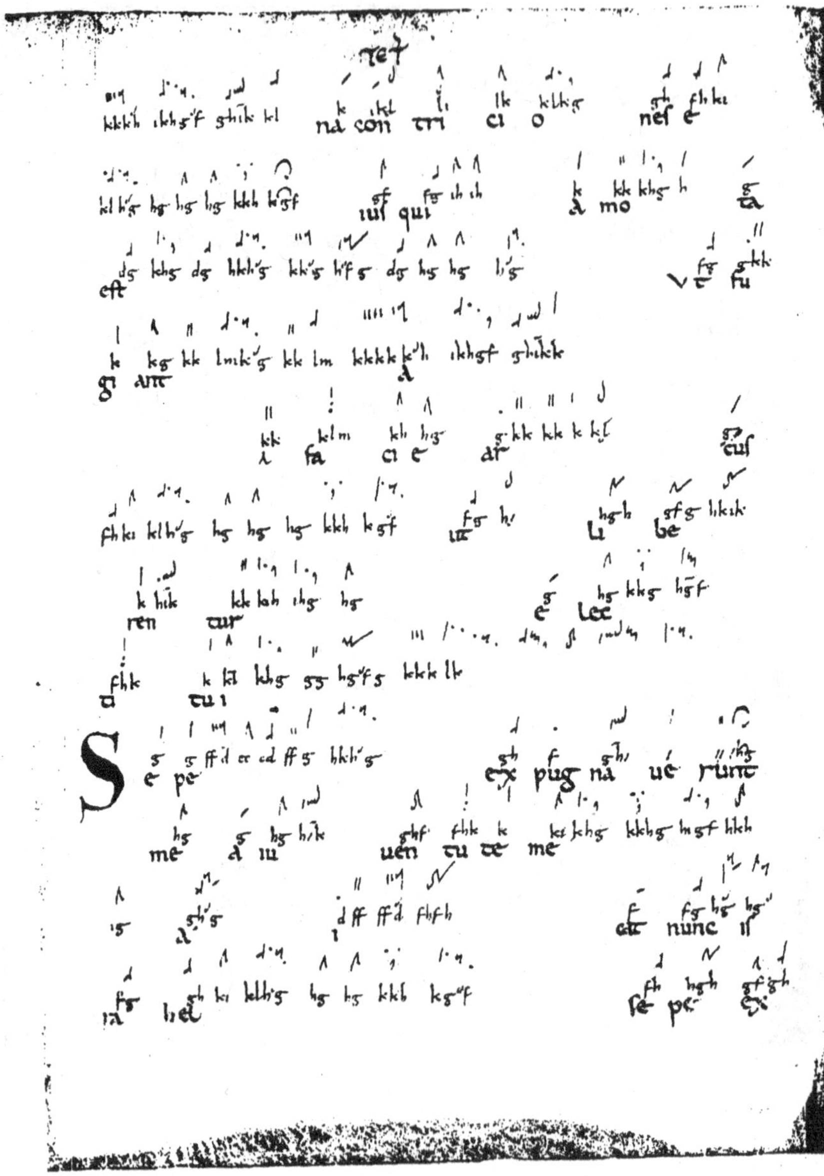

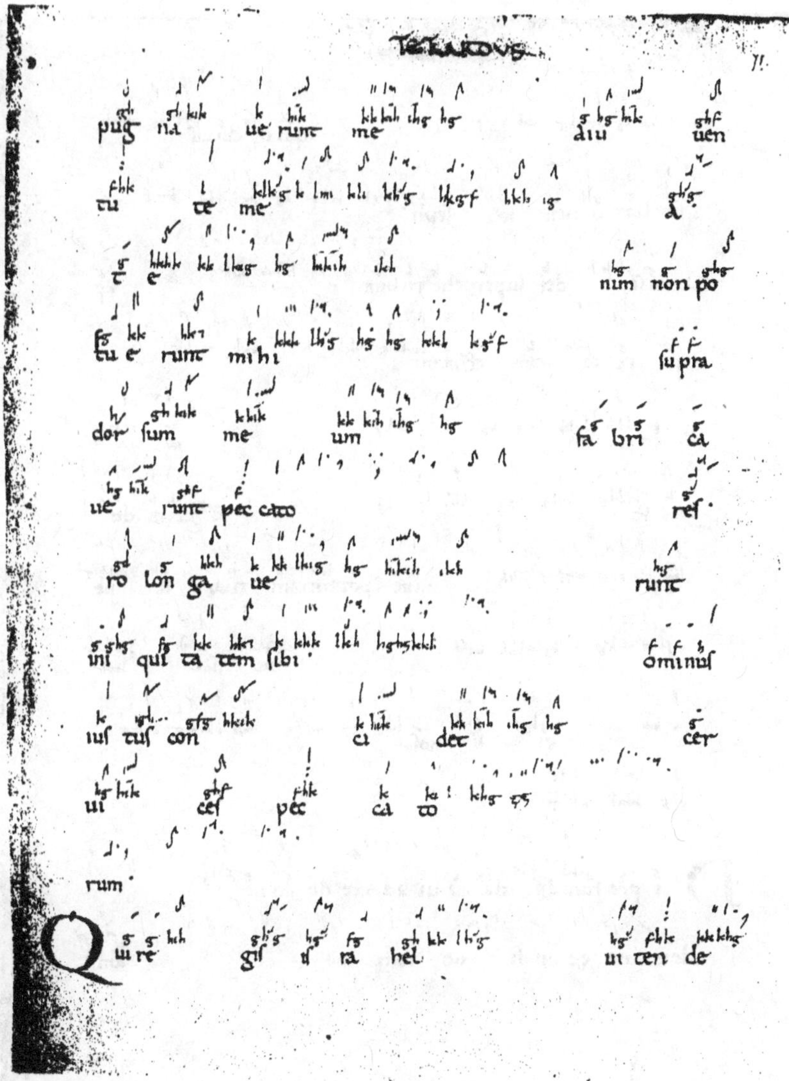

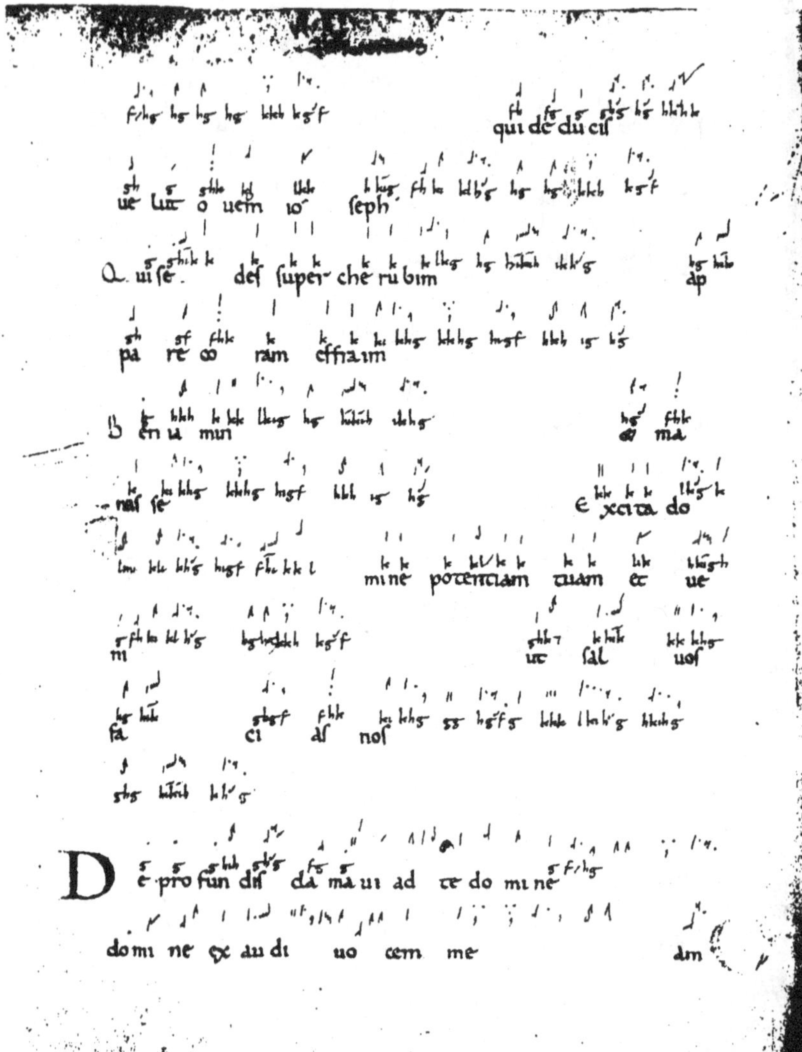

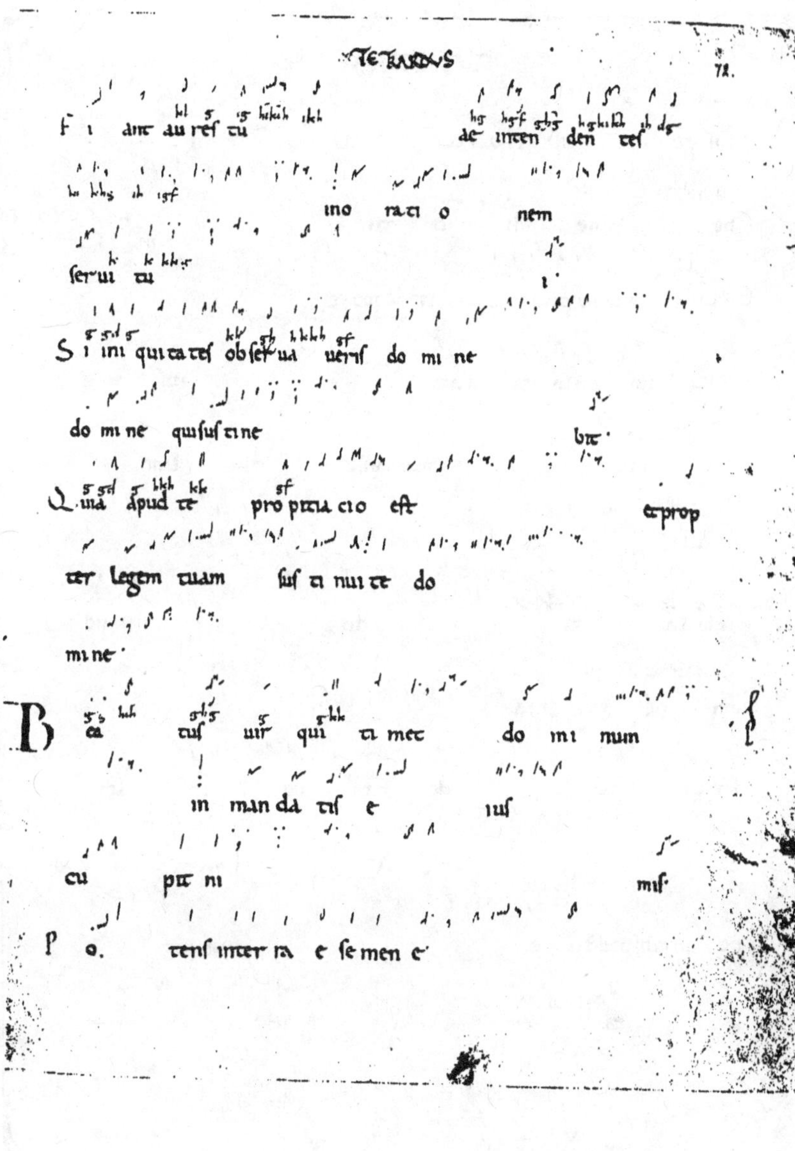

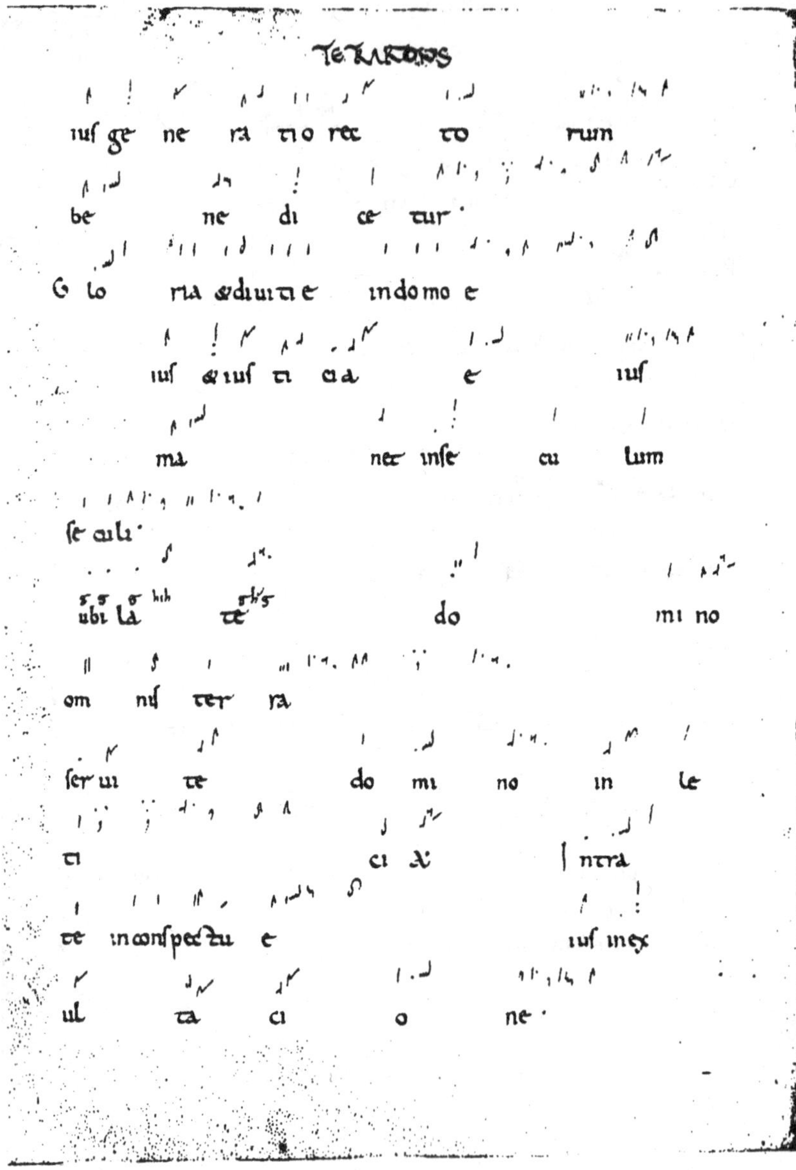

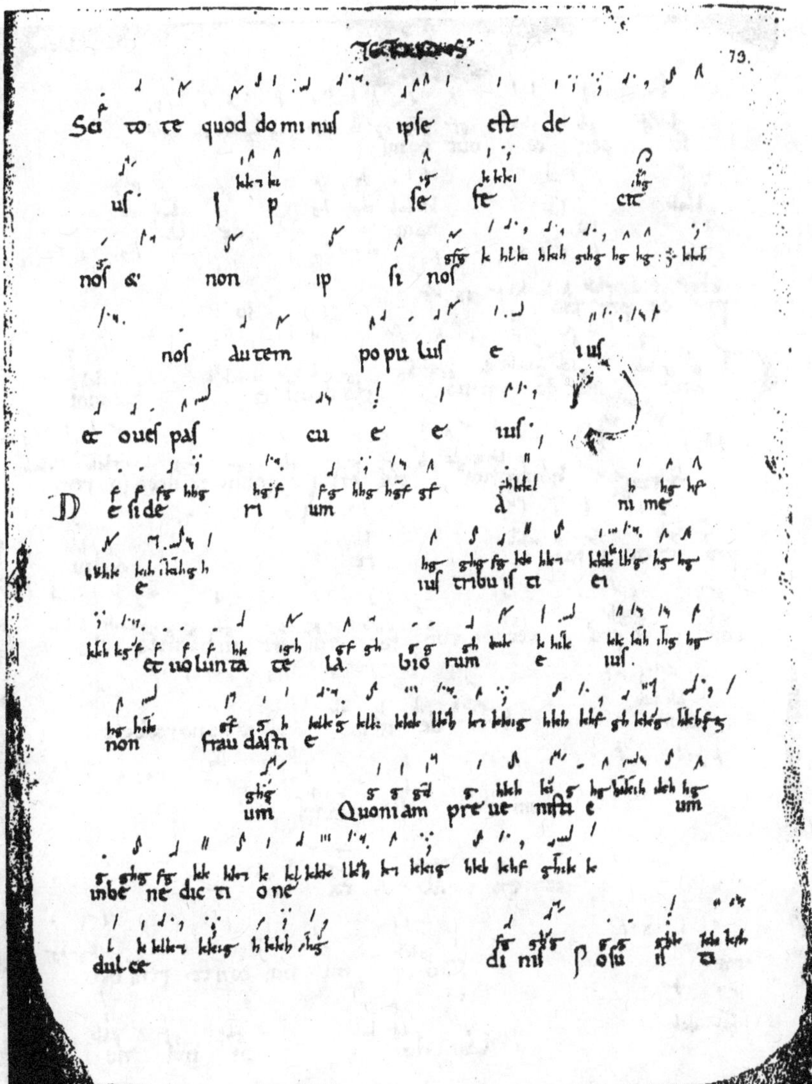
Sci to te quod do mi nus ipse est de
us ip se fe cit
nos et non ip si nos
nos autem po pu lus e ius
et oves pas cu e e ius
D e side ri um a ni me
e ius tribu is ti ei
et uo lunta te la bio rum e ius.
non frau dasti e
um Quoniam pre ue nisti e um
inbe ne dic ti one
dul ce di nis posu is ti

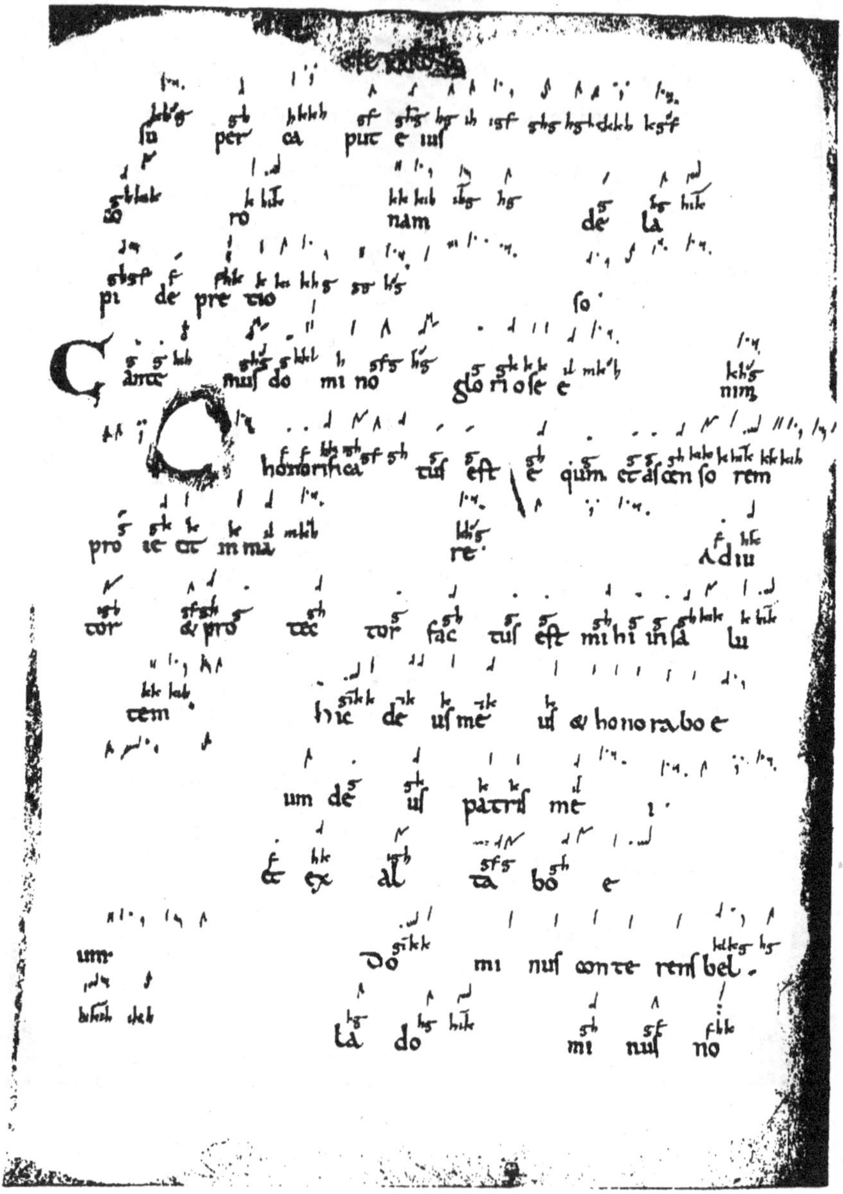

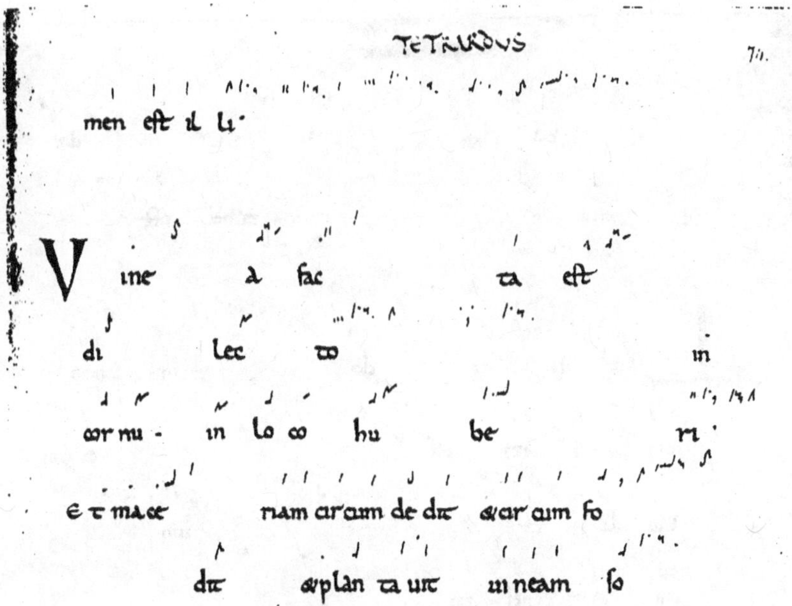
TETRARDUS
men est il li
Vine a fac ta est
di lec to in
cornu in lo co hu be ri
Et mace riam circum de dit et cir cum fo
dit et plan ta uit uineam so
reb Et edi fi ca uit tur rim in me
dio e ius et tor cu lar
fo dit ine
a
Vine a e nim do mi ni sa

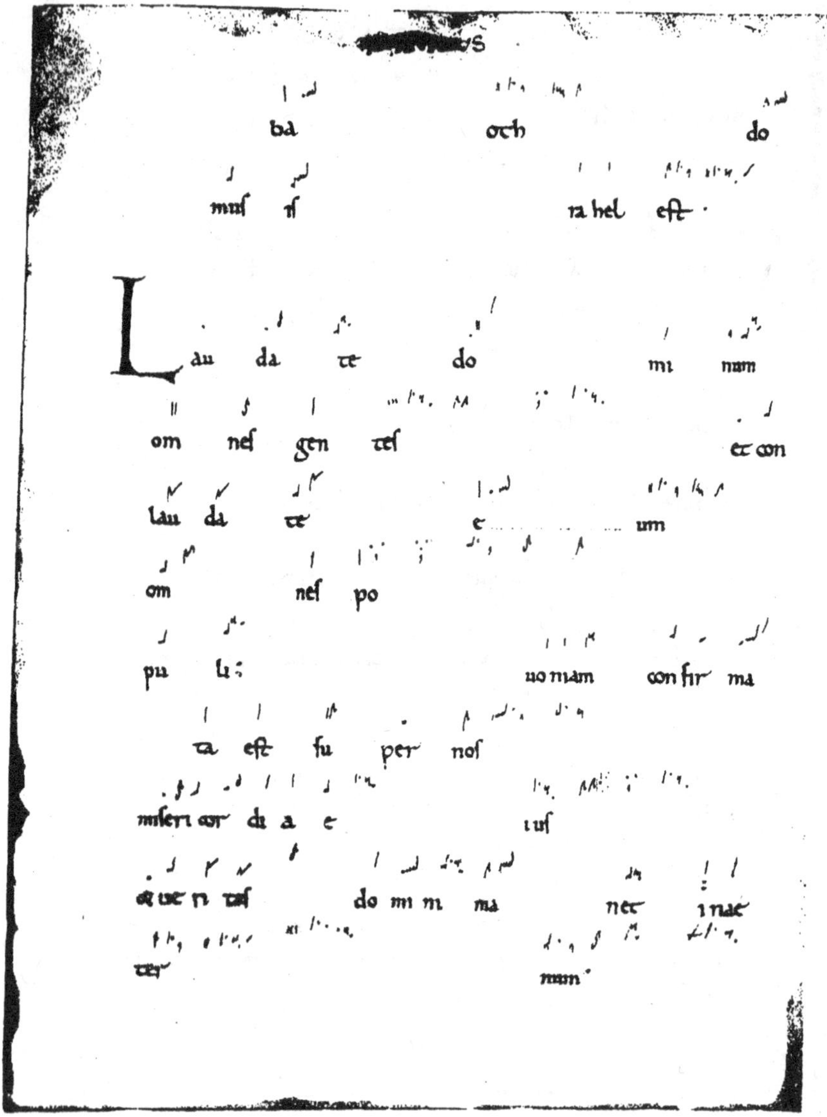
ba och do
mus is ra hel est
Lau da te do mi num
om nes gen tes et con
lau da te e um
om nes po
pu li uo mam con fir ma
ta est su per nos
miseri cor di a e ius
et ue ri tas do mi ni ma net in ae
ter num

Appendix 5
The Non-Standard Eighth-Mode Tracts

Absolve domine (LAV)

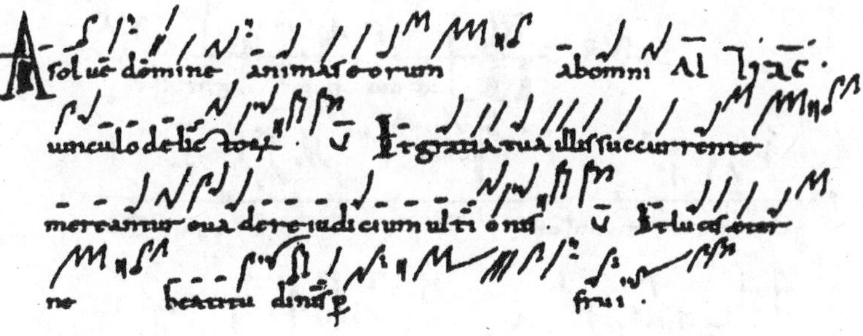

Adducentur (BEN5)

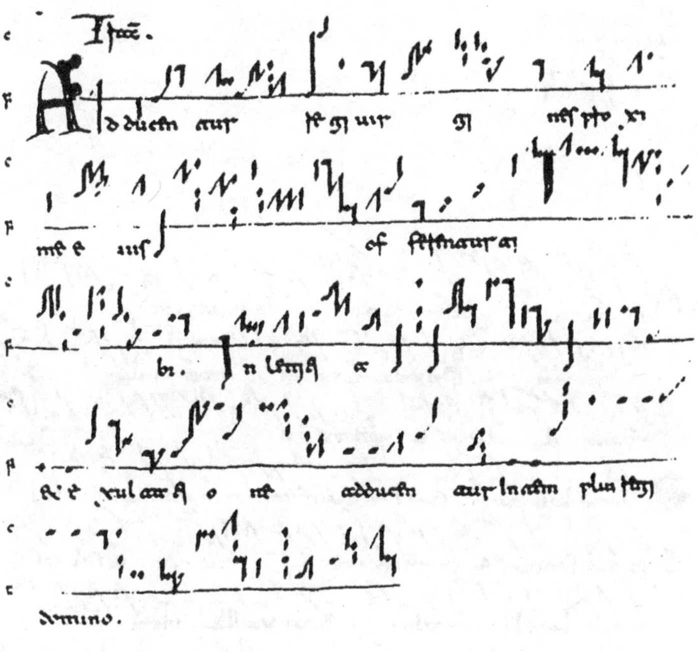

Aue Maria (BEN5)

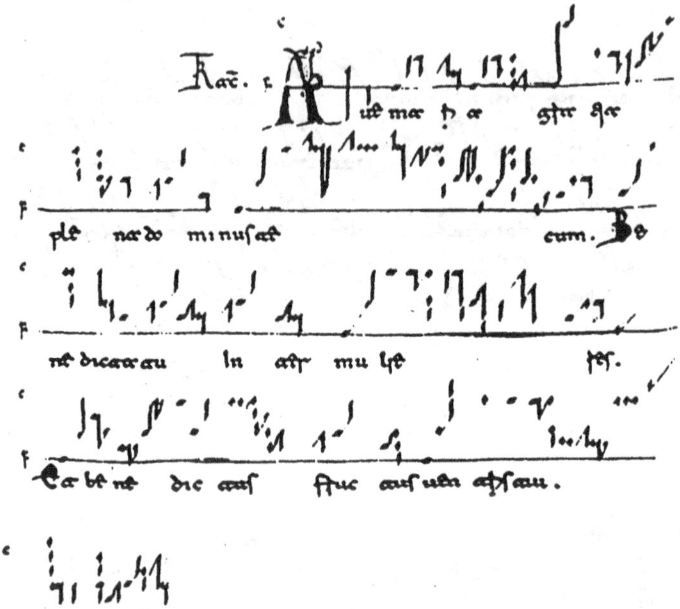

Aue Maria (LAV)

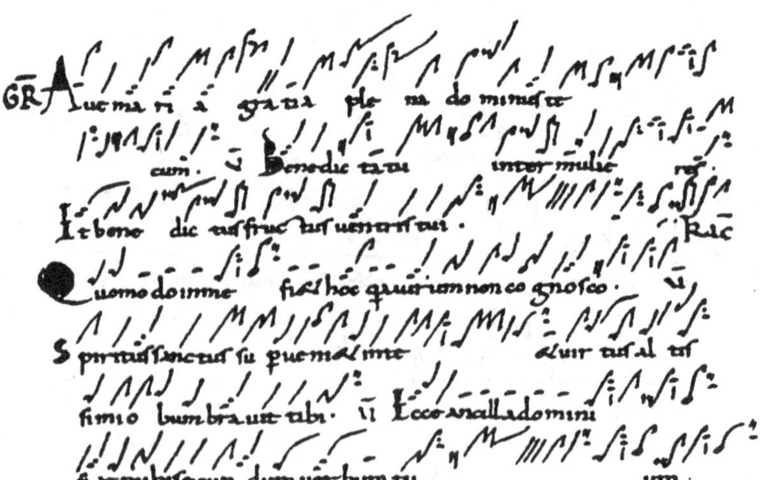

Benedicamus domino (BEN5)

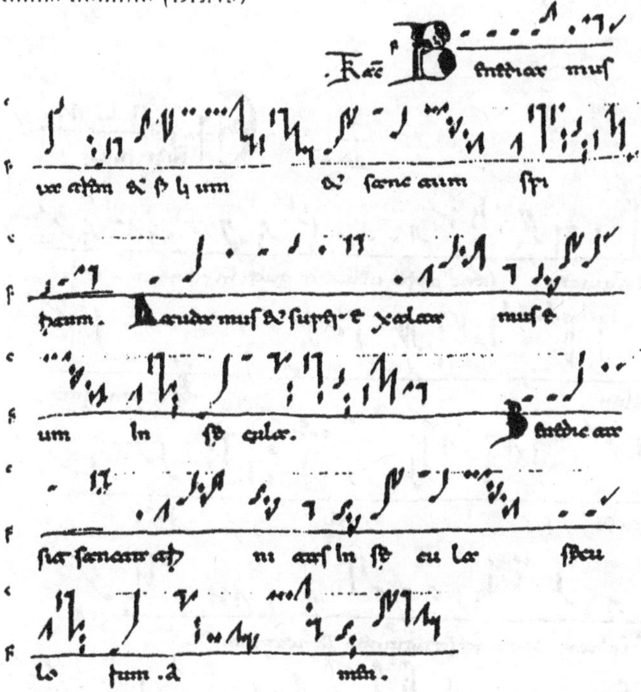

Conuertere (LAV)

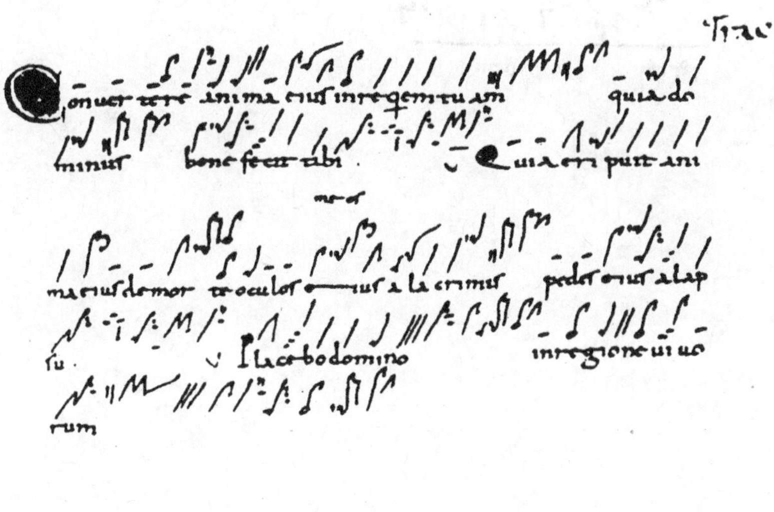

Effuderunt (BEN5)

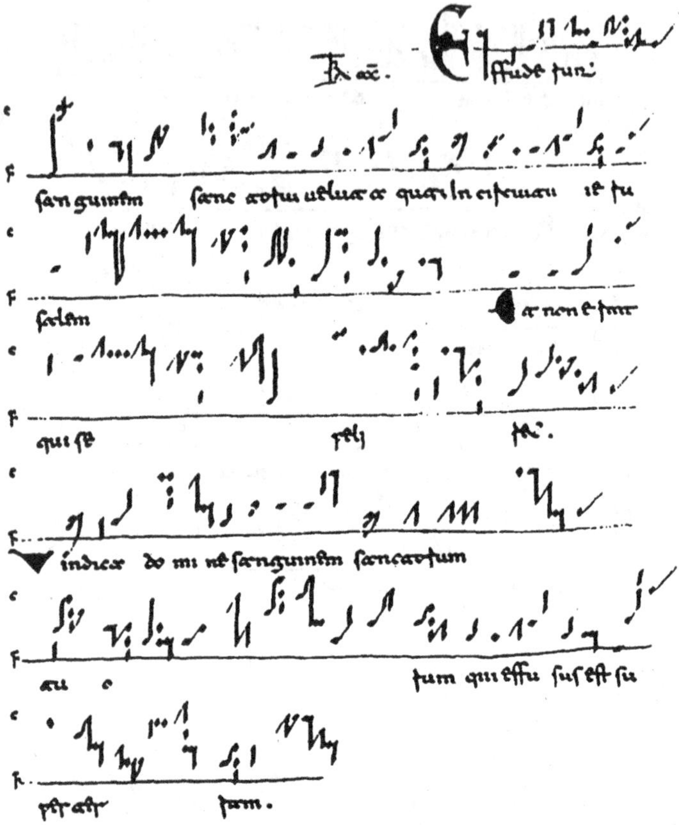

Effuderunt: significant variants

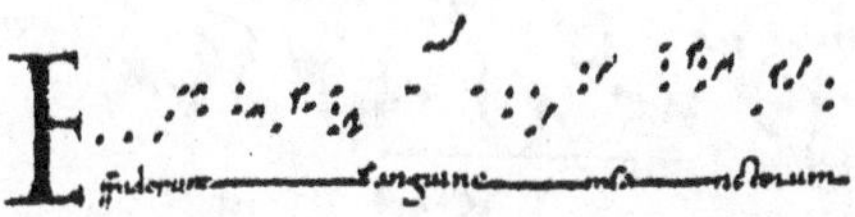

ALB

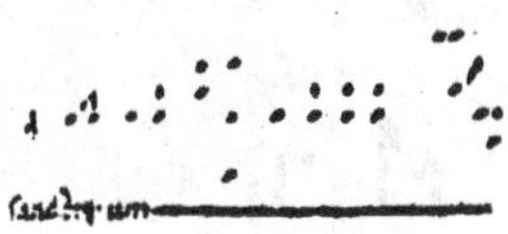

ALB

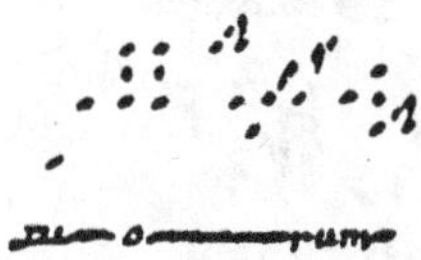

ALB

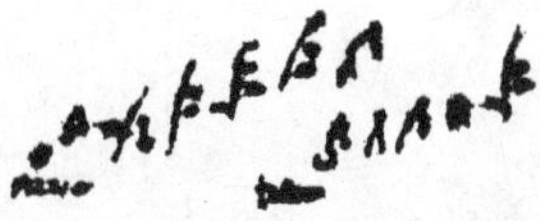

Chieti fragment

LAV

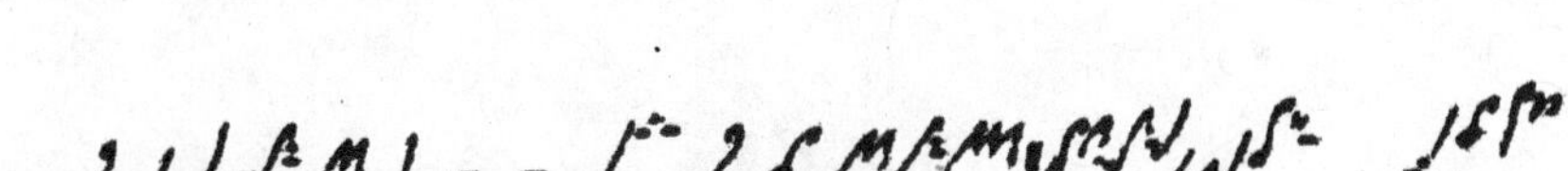

In columbe (BEN5)

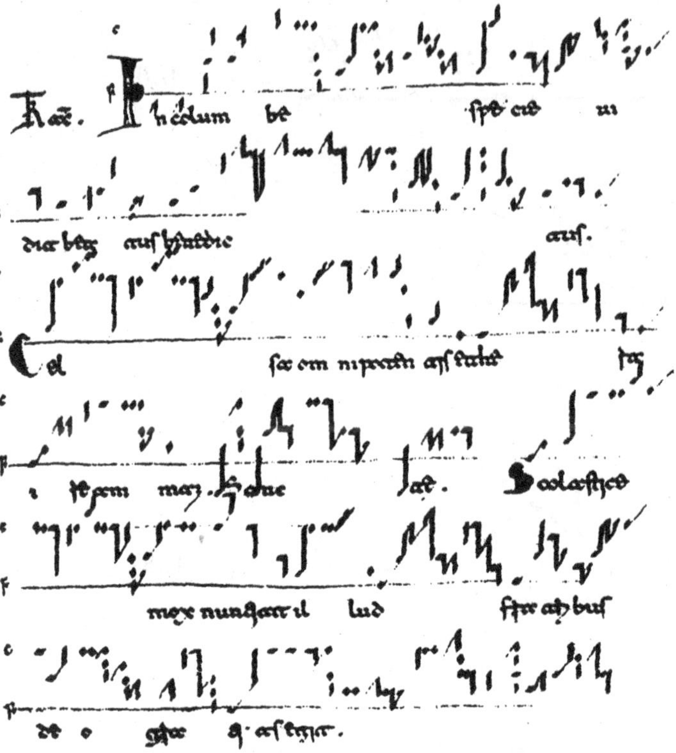

In columbe
(YRX)

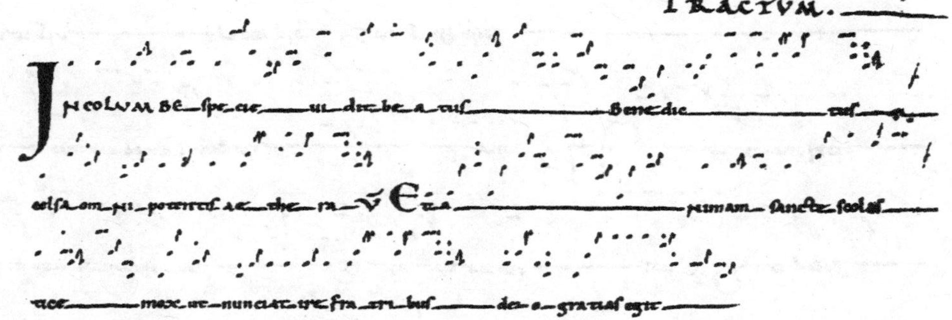

Iustorum anime
(BRE)

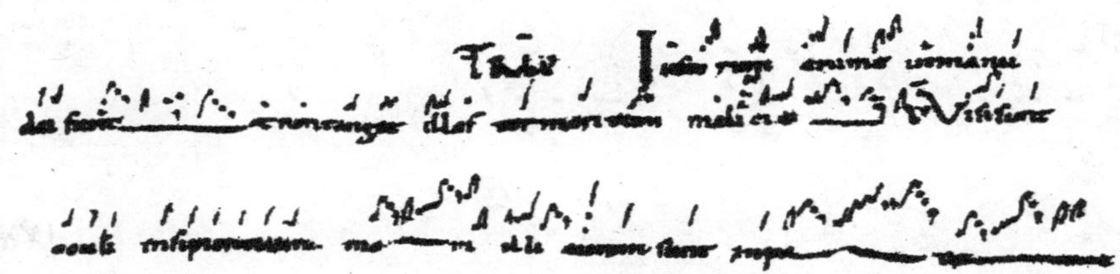

Nunc dimittis (YRX)

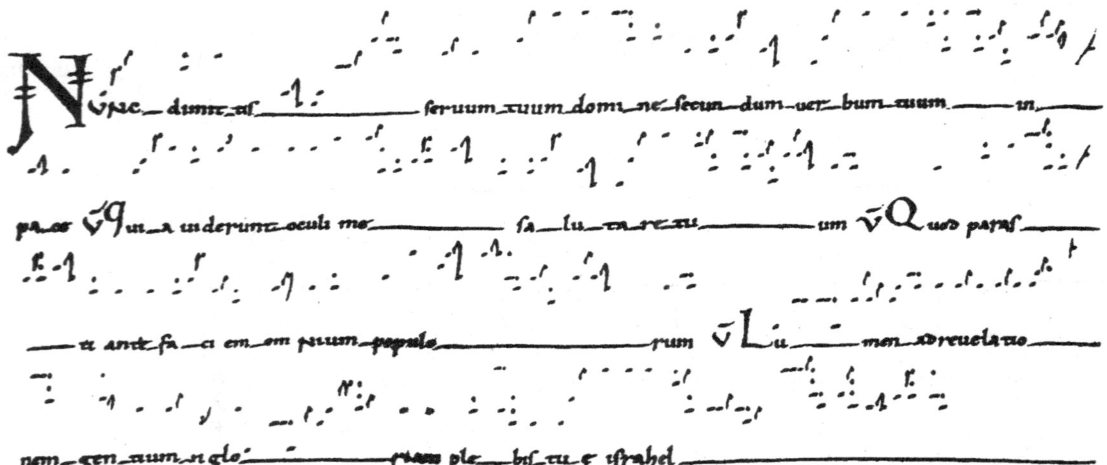

Nunc dimittis: significant variants

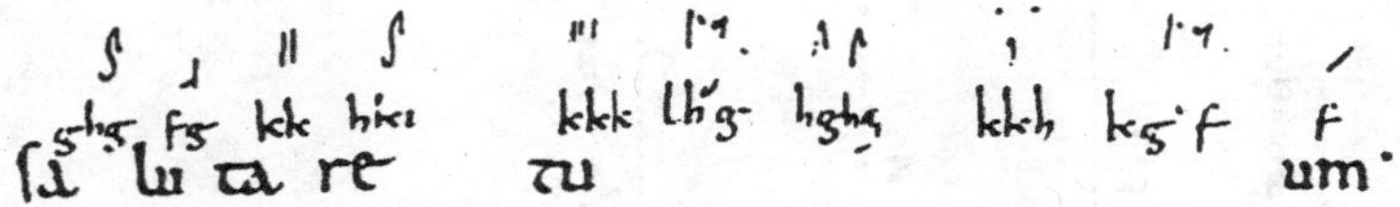

DIJ1

LAV

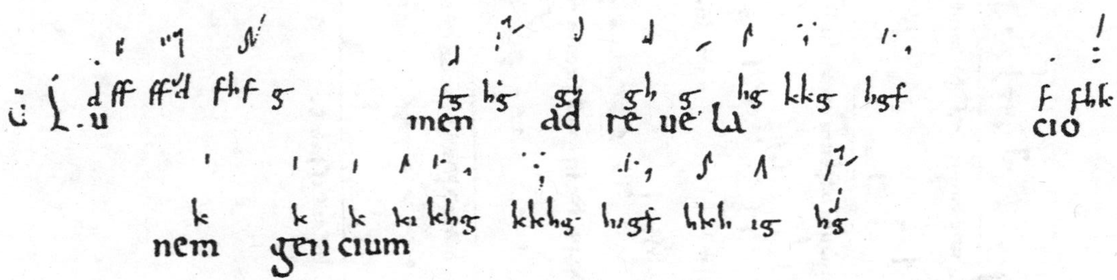

DIJ1

Nunc dimittis (BEN5)

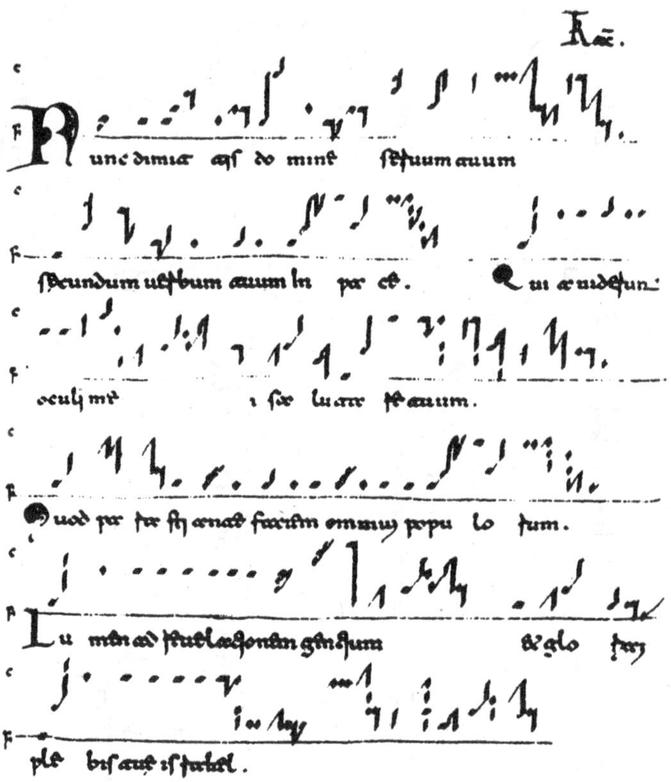

Posuisti (BEN5)

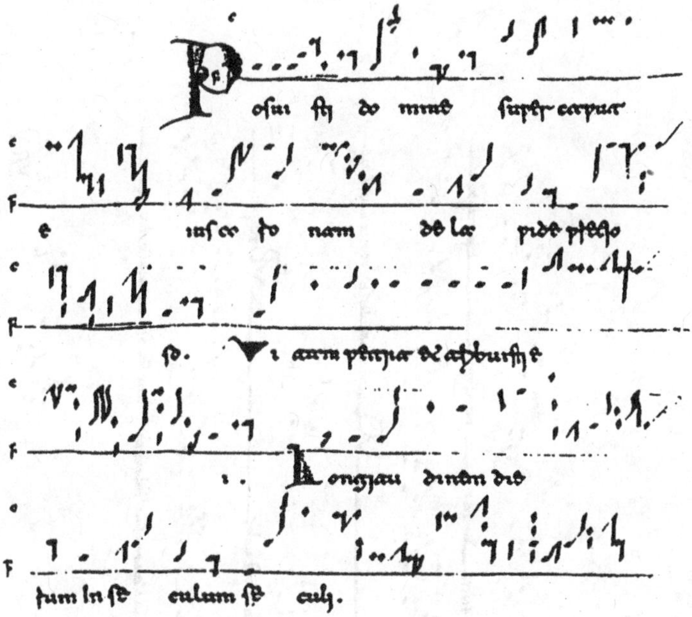

Sancti et iusti (BRE)

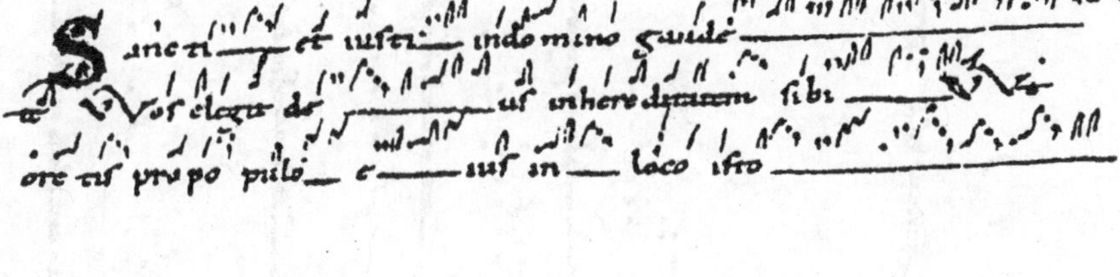

Venite (*ALB*, with significant variants found in *YRX*)

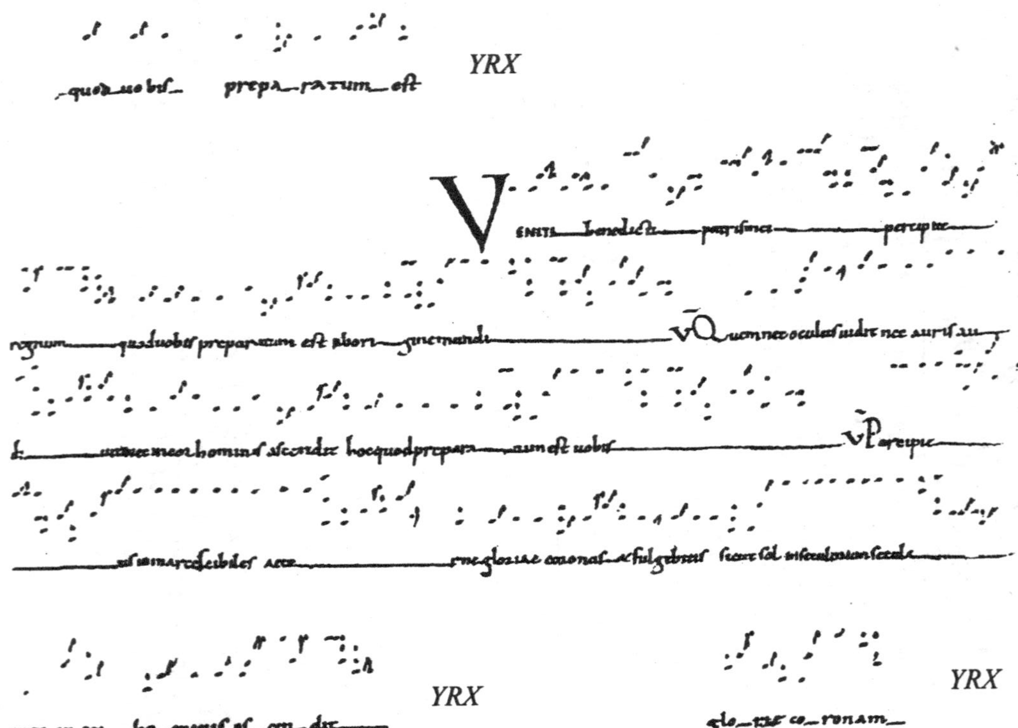

Adducentur (ORC)

Tract text	Phrase used and parallels
Adducentur	***A2*** like *Ad te leuaui*
regi	***A1*** intonation for second part of phrase, then hkihgh
virgines	***A1*** intonation for second part of phrase, then the end of the phrase ***B*** cadence
proxime	***D-A2***
eius	Low ***A2*** articulation as on '-cen-' in the first phrase, then ***D*** cadence
afferentur	***B2*** rise then ***B3*** figures
tibi	***B3-E3-F***
In letitia	g-l rise seen also in *Ad te leuaui 5*, ***E3*** then ***B3*** melismatic patterns
et exultatione	Recitation around k, phrase ***C*** material, then phrase ***C*** cadence
adducentur	fhk rise of ***B2***, then ***B3*** fall
in templum regis domino	***F***, with ***C*** cadence on '-plum', and much of final melisma missing

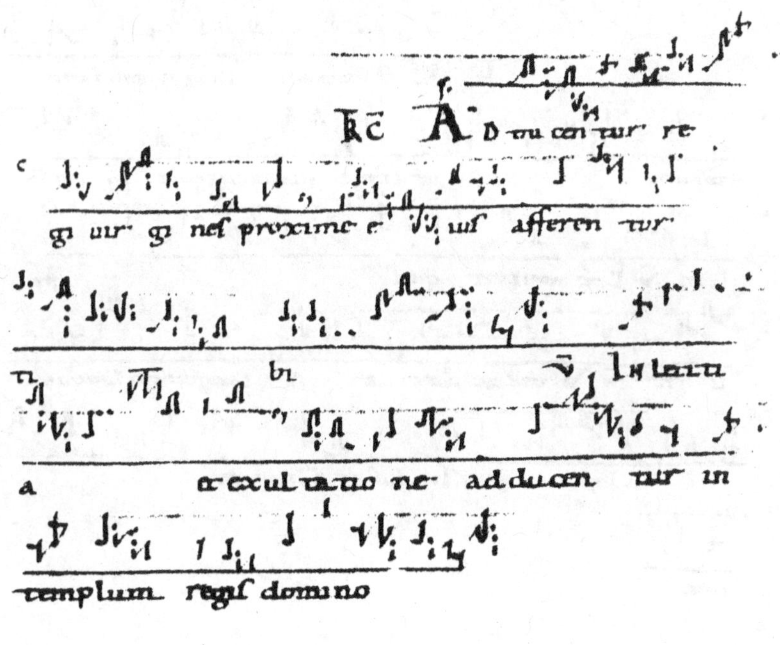

Effuderunt (ORC)

Tract text	Phrase used and parallels
Effuderunt sangiunem	***A2***, like *Desiderium*, but with abbreviated ending due to lack of text
sanctorum	***B1***, with material usually associated with last three syllables on '-um'
uelut aqua	***C1*** opening, pattern usually associated with second syllable in ***C2***, ***C*** cadence
in circuitu hierusalem	***D2/3*** opening, ***A2*** rise to l, ghgfgf seen in phrase ***F***, phrase ***F*** cadence (seen in *Ad te leuaui*)
Et non erat	***E1*** opening
qui sepeliret	***B3*** melismatic figures, then phrase ***F*** ending (see *Sepe*)
Vindica domine	***B4***, with middle section missing
sanguinem sanctorum tuorum	***B2*** rise, then ***B5*** figures seen on 'et non' in *Iubilate 9*, then ***C*** cadence
qui effusus est super terram	***F***

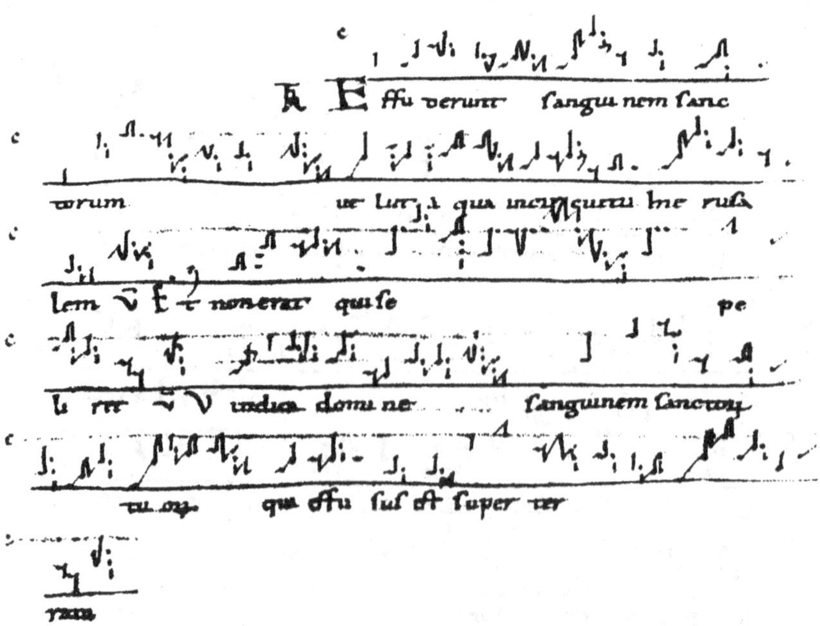

Nunc dimittis (ORC)

Tract text	Phrase used and parallels
Nunc dimittis domine	***A1***
seruum tuum	Beginning of ***B1***, then beginning of ***D1*** melisma
secundum uerbum tuum in pace	***B2*** opening, then abbreviated version of previous 'tuum', then unique oscillating cadence
Qui uiderunt oculi mei	***E3*** opening, then phrase ***C*** ending
salutare tuum	Abbreviated phrase ***F***
Quod parasti	***E3***
ante faciem	***A1*** figure, hkihg, ***D4*** opening
omnium populorum	***B2*** opening, then end of ***D1*** cadence
Lumen ad reuelationem	***E3*** opening, ***B3*** figures, ***C*** cadence
gentium	***D4*** opening, then ***A1*** cadence
et gloriam	***B2***, omitting middle
plebis tue israhel	***C2***, then ***F*** ending

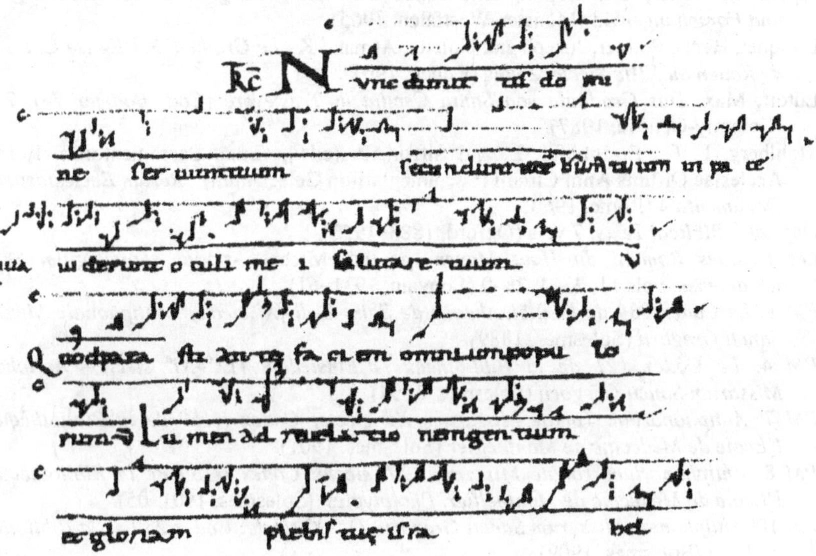

Bibliography

Primary Sources

Amalarius of Metz, *Opera Liturgica Omnia*, ed. Jean-Michel Hanssens, *Studi e Testi* 38–40 (Rome, 1948–50).

Codex 121 Einsiedeln, Commentary ed. Odo Lang (Weinheim, 1991).

Bezae Codex Cantabrigiensis, ed. Frederick Scrivener (Cambridge, 1899).

Echternacher Sakramentar und Antiphonar: Vollständige Facsimile-Ausgabe in Originalformat der Handschrift 1946... aus dem Besitz der Hessischen Landes- und Hochschulbibliothek Darmstadt with essays by Kurt Hans Staub, Paul Ulveling and Franz Unterkircher, *Codices Selecti* 74 (Graz, 1982).

Hesbert, René-Jean, 'Le Graduel de Saint-Denis', *Monumenta Musica Sacrae* 5 (Paris, 1981).

Hucbald, Guido and John on Music, ed. Warren Babb, with introductions by Claude Palisca, index of chants by Alejandro Planchart (New Haven, Conn., 1978).

Jülicher, Adolf, *Italia: das Neue Testament in Altlateinischer Überlieferung*, 3 vols (second edition; Berlin, 1970–76).

Liber Pontificalis, ed. Louis Duchesne, rev. Cyrille Vogel, 3 vols (Paris, 1955–57).

Lipphardt, Walter, 'Der karolingische Tonar von Metz', *Liturgiewissenschaftliche Quellen und Forschungen* 43 (Münster-Westfalen, 1965).

Loriquet, Henri, Pothier, Joseph and Colette, Armand K., *Le Graduel de l'Eglise Cathédrale de Rouen au XIIIe Siècle*, 2 vols (Rouen, 1907).

Lütolf, Max, *Das Graduale von Santa Cecilia in Trastevere (Cod. Bodmer 74)*, 2 vols (Cologny-Genève, 1987).

Mohlberg, L. C., Eizenhöfer, L. and Siffrin, P. (eds.), 'Liber Sacramentorum Romanae Aeclesiae Ordinis Anni Circuli (Sacramentarium Gelasianum)', *Rerum Ecclesiasticarum Documenta* 4 (Rome, 1960).

Old Latin Biblical Texts, 7 vols (Oxford, 1883–1923).

Les Ordines Romani du Haut Moyen-Age, ed. Michel Andrieu, *Spicilegium Sacrum Lovaniense*, vols 11, 23–4, 28–9 (Louvain, 1931–61).

PM 1: *Le Codex 339 de la Bibliothèque de Saint-Gall (Xe siècle): Antiphonale Missarum Sancti Gregorii* (Solesmes, 1889).

PM 4: *Le Codex 121 de la Bibliothèque d'Einsiedeln (IXe–XIe siècle): Antiphonale Missarum Sancti Gregorii* (Solesmes, 1894).

PM 7: *Antiphonarium Tonale Missarum, XIe siècle: Codex H159 de la Bibliothèque de l'École de Médecine de Montpellier* (Solesmes, 1901).

PM 8: *Antiphonarium Tonale Missarum, XIe siècle: Codex H159 de la Bibliothèque de l'École de Médecine de Montpellier. Phototypies* (Solesmes, 1901–05).

PM 10: *Antiphonale Missarum Sancti Gregorii, IXe–Xe siècle: Codex 239 de la Bibliothèque de Laon* (Solesmes, 1909).

PM 11: *Antiphonale Missarum Sancti Gregorii, Xe siècle: Codex 47 de la Bibliothèque de

Chartres (Solesmes, 1912).

PM 13: *Le Codex 903 de la Bibliothèque Nationale de Paris (XIe siècle): Graduel de Saint-Yrieix* (Solesmes, 1925).

PM 14: *Le Codex 10673 de la Bibliothèque Vaticane fonds latin (XIe siècle): Graduel Bénéventain* (Solesmes, 1931).

PM 15: *Le Codex VI.34 de la Bibliothèque Capitulaire de Bénévent (XIe-XIIe siècle): Graduel de Bénévent avec Prosaire et Tropaire* (Solesmes, 1937).

PM 16: *Le Manuscrit de Mont-Renaud, Xe siècle: Graduel et Antiphonaire de Noyon* (Solesmes, 1955).

PM 18: *Le Codex 123 de la Bibliothèque Angelica de Rome (XIe siècle): Graduel et Tropaire de Bologne* (Berne, 1969).

PM 19: *Le Manuscrit 807, Universitätsbibliothek Graz (XIIe siècle): Graduel de Klosterneuberg* (Berne, 1974).

PM 20: *Le Manuscrit VI–33, Archivio Arcivescovile Benevento: Missel de Bénévent (début du XIe siècle)* (Berne, 1983).

PM 21: *Le Chant Bénéventain* (Solesmes, 1992).

PM II/2: *Cantatorium, IXe siècle: N° 359 de la Bibliothèque de Saint-Gall* (Solesmes, 1924).

Thibaut, Jean Baptiste, *Monuments de la Notation Ekphonetique et Neumatique de l'Eglise Latine* (St. Petersburg, 1912).

Weber, Robert, 'Le Psautier Romain et les Autres Anciens Psautiers Latins', *Collectanea Biblica Latina* 10 (Rome, 1953).

Secondary sources

Apel, Willi, 'The Central Problem of Gregorian Chant', *JAMS* 9 (1956), 118–27.

Apel, Willi, *Gregorian Chant* (Bloomington, Ind., 1958).

Arlt, Wulf, 'Anschaulichkeit und Analytischer Charakter: Kriterion der Beschreibung und Analyse früher Neumenschriften', in Michel Huglo (ed.), *Musicologie Médievale: Notations et Séquences* (Paris and Geneva, 1987), 29–55.

Ashworth, Henry, 'Did St. Augustine bring the 'Gregorianum' to England?', *Ephemerides Liturgicae* 72 (1958), 39–43.

Atkinson, Charles M., 'From "Vitium" to "Tonus acquisitus": On the Evolution of the Notational Matrix of Medieval Chant', in *CP: Tihany*, 181–97.

Atkinson, Charles M., 'Further Thoughts on the Origin of the *Missa Graeca*', in Peter Cahn and Ann-Katrin Heimer (eds.), *De Musica et de Cantu: Helmut Hucke zum 60. Geburtstag* (Hildesheim, 1993), 75–93.

Atkinson, Charles M., 'Johannes Afflighemensis as a Historian of Mode', in Janka Szendrei and David Hiley (eds.), *Laborare Fratres in Unum: Festschrift László Dobszay* (Hildesheim and Zurich, 1995), 1–10.

Atkinson, Charles M., 'De Accentibus Toni Oritur Nota Quae Dicitur Neuma: Prosodic Accents, the Accent Theory, and the Paleofrankish Script', in Graeme Boone (ed.), *Essays on Medieval Music in Honor of David G. Hughes: Isham Library Papers* 4 (Cambridge, Mass., 1995), 17–42.

Avenary, Hanoch, 'The Northern and Southern Idioms of Early European Music: A New Approach to an Old Problem', *AM* 49 (1977), 27–49.

Bailey, Terence, *The Intonation Formulas of Western Chant* (Toronto, 1974).

Bailey, Terence, 'Ambrosian Chant in Southern Italy', *JPMMS* 6 (1983), 1–7.

Bailey, Terence, *The Ambrosian Cantus* (Ottawa, 1987).

Barezzani, Maria Teresa Rosa, *La Notazione Neumatica di un Codice Bresciano (Secolo XI)* (Cremona, 1981).

Baumann, Gerd (ed.), *The Written Word: Literacy in Transition: Wolfson College Lectures, 1985* (Oxford, 1986).

Baumstark, Anton, *Liturgie Comparée* (third edition; Chevetogne, 1953) .

Bellingham, Jane, *The Development of Musical Thought in the Medieval West from Late Antiquity to the Mid-Ninth Century* (DPhil, University of Oxford, 1998).

Bergeron, Katherine, *Decadent Enchantments: The Revival of Gregorian Chant at Solesmes* (Berkeley, 1998).

Bernard, Philippe, 'Sur un Aspect Controversé de la Réforme Carolingienne: «Vieux-Romain» et «Grégorien»', *Ecclesia Orans* 7 (Rome, 1990), 163–89.

Bernard, Philippe, *Du Chant Romain au Chant Grégorien* (Paris, 1995).

Bischoff, Bernhard, 'The Study of Foreign Languages in the Middle Ages', *Speculum* 36 (Cambridge, Mass., 1961), 209–24.

Bloch, Herbert, *Montecassino in the Middle Ages* (Rome, 1986).

Boe, John, 'The Beneventan Apostrophus in South Italian Notation A. D. 1000–1100', *EMH* 3 (1983), 43–66.

Boe, John, 'Chant Notation in Eleventh-Century Roman Manuscripts', in Graeme Boone (ed.), *Essays on Medieval Music in Honor of David G. Hughes: Isham Library Papers* 4 (Cambridge, Mass., 1995), 43–57.

Boe, John, 'Music Notation in Archivio San Pietro C 105 and in the Farfa Breviary, Chigi C. VI. 177', *Early Music History* 18 (1999), 1–45.

Boone, Graeme (ed.), *Essays on Medieval Music in Honor of David G. Hughes: Isham Library Papers* 4 (Cambridge, Mass., 1995).

Borders, James M., 'The Transmission of Franco-Roman Chant in Northern Italy', in *AMS: Abstracts of Papers Read at the Annual Meeting* (Louisville, 1983), 62–3.

Bower, Calvin, 'The Grammatical Model of Musical Understanding in the Middle Ages', in Patrick Gallacher and Helen Damico (eds.), *Hermeneutics and Medieval Culture* (Albany, NY, 1989), 133–45.

Brown, Giles, 'Introduction: The Carolingian Renaissance', in R. McKitterick (ed.), *Carolingian Culture: Emulation and Innovation* (Cambridge, 1994), 1–51.

Browne, Alma Colk, 'The a-p System of Letter Notation', *MD* 35 (1981), 5–54.

Bryden, John and Hughes, David, *An Index of Gregorian Chant*, 2 vols (Cambridge, Mass., 1969).

Cahn, Peter and Heimer, Ann-Katrin (eds.), *De Musica et de Cantu: Helmut Hucke zum 60. Geburtstag* (Hildesheim, 1993).

Cardine, Eugene, 'L'Edition Critique du Graduel: Nécessité, Avantages, Méthode', in Higini Anglès (ed.), *Congresso Internazionale di Musica Sacra, Rome, 1950* (Tournai, 1952), 187–91.

Carruthers, Mary, *The Book of Memory* (Cambridge, 1990).

Claire, Jean, 'Les Répertoires Liturgiques Latins avant l'Octoéchos. I. L'Office Férial Romano-Franc', *EG* 15 (1975), 5–192.

Claire, Jean, 'Le Répertoire Grégorien de l'Office. Structure Musical et Formes', in *Le Chant Grégorien, Patrimonie Artistique de l'Europe: Les Actes du Colloque International de Musicologie* (Louvain, 1980), 27–46.

Clanchy, Michael, *From Memory to Written Record: England 1066-1307* (second edition; Oxford, 1993).

Colette, Marie-Noël, 'L'Invention Musicale dans le Haut Moyen Age: Ponctuation et Transposition', *Analyse Musicale* (1990), 7–17.

Colette, Marie-Noël, 'La Notation du Demi-Ton dans le Manuscrit Paris, B. N. Lat. 1139 et dans Quelques Manuscrits du Sud de la France', in Claudio Leonardi and Enrico Menesto (eds.), *La Tradizione dei Tropi Liturgici* (Spoleto, 1990), 297–311.

Colette, Marie-Noël, 'Le Graduel-Antiphonaire, Albi, Bibliothèque Municipale 44 : une Notation Protoaquitaine Rhythmique', in *CP : Eger*, 117–39.

Colette, Marie-Noël, 'Grégorien et Vieux-Romain: Deux Méthodes Différentes de Collectage de Mélodies Traditionelles?', in Janka Szendrei and David Hiley (eds.), *Laborare Fratres in Unum: Festschrift Laszlo Dobszay* (Hildesheim and Zurich, 1995), 37–52.

Collins, Roger, *Early Medieval Europe, 300–1000* (London, 1991).

Connolly, Thomas, 'Introits and Archetypes: Some Archaisms of the Old Roman Chant', *JAMS* 25 (1972), 157–74.

Connolly, Thomas, 'The *Graduale* of S. Cecilia in Trastevere and the Old Roman Tradition', *JAMS* 28 (1975), 413–58.

Corbin, Solange, 'Valeur et Sens de la Notation Alphabétique, à Jumièges et en Normandie', in *Jumièges Congrès Scientifique du XIIIe Centenaire*, vol. 2 (Rouen, 1955), 913–24.

Corbin, Solange, 'La Cantillation des Rituels Chrétiens', *Revue de Musicologie* 67 (1961), 3–36.

Cowdrey, Herbert E. J., *The Cluniacs and the Gregorian Reform* (Oxford, 1970).

Cowdrey, Herbert E. J., *The Age of Abbot Desiderius: Montecassino, the Papacy and the Normans in the Eleventh and Early Twelfth Centuries* (Oxford, 1983).

Crocker, Richard, 'Thoughts on Responsories', in Graeme Boone (ed.), *Essays on Medieval Music in Honor of David G. Hughes: Isham Library Papers* 4 (Cambridge, Mass., 1995), 77–85.

Crosby, Ruth, 'Oral Delivery in the Middle Ages', *Speculum* 11 (1935), 88–110.

Cullin, Olivier, *Le Trait dans les Répertoires Vieux-Romain et Grégorien: un Témoin de la Psalmodie Sans Refrain* (PhD, University of Paris, Sorbonne, 1990).

Cullin, Olivier, 'L'*Office de Pâques* Comme Miroir du Chant Grégorien: du Concept Liturgique à la Réalisation Musicale', *Analyse Musicale* (1990), 19–25.

Cullin, Olivier, 'De la Psalmodie Sans Refrain à la Psalmodie Responsoriale: Transformation et Conservation dans les Répertoires Liturgiques Latins', *Revue de Musicologie* 77 (1991), 5–24.

Cullin, Olivier, 'Pour une Reévaluation des Formes Littéraires de la Psalmodie Sans Refrain: Canticum et Tractus', *Modus* 3 (Lisbon, 1989–1992), 41–8.

Cutter, Paul, 'The Old Roman Chant Tradition: Oral or Written?', *JAMS* 20 (1967), 167–81.

Cutter, Paul, 'The Question of the "Old Roman" Chant: A Reappraisal', *AM* 39 (1967), 2–20.

Cutter, Paul, 'Oral Transmission of the Old Roman Responsories?', *MQ* 62 (1976), 182–94.

Cutter, Paul, 'Musical Sources of the Old Roman Mass', *Musicological Studies and Documents* 36 (Neuhausen-Stuttgart, 1979).

Deshusses Jean, and Darragon, Benoit, *Concordances et Tableaux pour l'Etude des Grands Sacramentaires* (Fribourg, 1982–83).

de Vregille, Bernard, 'Aldebald the Scribe of Cluny and the Bible of Abbot William of Dijon', in Noreen Hunt (ed.), *Cluniac Monasticism in the Central Middle Ages* (London, 1971), 85–97.

Dobszay, László, 'Plainsong in Medieval Hungary', *JPMMS* 13 (1990), 49–78.

Dudley, Martin, '*Natalis innocentium*: The Holy Innocents in Liturgy and Drama', *Studies in Church History* (Ecclesiastical History Society; Oxford, 1994), 233–42.

Dunbabin, Jean, *France in the Making 843–1180* (Oxford, 1985).

Dyer, Joseph, 'Latin Psalters, Old Roman and Gregorian Chants', *KmJb* 68 (1984), 11–30.

Dyer, Joseph, 'Psalmody and the Roman Mass', *Studies in Music* 10 (London, Ontario, 1985), 1–24.

Dyer, Joseph, 'The Schola Cantorum and its Roman Milieu in the Early Middle Ages', in Peter Cahn and Ann-Katrin Heimer (eds.), *De Musica et de Cantu: Helmut Hucke zum 60. Geburtstag* (Hildesheim, 1993), 19–40.

Fassler, Margot, 'The Office of the Cantor in Early Western Monastic Rules and Customaries: A Preliminary Investigation', *EMH* 5 (1985), 29–51.

Ferrari, Guy, *Early Roman Monasteries: Notes for the History of the Monasteries and Convents at Rome from the V through the X Century* (Vatican City, 1957).

Ferreira, Manuel Pedro, 'The Cluny Gradual: its Notation and Melodic Character', in *CP: Eger*, 205–15.

Ferreira, Manuel Pedro, *Music at Cluny: The Tradition of Gregorian Chant for the Proper of the Mass. Melodic Variants and Microtonal Nuances* (PhD, Princeton University, 1997).

Fischer, Rupert, 'Das Graduale des Codex 121 der Stiftsbibliothek Einsiedeln', in Odo Lang (ed.), *Codex Einsiedeln 121: Kommentar* (Weinheim, 1991), 71–95.

Flotzinger, Rudolf, *Choralhandschriften österreichischer Provenienz in der Bodleian Library, Oxford* (Vienna, 1991).

Fouracre, Paul, 'Frankish Gaul to 814', in *NCMH*, 85–109.

Frere, Walter Howard, *Studies in Early Roman Liturgy, I: The Calendar* (Alcuin Club Collections, 28. Oxford, 1930).

Fry, Donald, 'Formulaic Theory and Old English Poetry', in *IMS 1977*, 169–73.

Ganz, David, *Corbie in the Carolingian Renaissance* (Sigmaringen, 1990).

Gellrich, Jesse, *The Idea of the Book in the Middle Ages: Language Theory, Mythology and Fiction* (Cornell, 1985).

Gushee, Lawrence, 'The *Musica Disciplina* of Aurelian of Réôme: a Critical Text and Commentary' (PhD, Yale University, 1963).

Gwynn, Aubrey, *The Irish Church in the Eleventh and Twelfth Centuries* (Dublin, 1992).

Gyug, Richard, *Missale Ragusinum: The Missal of Dubrovnik* (Toronto, 1990).

Haas, Max, *Mündlicher Überlieferung und altrömische Choral: historische und analytische computergestützte Untersuchungen* (Bern, 1997).

Hansen, Finn Egeland, *H159 Montpellier: Tonary of St. Bénigne of Dijon* (Copenhagen, 1974).

Hansen, Finn Egeland, 'Editorial Problems Connected with the Transcription of H159 Montpellier', *EG* (1977), 161–72.

Hansen, Finn Egeland, *The Grammar of Gregorian Tonality* (Copenhagen, 1979).

Harper, John, *The Forms and Orders of Western Liturgy from the Tenth to the Eighteenth Century* (Oxford, 1991).

Haug, Andreas, 'Zum Wechselspiel von Schrift und Gedächtnis im Zeitalter der Neumen', in *CP: Tihany*, 33–47.

Hen, Yitzhak, *Culture and Religion in Merovingian Gaul, AD 481–751* (Leiden, 1995).

Hiley, David, 'The Norman Chant Traditions – Normandy, Britain, Sicily', *PRMA* 107 (1980–81), 1–33.

Hiley, David, 'Recent Research on the Origins of Western Chant', *Early Music* 16 (1988), 203–13.

Hiley, David, 'Cluny, Sequences and Tropes', in Claudio Leonardi and Enrico Menesto (eds.), *La Tradizione dei Tropi Liturgici* (Spoleto, 1990), 125–38.

Hiley, David, 'The Sequence Melodies Sung at Cluny and Elsewhere', in Peter Cahn and Ann-Katrin Heimer (eds.), *De Musica et Cantu: Helmut Hucke zum 60. Geburtstag* (Hildesheim, 1993), 131–55.

Hiley, David, *Western Plainchant : A Handbook* (Oxford, 1993).

Holder, Stephen, 'The Noted Cluniac Breviary-Missal of Lewes: Fitzwilliam Museum Manuscript 369', *JPMMS* 8 (1985), 25–32.

Hourlier, Jacques, 'Remarques sur la Notation Clunisienne', *Revue Grégorienne* 30 (1951), 231–40.

Hourlier, Jacques, 'Le Bréviare de Saint-Taurin: Un Livre Liturgique Clunisien à l'Usage de l'Echelle-Saint-Aurin', *EG* (1953), 164–73.

Hourlier, Jacques, and Huglo, Michel, 'Notation Paléofranque', *EG* 2 (1957), 212–19.

Hucke, Helmut, 'Musikalisches formen der Offiziumsantiphonen', *KmJb* 37 (1953), 7–33.

Hucke, Helmut, 'Die Entwicklung des christlichen Kultgesangs zum Gregorianischen

Gesang', *Römische Quartalschrift* 48 (1953), 147–94.
Hucke, Helmut, 'Improvisation im Gregorianischen Gesang', *KmJb* 38 (1954), 5–8.
Hucke, Helmut, 'Die Einführung des gregorianischen Gesanges im Frankenreich', *Römische Quartalschrift* 49 (1954), 172–87.
Hucke, Helmut, 'Gregorianischer Gesang in altrömischer und Fränkischer Überlieferung', *Archiv für Musikwissenschaft* 12 (1955), 74–87.
Hucke, Helmut, 'Zu einigen Problemen der Choralforschung', *Die Musikforschung* 11 (1958), 385–414.
Hucke, Helmut, 'Tractusstudien' in Martin Ruhnke (ed.) *Festschrift Bruno Stäblein zum 70. Geburtstag* (Kassel, 1967), 116–20.
Hucke, Helmut, 'Der Übergang von mündlicher zu schriftlicher Musiküberlieferung im Mittelalter' in *IMS 1977*, 180–91.
Hucke, Helmut, 'Tract', *NG* vol. 19, 108–10.
Hucke, Helmut, 'Towards a New Historical View of Gregorian Chant', *JAMS* 33 (1980), 437–67.
Hughes, Andrew, *Mediaeval Music – the Sixth Liberal Art* (Toronto, 1974).
Hughes, Andrew, *Medieval Manuscripts for Mass and Office – A Guide to their Organization and Terminology* (Toronto, 1982).
Hughes, David, 'Variants in Antiphon Families: Notation and Tradition', in Marc Honegger and Paul Prévost (eds.), *La Musique et le Rite Sacré et Profane: Actes du XIIIe Congrès de la Société International de Musicologie Strasbourg, 1982* (Strasbourg, 1985), 29–47.
Hughes, David, 'Evidence for the Traditional View of the Transmission of Gregorian Chant', *JAMS* 40 (1987), 377–401.
Hughes, David, 'The Implications of Variants for Chant Transmission', in Peter Cahn and Ann-Katrin Heimer (eds.), *De Musica et Cantu: Helmut Hucke zum 60. Geburtstag* (Hildesheim, 1993), 65–74.
Huglo, Michel, 'Notes Historiques à Propos du Second Décret sur la Vigile Pascale', *Revue Grégorienne* 31 (1952), 121–36.
Huglo, Michel, 'Le Chant 'Vieux-Romain': Liste des Manuscrits et Témoins Indirects', *Sacris Erudiri* 6 (1954), 96–124.
Huglo, Michel, 'Le Tonaire de Saint-Bénigne de Dijon', *Annales Musicologiques* 4 (Paris, 1956), 7–18.
Huglo, Michel, *Les Tonaires: Inventaire, Analyse, Comparaison* (Paris, 1971).
Huglo, Michel, 'Tradition Orale et Tradition Ecrit dans la Transmission des Melodies Grégoriennes', in Hans Heinrich Eggebrecht and Max Lütolf (eds.), *Studien zur Tradition in der Musik: Kurt von Fischer zum 60. Geburtstag* (Munich, 1973), 31–42.
Huglo, Michel (ed.), *Musicologie Mediévale: Notations et Séquences. Actes de la Table Ronde du CNRS à l'Institut de Recherche et d'Histoire des Textes d'Orléans-La Source, 10-12 Septembre 1982* (Paris and Geneva, 1987).
Huglo, Michel, 'Les Formules d'Intonations "Noeane Noeagis" en Orient et en Occident', in Christian Meyer (ed.), *Aspects de la Musique Liturgique au Moyen Age: Actes des Colloques de Royaument de 1986, 1987 et 1988* (Paris, 1991), 44–53.
Hunt, Noreen, *Cluny under Saint Hugh 1049–1109* (London, 1967).
Hunt, Noreen, (ed.), *Cluniac Monasticism in the Central Middle Ages* (London, 1971).
Jammers, Ewald, *Tafeln zur Neumenschrift* (Tutzing, 1965)
Jeffery, Peter, 'The Oldest Sources of the *Graduale*: A Preliminary Checklist of MSS Copied before about 900', *JM* 2 (1983), 316–21.
Jeffery, Peter, *Re-Envisioning Past Musical Cultures: Ethnomusicology in the Study of Gregorian Chant* (Chicago, 1992).
Jeffery, Peter, 'Rome and Jerusalem: From Oral Tradition to Written Repertory', in Graeme Boone (ed.), *Essays on Medieval Music in Honor of David G. Hughes: Isham Library Papers* 4 (Cambridge, Mass., 1995), 207–47.

Joppich, Godehard, 'Der rhetorische Komponente in der Notation des Codex 121 von Einsiedeln', in Odo Lang (ed.), *Codex Einsiedeln 121: Kommentar* (Weinheim, 1991), 119–88.

Jounel, Pierre, *Le Culte des Saints dans les Basiliques du Latran et du Vatican au Douxième Siècle* (Rome, 1977).

Kainzbauer, Xavier, 'Der Tractus Tetrardus – eine centologische Untersuchung', *Beiträge zur Gregorianik* 11 (Regensburg, 1991), 1–132.

Kelly, Thomas Forrest, 'Montecassino and the Old Beneventan Chant', *EMH* 5 (1985), 53–83.

Kelly, Thomas Forrest, 'Non-Gregorian Music in an Antiphoner of Benevento', *JM* V (1987), 478–97.

Kelly, Thomas Forrest, 'Beneventan and Milanese Chant', *Journal of the Royal Musical Association* 112 (1987), 173–95.

Kelly, Thomas Forrest, *The Beneventan Chant* (Cambridge, 1989).

Kelly, Thomas Forrest, 'The Liturgical Rotulus at Benevento', in Janka Szendrei and David Hiley (eds.), *Laborare Fratres in Unum: Festschrift László Dobszay* (Hildesheim and Zurich, 1995), 167–86.

Kelly, Thomas Forrest, *The Exsultet in Southern Italy* (Oxford, 1996).

Lawrence, Clifford H., *Medieval Monasticism* (New York, 1984).

Leroquais, Victor, *Le Bréviare-Missel du Prieuré Clunisien de Lewes* (Paris, 1935).

Levy, Kenneth, 'The Italian Neophytes' Chants', *JAMS* 23 (1970), 181–227.

Levy, Kenneth, 'A Gregorian Processional Antiphon', *Schweizer Jahrbuch für Musikwissenschaft* 2 (1982), 91–102.

Levy, Kenneth, 'Toledo, Rome and the Legacy of Gaul', *EMH* 4 (1984), 49–99.

Levy, Kenneth, 'Charlemagne's Archetype of Gregorian Chant', *JAMS* 40 (1987), 1–30.

Levy, Kenneth, 'On the Origin of Neumes', *EMH* 7 (1987), 59–90.

Levy, Kenneth, 'The two Carolingian Archetypes of Gregorian Chant', in *IMS* (1987), 501–4.

Levy, Kenneth, 'Communication', *JAMS* 41 (1988) 566–75.

Levy, Kenneth, 'On Gregorian Orality', *JAMS* 43 (1990), 185–227.

Levy, Kenneth, 'Gregorian Chant and Oral Transmission', in Graeme Boone (ed.), *Essays on Medieval Music in Honor of David G. Hughes: Isham Library Papers* 4 (Cambridge, Mass., 1995), 277–86.

Lipphardt, Walter., 'Gregor der Grosse und sein Anteil am römischen Antiphonar', in Higini Anglès (ed.), *Congresso Internazionale di Musica Sacra, Rome, 1950* (Tournai, 1952), 248–54.

Lord, Albert Bates, *The Singer of Tales* (Cambridge, Mass., 1964).

Lord, Albert Bates, *Epic Singers and Oral Tradition* (Cornell, 1991).

McGee, Timothy, *The Sound of Medieval Song: Ornamentation and Vocal Style according to the Treatises* (Oxford, 1998).

McKinnon, James, 'On the Question of Psalmody in the Ancient Synagogue', *EMH* 6 (1986), 159–91.

McKinnon, James, 'The Fourth-Century Origin of the Gradual', *EMH* 7 (1987), 91–106.

McKinnon, James, 'The Eighth-Century Frankish-Roman Communion Cycle', *JAMS* 45 (1992), 179–227.

McKinnon, James, 'Antoine Chavasse and the Dating of Early Chant', *PMM* 1 (1992), 123–48.

McKinnon, James, 'Lector Chant versus Schola Chant: A Question of Historical Plausibility', in Janka Szendrei and David Hiley (eds.), *Laborare Fratres in Unum: Festschrift László Dobszay* (Hildesheim and Zurich, 1995), 201–11.

McKinnon, James, 'Properization: The Roman Mass', in *CP: Eger*, 15–22.

McKinnon, James, 'Vaticana Latina 5319: Witness to the Mid-Eighth-Century Roman

Proper of the Mass', in *CP: Sopron*, 403–11.

McKinnon, James, 'The Gregorian Canticle-Tracts of the Old Roman Easter Vigil', in C-H. Mahling and R. Seiberts (eds.), *Festschrift Walter Wiora zum 90. Geburtstag* (Tutzing, 1997), 254–70.

McKinnon, James, *The Advent Project: The Later-Seventh-Century Creation of the Roman Mass Proper* (Berkeley, 2000).

McKitterick, Rosamund, *The Frankish Church and the Carolingian Reforms, 789–895* (London, 1977).

McKitterick, Rosamund, *The Frankish Kingdoms under the Carolingians 751–987* (London, 1983).

McKitterick, Rosamund, *The Carolingians and the Written Word* (Cambridge, 1989).

McKitterick, Rosamund (ed.), *The Uses of Literacy in Early Medieval Europe* (Cambridge, 1990).

McKitterick, Rosamund (ed.), *Carolingian Culture: Emulation and Innovation* (Cambridge, 1994).

Maloy, Rebecca, *The Offertory Chant: Aspects of Chronology and Transmission* (Ph.D, Cincinnati University, 2001).

Mearns, James, *The Canticles of the Christian Church, Eastern and Western* (Cambridge, 1914).

Menache, Sophia, *The Vox Dei – Communication in the Middle Ages* (Oxford, 1990).

Möller, Hartmut, 'Deutsche Neumenschriften ausserhalb St. Gallens', in Peter Cahn and Ann-Katrin Heimer (eds.), *De Musica et de Cantu: Helmut Hucke zum 60. Geburtstag* (Hildesheim, 1993), 225–42.

Moreton, M. Bernard, *The Eighth-Century Gelasian Sacramentary: A Study in Tradition* (Oxford, 1976).

Nelson, Janet, 'Literacy in Carolingian Government', in Rosamund McKitterick (ed.), *The Uses of Literacy in Early Medieval Europe* (Cambridge, 1990), 258–96.

Nelson, Janet, 'Kingship and Royal Government', in *NCMH*, 383–430.

Nelson, Janet, 'Kingship and Empire in the Carolingian World', in R. McKitterick (ed.), *Carolingian Culture: Emulation and Innovation* (Cambridge, 1994), 52–87.

Nettl, Bruno, 'Some Notes on the State of Knowledge about Oral Transmission in Music', in *IMS* (1977), 139–44.

Nowacki, Edward, 'The Syntactical Analysis of Plainchant', in *IMS 1977*, 191–201.

Nowacki, Edward, *Studies on the Office Antiphons of the Old Roman Manuscripts* (PhD, Brandeis University, 1980).

Nowacki, Edward, 'The Gregorian Office Antiphons and the Comparative Method', *JM* 4 (1985), 243–75.

Nowacki, Edward, 'Text Declamation as a Determinant of Melodic Form in the Old Roman Eighth-Mode Tracts', *EMH* 6 (Cambridge, 1986), 193–225.

Nowacki, Edward, 'Constantinople-Aachen-Rome: The Transmission of *Veterem hominem*', in Peter Cahn and Ann-Katrin Heimer (eds.), *De Musica et de Cantu: Helmut Hucke zum 60. Geburtstag* (Hildesheim, 1993), 95–115.

Opie, Peter and Iona, *Children's Games* (Oxford, 1969).

Pinker, Stephen, *The Language Instinct* (London, 1995).

Planchart, Alejandro, 'Old Wine in New Bottles', in Peter Cahn and Ann-Katrin Heimer (eds.), *De Musica et de Cantu: Helmut Hucke zum 60. Geburtstag* (Hildesheim, 1993), 41–64.

Planchart, Alejandro, 'Notes on the Tropes in Manuscripts of the Rite of Aquileia', in Graeme Boone, (ed.) *Essays on Medieval Music in Honor of David G. Hughes: Isham Library Papers* 4 (Cambridge, Mass., 1995), 333–69.

Pognon, Edmond, *L'An Mille: Oeuvres de Liutprand, Raoul Glaber, Adémar de Chabannes, Adalberon et Helgaud* (Paris, 1947).

Raasted, Jorgen, 'The "Laetantis ad Verbia" of Aurelian's Greek Informant', in Christian Meyer (ed.), *Aspects de la Musique Liturgique au Moyen Age: Actes des Colloques de Royaument de 1986, 1987 et 1988* (Paris, 1991), 56–66.

Rankin, Susan, 'From Memory to Record: Musical Notations in Manuscripts from Exeter', *Anglo-Saxon England* 13 (1984), 97–112.

Rankin, Susan, 'Carolingian Music', in Rosamund McKitterick (ed.), *Carolingian Culture: Emulation and Innovation* (Cambridge, 1994), 274–316.

Rankin, Susan, 'Ways of Telling Stories', in Graeme Boone (ed.), *Essays on Medieval Music in Honor of David G. Hughes: Isham Library Papers* 4 (Cambridge, Mass., 1995), 371–94.

Reynolds, Leighton and Wilson, Nigel, *Scribes and Scholars* (third edition; Oxford, 1991).

Robertson, Anne Walters, *The Service Books of the Royal Abbey of Saint-Denis* (Oxford, 1991).

Roederer, Charlotte D., 'Can we Identify an Aquitanian Chant Style?', *JAMS* 27 (1974), 75–99.

Rollason, David W., *The Mildrith Legend: A Study in Early Medieval Hagiography in England* (Leicester, 1982).

Rubin, David, 'Cognitive Processes and Oral Traditions', in *IMS* (1977), 173–80.

Rubin, David, *Memory in Oral Traditions* (Oxford, 1995).

Santosuosso, Alma Colk, *Letter Notations in the Middle Ages* (Ottawa, 1989).

Schmidt, Hans, 'Die Tractus des zweiten Tones in Gregorianischer und stadtrömischer Überlieferung', in Dagmar Weise (ed.), *Festschrift Joseph Schmidt-Görg zum 60. Geburtstag* (Bonn, 1957), 283–302.

Schneider, Heinrich, 'Die altlateinischen biblischen Cantica', *Texte und Arbeiten*, 29–30 (Beuron, 1938).

Schwarzmaier, Hansmartin, 'The Monastery of St Benedict, Polirone, and its Cluniac Associations', in Noreen Hunt (ed.), *Cluniac Monasticism in the Central Middle Ages* (London, 1971), 123–42.

Sironi, Mauro, *Il Graduale Ms. Vallicelliana C52: Studio Storico-Liturgico e Musicologico* (PhD, U. Degli studi di Pavia, Scuola di Paleografia e filologia musicale, 1992–93).

Smits van Waesberghe, Joseph, 'Neues über die Schola Cantorum zu Rom', in *Zweiter Internationaler Kongres für Katholische Kirchenmusik* (Vienna, 1955), 111–19.

Southern, Richard, *The Making of the Middle Ages* (London, 1953).

Southern, Richard, *Western Society and the Church in the Middle Ages* (London, 1970).

Stäblein, Bruno, 'Zur Entstehung der gregorianischen Melodien', *KmJb* 35 (1951), 5–9.

Stäblein, Bruno,'Zur Frühgeschichte des römischen Chorals', in Higini Anglès (ed.), *Congresso Internazionale di Musica Sacra, Rome, 1950* (Tournai, 1952), 271–75.

Stäblein, Bruno, 'Die Gesänge des altrömischen Graduale Vat. Lat. 5319: Einführung', *Monumenta monodica medii aevi* 2 (1970), 3*–140*.

Stuart, Nicholas, 'Melodic "Corrections" in an Eleventh-Century Gradual (Paris, B. N., lat. 903)', *JPMMS* 2 (1979), 2–10.

Szendrei, Janka, 'The Introduction of Staff Notation into Middle Europe', *Studia Musicologica Academiae Scientiarum Hungaricae* 28 (Budapest, 1986), 303–19.

Szendrei, Janka and Hiley, David (eds.), *Laborare Fratres in Unum: Festschrift László Dobszay* (Hildesheim and Zurich, 1995).

Taft, Robert, *The Liturgy of the Hours in East and West* (Collegeville, Minnesota, 1986).

Talley, Thomas, *The Origins of the Liturgical Year* (New York, 1986).

Tomasello, Andrew, 'Ritual, Tradition, and Polyphony at the Court of Rome', *JM* 4 (1985), 447–71.

Treitler, Leo, 'Homer and Gregory: The Transmission of Epic Poetry and Plainchant', *MQ* 60 (1974), 333–72.

Treitler, Leo, '"Centonate" Chant: Übles Flickwerk or *E Pluribus Unus*?', *JAMS* 28 (1975),

1–23.

Treitler, Leo, 'Transmission and the Study of Music History', in *IMS 1977*, 202–11.

Treitler, Leo, 'Oral, Written, and Literate Process in the Transmission of Medieval Music', *Speculum* 56 (Cambridge, Mass., 1981), 471–91.

Treitler, Leo, 'Observations on the Transmission of some Aquitanian Tropes', *Forum Musicologicum* 3 (Winterthur, 1982), 11–60.

Treitler, Leo, 'From Ritual Through Language to Music', *Schweizer Jahrbuch für Musikwissenschaft* 2 (1982), 109–24.

Treitler, Leo, 'The Early History of Music Writing in the West', *JAMS* 35 (1982), 237–79.

Treitler, Leo, 'Reading and Singing: on the Genesis of Occidental Music-Writing', *EMH* 4 (Cambridge, 1984), 135–208.

Treitler, Leo, 'Paleography and Semiotics', in Michel Huglo (ed.), *Musicologie Mediévale: Notations et Séquences* (Paris and Geneva, 1987), 17–27.

Treitler, Leo, 'The "Unwritten" and "Written transmission" of Medieval Chant and the Start-up of Musical Notation', *JM* 10 (1992), 131–91.

Treitler, Leo, and Jacobsson, Ritva, 'Sketching Liturgical Archetypes: Hodie Surrexit Leo Fortis' in Peter Cahn and Ann-Katrin Heimer (eds.), *De Musica et de Cantu: Helmut Hucke zum 60. Geburtstag* (Hildesheim, 1993), 157–202.

Van der Werf, Hendrik, *The Emergence of Gregorian Chant. I: A Study of Modes and Melodies* (Rochester, New York, 1983).

Van der Werf, Hendrik, 'Oral and Written Transmission of the Gregorian Melodies for the Proprium Missae', *CP: Eger* 23–8.

Van Deusen, Nancy, *An Historical and Stylistic Comparison of the Graduals of Gregorian and Old Roman Chant* (PhD, Indiana University, 1972).

Van Dijk, Stephen J. P., 'The Urban and Papal Rites in Seventh- and Eighth-Century Rome', *Sacris Erudiri* 12 (Bruges, 1961), 411–87.

Van Dijk, Stephen J. P., 'Papal Schola "versus" Charlemagne', in Pieter Fischer (ed.), *Organicae Voces: Festschrift J. Smits van Waesberghe* (Amsterdam, 1963), 21–30.

Villetard, Henri, 'Catalogue et Description des Manuscrits de Montpellier Provenant du Département de l'Yonne', *Bulletin de la Société des Sciences Historiques et Naturelles de l'Yonne: 1900*, 54 (Paris, 1901).

Vogel, Cyrille, *Medieval Liturgy: an Introduction to the Sources,* trans. and rev. William Storey and Niels Rasmussen (Washington DC, 1986).

Vollaerts, Jan W. A., *Rhythmic Proportions in Early Medieval Ecclesiastical Chant* (Leiden, 1960).

Wagner, Peter, *Einführung in die gregorianischen Melodien* (Leipzig, 1921).

Wallace-Hadrill, John M., *The Frankish Church* (Oxford, 1983).

Wollasch, Joachim, 'A Cluniac Necrology from the Time of Abbot Hugh', in Noreen Hunt (ed.), *Cluniac Monasticism in the Central Middle Ages* (London, 1971), 143–90.

Yates, Frances, *The Art of Memory* (London, 1966).

Index